MACHINE LEARNING

Proceedings of the Tenth International Conference

University of Massachusetts, Amherst

June 27–29, 1993

Morgan Kaufmann Publishers, Inc.
San Mateo, California

Production, design, type, and manufacturing management
provided by Professional Book Center, Denver, Colorado

Morgan Kaufmann Publishers, Inc.
Editorial Office:
2929 Campus Drive, Suite 260,
San Mateo, CA 94403

ISBN 1-55860-307-7

Printed in the United States of America

96 95 94 93 4 3 2 1

CONTENTS

PREFACE

This volume contains the papers presented at the Tenth International Conference on Machine Learning, held at Amherst, Massachusetts, during June 27-29, 1993. Papers for the three informal workshops following the conference can be obtained from the workshop coordinators, whose names and affiliations are given on the following page.

The conference attracted 164 paper submissions, from which the 44 papers that appear here were selected by the program committee.

A great many people have contributed to the conference. I thank:

- The authors, who have taken time to produce and present their papers;
- The invited speakers, for sharing their research, insights, and perspective;
- The program committee members, who provided careful and constructive reviews;
- Those who served as adjunct members of the program committee by providing one or more essential reviews, namely Michael Cameron-Jones, Vijay Gullapalli, and Michael Jordan;
- The members of the program committee who met at Amherst in February to make the decisions regarding selection of papers, namely Andrew Barto, Haym Hirsh, Dennis Kibler, Pat Langley, Sridhar Mahadevan, Christopher Owens, Lorenza Saitta, and Steven Whitehead;
- The organizing committee members, who provided useful advice, namely Andrew Barto, Larry Birnbaum, Tom Dietterich, Edwina Rissland, and Derek Sleeman;
- The workshop organizers;
- Siemens Corporate Research, for providing financial support;
- Derek Sleeman, for the financial carry-forward from ML92;
- University Conference Services, particularly Todd Bryda and Mary McCulloch, for handling most of the local arrangements;
- Gwyn Mitchell for secretarial assistance;
- Professional Book Center, particularly Jennifer Ballentine, for producing this volume;
- Morgan Kaufmann Publishers, for serving as distributor of this volume.

Paul Utgoff, ML93 chair
Amherst, Massachusetts

ORGANIZING COMMITTEE

Andrew Barto, University of Massachusetts at Amherst

Larry Birnbaum, Northwestern University

Tom Dietterich, Oregon State University

Edwina Rissland, University of Massachusetts at Amherst

Derek Sleeman, University of Aberdeen

PROGRAM COMMITTEE

Andrew Barto, University of Massachusetts at Amherst

Larry Birnbaum, Northwestern University

Peter Cheeseman, NASA Ames Research Center

William Cohen, AT&T Bell Laboratories

Oren Etzioni, University of Washington

Usama Fayyad, Jet Propulsion Laboratory

Douglas Fisher, Vanderbilt University

John Grefenstette, Navy Research Laboratory

Haym Hirsh, Rutgers University

Robert Holte, University of Ottawa

Dennis Kibler, University of California at Irvine

Pat Langley, Siemens Corporate Research

Sridhar Mahadevan, IBM Watson

Ryszard Michalski, George Mason University

Tom Mitchell, Carnegie-Mellon University

Ray Mooney, University of Texas at Austin

Katharina Morik, University of Dortmund

Stephen Muggleton, The Turing Institute

Christopher Owens, University of Chicago

Michael Pazzani, University of California at Irvine

Leonard Pitt, University of Illinois at Champagne-Urbana

Ross Quinlan, University of Sydney

Larry Rendell, University of Illinois at Champagne-Urbana

Paul Rosenbloom, Information Sciences Institute, University of Southern California

Stuart Russell, University of California at Berkeley

Lorenza Saitta, University of Torino

Jude Shavlik, University of Wisconsin

Derek Sleeman, University of Aberdeen

Devika Subramanian, Cornell University

Richard Sutton, GTE Laboratories

Kurt VanLehn, University of Pittsburgh

Steven Whitehead, GTE Laboratories

Jan Zytkow, Wichita State University

WORKSHOPS

Reinforcement Learning: What We Know, What We Need
Coordinator: Richard Sutton, GTE Labs MS-44, 40 Sylvan Road, Waltham, MA 02254

Fielded Applications of Machine Learning
Coordinator: Pat Langley, Siemens Corporate Research, 755 College Road East, Princeton, NJ 08540

Knowledge Compilation and Speedup Learning
Coordinator: Devika Subramanian, Department of Computer Science, Cornell University, Ithaca, NY 14853

SCHEDULE—SUNDAY, JUNE 27

8:45	Welcome		
9:00	Combining Instance-Based and Model-Based Learning —*J. R. Quinlan*		
9:30	Addressing the Selective Superiority Problem: Automatic Algorithm/Model Class Selection—*Carla E. Brodley*		
10:00	SKICAT: A Machine Learning System for Automated Cataloging of Large Scale Sky Surveys—*Usama Fayyad, Nicholas Weir, S. Djorgovski*		
10:30	Break		
11:00	Invited Talk: Leo Breiman, University of California at Berkeley		
12:00	Lunch		
1:30	Efficiently Inducing Determinations: A Complete and Systematic Search Algorithm that Uses Optimal Pruning —*Jeffrey C. Schlimmer*	Database Mining of Subjective Agricultural Data—*R. Bharat Rao, Thomas B. Voigt, Thomas W. Fermanian*	Scaling Up Reinforcement Learning for Robot Control—*Long-Ji Lin*
2:00	Discovering Dynamics—*Saso Dzeroski, Ljupco Todorovski*	An Efficient Method for Constructing Approximate Decision Trees for Large Databases—*Ron Musick, Jason Catlett, Stuart Russell*	Adaptive Neurocontrol: How Black-Box and Simple Can it be?—*Jean-Michel Renders, Hugues Bersini, Marco Saerens*
2:30	Efficient Domain-Independent Experimentation— *Yolanda Gil*	An SE-Tree Based Characterization of the Induction Problem —*Ron Rymon*	Hierarchical Learning: Preliminary Results —*Leslie Pack Kaelbling*
3:00	Break		
3:30	Learning Search Control Knowledge for the Deep Space Network Scheduling Problem —*Jonathan Gratch, Steve A. Chien, Gerald F. DeJong*	Lookahead Feature Construction for Learning Hard Concepts —*Harish Ragavan, Larry Rendell*	Supervised Learning and Divide-and-Conquer: A Statistical Approach —*Michael I. Jordan, Robert A. Jacobs*
4:00	Constraining Learning with Search Control —*Jihie Kim, Paul S. Rosenbloom*	Using Decision Trees to Improve Case-Based Reasoning—*Claire Cardie*	Density-Adaptive Learning and Forgetting —*Marcos Salganicoff*
4:30	Learning Procedures from Interactive Natural Language Instructions —*Scott B. Huffman, John E. Laird*	Generalization under Implication by Recursive Anti-Unification —*Peter Idestam-Almquist*	Overcoming Incomplete Perception with Utile Distinction Memory —*R. Andrew McCallum*
5:00			
6:00	Reception		

SCHEDULE—MONDAY, JUNE 28

9:00	Using Qualitative Models to Guide Inductive Learning—*Peter Clark, Stan Matwin*		
9:30	Learning From Entailment: An Application to Propositional Horn Sentences—*Michael Frazier, Leonard Pitt*		
10:00	Learning from Queries and Examples with Tree-Structured Bias—*Prasad Tadepalli*		
10:30	Break		
11:00	Invited Talk: Micki Chi, University of Pittsburgh		
12:00	Lunch		
1:30	Explaining and Generalizing Diagnostic Decisions—*Paul O'Rorke, Yousri El Fattah, Margaret Elliott*	Learning DNF as Probabilistic Evidence Combination—*Steven W. Norton, Haym Hirsh*	Multi-Agent Reinforcement Learning: Independent vs. Cooperative Agents —*Ming Tan*
2:00	Better Learners Use Analogical Problem Solving Sparingly—*Kurt VanLehn, Randolph Jones*	Small Disjuncts in Action: Learning to Diagnose Errors in the Local Loop of the Telephone Network —*Andrea Danyluk, Foster J. Provost*	A Reinforcement Learning Method for Maximizing Undiscounted Rewards —*Anton Schwartz*
2:30	Automating Path Analysis for Building Causal Models from Data: First Results —*Paul Cohen, Adam Carlson, Lisa Ballesteros*	ELENA: A Bottom-Up Learning Method —*Pierre Brézellec*	ATM Scheduling with Queuing Delay Predictions—*Daniel B. Schwartz*
3:00			

SCHEDULE—TUESDAY, JUNE 29

9:00	Constructing Hidden Variables in Bayesian Networks via Conceptual Clustering—*Dennis Connolly*		
9:30	Learning Symbolic Rules Using Artificial Neural Networks—*Mark W. Craven, Jude Shavlik*		
10:00	Explanation Based Learning: A Comparison of Symbolic and Neural Network Approaches —*Tom M. Mitchell, Sebastian B. Thrun*		
10:30	Break		
11:00	Invited Talk: David Sandler, ThermoTrex		
12:00	Lunch		
1:30	Business Meeting		
2:00	Concept Sharing: A Means to Improve Multi-Concept Learning— *Piew Datta, Dennis Kibler*	Combinatorial Optimization in Inductive Concept Learning—*Dunja Mladenic*	Compiling Bayesian Networks into Neural Networks—*Eddie Schwalb*
2:30	Multitask Learning: A Knowledge-Based Source of Inductive Bias—*Richard A. Caruana*	The Evolution of Genetic Algorithms —*Shumeet Baluja*	Synthesis of Abstraction Hierarchies for Constraint Satisfaction by Clustering Approximately Equivalent Objects —*Thomas Ellman*
3:00	Online Learning with Random Representations —*Richard S. Sutton, Steve Whitehead*	Genetic Programming for Learning of Target Discrimination Functions—*Walter Alden Tackett*	GALOIS: An Order-Theoretic Approach to Conceptual Clustering—*Claudio Carpineto, Giovanni Romano*
3:30	Break		
4:00	Invited Talk: Pat Langley, Siemens		
5:00			
6:00	Dinner		

The Evolution of Genetic Algorithms:
Towards Massive Parallelism

Shumeet Baluja
Computer Science Department
Carnegie Mellon University
Pittsburgh, PA 15213
baluja@cs.cmu.edu

Abstract

One of the issues in creating any search technique is balancing the need for diverse exploration with the desire for efficient focusing. This paper explores a genetic algorithm (GA) architecture which is more resilient to local optima than other recently introduced GA models, and which provides the ability to focus search quickly. The GA uses a fine-grain parallel architecture to simulate evolution more closely than previous models. In order to motivate the need for fine-grain parallelism, this paper will provide an overview of the two preceding phases of development: the traditional genetic algorithm, and the coarse-grain parallel GA. A test set of 15 problems is used to compare the effectiveness of a fine-grain parallel GA with that of a coarse-grain parallel GA.

1 INTRODUCTION

The effectiveness of heuristic techniques used in machine learning, search, and function optimization, resides in the heuristic's ability to balance the need for a diverse set of sampling points with the ability to focus search quickly upon potential solutions. Genetic algorithms (GAs) are general purpose optimization tools designed to search irregular, poorly characterized search spaces. GAs are based upon the ideas of natural selection and genetic recombination. GAs combine the principles of survival of the fittest with a randomized information exchange. Although the information exchange is randomized, GAs are far different than simple random walks, having the ability to recognize trends toward optimal solutions, and to exploit such information by guiding the search toward them.

Genetic algorithms have evolved through three phases, their development motivated by the goal of balancing exploration with focusing. Each of these phases will be individually discussed in the next three sections. The first phase presented the traditional genetic algorithm. A single population of potential solutions is evolved through a series of generations. The second phase introduced the concept of parallel subpopulations. Only a limited amount of swapping of potential solutions is allowed between subpopulations. Each subpopulation evolves independently, with swapping at infrequent intervals. This has been termed coarse-grain parallelism, or the "island" model. The third phase, an extension of the second, introduced fine-grain parallelism. The GAs in this category differ from the previous by relaxing the boundaries between subpopulations. Swapping between subpopulations occurs frequently, and significantly contributes to the effectiveness of this form of genetic algorithm. This phase also differs from the previous two by evolving numerous small subpopulations; in the previous two phases, only a few large subpopulations are evolved.

2 TRADITIONAL GAs

Traditional genetic algorithms maintain a single population of potential solutions for the objective function being optimized. Although a large portion of GA research has been conducted with potential solutions encoded in binary notation, any encoding scheme can be used. The initial group of potential solutions is randomly selected. These potential solutions, termed "chromosomes", are allowed to evolve over a number of generations. At every generation, the fitness of each potential solution in terms of the objective function is calculated, and pairs of solutions are recombined to create the subsequent generation. Recombination is the method by which the parent chromosomes of the current generation donate parts of their potential solutions to the "children" chromosomes which appear in the subsequent generation. The probability that a solution will participate in this recombination increases with its fitness. Thus, although "good" chromosomes are more likely to be chosen for recombination, they are not guaranteed to be chosen. Further, the "children" chromosomes produced are not necessarily better than their parents. Nevertheless, because of the selective pressure applied through a number of generations, the overall trend is toward better chromosomes.

In order to perform expansive search, genetic diversity must be maintained. When diversity is lost, it is possible for the GA to settle into a local optimum. There are two fundamental mechanisms which the traditional GA uses to maintain diversity. The first, mentioned above, is a probabilistic scheme of selecting chromosomes for recombination. This insures that schemata, or common recurring patterns, other than those represented in the best chromosomes, appear in subsequent generations. Exclusively recombining good chromosomes will quickly converge the population without extensive exploration, thereby increasing the possibility of settling into a local optimum. The second mechanism, mutation, is a random change. For example, in binary encoded chromosomes, it is usually a random bit flip. In the traditional GA, the mutation rate is kept at a very small constant.

This algorithm is typically allowed to continue for an arbitrary number of generations. Upon completion, the best chromosome in the final population, or the best chromosome ever found, is returned.

Unlike the majority of other optimization heuristics, genetic algorithms do not work from a single point in the search space. Methods which only use a single point are susceptible to local optima. GAs continually maintain a population of points from which the search space is explored. This aids in searching multidimensional spaces, in which many variables must be optimized, and in locating global optima.

3 COARSE-GRAIN PARALLEL GAs

A coarse-grain parallel genetic algorithm (cgpGA) is based upon the theory of punctuated equilibria. In the paper *Distributed Genetic Algorithms for the Floor Plan Design Problem*, Cohoon et. al. describe the theory [Cohoon, 1988]:

> Punctuated Equilibria is based upon two principles: allopatric speciation and stasis. Allopatric speciation involves the rapid evolution of new species after a small set of members of species, peripheral isolates, becomes segregated into a new environment. Stasis, or stability, of a species, is simply the notion of lack of change. It implies that after equilibria is reached in an environment, there is very little drift away from the genetic composition of species. Ideally, a species would persist until its environment changes (or the species would drift very little). Punctuated Equilibria stresses that a powerful method for generating new species is to thrust an old species into a new environment, where change is beneficial and rewarded. For this reason we should expect a genetic algorithm approach based upon punctuated equilibria to perform better than the typical single environment scheme.

By implication, after some period of evolution, a large portion of the chromosomes in a single population will represent very similar schema. The children chromosomes produced thereafter will be similar to each other and to their parents, thereby rendering recombination operators largely ineffective for further search space exploration. One method of resolving this problem is to partition a single large population into separate subpopulations, each evolving its chromosomes independently from others. The fitness used to determine the probability of selection for recombination is measured relative only to the other members within the subpopulation. Independent evolutions, in separate subpopulations, should yield closely competitive, yet possibly unique results. In the context of a single subpopulation, in order to continue evolution after convergence has started, members of species from outside subpopulations can periodically be introduced. To ensure thorough mixing of chromosomes throughout the population, the swapping does not always occur between the same subpopulations.

Although the sudden injection of new material is an important aspect of these simulations, it is not always effective. It is possible that the subpopulation into which new material is introduced is entirely settled into an equilibrium state. If this is the case, new information may not be incorporated because of its incompatibility with the existing information.

Despite the problems associated with the sudden introduction of new material, parallel subpopulations have proven their effectiveness in two areas. The first is, as mentioned above, to preserve diversity and to ensure perpetual novelty in the population's "gene pool". Through the use of parallel subpopulations, GAs have been able to solve problems which could not be solved in a reasonable amount of time by single population GAs [Whitley & Starkweather, 1990] [Liepins & Baluja, 1991] [Muhlenbien, 1989]. The second use of the subpopulation structure is to emphasize various characteristics in the chromosome. For example, in multi-objective functions, the evaluations in each subpopulation can be used to emphasize different objectives. When members of separate subpopulations are mixed, the genetic information may be combined to reveal chromosomes which are strong with respect to more than a single objective. An exploration of multi-objective function optimization with parallel subpopulations can be found in [Husbands, 1991]. An interesting method of multi-objective optimization using only a single population with multiple fitness measures can be found in [Schaffer & Grefenstette, 1985].

4 FINE-GRAIN PARALLEL GAs

4.1 OVERVIEW & MOTIVATION

Unlike cgpGAs, the fine-grain parallel genetic algorithms (fgpGAs) examined here evolve numerous small, constantly interacting subpopulations. Variants of fgpGAs have been explored by [Davidor, 1991], [Spiessens and Manderick, 1991], [Muhlenbein, 1989] and [Schleuter, 1990]. One way in which to view the modified form of parallelism in fgpGAs is to conceptualize the populations as overlapping, as shown in Figure 1.

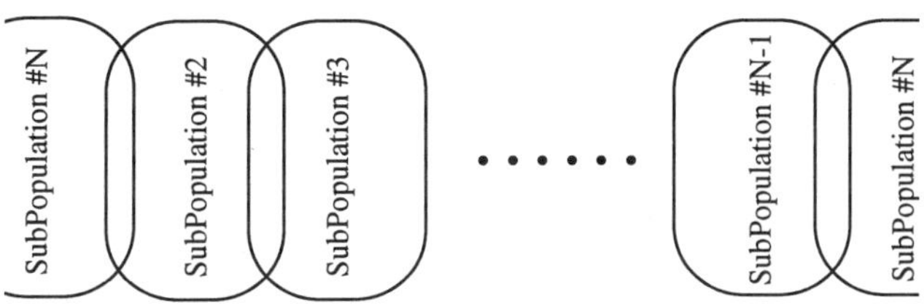

Figure 1: Overlapping Populations in a Fine Grain Parallel Genetic Algorithm.

The fine-grain population architecture offers three benefits which the other two models do not. First, the transfer of genetic information from one population to another is inherent in the architecture. In the traditional GA, there is no flow of information because there is only one population. In the cgpGA, the information is shared between subpopulations by swapping potential solutions at infrequent intervals. As pointed out earlier, the effectiveness of sudden infrequent swapping between subpopulations is limited because each subpopulation has the potential to evolve to incompatible local optima. The assimilation of genetic information across subpopulations is easier in the fine-grain parallel architecture as the exchange of information between subpopulations is continuous. A subpopulation cannot exist in a state of equilibrium until each subpopulation reaches equilibrium.

Second, the fine-grain model provides a more accurate representation of evolution. Instead of maintaining a large population from which any two chromosomes may recombine, recombination must be between two chromosomes from within the same neighborhood. This feature reveals a similarity to biological natural selection, in which a population is typically composed of relatively independent subpopulations which interact. Although the similarity with natural selection may not be important directly within the context GAs are used, the constant interaction can significantly help subpopulations escape from local minima.

The third benefit is a gain of speed. In the traditional genetic algorithm each potential solution must be assigned a fitness value with respect to all other potential solutions within the current population. This value is used to determine probabilistically which chromosomes will be chosen for recombination. Global ranking slows the GA considerably. Although the cgpGA does not require a global ranking of each potential solution, it requires a ranking within each individual subpopulation. In the fine-grain parallel model, the ranking required is local; ranking is relative to the other chromosomes within the neighborhood. As the population and neighborhood size can be kept small, the time required to perform local ranking is not as severe as in the two earlier models.

The fine-grain parallel organization and the cgpGA organization share the advantages of the model presented in the theory of punctuated equilibria: subpopulations which are a large distance apart will evolve comparatively unique chromosomes in a manner similar to simple, disjoint, parallel subpopulations. However, the fgpGA's higher connectivity allows all subpopulations within a close proximity to each other to have a greater influence on each other than those a large distance apart. As with cgpGAs, the larger the number of subpopulations, the greater the potential diversity in individual evolutions.

The danger of reaching a suboptimal state in fine-grain parallel genetic algorithms can be greater than that in cgpGAs for two reasons. First, the fgpGA structure employs a greater degree of swapping between subpopulations than the cgpGA's. Therefore, strong local optima can quickly spread throughout the entire population. Second, because there are significantly fewer chromosomes per subpopulation in the fgpGA model than in the cgpGA model, the diversity of information within subpopulations is more limited. In order to address this problem, fgpGAs rely upon the size of the group of genetic algorithms and the controlled degree of overlap to allow unique evolutions in different portions of the total population.

One question which must be answered under the fgpGA model is the extent and nature of overlap between subpopulations [Muhlenbein, 1989] [Schleuter, 1990] [Baluja, 1992]. If the overlap spans many subpopulations, good chromosomes could rapidly flow throughout the GA structure. However, with a fast flow, the advantages of punctuated equilibria may be lost, and niche formation may be hindered. Many different issues regarding topology need to be addressed, such as whether the subpopulations should be connected in a linear manner or whether the overlapping subpopulations should be virtual, almost simulating neural network connections. Furthermore, should the connections between subpopulations be fixed, or time-varying? These topics are among those to be addressed by future research within this area.

4.2 fgpGA: POPULATION ARCHITECTURE

As described in the previous section, there are many possible population topologies. The fgpGA examined throughout the remainder of this paper uses a two dimensional toroidal array of subpopulations. See Figure 2. Each subpopulation evolves only 2 chromosomes per generation. The 2 parent chromosomes are chosen from a group of 10 chromosomes. The group of 10 is comprised of 1 chromosome from each of the 8 surrounding neighbors and the 2 chromosomes which were evolved in the previous generation. The chromosome selected from a neighbor is chosen randomly from the 2 evolved at the neighbor. The fitness of each chromosome is determined relative to the other chromosomes in the group of 10. Two chromosomes from this set of 10 are probabilistically chosen for recombination based upon their fitness; the other 8 are discarded. In the subsequent generation, the 2 "children" chromosomes produced, through crossover and mutation (described in the next section) of the selected parents, are available for recombination, either within the population in which they are located, or by its neighbors.

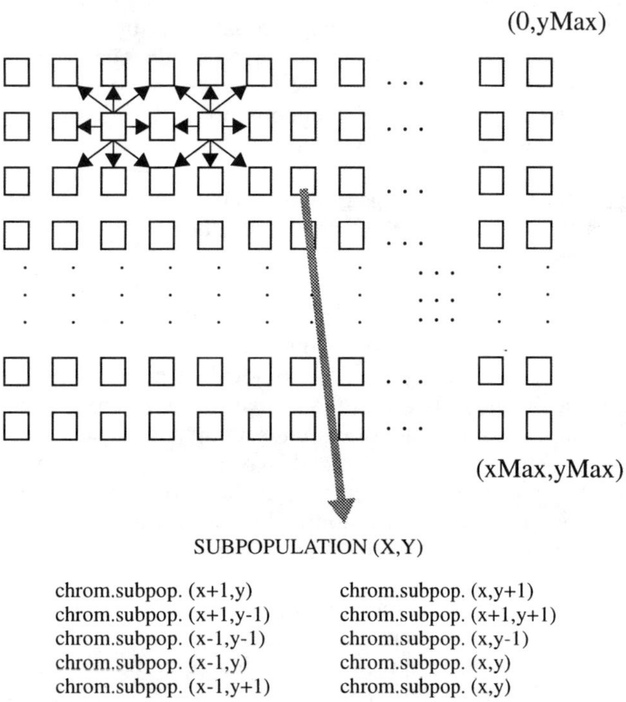

Figure 2: Each subpopulation contributes one of its two chromosomes to each of its 8 nearest neighbors. The composition of subpopulation (x,y) is shown. Both of the chromosomes evolved at population(x,y) are included. The subpopulations form a toroid.

4.3 fgpGA: IMPLEMENTATION SPECIFICS

This section describes the recombination, mutation, and elitist selection mechanisms used. The recombination operator used for testing this algorithm is a standard two point crossover, in which a randomly chosen subsection of one parent chromosome is swapped with the corresponding subsection of the second parent chromosome. This is a general crossover operator that has been shown to be effective in GA literature. For a discussion of the merits and drawbacks of two point crossover, the reader is referred to [DeJong, 1990] [Syswerda, 1990]. Mutation is implemented as a simple random bit flip which occurs in the "children" chromosomes after the crossover has taken place with the parents, and before the chromosome is evaluated. The mutation rate is kept at a constant 1%.

Elitist selection is a commonly employed tool to ensure that the progress made by a GA is not lost due to random chance. Because a GA's selection of parent chromosomes is probabilistic, it is not guaranteed that the best chromosome in a particular generation will survive to the subsequent generation. It is also possible that if the chromosome is selected for recombination, some of the good genetic material may not survive through the crossover and mutation operators. A modest form of elitist selection is used to address this problem. Elitist selection carries the best chromosome, from the population of 10 candidates for recombination, from generation **g** to **g+1**. This does not imply that the best chromosome will be selected for recombination; rather, it means that the chromosome will be in the population of 10 which are candidates for recombination. Since the population size is limited to 10, the best chromosome from the previous generation replaces the chromosome with the lowest relative fitness in the current generation. Although this aids in preventing repetitive search, it may be detrimental when the GA is caught in a local optima, as elitist selection may preserve the local optima in the population's candidates for recombination.

5 FINE VS. COARSE-GRAIN PARALLELISM

The remainder of this paper is devoted to comparing fine-grain and coarse-grain parallel GAs. This paper does not compare results with traditional GAs since a large amount of work has already been conducted towards quantifying the differences in structure and performance between cgpGAs and traditional GAs [Pettey et. al. 1987] [Cohoon et. al. 1988] [Whitley & Starkweather, 1990] [Tanese, 1987].

5.1 ALGORITHMS TESTED

Two GAs were tested, the fgpGA described in the previous section and the cgpGA described below. The cgpGA was very loosely based upon the cgpGA described in [Whitley & Starkweather, 1990]. Two point crossover and a 1% mutation rate were used. Like the fgpGA described above, the cgpGA employed modest elitist selection, in which the single best chromosome from each generation was carried to the subsequent generation. The best chromosome replaced the worst chromosome in the subsequent generation. Forty subpopulations were evolved. Each subpopulation contained 100 chromosomes, for a total of 4000 chromosomes evaluated simultaneously.

The cgpGA implemented a small amount of communication between the subpopulations. Assuming a circular ordering of subpopulations, after every 100 generations, the best chromosome from each subpopulation migrated to a subpopulation **e** subpopulations away, where **e** is defined to be the number of generations divided by 100 that have passed. Because the population was a set size, the migrating chromosome replaced the worst chromosome in the target subpopulation.

Although the parameters for both the cgpGA and the fgpGA were not optimized for any single problem, they were chosen to work satisfactorily on a variety of different problems. When comparing results, it should be considered that the fgpGA evaluated 8192 chromosomes per generation, and the cgpGA evaluated 4000. The discrepancies in the number of evaluations per generation can be attributed to the mapping of the algorithm onto the hardware architecture on which these tests were attempted.

5.2 TEST PROBLEMS

This section presents the test problems which are used to compare the effectiveness of fine and coarse-grain parallel genetic algorithms. Fifteen test problems were attempted: DeJong's five function test suite, three subset-sum problems, two orderings of fully and partially deceptive order 4 problems, and three versions of all-ones problems.

5.2.1 DeJong's Test Suite

DeJong's test suite is comprised of five minimization problems commonly used to test the effectiveness of GAs [DeJong, 1975]. The test suite was designed to incorporate functions with the following characteristics: continuous/discontinuous, convex/nonconvex, unimodal/multimodal, quadratic/nonquadratic, low dimensionality/high dimensionality, and deterministic/stochastic [Goldberg, 1989]. The functions were encoded in standard binary notation.

5.2.2 Subset-Sum

The problems can be stated as follows: given S elements, each of a possibly unique weight, is there a subset of S that adds up exactly to an arbitrary number, T. The subset sum problems are NP-Complete. This problem was implemented as a 120 bit chromosome. Each bit represented a unique object, with weight randomly assigned between 1 & 200. The weight T was selected to be either 1/4, 1/20, or 1/40 of the sum of the weights of the objects. The only addition to the problem was that the sum of the weights was guaranteed to be divisible by 4, 20 & 40, respectively.

5.2.3 Fully and Partially Deceptive Order 4

The fully deceptive problem is a 40 bit maximization problem. The problem was defined in Whitley & Starkweather's paper GENITOR II [Whitley & Starkweather, 1990]. The problem is comprised of 10 subproblems, each 4 bits long. The subproblems use the lookup table shown in Table 1. The partially deceptive problem uses the same evaluations, with the exceptions of the evaluations corresponding to 1111 and 0101, which are reversed.

Table 1: Order 4 Fully Deceptive Problem

Chrom.	Eval.	Chrom.	Eval.
1111	30	**0110**	14
0000	28	**1001**	12
0001	26	**1010**	10
0010	24	**1100**	08
0100	22	**1110**	06
1000	20	**1101**	04
0011	18	**1011**	02
0101	16	**0111**	00

Both the fully deceptive and partially deceptive problems were attempted using two orderings of bits. The first encoding is block encoding; the placement of the 4 bits which comprise a subproblem are located next to each other. The second encoding is interleaved; the bits which comprise each subproblem are uniformly spread throughout the chromosome. With the use of two point crossover, the first encoding is much easier for the GA to solve than the second. The encodings are shown in Figure 3.

Block Encoding: aaaabbbbccccddddeeeeffffgggghhhhiiiijjjj

Interleaved: abcdefghijabcdefghijabcdefghijabcdefghij

Figure 3: Two encodings of the order 4 deceptive problem & partially deceptive problems.

5.2.4 Three "All-Ones" Problems

Three versions of the all-ones problem were tried [Syswerda, 1990]. The first version was the straight all-ones problem. The objective of this problem is to find the chromosome which contains a 1 in each bit position.

The second version of the all-ones problem contains bits which are meaningless. This problem was encoded as a 180 bit problem, but only the first 120 bits were counted toward the evaluation.

The third all-ones problem is the contiguous bits problem. In evaluating the chromosome, points are only given for 1s which also have at least one other neighbor which has a value of 1. If there exists a 1 which has zeros as its two neighbors, no points are given for the bit.

5.3 RESULTS & DISCUSSION

The results are shown for the 15 test problems in Table 2. They are the average of 10 runs per problem for each algorithm. Each run was started with a different randomly chosen initial population of chromosomes. The maximum number of allowed generations for the cgpGA is 3000; after 3000 the attempt is considered a failure. The maximum number of generations before failure for the fgpGA is 1400.

For many problems, especially the all-ones problem, on which the cgpGA did comparatively poorly, cgpGAs can do significantly better if the population size, mutation rate, and swap interval parameters are tuned for the problem. For example, because the all-ones problem is relatively "easy" for the GA to solve, it can be solved very efficiently using a population size of 10 rather than 100. However, to measure the ability of the algorithms to perform on a variety of problems without parameter tuning, the parameters were held constant throughout all of the test runs.

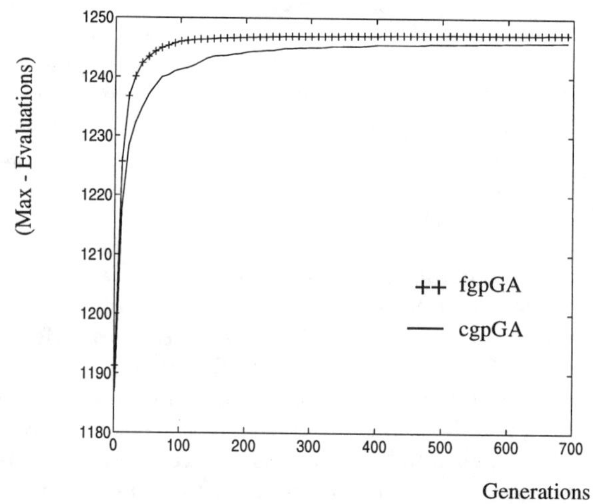

Figure 4: Average evaluations for 10 runs of the cgpGA and fgpGA on DeJong's F4. Due to memory restrictions, the cgpGA was run with 80 subpopulations with 50 chromosomes per population. F4 is shown graphically to aid in quantifying performance in the presence of the random gaussian factor [DeJong, 1975], [Ingber, 1992]. Note that generations 200-700 yield only very small improvements. (Samples taken at every 10 generations.)

Table 2: Results for the 15 test problems. Each entry represents the average number of generations before the optimal solution was found. The fgpGA evaluated 8192 chromosomes per generation, the cgpGA 4000.

Test Function	Size (Bits)	fgpGA	cgpGA 40 subpop.
DeJong Function #1	30	29.8	79.0
DeJong Function #2	24	38.6	111.8
DeJong Function #3*	50	19.5	64.5
DeJong Function #4	240	See Figure 4	
DeJong Function #5**	34	18.0	18.0
Subset Sum (1/4)	120	14.0	35.6
Subset Sum (1/20)	120	55.0	344.5
Subset Sum (1/40)	120	76.8	629.0
Partially Deceptive (A)	40	32.0	95.1
Partially Deceptive (B)	40	53.0	252.5
Fully Deceptive (A)	40	57.5	305.9
Fully Deceptive (B)	40	742.5	1634.7
All-Ones	120	90.5	648.2
Sparse All-Ones***	180	94.8	342.0
Contiguous All-Ones	120	90.8	609.1

* The stopping criterion for DeJong's F3 was an evaluation of -30.

** The stopping criterion for DeJong's F5 was an evaluation of 0.998004.

*** Due to memory restrictions, this problem was attempted with 90 significant bits, and 30 extra bits (cgpGA only). The fgpGA was attempted with 120 significant bits and 60 extra.

One of the reasons the fgpGA performed better than the cgpGA is the ability of good chromosomes to spread rapidly through the population. A large portion of the population has access to the best chromosome very shortly after it is found. A sample run, shown in Figure 5, displays the number of populations which "have seen" the best chromosome found in each generation. The term "has seen" does not imply that the populations have selected the chromosome for recombination, rather that the chromosome is a candidate for selection. The sudden drops of the number of populations, in Figure 5, represent generations in which a better chromosome is found.

The fgpGA implementation allows a good chromosome to be accessed immediately by the 8 surrounding subpopulations. In order for more than the original 9 populations to incorporate the chromosome, it must again be selected for recombination. Assuming that it is selected, valuable schemata must not be destroyed by crossover or mutation operators. Although the populations which surround the original 9 will incorporate the resultant chromosomes into their population, for it to spread further, they must also select them for recombination based upon their evaluation, which may not be as good as their parents. Further, if the crossover and mutation operations have destroyed valuable schemata, the children produced may not be preserved by elitist selection. If the important schemata are a small part of the total chromosome, the chances of the chromosomes spreading throughout the population with the schemata intact is much greater, since in this case,

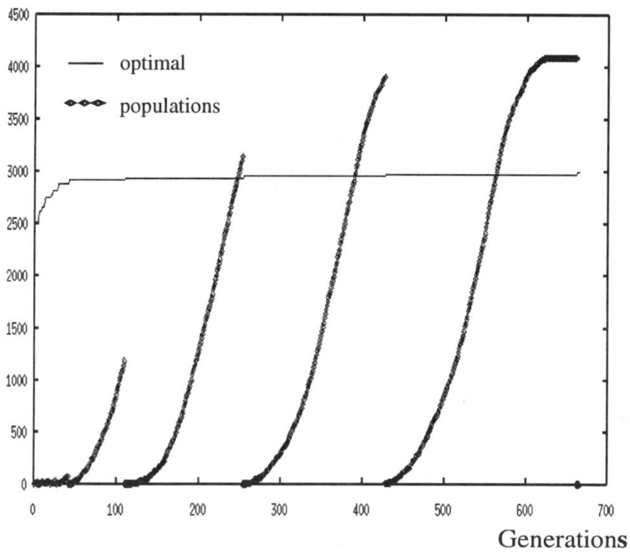

Figure 5: The Number of populations which contain the best chromosome using the fgpGA to optimize the order 4 fully deceptive problem, interleaved. Also plotted is the best value * 10, for comparison. The sudden drops in the number of populations correspond to a new best solution found in one of the populations.

crossover and mutation operators have a smaller chance of destroying valuable schemata.

The choice of how subpopulations should overlap plays a significant role in how fast the chromosomes spread through the subpopulations. For certain classes of problems, it may be important to ensure that the flow of chromosomes is slow, in order to allow for extremely different evaluations in different portions of the model. However, in other applications, in which the search space is not deceptive and does not contain many local minima, a fast flow may yield good answers quickly, as good chromosomes can rapidly dominate the "gene pool".

6 SUMMARY & FUTURE DIRECTIONS

Preliminary results on fifteen test problems have shown the fgpGA to be able to solve problems more efficiently than a cgpGA. To evaluate fine-grain parallelism further, both harder test problems and different population topologies should be explored.

One of the difficulties inherent in comparing parallel genetic algorithms with each other, and with traditional GAs, is choosing the best criteria. Although the number of evaluations is commonly used, parallel evolutions show extensive overlap in the evaluations performed. For problems which are "easy" for the GA to solve, parallel subpopulations may perform too broad a search, as the search performed by a traditional, single population GA may be enough. However, on harder problems, it often happens that parallel populations find solutions both more often and faster than traditional GAs. Another measure, generations to find optimal solutions, has a bias in favor of parallelism because more chromosomes are evaluated per generation. Another candidate criterion is cpu-speed; however, implementations of different algorithms may use the same hardware with varying degrees of effectiveness. In this paper, both evaluations and generations were presented. Although the results were in favor of the fgpGA, the parameters in the cgpGA and the fgpGA were not tuned per problem. As stated earlier, it is suspected that with a little tuning, both GAs could improve performance.

Perhaps the most interesting topic for future research is the need to design subpopulation topologies which maximally exploit the parallelism inherent in these GAs. Two interesting structures to examine in the future would be one in which each population is only connected to 1 of its nearest neighbors and a second in which the connections are made randomly, perhaps with a set maximum reaching distance.

One of the important applications of parallel genetic algorithms, which was not explored here, is the use of sets of populations to optimize different objectives in multi-objective functions. For this type of problem, each subpopulation evolves under the pressures of individual subgoals of the complete problem. As stated in [Husbands, 1991] "...the solution to a complex problem is allowed to emerge from the simultaneous solution of a number of simpler, related sub-problems. Using this variation of divide and conquer, the inherent parallelism in a problem is brought out and thoroughly exploited." This method is directly applicable to the fgpGA described here: individual populations can work towards individual sub-goals. It will be interesting to determine the role that the position of sub-goal assignment to individual populations has on the overall effectiveness of the GA.

Acknowledgments

I would like to thank Dean Pomerleau, Chuck Thorpe, Stephen Smith, Dayne Freitag, and Todd Jochem for their helpful comments and suggestions throughout the development of this paper.

This research was partly sponsored by Defense Advanced Research Projects Agency, under contracts "Perception for Outdoor Navigation" (contract number DACA76-89-C-0014, monitored by the US Army Topographic Engineering Center) and "Unmanned Ground Vehicle System" (contract number DAAE07-90-C-R059, monitored by TACOM). It was also partially sponsored by the National Science Foundation, under NSF Contract BCS-9120655, titled "Annotated Maps for Autonomous Underwater Vehicles", and the NSF grant titled "Massively Parallel Real-Time Computer Vision". The views and conclusions contained in this document are those of the author and should not be interpreted as representing the official policies, either expressed or implied, of the Defense Advanced Research Projects Agency, the National Science Foundation, or the U.S. Government.

References

Baluja, S. (1992) A Massively Distributed Parallel Genetic Algorithm. CMU-CS-92-196R. School of Computer Science, Carnegie Mellon University.

Caruana, R. and J. Schaffer (1988) Representation and Hidden Bias: Gray Vs. Binary Coding for Genetic Algorithms. *Proceedings of the 5th International Conference on Machine Learning*. Morgan Kaufmann. Los Altos. CA. June 1988 152-161

Cobb, H. (1990) An Investigation Into the Use of Hypermutation as an Adaptive Operator in Genetic Algorithms Having continuous, Time Dependent Nonstationary Environments. NCARAI Library. AIC-90-001.

Cohoon, J.P, S.U. Hedge, W.N. Martin & D. Richards (1988), Distributed Genetic Algorithms for the Floor Plan Design Problem. Technical Report TR-88-12. School of Engineering and Applied Science, Computer Science Department, University of Virginia.

Davidor, Y (1991) A Naturally Occurring Niche & Species Phenomenon: The Model and First Results. *Proceedings of the Fourth International Conference on Genetic Algorithms.* Morgan Kaufmann, San Mateo, CA.

DeJong, K.A. (1975) *An Analysis of the Behavior of a Class of Genetic Adaptive Systems.* (Doctoral dissertation, University of Michigan). Dissertation Abstracts International 36-10, 5140B.

DeJong, K.A. and W. Spears (1990) An Analysis of Multi-Point Crossover. NCARAI Library. AIC-90-014.

Eshelman, L. (1990). The CHC Adaptive Search Algorithm: How to have safe search when engaging in nontraditional genetic recombination. *Foundations of Genetic Algorithms*, Bloomington, IN.

Goldberg, D.E. (1989) *Genetic Algorithms in Search, Optimization, and Machine Learning*. Addison-Wesley.

Husbands, P., F. Mill & S.Warrington (1991), Genetic Algorithms, Production Plan Optimisation and Scheduling. *Parallel Problem Solving from Nature*, H.P. Schwefel & R. Manner Eds. Springer Verlag, Berlin.

Ingber, L and B. Rosen (1992) Genetic Algorithms and Very Fast Simulated Reannealing: A comparison. To be published in *Mathematical and Computer Modelling.*

Liepins, G.E. and S. Baluja (1991) apGA: an Adaptive Parallel Genetic Algorithm. *Computer Science and Operations Research, New Developments in Their Interfaces.* Balci, Sharda & Zenios eds. Pergamon Press.

Liepins, G. E. and M. D. Vose (1990). Representational Issues in Genetic Optimization, *Journal Expt. Theor. Artificial Intelligence.*, 2, 101-115

Muhlenbein, H (1989) Parallel Genetic Algorithms, Population Genetics and Combinatorial Optimization. *Proceedings of the Third International Conference on Genetic Algorithms.* Morgan Kaufmann. San Mateo, CA.

Petty, C, M. Leuze, J. Grefenstette (1987) A Parallel Genetic Algorithm, *Proceedings of the Second International Conference on Genetic Algorithms.* Lawrence Erlbaum Associates. N.J.

Schaffer, J.D. and J.J. Grefenstette (1985) Multi-Objective Learning Via Genetic Algorithms, *Proceedings of Ninth International Joint Conference on Artificial Intelligence.*

Schaffer, J.D., R.A. Caruana, L.J. Eshelman, and R. Das (1989). A Study of Control Parameters Affecting Online Performance of Genetic Algorithms for Function Optimization, *Proceedings of the Third International Conference on Genetic Algorithms.* Morgan Kaufmann, San Mateo, CA.

Schleuter, M.G. (1990), Explicit Parallelism of Genetic Algorithms through Population Structures. *Parallel Problem Solving from Nature*, H.P. Schwefel & R. Manner Eds. Springer Verlag, Berlin.

Spiessens, P. and B. Manderick (1991), A Massively Parallel Genetic Algorithm: Implementation and First Results. *Proceedings of the Fourth International Conference on Genetic Algorithms.* Morgan Kaufmann, San Mateo, CA.

Syswerda, G. (1989) Uniform Crossover in Genetic Algorithms, *Proceedings of the Third International Conference on Genetic Algorithms.* Morgan Kaufmann. San Mateo, CA.

Tanese, R. (1987) A Parallel Genetic Algorithm for a Hypercube. *Proceedings of the Second International Conference on Genetic Algorithms.* Lawrence Erlbaum Associates. N.J.

Whitley, D. and T. Starkweather (1990). GENITOR II: a Distributed Genetic Algorithm, *Journal Expt. Theor. Artificial Intelligence*, 2, 189-214.

ÉLÉNA : A BOTTOM-UP LEARNING METHOD

Pierre Brézellec
Laboratoire d'Informatique Université Paris Nord
CNRS URA 1507
Avenue J-B Clément 93430 Villetaneuse
France
brezel@lipn.univ-paris13.fr
&
Atelier de Bio-Informatique Institut Curie
section Physique-Chimie,
11, rue Pierre et Marie Curie 75005 Paris .

Henry Soldano
Laboratoire d'Informatique Université Paris Nord
CNRS URA 1507
Avenue J-B Clément 93430 Villetaneuse
France
soldano@lipn.univ-paris13.fr
&
Atelier de Bio-Informatique Institut Curie
section Physique-Chimie,
11, rue Pierre et Marie Curie 75005 Paris.

ABSTRACT

This paper presents a description and an experimental evaluation of ÉLÉNA, a learning system which induces characteristic and discriminant concept descriptions from positive instances, negative instances, and a background knowledge theory. The resulting concept description is expressed as a disjunction of conjunctive terms in a propositional language. Each conjunctive term is the maximal specific generalisation of a subset of the positive instances. ÉLÉNA works in three steps. The first step consists in an exhaustive use of the theory in order to extend the instances representation. Then the learning component performs a bottom-up beam search through the concept description space. During the final step, the theory is used again in order to reduce each conjunctive term of the resulting formula to a minimal representation. Basically, ÉLÉNA has the same features as our previous system SAMIA but its learning component is different. The paper reports the results of several experiments and compares the performance of ÉLÉNA with two other learning methods, namely ID and CN. Accuracies on test instances and concept description sizes are compared. The experiments indicate that ÉLÉNA's classification accuracy is roughly equivalent to the two previous systems. Morever, as the results of the learning algorithms can be expressed as a set of rules, one can notice that the number of rules of ÉLÉNA's concept descriptions is lower than both ID's and CN's one.

INTRODUCTION

During the past few years various systems have been proposed to perform concept learning from examples (CN2 (Clark 1989), ID3 (Quinlan 1986), AQ (Zhang 1989)). These systems perform a partial exploration of the concept space to be searched, using various heuristics and some statistical criteria (as in CN2 and ID3), or truncation and flexible matching (as in AQ). The concept representations used are either decision trees (ID3), decision lists (CN2) or disjunctive formulas (AQ). The search is performed by a top-down generate and test procedure using specialisation operators[1]. For the class of learning problems addressed by these systems, little attention has been paid to bottom-up strategies which were considered as inefficient. The system we propose here uses a bottom-up strategy. It is devoted to concept acquisition from positive and negative instances. It describes instances as conjunctions of literals and uses a theory composed of a set of rules. The theory is used during a preprocessing step in order to extend the description of instances. During the learning step, ÉLÉNA searches for a disjunctive formula, each conjunctive term of which is a maximal specific generalisation of positive instances. A postprocessing step is then performed in order to obtain minimal representations of the conjunctive terms of the formula. This formula is a characteristic and discriminant representation of the concept and not only a discriminant one as in top-down methods above-mentioned.

Section 1 presents knowledge representation, properties of the concept representation space, the preprocessing and postprocessing steps, and some issues about the learning bias. Section 2 is devoted to the learning component of ÉLÉNA. Section 3 presents experiments in which ÉLÉNA is compared to CN and ID. Section 4 reviews related work and presents the differences between the

[1] It should be noticed that AQ uses a data-driven mixed strategy.

learning components of SAMIA (Brézellec 1993) and ÉLÉNA. The paper ends with a summary and outline of our projects.

1 PRESENTATION OF THE SYSTEM

1.1 DESCRIPTION OF THE LEARNING MECHANISM

Let A be the set of atoms of a given propositional language. A is divided into a set P of primitive atoms and a set S of non primitive atoms. Moreover a theory T is given expressed as an unordered set of rules. The left part of each rule is a conjunction of literals of A, and the right part (i.e., the conclusion) is a literal of A. As usual, an instance is defined by the assignation of the values True or False to every atom of A. However each instance is initially described as the conjunction of the corresponding literals of P. The first step of the overall learning mechanism consists of a saturation of every instance with respect to the theory T. After the preprocessing step, each instance is represented as the conjunction of the positive literals, where a positive literal is a primitive or a non primitive atom whose value is True. Then, the second step consists in searching for a concept representation f from a set E_p of positive instances and a set E_n of negative instances. Each element of the search space is a disjunction of conjunctive terms. However only particular conjunctive terms, hereafter denoted as prototypes, are considered. Such terms are maximal specific generalisations of subsets of the set E_p of positive instances. In our framework prototypes are recursively defined by an instance or the result of the maximal specific generalisation (msg for short) of two prototypes using an intersection operator msg. Let e_1 and e_2 be two prototypes, then msg(e_1,e_2) is defined as the conjunction of positive literals[2] belonging to both e_1 and e_2. The justification of the restriction of conjunctive terms to maximal specific generalisations relies on the following property :

Proposition 1: For any term t (i.e., any conjunction of positive literals of A), there exists a prototype p such that p covers[3] exactly the positive instances covered by t and a subset of the negatives instances covered by t.
The prototype p is simply the maximal specific generalisation of the positive instances covered by t, and thus is more specific or equal than t. This prototype space, together with the general-to-specific partial ordering, defines a "Galois lattice" (E_p, A) (i.e., an algebraic structure (Ganter 1986)). Another useful property of the prototypes is related to the logical dependencies between atoms. Such relations may be either explicit ones (i.e., represented inside the theory T) or implicit ones.

Proposition 2 : Let a_1 ,..., a_k be atoms of A, and assume that the following implication '$a_1 \wedge ... \wedge a_{k-1}$ ---> a_k' holds for a subset E of the positive instances. Then if a prototype, resulting from the maximal specific generalisation of a subset of E contains a_1 ,..., a_{k-1}, it contains a_k.
Notice that if E = E_p, then a_k belongs to any prototype containing a_1 ,..., a_{k-1}. As a consequence of the last proposition, we have the following corollary :

Corollary : Let us consider a rule of T containing only positive literals. If the left part of this rule belongs to a given prototype, then its conclusion also belongs to it.
The property described by the last corollary is the basis of the last step of the learning mechanism. Let f be the formula resulting from the search through the concept representation space. During the postprocessing step, each prototype p of f is rewritten as a conjunctive term with a minimum size and logically equivalent to p. This is simply performed by removing from p every atom which is logically deduced from other atoms of p and rules of the theory. This process has been designed for theories seen as acyclic AND/OR graphs as in (Drastal 1989). A simple example is used in order to illustrate the whole learning mechanism :

Example :
P={triangle, square, circle, color_black, color_red},
S={polygone, ellipse},
T={triangle --> polygon, square --> polygon, circle --> ellipse}
E_p={i_1=(triangle, color_red), i_2=(square, color_red), i_3=(square, color_black)}

E_n is not represented here.

1. Preprocessing step : Both positive and negative instances are extended. E_p={i_1=(triangle, polygon, color_red),i_2=(square, polygon, color_red),i_3=(square, polygon, color_black)}.

2. Searching for a concept representation : Let us suppose that the result f is as follows : f=$e_1 \vee e_2$, e_1=msg(i_1,i_2) = (polygon, color_red), e_2=msg(i_2,i_3) = (square, polygon).

3. Postprocessing step : Prototypes are reduced to a minimal form. "e_1" is unchanged, but 'polygon' is removed from e_2 since 'polygon' follows from 'square' and

---

[2]We will give hereafter an explanation of why negative literals are not allowed in generalizations (It is related to the flexibility of the concept representation).

[3]A prototype p covers an instance e iff $e \Rightarrow p$, i.e., p is more general than e.

'square --> polygon'. So, we obtain : f = (polygon, color_red) ∨ (square).

1.2 INDUCTIVE BIAS[4]

Prototypes are conjunctions of positive literals of A. If necessary, negative literals are explicitly added to the language A as new atoms (denoted as negative atoms). In the case of boolean functions learning, all negative literals have to be represented. In the case of a non structured value domain D for which no bias is defined, each value x of D is associated with an atom X representing the subset D-{x}. More precisely, in order to have a unique definition of maximal specific generalisation, the structure of the value domain D has to be a lattice according to the specific to general ordering of the subsets of D. Then the maximal specific generalisation of two subdomains D1 and D2 is simply their upperbound in this lattice. Such a lattice is implicitly generated by defining a set of atoms. This defines an inductive bias about the attribute. As an example when considering a hierarchy, selective addition of negative atoms allows to control the inductive bias. The example described in the previous paragraph is a case of a hierarchy. Adding selected negative atoms, which correspond -for instance- to the highest nodes of the hierarchy, modifies the inductive bias.
Defining prototypes as conjunctions of positive literals, adding negative literals as new atoms when necessary, and using a theory in order to extend the language, allows a user-defined flexible handling of inductive bias. Furthermore it should be pointed out that the <u>msg</u> operator clearly has a linear computational complexity relatively to the size of the language A. As a consequence, the size of the language may be as large as necessary.

2 THE LEARNING COMPONENT

ÉLÉNA represents acquired knowledge in the form of disjunctive formulas. Hereafter we present a summary of the ÉLÉNA algorithm which is based on a "standard greedy set-covering algorithm". It works in an iterative fashion. Each iteration searches for a single prototype which is consistent with respect to a user-defined consistency threshold and which maximises the sum of positive instances covered. Then, the positive instances covered by the "best prototype" are removed from the current training set. This step iterates until the training set is empty or no more satisfactory prototypes can be found. This "find a best conjunct and remove covered examples" scheme is clearly analogous to strategies used in AQ and CN.
ÉLÉNA searches for prototypes by carrying out a pruned specific to general search. At each stage in the search, ÉLÉNA retains a size-limited set of "best prototypes found so far". ÉLÉNA examines only generalisations of this set, carrying out a beam search of the space of prototypes. A prototype is generalised using the <u>msg</u> operator. Each prototype can be generalised in several ways (i.e., a prototype can be generalised with every current positive instances) and ÉLÉNA generates all such generalisations. After the completion of this step, ÉLÉNA removes the lowest ranking elements as measured by the evaluation function. We give hereafter the ÉLÉNA algorithm :

```
Let POS be a set of positive instances.
Let NEG be a set of negative instances.
Let pcex be a consistency threshold.
Let maxstar be an upper bound.
Procedure ÉLÉNA(POS,NEG)
Let DISJUNCTIVE_FORMULA be the empty disjunct.
Repeat until BEST_PROTOTYPE is nil or POS is
empty:
   Let BEST_PROTOTYPE be Find_Best(POS,NEG)
   If BEST_PROTOTYPE is not nil Then
       Let POS_N be the positive instances
       covered by BEST_PROTOTYPE.
       Remove from POS the instances POS_N.
       Add BEST_PROTOTYPE as an extra disjunct
       to DISJUNCTIVE_FORMULA.
Return(DISJUNCTIVE_FORMULA).

Procedure Find_Best(POS,NEG)
Let STAR be POS.
Let BEST be nil.
While STAR is not empty,
   Let NEWSTAR be Compute_Star(STAR,POS,NEG).
   Let BEST_N be the best prototypein NEWSTAR.
   If BEST_N is better than BEST Then
       Let BEST be BEST_N.
       Let STAR be NEWSTAR.
Return(BEST).

Procedure Compute_Star(STAR,POS,NEG)
Let STAR_N be the set :
   {msg(star_i, pos_j)/star_i ∈ STAR, pos_j ∈ POS}
Remove all the elements of STAR_N that cover
more than pcex ×|NEG| instances of NEG.
Repeat until size of STAR_N ≤ maxstar:
   Remove the worst prototype from STAR_N.
Return(STAR_N).
```

[4]A more detailed presentation can be found in (Brézellec 1993).

3 EXPERIMENTS

The learning component of ÉLÉNA together with ID and CN[5] have been tested on several problems : the 11-multiplexer problem, the 11-multiplexer problem with irrelevant attributes, the 20-multiplexer problem, the "even parity" concept problem, and a natural domain problem issued from DNA sequence analysis (learning 5'-splice sites). Two aspects of the algorithms' behaviour have been used to assess them :

1°) *Classification accuracy* : Number of correct classifications divided by the number of instances tested (here denoted as ACC).

2°) *Syntactic complexity of the concept representation (Zhang 1989)* : ÉLÉNA, ID, and CN have different concept description languages. These are the Disjunctive Formulas, Decision Trees, and Decision Lists. The syntactic complexity of the descriptions are computed as follows :

- Disjunctive Formula : NT is the averaged number of terms of the disjunctive formulas and ANS is the averaged number of literals in the conjunctive terms,
- Decision Tree : NL is the averaged number of the leaves of the decision trees ; NN is the averaged number of their nodes (including leaves),
- Decision List : NR is the averaged number of rules of the decision lists and ANS is the averaged number of selectors in the rules.

We enumerate below ID's (with and without pruning), CN's and ÉLÉNA's user-variable parameters which are used in our experiments :

-ID without pruning (see (Quinlan 1986)) : Prune threshold=0%, Variance termination threshold=10%,

-ID with pruning : Prune threshold=10%, Variance termination threshold=10%,

-CN (see (Clark 1989)) : Threshold of significance=1, Star size=80. We must point out that "Star size" has been set up to a value which is fair : A lower value slightly decreases the accuracy (in particular in the case of the 11-multiplexer with irrelevant attributes problem) ; a greater value increases time complexity without significant improvements of the accuracy.

-ÉLÉNA : pcex=0.0, maxstar = 40.

3.1 THE 11-MULTIPLEXER PROBLEM

The 11-multiplexer boolean function has often been used to evaluate learning methods ((Quinlan 1988), (Van de Velde 1989), (Zhang 1989), (Brézellec 1993)). Each object is a boolean vector of length 11. The 11-multiplexer function can be represented as a normal disjunctive form (8 terms of 4 literals each). In order to evaluate ÉLÉNA, ID, and CN in noisy environments, two kinds of noises have been introduced ((Rendell 1990), (Brézellec 1993)) : *Noise of level n on class membership values* and *Noise of level n on attributes values*[6]. The basic evaluation procedure consists in a random selection of 200 positive and 200 negative learning instances, the corruption of these learning instances according to the kind and level of noise (the test instances are not corrupted (Rendell 1990)), learning, and then the classification of the remaining 824 positive and 824 negative test instances. This procedure is repeated 40 times. Table 1 presents the results of each algorithm for varying degrees of corruption of class membership values. In each case we present the average accuracy on the test data and the average syntactic complexity of the resulting concept descriptions.

Table 1

class error	ÉLÉNA			ID without pruning			ID with pruning			CN		
	ACC	NT	ANS	ACC	NL	NN	ACC	NL	NN	ACC	NR	ANS
5	0.881	17.2	5.5	0.824	122	244	0.827	110	219	0.876	36.9	3.3
10	0.812	20.8	5.7	0.78	145	289	0.785	130	259	0.803	46.7	3.6
15	0.761	24.4	6	0.734	164	327	0.741	152	303	0.748	53.7	3.8
20	0.715	27	6.1	0.692	179	358	0.697	168	335	0.713	57.3	3.9

Table 2 presents the results of each algorithm for varying degrees of corruption of attributes values.

Table2

attribute error	ÉLÉNA			ID without pruning			ID with pruning			CN		
	ACC	NT	ANS	ACC	NL	NN	ACC	NL	NN	ACC	NR	ANS
5	0.953	12.6	5	0.903	94	187	0.896	84	168	0.963	23.6	2.8
10	0.933	13.7	5.1	0.888	100	200	0.884	88	175	0.928	29.3	3.1
15	0.908	15.1	5.3	0.861	110	220	0.86	92	183	0.904	33.1	3.3
20	0.888	16.6	5.5	0.852	113	225	0.854	93	185	0.88	37	3.4

3.2 THE 11-MULTIPLEXER PROBLEM WITH IRRELEVANT ATTRIBUTES

To assess the behaviour of the learning algorithms in the presence of irrelevant attributes, we have added to the description of the 11-multiplexer problem, 11, 22, and 33 irrelevant attributes whose values are randomly generated. Table 3 presents the results of each algorithm.

[5] ID and CN are R. Boswell's implementations of ID3 and CN2 ((Boswell 19900), (Clark 1991)).

[6] A class error of level 10 means that the class of 10 percent of randomly selected positive instances and 10 percent of randomly selected negative instances is modified. An attribute error of level 10 means that 10 percent of positive instances and 10 percent of negative instances are randomly selected ; then, the value of a randomly chosen attribute of each selected instance is modified.

(The evaluation procedure used here is similar to the previous one (i.e., 200 positive and 200 negative learning instances are randomly generated ; 824 positive and 824 negative test instances are randomly generated. This procedure is repeated 40 times ...)).

Table 3

irrelevant attributes	ÉLÉNA			ID without pruning			ID with pruning			CN		
	ACC	NT	ANS	ACC	NL	NN	ACC	NL	NN	ACC	NR	ANS
0	0.991	10.3	4.5	0.934	86	171	0.921	81	161	0.996	14.8	2.7
11	0.983	10.4	4.6	0.82	86	172	0:81	79	158	0.991	14.7	2.7
22	0.943	11.8	4.8	0.739	86	172	0.738	80	159	0.977	15.6	2.7
33	0.816	16	5.4	0.70	85	169	0.699	78	155	0.947	16.4	2.8

Note : If "maxstar" is set up to 80, ÉLÉNA's accuracy is 0.91 in the 33 irrelevant attributes problem.

3.3 THE 20-MULTIPLEXER PROBLEM

Here, each object is a boolean vector of length 20. Thus, it can be noticed that there are 2^{20} different objects. The 20-multiplexer function can be represented as a normal disjunctive form (16 terms of 5 literals each). The basic evaluation procedure consists in a random generation of 300 positive and 300 negative learning instances, and then the classification of 1000 positive and 1000 negative randomly generated test instances. This procedure is repeated 40 times. Table 4 presents the results of each algorithm.

Table 4

20-mul.	ÉLÉNA			ID without pruning			ID with pruning			CN		
	ACC	NT	ANS	ACC	NL	NN	ACC	NL	NN	ACC	NR	ANS
	0.955	20.3	5.5	0.659	181	361	0.659	169	337	0.95	30	3.5

3.4 THE "EVEN PARITY" CONCEPT

To emphasize one of the drawbacks of the Top-Down learning algorithms, we have run experiments on the "even parity" concept. Let us assume that an object is described by 40 binary value attributes ; then, the "even parity" concept is defined by the normal disjunctive formula $((x1=0 \wedge x2=0 \wedge x3=0) \vee (x1=0 \wedge x2=1 \wedge x3=1) \vee (x1=1 \wedge x2=0 \wedge x3=1) \vee (x1=1 \wedge x2=1 \wedge x3=0))$ where x1, x2, x3 are the name of the first three attributes ; the values of the 37 other attributes are randomly generated. Top-Down learning algorithms cannot easily tame this kind of concept. Indeed, at the beginning of the search, the entropy of the relevant selectors (i.e., x1=0, x1=1, ..., x3=0, x3=1) is not greater than the entropy of the others. Thus, these algorithms select irrelevant selectors, and then fail to learn such a concept. On the other hand, from the outset of the learning process, Bottom-Up algorithms' search strategy allows to generate prototypes which combine several selectors providing relevant search space instances. Therefore, Bottom-Up algorithms quickly learn this kind of concept. We give below the description of the experimental procedure and the obtained results.

The basic evaluation procedure consists in a random selection of 55 positive instances and 55 negative instances, learning, and then the classification of 500 positive and 500 negative randomly generated test instances. This procedure is repeated 40 times. Table 5 presents the results of each algorithm.

Table 5

even parity concept	ÉLÉNA			ID without pruning			ID with pruning			CN		
	ACC	NT	ANS	ACC	NL	NN	ACC	NL	NN	ACC	NR	ANS
	0.99	4.5	3.2	0.536	32	63	0.539	31	61	0.809	9.4	2.5

3.5 A DNA SEQUENCE ANALYSIS PROBLEM : THE 5'-SPLICE SITES

The genes of the Eukaryotes (i.e., humans and leeks for instance) are split. Thus, these genes are composed of coding regions -called exons- and non coding regions -called introns-. A "5'-splice site" is a region that directs the excision of the introns (Brunak 1991). The training set used here contains 302 positive instances and 600 negative instances of 5'-splice sites. A test set containing 118 positive instances and 600 negative instances is also provided. Each instance is described using 18 attribute-value pairs whose value domains are {A,T,G,C}. In this problem, in order to allow fair comparison of syntactic complexities, ÉLÉNA's prototypes are translated from the propositional language to constraints on the value domain of the attributes. Thus, a prototype is a conjunction of constraints $\{a_i \in S_i\}$, where S_i denotes a subset of {A,T,G,C}, and a_i the ith attribute. Comparison with ID is still unfair since each node is associated with four possible outcomes, namely {A}, {T}, {G}, {C}. Table 6 summarizes the experimental results.

Table 6

5'-splice sites	ÉLÉNA			ID without pruning			ID with pruning			CN		
	ACC	NT	NCT	ACC	NL	NN	ACC	NL	NN	ACC	NR	ANS
	0.859	12	13	0.84	214	285	0.89	121	161	0.85	56	2.5

3.6 DISCUSSION

The first comment is that, roughly speaking, the accuracies of ÉLÉNA and CN are equivalent. Comparing the sizes of the concept representation learned by the three systems, it should be noticed that ÉLÉNA produces less rules (comparing NT, NR, NL). Concerning the 5'-splice sites, full comparison of syntactic complexities is difficult. However, the average number of components in ÉLÉNA's rules is larger than CN's one. This is not surprising since ÉLÉNA searches for characteristic concepts descriptions. Morever trading off less disjunction for more conjunction might make the rules more comprehensible to people but this statement needs to be carefully evaluated. In the case of the "even parity" concept, we have shown that a bottom-up search strategy is more accurate than a top-down one. Indeed, any top-down induction system looks for relationships between the value of a single attribute and a class membership. Unfortunately, at the beginning of the learning process, the entropy of the relevant attributes is not better than the others ; therefore such systems fail to learn the concept. On the other hand, a bottom-up strategy seems more appropriate. It seems mainly due to the fact that the evaluation function only provides a good "pointer" for overly-specific rules.Thus approaching the concept from the most-specific part of the search space will work, but starting from the most general will not as it has been pointed out earlier. Such a case is not the only one. Thus, if -for instance- the description of a conjunctive concept is made of the conjunction of a lot of features, a bottom-up approach can especially be well suited : Right at the start of the learning process, the msg operator generates descriptions that combine at one go several features ; therefore, a bottom-up algorithm can quickly converge towards the good description. However situations may occur in which each maximal specific generalisation of two instances covers the same small number of instances ; in this case, the beginning of ÉLÉNA's search may also be difficult.

More generally, the "even parity" concept clearly shows that bottom-up methods can be very useful for learning certain concepts. This problem also arisen in the ILP (Inductive Logic Programming) literature where again top-down learning can run into difficulties when using information gain as a heuristic. Thus, in (Botta 1992), the authors show that the heuristic based on the information gain criterion coupled with an hill climbing search strategy may be misleading. They have designed a domain in which predicates with high information gain are irrelevant and in which relevant predicates have low information gain. The algorithms based on the previous heuristic fail to learn the concept since they are misleaded in wrong directions when combining several predicates in one shot as in a bottom-up approaches will probably lead them to the correct solution[7].

Finally, we report hereunder the average elapsed cpu time (seconds), during learning[8]. It clearly shows that the time complexity of ÉLÉNA is linked to the number of the positive instances :

cpu time	11-mul.	11-mul. + 11	11-mul. + 22	11-mul. + 33	20-mul.	Even Par.	5'-splice
ID	1	2	2.5	3.7	3	1	2
CN	43	183	491	993	384	355	571
ÉLÉNA	240	519	858	1439	2208	58	5250

4 RELATED WORK

Concerning the concept representation space, our approach is close to the work of (Kudo 1989). In this work, the authors search for all maximal subsets of the positive instances where the maximal specific generalisations cover no negative instances. Their algorithm seems efficient but still has exponential complexity with the number of positive instances since it performs an exhaustive search. In another related work, learning is performed by constructing a Galois lattice (Liquière 1990). The construction is only partial thanks to the use of a consistency criterion. As a matter of fact the nodes of the lattice represent prototypes as defined here. Unfortunately, here again exhaustive search leads to untractable computational complexity. From this point of view, the beam search strategy is efficient : The generalisation of the prototypes which is the basic operation in ÉLÉNA is bounded by $O(|POS|^2)$ where $|POS|$ is the number of the positive instances of the current training set. Nevertheless, reducing ÉLÉNA's time complexity is one of our goal : Since it is linked to the number of positive instances, we have implemented a new version of ÉLÉNA in which each element of Star_N (see algorithm) is generalised with a set number of randomly selected positives instances.

Another learning system, EACH (Salzberg 1991), also builds maximal specific generalisations referred to as hyperrectangles. However comparison with ÉLÉNA is difficult since EACH is mainly an instance based-learning system. The learning yields in partitionning the instance space. EACH classifies a new instance by computing the closest hyperrectangle according to an incrementally modified distance.

In a previous work (Brézellec 1993), we have described SAMIA, a bottom-up learning system close to ÉLÉNA except that its learning component uses a simulated annealing search strategy. We have shown that simulated annealing (an optimisation algorithm) is an interesting alternative to classical search strategies as CN's beam search or ID's depth first search. In short, SAMIA applies building operators (*extension*, *contraction*, *generalisation*) to a disjunction of prototypes which represents the whole concept. Experimental results of SAMIA were fine but further experiments showed that the accuracies were disappointing when adding irrelevant attributes as in experiment 3.2. Our opinion is that this was related to

[7] They also show that a domain theory -which combines in rules relevant predicates- leads the algorithm to the good solution.

[8] ÉLÉNA, ID and CN were run on a Sparc 2 workstation.

the fact that SAMIA works by refining a whole disjunction of prototypes. To overcome this drawback, we have designed the learning component of ÉLÉNA which iteratively searches for a "best prototype", and thus incrementally builds the description of the concept to learn. As shown in section 3.2 this leads to satisfying results on the irrelevant attributes problem. Now, we think that one of the most obvious improvement to ÉLÉNA is to replace its beam search strategy by a simulated annealing one. Thus, our next bottom-up algorithm should combine features of both ÉLÉNA's and SAMIA's learning components.

CONCLUSION

The most significant aspects of our method is that 1) it is a bottom-up approach, 2) the concept representation space is restricted to disjunctions of prototypes, i.e., maximal specific generalisations of subsets of instances, 3) it uses background knowledge in a preprocessing level in order to extend instances description as do other various learning systems ((Rouveirol 1990), (Bisson 1992)), 4) it uses background knowledge in a postprocessing level in order to obtain a minimal representation of the conjunctive terms of the concept description. One could notice that this step tends to produce "operational prototypes" (e.g., transforming "triangle and polygone" into "triangle").
The experiments we have conducted show that ÉLÉNA and CN have comparable performance[9] (except CPU time) and that bottom-up methods can be accurate and in some cases even more accurate than top-down methods. Moreover, since ÉLÉNA's msg operator has linear computational complexity relatively to the size of the language, we think that it will be well suited to situations in which an exhaustive deductive step is applied to the learning instances.
Concerning the use of background knowledge, and the control of learning bias, full evaluation of our method has not been yet performed. In the future, we intend to compare our system to MIRO (Drastal 1989) in which the theory is used to move the description language towards a more abstract one, rather than extending the language as it is done here.

Acknowledgements

We thank LRI at Orsay (France) for giving us ID and CN. Special thanks go to Alain Viari (Institut Curie/CNRS) for his invaluable assistance in understanding the biological problem. We also want to thank the referees for their thoughtful criticisms which improved the paper considerably. This work has been supported by a grant from ORGANIBIO (Cm2aO program).

[9] In several experiments ID showed weaker results. However converting decision trees into set of rules, should overcome such limitations as shown in (Quinlan 1988).

References

Bisson, S., "Conceptual Clustering in a First Order Logic Representation", Proceedings of the Tenth European Conference on Artificial Intelligence, Vienna 1992, Neumann, pp 458-468.

Boswell, R., "Manual for NewID version 2.1", The Turing Institute, January 1990.

Clark, P., Boswell, R. ,"Rule Induction with CN2 : Some Recent Improvements", Proceedings of the Fith European Working Session on Learning, Berlin 1991, Springer Verlag, pp 151-163.

Botta, M. , Giordana, A., Saitta, L., "Comparison of Search Startegies in Learning Relations", Proceedings of the Tenth European Conference on Artificial Intelligence, Vienna 1992, Neumann, pp 451-455.

Brézellec, P., Soldano, H., "SAMIA : A Bottom-Up Learning Method using a Simulated Annealing Algorithm", Proceedings of The First European Conference on Machine Learning, Vienna 1993, Springer Verlag, pp 297-309.

Brunak, S., Engelbrecht J., Knudsen S., "Prediction of Human mRNA Donor and Acceptor Sites from the DNA Sequence", Journal of Molecular Biology (n° 220, 1991), pp 49-65.

Clark, P., Niblett, T., "The CN2 Induction Algorithm", Machine Learning (vol 3, n° 4, 1989), Kluwer Academic Publishers, pp 261-283.

Drastal, G., Czako, R., Raatz, S., "Induction in an abstraction space : A form of constructive induction", Proceedings of the Eleventh International Joint Conference on Artificial Intelligence, Detroit 1989, Morgan Kaufmann, pp 708-712.

Ganter B., Rindefrey K., Skorsky M., "Software for a formal concept analysis", Classification as a tool of Research, North Holland 1986.

Kudo, M., Shimbo, M., "Optimal subclasses with dichotomous variables for features selection and discrimination", IEEE Trans. Systems, Man, Cybern (n° 19, 1989), pp 1194-1199.

Liquière, M., Méphu Nguifo, E., "LEarning with GALois Lattice : Un système d'apprentissage de concepts à partir d'exemples", Cinquième Journées Française d'Apprentissage, Lannion 1990, pp 93-113.

Quinlan, J.R., “Induction of Decision Trees”, Machine Learning (vol 1, n° 1, 1986), Kluwer Academic Publishers, pp 81-106.

Quinlan, J.R., "An Empirical Comparison of Genetic and Decision-Tree Classifiers", Proceedings of the Fifth International Conference on Machine Learning, Ann Arbor 1988, pp 135-141.

Rendell, L., Cho, H., "Empirical Learning as a Function of Concept Character", Machine Learning (vol 5, n° 3, 1990), Kluwer Academic Publishers, pp 267-276.

Rouveirol, C., Puget, J.F., "Beyond inversion of resolution", Proceedings of the Seventh International Conference on Machine Learning, Austin 1990, pp 557-562.

Salzberg, S., "A Nearest Hyperrectangle Learning Method", Machine Learning (vol 6, n° 3, 1991), Kluwer Academic Publishers, pp 251-283.

Van de Velde, W., "IDL, or Taming the Multiplexer", Proceedings of the Fourth European Working Session on Learning, Montpellier 1989, Morgan Kaufmann, pp 211-225.

Zhang, J., Michalski, R.S., "Rule Optimisation Via SG-Trunc Method", Proceedings of the Fourth European Working Session on Learning, Montpellier 1989, Morgan Kaufmann, pp 251-262.

Addressing the Selective Superiority Problem: Automatic Algorithm/Model Class Selection

Carla E. Brodley
Department of Computer Science
University of Massachusetts
Amherst, MA 01003
brodley@cs.umass.edu

Abstract

The results of empirical comparisons of existing learning algorithms illustrate that each algorithm has a *selective superiority*; it is best for some but not all tasks. Given a data set, it is often not clear beforehand which algorithm will yield the best performance. In such cases one must search the space of available algorithms to find the one that produces the best classifier. In this paper we present an approach that applies knowledge about the representational biases of a set of learning algorithms to conduct this search automatically. In addition, the approach permits the available algorithms' model classes to be mixed in a recursive tree-structured hybrid. We describe an implementation of the approach, MCS, that performs a heuristic best-first search for the best hybrid classifier for a set of data. An empirical comparison of MCS to each of its primitive learning algorithms, and to the computationally intensive method of cross-validation, illustrates that automatic selection of learning algorithms using knowledge can be used to solve the selective superiority problem.

1 THE PROBLEM OF SELECTIVE SUPERIORITY

Several dozen inductive learning algorithms have been developed over the last few decades, including versions of perceptron, DNF cover, decision tree, instance-based, and neural-net algorithms. In every case, the algorithm can boast one or more superior learning performances over the others, but none is always better. The results of empirical comparisons of existing learning algorithms illustrate that each algorithm has a *selective superiority*: it is best for some but not all tasks (Weiss & Kapouleas (1989), Aha, Kibler & Albert (1991), Shavlik, Mooney & Towell (1991), Salzberg (1991).) This is because each algorithm is biased, leading to a good fit for some learning tasks, and a poor fit for others.

An algorithm's success in finding a good generalization for a given data set depends on two factors. The first is whether the algorithm's representation space contains a good generalization. In statistics, this space is called the algorithm's *model class*. For example, the model class of a symbolic, univariate decision tree algorithm is the Disjunctive Normal Form. The model class of a perceptron learning algorithm is the class of linear discriminant functions. Because an algorithm's model class defines the space of possible generalizations, not even an exhaustive search strategy can overcome a poor choice of model class. The second factor of an algorithm's success is its search bias. Even algorithms that search the same model space have shown selective superiority. For example, if a set of instances is not linearly separable then the Least Mean Squares (LMS) training rule provides a better solution than the Absolute Error Correction rule (ACR) for learning the weights of a linear discriminant function (Duda & Hart, 1973). However, when the instances are linearly separable the situation is reversed; LMS is not guaranteed to find a separating hyperplane, whereas ACR is. In many cases, the choice of learning algorithm can be made on subject matter considerations. However, when such prior knowledge is not available, the choice can be made by comparing each algorithm's performance on the data.

2 AUTOMATIC ALGORITHM SELECTION

Selecting the best algorithm for a data set in the absence of prior knowledge is a search problem. One well-known approach from statistics is to use cross-validation (Linhart & Zucchini, 1986). Given a set of data, an n-fold cross-validation splits the data into n equal parts. Each candidate algorithm is run n times; for each run, $n-1$ parts of the data are used to form a classifier, which is then evaluated using the remaining part. The results of the n runs are averaged and the algorithm that produced classifiers with the highest average classification accuracy is selected. Recently, Schaffer (1993) applied this idea to selecting a classification algorithm. The results of an empirical comparison of a cross-validation method (CV) to each algorithm considered by CV, illustrated that on average, across the test-suite of domains, CV performed best.

A cross-validation strategy performs an exhaustive search through the space of candidate methods. As the number of alternatives increases, the time required to search for the best algorithm may become impractical due to the computational expense of performing a cross-validation. One of the oldest methods in Artificial Intelligence for reducing search effort is to use knowledge about the problem domain. Here the problem domain is selection of the best learning algorithm for a given set of data. The search space is defined by the data set and the set of candidate algorithms. In this domain, knowledge stems from understanding the biases of the candidate algorithms and how this can be applied to guide the search for the best algorithm/model class for a given set of data.

A recent focus of research in machine learning is to understand the tasks for which a particular algorithm will perform better than some specified set of alternatives (Feng, Sutherland, King, Muggleton & Henry, 1993; Aha, 1992; Shavlik, Mooney & Towell, 1991; Rendell & Cho, 1990). Systems that allow the user to specify an inductive policy, require that the biases of the available learning algorithm be known and be represented explicitly (for manipulation during search) (Provost & Buchanan, 1992). The knowledge resulting from such efforts can be used to form a heuristic search procedure for automatic algorithm selection. To this end, we present a knowledge-based approach to algorithm/model class selection. Our approach differs from cross-validation in two fundamental ways. Firstly, algorithm selection is guided by various kinds of hypothesis pathology that develop when using an algorithm that is a poor choice. We define hypothesis pathology to be the recognizable symptoms of when a hypothesis fits the data poorly. When an algorithm and its underlying model class is inappropriate, one needs to find a different one that is appropriate. The ability to do this depends both on recognizing whether and why the algorithm is a poor choice, and on using this information to select a better one. We have encoded this knowledge as a set of heuristic rules. Secondly, our approach is applied recursively, providing a mechanism for mixing the available model classes to form a hybrid classifier.

3 KNOWLEDGE-BASED SEARCH

Our approach of using hypothesis pathology to guide the search has the ability to assess why a particular model class or search bias is inappropriate and from this assessment can make an informed choice as to which to try next. If a hypothesis representation is judged inappropriate, then we want to redirect the search to a part of the space that will produce a good generalization. The type of pathology dictates where in the space to redirect the search.

A simple approach was illustrated in the work on perceptron trees (Utgoff, 1989). The algorithm first tried a simple perceptron as the test, but if it was doing poorly, it was replaced by a single variable test. This approach detected hypothesis pathology, and selected a new representation, but the pathology was not used to guide the selection, because there was only a single alternate choice.

FRINGE (1990) uses a different approach. The concept representation is changed by adding compound terms, based on those found at the fringe of the decision tree, and rebuilding the tree. When a compound term would be useful, and is missing, the tree contains many replicated subtrees. When such pathology exists, the terms that would be useful in a compound term often appear near the fringe of the tree. Thus, the hypothesis pathology indicates a specific change in bias through the addition of compound terms.

Our approach to searching the model space is dynamic; given a set of training instances, a best-first search for the appropriate classifier is performed. A set of heuristic rules is used to decide which model class to try next, which search bias to use, and to determine when the best classifier has been found. The best classifier found is then used to partition the instance space, and the search is applied recursively to each resulting partition. If during the best-first search, a *subtree* of the partially formed classifier exhibits some type of pathology, the approach can backtrack and replace the subtree with a different classifier.

The heuristic rules are created from practical knowledge about how to detect when a generalization is a good fit, or whether a better one could be found by changing the model class or search bias. For example, the model class of a univariate decision tree is a poor choice when the features are related numerically. In this case, the features will be tested repeatedly in the decision tree, giving evidence that a series of tests are being used to approximate a non-orthogonal partition of the data that is not easily represented by a series of hyper-rectangles. The following rule not only detects this situation, but also directs the search to the appropriate model class.

IF two or more features are tested repeatedly
in a path of the tree
THEN switch from univariate test to linear test
AND fit a linear test of these features to the
instances at the top of the path

4 RECURSIVE COMBINATION OF MODEL CLASSES

Our method builds a hybrid decision tree, with the test at a node being created by selecting and applying a primitive learning algorithm, each with a different underlying model class. The ability to combine the different model classes and apply different learning algorithms allows for the possibility that the data set is not best represented by a homogeneous classifier. For some data sets, combining heterogeneous model classes will produce the best classifier. The ability to combine model classes in a single tree structure allows a space of classifiers that is strictly richer than the union of its constituent primitive model classes. The case of picking a single model class is not lost, but the approach also permits hybrid classifiers. In our approach, each model class is permitted anywhere in the recursive tree structure. Both perceptron trees (Utgoff, 1989) and CRL (Yerramareddy, Tcheng, Lu & Assanis, 1992) restrict where in the tree certain model classes are permitted. For example, in perceptron trees, internal test nodes must be univariate and symbolic, whereas leaf-node tests (tests right above the leaves) must be perceptrons.

5 MCS: A MODEL CLASS SELECTION SYSTEM

We have implemented the approach in a system that we call the *Model Class Selection (MCS) System*. Given a set of data, MCS builds a hybrid classifier using a set of heuristic rules to guide a best-first search for the best model class for each node in the hybrid classifier. To avoid overfitting, the classifier is pruned back to reduce the estimated classification error, as computed for an independent set of instances (Breiman, Friedman, Olshen & Stone, 1984). MCS's pruning procedure differs from the traditional pruning phase of decision tree algorithms. During MCS's tree-formation stage, if an alternative classifier to the one selected appears almost as good, it is stored for the pruning phase. When considering whether to prune back a subtree in the hybrid classifier, MCS computes the classification errors of both the subtree and the alternative classifier. MCS compares the error rates to choose among: keeping the subtree, replacing it with the alternative classifier or replacing it with a leaf node containing the most frequently observed class for the instances used to form the subtree. In the next two sections we describe MCS's model classes and rule base.

5.1 MODEL CLASSES

MCS combines three primitive representations that have been used extensively in both machine learning and statistics algorithms: linear discriminant functions, decision trees and instance-based classifiers. A set of R linear discriminant functions defines a set of R regions in the instance space, separated by hyperplanes, each labeled with a different class name. A univariate decision tree splits the instance space with cuts orthogonal to each of the axes, forming a set of hyperrectangular regions, each labeled with a class name. An instance-based classifier defines a piece-wise linear partition of the instance space; the number of pieces is determined by the number and distribution of the instances. The result is a set of regions, each labeled by a different class name, separated by piece-wise linear boundaries.

Each of the three model classes is a subclass of the model class of piece-wise linear partitions. A univariate test in a decision tree is a special case of a linear discriminant function: a linear discriminant function can be based on all n of the input features, only one feature or some subset of the n input features. A linear discriminant function defines only one hyperplane boundary in the instance space, whereas an instance-based classifier forms a series of hyperplane boundaries. In Figure 1a we show an instance space for which classifiers from each of the three model classes would define an identical partition of the instance space.

For many data sets, classifiers from each of the three model classes will define different partitions. Figures 1b, 1c, and 1d illustrate the type of partition each model class might define for a simple instance space consisting of five negative and three positive examples of the concept to be learned. Which of these concept representations is best depends on where in the instance space the true concept boundary lies.

For each model class there are many different algorithms for searching for the classifier that best fits the data. The *fitting algorithms* for each model class that MCS uses are:

Univariate Decision Trees: To build a univariate decision tree, MCS uses the information gain-ratio metric (Quinlan, 1986).

Linear Discriminant Functions: For two-class tasks the system uses a linear threshold unit, and for multiclass tasks it uses a linear machine (Nilsson, 1965). To find the weights of a linear discriminant function the system uses the Recursive Least Squares procedure (Young, 1984) for two-class tasks and the Thermal Training rule (Frean, 1990; Brodley & Utgoff, 1992) for multiclass tasks. To select the terms to use with a linear discriminant function, one of four search procedures is used: sequential backward elimination (SBE) (Kittler, 1986), a variation of SBE that uses the form of the function to determine which terms to eliminate (Brodley & Utgoff, 1992), sequential forward selection (SFS) (Kittler, 1986), and a method that examines a decision tree for replicated tests of a subset of the features, to suggest which terms to consider. The choice of which of these search biases to use

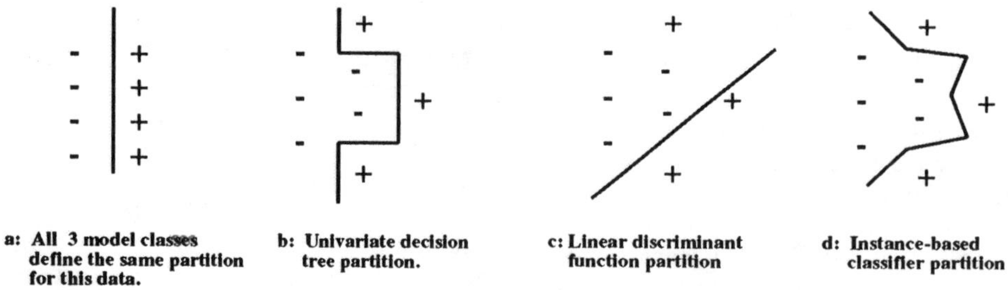

Figure 1: Partitions of the Instance Space

is determined dynamically during learning, depending on the hypotheses that have already been formed and what their pathologies suggested.

Instance-Based Classifiers: MCS uses two algorithms for fitting an instance-based classifier to the data. The first is the k-nearest neighbor algorithm (Duda & Hart, 1973), which stores each instance of the training data. To find k, the system uses the following measure of accuracy: for each instance in the training data, classify that instance using the remaining instances. MCS searches for the value of k that produces the most correct classifications on the training data. The second algorithm tries to eliminate instances that do not contribute to the classifier's accuracy and is similar in spirit to IB3 (Aha, Kibler & Albert, 1991). To this end, when the accuracy of the k-NN is computed MCS keeps track, for each instance, of the number of times it was a k-nearest neighbor and whether its class matched that of the instance being classified. Instances for which the number of incorrect matches was higher than the number of correct matches are removed.

5.2 RULE BASE

The heuristic rules use several types of pathology detection criteria to guide the search for the best classifier. The following criteria are used in the rules to detect the success or failure of a hypothesis and provide information about the reasons of failure:

1. **Information Gain-Ratio:** This measure is used to compare any two partitions of the instances; a partition can be defined by a univariate test, a linear discriminant function, a k-NN classifier, or even an entire subtree.
2. **Codelength:** Our use of this measure is based on the Minimum Description Length Principle, which states that the best "hypothesis" to induce from a data set is the one that minimizes the length of the hypothesis plus the length of the exceptions (Rissanen, 1989). The *codelength* of a classifier (the hypothesis) is the number of bits required to code the classifier and the the error vector resulting from using the classifier to classify the instances. This metric is used to determine by how much a symbolic or linear test *compresses* the data. We define the amount of compression to be the codelength of the errors without the test minus the codelength of the test plus the codelength of the errors resulting from using the test to classify the data. We use the exact error code for exceptions given in Rissanen and encode integers using Elias's asymptotically optimal encoding (Rissanen, 1989).
3. **Concept Form:** Analysis of a classifier's form can be used to guide the search for the best classifier. For example, MCS examines a partially formed tree to determine whether a set of univariate tests is tested repeatedly in the tree. The action that is taken depends on the form of the replication. Examination of a linear combination test yields information about the relative importance of the different features to classification, which in turn yields information about which search bias and model class will be most appropriate.
4. **Information about the Data Set:** We use one measure of training instances: the number of instances relative to the number of features.

The process of selecting an algorithm to apply to a data set, often requires knowledge about how to determine whether the best classifier has been found, and if not, which algorithm to try next. Many learning practitioners and statisticians make these decision by using statistics (diagnostics) computed about the resulting classifier and by examining the classifier's form. In MCS this knowledge is encoded explicitly in the rule base. In Table 1 we show a selection of rules from MCS. Rule 1 begins the search and is based on Duda and Hart's (1973) observation that when there are fewer than $2n$ instances (the capacity of a hyperplane) a linear test will *underfit* the training instances; the fewer the instances, the higher the probability that the data will be fit by chance. Rule 2 examines the univariate test to determine whether the initial decision was correct. If the test is not 100% accurate, then MCS searches for a multivariate test using SFS if the average squared difference between the informa-

Table 1: A Selection of Rules from MCS's Rule Base

1.) IF the number of instances is less than the capacity of a hyperplane
THEN find the best univariate test
ELSE form linear test LT_n of all n features

2.) IF the best univariate test is 100% accurate
THEN select it and recurse.
ELSE
IF the test does not compress the data
THEN fit a k-NN (k=2)
ELSIF the average difference in info-score of each feature to best feature is $< \epsilon$
THEN start with best feature and search for a better test using SFS
ELSE select the univariate test and recurse

3.) IF the instances are linearly separable (determined by accuracy of LT_i)
THEN continue trying to eliminate noisy and irrelevant features
ELSE examine the magnitudes of the weights of the linear test:
IF a few weights are larger than the others
THEN find best univariate test
ELSIF many of the weights are close to zero
THEN use greedy SBE
ELSE use SBE to find the best linear test based on the fewest features

4.) IF info-score(LT_i) > info-score(LT_i) OR $i = 1$
THEN IF best linear test compresses data
THEN select that test and recurse
ELSE find the best univariate test
ELSE continue trying to eliminate noisy and irrelevant variables

5.) IF neither a univariate nor a linear test compress the data (based on MDLP)
THEN find the best value of k for an instance based classifier AND select from available tests, the one with max info-score, recurse

6.) IF the best univariate test's info-score is > than that of a linear test of n features
THEN search for a better test starting with the univariate test and using SFS
ELSE examine form of the linear test to choose SBE or greedy SBE (see Rule 3)

tion score of each of the other features and the best feature is less than a threshold (10% of the magnitude of the best score). Using Rules 2 and 5, MCS checks to see that the best test found thus far compresses the training data, which occurs when the codelength of the test plus the codelength of the error vector, resulting from using the test to classify the data, is less than the codelength of the error vector of the instances. If the number of bits to code the test is not less than the number of bits to code the errors that the test corrects, then MCS fits a k-NN classifier to the data. Rule 3 determines whether the initial selection of a linear test was appropriate. If the instances are linearly separable then MCS tries to eliminate any noisy or irrelevant features from the test; otherwise MCS examines the form of the test to decide where next to direct the search. Rule 4 evaluates the best linear test found in the search; if the test compresses the data then it is selected; otherwise a search for the best univariate test is conducted (if one has not been found yet). Rule 6 starts a SFS for the best linear test if the information score of a univariate test is higher than that of a multivariate test based on all n features.

Currently, MCS's rule base contains twenty-five rules, built using an iterative approach. Candidate rules were derived based on the author's knowledge of how to detect hypothesis pathology and whether a hypothesis is a good fit to the data. Each rule was then tested using a set of four development data sets (the Breast, Bupa, Cleveland and Segmentation data sets from the UCI data base). Based on statistics kept of the rule's usage, in comparison to the other rules' usage, and on a detailed trace of the search through the generalization space, the rule was either kept, rejected, or altered and re-evaluated for inclusion into the rule base. The rules were constructed such that only one rule will match; no conflict resolution is required. The author makes no claim that the current set of rules is complete or that better rules do not exist. However, as the results of the next section illustrate, general rules can be found that work well across many data sets.

6 ILLUSTRATION

To illustrate that knowledge about the biases of learning algorithms can be used successfully by an automatic algorithm selection system, we compare MCS to each of the individual model classes: a k-NN, a linear test based on all of the input features (LT) and a univariate decision tree (Utree). In addition, we include a hybrid algorithm LMDT (Brodley & Utgoff, 1992), which combines linear machine tests with decision trees. To determine how a knowledge-based approach compares to the traditional cross-validation scheme we report results for an algorithm that we call CV-10, which performs a ten-fold cross-validation on the training data to select the best of k-NN, LT, Utree or LMDT. CV-10 chooses the algorithm that achieves

Table 2: Accuracy for Test Data (Percent Correct)

Method	Hep.	LED	Road	Votes	Vowel
k-NN	82.63	62.12	78.95	93.24	94.66
LT	83.95	68.80	70.69	95.46	45.22
LMDT	83.42	72.56	83.01	95.37	75.18
Utree	78.95	73.36	83.19	95.09	68.02
CV-10	81.58	72.40	83.19	94.63	94.66
MCS	82.89	72.76	82.79	95.28	94.66

the highest average accuracy and then runs that algorithm on the entire training set.

None of the data sets used in this illustration were used during development of the rule base. The data sets (all available in the UCI repository) are:

Hepatitis: The task for this domain is to predict from test results whether a patient will die from hepatitis. There are 155 instances described by 19 numeric and Boolean attributes.

LED: The data for the digit recognition problem consists of ten classes representing whether an LED display shows a 0-9. Each of seven Boolean attributes has a 10% probability of having its value inverted. There are 500 instances.

Road: The data come from four images of country roads in Massachusetts. Each instance represents a 3X3 grid of pixels described by three color and four texture features. The classes are road, road-line, dirt, gravel, foliage, trunk, sky, tree and grass. There are 8212 instances in this data set and 381 values are missing.

Votes: In this domain the task is to classify each of 435 members of Congress, in 1984, as Republican or Democrat using their votes on 16 key issues. There are 392 values missing.

Vowel: The task is to recognize the eleven steady state vowels of British English. There are ten numeric features describing the 990 instances.

To compare the performance of the six learning methods we ran each ten times. For each run, the data were split randomly into a training and a test set, with 75% of the data in the training set and 25% in the test set. To determine the significance of the differences among the learning methods we used paired *t*-tests. Because the same random splits of each data set were used for each method, the variances of the errors for any two methods are each due to effects that are point-by-point identical. For algorithms that require a separate data file for pruning (Utree, LMDT and MCS) one third of the training data was reserved for pruning.

Table 2 shows the sample average of each method's classification accuracy on the independent test sets.

Table 3: Time Used to Select a Classifier (Seconds)

Method	Hep.	LED	Road	Votes	Vowel
CV-10	390	598	29,593	838	1,263
MCS	174	130	12,237	246	218

Table 4: Model Classes in the MCS Classifiers

Model Class	Hep.	LED	Road	Votes	Vowel
k-NN	0.5	1.7	4.0	0.1	1.0
Linear	0.6	3.5	9.3	1.0	0.0
Univariate	1.7	2.2	23.4	0.9	0.0

Looking first at the individual algorithms, we observe typical selective superiority results. Each of *k*-NN, LT and UTree was best for at least one of the data sets (LMDT was close to the best for several data sets), and each was statistically significantly worse (at the 0.05 level) than the best method for other data sets. MCS's and CV-10's performances on the other hand, do not show a selective superiority for these data sets - they are robust across the set of tasks. Both CV-10 and MCS outperform each of the other methods *on average*. MCS yields slightly higher accuracies than CV-10 for four data sets, but these differences are not significant. For the Hepatitis, LED and Votes data sets, one of the individual methods achieved slightly higher accuracy, but in each case the difference between the best individual method and MCS is not significant. However both CV-10 and MCS are always statistically significantly more accurate than the worst methods for each data set.

MCS required far less time than CV-10 and achieved the same level of accuracy on all test problems. In Table 3 we report the number of CPU seconds used by CV-10 and MCS on a DEC Station 5000/200. This result illustrates that applying knowledge reduces the search required to find the best classifier without compromising the quality of the solution.

The main point to take away from this comparison is not that MCS "beats" the individual algorithms in terms of accuracy. MCS achieves significantly better accuracies than the worst methods and is competitive with the best method for each data set. Therefore, we conclude from this comparison that MCS's performance demonstrates that knowledge can be successfully applied to solve the selective superiority problem and at a much lower cost than cross-validation.

One issue that requires further investigation is why the hybrid classifiers are not significantly more accurate than the individual model classes. In Table 4 we show the average number of test nodes from each model class in the classifiers found by MCS. For four out of the five data sets, MCS selected hybrid classifiers. This

Table 5: Classification Overlap (Percentage)

Pair	Hep.	LED	Road	Votes	Vowel
MCS-k-NN	86	66	83	94	**100**
MCS-LT	**91**	80	72	**99**	43
MCS-Utree	84	**85**	**85**	**99**	66
LT-Utree	84	75	70	**99**	26
LT-k-NN	86	58	66	94	43
Utree-k-NN	78	64	79	94	66

raises the question of why the hybrid classifiers did not achieve *higher* accuracy than each of the homogeneous classifiers for these four data sets.

There are several possible answers. Firstly, for these data sets it may be impossible to achieve higher accuracy than that obtained by the best individual method due to noise in the instances. A second possibility is that MCS needs better rules to show the advantages of a hybrid classifier. Finally, MCS's model classes may be too similar to show a difference. MCS creates hybrid classifiers that are piece-wise linear. Each of the primitive model classes is also piece-wise linear, albeit with different restrictions on how they can partition the instance space and with different search biases.

To cast insight into which of the possible explanations seems most likely, we examine the differences among the decision boundaries each classifier forms. To this end, we compute a heuristic measure of the similarity between two classifiers' boundaries: we compute the percentage overlap in the classification decisions that each makes. Although this does not tell us the exact difference in the decision boundaries, it gives a rough measure of how different these boundaries are for classification of the types of instances observed.

After each algorithm was run on a random partition of a data set, we computed the overlap between the classification decisions made by each pair of learning algorithms; we counted the number of instances that were classified the same way by each of two classifiers constructed using different algorithms. In Table 5 we report the average for each data set, over the ten runs, of the classification overlap percentage between each pair of classifiers. The higher the percentage, the closer the decision boundaries are for classification of instances likely to be observed in the domain. For example, the largest pair-wise overlap for the Hepatitis data set is between MCS and LT. This indicates that MCS defines decision boundaries that are more similar to LT's boundaries than Utree's or k-NN's. Combining the results reported in Tables 2 and 5, we observe that MCS's classification overlap is highest with the best individual method and therefore its decision boundaries are in highest agreement with those of the best individual method. In addition, MCS's overlap with the best method was higher than any pair-wise overlap between the primitive algorithms for four of the data sets. The one exception is the Votes data set; both LT and Utree have an almost perfect overlap with MCS and therefore show a similarly high pair-wise overlap.

Given that, on average, the hybrid classifiers classify test instances most similarly to the best of the primitive algorithms for each data set, we find that the two most likely explanations for why the hybrid classifiers did not outperform the best of LT, Utree and k-NN on each data set are: it is impossible to achieve higher accuracies on these data sets than the best of the homogeneous classifiers or MCS's *model classes* are too similar to improve classification performance over the best homogeneous classifier for a given data set.

7 FUTURE WORK

In our experiments the hybrid classifiers produced by MCS did not achieve higher accuracy than the best homogeneous classifier for each of the five data sets. Therefore, we were not able to demonstrate that using different *model classes* for different subspaces of a learning task (to form a hybrid classifier) leads to the best classifier. Our classification overlap analysis suggests two possible explanations that need further investigation. Firstly, greater benefits of hybrid classifiers may be realized through the inclusion of model classes that do not form piece-wise linear partitions; with the inclusion of classes such as splines or quadratic discriminant functions, the benefits of heterogeneous classifiers may be more clearly illustrated. A second issue to investigate is whether data sets exist that are best represented by a hybrid classifier. Certainly, we can create artificial data sets for which this is true, but from the results of the illustration it is unclear whether better accuracies can be achieved for the five data sets, than the accuracy of the best of the set of classifiers constructed using the primitive algorithms.

As more knowledge about the biases of machine learning, symbolic and statistical classification algorithms becomes available, the efficiency of the search and the quality of the solutions will improve. One direction in which to extend the recursive knowledge-based is to incorporate the results of efforts such as the StatLog project to reduce the amount of search required. One of the results of the StatLog project is a study that relates statistical measures of a data set to the performance of different algorithms (Feng, et al. 1993). Measures such as homogeneity of covariances and skewness were used to explain differences in the performances of a set of machine learning, statistical and neural net algorithms on a test-suite of classification tasks. The knowledge resulting from this type of study could be used to begin the best-first search. By starting the search from a promising part of the space, it stands to reason that the time required to find the best classifier would be greatly reduced.

8 CONCLUSION

In this paper we have presented a recursive heuristic approach to algorithm selection for classifier construction. We illustrated empirically that an automated algorithm selection system, MCS, can use knowledge about the biases of machine learning algorithms and representations to solve the selective superiority problem. Clearly, when prior knowledge of which model class will be best for a data set exists, it should be applied. Such knowledge does not preclude the use of systems such as MCS; it can be used to focus the search in the most promising areas, thereby reducing the amount of search required. As we as researchers gain more insight into the biases of the algorithms that we create, we will be able to improve the performance of systems that use knowledge to perform automatic algorithm selection.

Acknowledgments

This material is based upon work supported by the National Aeronautics and Space Administration under Grant No. NCC 2-658. The Hepatitis, LED, Votes and Vowel data sets are from the UCI machine learning database. B. Draper provided the Road data. Discussions with J. Callan, J. Clouse, T. Fawcett, C. Schaffer and P. Smyth helped to clarify the issues presented in this paper. Thanks to Paul Utgoff, whose comments improved both the content and presentation of this paper, and for providing the inspiration for this research.

References

Aha, D. W., Kibler, D., & Albert, M. (1991). Instance-based learning algorithms. *Machine Learning, 6*, 37-66.

Aha, D. W. (1992). Generalizing from case studies: A case study. *Machine Learning: Proceedings of the Ninth International Conferencc* (pp. 1-10). San Mateo, CA: Morgan Kaufmann.

Breiman, L., Friedman, J. H., Olshen, R. A., & Stone, C. J. (1984). *Classification and regression trees.* Belmont, CA: Wadsworth International Group.

Brodley, C. E., & Utgoff, P. E. (1992). *Multivariate versus univariate decision trees*, (Coins Technical Report 92-8), Amherst, MA: University of Massachusetts, Department of Computer and Information Science.

Duda, R. O., & Hart, P. E. (1973). *Pattern classification and scene analysis.* New York: Wiley & Sons.

Feng, C., Sutherland, A., King, R., Muggleton, S., & Henry, R. (1993). Comparison of machine learning classifiers to statistics and neural networks. *Preliminary Papers of the Fourth International Workshop on Artificial Intelligence and Statistics* (pp. 41-52).

Frean, M. (1990). *Small nets and short paths: Optimising neural computation.* Doctoral dissertation, Center for Cognitive Science, University of Edinburgh.

Kittler, J. (1986). Feature selection and extraction. In Young & Fu (Eds.), *Handbook of pattern recognition and image processing.* New York: Academic Press.

Linhart, H., & Zucchini, W. (1986). *Model selection.* NY: Wiley.

Nilsson, N. J. (1965). *Learning machines.* New York: McGraw-Hill.

Pagallo, G. M. (1990). *Adaptive decision tree algorithms for learning from examples.* Doctoral dissertation, University of California at Santa Cruz.

Provost, F. J., & Buchanan, B. G. (1992). Inductive policy. *Proceedings of the Tenth National Conference on Artificial Intelligence* (pp. 255-261). San Jose, CA: MIT Press.

Quinlan, J. R. (1986). Induction of decision trees. *Machine Learning, 1*, 81-106.

Rendell, L., & Cho, H. (1990). Empirical learning as a function of concept character. *Machine Learning, 5*, 267-298.

Rissanen, J. (1989). *Stochastic complexity in statistical inquiry.* New Jersey: World Scientific.

Salzberg, S. (1991). A nearest hyperrectangle learning. *Machine Learning, 6*, 251-276.

Schaffer, C. (1993). Selecting a classification method by cross-validation. *Preliminary Papers of the Fourth International Workshop on Artificial Intelligence and Statistics* (pp. 15-25).

Shavlik, J. W., Mooney, R. J., & Towell, G. G. (1991). Symbolic and neural learning algorithms: An experimental comparison. *Machine Learning, 6*, 111-144.

Utgoff, P. E. (1989). Perceptron trees: A case study in hybrid concept representations. *Connection Science, 1*, 377-391.

Weiss, S. M., & Kapouleas, I. (1989). An empirical comparision of pattern recognition, neural nets, and machine learning classification methods. *Proceedings of the Eleventh International Joint Conference on Artificial Intelligence* (pp. 781-787). Detroit, Michigan: Morgan Kaufmann.

Yerramareddy, S., Tcheng, D. K., Lu, S. , & Assanis, D. N. (1992). Creating and using models for engineering design. *IEEE Expert, 3*, 52-59.

Young, P. (1984). *Recursive estimation and time-series analysis.* New York: Springer-Verlag.

Using Decision Trees to Improve Case-Based Learning

Claire Cardie
Department of Computer Science
University of Massachusetts
Amherst, MA 01003
E-mail: cardie@cs.umass.edu

Abstract

This paper shows that decision trees can be used to improve the performance of case-based learning (CBL) systems. We introduce a performance task for machine learning systems called semi-flexible prediction that lies between the classification task performed by decision tree algorithms and the flexible prediction task performed by conceptual clustering systems. In semi-flexible prediction, learning should improve prediction of a specific set of features known a priori rather than a single known feature (as in classification) or an arbitrary set of features (as in conceptual clustering). We describe one such task from natural language processing and present experiments that compare solutions to the problem using decision trees, CBL, and a hybrid approach that combines the two. In the hybrid approach, decision trees are used to specify the features to be included in k-nearest neighbor case retrieval. Results from the experiments show that the hybrid approach outperforms both the decision tree and case-based approaches as well as two case-based systems that incorporate expert knowledge into their case retrieval algorithms. Results clearly indicate that decision trees can be used to improve the performance of CBL systems and do so without reliance on potentially expensive expert knowledge.

1 INTRODUCTION

The ability or inability of a natural language processing (NLP) system to handle gaps in lexicon coverage ultimately affects the system's performance on novel texts. Suppose, for example, that a natural language system processes a text with the goal of summarizing it or extracting relevant information, but unexpectedly encounters an unknown word. Rather than stop and wait for a knowledge engineer to enter the missing lexical information, or skip the offending word altogether, a robust sentence analyzer should infer the necessary syntactic and semantic knowledge for the unknown word and then continue processing the text. Consider the following sentence for which an NLP system finds no entry in its lexicon for "Malaysia:"[1]

> Sanyo Electric Co. and Ford Motor Co. have agreed to set up a joint venture by the end of this year to produce car audio parts in **Malaysia**, they said Thursday.

Before the NLP system can continue beyond "Malaysia," it may need to know a specific set of features for the unknown word including its

- part of speech (e.g., noun),
- general semantic class (e.g., location),
- specific semantic class (e.g., country),
- associated concepts (e.g., "Malaysia" may activate a company-location concept in this context),
- relationship to other entities in the sentence (e.g., the joint venture company will be located in Malaysia),
- relationship to entities in a database (e.g., Ford may be a party to another joint venture in Malaysia), etc.

Although the exact types of knowledge required vary tremendously from system to system, all NLP systems are faced with the problem of inferring a number of predetermined features for each unknown word encountered in a text.

When viewed as a problem in machine learning, this lexical acquisition task does not fit neatly into existing paradigms. Because it requires classification along multiple, sometimes related, dimensions, lexical acquisition isn't simply a *classification* problem of the type typically handled by decision tree algorithms (Quinlan 1986). However, because the features to be predicted are known beforehand, neither

[1] This sentence was taken from the TIPSTER joint ventures corpus.

is it a pure example of the *flexible prediction* task (e.g., Fisher 1989; Fisher 1987) performed by conceptual clustering algorithms (Fisher 1987; Michalski & Stepp 1983). Instead, the lexical acquisition problem seems to fall naturally somewhere between the two, in a paradigm we will call *semi-flexible prediction.* In semi-flexible prediction tasks, **learning should improve prediction of a set of features known a priori** rather than a single feature (as in classification) or an arbitrary set of features (as in flexible prediction). This paper describes a hybrid learning technique for semi-flexible prediction tasks that combines case-based learning (CBL)[2] and decision trees: for each feature to be predicted, we rely on a decision tree algorithm to choose the attributes to be included in a simple k-nearest neighbor case retrieval mechanism. We evaluate the approach on the lexical acquisition task described above and show that the hybrid learning algorithm outperforms a pure decision tree solution, a k-nearest neighbors CBL algorithm, and two CBL algorithms that ostensibly encode expert knowledge in their similarity functions. Given the results of our experiments, we conclude that a combination of case-based learning and decision tree algorithms may offer a solution for semi-flexible, knowledge-based prediction. In addition, we believe that the hybrid technique offers an automated alternative to the usually time- and knowledge-intensive design of usable similarity functions for case-based reasoning systems.

In the next section, we first outline a simplified version of the lexical acquisition problem that will be used as the semi-flexible prediction task in all experiments. We then briefly describe the instance representation used across all solutions. Section 3 compares solutions to the problem using a decision tree algorithm, three case-based learning variations, and the hybrid CBL-decision tree algorithm. We conclude with a discussion of related work the contributions of this research (section 4).

2 LEARNING THE DEFINITION OF UNKNOWN WORDS

In the experiments of section 3, we use a semi-flexible prediction task that is a simplification of the the lexical acquisition task described above:

> *Given the context in which an unknown word occurs, learn just three features of the unknown word — the word's*
> 1. *part of speech,*
> 2. *general semantic class, and*
> 3. *specific semantic class.*

[2]The term "case-based learning" is essentially equivalent to "instance-based learning" (Aha, Kibler, & Albert 1991; Aha 1989), but the former term is preferred here because it implies the possibility of a case adaptation phase.

In addition, we focus only on learning the definitions of open class words and assume that information for all closed class words is known. Closed class words are function words like prepositions, auxiliaries, articles, and connectives, whose meanings vary little from one domain to another. All other words (e.g., nouns, verbs, adjectives) are open class words. Focusing on open class words is a legitimate simplification of the original problem because it is likely that the lexicon employed by any natural language processing system will contain entries for all closed class words.[3]

In addition, all training and test instances are lists of attribute-value pairs and are derived from sentences in the TIPSTER JV corpus. This corpus currently contains over 1300 texts that recount world-wide activity in the area of business joint ventures. The next section describes the instance representation used for this language learning problem.

2.1 THE INSTANCE REPRESENTATION

Each training instance is a list of 38 attribute-value pairs and represents the definition of a single open class word as well as the context in which it occurs. Figure 1 shows the training instance for the word "venture" in a sentence taken directly from the TIPSTER JV corpus. Features are divided into three groups: word definition features, local context features, and global context features. First, there are 5 *word definition features* that encode information about the unknown word: the word itself, its part of speech, general and specific semantic attributes, and morphology. Values for the part of speech (**p-o-s**), general attribute (**gen-att**), and specific attribute (**spec-att**) are taken from taxonomies developed for use with the corpus and contain 18, 17, and 45 entries, respectively. "Venture," for example, is a *noun modifier (nm)*[4] and has been assigned the most general semantic attribute, *entity*, but no specific semantic attribute. It has no associated morphological information.

Next, we represent the context via 20 local context features and 13 global context features. The *local context features* describe semantic and syntactic knowledge for the two words preceding (**prev1** and **prev2**) and the two words following (**fol1** and **fol2**) the current word. Again, we draw from the taxonomies to describe each word's part of speech, and general and specific attributes. We also include a feature that indicates the domain-specific **concept** activated by each word in the current context. Most knowledge-based sentence an-

[3]The UMass NLP systems that process texts in the domains of Latin American terrorism, business joint ventures, and microelectronics, for example, rely on the same set of approximately 130 closed class words.

[4]The *noun modifier(nm)* category covers both adjectives and nouns that act as modifiers. We reserve the *noun* category for head nouns only.

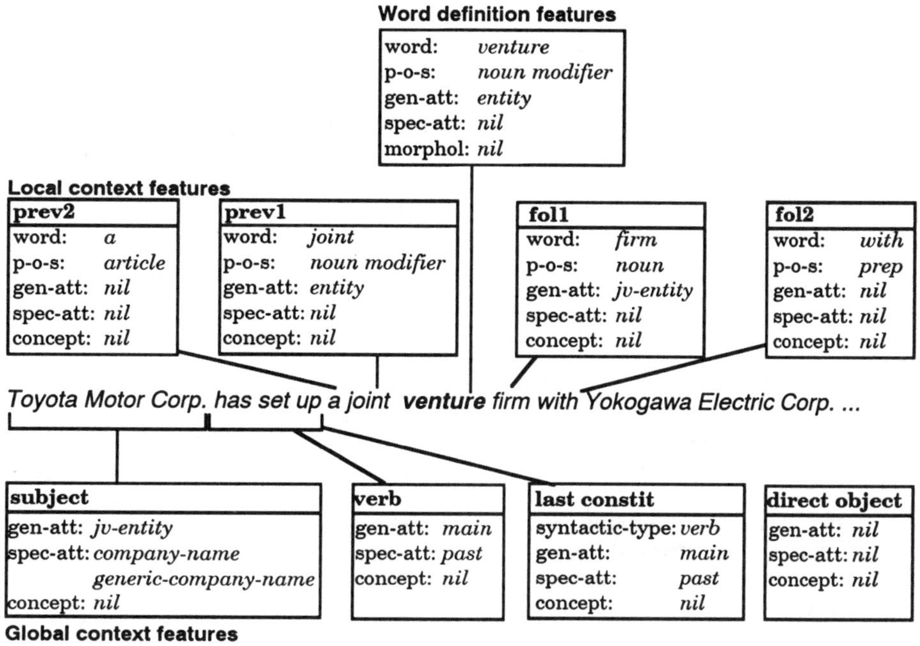

Figure 1: Case for "venture"

alyzers rely on such domain-specific concept activation to indicate when important information has been encountered. In the terrorism domain, for example, "killed" should activate a terrorist-murder concept in the sentence, "Terrorists killed President Gorka," but not in the sentence, "The cancer had effectively been killed." There are currently 11 possible values for concept attributes. In Figure 1, none of the words in the local context of "venture" activates a domain-specific concept.

Finally, the *global context features* represent the state of the parser at the unknown word and include semantic information for each major syntactic constituent (i.e., subject, verb, direct object) and for the most recent low-level constituent, **last constit**. **Last constit** refers to the most recent noun phrase, prepositional phrase, or verb phrase, and often overlaps with one of the major syntactic constituents. Note that all features for the direct object are empty because that constituent has not yet been recognized at the point of the unknown word.

The intent of this representation of global and local context is to include an attribute-value pair for essentially every piece of knowledge that the parser might access to determine the definition of an unknown word when one is encountered as it analyzes a text. In particular, the representation is based on the kinds of knowledge available to the CIRCUS conceptual sentence analyzer (Lehnert 1990) that was used to process the TIPSTER JV corpus. A more detailed description of the instance representation, the taxonomies, and the semi-automated method used to generate the training instances is described in (Cardie 1993).[5]

Every training instance in the experiments below is based on the the 38-attribute feature set described here. In all test instances, however, we omit the **p-o-s**, **gen-att**, and **spec-att** word definition features we are trying to predict. These features represent the part of speech and semantic classes of the unknown word and will be inferred by the learning algorithm. In the next section, we present experiments using decision tree, CBL, and hybrid solutions to the unknown word problem and compare them to each other and to additional performance baselines.

3 COMPARING THE DECISION TREE, CBL, AND HYBRID APPROACHES

In each of the following experiments, we draw the training and test instances from a base set of 2056 38-attribute instances, one for each occurrence of an open class word in 120 sentences of the TIPSTER JV corpus. In addition, all experiments use a 10-fold cross validation evaluation scheme in which we randomly choose a different, non-overlapping set of 205 test cases

[5]In that paper we learn 4 features for each unknown word instead of 3 and focus on the task from a natural language processing perspective. As a result, there are minor differences in the instance representations described in each paper. Verbs, for example, take on semantic features in the representation used here, but do not in (Cardie 1993).

from this base set and use the remaining instances for training in each of 10 runs. We emphasize that the same 10 training and test set combinations were used in the 10-fold cross validation of each experiment below.

3.1 DECISION TREE APPROACH

The decision tree approach to the semi-flexible prediction problem described in section 2 consists of generating 3 decision trees, one for each class of knowledge to be learned for an unknown word — its part of speech (**p-o-s**), general semantic attribute (**gen-att**), and specific semantic attribute (**spec-att**). We will refer to these as the *missing features* of the unknown word. To generate the decision tree for feature x, we present the training instances to the C4.5 decision tree system (Quinlan 1992) after removing the 3 missing features and augmenting the training instance with the value for x as its supervisory class information. The missing features were also removed from the test instances.

Table 1 shows the average performance of C4.5 in predicting each of the missing features across 10 runs and compares it to two baselines.[6] The first baseline indicates the expected accuracy of a system that randomly guesses a legal value for each missing feature based on the distribution of values across the test set. The second baseline shows the performance of a system that always chooses the most frequent value as a default. Chi-square significance tests on the associated frequencies show that the decision tree approach performs significantly better than both of the baselines ($p = .01$).

Table 1: Results for the Decision Tree Approach (% correct)

Missing Feature	Decision Tree	Random Selection	Default
p-o-s	89.0	34.3	81.5
gen-att	66.0	15.9	25.6
spec-att	69.9	24.7	45.3

3.2 CASE-BASED APPROACH

In CBL, the case base is effectively a set of training examples, each of which describes a single problem-solving episode. After training, when a new problem arises, a case retrieval algorithm compares the new problem to those stored in the case base, finds the most similar training case, and then uses it to solve the current problem. In the case-based solution to the NLP problem described above, we create a flat case base of training instances, each of which contains all 38 attribute-value pairs. Then, given a test case from which the 3 missing features have been removed, the case retrieval algorithm searches the case base, finds the training cases that best match it, and then uses them to predict values for the missing features of the unknown word. We use the following case retrieval algorithm for this task:

1. Compare the test case to each case in the case base, counting the number of features that match (i.e., match = 1, mismatch = 0). Do not include the missing features in the comparison. Only give partial credit (.5) for matches on *nil*'s.[7]
2. Keep the k highest-scoring cases.
3. Of these, return the case(s) whose **word** matches the unknown word, if any exist (i.e., prefer instances of the unknown word seen during training). Otherwise, return all k cases.[8]
4. Let the retrieved cases vote on the values for the missing features.

The case retrieval algorithm is essentially a k-nearest neighbors (*k-nn*) matching algorithm with a bias toward examples of the unknown word encountered during training. Table 2 shows the averaged results of the case-based runs (for k= 1, 5, 10) and compares them to the decision tree results. Significant differences in performance with respect to the decision tree approach are indicated in the table by $*$'s. Generally, the decision tree performs better than the CBL approach for k=1, worse than the CBL approach for k=10, and is indistinguishable from the case-based approach for k=5.

The problem with the CBL solution as presented is the difficulty of defining a similarity function for case retrieval that can be used to accurately predict all of the missing features of the unknown word. The k-nn routine in the case retrieval algorithm described above (step1) assumes that all features are equally important for predicting each of the missing features. But intuitively it seems that accurate prediction of each class of missing information for the unknown word may actually rely on very different subsets of the feature set. In fact, it is well known that k-nn algorithms perform poorly in the presence of irrelevant features (Aha, Kibler, & Albert 1991; Aha 1989).

One method for optimizing the similarity metric for each missing feature is to employ expert knowledge. We can incorporate informed intuitions about the nature of each class of missing knowledge into the case retrieval algorithm by letting an expert decide which

[6]In all experiments described in this paper, we allow mismatches between the noun and noun modifier parts of speech because the parser can fix these errors.

[7]This is because a *nil* value indicates that an attribute did not apply in the current context and the matching process should focus on relevant features rather than omitted features.

[8]More than k cases will be returned if there are ties.

Table 2: Results for the Baseline Case-Based Approach (% correct). (* and ** indicate significance with respect to the decision tree results, $* \rightarrow p = .01$ and $** \rightarrow p = .05$.)

Missing Feature	Case-Based (k = 1)	Case-Based (k = 5)	Case-Based (k = 10)	Decision Tree
p-o-s	86.6*	88.8	89.4	89.0
gen-att	58.5*	66.2	69.1*	66.0
spec-att	62.9*	70.4	72.2**	69.9

features to include in the k-nn calculations. Some successful part of speech taggers, for example, make decisions based only on knowledge of the words in a window to either side of the unknown word. This implies that the k-nn routine should only include the local context features in its calculations. Adding the global context features may only hurt performance. On the other hand, the semantic features of an unknown word seem to depend partially on local context and partially on knowledge about the global state of the sentence. For example, the semantic class of a noun that follows a verb may depend on the semantic class of the clause's subject. Therefore, when predicting semantic features, it might be better first to find the most similar cases using the local context features and then choose from these the cases that match best along both the local and global context dimensions.

We incorporated these observations into two variations of the baseline CBL system. The first variation, referred to as the "p-o-s" CBL system, was designed to improve **p-o-s** prediction and uses only the local context features in its k-nn comparisons. The second variation, referred to as the "semantic class" CBL system, was designed to improve prediction of the **gen-att** and **spec-att** features. It submits those cases initially selected using just local context features to an additional k-nn filter that includes the global context features as well. Like the baseline CBL system, both intuitive variations also prefer cases whose **word** feature matches the unknown word.

Table 3 shows the results of the intuitive CBL variations and compares them to the baseline CBL algorithm and the decision tree results. Only the results for k=10 are shown, but runs using k=1, 5 exhibited similar behavior. All results are averaged over 10 runs. Also shown in the table are annotations for statistical significance. (*'s indicate the performance of all case-based systems as compared to the decision tree results and ◇'s indicate performance of the intuitive CBL variations as compared to the CBL baseline.) As expected, focusing on local features improved part of speech prediction and the semantic class CBL variation improved performance across the general and specific semantic attributes. However, the p-o-s CBL method also unexpectedly improved the prediction of both semantic class attributes.

3.3 HYBRID APPROACH

The preceding experiments show that it is possible to use informed intuitions to discard irrelevant attributes from the feature set and thus improve performance of the k-nn case retrieval algorithm. Given that feature set specification is a notoriously time-consuming and knowledge-intensive task however (Quinlan 1983), it would be better if the feature set could be chosen systematically and automatically. This problem is addressed in the hybrid approach to semi-flexible prediction in which decision trees aid in the definition of a similarity metric that focuses on an appropriate subset of features by isolating the attributes most important for accurate prediction of each class of missing knowledge. In the hybrid approach, we let C4.5 select the features to be included for k-nn case retrieval:

1. *For each training set used in the decision tree experiments (section 3.1), note the features that occurred in the corresponding C4.5 decision tree.*[9] This essentially produces, for each of the missing attributes, a list of all features that C4.5 found useful for predicting its value.
2. *Run the baseline case retrieval algorithm (section 3.2) with the following modification: instead of invoking the case retrieval algorithm once for each test case, run it three times, once for each missing attribute to be predicted.* In the retrieval for attribute a, however, include only the features C4.5 found to be important for predicting a in the k-nn calculations.[10]

When predicting the part of speech of the unknown word, for example, only those features C4.5 found to be important for **p-o-s** prediction are included in the k-nn matching routine (step 1 of the case retrieval algorithm). In contrast to the expert knowledge required to devise the intuitive CBL approaches, case retrieval is automatically tuned in the hybrid system by using C4.5 for feature specification. The feature sets proposed by C4.5 reduce the number of attributes used in

[9] We use the pruned decision trees produced by C4.5 for this experiment as well as for the original decision tree experiments. Note also that as part of the 10-fold cross validation scheme, we created 10 decision trees for each missing feature — one for each training set. We use these same decision trees for the current experiment.

[10] We actually only compare each test case to the entire case base once (not three times) and use the results of that comparison for each of the three k-nn calculations.

Table 3: Results for Intuitive CBL Variations (% correct, $k = 10$). (* and ** indicate significance with respect to the decision tree results, $* \rightarrow p = .01$ and $** \rightarrow p = .05$. $\diamond$ and $\diamond\diamond$ indicate significance with respect to the baseline CBL system, $\diamond \rightarrow p = .01$ and $\diamond\diamond \rightarrow p = .05$.)

Missing Feature	Case-Based (p-o-s)	Case-Based (semantic class)	Case-Based (baseline)	Decision Tree
p-o-s	91.4*◇	90.4**	89.4	89.0
gen-att	73.9*◇	72.1*◇	69.1*	66.0
spec-att	75.0*◇	74.2*◇◇	72.2**	69.9

the case retrieval algorithm from 35 to an average of 14 (**p-o-s**), 11 (**gen-att**), and 15 (**spec-att**) features.[11]

Table 4 shows the average performance of the hybrid approach across 10 runs and compares it to identical runs for the baseline CBL system and the best of the intuitive T approaches, i.e., the approach that relied only on local context features. Again, only results for k=10 are shown although results for k=1, 5 were much the same. The table also compares the results to a system that randomly chooses the features to be used in the k-nn calculations while controlling for feature set size (i.e., we use the same number of features that were used in the corresponding run for the hybrid approach). In all but one case, the hybrid approach significantly outperforms the other approaches ($p = .05$). The only exception was prediction of the **gen-att** feature, for which the p-o-s CBL system did as well as the hybrid approach. As noted above, however, the p-o-s CBL system that focused on local context features was designed to improve prediction of part of speech, not general semantic class.

In spite of the promising performance demonstrated by the hybrid learning system, there are problems with our current approach. The speed of the algorithm degrades linearly with the size of the case base and modifications would be required before the approach could be tested using a hierarchical case base. Methods described in (Aha, Kibler, & Albert 1991) to reduce the storage requirements of T algorithms provide an alternative to construction of a hierarchical case base, however. In addition, it is not feasible to tune the case retrieval mechanism (i.e., to determine the relevant attributes associated with each missing feature) after every incoming instance because the costs associated with running a decision tree algorithm are too great. Instead, one might wait until the case base was relatively stable before employing the hybrid CBL approach or tune the similarity metrics only occasionally. In both solutions, however, we lose some of the inherent advantages associated with the incremental nature of CBL algorithms. Finally, we should test the approach on additional data sets, or find a method for automatically recognizing problems that will respond favorably to this hybrid technique.

[11]These are averages across the 10 experiments run for each missing feature as part of the 10-fold cross validation evaluation.

4 RELATED WORK AND CONCLUSIONS

4.1 RELATED WORK IN LEXICAL ACQUISITION

Although the problem of automating lexical acquisition has been addressed before, previous approaches often focus on learning either syntactic or limited semantic knowledge but not both (e.g., (Brent 1990; Grefenstette 1992; Resnik 1992; and Zernik 1991)). Moreover, the approaches tend to fall into one of two categories: statistically-based methods that acquire (usually syntactic) lexical knowledge (e.g., (Brent 1991; Church & Hanks 1990; Hindle 1990; Resnik 1992; Yarowsky 1992; and Zernik 1991)), or knowledge-intensive methods that acquire syntactic and/or semantic lexical knowledge, but rely heavily on hand-coded world knowledge (e.g., (Berwick 1983; Granger 1977; Hastings et al. 1991; Lytinen & Roberts 1989; and Selfridge 1986)) or hand-coded heuristics that describe how and when to acquire new word definitions (e.g., Jacobs & Zernik 1988 and Wilensky 1991). Our approach differs from all of these in that

- it uses a novel combination of two existing machine learning paradigms
- the same learning algorithm and instance representation are used to simultaneously learn both syntactic and semantic lexical knowledge
- the approach does not rely on hand-coded heuristics, and
- relatively little training is needed.[12]

[12]For a more detailed description of this work from an NLP perspective, see (Cardie, 1993). In that paper, we incorporate the hybrid learning algorithm described here into a working sentence analyzer that processes text from a variety of corpora. We then evaluate the approach for learning the definitions of unknown words in two practical language processing applications.

Table 4: Results for Hybrid Approach (% correct). (^ indicates results not significantly different than the hybrid system. The hybrid system significantly outperforms all other variations, $p = .05$.)

Missing Feature	Hybrid (DT + CBL) $k = 10$	Case-Based (baseline) $k = 10$	Case-Based (p-o-s) $k = 10$	Random Features $k = 10$	Decision Tree
p-o-s	92.5	89.4	91.4	89.7	89.0
gen-att	73.4	69.1	73.9^	62.9	66.0
spec-att	76.7	72.2	75.0	71.1	69.9

4.2 ADDITIONAL RELATED WORK AND CONCLUSIONS

In this paper, we have compared three approaches to problems in semi-flexible prediction: decision trees, case-based learning, and a hybrid technique that combines the two. In the hybrid approach, decision trees specify the features to be included in k-nearest neighbor case retrieval. In related work, (Aha 1989) presents a method for learning concept-dependent attribute relevancies in a case-based paradigm. He dynamically updates the similarity function for each concept by modifying an attribute weight vector associated with the concept in response to classification performance. Here we use decision trees essentially to create an attribute weight vector for each concept where the weights are either 0 or 1. However, one possibility which we have not yet explored is to use the position of an attribute in the decision tree to derive attribute weights between 0 and 1. This would make our weight vector more similar to Aha's real-valued weights that range between 0 and 0.5. In addition, Aha's method differs from ours in that (1) it is completely incremental, i.e., the similarity function for each concept must be updated for every incoming instance, and (2) it is designed for boolean-valued concepts rather than the multi-valued concepts used here. Although, in theory, the incremental method seems ultimately more appropriate, it may not be feasible when the number of concepts to be learned is large and/or there are multi-valued concepts involved.

Given the results of the experiments outlined in section 3 that compare the decision tree, cased-based, and hybrid approaches to semi-flexible prediction, we conclude that the hybrid technique performs significantly better than the pure decision tree and CBL algorithms for a language learning task. It also performed better than two CBL systems that incorporated expert knowledge for the feature specification task. This result has important implications for work in case-based paradigms because it clearly indicates that decision tree algorithms can be used to improve the performance of some CBL systems without reliance on potentially expensive expert knowledge. On one hand, these results may not seem surprising since previous research has found the converse to be true — (Skalak & Rissland 1990) show that a case-based reasoning system can successfully perform the feature specification task for a decision tree classification system. However, (Almuallim & T 1991) show that ID3 (Quinlan 1986) is not particularly good at selecting a minimum set of features from an original set containing possibly many irrelevant attributes. While their results may hold in general, we claim that there is at least one important class of problem for which decision tree algorithms can perform feature specification reasonably well.

Acknowledgments

Many thanks to Professor J. Ross Quinlan for supplying the C4.5 decision tree system. Thanks also to Carla Brodley, Ellen Riloff, Wendy Lehnert, and David Skalak for helpful comments and discussions. This research was supported by the Office of Naval Research Contract N00014-92-J-1427 and NSF Grant no. EEC-9209623, State/Industry/University Cooperative Research on Intelligent Information Retrieval.

References

Aha, D., Kibler, D., & Albert, M. (1991). Instance-Based Learning Algorithms. *Machine Learning 6* (1): pp. 37-66.

Aha, D. (1989). Incremental, Instance-Based Learning of Independent and Graded Concept Descriptions. *Proceedings, Sixth International Workshop on Machine Learning*, pp. 387-391. Cornell University, Ithaca, NY. Morgan Kaufmann.

Almuallim, H., & Dietterich, T. G. (1991). Learning With Many Irrelevant Features. *Proceedings, Ninth National Conference on Artificial Intelligence*, pp. 547-552. Anaheim, CA. AAAI Press / The MIT Press.

Berwick, R. (1983). Learning word meanings from examples. *Proceedings, Eighth International Joint Conference on Artificial Intelligence*, pp. 459-461. Karlsruhe, Germany.

Brent, M. (1991). Automatic acquisition of subcategorization frames from untagged text. *Proceedings, 29th Annual Meeting of the Association for Computational Linguistics*, pp. 209-214. University of California, Berkeley. Association for Computational Linguistics.

Brent, M. (1990). Semantic classification of verbs from their syntactic contexts: automated lexicography with implications for child language acquisition. *Proceedings, Twelfth Annual Conference of the Cognitive Science Society*, pp. 428-437. Cambridge MA. The Cognitive Science Society.

Cardie, C. (1993). A Case-Based Approach to Knowledge Acquisition for Domain-Specific Sentence Analysis. To appear in *Proceedings, Eleventh National Conference on Artificial Intelligence.* Washington, DC.

Church, K., & Hanks, P. (1990). Word association norms, mutual information, and lexicography. *Computational Linguistics, 16.*

Fisher, D. (1989). Noise-Tolerant Conceptual Clustering. *Proceedings, Eleventh International Joint Conference on Artificial Intelligence*, pp. 630-635. Detroit MI. Morgan Kaufmann.

Fisher, D. H. (1987). Knowledge Acquisition Via Incremental Conceptual Clustering. *Machine Learning 2*: 139-172.

Granger, R. (1977). Foulup: A program that figures out meanings of words from context. *Proceedings, Fifth International Joint Conference on Artificial Intelligence*, pp. 172-178. Morgan Kaufmann.

Grefenstette, G. (1992). SEXTANT: Exploring unexplored contexts for semantic extraction from syntactic analysis. *Proceedings, 30th Annual Meeting of the Association for Computational Linguistics*, pp. 324-326. University of Delaware, Newark, DE. Association for Computational Linguistics.

Hastings, P., Lytinen, S., & Lindsay, R. (1991). Learning Words from Context. *Proceedings, Eighth International Conference on Machine Learning*, pp. 55-59. Northwestern University, Chicago, IL. Morgan Kaufmann.

Hindle, D. (1990). Noun classification from predicate-argument structures. *Proceedings, 28th Annual Meeting of the Association for Computational Linguistics*, pp. 268-275. University of Pittsburgh. Association for Computational Linguistics.

Jacobs, P., & Zernik, U. (1988). Acquiring Lexical Knowledge from Text: A Case Study. *Proceedings, Seventh National Conference on Artificial Intelligence*, pp. 739-744. St. Paul, MN. Morgan Kaufmann.

Lehnert, W. (1990). Symbolic/Subsymbolic Sentence Analysis: Exploiting the Best of Two Worlds. In J. Barnden, & J. Pollack (Eds.), *Advances in Connectionist and Neural Computation Theory*, pp. 135-164. Norwood, NJ: Ablex Publishers.

Lytinen, S., & Roberts, S. (1989). Lexical Acquisition as a By-Product of Natural Language Processing. *Proceedings, IJCAI-89 Workshop on Lexical Acquisition.*

Michalski, R. S., & Stepp, R. (1983). Learning from observation: conceptual clustering. In R. S. Michalski, J. G. Carbonell, & T. M. Mitchell (Eds.), *Machine Learning: An Artificial Intelligence Approach.* Morgan Kaufmann.

Quinlan, J. R. (1992). *C4.5: Programs for Machine Learning.* Morgan Kaufmann.

Quinlan, J. R. (1986). Induction of decision trees. *Machine Learning, 1*: 81-106.

Quinlan, J. R. (1983). Learning Efficient Classification Procedures and Their Application to Chess End Games. In R. S. Michalski, J. G. Carbonell, & T. M. Mitchell (Eds.), *Machine Learning: An Artificial Intelligence Approach.* Palo Alto: Morgan Kaufmann.

Resnik, P. (1992). A class-based approach to lexical discovery. *Proceedings, 30th Annual Meeting of the Association for Computational Linguistics*, pp. 327-329. University of Delaware, Newark, DE. Association for Computational Linguistics.

Selfridge, M. (1986). A computer model of child language learning. *Artificial Intelligence, 29*: 171-216.

Skalak, D. and Rissland, E. (1990). Inductive Learning in a Mixed Paradigm Setting. *Proceedings, Eighth National Conference on Artificial Intelligence*, pp. 840-847. Boston, MA. AAAI Press/MIT Press.

Wilensky, R. (1991). Extending the Lexicon by Exploiting Subregularities. *Tech. Report No. UCB/CSD 91/618.* Computer Science Division (EECS), Univ. of California, Berkeley.

Yarowsky, D. (1992). Word-Sense Disambiguation Using Statistical Models of Roget's Categories Trained on Large Corpora. *Proceedings, COLING-92.*

Zernik, U. (1991). Train1 vs. Train 2: Tagging Word Senses in Corpus. In U. Zernik (Ed.), *Lexical Acquisition: Exploiting On-Line Resources to Build a Lexicon*, pp. 91-112. Hillsdale, NJ: Lawrence Erlbaum Associates, Inc.

GALOIS : An order-theoretic approach to conceptual clustering

Claudio Carpineto and **Giovanni Romano**
Fondazione Ugo Bordoni
Via B. Castiglione 59, 00142 Rome (Italy)
fubdpt5@itcaspur.bitnet

Abstract

The theory of concept (or Galois) lattices provides a natural and formal setting in which to discover and represent concept hierarchies. In this paper we present a system, GALOIS, which is able to determine the concept lattice corresponding to a given set of objects. GALOIS is incremental and relatively efficient, the time complexity of each update ranging from O(n) to O(n^2) where n is the number of concepts in the lattice. Unlike most approaches to conceptual clustering, GALOIS represents and updates all possible classes in a restricted concept space. Therefore the concept hierarchies it finds are always justified and are not sensitive to object ordering. We experimentally demonstrate, using several machine learning data sets, that GALOIS can be successfully used for class discovery and class prediction. We also point out applications of GALOIS in fields related to machine learning (i.e., information retrieval and databases).

1 INTRODUCTION

Much of recent work on conceptual clustering has focused on incremental construction of concept hierarchies from a collection of unlabelled objects (e.g., Lebowitz 1986, Fisher 1987, Hanson and Bauer 1987, Hadzikadic&Yun 1989, Langley 1991). Although these approaches differ in many respects (e.g., the concept representation, the hierarchy evaluation criteria, the use of the hierarchy for learning), they usually tackle the problem in the same manner, i.e. defining a set of hierarchy change operators and carrying out a hill-climbing search through a space of possible concept hierarchies aimed at finding a "good" hierarchy (Gennari et al 1989). The operators are applied whenever a new object is presented, and they either incorporate the new object into an existing class, or create new classes, or delete old classes, depending on evaluation of some heuristic criterion associated to the resulting hierarchies. These systems perform well in many experimental settings, but, because the criteria used to modify and evaluate the hierarchy are mostly local and/or heuristic, they have some drawbacks. One main problem is the lack of a clear semantics, by which to characterize or explain the whole hierarchy in terms of the object description. In fact, it may sometimes be difficult to understand why certain nodes have been generated and others have been omitted. Another related limitation is the sensitivity to order of presentation of objects. To illustrate these points consider the following collection of four objects (a, b, c, d), each described by four binary attributes:

a = (0 0 0 1)
b = (0 0 1 1)
c = (1 1 0 0)
d = (1 0 0 0)

If Fisher's COBWEB (Fisher, 1987) - taken as a representative of the hierarchical conceptual clustering systems - were presented with the sequence (a, b, c, d), it would produce, as could be easily checked, the hierarchy: (root (a b (c&d (c d)))).
This hierarchy, however, does not seem to reflect the actual object description, in that while it contains the class c&d it does not contain the perfectly symmetrical class a&b. Furthermore, if COBWEB were given the reversed sequence (d, c, b, a) it would produce a different asymmetrical hierarchy : (root (d c (b&a (b a)))).

In this paper we present an approach to conceptual clustering that helps overcome such limitations. Rather than finding and updating a particular subset (i.e., the output hierarchy) of the concepts, we keep and update *all* the classes that can be generated in a restricted concept language. This strategy is similar to the version space approach (Mitchell 1982) in concept induction from labelled examples. Our approach relies on a theory - the theory of concept (or Galois) lattices - which has received little attention in artificial intelligence approaches to clustering (Carpineto&Romano 1992). We believe it offers a formal and natural tool for restricting, representing, and ordering the set of concepts that can be induced over a collection of unlabelled objects. Its best features are that the concept hierarchies produced are globally related to the object description and that they are not sensitive to object ordering. In the paper we build on the theory of concept lattices, tackling the problem of its automatization and use in a performance system. We define an algorithm for incremental construction of the concept lattice, implemented in a system named GALOIS[1], and show that its time complexity ranges from O(n) to $O(n^2)$ where n is the number of concepts in the lattice. We experimentally demonstrate that the resulting lattice permits to do both class discovery and class prediction with very good results.

The rest of the paper is organized as follows. First we introduce the basics of the theory of concept lattices. Then we describe the algorithm for incrementally finding the concept lattice and discuss its computational complexity. Next we evaluate GALOIS' learning ability on several domains (soybean, congressional voting, breast cancer, iris). Finally we outline extensions and further applications of GALOIS, such as automatic keywords classification in information retrieval and inferencing of implication rules in databases.

2 THE CONCEPT LATTICE: BACKGROUND

A context is a triple (O,D,I) where O is a set of objects, D is a set of descriptors, and $I \subseteq OxD$. We write *oId*, meaning the object *o* has the descriptor *d*. We can think of the set of descriptors associated with an object as a bit vector. Each bit (descriptor) corresponds to a possible value of a particular attribute and is on or off depending on whether an object has that value for that attribute.
A concept is considered to be determined by its extent and its intent: the extent consists of all objects belonging to the concept while the intent is the collection of all descriptors shared by the objects. For $A \subseteq O$ and $B \subseteq D$, define

$$A' = \{d \in D \mid (\forall o \in A)\ oId\}$$
$$B' = \{o \in O \mid (\forall d \in B)\ oId\}$$

so A' is the set of descriptors common to all objects in A and B' is the set of objects possessing the attributes in B. Then a concept of the context (O,D,I) is defined to be a couple (A, B) where $A \subseteq O$, $B \subseteq D$, A' = B, B' = A. The extent of the concept is A while the intent is B. Therefore only some couples (A,B) - i.e., the couples that are complete with respect to I according to the given definition - represent admissible concepts. Note that a subset B of D is the intent of some concept if and only if B''=B in which case the unique concept of which B is an intent is (B',B); a dual statement holds for the extent of a concept.
The set of all concepts of the context (O, D, I) is denoted by C(O, D, I). An ordering relation ($\leq$) is easily defined on this set of concepts by

$$(A_1, B_1) \leq (A_2, B_2) \leftrightarrow A_1 \subseteq A_2$$

or, equivalently, by

$$(A_1, B_1) \leq (A_2, B_2) \leftrightarrow B_1 \supseteq B_2.$$

C(O, D, I) along with $\geq$ form an ordered set. It can be characterized in the following way (see (Davey and Priestley 1990) for the complete theorem and its proof)).

The Fundamental Theorem on Concept Lattices (C(O, D, I) ; $\leq$) is a complete lattice[2] in which the least upper bound (*Sup*) and the greatest lower bound (*Inf*) are given by

$$Sup_{j \in J}\ (A_j, B_j) = ((\bigcup_{j \in J} A_j)'', \bigcap_{j \in J} B_j)$$
$$Inf_{j \in J}\ (A_j, B_j) = (\bigcap_{j \in J} A_j, (\bigcup_{j \in J} B_j)'').$$

So for any subset of concepts there is a least upper bound whose intent is given by the intersection of the intents of the concepts in the subset (a dual statement holds for the extent of a greatest lower bound).

If we consider again the context introduced earlier, consisting of the four objects a b c d, it is straightforward to see that independently of order of presentation the corresponding concept lattice is the (symmetrical) hierarchy: (root((a&b(a b)) (c&d(c d))). In table 1 a more expressive example representing a simple context for the planets of our solar system is shown. The corresponding concept lattice is illustrated in figure 1 (ss stands for size-small, my for moon-yes,etc).

	size			distance from sun		moon	
	small	medium	large	near	far	yes	no
Mercury	x			x			x
Venus	x			x			x
Earth	x			x		x	
Mars	x			x		x	
Jupiter			x		x	x	
Saturn			x		x	x	
Uranus		x			x	x	
Neptune		x			x	x	
Pluto	x				x	x	

Table 1: A context for the planets

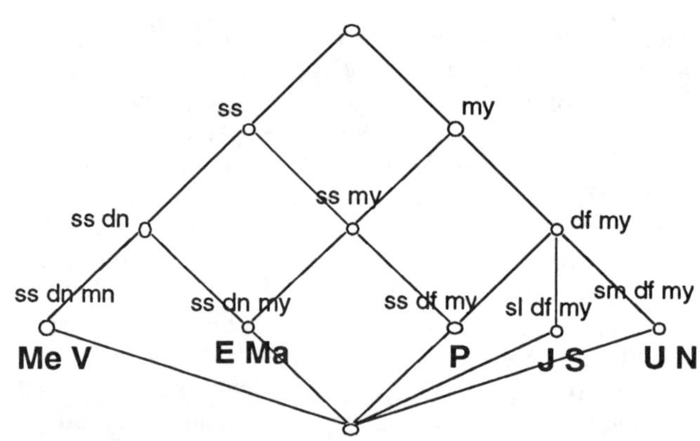

Figure 1: The concept lattice of the planet context

[1]GALOIS has been implemented in Common Lisp on a Symbolics Lisp Machine.

[2]Recall that given a non-empty ordered set P, if for all $S \subset P$ there exist a least upper bound and a greatest lower bound then P is called a complete lattice.

In the graph representing the concept lattice, also called Hasse diagram, there is an edge between two concepts if they are ordered and there is no other intermediate concept in the lattice. The top concept contain all objects and is defined by their common descriptors (none in this case), the bottom concept is defined by the set of all descriptors and contains no objects. The labels in fig.1 indicate the intent of each concept; for the most specific concepts the extents are also shown. Note that many couples are not admissible in this context; the concept *df,* for instance, does not belong to the lattice in that all objects having df have also my. Note also that the intent (or, dually, the extent) of a concept in the lattice is sufficient to characterize the concept.

3 AN ALGORITHM FOR THE INCREMENTAL DETERMINATION OF THE CONCEPT LATTICE

Determining the concept lattice along with the Hasse diagram is a computationally difficult problem (Guénoche 1990). Furthermore the algorithms that have been proposed are - with one notably exception (Godin et al 1991) - non-incremental, whereas an important requirement posed by many real problems, including most conceptual clustering tasks, is incrementality. In this section we describe the incremental algorithm used by GALOIS to build the concept lattice. We start by informally discussing the effect of adding a new object to a given lattice. First of all we have to note that old concepts are never removed from the lattice. In fact, either they are incomparable to (the concept corresponding to) the new object and therefore are not affected by its introduction, or they include (or are equal to) the new object and therefore have just their extent augmented by the new object. In addition to modifying the extent of the concepts in which it is contained, the new object in general causes new concepts to be added to the lattice. This happens whenever the intersection of the new object with any set of *objects* with which it shares some attribute is not already present in the lattice. Any new concept introduced in the lattice has to be then consistently linked to the other concepts, including the other new concepts. This will in general cause the elimination of some edges (i.e., the edges betwccn all couples of concepts C_1 and C_2 such that $C_1 > C_{new} > C_2$).

The algorithm we propose relies on two basic ideas. The first is that in order to find the concepts in the updated lattice it suffices to consider the intersections of the new object with the concepts[3] in the old lattice. The second is that the ordering of the old concept lattice can be exploited to delay the generation of each new concept and its relative edges until it is really necessary, thus avoiding much concept duplication and edge consistency checking.

We shall explain both ideas in turn.

To generate the concepts in the updated lattice it is not necessary to intersect the new object with all possible combinations of the old *objects.* By contrast, intersecting the new object with the concepts in the old lattice is sufficient to guarantee that *all* updated concepts will be generated, including those resulting from the intersection of *new* concepts (the new concepts being those generated intersecting the new object with some old concept). This can be proved as follows.

Given any two new nodes C_1 and C_2 we have to show that there exist a (new) node C_k such that $C_k = C_1 \cap C_2$. Since C_1 and C_2 are new nodes then there exist two old nodes C_{11} and C_{22} such that

$C_1 = C_{new\text{-}ob} \cap C_{11}$, $C_2 = C_{new\text{-}ob} \cap C_{22}$,

where $C_{new\text{-}ob}$ is the node corresponding to the new object. We have

$C_1 \cap C_2 = C_{11} \cap C_{new\text{-}ob} \cap C_{22} \cap C_{new\text{-}ob} = (C_{11} \cap C_{22}) \cap C_{new\text{-}ob}$.

Since $(C_{11} \cap C_{22})$ belongs to the old lattice then $C_k = (C_{11} \cap C_{22}) \cap C_{new\text{-}ob}$.

The main loop of the algorithm therefore consists of adding the intersections of the new object with old concepts, and their relative edges, to the lattice.

At this point the second idea comes to place. If we were going to examine each node in the lattice independently of each other, then for any intersection with the new object we would have to spend much effort to check whether the intersection has already been generated. However, if we exploit the old lattice's structure we can avoid such operation. For each node in the lattice GALOIS compares the (intents of the) fathers of the node to the intersection of (the intent of) the node with (the intent of) the new object. Basically there are four possible cases:

1) there is a father < intersection;
2) there is a father = intersection;
3) there is a father > intersection;
4) all fathers are incomparable to intersection.

In case 1) GALOIS does not create the new concept, in that the same concept will be generated when we intersect the new object with the father of the node. In case 2) it does not create the new concept because it is already present in the lattice. In cases 3) and 4) it actually adds the new concept to the lattice. By doing so GALOIS is guaranteed to never generate two concepts equal. The prove goes as follows.

Consider two concepts C_1 and C_2 such that the intersection with the new object is the same:

$C_1 \cap C_{new\text{-}ob} = C_2 \cap C_{new\text{-}ob}$.

It follows:

$$C_1 \cap C_2 \leq (C_1 \cap C_2) \cap (C_{new\text{-}ob} \cap C_{new\text{-}ob}) = (C_1 \cap C_{new\text{-}ob}) \cap (C_2 \cap C_{new\text{-}ob}) = (C_1 \cap C_{new\text{-}ob}).$$

So $C_1 \cap C_2 \leq C_1 \cap C_{new\text{-}ob}$. Now, if $C_1 \cap C_2 < C_1 \cap C_{new\text{-}ob}$ then there exists a father of C_1 (i.e., C_1

[3]From now on, when we refer to a concept (sometimes called node) we usually mean its intent.

$\cap C_2$) more specific than the intersection ($C_1 \cap C_{new\text{-}ob}$) and therefore the generation of the new node is ruled out by case 1); else, if $C_1 \cap C_2 = C_1 \cap C_{new\text{-}ob}$ then there exists a father of C_1 (i.e., $C_1 \cap C_2$) equal to the intersection ($C_1 \cap C_{new\text{-}ob}$) and therefore the generation of the new node is ruled out by case 2). In any case the new node is generated only once.

After a new node has been added to the lattice we have to create the relative edges. For this problem there is no simple solution because the new node has to be consistently linked also to the other new nodes, and the new nodes to be added to the lattice cannot be generated in an ordered fashion. The procedure GALOIS uses (which will be referred to as LINK) works on the current lattice, i.e. it considers also the nodes that have been added to the input lattice until that point. It determines for any new node two boundary sets, the lower boundary set S containing the most general concepts more specific than the new node, and the upper boundary set G containing the most specific concepts more general than the new node. Then it links the new node to each element in S and G, and remove the edges between S and G (if any). The sets S and G are determined considering only a subset of the whole current concept lattice; because the new node is the intersection of the new object with an old concept, the concepts to which it may be linked have necessarily to be more general than the old node or more general than the new object.

In table 2 the complete description of the algorithm is given. For each new object the algorithm is initialized adding the concept corresponding to the new object to the lattice. The function LINK realizes the procedure we described above; it takes as arguments the concept to be linked and the two concepts which determine the subset of the *current* concept lattice to be searched. To see the algorithm at work, consider again the concept lattice shown in fig. 1 and suppose to introduce the new planet X?=(size-medium,distance-near,moon-no). GALOIS returns the updated lattice shown in figure 2. The detailed working is as follows. All the concepts in the old lattice having an empty intersection with X? are processed by case a) and do not modify the lattice. There are only four remaining concepts: UN, EMa, MeV, ss-dn. Concept UN (case f) returns the node sm, the sets S=[UN, X?], G=[top] and the relative edges (UN,sm), (X?,sm), (sm,top). Concept EMa (case c) does not modify the lattice. Concept MeV (case f) returns the node mn-dn, the sets S=[MeV, X?], G=[top] and the edges (MeV,mn-dn), (X?,mn-dn), (mn-dn,top). Concept ss-dn (case f) returns the node dn, the sets S=[mn-dn, ss-dn], G=[top] and the edges (mn-dn,dn), (ss-dn,dn), (dn,top), *and eliminates the edge (mn-dn,top).*

Table 2: The algorithm for incremental update of the concept lattice

```
For each concept in lattice
  do
  intersection ¨ concept ( new-object
  select-case
     <<intersection = empty>>                         ;a
        do-nothing
     <<intersection = concept>>                       ;b
        do-nothing
     <<there is father(concept) < intersection>>      ;c
        do-nothing
     <<there is father(concept) = intersection>>      ;d
        LINK(father(concept), new-object, concept)
     <<there is father(concept) > intersection>>      ;e
        add intersection to lattice
        LINK(intersection, new-object, concept)
        for each father(concept) > intersection>
           eliminate edge (concept,father(concept))
     <<otherwise>>                                    ;f
        add intersection to lattice
        LINK(intersection, new-object, concept)
```

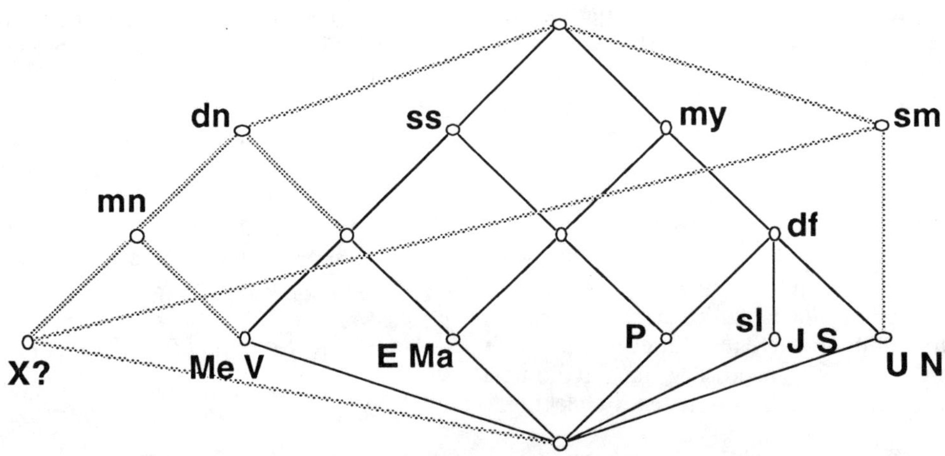

Figure 2: The concept lattice after the introduction of the new planet

4 COMPUTATIONAL COMPLEXITY

In this section we evaluate the space and time complexity of GALOIS.

4.1 SPACE COMPLEXITY

For the number of concepts present in the lattice there is a theoretical upper bound which is dependent on the number of descriptors. Assuming the attribute space used to describe the objects consists of m v-valued attributes, the conjunctive concept language on which GALOIS operates contain $(v+1)^m$ admissible concepts. For practical values of v and m this bound may be very high, so it is significant to see how the number of concepts varies with the number of objects. The experimental evaluations we have done on several machine learning datasets reveal that the growth of concepts ranges from linear to quadratic with respect to the number of objects. The lower bound was obtained with the dataset Iris (150 objects, 363 concepts), the upper bound with the dataset Soybean (47 objects, 3593 concepts).

4.2 TIME COMPLEXITY

For each object GALOIS iterates on the concepts in the lattice, which - assuming there are m binary attributes - are at most 3^m. In each iteration it may then have to apply the function LINK, which at most requires the examination of all concepts greater than the new object (2^m concepts).Therefore the worst-case time complexity is $O(3^m 2^m N) < O(3^{2m} N)$ where N is the number of objects. If the number of attributes is upper bounded, as it usually happens, the asymptotical behavior is linear in the number of objects. In practice, however, the constant factor relative to each update may be very large. While we have seen that it theorctically ranges from l to l^2 where l is the number of concepts in the lattice, it may be interesting to evaluate its experimental behavior. For this purpose we plotted the number of nodes examinated in each update by the key operation of GALOIS (i.e., determination of the lower boundary set S within the function LINK) as a function of the number of concepts in the lattice. We found (for the datasets Soybean, Congressional voting, Breast cancer, Iris) that although the complexity of each update varied between the two theoretical extremes with many oscillations, it never exceeded a small fraction of the square of the number of concepts. We have planned further experiments that may help clarify the actual behavior of the algorithm and may give clues as to reducing its overall complexity.

5 EMPIRICAL EVALUATION OF GALOIS AS A LEARNING SYSTEM

The concept lattice corresponding to a given set of objects may contain a large number of concepts. As all concepts in the lattice are formally justified they are equally good, in a sense. Also, their number monotonically grows as more objects are seen. Therefore GALOIS, like other hierarchical conceptual clustering systems, needs further information and/or concept selection mechanisms to be applied as a learning system. In this section we explore this issue, presenting the two current learning modes of GALOIS.

5.1 GALOIS FOR CLASS DISCOVERY

GALOIS can be applied to datasets containing objects which are assigned to two or more "natural" classes. When working in the discovery mode GALOIS takes as input growing samples of objects. Each sample reflects the natural distribution of the objects in the dataset, which is assumed to be known. For any sample GALOIS constructs out of the concepts in the lattice all possible partitions satisfying the given distribution. As we shall see experimentation demonstrates that as the sample grows the set of partitions may converge to the natural partition. Sometimes the system cannot find any partition with the given distribution. This kind of information is also useful because it reveals that the structure of the data set is such that the sought concepts lack logical descriptions.

5.2 GALOIS FOR CLASS PREDICTION

A typical experiment to evaluate a clustering system (e.g., Fisher 1987, Hadzikadic&Yun 1989, McKusick&Langley 1991, Anderson&Matessa 1992) is to let the system predict the class of new objects. The system is first given a training set of objects having their class labels hidden, so that concepts are determined as if the objects were unlabelled. Afterwards the system is given access to the class label of the objects stored under each concept and it may use this information to predict the class name of new unlabelled objects. We have provided GALOIS with different procedures for predicting class membership based on the properties of the dataset to which it is applied. They are illustrated in the following.

The two learning modes we have just described were evaluated on four datasets. The datasets we chose represent on the whole a difficult testbed for any inductive learning program, in that they feature most problems encountered with real data (e.g., multiple classes, missing attributes, noise, numeric attributes). We now describe in detail the result we obtained with each dataset.

5.3 SOYBEAN

We used the small Soybean data set, consisting of 47 objects (descriptions of soybean diseases) partitioned in 4 classes (disease categories). The distribution is (0.21,0.21,0.21,0.37). Each object is described by 35 attributes with no missing values. The number of partitions found by GALOIS in the discovery mode decreased from 279 to 4, including the natural partition.

We also ran GALOIS on the subsets of the small Soybean data set containing only two classes, and in these cases we obtained just the natural partitions. In the prediction mode we split the whole data set into two random halves and let GALOIS build the lattice on a half and predict the class on the other half. The procedure to assign objects to classes is as follows. After GALOIS has been trained it finds for each class the best consistent concepts (i.e., the concepts which are consistent and maximally complete) in the lattice. Then for any test object GALOIS computes the similarity[4] between the object and each best consistent concept and assign the object to the class with the highest score. We ran GALOIS on ten random samples. Usually the predictive accuracy on the test set reached its asymptote (100%) after few training objects. Only in one run it did not raise to 100% quickly (i.e., until the 21st training object).

5.4 CONGRESSIONAL VOTING

This data set consists of 435 objects described by 16 binary attributes with missing values (the votes of members of Congress on key issues in 1984). Objects are partitioned into two classes (Democrats and Republicans). When there is an attribute with missing value, as in this case, we give each occurrence of the missing value a unique, unmatchable value. We made the experiments on a subset containing 100 objects, with 50 random objects for each class. In the discovery mode, GALOIS became unable to find any partition with the given distribution after seeing the first small samples[5]. Therefore we relaxed the constraint on the degree of coverage of each concept in the partition introducing a tolerance value (Δ). We found that for small values of Δ GALOIS converged to a very limited number of partitions which were good approximation of the natural partition. To use GALOIS in the predicton mode we defined another mechanism for assigning objects to classes. In fact, the performances of the procedure used for the Soybean dataset degrade as the partitions found by Galois diverge from the natural partition (this is a case in point, although the results for this data set are still good). The new procedure is as follows. For any test object GALOIS finds all concepts in the lattice which are consistent *and more general than the object*. Next it assigns the object to the more numerous class in the previous set. The experiments were made presenting GALOIS with a random set of 100 objects (50 for training and 50 for test). We repeated the experiments ten times. The predictive accuracy on the test set ranged from 88% to 100% ($\sigma = 4.4$).

5.5 BREAST CANCER

This data set consists of 286 objects (clinical records) described by 9 attributes with missing values Objects are partitioned into two classes (recurrence and no-recurrence of breast cancer). The data set is intrinsically noisy, in that there are six pairs of objects with equal description and different class label. When we ran GALOIS in discovery mode on this data set the results were poor. Even introducing the tolerance value for the coverage degree, the results did not improve much, in that the partitions we found bore a little resemblance to the natural partition. By contrast, the prediction mode, which does not rely on existence of concepts consistent and complete, worked fairly well. We used a slightly modified version of the procedure we introduced above[6], and ran GALOIS on a random sets of 100 objects (50 for training and 50 for test) ten times. The predictive accuracies we obtained ranged from 72% to 86% ($\sigma = 5.3$).

5.6 IRIS

This data set consists of 150 objects (exemplars of Iris) described by 4 numeric attributes. The objects are partitioned into three classes (species of Iris). If we consider the numeric values in the object description as if they were nominal values then the concept lattice corresponding to the data set contains few objects, none of which cover more than 28 objects. Therefore it was impossible for the discovery mode of GALOIS to find partitions containing concepts with a sufficient degree of coverage.We tried to overcome this difficulty discretizing the attributes (thus increasing the object similarity). As a result, however, the concepts in the lattice did not increase.Neither did the results for class discovery improve. We found that strong discretizations (e.g., binary attributes) have the effect of reducing the concept space too much, whereas weak discretizations do not help increase object similarity. By contrast, discretizing (we partitioned the numeric range of each attribute in 10 intervals) turned out to be useful when we ran GALOIS in prediction mode. The training and test set used in the experiments were generated by randomly selecting 100 instances as training set and using the remaining 50 instances as test set. To predict the class membership we applied the same procedure used for the congressional voting data base. The predictive accuracy we obtained varied between 88% and 100% ($\sigma = 3.5$).

In figure 3 the complete results obtained for each data set are depicted. The results are averaged over ten runs The predictive accuracies we obtained are usually comparable to the best accuracies reported in the literature, including

[4]The similarity between an object and a concept is given by the number of concept descriptors equal to or more general than the object descriptors.

[5] Consider that a concept lattice is such that if there is no partition with a given distribution for a sample S, then there is no partition with the same distribution for any sample $S' \supset S$.

[6]In this data set, unlike the congressional voting data base, there are some inconsistently labelled objects. To account for this, when GALOIS searches the lattice to collect the concepts more general than the object it also considers partially inconsistent concepts, i.e., concepts that contain a small percentage (10%) of objects with a different class label.

probabilistic clustering systems (see (Anderson&Matessa 1992) for a detailed comparison).

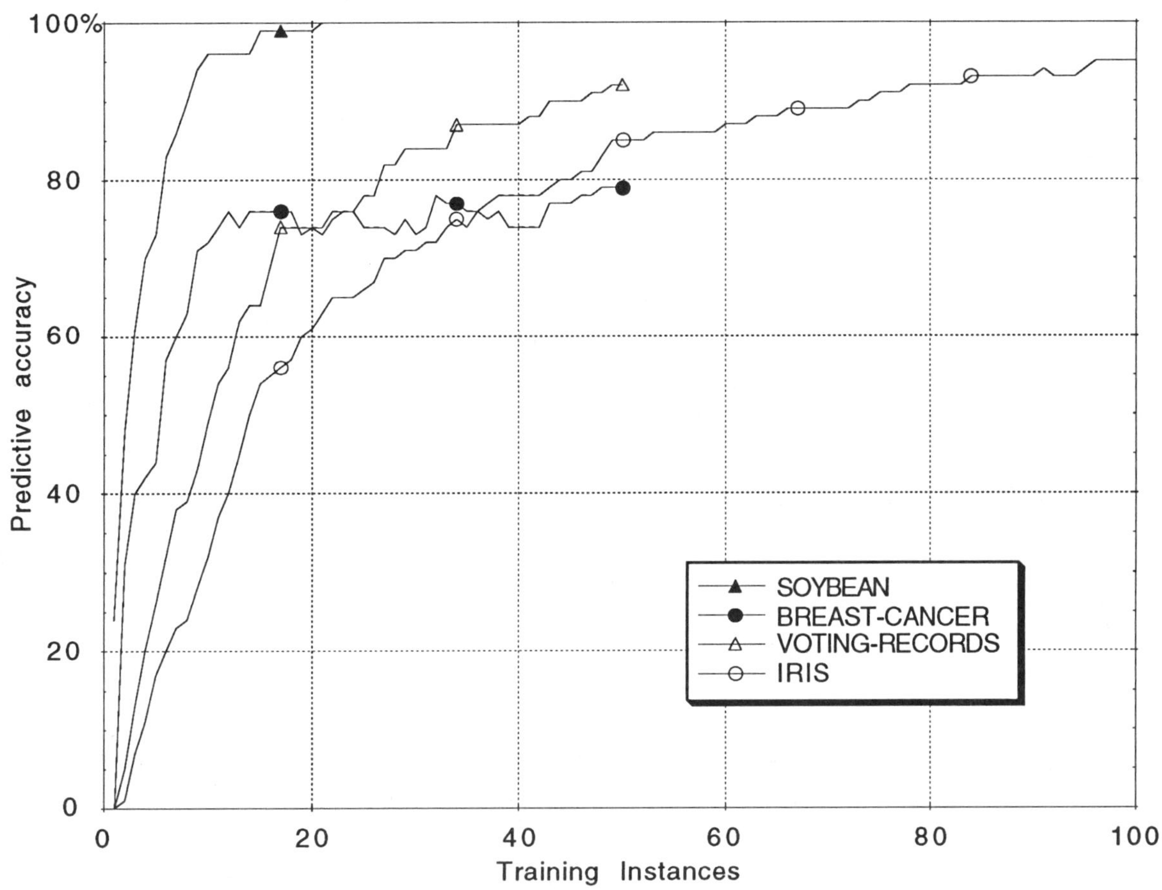

Fig.3. Prediction performance of GALOIS on four data sets

6 RELATED WORK

The only other algorithm for incremental determination of concept lattices we are aware of is reported in (Godin et al 1991). It is substantially different from GALOIS. It is based on partitioning the concepts in the lattice according to the cardinality of their intents, and subsequently processing the obtained subsets (at most m, where m is the number of attributes) in ascending cardinality order. While the asymptotic behavior of its time complexity is the same as GALOIS, in practice it may be less efficient. In fact, on one hand the sets in the partition are in general larger than the lattice subset explored by the function LINK in GALOIS:

$$(\max \| S_i \| = \max_i \binom{m}{i} 2^{m-i} > 2^m);$$

on the other hand, for each concept the algorithm in (Godin et al 1991) has to examine all elements in such set twice, once to check concept duplication and once to properly set the edges. By contrast, GALOIS applies the function LINK at most once for each concept. Another major difference between this work and the work by Godin et al is application of concept lattices. They apply concept lattices to the information retrieval domain, where objects are documents, descriptors are keywords, and a context is the indexing relationship between documents and keywords. In this context the concept lattice is seen as an automatic keyword classification structure supporting a browsing interface. Another suggested application is discovery of implication rules between object attributes, which turns out to be closely related to the theory of functional dependencies developed in databases. However, they do not explore the potentials of concept lattices for inductive learning tasks, as we do.

The major advantages of GALOIS over other incremental hierarchical conceptual clustering systems (e.g., Lebowitz 1986, Fisher 1987, Hanson and Bauer 1987, Hadzikadic&Yun 1989, Langley 1991) are clarity and generality. A concept lattice represent a virtually "unbiased" set of clusters - i.e., all complete classes of objects having a conjunctive description - and has therefore a clear and simple semantics. Unlike the concept hierarchies produced by other systems, it can be easily explained and manipulated, and it lends itself to several applications. The applications include, but are not limited to, inductive learning tasks. The major disadvantage of GALOIS is its relative efficiency, especially when, as for the Soybean data set, the number of concepts in the lattice become very large. There are also other differences. While GALOIS' concepts are strict conjunctive logical descriptions, other systems employ more flexible formalisms, such as probabilistic concepts (Fisher 1987, McKusick&Langley 1991), contingency tables (Hanson&Bauer 1989), prototype schemata (Hadzikadic&Yun 1989). Also, constraints on the classification structure are different: while most clustering systems (one exception is Lebowitz's UNIMEM) can only find disjoint classes, GALOIS can also generate overlapping classes. This may be an important requirement for many applications, even though data sets with non-disjoint classes are rare in the machine learning field (in fact, we regret we could get none).

7 CONCLUSION AND FUTURE WORK

We presented GALOIS, a system for conceptual classification based on the theory of concept lattices. GALOIS implements a new incremental algorithm for determining the concept lattice corresponding to a set of objects. For each update the algorithm takes time ranging from O(n) to O(n^2) where n is the number of concepts in the lattice. In the paper we focused on the application of concept lattices to conceptual clustering tasks, presenting several experimental results.

This work can be extended in several directions. We are currently investigating the following.

- Generalizing Galois lattices to include richer concept representations (e.g., conjunctive languages on tree-structured attributes).
- Adding domain knowledge to constrain the growth of the lattice or to improve the learning ability.
- Characterizing the relationships between the performances of the different prediction methods used by GALOIS and the properties of the data sets.
- Factorizing the concept language to reduce the complexity of the algorithm.
- Applying GALOIS to other tasks and/or domains.

Acknowledgements

We would like to thank Attilio Giordana and Lorenza Saitta for providing us with the data sets. We would also like to thank Jan Zytkow for his comments on an earlier version of this paper. This work was carried out in the framework of the agreement between the Italian PT Administration and the Fondazione Ugo Bordoni.

References

Anderson, J., Matessa, M. (1992). Exploration of an Incremental, Bayesian Algorithm for Categorization. *Machine Learning*, 9, 275-308.

Carpineto, C., Romano, G. (1992). Concept Lattices and Conceptual Clustering. In *Proc. of GAA-92 (Italian Workshop on Machine Learning)*, Rome.

Davey, B., Priestley, H. (1990). *Introduction to Lattices and Order*. Cambridge University Press.

Fisher, D. (1987). Knowledge acquisition via incremental conceptual clustering. *Machine Learning*, 2, 139-172.

Gennari, J., Langley, P., Fisher, D. (1989). Model of Incremental Concept Formation. *Artificial Intelligence*, 40, 12-61.

Godin, R., Missaoui, R., Alaoui, H. (1991). Learning Algorithms using a Galois Lattice Structure. In *Proc. of the 1991 IEEE International Conference on Tools for AI.* San Jose, CA.

Guénoche, A. (1990). Construction du Treillis de Galois d'une Relation Binaire. *Mathématiques et Sciences Humaines*, 109, 41-53.

Hadzikadic, M., Yun, D. (1989). Concept Formation by Incremental Conceptual Clustering. In *Proc of 11th IJCAI*, Detroit.

Hanson, S., Bauer, M. (1989). Conceptual Clustering, Categorization, and Polymorphy. *Machine Learning*, 3, 343-372

Lebowitz, M. (1986). Concept learning in a rich input domain: Generalization-based memory. In R. Michalski et al. (Eds.), *Machine Learning: An Artificial Intelligence Approach 2*. Morgan Kaufmann.

McKusick, K, Langley, P. (1991). Constraints on Tree Structure in Concept Formation. In *Proc.of 12th IJCAI*, Sidney.

Mitchell, T. (1982). Generalization as search. *Artificial Intelligence*, 18, 203-226.

Multitask Learning: A Knowledge-Based Source of Inductive Bias

Richard A. Caruana
School of Computer Science
Carnegie Mellon University
Pittsburgh, PA 15213
caruana@cs.cmu.edu

Abstract

This paper suggests that it may be easier to learn several hard tasks at one time than to learn these same tasks separately. In effect, the information provided by the training signal for each task serves as a domain-specific inductive bias for the other tasks. Frequently the world gives us clusters of related tasks to learn. When it does not, it is often straightforward to create additional tasks. For many domains, acquiring inductive bias by collecting additional teaching signal may be more practical than the traditional approach of codifying domain-specific biases acquired from human expertise. We call this approach Multitask Learning (MTL). Since much of the power of an inductive learner follows directly from its inductive bias, multitask learning may yield more powerful learning. An empirical example of multitask connectionist learning is presented where learning improves by training one network on several related tasks at the same time. Multitask decision tree induction is also outlined.

1 INTRODUCTION

Inductive bias is anything that causes an inductive learner to prefer some hypotheses over other hypotheses. Bias-free learning is impossible; in fact, much of the power of an inductive learner follows directly from the power of its inductive bias (Mitchell 1980). Though many different sources of inductive bias have been used, these do not yet appear to be powerful enough to enable machine learning to develop inductive systems that scale to complex real-world tasks.

The standard methodology in machine learning is to break large problems into small, reasonably independent subproblems, learn the subproblems separately, and then recombine the learned pieces (Waibel 1989). This paper suggests that part of this methodology may be wrong. The reductionist method has caused us to attempt learning on simple, isolated tasks before earnestly attempting learning on larger, richer tasks. By adhering to this method we may be ignoring a critical source of inductive bias for real-world problems: the inductive bias inherent in the similarity of related tasks drawn from the same domain. If an inductive learner is given several related tasks at the same time, these tasks can be used as valuable sources of inductive bias for each other. This may make learning faster or more accurate and may allow hard tasks to be learned that are not learnable in isolation. We call this approach Multitask Learning (MTL).

First we introduce multitask learning at an abstract level and explain how related tasks can be used as sources of mutual inductive bias. Then we present a concrete example of MTL applied to artificial neural networks. After this demonstration we discuss multitask connectionist learning in more detail. Then we briefly describe multitask decision-tree learning. After this we discuss related work, most notably that on giving hints to networks and on transferring knowledge between related tasks learned one at a time. Finally, we summarize the MTL methodology and highlight the research problems that will have to be tackled for MTL to succeed on complex, real-world tasks.

2 MULTITASK LEARNING AND INDUCTIVE BIAS

We learn embedded in a world that simultaneously tasks us to learn many related things. These things obey the same physical laws, derive from the same human culture, are preprocessed by the same sensory hardware, etc. Perhaps it is the similarity of the tasks we learn that enables us to learn so much with so little experience.

A child trained from birth on a single, isolated, complex task—and nothing else—would be unlikely to learn it. If you were trained from birth to play tennis—and nothing else—you would probably not learn tennis. Instead, you learn to play tennis in a world that tasks you to learn many other things. You also learn to walk, to run, to jump, to exercise, to grasp, to throw, to swing, to recognize objects, to predict trajectories, to rest, to talk, to study, to practice, etc. These tasks are not all the same: running in tennis is different from running on a track, yet they are related. Perhaps the similarities between the thousands of tasks you learn are what enable you to learn any one of them—including tennis.

An artificial neural network (or a decision tree) trained tabula rasa on a single, isolated, complex task is unlikely to learn it. For example, a neural network with a 1000 by 1000 pixel input retina will be unlikely to learn to recognize complex objects in the real world given the number of training patterns and the amount of training time we likely can afford. Instead, it may be better to embed the inductive learner in an environment that simultaneously tasks it to learn many related tasks. If these tasks share computed subfeatures or learnable subprocesses, the inductive learner may find that it is easier to learn them together than to learn them in isolation. Thus if we simultaneously train the neural network to recognize objects and object outlines, shapes, edges, regions, subregions, textures, reflections, highlights, shadows, text, orientation, size, distance, etc., it may be better able to learn to recognize complex objects in the real world. This is Multitask Learning (MTL).

MTL is predicated on the notion that tasks can serve as mutual sources of inductive bias for each other. Inductive bias is anything that causes an inductive learner to prefer some hypotheses over others. MTL is one particular kind of inductive bias. MTL uses the information contained in the training signal of related tasks to bias the learner to hypotheses that benefit multiple tasks. One does not usually think of training data as a bias; but when the training data contains the teaching signal for more than one task, it is easy to see that, from the point of view of any one task, the other tasks may serve as bias. For this multitask bias to exist, the inductive learner must also be biased (typically via a simplicity bias) to prefer hypotheses that have utility across multiple tasks.

Inductive biases can be categorized by their strength, explicitness, and domain specificity. The strength of the multitask bias depends on how the tasks are related and how strongly the inductive learner is biased towards sharing learned structure across the tasks. The multitask bias is explicit in that the information provided in the teaching signal is explicit. It can also be implicit, however, because the simplicity bias it depends on is, in many inductive systems, only implicitly specified. The multitask bias is domain specific if the tasks are drawn from one domain. It is a *knowledge-based* inductive bias because the training signal for the tasks can be knowledge rich. That is, from the point of view of any one task, the information contained in the training signal for the other tasks can provide additional domain knowledge to the learner that it would not have received if it were working on one task at a time.

Bias-free learning is impossible; much of the power of an inductive learner follows directly from its inductive bias (Mitchell 1980). Most inductive systems rely on weak biases because there exist weak biases with broad applicability that are easy to use on new problems (e.g., syntactic simplicity). Strong inductive biases are usually domain specific. Unfortunately, domain-specific inductive biases are often costly, typically requiring a domain theory manually encoded by a human expert. MTL may provide an effective source of domain-specific, knowledge-rich, inductive bias that requires less effort from the domain expert.

3 AN EXAMPLE OF MULTITASK CONNECTIONIST LEARNING

The simplest way to introduce multitask connectionist learning is with an example. Consider the following four boolean functions defined on 8 bit inputs:

```
Task 1  =  B1   OR   Parity(B2-B8)
Task 2  =  B1   OR   Parity(B2-B8)
Task 3  =  B1  AND   Parity(B2-B8)
Task 4  =  B1  AND   Parity(B2-B8)
```

where Bi represents the ith bit (leftmost bit is B1), and Parity(B2–B8) is the parity (number of bits set, mod 2) of bits 2–8

For example, if the input pattern is 10001101 then Task1(10001101) = 1 OR Parity(0001101) = 1 OR 1 = 1. Similarly Task4(10001101) = 0.

These four tasks are related in several ways. First, all the tasks are defined on the same inputs: eight binary bits. Second, each task is defined using a common computed subfeature: the parity of bits 2 through 8. Third, on those inputs where Task 1 must compute the parity of bits 2 through 8, Task 2 does not need to compute parity, and vice versa. That is, if B1 = 0, then Task 1 = Parity(B2–B8) but Task 2 = 1 independent of the value of Parity(B2–B8). Task 3 and Task 4 are related similarly: Task 3 needs Parity(B2–B8) when B1 = 1, but Task 4 does not, etc.

Backpropagation (Rumelhart et al. 1986) can be used to train artificial neural networks to learn these tasks. Figure 1 shows the networks one would typically use. Since the tasks are independent, a separate network is used for each task. This is single task learning (STL). But it is also possible, as shown in Figure 2, to use a single network to learn the four tasks at the same time. This is multitask learning (MTL).

The four graphs in Figure 3 show the generalization performance for single and multitask networks trained on Tasks 1–4. Each graph contains three generalization performance curves, one for that task trained in isolation, one for that task trained paired with another task (i.e., MTL with two tasks), and one for that task when all four tasks are trained together (i.e., MTL with four tasks). To simplify the presentation of the two-task multitask data, we present curves only for Tasks 1 and 2 trained together and for Tasks 3 and 4 trained together.

All runs use fully connected feed-forward networks with 8 input units, 160 hidden units, and 1–4 output units. (Networks with fewer than 20 hidden units are adequate for these tasks. The networks are large to minimize capacity effects when different *numbers* of tasks are trained on one network.

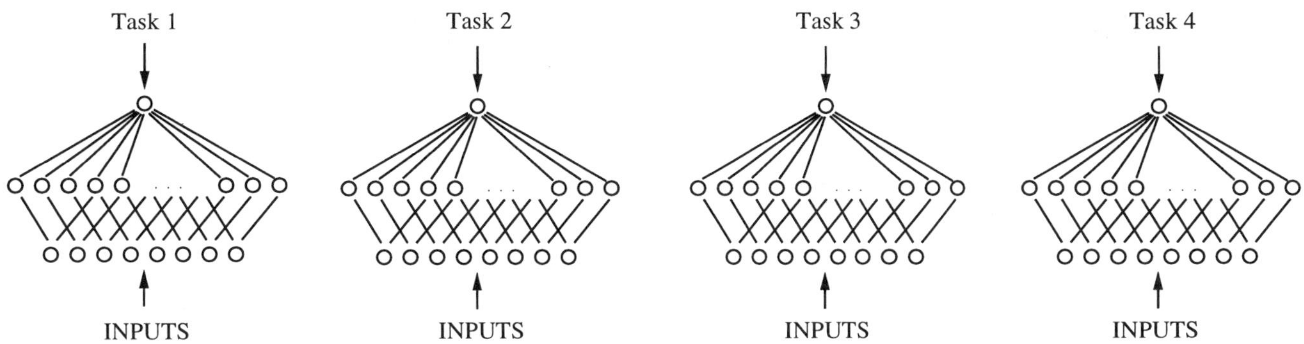

Figure 1: Connectionist Single Task Learning (STL) of Four Functions Defined on the Same Inputs

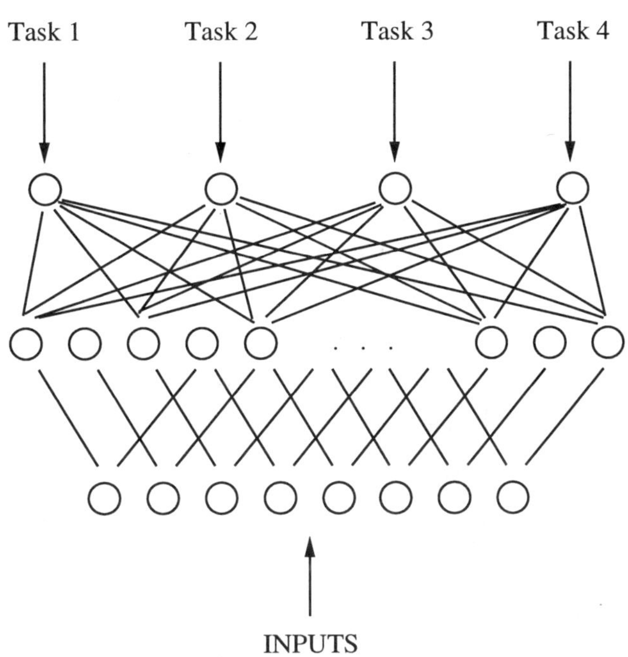

Figure 2: Connectionist Multitask Learning (MTL) of Four Related Functions Defined on the Same Inputs

Other experiments we have run suggest that the generalization performance on these tasks is not injured by the excess capacity.) All networks were trained with backpropagation using MITRE Corporation's Aspirin/MIGRAINES 5.0 with learning rate = 0.1, momentum = 0.9, and per-pattern updating. The training sets contain 64 patterns selected randomly from the 256 possible patterns. The remaining 192 patterns are used as a cross-validation hold-out set to measure generalization performance. The training set was kept small to make generalization challenging, to prevent a training set from including most of the 128 possible examples of the parity subfunction, and to insure that the hold-out set is large enough to yield reliable generalization measures. Each plot is the average of 20 runs.

Let's carefully examine the graphs in Figure 3. The first graph shows the average generalization performance during training for Task 1. The three curves represent the performance for Task 1 when trained alone, when trained with Task 2, and when trained with Tasks 2, 3, and 4. The poorest performance occurs when Task 1 is trained by itself. This is single task neural network learning. Better generalization performance on Task 1 is achieved when a single network is trained on both Tasks 1 and 2 at the same time. And even better generalization performance is achieved by training all four tasks together on a single network. Similar results are found for the other tasks: for each task, better performance is achieved if that task is trained on a network that is trained simultaneously on the other tasks. Note also that better generalization performance is obtained without the need for additional training passes. (In fact, the MTL run is computationally more efficient than the four STL runs it replaces.) To check the results presented graphically in Figure 3, an analysis of variance (ANOVA) of the peak generalization performances from each of the 20 training runs was also performed. This analysis confirms that MTL statistically outperforms STL at the .05 level.

Why is each task learned better if it is trained in the context of a network that is learning the other related tasks at the same time? We have run experiments to verify that the improved generalization performance of MTL is the result of multitask inductive bias. Specifically, we have done experiments to rule out two effects that do not depend on the tasks being related. The first effect is that adding noise to neural net learning sometimes improves generalization performance (Holmstrom & Koistinen 1992). To the extent that the tasks are uncorrelated, their contribution to the aggregate gradient (the gradient that sums the error fed back from each layer's outputs) will appear as noise for other tasks. Thus the uncorrelatedness of the tasks might improve generalization performance by acting as a source of noise. To test for this effect we trained nets on the tasks using random additional tasks. For example, we trained a four output net on Task 1 and three different random tasks. (Each random task was was held constant during training—the random tasks are true functions.)

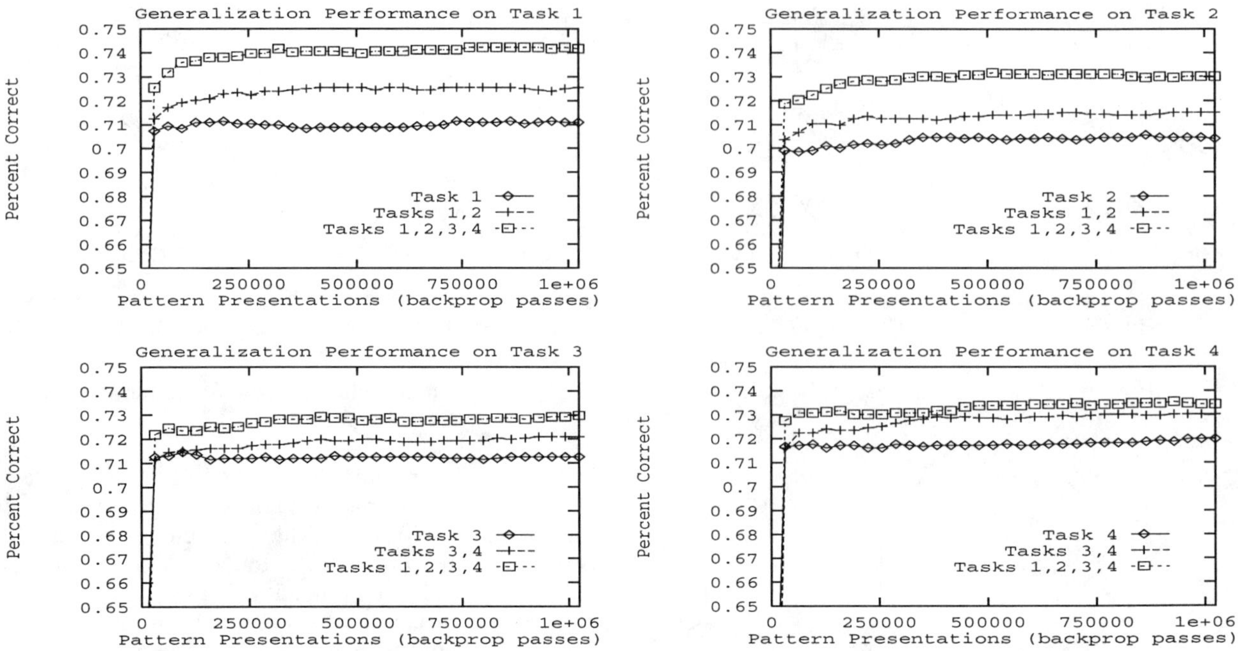

Figure 3: Generalization Performance of Single Task Learning and Multitask Learning on Tasks 1–4

The second effect we tested for is the possibility that adding tasks merely changes the weight updating dynamics to somehow favor nets with more tasks. To test for this we trained nets on four "replicated" tasks at one time. For example, a single net was trained on four copies of Task 1; each of its four outputs received exactly the same training signal. In this degenerate form of MTL, each task correlates perfectly with the others and contributes no additional information, thus cannot serve as a source of knowledge-based inductive bias.

Figure 4 shows the generalization performance for Task 1 when it is multitask trained with three random functions. The performance for Task 1 when it is trained alone, with Task 2, and with Tasks 2–4 is shown for comparison. The performance for Task 1 when it is trained on networks simultaneously trained on random functions is similar to the performance for Task 1 trained alone. (When the other tasks are multitasked with random functions their performance actually drops a little.) We conclude that it is unlikely that the MTL effect is due to the uncorrelatedness of the multiple tasks serving as a beneficial source of noise. (To rule out the possibility that net capacity might artificially limit performance when learning random functions, we verified that networks with as few as 20 hidden units are able to train to 100 percent accuracy on one task and three random tasks.)

Figure 4 also shows the performance of nets trained on four copies of Task 1. (The figure shows the performance for one output selected at random.) Surprisingly, performance is better than that for Task 1 trained in isolation. This improvement is gained without any additional information

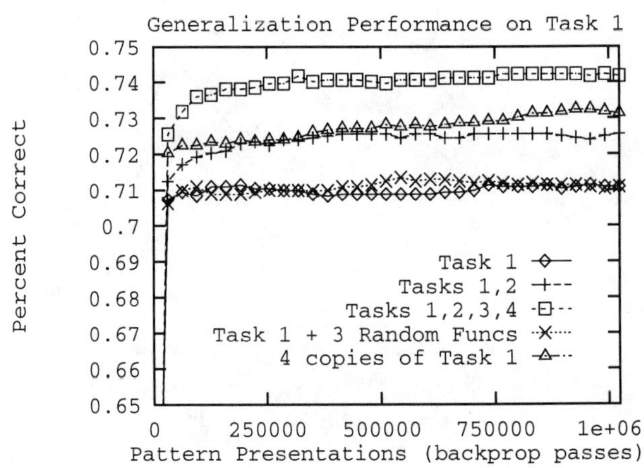

Figure 4: Performance of MTL Variants on Task 1

being given to the system. We can think of three explanations: 1) the extra copies may increase the effective learning rate on the weights from the input layer to the hidden layer because their backpropagated error signals add; 2) the four copies may provide a better signal-to-noise ratio early in training when error signals are backpropagated through initially random weights because there are four times as many random weights backpropagating from the output layer to the hidden layer; and 3) having more weights connected to the same signal increases the odds that one of the weights will be close to a "good" value. We have yet to determine what mechanism accounts for the observed performance increase. Fortunately, the replication effect is not large enough to explain the MTL performance increase observed on Tasks 1–4 even if we assume it is somehow able to confer the same magnitude advantage for tasks as different as Tasks 1–4.

One final comment is necessary here. Is the MTL bias effect we observe large enough to be interesting? There are several answers to this. First, performance increased as the number of related tasks increased. In many domains it is surprisingly easy to add more tasks. The accumulated benefit of MTL might be significant in some domains. Second, parity is a hard function to learn, so hard that it is rarely used in generalization studies. (Most studies using parity try to learn parity by training on the complete set of patterns.) The fact that we see improved generalization on tasks that compute parity internally (but are not trained on any explicit information about the parity function itself) is remarkable. Third, the networks have not been "told" that the tasks share a common computable subfeature. Moreover, the tasks differ significantly in how they use this subfeature. This represents a challenging case for MTL because the relationship between the tasks is deeply buried. Yet measurable improvement does occur.

4 MULTITASK CONNECTIONIST LEARNING IN MORE DETAIL

4.1 Advantages and Disadvantages

What are the advantages and disadvantages of using one net to learn several tasks compared with separate nets for each task? Let's begin by examining the possible disadvantages:

1. The MTL net will probably need additional capacity if it is to learn all the tasks.
2. Because the MTL net is doing several potentially competing jobs at the same time, the gradients computed from the error signal for each task may interfere (i.e., cause the aggregate gradient to be flatter or less directional), so learning might be slower for some MTL tasks.
3. The MTL net may begin to overtrain on different tasks at different times. If overtraining is prevented by halting training when the cross-validation generalization performance begins to drop, there may be no one place to stop training the MTL net to achieve peak generalization on all tasks.
4. MTL will sometimes require that new tasks be defined and that training signal for these new tasks be acquired. This places additional burden on the domain expert.
5. If the learning parameters (e.g., learning rate, momentum, initial weight ranges, etc.) must be set differently for different tasks, there may be no one setting appropriate to all the tasks.

The advantages of MTL stem from the possibility that, if the tasks are related, information from the teaching signal of one task might aid learning the other tasks. If the benefit from this mutual inductive bias is strong enough, most of the disadvantages described above can be mitigated:

1. If the tasks can share weights, the MTL net, while bigger than any one net required for the individual tasks, will be smaller than the individual nets combined.
2. Although the MTL aggregate gradient may be flatter, it may be less susceptible to noise. It may also point in better directions because early in search the gradients will point in directions beneficial to several tasks, i.e., towards more generally useful subfeatures.
3. Although tasks will overtrain at different times, this is not really a problem. MTL requires that tasks are trained in the context of other tasks, not that learning produce a single net to use for all tasks. MTL can produce separate nets for each task, each representing the point where generalization performance peaked on that task. (We did this for the ANOVA in Section 3.)
4. Devising new tasks and acquiring the training signal will not always be easy, but it will often be easier than the alternative: acquiring and codifying domain-specific inductive biases acquired from human expertise. We conjecture that MTL provides a convenient "pipe" through which to add domain-specific inductive bias.
5. Where tasks require tweaking the learning parameters, it may be impossible to train the tasks at one time. This may limit MTL's use in some domains.

4.2 How MTL Can Improve Generalization

There are several reasons why multitask nets may generalize better. MTL can provide a data amplification effect, can allow tasks to "eavesdrop" on patterns discovered for other tasks, and can bias the network towards representations that might be overlooked if the tasks are learned separately. Let's examine each of these more closely.

The data amplification effect is best explained using Tasks 1–4 from Section 3. Both Task 1 and 2 need to compute the parity subfeature on half of the patterns, but Task 1 needs parity only on those patterns for which Task 2 does not, and vice versa. Thus the teaching signal for Task 1 provides information about parity half of the time and the teaching signal for Task 2 provides information about parity the other half of the time. A net trained on one of these tasks receives information about the parity subfeature only about half the time, whereas a net trained on both Tasks 1 and 2 gets information about the parity subfeature on every training pattern. Both nets see exactly the same training patterns, but the multitask net is getting more information with each training pattern. This can increase the effective sample size for a computed subfeature. To any one task, the other tasks are providing an inductive bias, i.e., a preference for hypotheses that more accurately compute common subfeatures. (This effect cannot explain all the MTL performance observed on Tasks 1–4 because performance increases if Tasks 1 and 2 are trained with Tasks 3 and 4, yet Tasks 1 and 2 already "require" the parity subfeature for all patterns.)

"Eavesdropping" will be a common benefit of MTL. If tasks are related, it is likely that the computed subfeatures needed by some tasks will sometimes be useful to other tasks. These subfeatures may not be learnable by the tasks that eavesdrop on them if they are trained separately, but might prove valuable sources of information when they are learned for other tasks.

At its best, MTL will bias nets to learn internal representations they would not have learned if trained on the tasks in isolation. Consider a set of 100 tasks for which there are 100 training patterns. Assume each task could benefit by computing a function F of its inputs. Further assume that each task needs F for only one of the 100 training patterns and that each task needs F for a different pattern. Nets trained on the tasks one a time will not learn F because they receive insufficient information to recognize F exists. A net trained on all 100 tasks, however, might learn F. MTL may allow nets to discover internal representations that STL nets could not. MTL may also bias nets towards one of several different internal representations if one representation benefits several tasks.

4.3 Where Multiple Tasks Come From

Tasks 1–4 were devised to be related in carefully chosen ways. Where will the additional tasks MTL requires come from for real-world problems? Often the real world gives us related tasks to learn at the same time. For example, in the Calendar Apprentice System (Dent et al. 1990) inductive learning is used to predict the location, time of day, day of the week, and duration for the meetings it schedules. These tasks are related; they are functions of the same data and probably share some common subfeatures. The Calendar Apprentice currently learns these tasks independently. (Actually, it learns the tasks in a specified order so it can *feed* the output of one task as an input feature to the next.) The MTL approach is to induce a single model for all four tasks at the same time. MTL does not need to define an order for task induction to enable tasks to feed information to each other.

Many real-world domains are "natural" multitask domains if one avoids reductionism. But it is not essential that a domain "naturally" present multiple tasks to use MTL. MTL is a means of adding domain-specific inductive bias to an inductive system via additional teaching signal. For many domains it is surprisingly easy to devise additional related tasks. These might be semi-modular pieces of the larger task (e.g., tasking a robot to predict the trajectory of a ball when the full task requires the robot to catch the ball) or might be tasks that appear to require similar abilities as the given task(s). Acquiring the additional training signal is not trivial, but it is probably easier than asking domain experts to provide other forms of domain-specific inductive bias: domain experts excel at using their knowledge, but usually find codifying their knowledge difficult. Note that MTL does not require that the training signals be available at run time. The training signals are needed only during training because they are outputs—not inputs—of the MTL net. Thus one is free to specify any feature or task that might be useful even if there will be no operational procedure to compute it later.

5 MULTITASK DECISION TREES

MTL can be applied to other learning techniques, even to techniques like decision trees that are not usually used for multiple tasks. Typically, a leaf in a decision tree provides a single class assignment to the instances that reach it. Sometimes leaf nodes refer to multiple classes within a single task, e.g., by assigning probabilities for each class, but separate decision trees are usually built for different tasks. This need not be the case. We can create multitask decision trees containing nodes that assign membership for all the tasks the decision tree is trained on. That is, a single decision tree might have a leaf node that corresponds to class A for Task 1, class C for Task 2, etc.

An example will clarify why one would do this. Suppose we wish to learn several related medical diagnosis tasks. Task 1 is to determine if the patient has retinal degeneracy, Task 2 is to determine if the patient has diabetes, Task 3 is to determine if the patient has reduced peripheral circulation, and Task 4 is to determine if the patient has pulmonary disease. These tasks are strongly related, but the relationship between them is convoluted. Diabetes often causes retinal degeneration and reduced peripheral circulation, and increases the risk of pulmonary disease. Retinal degeneration and reduced peripheral flow are common first symptoms of diabetes. Pulmonary disease, if it is linked to diabetes, is usually a long-term consequence of diabetes, not a diagnostically useful symptom. But any of these conditions can also derive from other dysfunctions and they also often occur in isolation.

The web relating these conditions is tangled. And we can easily imagine a larger web that would bring in dozens of other related symptoms and ailments. The classic decision tree induction approach (Quinlan 1986) is to induce a separate decision tree for each malady. If it is known that some diagnoses might benefit from other diagnoses, we might learn the decision trees in some order and use the outputs from earlier trees as input features to subsequent trees. This is awkward given the number of tasks and the complex web that relates them. The MTL approach is to grow a single decision tree that predicts all the conditions at the same time. To do this we must devise a new greedy splitting rule so that multitask decision trees may be efficiently grown in traditional top-down fashion. One such rule is the average information gain (or entropy decrease) over all the tasks. This will favor attribute splits high in the decision tree that provide discrimination for several tasks. Thus early in its search the decision tree will be biased towards categorizations that have broad utility. As in MTL networks, this bias will cause learning to develop clusters that represent more meaningful subgroups of the domain. In the diabetes example, the MTL decision tree will be more likely to learn the class *brittle diabetics* because this class is useful to all the tasks.

6 RELATED WORK

It is common to train neural nets with many outputs. Usually these outputs encode a single task. For example, in classification tasks it is common to use one output for each class, the output with the highest activation being the classification. But using one net for a few strongly related tasks is also not new. The classic NETtalk (Sejnowski & Rosenberg 1986) application uses one net to learn both phonemes and their stresses. This multitask approach is natural for problems like NETtalk because the goal of NETtalk is to learn to control a synthesizer that needs both phoneme and stress commands at the same time for every input. NETtalk is an example of multitask learning. (Experiments are currently underway to see if STL NETtalk would perform worse than MTL NETtalk.)

Transferring learned structure between related tasks is not new. The main differences between this work and previous work on knowledge transfer are the emphasis here on learning the tasks at the same time and the realization that using many additional tasks might make learning substantially easier. These differences are significant. The work on transferring learned structure between neural nets trained on similar tasks (Pratt et al. 1991)(Pratt 1992)(Sharkey & Sharkey 1992) demonstrates one can use what is learned on one task as a bias for another task. The problem with this is that nets are trained on the tasks sequentially. The operator must devise an appropriate training sequence. One also needs a means of causing the net to retain what it learned before while still enabling it the flexibility to learn anew and modify what was learned before. Because of these difficulties it is unlikely this approach would scale to many tasks. And even if it could, there is no opportunity for a system that trains tasks one at a time to discover representations apparent only when several tasks are viewed together.

This work is most similar to that on providing hints to networks (Abu-Mostafa 1989)(Suddarth & Kergosien 1990)(Suddarth & Holden 1991). The hints approach uses additional tasks that are semi-modular decompositions of the main task. This is definitely MTL. This paper advances the work on hints in four ways: 1) by recognizing that multiple tasks serve as mutual sources of inductive bias; 2) by showing that tasks can be related in more diverse ways than hints yet still yield beneficial bias; 3) by further exploring the ways in which tasks can bias each other; and 4) by suggesting that creating new related tasks may be an efficient way of providing domain-specific inductive bias to learning systems. The empirical results we present demonstrate the first three of these contributions: Tasks 1–4 are not easily viewed as providing hints for each other, yet generalization performance increases when they are trained together.

MTL decision trees are related to some conceptual clustering techniques, most notably COBWEB (Fisher 1987). In fact, a simple modification to the indices in COBWEB's probabilistic information metric yields a metric suitable for judging multitask decision tree splits. COBWEB considers all features as tasks to predict. MTL decision trees allow the user to specify which signals are features and which are training signal, thus making it easier to create additional tasks without committing to extra training information being available later at run time.

7 SUMMARY

Acquiring domain-specific inductive bias is subject to the knowledge acquisition bottleneck. We suggest that domain-specific inductive bias can more easily be acquired in some domains by acquiring teaching signal for additional tasks in that domain. We describe several mechanisms by which this teaching signal can serve as an inductive bias when combined with a bias that prefers hypotheses that benefit several tasks.

We introduce multitask learning (MTL) in connectionism because there is an established methodology for training artificial neural networks that have multiple outputs. In fact, the classic NETtalk application and previous work on supplying hints to neural networks are instances of MTL in connectionism. We provide an empirical demonstration that shows that even when the similarity between multiple tasks is difficult to learn and recognize, MTL can still improve generalization performance. We further demonstrate that this improvement is not easily attributable to effects other than a mutual inductive bias based on the similarity of the tasks.

To show the generality of the MTL methodology, we briefly outline how to do top-down induction of multitask decision trees. This is significant because decision trees are not usually used to learn multiple tasks. Doing this results in a system that generalizes some conceptual clustering techniques so as to make them more useful in domains where the distinction between features (information that will be available in the future) and classes (things that we want to predict) must be retained.

Precisely what conditions are required for MTL to succeed are not yet known. Perhaps it will be sufficient to give multiple tasks to inductive systems and allow their existing simplicity biases to exploit the relatedness. Or perhaps we will have to devise new ways to help the inductive systems recognize common substructure and then "coerce" them to share representations for this substructure. Much work remains to be done. We need more effective ways to "open up" complex networks so that we can see what inside. In particular, we need to devise methods for detecting when "eavesdropping" is occurring or when a new (or modified) internal representation has been developed. We need to better understand how tasks should be related for MTL to succeed and how to recognize these traits in real-world tasks. We need to empirically demonstrate that MTL can provide a strong enough inductive bias to be useful in complex tasks. We need to evaluate how hard it will be to build useful additional tasks for domains of interest (e.g., vision). We conjecture that as the complexity of the domain scales, so too will the opportunity for creating additional related tasks. If this is true, MTL may provide a practical method of acquiring domain-specific inductive bias that scales naturally with the complexity of the task.

Acknowledgements

Thanks to Wray Buntine, Lonnie Chrisman, Jeff Jackson, Tom Mitchell, Herb Simon, and Sebastian Thrun for their help in refining the ideas presented here. Special thanks to the reviewers and to Lonnie Chrisman, Rich Goodwin, Tom Mitchell, and Diane Staub for their careful review of drafts of this paper.

This research was sponsored in part by the Avionics Lab, Wright Research and Development Center, Aeronautical Systems Division (AFSC), U. S. Air Force, Wright-Patterson AFB, OH 45433-6543 under Contract F33615-90-C-1465, Arpa Order No. 7597. The views and conclusions contained in this document are those of the authors and should not be interpreted as representing the official policies, either expressed or implied, of the U.S. Government.

References

Abu-Mostafa, Y. S. (1990) Learning From Hints in Neural Networks. *Journal of Complexity* **6**(2):192-198.

Dent, L., Boticario, J., McDermott, J., Mitchell, T. & Zabowski, D. (1992). A Personal Learning Apprentice. *Proceedings of 1992 National Conference on Artificial Intelligence.*

Fisher, D. H.(1987) Conceptual Clustering, Learning From Examples, and Inference. *Proceedings of the 4th International Workshop on Machine Learning.*

Holmstrom, L. & Koistinen, P. (1992) Using Additive Noise in Back-propagation Training. *IEEE Transactions on Neural Networks.* **3**(1):24-38.

Mitchell, T. M. (1980) The Need for Biases in Learning Generalizations. Rutgers University: *CBM-TR-117.*

Quinlan, J. R. (1986) Induction of Decision Trees. *Machine Learning.* **1**:81-106.

Pratt, L. Y., Mostow, J. & Kamm, C. A. (1991) Direct Transfer of Learned Information Among Neural Networks. *Proceedings of AAAI-91.*

Pratt, L. Y. (1992) Non-literal Transfer Among Neural Network Learners. Colorado School of Mines: *MCS-92-04.*

Rumelhart, D. E., Hinton, G. E. & Williams, R. J. (1986) Learning Representations by Back-propagating Errors. *Nature.* **323**:533-536.

Sejnowski, T. J. & Rosenberg, C. R. (1986) NETtalk: A Parallel Network that Learns to Read Aloud. John Hopkins: *JHU/EECS-86/01.*

Sharkey, N. E. & Sharkey, A. J. C. (1992) Adaptive Generalisation and the Transfer of Knowledge. University of Exeter: *R257.*

Suddarth, S. C. & Holden, A. D. C. (1991) Symbolic-neural Systems and the Use of Hints for Developing Complex Systems. *International Journal of Max-Machine Studies* **35**:3:291-311.

Suddarth, S. C. & Kergosien, Y. L. (1990) Rule-injection Hints as a Means of Improving Network Performance and Learning Time. *Proceedings of the 1990 EURASIP Workshop on Neural Networks.* 120-129.

Waibel, A., Sawai, H. & Shikano, K. (1989) Modularity and Scaling in Large Phonemic Neural Networks. *IEEE Transactions on Acoustics, Speech and Signal Processing.* **37**(12):1888-98.

Using Qualitative Models to Guide Inductive Learning

Peter Clark
Knowledge Systems Laboratory
National Research Council
M-50 Montreal Road
Ottawa, Canada
pete@ai.iit.nrc.ca

Stan Matwin
Ottawa Machine Learning Group
Computer Science
University of Ottawa
Ottawa, Canada
stan@csi.uottawa.ca

Abstract

This paper presents a method for using qualitative models to guide inductive learning. Our objectives are to induce rules which are not only accurate but also explainable with respect to the qualitative model, and to reduce learning time by exploiting domain knowledge in the learning process. Such explainability is essential both for practical application of inductive technology, and for integrating the results of learning back into an existing knowledge-base. We apply this method to two process control problems, a water tank network and an ore grinding process used in the mining industry. Surprisingly, in addition to achieving explainability the classificational accuracy of the induced rules is also increased. We show how the value of the qualitative models can be quantified in terms of their equivalence to additional training examples, and finally discuss possible extensions.

1 INTRODUCTION

1.1 OVERVIEW

This paper presents and evaluates a technique for using qualitative models to guide inductive learning from examples. Our objective is to induce rules which are not only accurate but also explainable using this qualitative background knowledge, a requirement both for practical application of machine learning and for integrating the results of learning back into a wider body of existing knowledge. The research can be viewed as developing and evaluating a special case of the general theory-guided learning paradigm (e.g. [Bergadano and Giordana, 1988, Pazzani and Kibler, 1992]), in which the theory is a qualitative model and the learning technique is rule induction from data. Our method is based on defining a notion of consistency of a rule with a qualitative model, and then restricting the specialisation operator in an induction system (CN2) to only investigate specialisations consistent with the QM during search. We describe the application of this method to two learning problems in process control. Our evaluation shows that this method, in addition to achieving consistency of learned knowledge with background knowledge, can also improve overall classificational accuracy. We show how a metric can be defined which quantifies the value of the qualitative model in terms of its equivalence to extra training examples, and finally speculate how empirically learned knowledge might feed back to modify the qualitative model itself.

1.2 MOTIVATION

It is now well recognised that applying standard inductive learning tools such as ID3, C4.5 or CN2 is somewhat of a skill. Their inability to exploit background knowledge leaves the knowledge engineer with substantial work to perform in order to generate rules which both perform well and which are sufficiently 'sensible' that they can enhance the knowledge of domain experts, and be relied upon for real-world performance tasks. Gillian Mowforth, a former employee of Intelligent Terminals Ltd. and with substantial experience of commercially applying rule induction, estimates that in typical commercial applications of ExTran (an ID3 derivative) around 30% of the final decision tree installed for the customer would have been hand-engineered rather than induced [Mowforth, 1992]. She reports typical applications would involve data collection, rule induction, and then analysis of the induced tree in collaboration with the experts to see if it "made sense". This latter process was time consuming, and would be followed by modifying the induction procedure e.g. by removing/adding training examples, by modifying the example description language, or by re-running the induction system in interactive mode to force certain attribute tests to be included/excluded in parts of the tree. Then a new tree would be induced and the process iterated until the tree was acceptable to the experts, the whole application taking several months to complete. Similar experiences have been reported by others involved in machine learning applications.

The complete process is thus interactive, involving

substantial domain expertise in addition to use of an inductive tool. In this process, statistically justified rules are being compared against domain knowledge, and the results used to refine learning. Domain knowledge can be viewed as a compiled version of many training examples (i.e. all previous empirical evidence), above and beyond the data set immediately available. Ideally, this knowledge will prune out rules which by chance perform well on the training data, but in general have poor performance.

In this paper we model this process using a qualitative model to represent background knowledge and restrict the choices available to an inductive engine. At the end of the paper we also speculate on extending our method to perform the reverse process, which Mowforth also reports was common: namely where strong statistical evidence may cause experts to revise their domain knowledge.

2 CONTEXT & RELATED WORK

While it is widely accepted that background knowledge is necessary for all but the simplest learning tasks, we note that there are two principle ways in which background knowledge can be used:

1. To expand the hypothesis language by introducing extra terms (e.g. in Foil [Quinlan, 1990] and Golem [Muggleton and Feng, 1990]).
2. To constrain search (our objective in this paper).

These two methods have significantly different outcomes: in the first case background knowledge actually aggravates the search problem as the search space is expanded, whereas in the second the hypothesis space is restricted, reducing search. We highlight this to clearly distinguish this work from other systems which use background knowledge in the former sense.

The general paradigm of using domain knowledge to guide learning has been advocated by numerous authors (e.g. [Bergadano and Giordana, 1988, Pazzani and Kibler, 1992, Clark and Matwin, 1993, Flann and Dietterich, 1990]). Our work here can be viewed as developing and evaluating a special case of this theory-guided learning paradigm, in which the theory is a qualitative model (QM) and the learning is rule induction from data. Within the general paradigm, abstract background knowledge specifies constraints on which hypotheses should be explored during inductive search. We apply this to a qualitative model by defining a notion of consistency of a rule with the model, and then constraining search to examine only consistent rules. The qualitative model can thus be viewed as indirectly specifying a domain-specific grammar for induced knowledge [Cohen, 1992, DeJong, 1989], or as encoding a set of 'rule models' for the inductive component to search [Kietz and Wrobel, 1992].

We finally note that this work of course differs from machine learning research in compiling qualitative

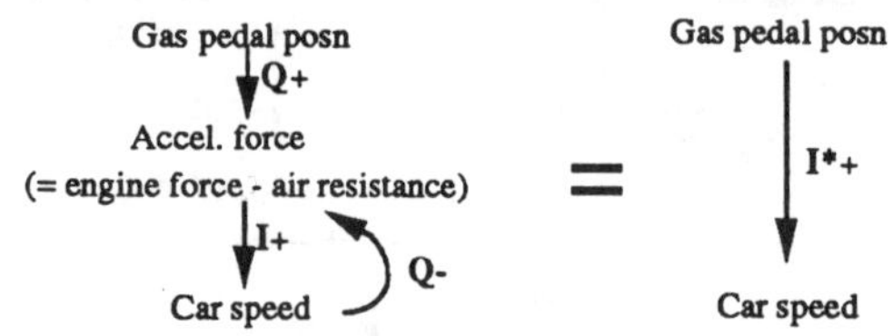

Figure 1: The `I*` relation, a syntactic shorthand for a self-stabilising feedback loop.

models into rules (in this paradigm, there is no independent training data and the QM does not directly constrain induction e.g. [Bratko et al., 1989]), and in learning QMs themselves from examples (e.g. [Bratko et al., 1991, Mozetic, 1987]).

3 LEARNING METHOD

3.1 KNOWLEDGE REPRESENTATION

Our learning method takes as input a set of training examples and a qualitative model, and as output produces classification rules explainable by that model.

A QM comprises nodes, representing parameters of the application domain, and arcs, representing their relationships (arrows indicating temporal precedence). As in Qualitative Process theory (QPT) [Forbus, 1984], we label arcs as either `I+`, `I−`, `Q+` or `Q−`. The link $X \xrightarrow{Q+} Y$ denotes that `Y` varies monotonically with `X` (e.g. if `X` increases then so does `Y`), while the link $X \xrightarrow{I+} Y$ denotes that `Y`'s rate of change `dY/dt` varies monotonically with `X`. Similarly, the $\xrightarrow{Q-}$and $\xrightarrow{I-}$links denote inverse monotonic relationships.

As a syntactic shorthand, we introduce a third label `I*`, shown in Figure 1, to denote a self-stabilising feedback loop. $X \xrightarrow{I*+} Y$ also denotes that if `X` is increased then initially `Y` will rise; however, as `Y` subsequently increases, it's rate of increase `dY/dt` will eventually fall until `Y` reaches a new constant value. For example, the gas pedal position `P` in a car is related to the car's speed `S` by $P \xrightarrow{I*+} S$. Initially depressing the pedal causes `dS/dt` to rise; however, the car will not increase speed indefinitely but eventually reach a new, higher constant speed. Thus at short time-scales the `I*` relationship behaves as $P \xrightarrow{I+} S$, while for long time-scales it behaves as $P \xrightarrow{Q+} S$ (every gas pedal position eventually produces a corresponding speed for the car).

While similar to QPT models, it should be noted that our QMs differ in that they are *incompletely specified.* We have not stated (i) the distinguished or 'landmark' values for each parameter, nor (ii) how to resolve conflicting influences during simulation. As a result, our models *on their own* cannot be used for simulation or prediction. Instead, their role is to constrain induction of quantitative rules from examples, and to provide explanations of those rules. The QM concisely represents the space of relationships which are considered credible in the domain by the model's constructor.

3.2 USING THE QUALITATIVE MODEL TO CONSTRAIN INDUCTION

The application of the QM to rule induction is simple; rather than the inductive tool searching the space of all possible rules, it searches only those which are consistent with the QM. The inductive tool is thus constrained to search only a subset of its original search space. To effect this, we first define when a rule is 'consistent with the QM'. Second, we modify the search operator in the inductive tool to only search rules which satisfy this definition.

Our implementation is as follows. First, we define a rule extraction algorithm which exhaustively enumerates (schemata for) all rules (up to some maximum length) consistent with the QM. This enumeration is stored in a lookup table. Second, an induction tool is used to induce classification rules using a set of training examples, while prevented from searching rules not represented in this lookup table. To do this, we modify the learner so that each time it generates a new hypothesis rule to test, it additionally checks that it is in this table. If it is not, the hypothesis is discarded without further work.

The inductive tool we used was CN2, which induces (in unordered mode) a set of "if...then..." rules given a set of training examples. CN2 executes a greedy set covering algorithm, performing a general-to-specific beam search for a rule at each step [Clark and Niblett, 1989, Clark and Boswell, 1991]. It was modified so that as it specialises hypothesis rules in its beam, it additionally performs this check on specialisations generated. A similar approach can be envisaged for ID3; rather than evaluating all possible attribute tests when expanding a node in the tree, evaluate only those such that the resulting decision tree branch was contained in the table of consistent rules.

3.3 EXTRACTING RULES FROM THE QM

Before defining a decision procedure to identify which rules are consistent with a QM, we first note that this notion of 'consistency' is not as easy to formalise as might be expected. Informally, the decision procedure should identify all and only those rules which an expert will consider 'sensible', given the QM. This requires an interpretation of what should be considered acceptable evidence for a prediction, given the QM. Below we describe our definition of which rules are 'consistent' with a QM, while noting that alternatives might also be acceptable.

We define a **rule** as a structure:

$$\textbf{if } T_1 \textbf{ and } \ldots \textbf{ and } T_n \textbf{ then } C$$

where each T_i is a test on some observable parameter P_i (testing either $P_i > k$ or $P_i < k$, where k is some constant), and the conclusion C asserts either "P_{conc} will increase" or "P_{conc} will decrease" for some observable parameter P_{conc}. The interpretation of the rule is that if the conditions hold at some time T, then P_{conc} will have increased/decreased by time $T + \Delta T$ (where ΔT is a constant, representing how far ahead the user wishes to predict). A **rule schema** is a rule with the constants k_i replaced by universally quantified variables, representing a set of rules.

We wish to know which conjuncts of tests T_i 'sensibly' predict a change in C, given the QM. For example, given the two-node QM for a car: "**gas** $\xrightarrow{\texttt{I*+}}$**speed**", we consider rules or the form

"**if gas** $> k_1$ **then speed** will increase"

consistent with this QM, while rules of the form

"**if gas** $< k_1$ **then speed** will increase"

would not be (where k_1 is some constant).

In general, considering the three different qualitative relations `I`, `I*` and `Q` in isolation, the corresponding structures of consistent rules are:

Reln	Corresponding rule schema
`A`$\xrightarrow{\texttt{I+}}$`B`	**if** `A` $> k_A$ **then** `B` will increase.
`A`$\xrightarrow{\texttt{I*+}}$`B`	**if** `A` $> k_A$ **and** `B` $< k_B$ **then** `B` will increase.
`A`$\xrightarrow{\texttt{Q+}}$`B`	(no rule).

The rule schema for `I*` above expresses a condition of disequilibrium, resulting (by definition, Section 3.1) in a rise in `B` to re-establish equilibrium. For the `Q` relation, knowing the value of `A` alone does not tell us how `B` might change in future.

We now generalise these schemata to apply to QMs which contain more than just two nodes and one arc. To find a plausible explanation of why our target P_{conc} will change, we simply find a path in the QM from some node (which we call the **source** of the change) to P_{conc} which traverses at least one `I` or `I*` arc. One of these I/I* arcs is then nominated as responsible for P_{conc}'s future change; nodes upstream of this arc are considered **causes** of this future change, in that they are either the source or correlated with the source. These nodes together correspond to the `A` node in the three schemata mentioned earlier. Nodes downstream of the I/I* arc are called the **effects**, and together correspond to the `B` node in the earlier mentioned schemata. Rules which are consistent with this path are thus those which:

1. test that some subset of observable parameters upstream of the nominated `I/I*` arc are greater than some constant,
2. (for `I*` only) test that some subset of observable parameters downstream of the arc are less than some constant,
3. conclude that P_{conc} will increase.

Thus there would be 9 rules[1] consistent with the following path from a QM of a car:

$$fp \text{ (foot position) } \xrightarrow{\texttt{Q+}} gas \xrightarrow{\texttt{I*+}} revs \xrightarrow{\texttt{Q+}} speed$$

[1] i.e. rule schemata; we will just use the word 'rule' from now on to simplify the presentation.

namely: {
if $fp > k_{fp}$ and $revs < k_r$ then speed ↑,
if $gas > k_g$ and $revs < k_r$ then speed ↑,
if $fp > k_{fp}$ and $gas > k_g$ and $revs < k_r$ then speed ↑,
: : : : : : : : : : : :
if $fp > k_{fp}$ and $speed < k_s$ then speed ↑,
: : : : : : : : : : : :
if $fp > k_{fp}$ and $gas > k_g$ and $revs < k_r$ and $speed < k_s$ then speed ↑ }.

This example uses just positive arcs (e.g. Q+). Negative arcs are handled in the obvious way, namely by inverting the greater-than and less-than tests as each negative arc is traversed. Rules predicting a decrease in the target parameter are generated by inverting the greater-than and less-than tests in rules predicting an increase.

This method of extracting consistent rules is still incomplete:

1. It ignores parameters not in the path used, but nevertheless correlated with parameters on the path (e.g. via Q relations). These off-path parameters might provide useful evidence of values of on-path parameters, particularly if none of the on-path parameters are directly observable.
2. It assumes just one source.

To overcome the first point, the full rule extraction algorithm also allows off-path parameters, affected by on-path parameters via a chain of Q or I* relations, to be included in a rule's condition. The net result is to extract a tree from the QM, whose root node is the source and with P_{conc} as one of its leafs. To allow multiple sources, we combine rules together (by conjoining their conditions) to produce new rules, checking that we do not treat any parameter in the new rule as both a cause and an effect simultaneously.

4 EXPERIMENTAL EVALUATION

4.1 APPLICATION DOMAINS

We evaluated our method by applying it to two process control problems: a water tank system containing feedback, and a real-world process of ore grinding, in which rock is crushed into small particles for mineral extraction. For each of these systems, there is a particular **parameter of interest** whose movement we wish to predict (the water level in the lowest tank, and the efficiency of the grinding process respectively). To generate training data, numeric simulators of the real physical processes were constructed.

4.2 THE WATER TANK SYSTEM

The water tank system is shown in Figure 2. Water enters the circuit through the upper pipe, and fills the first tank (with level L1). The flow of water out of a tank is proportional to the tank's water level (the higher the level, the greater the pressure at the base of the tank and the faster the out-flow; there is no reflux). In addition, there is feedback from some tanks to

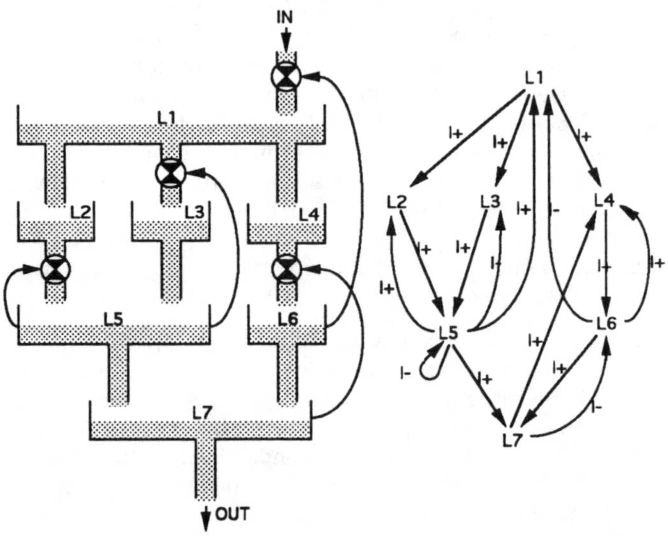

Figure 2: The water tank system (left), and its QM (right). (See text for description).

control valves earlier in the circuit as illustrated. As a valve-controlling tank becomes full, the controlled valve closes thus reducing water flow earlier in the pipe network. There are seven observable parameters, namely the levels in each of the seven tanks. The learning task is to predict whether the level L7 in the last tank will have increased or decreased by some time $T + \Delta T$ in the future given observations at time T. There is one operator-controllable parameter to this system, namely the flow rate of water into the system. A simple numeric simulator was used to model the behaviour of the system with time. The qualitative model of the system which we constructed, intended to reasonably describe the (simulated) physical system, is also shown in Figure 2.

4.3 THE ORE GRINDING CIRCUIT

The grinding circuit (Figure 3) is substantially more complex, and is a simplified version of a similar circuit used in the mining industry [JKTech Ltd., 1991]. Ore enters along a feed conveyor belt, and accumulates in ball mill one. A ball mill is a large, rotating drum which breaks up the rock into smaller components. A fraction of the contents of the ball mill leaves during each time step, and arrives at the screen. The screen is a metal mesh with holes in, allowing smaller rock to pass through while larger rock is fed back into ball mill one. Ore which passes through the screen reaches and accumulates in a large centrifuge called a cyclone. The smaller contents of the centrifuge are filtered out and leave the system. Larger ore in the centrifuge is also removed (the underflow) and enters a second ball mill, where it is further crushed and then returns to the cyclone. Water can be added to both ball mills, increasing the out-flow from the mills but also reducing the mills' efficiency as energy is then spent 'grinding' water. There are four operator-controllable parameters, namely: the feed rate and size distribution of ore

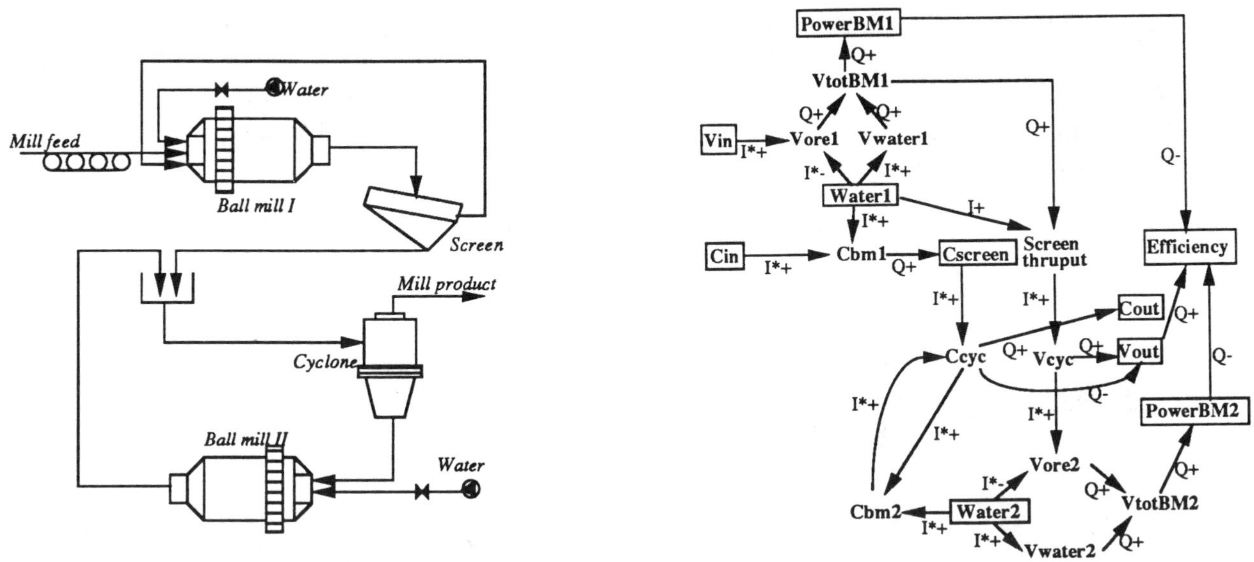

Figure 3: The ore grinding circuit (left), and its QM (right). (See text for description).

into the system, and the rate of water addition into the two ball mills.

The grinding circuit simulator was a simplified version of a more complex, commercial simulator used in the mining industry [JKTech Ltd., 1991]. The QM we constructed of this process is shown in Figure 3. As in the water circuit, the QM is to a large extent our 'guess' at a reasonable qualitative description of the (simulated) physical circuit. The ten observable parameters of the physical system, also contained in the QM (shown in boxes), are: the coarseness and feed rate of ore into the system ($\mathtt{C_{in}}$ and $\mathtt{V_{in}}$), the rate of water addition to each ball mill ($\mathtt{Water_1}$ and $\mathtt{Water_2}$), the power drawn by each ball mill ($\mathtt{Power_{BM1}}$ and $\mathtt{Power_{BM2}}$), the coarseness of ore at the screen ($\mathtt{C_{screen}}$), the coarseness and output rate of ore leaving the system ($\mathtt{C_{out}}$ and $\mathtt{V_{out}}$) and the overall volume/power efficiency of the circuit (`Efficiency`). The learning task is to predict if the overall efficiency will increase or decrease by time $T + \Delta T$ given values of the observables at time T.

4.4 GENERATING DATA SETS

For both applications, data sets were generated using the numeric simulators (NB. not the QMs). Each example in a data set is a snapshot of the system's state at some time T, described by values of the observable parameters, plus an extra qualitative value ('`increase`' or '`decrease`') stating whether the parameter of interest was observed to have increased or decreased by time $T + \Delta T$. ΔT was taken as 10 and 100 time steps for the water and ore systems respectively, corresponding to approximately 1 second and 1 minute real-time.

To generate an example of each process in a random but still physically plausible state, the simulator was run for 500 time steps with the controllable parameter(s) being randomly perturbed at intervals. After 500 time steps, the perturbations were stopped, values of observable parameters recorded, and the simulation continued for another ΔT steps to see if the parameter of interest increased or decreased. These observations formed one example. This process was repeated approximately 500 times for each application to generate two data sets.

4.5 RULE INDUCTION

For each of the two applications, the data set was split randomly into a training and testing set of controlled sizes. Rules were induced by CN2 using the training data, and then tested on the testing data. In normal (no qualitative model) mode, CN2 heuristically searches the rule space for good rules. In constrained (qualitative model) mode, only rules consistent with the qualitative model were explored as described in Section 3.2.

CN2 has two parameters which control the extent of search conducted, namely the beam width and the depth limit of search. CN2 was run with beam widths of 1, 3, 5 and 7, and with depth limits of 2 and 3 (water tanks) or 2, 3 and 4 (ore circuit)[2], and the results averaged. Experiments with five different training set sizes were conducted, the algorithm run in both no-QM and QM modes, and the experiments repeated 30 times (for the water tanks) and 10 times (for the ore circuit). This represents a total of 2400 runs for the water tanks and 1200 runs for the ore circuit. We recorded the CPU time and improvement in classificational accuracy compared with the default accuracy (61.8% water, 61.5% ore) for each run of the algorithm.

4.6 RESULTS

The results (Tables 1 and 2) show averages and their

[2]corresponding to the maximum lengths of 3 (water) and 4 (ore) we imposed when pre-enumerating rule schemata consistent with the QMs (Section 3.2).

Table 1: Effect of qualitative knowledge on learning (water tank application).

No. training examples	Accuracy increase (%)		CPU time (sec)		'Explainability'	
	no QM	QM	no QM	QM	no QM	QM
20	13.4 ±0.5	13.6 ±0.5	5.3 ±0.2	2.2 ±0.1	39%	100%
40	18.9 ±0.4	21.0 ±0.3	12.8 ±0.3	5.9 ±0.1	35%	100%
81	23.9 ±0.2	26.3 ±0.2	34.3 ±0.8	16.0 ±0.3	37%	100%
121	25.8 ±0.1	27.7 ±0.2	61.4 ±1.5	29.3 ±0.6	39%	100%
162	26.9 ±0.2	28.8 ±0.1	93.5 ±2.1	44.4 ±1.0	41%	100%

Table 2: Effect of qualitative knowledge on learning (grinding circuit application).

No. training examples	Accuracy increase (%)		CPU time (sec)		'Explainability'	
	no QM	QM	no QM	QM	no QM	QM
26	5.7 ±0.6	6.0 ±0.6	8.2 ±0.4	8.9 ±0.4	48%	100%
53	12.0 ±0.3	12.2 ±0.4	22.6 ±0.8	26.3 ±1.1	53%	100%
107	14.8 ±0.3	16.3 ±0.2	68.1 ±2.2	79.2 ±3.1	57%	100%
161	16.0 ±0.3	17.0 ±0.3	128.6 ±4.1	154.3 ±6.5	58%	100%
215	17.7 ±0.2	18.3 ±0.2	205.5 ±6.0	240.4 ±10.0	54%	100%

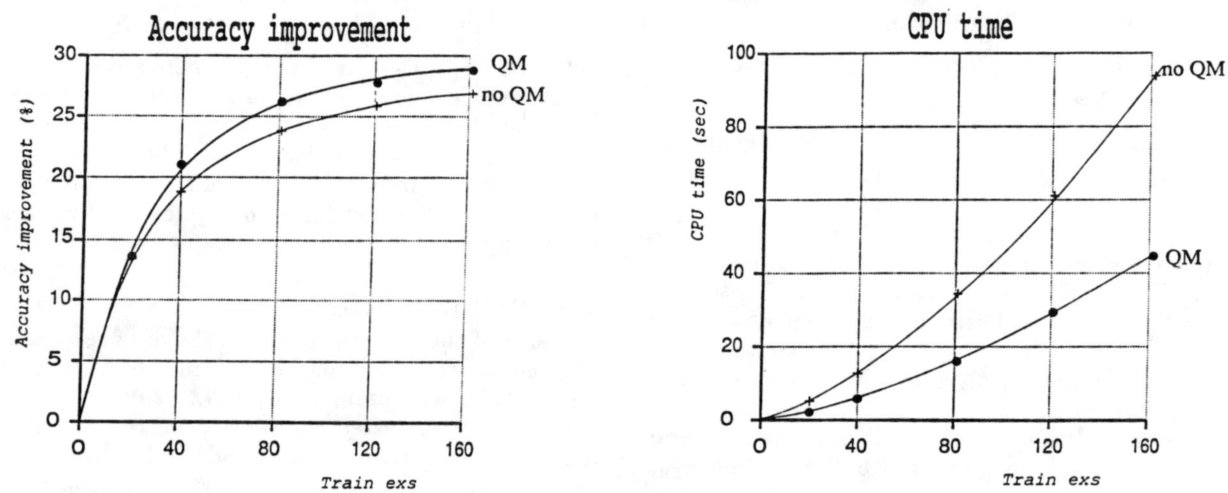

Figure 4: **Water Tank System:** Variation of classificational accuracy and CPU time with number of training examples, comparing learning without and with the QM (plot of data from Table 1).

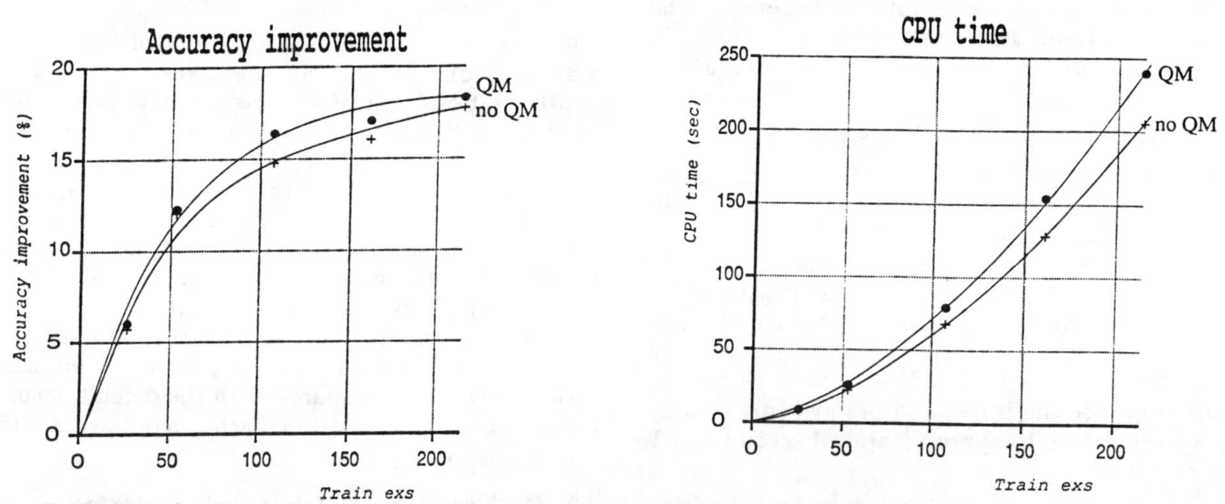

Figure 5: **Ore Grinding Circuit:** Variation of classificational accuracy and CPU time with number of training examples, comparing learning without and with the QM (plot of data from Table 2.

standard errors (denoted by $\pm$). The column 'explainability' shows the (average) percentage of induced rules which were consistent with, and hence deemed explainable by, the QM (by definition, this figure will be 100% for QM-constrained learning). The same results are plotted in Figures 4 and 5.

4.7 ANALYSIS AND DISCUSSION

We consider one of the most significant benefits of this method is the explainability of induced rules. All rules induced with the QM 'make sense' (compared with only about 50% without the QM), in that an expert (or indeed the computer itself, using the QM) can construct a causal explanation describing how the state of the system (as revealed by observable parameter values) might cause the parameter of interest to change in the way the rule describes. Such explainability is an essential aspect of learning, as discussed earlier.

Having said this, several other surprising and positive results were observed. First, in both applications classificational accuracy is increased by use of the qualitative models, even though the QM restricts rather than expands the space of rules available to the learner. It thus appears that, without the QMs, the learning algorithm sometimes selects rules which by chance perform well on the training data, but which do not predict well and which are not consistent with the QMs. This result thus illustrates that the QM is injecting extra knowledge into the final rule sets produced, improving performance.

In the water tank application, CPU time is also reduced using the QM, as the induction algorithm has fewer possibilities to explore. In the ore grinding application, however, CPU time is slightly increased by using the QM. This is also surprising, as the QM reduces the size of the total search space. However, two factors may contribute to the increased CPU. First, CN2's specialisation operator has to perform an extra lookup operation to verify a specialisation is in the set of specialisations consistent with the QM. Second, the high connectivity of the ore grinding QM results in a large number of rules being considered consistent, thus only imposing moderate constraint on search. Third, constraining the total search space size does not necessarily constrain the size of the space heuristically searched. CN2's beam search follows the $N_{beamwidth}$ best hypotheses in parallel. So long as there are at least $N_{beamwidth}$ possible options, the CPU time will be unaffected by constraining the space. In addition, the QM may guide the algorithm into richer portions of the space where many possibilities merit exploration, whereas without the QM several 'dead ends' may be explored where search is abandoned earlier.

4.8 QUANTIFYING THE QM'S VALUE

From the plots in Figures 4 and 5, we can define a useful metric of the qualitative models' value, based on its equivalence to an increased number of training examples. This allows us to compare the value of different qualitative models against a common scale.

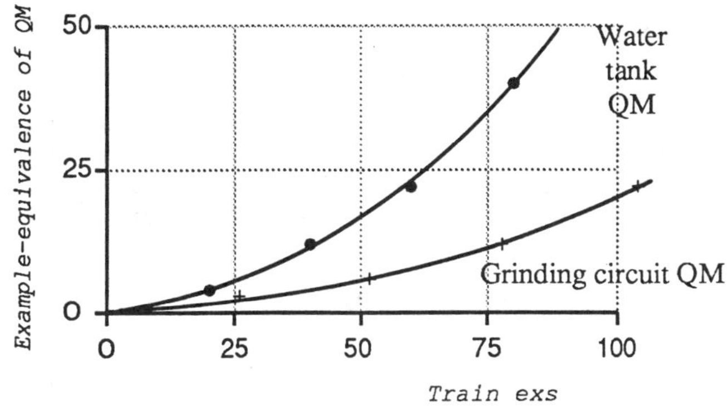

Figure 6: Equivalence of the two QMs to extra training examples.

If a classificational accuracy A can be achieved using N training examples with the QM, or with $N + \Delta N$ examples without the QM, then we define ΔN as the **example-equivalence** of the QM (for classificational accuracy, for N training examples). We similarly define the **CPU example-equivalence** of the QM as the number of extra examples which the QM-constrained algorithm can process in the same time.

Using the plots in Figures 4 and 5, we can plot the example-equivalence of the two QMs as shown in Figure 6. Approximating these curves as straight lines, we can take their slopes as an overall value metric for each QM:

	Approximate example-equivalence ($0 \leq N_{train\_exs} \leq \sim 200$)
Water QM	+0.5 examples per training example
Ore QM	+0.2 examples per training example

(Similarly, the CPU example-equivalences are +0.6 and −0.1 examples per training example respectively). While this provides an appealing metric for a QM, it should be interpreted carefully:

1. As is well known, training set size and accuracy improvement are not linearly related. Thus the monotonically increasing example-equivalence with training size does not imply a monotonically increasing accuracy improvement. In fact, accuracy improvement rises, reaches a maximum and then falls again as training set size increases (Tables 1 and 2). This is because the value (in terms of improved accuracy) of an extra example becomes less and less as the training set size grows.
2. The QM on its own (i.e. with zero training examples) does not contribute to an accuracy improvement. This is because our method does not use the QM directly for prediction, but solely as a filter for inductive hypotheses. (In fact it cannot, as our QMs do not specify parameters' distinguished or 'landmark' values. It is precisely the inductive learner's task to identify these values).
3. It is not clear how far the curves in Figure 6 can

be meaningfully extrapolated. For larger training set sizes, the no-QM curves in Figures 4 and 5 may eventually touch the QM curves (resulting in an example-equivalence of zero for the QM), or even cross them (resulting in a negative-example equivalence). Thus we qualify our 'examples per training example' values as only being valid within a certain range of training set sizes.

5 DISCUSSION AND CONCLUSION

We have presented and evaluated a technique for using qualitative models to guide inductive learning. The learning algorithm produces rules which not only have improved performance but which are explainable by this background knowledge, reflecting the normally manual knowledge engineering which accompanies application of machine learning algorithms. This is significant as qualitative knowledge is a ubiquitous component of common-sense knowledge; being able to harness it to positive effect offers a means for both improved learning performance and for better integration of learning and reasoning systems in the future.

We have also defined the notion of an example-equivalence metric for qualitative models, by which a model's value for learning can be quantified and hence different models compared. In both the applications investigated, the models had a positive example-equivalence, i.e. produced an overall improvement in learning behaviour.

Our method assumes the existence of a reasonable qualitative model of the domain under investigation, and thus imposes a cost as well as saving in knowledge engineering. It can perhaps best be viewed as providing a solid framework for incorporating domain knowledge in induction, which otherwise has to be incorporated by rather ad hoc means (Section 1.2). In addition to explainability, it offers a practical way in which domain knowledge can reduce required search, helping to solve the ubiquitous tractability problems faced by knowledge-poor learning systems in non-trivial domains.

We note also that the benefits of our method depend on the quality of the QM used; a QM poorly approximating the physical system may harm rather than improve accuracy (i.e. have a negative example-equivalence). This fact, combined with the ability to quantify the QM's value, suggests the exciting possibility of including the reverse process reported by knowledge engineers, in which the QM itself could be revised based on strong correlations in the data. The example-equivalence suggests one way in which this could be done, based on heuristically searching the space of perturbations to the original qualitative model using example-equivalence as a search heuristic.

Acknowledgements: We are greatly indebted to Rob Holte, Peter Turney, Donald Michie and Claude Sammut for valuable contributions and comments.

References

Bergadano, F. and Giordana, A. (1988). A knowledge-intensive approach to concept induction. In Laird, J., editor, *ML-88 (Proc. Fifth Int. Machine Learning Conference)*, pages 305–317, Ca. Kaufmann.

Bratko, I., Mozetic, I., and Lavrač, N. (1989). *Kardio: A Study in Deep and Qualitative Knowledge for Expert Systems.* MIT Press, Cambridge, Ma.

Bratko, I., Muggleton, S., and Varsek, A. (1991). Learning qualitative models of dynamic systems. In *ML91 (Proc. Eigth Int. Machine Learning Workshop)*, pages 385–388, Ca. Kaufmann.

Clark, P. and Boswell, R. (1991). Rule induction with CN2: Some recent improvements. In Kodratoff, Y., editor, *Machine Learning – EWSL-91*, pages 151–163, Berlin. Springer-Verlag.

Clark, P. and Matwin, S. (1993). Learning domain theories using abstract background knowledge. In Brazdil, P., editor, *Proceedings of the Sixth European Conference in Machine Learning (ECML-93).* Springer-Verlag. (in press).

Clark, P. and Niblett, T. (1989). The CN2 induction algorithm. *Machine Learning Journal*, 3(4):261–283.

Cohen, W. W. (1992). Compiling prior knowledge into an explicit bias. In Sleeman, D. and Edwards, P., editors, *Proc. Ninth Int. Machine Learning Conference (ML-92)*, pages 102–110, CA. Kaufmann.

DeJong, G. (1989). Explanation-based learning with plausible inferencing. In *Proc. 4th European Machine Learning Conference (EWSL-89)*, pages 1–10, London. Pitman.

Flann, N. S. and Dietterich, T. G. (1990). A study of explanation-based methods for inductive learning. In Shavlik, J. W. and Dietterich, T. G., editors, *Readings in Machine Learning*, pages 808–827. Kaufmann, CA.

Forbus, K. D. (1984). Qualitative process theory. *Artificial Intelligence*, 24:85–168.

JKTech Ltd. (1991). *The JKSimMet Steady State Mineral Processing Simulator.* JKTech, QLD, Australia.

Kietz, J. U. and Wrobel, S. (1992). Controlling the complexity of learning in logic through syntactic and task-oriented models. In Muggleton, S., editor, *Inductive Logic Programming*, pages 335–359. Academic Press, London.

Mowforth, G. (1992). Personal communication (taped interview).

Mozetic, I. (1987). The role of abstractions in learning qualitative models. In Langley, P., editor, *Proc. 4th International Workshop on Machine Learning*, CA. Kaufmann.

Muggleton, S. and Feng, C. (1990). Efficient induction of logic programs. In *First International Conference on Algorithmic Learning Theory*, pages 369–381, Tokyo, Japan. Japanese Society for Artificial Intelligence.

Pazzani, M. and Kibler, D. (1992). The utility of knowledge in inductive learning. *Machine Learning Journal*, 9(1):57–94.

Quinlan, J. R. (1990). Learning logical definitions from relations. *Machine Learning*, 5(3):239–266.

Automating Path Analysis for Building Causal Models from Data

Paul R. Cohen Adam Carlson Lisa Ballesteros Robert St.Amant
Experimental Knowledge Systems Laboratory
Department of Computer Science
University of Massachusetts, Amherst
cohen@cs.umass.edu carlson@cs.umass.edu balleste@cs.umass.edu stamant@cs.umass.edu

Abstract

Path analysis is a generalization of multiple linear regression that builds models with causal interpretations. It is an *exploratory* or *discovery* procedure for finding causal structure in correlational data. Recently, we have applied statistical methods such as path analysis to the problem of building models of AI programs, which are generally complex and poorly understood. For example, we built by hand a path-analytic causal model of the behavior of the Phoenix planner. Path analysis has a huge search space, however. If one measures N parameters of a system, then one can build $O(2^{N^2})$ causal models relating these parameters. For this reason, we have developed an algorithm that heuristically searches the space of causal models. This paper describes path analysis and the algorithm, and presents preliminary empirical results, including what we believe is the first example of a causal model of an AI system induced from performance data by another AI system.

1. INTRODUCTION

Because machine learning techniques search for structure in data, they often closely parallel statistical techniques for exploratory data analysis, such as clustering, factor analysis and regression. This paper describes a statistical *discovery procedure* for finding causal structure in correlational data, called *path analysis* [Asher, 83; Li, 75] and an algorithm that builds path-analytic models automatically, given data. This work has the same goals as research in function finding and other discovery techniques, that is, to find rules, laws, and mechanisms that underlie nonexperimental data [Falkenhainer & Michalski 86; Langley et al., 87; Schaffer, 90; Zytkow et al., 90].[1] Whereas function finding algorithms produce functional abstractions of (presumably) causal mechanisms, our algorithm produces explicitly causal models. Our work is most similar to that of Glymour et al. [87], who built the TETRAD system around the analysis of structural equations—essentially path analysis. Pearl [91; 93] and Spirtes [93] have recently developed a causal induction algorithm with a more general mathematical basis than path analysis; it relies on evidence of nonindependence, a weaker criterion than path analysis, which relies on evidence of correlation.

We developed the algorithm to help us discover causal explanations of how a complex AI planning system works. The system, called Phoenix [Cohen et al., 89], simulates forest fires and the activities of agents such as bulldozers and helicopters. One agent, called the fireboss, plans how the others, which are semi-autonomous, should fight the fire; but things inevitably go wrong, winds shift, plans fail, bulldozers run out of gas, and the fireboss soon has a crisis on its hands. At first, this chaos was appealing and we congratulated ourselves for building such a realistic environment. However, we soon realized that we could explain very little about the behavior of the fireboss. We turned to regression analysis to answer some questions, such as, "Which has more impact on the time to contain a fire: the wind speed or the number of times the fireboss must replan?" But although regression assumed these factors interacted, it provided no explanation of their causal relationship. For example, we knew that the wind speed could affect the incidence of replanning and not vice versa, but this causal, explanatory knowledge was not to be found in regression models. Nor would automated regression procedures (e.g., stepwise multiple regression) find causal models of our planner. Path analysis, however, is a generalization of regression analysis that produces explicitly causal models. We built one such model of Phoenix by hand, and by automating path analysis as we describe below, we have been able to discover other causal explanations of how the Phoenix fireboss works.

Readers who are familiar with regression analysis might skip to Section 3, where we introduce path analysis, or Section 4 where we illustrate a path analysis of Phoenix. Section 5 describes our algorithm. Section 6 discusses two experiments, an informal one in which we applied the algorithm to Phoenix data, and a factorial experiment in which the behavior of the algorithm was probed by applying it to artificial data.

[1] The term "nonexperimental" is perhaps confusing, because data are usually collected in an experiment. Nonexperimental means that the experiment is over and the opportunity to manipulate variables to see effects has passed. Causal hypotheses must therefore be generated and tested with the data, alone.

2. BACKGROUND: REGRESSION

Path analysis is a generalization of multiple linear regression, so we will begin with regression. Simple linear regression finds a *least-squares* line relating a single predictor variable x to a performance variable y. A least-squares line is one that minimizes the sum of squared deviations of predicted values from actual values. That is, simple linear regression finds a line $\hat{y} = bx + a$ that minimizes $\sum_i (\hat{y}_i - y_i)^2$.

Multiple linear regression finds least-squares rules (i.e., planes and hyperplanes) for more than one predictor variable, rules of the form $\hat{y} = b_1x_1 + \ldots + b_kx_k + a$. The interpretation of such a rule is that a unit change in a predictor variable x produces b units change in $\hat{y}$. Thus, the regression coefficients depend on the units of measurement of the predictor variables; for example, if x is measured in feet then b will be a factor of 5280 larger than if x is measured in miles. For this and other reasons, regression models are often constructed for standardized variables. A standardized variable is what you get by subtracting from the variable its mean and dividing by its standard deviation. For concreteness and simplicity, we will show how to solve for coefficients in a standardized linear regression model with three predictor variables. Here is the *prediction model:* $\hat{Y} = \beta_1 X_1 + \beta_2 X_2 + \beta_3 X_3$ (standardized variables are denoted with uppercase letters). The interpretation of this model is that a change in X_1 of one standard deviation, s_1, produces β_1 standard deviations change in $\hat{Y}$. Thus, beta coefficients are comparable: if $\beta_1 = .4$, $\beta_2 = .8$, then a standard deviation change in X_2 has twice the influence on Y as a standard deviation change in X_1.

Multiple linear regression finds beta coefficients to construct a least-squares rule. First, multiply the prediction model through by each of the terms on the right hand side, producing three equations:

$$\hat{Y}X_1 = \beta_1 X_1^2 + \beta_2 X_2 X_1 + \beta_3 X_3 X_1$$
$$\hat{Y}X_2 = \beta_1 X_1 X_2 + \beta_2 X_2^2 + \beta_3 X_3 X_2$$
$$\hat{Y}X_3 = \beta_1 X_1 X_3 + \beta_2 X_2 X_3 + \beta_3 X_3^2$$

then take sums:

$$\sum \hat{Y}X_1 = b_1 \sum X_1^2 + b_2 \sum X_2 X_1 + b_3 \sum X_3 X_1$$
$$\sum \hat{Y}X_2 = b_1 \sum X_1 X_2 + b_2 \sum X_2^2 + b_3 \sum X_3 X_2$$
$$\sum \hat{Y}X_3 = b_1 \sum X_1 X_3 + b_2 \sum X_2 X_3 + b_3 \sum X_3^2$$

Now, because the sum of the product of two standardized variables is their correlation (divided by N, which we can ignore here) and the square of a standardized variable (divided by N) is the variance, the previous equations can be written in terms of correlations:

$$\begin{aligned} r_{YX_1} &= \beta_1 + \beta_2 r_{X_2X_1} + \beta_3 r_{X_3X_1} \\ r_{YX_2} &= \beta_1 r_{X_2X_1} + \beta_2 + \beta_3 r_{X_3X_2} \\ r_{YX_3} &= \beta_1 r_{X_3X_1} + \beta_2 r_{X_3X_2} + \beta_3 \end{aligned} \qquad (1)$$

Clearly, with these three equations we can solve for the three unknown beta coefficients. We have not shown that these coefficients guarantee that $\hat{Y} = \beta_1 X_1 + \beta_2 X_2 + \beta_3 X_3$ is a least-squares rule, but the interested reader can find this demonstration in [Li, 75] or any good statistics text.

The three equations (1) are called the *normal equations*, and they have an interesting interpretation, illustrated in Figure 1. Consider the first normal equation, $r_{YX_1} = \beta_1 + \beta_2 r_{X_2X_1} + \beta_3 r_{X_3X_1}$. The β_1 term is represented in Figure 1 by the direct path between X_1, and Y; the second term is represented by the indirect path from X_1, through X_2 to Y; and the third term is represented by the indirect path through X_3. Thus, the correlation r_{YX_1} is given by the sum of the weights of three paths in Figure 1, where the weight of a path is the product of the coefficients (either correlations or betas) along the constituent links of the path. The second and third normal equations have similar interpretations in Figure 1. By convention, curved arcs without arrows represent correlations and directed arcs represent causes. The causal interpretation of beta coefficients is plausible because betas are standardized *partial* regression coefficients; they represent the effect of a predictor variable on Y when all the other predictor variables are fixed. You can interpret β_1 as what happens to Y when *only* X_1 is systematically varied. In this sense, beta coefficients provide a statistical version of the control you get in an experiment in which X_2 and X_3 are fixed and X_1 is varied; in such an experiment, the effect on Y is attributable to X_1. (Alternatively, the effects might be due to an unmeasured or *latent* variable that is correlated with X_1; we will not consider this case here.)

So far we have described how a prediction model $\hat{Y} = \beta_1 X_1 + \beta_2 X_2 + \beta_3 X_3$ gives rise to a set of normal equations, and to beta coefficients that make the prediction model a least-squares fit to our data. We also gave a causal interpretation of the normal equations in terms of the path model in Figure 1. If this were all we could do, path analysis would be identical to linear regression and not worth the effort.

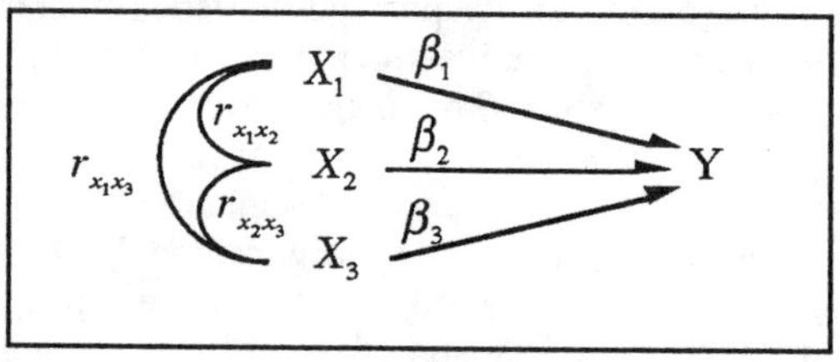

Figure 1: The path model that corresponds to the multiple linear regression of Y on X_1, X_2 and X_3.

3. PATH ANALYSIS

The power of path analysis is that we can specify virtually any prediction model we like, and then solve for beta coefficients that ensure the model is a least-squares fit to our data. For example, Figure 2 shows a model in which X_1 and X_2 directly cause Y, and X_2 also indirectly influences Y through X_3, and no intercorrelations between

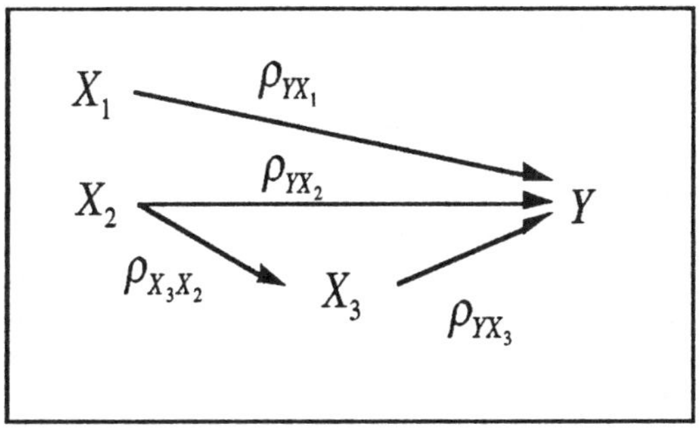

Figure 2: A path model that does not correspond to a multiple linear regression of Y on X_1, X_2 and X_3.

X_1, X_2 and X_3 exist. The corresponding prediction model is $\hat{Y} = \rho_{YX_1}X_1 + \rho_{YX_2}X_2 + \rho_{YX_3}X_3$. The arcs are labeled with *path coefficients*, denoted ρ. Path analysis tells us whether these coefficients are correlations or betas, and if the latter, path analysis solves for the values that make the prediction model a least-squares fit to the data.

What follows is an informal description of the steps in path analysis. See [Cohen] for a more formal discussion of why these steps yield path coefficients that ensure that the prediction model is a least-squares fit to the data. The first step is to propose a prediction model and a corresponding path diagram. Imagine Figure 2 is the result. The second step is to tag each arc as a correlation or a beta coefficient. If several variables $A, B, \ldots$ all point to another variable K (as X_1, X_2, X_3 point to Y in Fig. 2) then

- If $A, B, \ldots$ are independent causes of K, then the path coefficients $\rho_{KA}, \rho_{KB}, \ldots$ are just the correlation coefficients $r_{AK}, r_{BK}, \ldots$, respectively.
- If $A, B, \ldots$ are dependent causes of K, then $\rho_{KA}, \rho_{KB}, \ldots$ are the standardized partial regression coefficients $\beta_{AK}, \beta_{BK}, \ldots$, respectively, obtained from the multiple regression of K on $A, B, \ldots$

By these rules, $\rho_{YX_1} = r_{X_1Y}$ because X_1 is independent of all other causes of Y; $\rho_{YX_2} = \beta_{X_2Y}$ and $\rho_{YX_3} = \beta_{X_3Y}$ because X_2 and X_3 are dependent causes of Y; and $\rho_{X_3X_2} = r_{X_2X_3}$ because X_2 is independent of all other causes of X_3.

The next step is to solve for the path coefficients. Because ρ_{YX_1} and $\rho_{X_3X_2}$ are correlations, they are calculated directly from our data. To find the other path coefficients we first run a multiple regression of Y on X_2 and X_3, or, equivalently, solve two normal equations, $r_{YX_2} = \beta_{YX_2} + \beta_{YX_3}r_{X_2X_3}$ and $r_{YX_3} = \beta_{YX_2}r_{X_2X_3} + \beta_{YX_3}$, for β_{YX_2} and β_{YX_3}.

Finally we can estimate the correlations between X_1, X_2, X_3 and Y. This involves finding paths between the X variables and Y, and summing the weights of the paths. In 1929, Sewall Wright [Asher, 83; Li, 75;] specified three rules for legal paths. We found that it was possible to reduce Wright's rules to a more compact form by introducing the idea of entering or leaving a node by an arrowhead. In the following rules, entering a node by an arrowhead means to follow a forward arrow or a correlation link to the node. Leaving a node by an arrowhead means to follow a backward arrow or correlation link from a node. These rules for are:

1) A path cannot go through a node twice
2) Once a node has been entered by an arrowhead, no node can be left by an arrowhead

This is significantly easier to implement than Wright's rules.

The weight of a path comprising multiple links is the product of the coefficients along the path. By these rules, the estimated correlation $\hat{r}_{X_1Y}$ is just the path coefficient ρ_{YX_1}, which is the empirical correlation r_{X_1Y}. However, $\hat{r}_{X_2Y} = \beta_{YX_2} + r_{X_2X_3}\beta_{YX_3}$ because there are two paths between X_2 and Y, the first direct and the second indirect through X_3. Similarly, $\hat{r}_{X_3Y} = \beta_{YX_3} + r_{X_2X_3}\beta_{YX_2}$ because there are two paths between X_3 and Y, one going backward through X_2.

4. PATH ANALYSIS OF PHOENIX DATA

Let us illustrate these steps with an example from the Phoenix system [Cohen & Hart, 93; Cohen et al., 89; Hart & Cohen, 92]. We ran Phoenix on 215 simulated forest fires and collected many measurements after each trial, including:

WindSpeed	The wind speed during the trial
RTK	The ratio of fireboss "thinking speed" to the rate at which fires burn
NumPlans	The number of plans tried before the fire is contained
FirstPlan	The name of the first plan tried
Fireline	The length of fireline dug by bulldozers
FinishTime	The amount of simulated time required to contain the fire

We specified a prediction model and the path model shown in Figure 3, and solved for the path coefficients on each link. You can see that the estimated correlation between, say, *FirstPlan* and *FinishTime* is the sum of three paths

$$\hat{r}_{FirstPlan,\ FinishTime} = (-.432 \times .287) + (.219 \times .506) + (-.432 \times .843 \times .506) = -.19$$

As it happens, this estimated correlation is very close to the actual empirical correlation, calculated from our data.

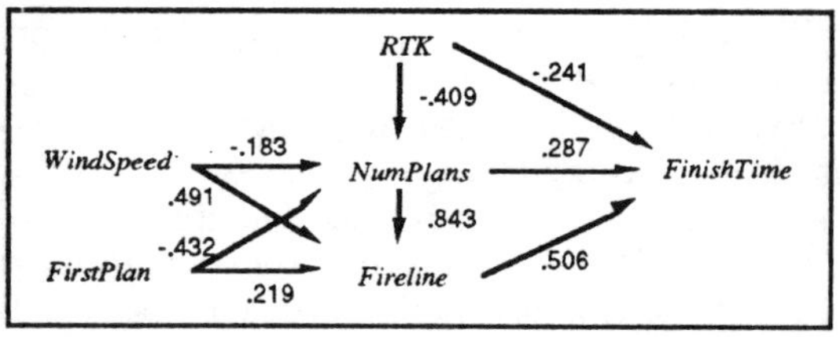

Figure 3: The result of a path analysis of Phoenix data

The disparities or *errors* between estimated and actual correlations of *FinishTime* with all the other factors are shown in Table 1. With the exception of the disparity between the correlations of *WindSpeed* and *FinishTime*, the estimated and actual correlations accord well, suggesting that Figure 3 is a good model of our data.

Table 1: Errors in estimated correlations. The first row is the estimated correlation of *FinishTime* and the factor listed in each column; the second row is the actual, empirical correlation.

	WS	*RTK*	*# Pln*	*First*	*Fline*
$\hat{r}_{Factor\ FinishTime}$	.118	-.488	.704	-.197	.765
$r_{Factor\ FinishTime}$	-.053	-.484	.718	-.193	.755

5. AUTOMATIC GENERATION OF PATH MODELS

The question that motivated the current research is whether models like the one in Figure 3 can be generated automatically by a heuristic search algorithm. This section describes such an algorithm.

The search space for the algorithm is the set of all possible path models. Path models are graphs which satisfy the constraints described in section 3. We can represent any path model then as an adjacency matrix of size N x N, where n is the number of variables in the model. Thus the search space is of size 2^{N^2}.

The algorithm uses a form of best-first search. A single path model constitutes a state, while the sole operator is the addition of an arc to one variable in the model from another (possibly new) variable. We begin with a graph consisting of just the dependent variables. During the search we maintain a list of all the models and all possible modifications to those models. Attach step in the search we select the best modification in the list, apply it to its target model, evaluate the new model, and add it to the list. We continue until either we have reached an acceptable model or we can make no more significant improvements. The most complex issue to be addressed in applying this algorithm is constructing the evaluation function.

We must first distinguish two senses in which a model can be "good." A common *statistical* measure of goodness is R^2, the percentage of variance in the dependent variable, Y, accounted for by the independent variables $X_1, X_2, \ldots$. If R^2 is low, then other variables besides $X_1, X_2, \ldots$ influence Y, and our understanding of Y is therefore incomplete. However, for any set of independent variables, no model accounts for more of the variance in Y than the regression model, in which all independent variables are correlated and all point directly to the dependent variable (e.g., Fig. 1). No wonder this model accounts for so much variance: every variable directly influences Y! It is not a parsimonious model. Nor is it likely to be a plausible causal model of any system we analyze. For example, a regression analysis of the Phoenix data treats *WindSpeed* and *Fireline* as causes at the same "level," that is, both pointing directly to *FinishTime*, but we know that *WindSpeed* is "causally upstream" of *Fireline*. In fact, we know that wind speed influences the rate at which fires burn, and, so, probably influences the amount of fireline that is cut. So R^2, the statistical measure of goodness, is not necessarily the researcher's *pragmatic* measure of goodness. The researcher wants a model that is a plausible causal story, and that includes as few correlational and causal relations among variables as possible, so causal influences are localized, not dissipated through a network of correlations. Such a model will necessarily have a lower R^2 than a highly-connected model, but will often be preferred. In fact, when we constructed the Phoenix model by hand, an important measure of goodness was the errors between estimated and empirical correlations, and we never even calculated R^2.

Another distinction is between modification evaluation and model evaluation. Assuming that good models are clustered together in model space, a few heuristics can move the search into that general region of the space. These are the modification heuristics. A model evaluation function should dominate the search once the modification evaluation heuristics have brought the search into the right neighborhood. This is achieved by including the model evaluation function as a term in the modification evaluation function.

We rely on a variety of heuristics to guide search toward good models and to evaluate a path model. We can group heuristics into three general classes. The first class contains what we might call syntactic criteria:

- no cycles are allowed;
- there must be a path (in the sense of Wright's rules) from every variable to a dependent variable;
- a dependent variable may have no outgoing arcs.

The second class contains domain independent heuristics. These apply to any path analysis problem; however, the weighting of the heuristic may depend on the particular problem. Some heuristics we have tried are

- R^2, the statistical measure of goodness;

- the predicted correlation error (minimize the total squared error between the actual correlation matrix and the predicted correlation matrix for the model);
- parsimony (i.e. the ratio of variables to arcs, or the number of arcs which don't introduce a new variable);
- the correlation between the variables being connected by a new link;
- the total number of variables and arcs.

Others which we have considered, but not yet implemented are

- the "attenuation" of the variables and arcs in the model (the "stretchiness" of the model);
- bandwidth;
- Various adjustments to R^2 .

The third class represents domain/problem dependent forms of knowledge. These include knowledge that

- particular variables are independent;
- particular variables are likely/unlikely causes of others;
- a particular range of values for a domain independent heuristic is appropriate for the problem.

Our evaluation of a modification is a function of these heuristics. In the current implementation we use a weighted sum of the actual correlation between the variables to be linked, the predicted correlation error and the evaluation of the resulting model.

The modification evaluation step hides a good deal of computation required for the heuristic evaluation functions, including path coefficients in the model and the correlation estimates between variables. In the basic algorithm we calculate these parameters from scratch for each newly generated model. Because these calculations dominate search cost, we are currently working on improving the algorithm by incrementally calculating changes to each model's evaluation. This should greatly increase efficiency.

6. EXPERIMENTS

We have run several experiments to demonstrate the performance of our algorithm and probe factors that affect performance. In the first experiment we tested whether the algorithm could generate a model from the Phoenix data. The second experiment was more exhaustive; for this we used artificial data.

6.1. EXPERIMENT 1

We provided the algorithm with data from 215 trials of the Phoenix planner, specifically, *Windspeed RTK NumPlans Fireline*, and *FinishTime* (we dropped *FirstPlan* from the data set). We designated *FinishTime* the dependent variable. The search space of models was large, $2^{N^2-N} = 1,048,576$, but the model-scoring and modification-scoring functions were sufficiently powerful to limit the solution space to 6856 models. When the algorithm terminated, after four hours work on a Texas Instruments Explorer II+ Lisp Machine, its best two models were the ones shown in Figure 4. These models have much to commend them, but they are also flawed in some respects. A good aspect of the models is that they get the causal order of *WindSpeed*, *NumPlans*, and *Fireline* right: the wind speed is causally upstream of the other factors, which are measures of behavior of the Phoenix planner. A bad aspect of the models is that both say *WindSpeed* causes *RTK* when, in fact, these are independent variables set by the experimenter. However, probing this curiosity we realized that due to a sampling bias in our experiment, *WindSpeed* and *RTK* covary, so connecting them is not absurd. A disappointing aspect of the models is that neither recognizes the important influence of *RTK* on *NumPlans* and the influence of *NumPlans* on *Fireline*. In defense of the algorithm, however, we note that the algorithm used model scoring and modification scoring functions that valued R^2, while we, when we built Figure 3 by hand, were concerned primarily about the errors between estimated and empirical correlations, and not concerned at all about R^2. Thus we should not be too surprised that the algorithm did not reproduce our model in Figure 3.

Although the algorithm ran slowly, and is in some ways disappointing, it did produce what we believe is the first causal model of a complex software system ever generated automatically.

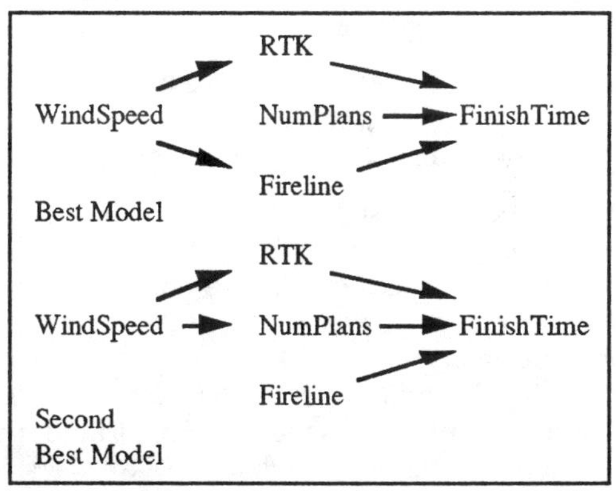

Figure 4: The best and second best Phoenix models found by the algorithm.

6.2. EXPERIMENT 2

The first experiment raised more questions than it answered: Does the performance of the algorithm depend on the sample variance for each variable? Does performance depend on the number of data for each variable? How do we know whether the algorithm is finding the "right" model? To address these and other questions we ran an experiment in which we constructed path models that represented "truth" and tested how frequently our algorithm could discover the true models. Specifically, we followed these steps:

1. Randomly fill some cells in an adjacency matrix to produce a path model.
2. Randomly assign weights to the links in the path model subject to the constraint that the R^2 of the resulting model should exceed .9.
3. Generate data consistent with the weights in step 2.
4. Submit the data to our algorithm and record the models it proposed.
5. Determine how well our algorithm discovered the true model.

Steps 3 and 5 require some explanation. Imagine someone asks you to generate two samples of numbers drawn from a normal (Gaussian) distribution with mean zero such that the correlation of the samples is a particular, specified value, say, .8. Now make the problem more difficult: generate N columns of numbers so that all their pairwise correlations have particular, specified values. Solving this problem (step 3, above) ensures that we generate data with the same correlational structure as the path model specified in step 2. The details of the process are sketched in the Appendix.

We evaluated the performance of our algorithm (step 5, above) by two criteria:

Shared path score: For each true model, make a list of all the paths from each independent variable to the dependent variable; what fraction of these paths exist in the model discovered by our algorithm?

Shared link score: For each true model, make a list of all the links between variables; what fraction of these links exist in the model discovered by our algorithm?

Our experiment was designed to test the effects of sample size on the performance of the algorithm. The Phoenix data included 215 values of each variable, but for this experiment we looked at four levels of the factor: 10, 30, 50, and 100 data per sample. We thought that the performance of the algorithm might deteriorate when sample sizes became small, because the effects of outlier values in the samples would be exacerbated. We generated five true path models with four variables, shown in Figure 5. For each model we generated 12 variants, that is, 12 sets of data for variables A,B,C and D that conformed to the correlation structure established in step 2, above. This produced 60 models. We ran our algorithm on these variants in each of the 4 conditions just described. Thus, the algorithm ran 240 times.

The algorithm found the true model in 109 of the 240 trials. Summary statistics for these trials, and trials in which the algorithm did not find the true model, are presented in Table 2. When the algorithm did find the true model, it explored 174.6 models, on average. This is about four percent of the 4096 models that were possible. Trials that did not find the true model explored only 86.96 models,

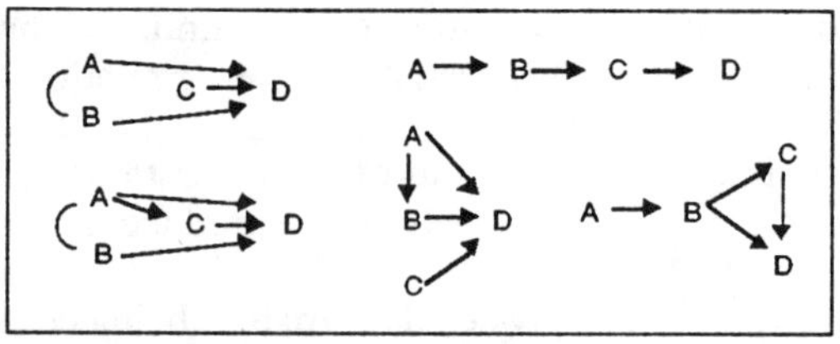

Figure 5: Five path models used to test the algorithm.

which suggests that one reason they failed to find the true model is they gave up too soon. This in turn suggests that our criteria for terminating a search can be improved.

In all trials, the average score of the best model found by the algorithm was better than the average score of the true model. Our immediate inclination was to say the scoring criteria led the algorithm astray, away from the true model. However, the disparity between the best model score and the true model score was less in the trials that found the true model, which casts doubt on this explanation. The reason for the disparity is actually quite subtle: when we generate data to match the correlation structure of each path model (as described in the Appendix), we do, in fact, generate data that have the expected correlations, but if we fit the path model to those data, the resulting R^2 is lower than expected. Said differently, after assigning link weights to the true model (step 2, above), the model R^2 might be, say, .95, but after we generate data (step 3) and fit the data to the model, we find that the model only accounts for, say, 80% of the variance in the data. This is an artifact of our procedure for generating data. Consequently, in most of our trials, the model from which we generated the data is not the model with the highest score. This problem will have to be solved before we can claim that our algorithm found or failed to find the "best" model.

Table 2. Summary statistics from 240 trials.

	Trials that did find the true model		Trials that did not find the true model	
	Mean	Std.	Mean	Std.
Number of models	174.600	93.300	86.962	72.770
Best model score	.974	.027	.954	.018
True model score	.847	.258	.708	.417
Shared path score	.612	.202	.565	.133
Shared link score	.542	.193	.501	.144

We would like to place more stock in two measures of structural similarity between the true model and the best found model. The shared path score is the proportion of paths in the best found model that also exist in the true model. For example, the top-left model in Figure 5 has 5 paths from A, B and C to D, so if the best found model was, say, the top-right model, which has only three paths from A, B and C to D, then the shared path score would be 0.6. Another criterion is the shared link score, which is the fraction of the links connecting variables in the true model that are also in the best found model. Unfortunately, neither score strongly differentiates trials in which the true model was found from those in which it wasn't. On average, 56-61% of the paths, and 50-54% of the links, in the true model are also in the best found model. These numbers are not high. On the other hand, if the disparity between the true model and the best found model was just two links, then the average shared link score would be 52%. So although the shared path and shared link scores are low, they suggest that the best found model differed from the true one by little less than two links on average. Clearly, the algorithm can be improved, but it performs better than the first impression given by the shared path score and shared link score.

We ran a one-way analysis of variance to find the effects of the number of data points in our samples. The dependent variables were the five measures in Table 2. Happily, sample size appears to have no impact on the number of models expanded by the algorithm, the score of the best found model, or the shared path or shared link scores. But the sample size has a large significant effect on the score of the true model. This effect turned out to be a statistical artifact, due entirely to the sensitivity to sample size of the method for generating data. Thus, it appears that the algorithm can work even with relatively few data.

7. CONCLUSION

We have described an algorithm for path analysis and first results from experiments with the algorithm. In a crude sense the algorithm "works," that is, it generates causal models from data. It works slowly, however, and we have yet to establish criteria for demonstrating clearly that it works well. The algorithm's speed can certainly be improved; for example, we keep all models that have been generated, which takes a lot of space, so paging contributes significantly to the run time. Still, the complexity of the search space is exponential in the square of the number of variables. It remains to be seen whether we can improve the algorithm enough to build large causal models in a reasonable time.

More important in the near term is whether the algorithm produces good models. As we noted earlier, goodness can be evaluated by both statistical and pragmatic criteria. The algorithm is currently parameterized, which enables us to adjust the relative importance of the criteria. As you might expect, if R^2 is weighted heavily and parsimony is devalued, then the algorithm will always generate regression models, in which all variables point directly to the dependent variable and are fully intercorrelated. If parsimony is also weighted heavily, the algorithm tends to keep the flat causal structure of regression models, but drops the intercorrelations among the predictor variables. If errors between expected and empirical correlations and parsimony are weighted heavily, then the algorithm will produce causal models with nodes between the predictor and dependent variables, such as the models in Figure 4. All of these kinds of models are good by some criteria.

If by good we mean that the algorithm finds the "correct" model—the model that corresponds to the system that generated the data—then evaluation of goodness is technically challenging. Our procedure was to first decide upon a path model, then generate data consistent with the correlation structure of the model, then see whether our algorithm could find the original model. While the logic of the experiment is sound, two technical problems arose. First, it often happened that we generated data that were better explained by a model other than the original model. In this case, the "correct" model, that is, the one from which we generated the data, might be given a low score by the statistical component (i.e., R^2) of the model scoring function. Second, in the event that the algorithm does not find exactly the "correct" model, but one very like it, how should we measure closeness? Our criteria, shared paths and shared links, were not ideal. More needs to be done to solve both of these problems.

We have yet to answer many questions about factors that affect the performance of the algorithm. For example, we ran an experiment to see whether the variance of our sample data affects performance, but the results were inconclusive. We also need to know how the solution space increases with the number of variables. With four variables, the algorithm searched roughly 100 models on average, but with five variables it searched thousands of models. Clearly, we would prefer this curve to rise less steeply.

Still, we are encouraged by our results, and by the promise the algorithm holds for automatically finding causal models of systems. However ponderous it is, however difficult it is to evaluate, the fact remains that the algorithm generated causal models of a complex AI planning system, and promises to be a valuable tool for those who seek to understand AI systems with statistical methods.

APPENDIX: DATA GENERATION

Every path model has associated with it a predicted correlation matrix, calculated from its path weights, which describes the relationships among its variables. For the purpose of data generation, the path weights of a given model are randomly generated under the following constraints:

- $.15 \leq$ causal path weights < 1
- $.5 \leq$ correlational path weights < 1
- all predicted correlations for the model must be less than one
- $.9 < R^2 \leq 1.0$

After initialization of the path weights, the predicted correlation matrix is calculated. It is essential that data generated for a model have the same correlational structure as the model. The technique for the generation of variates from a multivariate normal distribution was chosen for its efficiency and because it returns a variate having the correlational structure underlying the variance-covariance matrix used to calculate that variate.

A p-dimensional random vector $\bar{x}$ is defined to have a multivariate normal distribution if and only if every nontrivial linear combination of the p components of $\bar{x}$ has a univariate normal distribution. The p-variate normal distribution having mean $\bar{\mu}$ and variance-covariance matrix V (nonsingular) is defined by the pdf

$$f(x) = (2\pi)^{\frac{-p}{2}} |V|^{\frac{-1}{2}} \exp\{-.5(\bar{x} - \bar{\mu})' V^{-1} (\bar{x} - \bar{\mu})\} \quad (1)$$

The distribution of $\bar{x}$ can be represented as a linear transformation of p independent normal variates in $\bar{z}$, such that

$$\bar{x} = A\bar{z} + \bar{\mu} \quad (2)$$

The method for generating $\bar{x}$ from this distribution involves generating $z_1, z_2, ..., z_p$ independent normal variates and forming $\bar{z}$ from them. Since each z_p is sampled from the normal distribution with standard deviation 1, the variance-covariance matrix is equal to the correlation matrix. A is formed from a Choleski decomposition of V and $\bar{\mu}$ is chosen to be a zero vector. These values are substituted into equation (2) to calculate $\bar{x}$. The process is repeated n times, each vector $\bar{x}$ forming the columns of a $p \times n$ data matrix having n data points for each variable.

Acknowledgments

We would like to thank Glenn Shafer for his help with the development of these ideas.

This research was supported by DARPA-AFOSR contract F30602-91-C-0076. The United States Government is authorized to reproduce and distribute reprints for governmental purposes notwithstanding any copyright notation hereon.

References

Asher, H.B. 1983. *Causal Modeling*. Sage Publications, Newbury Park, CA.

Cohen, P.R. *Empirical Methods for Artificial Intelligence*. Forthcoming.

Cohen, P.R & Hart, D.M., 1993. Path analysis models of an autonomous agent in a complex environment. To appear in *Proceedings of The Fourth International Workshop on AI and Statistics*. Ft. Lauderdale, FL. 185–189.

Cohen, P.R., Greenberg, M.L., Hart, D.M. & Howe, A.E., 1989. Trial by fire: Understanding the design requirements for agents in complex environments. *AI Magazine*, 10(3): 32-48.

Falkenhainer, B.C. & Michalski, R.S., 1986. Integrating quantitative and qualitative discovery: the ABACUS system. *Machine Learning* 1(1): 367-401.

Glymour, C., Scheines, R., Spirtes, P. & Kelly, K., 1987. *Discovering Causal Structure*. Academic Press.

Hart, D.M. & Cohen, P.R., 1992. Predicting and explaining success and task duration in the Phoenix planner. *Proceedings of the First International Conference on AI Planning Systems*. Morgan Kaufmann. 106-115.

Langley, P., Simon, H.A., Bradshaw, G.L. & Zytkow, J.M., 1987. *Scientific Discovery: Computational Explorations of the Creative Processes*. The MIT Press.

Li, C.C. 1975. *Path Analysis–A Primer*. Boxwood Press.

Pearl, J. & Verma, T.S., 1991. A theory of inferred causation. *Principles of Knowledge Representation and Reasoning: Proceedings of the Second International Conference*, J. Allen, R. Fikes, & E. Sandewall (Eds.). Morgan Kaufman. 441–452.

Pearl, J. & Wermuth, N., 1993. When can association graphs admit a causal interpretation? *Preliminary Papers of the Fourth International Workshop on AI and Statistics*. Ft. Lauderdale, FL. 141–150.

Schaffer, C., 1990. A proven domain-independent scientific function-finding algorithm. In *Proceedings of the Eighth National Conference on Artificial Intelligence*. The MIT Press. 828–833.

Spirtes, P., Glymour, C. and Scheines, R. (1993) *Causation, Prediction and Search*. Springer-Verlag.

Zytkow, J.M., Zhu, J. & Hussam, A., 1990. Automated discovery in a chemistry laboratory. In *Proceedings of the Eighth National Conference on Artificial Intelligence*. The MIT Press. 889–894.

Constructing Hidden Variables in Bayesian Networks via Conceptual Clustering

Dennis Connolly
The MITRE Corporation
Burlington Road
Bedford, MA 01730
(decon@linus.mitre.org)

Abstract

This paper describes a learning algorithm for constructing Bayesian networks. A major feature of this approach is the use of conceptual clustering to construct hidden variables in the network. These ideas have been implemented in a system called *Tantra*.

1 INTRODUCTION

This paper describes a learning algorithm for constructing Bayesian networks. An important feature of this approach is the use of conceptual clustering to construct hidden variables in the network. Clustering is also used to derive network topology. Both clustering algorithms employ metrics based upon mutual information. This paper will focus primarily on the learning of hidden variables. These ideas have been implemented in a system called *Tantra*.

By using learning to derive the network structure empirically, we hope to reduce knowledge engineering, while improving and generalizing our understanding of complex phenomena. Our approach has the following advantages:

- Our approach supports learning networks with hidden variables.
- The use of AI learning techniques allows us to search for networks which approximate a distribution, when no exact solution exists.
- Our constructive approach allows us to avoid assumptions about the structure of hidden variables being searched for. (e.g., The cardinality of the variable is binary or known *a priori.*)
- Each phase of the learning is incremental and requires maintaining second-order statistics, eliminating the need for storing the complete joint distribution.

In Section 2 we discuss how Bayesian networks can be used to impose structure on complex environments and the role of hidden variables in this enterprise. In Section 3 we describe the learning algorithm. In Section 4 we show some preliminary results from applying this algorithm to some simple problems. Section 5 discusses some related work. Finally, in Section 6 we discuss some of the limitations of this approach and some of our plans for future research.

2 HIDDEN VARIABLES

When scientists and engineers confront a new problem, they often make the assumption of conditional independence. This simplifies problems and often makes problems linear, allowing decomposition. Bayesian networks, themselves, rely on this assumption. In a Bayesian network, all dependencies are represented explicitly as links. This allows probabilities at nodes to be computed via a relatively simple and local updating algorithm and eliminates the need for maintaining large joint distributions.

A natural assumption is that probabilistic models which rely on these independence assumptions are only applicable when this independence actually holds in nature. As Pearl [13] points out, however, this need not be the case. Rather than passively waiting for situations in which this independence is exhibited on the surface, the expressiveness of Bayesian networks allows us to actively structure the environment. Two variables which would not otherwise be independent, could be so with respect to a third variable. In a Bayesian network, this corresponds to making the third variable separate the other two in the network topology. When no such variable is directly observable, a variable may be invented for this purpose. Such variables are referred to as *hidden variables* and can be thought of as reflecting "hidden" causes in nature. From this perspective, we are not so much inventing hidden variables as discovering these hidden causes. Pearl argues that in many situations, this distinction is artificial, since many familiar hidden causes are in fact inventions of the human mind, whose purpose is precisely to make computation tractable. In the work described in this paper, we adopt a constructive approach to searching for these hidden relationships.

3 LEARNING IN TANTRA

Tantra is a learning algorithm which uses conceptual clustering to construct Bayesian networks containing hidden variables from empirical data. *Tantra* takes as input, a training set consisting of attribute-value vectors and produces as output, a tree-structured Bayesian network whose leaves are variables representing the *observables* (i.e., the attributes actually present in the training data) and whose interior nodes are hidden variables which capture hidden relationships between the observables. Mutual information clustering is used to determine the topology of this tree and conceptual clustering is used to construct the hidden variables at the interior nodes.

3.1 LEARNING TOPOLOGY

The topology of the Bayesian network is determined via clustering. The central idea behind this clustering is to group those variables which exhibit the strongest dependencies together and find hidden variables which will render them conditionally independent. These groups, in turn, are organized into larger groups which are themselves rendered independent via further hidden variables. This is done by performing agglomerative clustering[5] on the set of variables representing the observables. Clustering is performed hierarchically to form a tree whose leaves are these observable variables and whose interior nodes will be assigned hidden variables by the process described in the following subsection.

In order to measure the degree of conditional independence between two variables, X and Y, we use mutual information:

$$\sum_i \sum_j P(X_i, Y_j) \log \frac{P(X_i, Y_j)}{P(X_i)P(Y_j)}$$

which is zero when the two variables are conditionally independent and becomes larger as the dependency between the variables grows. With this similarity measure, we can define our criterion function to maximize intra-cluster similarity and minimize inter-cluster similarity as in traditional clustering. The criterion function that we currently use is the average pairwise inter-cluster mutual information divided by the average pairwise intra-cluster mutual information.[1] By minimizing this criterion function, we seek to group

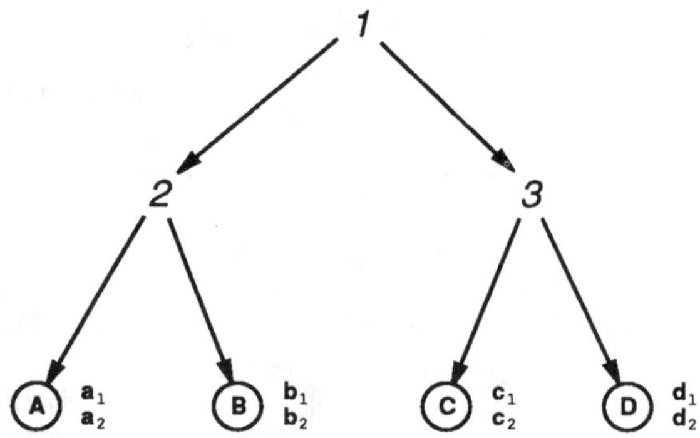

Figure 1: Induced topology.

those variables which exhibit the strongest dependencies as suggested earlier. We then seek to discover the hidden causes which "explain" these dependencies[2] and render the affected variables conditionally independent.

Figure 1 shows the results of applying this procedure to the four observables, A, B, C, and D, with dependencies reflected by the following mutual information values:

$<D \quad C>$	0.50769246
$<B \quad A>$	0.50769246
$<D \quad A>$	0.18738641
$<D \quad B>$	0.18738641
$<C \quad A>$	0.18738641
$<C \quad B>$	0.18738641

We see that the clustering forms two clusters reflecting the strong dependencies between A and B and between C and D. These dependencies will be mitigated by introducing hidden variables at vertices 2 and 3, while introducing a hidden variable at vertex 1 will handle the dependencies between the clusters. The actual construction of these hidden variables is described in the following subsection.

3.2 CONSTRUCTING HIDDEN VARIABLES

We use conceptual clustering to construct hidden variables. Conceptual clustering allows us to learn new

[1] We are still experimenting with stopping conditions for clustering at each level. We currently use a combination of heuristics including a monotonicity condition (stop when the criterion function starts increasing) and a threshold. A more principled approach would be to use statistical significance tests (e.g., χ^2) to determine if the dependencies between variables in a proposed cluster are significant enough to justify the introduction of a new hidden variable. We are also considering adopting a minimum description length criterion.

[2] Strictly speaking, hidden causes are not always needed to model such dependencies. In some cases, dependencies may be modeled via connections solely among observable variables. This research is focused upon those situations when this is not the case. This issue is discussed further in Section 6

concepts which can be used to define a hidden variable to render other variables in the Bayesian network independent. Furthermore, it allows us to learn these concepts in an unsupervised fashion.

In order to construct a hidden variable, we need to determine the values that the constructed variable can take (i.e., its domain) and the conditional probabilities of these values with respect to the values of other variables. In principle, knowing only the number of values that the hidden variable can take (the cardinality) and the conditional probabilities, effectively defines the domain. In practice, seeking a hidden variable by searching for these values is a difficult proposition without some type of assumptions about the structure of the variable to constrain the large search space. Pearl[13] showed how to solve for the probabilities, provided that all variables are binary, that the network is tree-structured, and that an exact solution exists. In [2], an approach analogous to neural network backpropagation is used to derive the conditional probabilities in Bayesian networks using gradient descent. This approach, however, requires that the structure of the Bayesian network, including cardinality of the hidden variables, is known *a priori*.

Tantra's approach is to choose a representation for the hidden variable itself which permits us to search hypotheses about its structure directly. We seek a representation which is expressive enough to represent useful intermediate search states but which is restricted enough to constrain search (i.e., inductive bias). By representing the values of hidden variables as probabilistic concepts, we can transform our search problem into one of searching for partitions of the training data using conceptual clustering similar to the approach used in Fisher's well known COBWEB algorithm[7].

In COBWEB, classes are formed by hierarchically clustering objects to maximize class predictiveness. Describing each class is a *probabilistic concept* description, containing conditional probabilities of each attribute-value assignment, given the class. These descriptions are derived from frequency counts which are updated as new instances are added to the class. Clustering involves searching for partitions which maximize a function called *category utility* which measures the average predictiveness of features given class and class given feature. COBWEB is an incremental algorithm in which new instances are placed into the new or existing class which maximizes category utility, with additional operators to permit the merging and splitting of resulting clusters.

We use clustering similar to COBWEB to learn concepts which are used to define new hidden variables. By requiring our clustering to be mutually exclusive, we may interpret the partition at any level in the hierarchy as a variable in a Bayesian network, with values corresponding to the classes in the partition. For each hidden variable being constructed in the Bayesian network, we induce a COBWEB-style hierarchy whose top level classes form the values of that variable. As in COBWEB, each class is described by a probabilistic concept. In our case, the attribute-value assignments for which conditional probabilities are maintained correspond to values of other variables in the Bayesian network. For those variables which are themselves hidden variables, the COBWEB classes induced for these variables provide these values. For reasons which will become apparent, we include second-order statistics, $P(X_i, Y_j \mid C_k)$, in the probabilistic concept descriptions. Figure 2 shows the top level of the COBWEB hierarchy used to construct the hidden variable at vertex 2 of the induced topology in Figure 1.

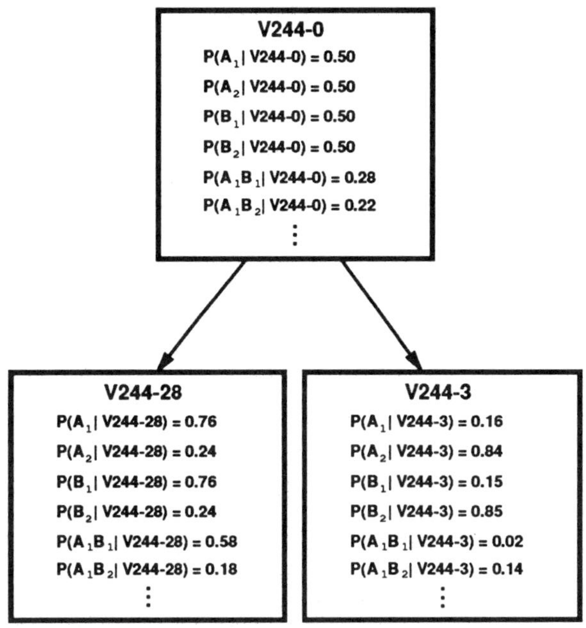

Figure 2: COBWEB hierarchy for variable $V244$.

While COBWEB attempts to learn concepts which optimize class predictiveness, the concepts which we are searching for are those which render other variables in the Bayesian network conditionally independent. In order to accomplish this, we replace category utility with a criterion function based upon mutual information[3]:

$$\sum_{<XY>} \sum_{k} \sum_{i} \sum_{j} P(X_i, Y_j, C_k) \log \frac{P(X_i, Y_j \mid C_k)}{P(X_i \mid C_k) P(Y_j \mid C_k)}$$

This criterion function computes the mutual information between each pair of variables <X Y> separated by the variable being constructed, summed across all

[3]The criterion function currently used in *Tantra* includes an additional term which rewards partitions with fewer classes.

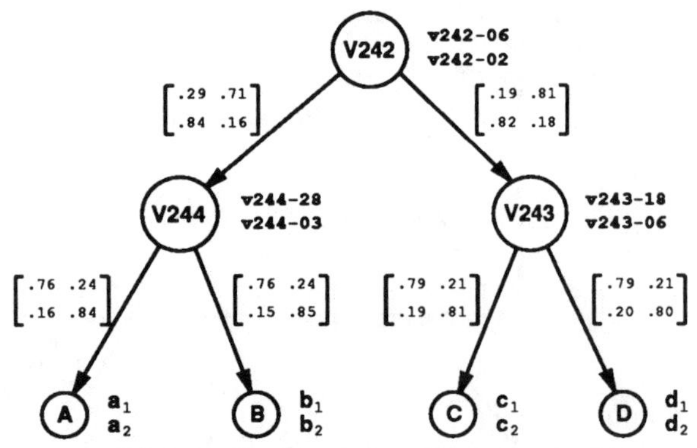

Figure 3: Final Bayesian network.

such pairs. Two variables, X and Y, are separated by Z when Z lies on the path between X and Y in the Bayesian network topology. When constructing the hidden variable at vertex 2 in Figure 1, for example, our criterion function would sum over the mutual information computed for each of the following pairs:

$<A \;\; B>$, $<A \;\; C>$, $<A \;\; D>$, $<A \;\; V243>$, $<A \;\; V242>$, $<B \;\; C>$, $<B \;\; D>$, $<B \;\; V243>$, and $<B \;\; V242>$.

The mutual information in this function is conditioned upon the COBWEB classes, C_k, of the variable being constructed. As in standard COBWEB, the conditional probabilities are taken from the probabilistic concepts for the classes. Note that computing mutual information requires the second-order statistics stored in the probabilistic concept. By minimizing this criterion function, we seek to find the partition which is best capable of rendering those variables separated by this hidden variable conditionally independent.

The final output of this process is a Bayesian network whose topology is that induced by the hierarchical clustering described in the previous sub-section and whose hidden variables have values which are simply the names of the top level classes in the induced COBWEB hierarchies. The conditional probabilities are taken directly from the probabilistic concepts for these classes. Figure 3 shows the final Bayesian network produced for our example.

3.3 SEARCH CONTROL

In the previous discussion, we have disregarded an important issue. For a particular hidden variable, the learning of classes is influenced by the attribute values appearing in the probabilistic concepts for those classes. As described in the previous sub-section, these attribute values come from other variables in the Bayesian network. When these variables are observable, this presents no problem, since the value assignments for these attributes for training instances are known and are stable. For those variables which are themselves hidden variables, however, these values are themselves induced classes. This presents the obvious dilemma that no single hidden variable can be learned, until all others are learned first. There are several possible strategies for addressing this issue:

- We may search for classes which explicitly render only observable variables independent. Our criterion function would not include pairs of variables containing hidden variables in its summation. For some hidden variables in some topologies this provides sufficient constraint on the induced class to also render pairs containing hidden variables independent.
- We may construct hidden variables one at a time. As each new hidden variable is constructed, it is expected to render independent observable variables and those hidden variables which have already been constructed. For each hidden variable, we must reprocess the entire training set.
- We may construct the hidden variables in parallel. As each training instance is processed its attribute assignments are first augmented with initial assignments for each of the hidden variables. These assignments are computed by classifying the instance in the COBWEB hierarchy for each hidden variable, ignoring other hidden variables (i.e., seeking to render only observable variables independent as in the first strategy). With these initial assignments, the instance is reclassified in the COBWEB hierarchies without ignoring other hidden variables. If any of the classifications changes, the attribute assignments of the instance are updated and this step is repeated, iterating until the classifications stabilize.[4] Once stable classifications are made, another more serious problem presents itself. If the classification resulted in a split or a merge as described in Fisher[7], the attribute assignments are no longer valid for all previous training instances which were classified under the affected nodes. This requires reorganizing each COBWEB hierarchy to reflect statistics consistent with the new assignments.

We have experimented with each of these strategies. Thus far we have found the last two approaches to perform the best, providing very similar results. The results reported in this paper were obtained using the second strategy. While the rather simple-minded strategies described above have done well on the problems we have examined thus far, we expect further

[4] The classification performed during each of these steps is actually a restricted form in which the instance is classified into one of the existing top level classes without permanently altering statistics. Once stable assignments are found, the training instance is permanently classified in each COBWEB hierarchy, allowing the full range of splitting, merging, and node addition operations.

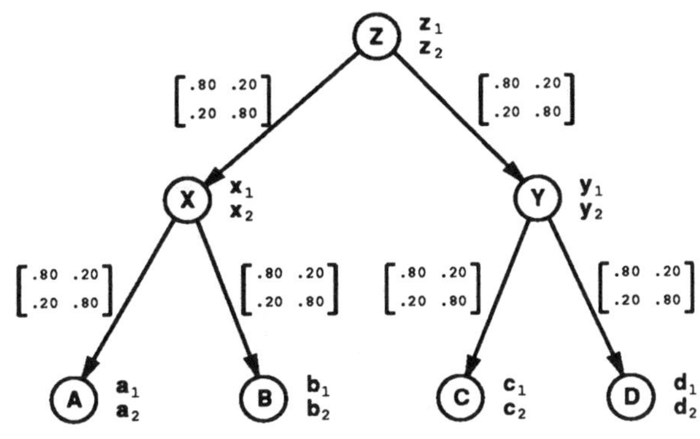

Figure 4: Hand-coded Bayesian network.

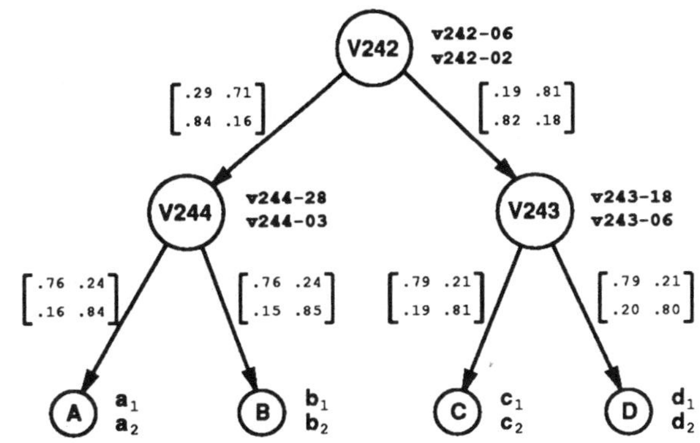

Figure 5: Learned Bayesian network.

work in this area will be required as we investigate more complicated networks.

4 RESULTS

This section shows some preliminary results. One way of evaluating *Tantra* is by examining its behavior for a distribution for which a corresponding tree structured Bayesian network containing hidden variables is known to exist. Such a distribution can be generated from a known Bayesian network. We start by manually creating a tree structured Bayesian network. From such a network, we can derive the probability of any event (i.e., Boolean combination of variables), as described in Pearl[13]. We can treat the interior variables in this hand-coded network as hidden variables by generating the joint distribution for only those variables at the network's leaves. From this distribution, we draw our training instances (which also contain only the variables at the leaves of the hand-coded network). Using this training data we construct a learned network using *Tantra*. This network can then be compared against the original hand-coded network. The goal is to produce a learned network which generates the same joint probability distribution for the observable variables (i.e., the variables at the leaves of the hand-coded network) as the hand-coded network. Of course one way of doing this is to produce a learned network which recovers the structure of the original network.

Consider the hand-coded Bayesian network shown in Figure 4. From this network we derived a joint distribution and training set for the variables A, B, C, and D, treating X, Y, and Z as hidden variables. Figure 5 shows the Bayesian network produced by *Tantra* from this data. The variables $V242$, $V244$, and $V243$ are hidden variables constructed by *Tantra*. Figure 6 shows a comparison of the joint distributions for the learned network and the hand-coded network. Figure 7 shows the learning curve for this problem.

Figures 8 and 10 show some slightly more difficult

sample space event	*original network*	*learned network*	*absolute error*
$A_1B_1C_1D_1$	0.1480	0.1416	0.0064
$A_1B_1C_1D_2$	0.0544	0.0545	0.0001
$A_1B_1C_2D_1$	0.0544	0.0542	0.0002
$A_1B_1C_2D_2$	0.0832	0.0867	0.0035
$A_1B_2C_1D_1$	0.0544	0.0561	0.0017
$A_1B_2C_1D_2$	0.0256	0.0256	0.0000
$A_1B_2C_2D_1$	0.0256	0.0256	0.0000
$A_1B_2C_2D_2$	0.0544	0.0524	0.0020
$A_2B_1C_1D_1$	0.0544	0.0567	0.0023
$A_2B_1C_1D_2$	0.0256	0.0256	0.0000
$A_2B_1C_2D_1$	0.0256	0.0256	0.0000
$A_2B_1C_2D_2$	0.0544	0.0517	0.0027
$A_2B_2C_1D_1$	0.0832	0.0817	0.0015
$A_2B_2C_1D_2$	0.0544	0.0544	0.0000
$A_2B_2C_2D_1$	0.0544	0.0548	0.0004
$A_2B_2C_2D_2$	0.1480	0.1526	0.0046
average error			0.0015

Figure 6: Comparison of the joint distributions for the learned network and the hand-coded network.

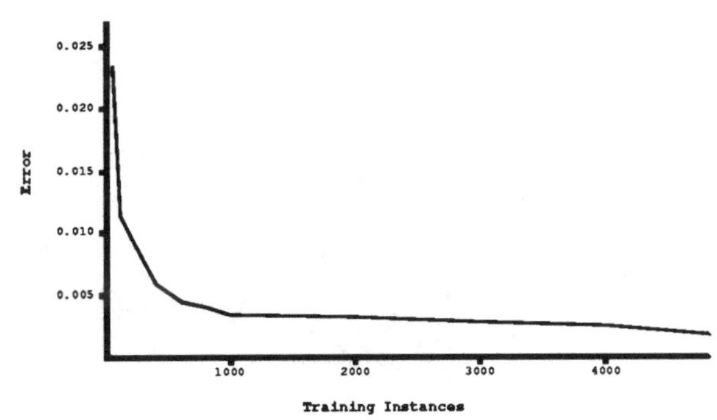

Figure 7: Learning Curve.

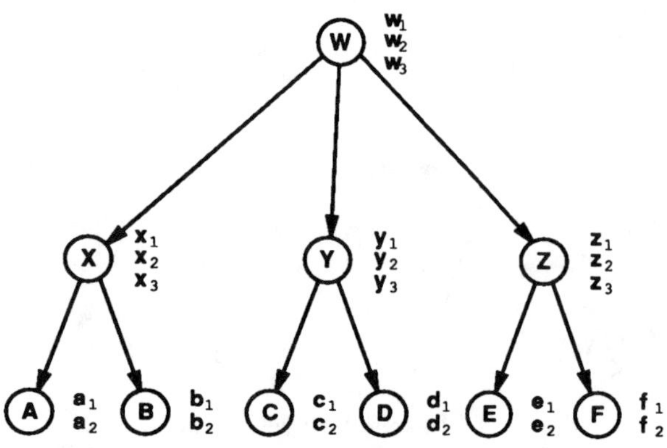

Figure 8: Three Value Bayesian network.

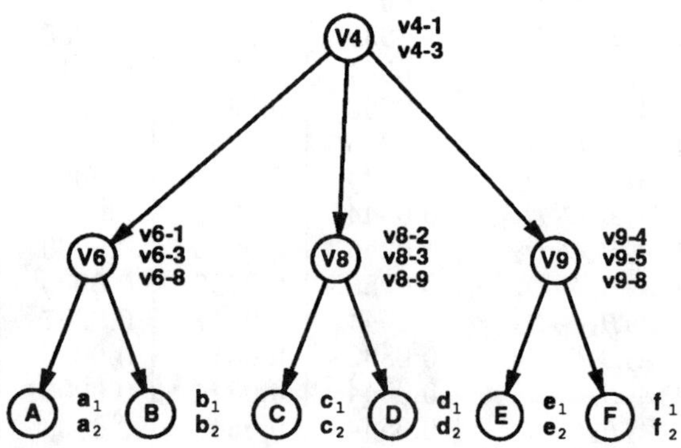

Figure 9: Learned Bayesian network for Three Value Problem.

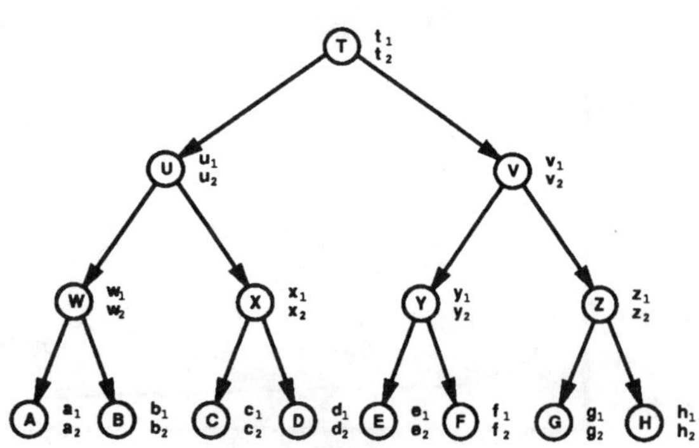

Figure 10: Four Layer Bayesian network.

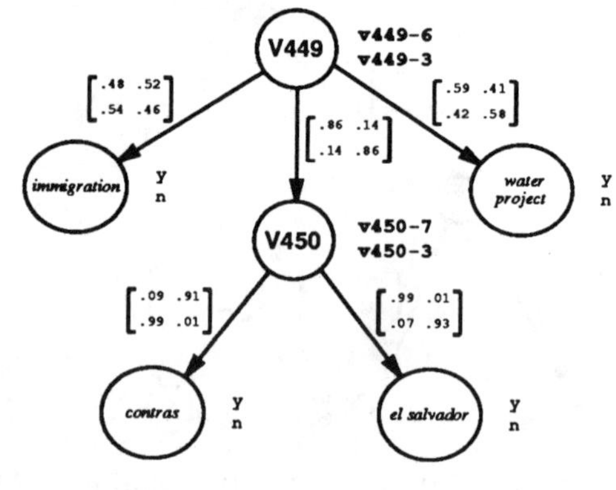

Figure 11: Network derived from Congressional voting data.

networks. Note that the network in Figure 8 contains hidden variables with three values. The learned network for this case is shown in Figure 9. The average error for this network was 0.0014. The hidden variables constructed by *Tantra* in the first layer of the learned network also contain three values, corresponding to three top level partitions produced by the clustering algorithm. For the top variable *Tantra* was able to find a two partition solution. This example demonstrates that *Tantra* is not limited to binary variables, supporting our claim that this approach avoids assumptions about the structure of hidden variables. We have also tested *Tantra* on networks with non-binary observables, obtaining similar results. The network in Figure 10 is a larger network, containing 7 hidden variables and an additional layer. The network which *Tantra* learned for this problem is not shown but contained the same topology but with two three-value hidden variables in the first layer. The error for this network was 0.0004. It should be pointed out that while we have not yet produced learning curves for the networks in Figures 8 and 10, that the number of training instances used to derive the learned networks described above were 1000 and 2000, respectively.

We have also tested *Tantra* on natural data. Figure 11 shows a network constructed from congressional voting data.[10] This data consists of votes on key issues by members the U.S. House of Representatives. Unlike the generated data, this data contains dependencies that are only approximately tree-structured and which do not exhibit the symmetries of the hand-coded network. The error for this network was 0.0087.

5 RELATED WORK

There have been a number of systems which construct Markov networks or Bayesian networks from probability distributions[1, 14, 8]. Few approaches however, learn networks with hidden variables. Pearl and Verma[11] have developed an algorithm to determine causal structure when hidden causes are present by distinguishing between "genuine" causation and "spurious" association, while Glymour and Spirtes[9] have demonstrated how constraints on the correlation matrix can be used to determine the presence of hidden variables in networks with real-valued variables. The primary emphasis of much of this work has been the detection of the *presence* of hidden variables (i.e., network topology) rather than the construction of these variables.

Pearl[13, 12] developed an algorithm for discovering hidden variables in Bayesian networks provided that all variables are binary, that the network is tree-structured, and that an exact solution exists. Our approach is an attempt to relax these restrictions (at the cost of mathematical rigor) by adopting a constructive approach that is more heuristic in nature.

Cooper and Herskovits[3] describe an approach to finding the likely structure of probabilistic networks given data. The primary contribution of this work is the derivation of a Bayesian method for computing the posterior probability of a particular network structure by integrating over all possible assignments of conditional probabilities to that structure. These posterior probabilities can then be used to search for the most likely network structure. Once such a structure is discovered, the expected value of the conditional probabilities are computed. Hidden variables are treated as missing values which are handled by summing over all possible assignments of this variable for each instance in the data set, a process which is exponential in the size of the data set.

The conceptual clustering used to construct hidden variables in our approach is based upon Fisher's COBWEB[7]. The primary difference in our approach, is that we use the concepts learned by this clustering to construct hidden variables in Bayesian networks, and that to support this we use a criterion function based upon mutual information rather than category utility. In [6] Fisher suggests a relationship between COBWEB classes and hidden variables.

Others have used conceptual clustering to induce internal representations. Day[4], for example, has used COBWEB-style clustering to induce generalizations of variables for constraint satisfaction problems.

6 DISCUSSION

This paper has described an approach for constructing Bayesian networks from empirical data. This approach uses conceptual clustering to construct networks with hidden variables.

A major limitation of the current system is that it learns only tree-structured networks. While the increased expressiveness afforded by networks containing hidden variables may make it possible to approximate non-tree-structured dependencies with tree-structured networks, it may be at the cost of unnecessary complexity. It would clearly be desirable to learn networks which support both hidden variables and more general topologies, allowing us, at least in principle, to find the network representation which is best suited to each particular problem. This will be a major thrust of upcoming research. This limitation is primarily a result of the strictly hierarchical clustering used to induce topology. One line of inquiry is to explore clustering approaches which allow clusters to overlap. While the current approach to learning *topology* supports only trees, we see no reason to suppose that our approach to constructing hidden variables, which has been the major emphasis of this research, is inherently limited in this way. The task is still to find a partition which minimizes the average mutual information between all separated nodes. We plan to test this hypothesis by using the clustering algorithm to construct variables in non-tree networks where the topology is known but the structure of hidden variables and conditional probabilities must be discovered.

Another useful generalization of the current system would be to support real-valued variables. The idea of clustering to form intermediate concepts in hidden variables suggests that we might attack real-valued variables similarly by forming partitions in these linearly ordered spaces such that individual values are independent given the partition.

As suggested earlier, the current system models all dependencies by introducing hidden variables. Clearly this is a deficiency since some dependencies may be modeled via connections solely among observable variables as is done in the Chow and Liu algorithm[1]. While the emphasis of this research is the construction of hidden variables when this is not the case, we would clearly like to handle such situations without adding unnecessary complexity to our model. We have considered a number of heuristic methods for addressing this issue (e.g., seeking conditions under which a hidden variable may be replaced by one of the observables that it subsumes) but have yet to address this issue in a satisfactory way in the general case. Hopefully, some of the work by Pearl and others[11, 9] on causality and the evidence for hidden causes can be brought to bear upon this problem.

Another area requiring further research is the top-level search control for the algorithm. As discussed in Section 3.3, the partitions chosen for each constructed hidden variable are dependent on those partitions chosen for other hidden variables. While some of the strategies described in Section 3.3 have been successful for the simple problems we have investigated thus far, we have not yet found a completely satisfactory approach and plan further work in this area. In addition to inter-variable dependencies, the determination of topology and hidden variable structure are also inter-dependent. While we currently determine topology solely on the basis of mutual information and then search for hidden variables which effect the dependencies dictated by this topology, in the future, we hope to more tightly couple the learning of topology with construction of hidden variables.

A related goal is to make our algorithm truly incremental. Currently, each step of the algorithm (learning topology and constructing each hidden variable) is incremental. The advantage of this is that it requires us to maintain only second-order statistics rather than the complete joint distribution. However, each step must process the entire training set, making the overall algorithm not truly incremental.

While the above limitations are important, another deserves equal attention. Unlike the techniques rigorously derived and analyzed in Pearl[13], the formal properties of our system remain unproven. While the nature of our approach, like many AI techniques involving search, may elude the formal treatment we might desire, we would like to place much of this work on a sounder theoretical footing. We would like a better understanding, for example, of the expressiveness of our probabilistic concept representation for hidden variables. In particular, we would like to evaluate the adequacy of this representation for its intended task of defining concepts which render other variables independent and its effectiveness as a search bias. We would also like to more precisely characterize the tradeoff between model accuracy and complexity and examine the issue of overfitting. As suggested earlier, our current heuristic approach to controlling model fit would benefit greatly from a firmer theoretical grounding, including an examination of statistical significance tests. We also feel that the central role of mutual information in our approach would make the minimum description length criterion a promising candidate to address some of these issues while removing many of the thresholds and heuristics that have crept into the system.

In the meanwhile, we plan to do more extensive empirical testing of the approach, testing its generality and testing it on more natural data sets. We also plan to conduct experiments involving the application of constructed networks to perform classification tasks.

Acknowledgments

Much of the COBWEB implementation was provided by David Day. The congressional voting data was provided by the UCI Repository of machine learning databases[10]. Discussions with John Burger, Marc Vilain, and David Day have helped to refine many of the ideas in this paper. Thanks to Marc Vilain, John Burger, and the anonymous reviewers for their helpful comments on the draft of this paper.

References

[1] C.K. Chow and C.N. Liu. Approximating discrete probability distributions with dependence trees. *IEEE Transactions on Information Theory*, 14:462–467, 1968.

[2] D. Connolly. Learning weights in Bayesian networks via backpropogation. In progress.

[3] G.F. Cooper and E. Herskovits. A bayesian method for the induction of probabilistic networks from data. *Machine Learning*, 9:309–347, 1992.

[4] Day, D. S. Learning variable descriptors for applying heuristics across CSP problems. In *Proceedings of the Eighth International Workshop on Machine Learning*, San Mateo, CA, 1991. Morgan Kaufmann Publishers.

[5] Richard O. Duda and Peter E. Hart. *Pattern Classification and Scene Analysis.* John Wiley and Sons, Inc., New York, 1973.

[6] Douglas H. Fisher. Improving inference through conceptual clustering. In *Proceedings of the National Conference on Artificial Intelligence*, 1987.

[7] Douglas H. Fisher. Knowledge acquisition via incremental conceptual clustering. *Machine Learning*, 2:139–172, 1987.

[8] R.M. Fung and S.L. Crawford. Constructor: A syswtem for the induction of probabilistic models. In *Proceedings of the National Conference on Artificial Intelligence*, 1990.

[9] Glymour, C. and Spirtes, P. Latent Variables, Causal Models and Overidentifying Constraints. *Journal of Econometrics*, 39:175–198, 1988.

[10] Murphy, P.M., Aha, D.W. *UCI Repository of machine learning databases* [Machine-readable data repository]. Irvine, CA: University of California, Department of Information and Computer Science., 1991.

[11] J. Pearl and T.S. Verma. A theory of inferred causation. In *Proceedings of the Second International Conference On Principles of Knowledge Representation and Reasoning*, pages 441–452, 1991.

[12] Judea Pearl. Fusion, propagation, and structuring in belief networks. *Artificial Intelligence*, 29:241–288, 1986.

[13] Judea Pearl. *Probabilistic Reasoning in Intelligent Systems: Networks of Plausible Inference.* Morgan Kaufmann, 1988.

[14] G. Rebane and J Pearl. The recovery of causal poly-trees from statistical data. In *Proceedings of the Workshop on Uncertainty in Artificial Intelligence*, 1987.

Learning Symbolic Rules Using Artificial Neural Networks

Mark W. Craven and Jude W. Shavlik
Computer Sciences Department
University of Wisconsin
1210 West Dayton St.
Madison, WI 53706
email: {craven, shavlik}@cs.wisc.edu

Abstract

A distinct advantage of symbolic learning algorithms over artificial neural networks is that typically the concept representations they form are more easily understood by humans. One approach to understanding the representations formed by neural networks is to extract symbolic rules from trained networks. In this paper we describe and investigate an approach for extracting rules from networks that uses (1) the NofM extraction algorithm, and (2) the network training method of soft weight-sharing. Previously, the NofM algorithm had been successfully applied only to *knowledge-based* neural networks. Our experiments demonstrate that our extracted rules generalize better than rules learned using the C4.5 system. In addition to being accurate, our extracted rules are also reasonably comprehensible.

1 INTRODUCTION

Artificial neural networks (ANNs) have been successfully applied to real-world problems as varied as steering a motor vehicle (Pomerleau, 1991) and learning to pronounce English text (Sejnowski & Rosenberg, 1987). In addition to these practical successes, several empirical studies have concluded that neural networks provide performance comparable to, and in some cases, better than common symbolic learning algorithms (Atlas et al., 1989; Fisher & McKusick, 1989; Mooney et al., 1989). A distinct advantage of symbolic learning algorithms, however, is that the concept representations they form are usually more easily understood by humans than the representations formed by neural networks. In this paper we describe and investigate an approach for extracting symbolic rules from trained neural networks. Our approach uses the NofM algorithm (Towell & Shavlik, 1991) to extract rules from networks that have been trained using Nowlan and Hinton's (1992) method of *soft weight-sharing*. Although soft weight-sharing was designed as a technique for improving generalization in neural networks, we explore it here as a means for facilitating rule extraction. We present experiments that demonstrate, for two difficult learning tasks, our method learns rules that are more accurate than rules induced by Quinlan's (1993) C4.5 system. Furthermore, the rules that are extracted from our trained networks are comparable to rules induced by C4.5 in terms of complexity and understandability.

Towell and Shavlik (1991) demonstrated that concise and accurate symbolic rules can be extracted in the restricted case of *knowledge-based* neural networks. In a knowledge-based network, the topology and initial weights of the network are specified by a domain theory consisting of symbolic inference rules. Since these networks initially encode symbolic rules, training is more a process of rule refinement than of *tabula rasa* learning. This paper describes work that involves using Towell and Shavlik's NofM algorithm to extract rules from ANNs which have *not* been initialized by a domain theory. Because the NofM algorithm assumes that the weights in a trained network are clustered, we modify the training process to encourage such a network state after training. Previously, Towell (1991) reported that the NofM algorithm failed to extract accurate rules from conventional networks.

We use two problem domains to investigate the effectiveness of our approach. The first domain involves recognizing *promoters* in DNA (Towell et al., 1990). Promoters are short nucleotide sequences that occur before genes and serve as binding sites for the protein *RNA polymerase* during gene transcription. Identifying promoters is an important step in locating genes in DNA sequences. The second problem domain that we investigate is a simplified version of the NetTalk task of mapping English text to its pronunciation (Sejnowski & Rosenberg, 1987). Our scaled-down version of this domain involves learning only the stresses (but not the phonemes) from a corpus of the 1000 most common English words.

2 EXTRACTING RULES FROM NEURAL NETWORKS

An important criterion by which a machine learning algorithm should be judged is the comprehensibility of the representations formed by the algorithm. That is, does the algorithm encode the information it learns in such a way that it may be inspected and understood by humans? There are at least five reasons why this is an important criterion.

- *Validation.* If the designers and end-users of a learning system are to be confident in the performance of the system, then they must understand how it arrives at its decisions.
- *Discovery.* Learning algorithms may discover salient features in the input data whose importance was not previously recognized. If the representations formed by the learner are comprehensible, then these discoveries can be made accessible to human review.
- *Explanation.* If the representations are understandable, then an explanation of the classification made on a particular case can be garnered.
- *Improving generalization.* The feature representation used for an inductive learning task can have a significant impact on generalization performance. Understanding learned concept representations may facilitate the design of a better feature representation for a given problem.
- *Refinement.* Some researchers use inductive learning systems to refine approximately-correct domain theories (Ourston & Mooney, 1990; Pazzani & Kibler, 1992; Towell et al., 1990). When a learning system is used in this way, it is important to understand the changes to the knowledge base that have been imparted during the training process.

2.1 RULE EXTRACTION METHODS

A significant limitation of artificial neural networks is that the concepts they learn are usually impenetrable to human understanding because concepts are represented by a large number of real-valued parameters: the weights and biases of the network. One approach toward understanding the representations formed by a neural network is to extract symbolic rules from the network (Fu, 1991; McMillan et al., 1991; Saito & Nakano, 1988).

The underlying premise of these rule-extraction methods is that each hidden and output unit in the network can be thought of as implementing a symbolic rule. The concept associated with each unit is the consequent of the rule, and certain subsets of the units that feed into this unit represent the antecedents of

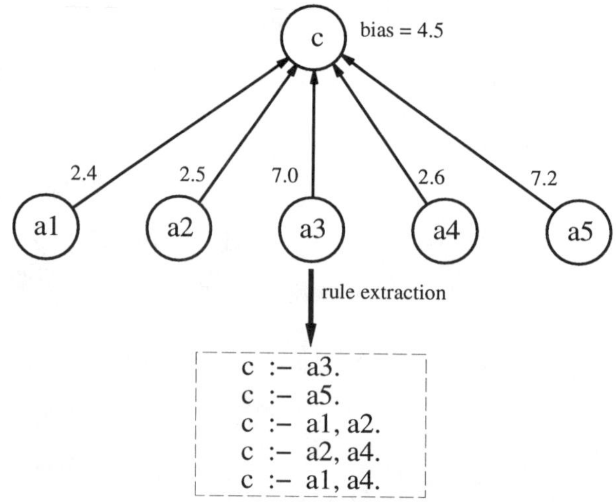

Figure 1: **Extracting Rules from a Unit in a Neural Network.** The extracted rules show the combinations of antecedent units which must be active for the consequent unit's bias to be exceeded.

the rule. As shown in Figure 1, the process of rule extraction involves finding the *sufficient* conditions for each consequent. In order to find such sets of sufficient conditions, rule-extraction methods assume that, after training, hidden and output units tend to be either maximally active (i.e., have activation near one), or inactive (i.e., have activation near zero). Given this assumption, a rule-extraction algorithm can search for minimal sets of antecedent units that, when maximally active, cause the consequent unit to become maximally active. The process of searching for rules is problematic because of the combinatorics involved. The complexity of this search is $O(2^n)$ where n is the number of connections impinging on the consequent unit. Moreover, these algorithms tend to extract a large number of rules, even for networks of moderate complexity.

2.2 THE NofM ALGORITHM

Towell and Shavlik previously described an algorithm, called NofM, that avoids the combinatoric and rule-set size problems of other rule-extraction algorithms by clustering weights into equivalence classes. They have demonstrated that their NofM algorithm is able to extract accurate and concise rules from trained knowledge-based neural networks; that is, networks for which the topology and initial weights have been specified by an approximately-correct domain theory. The algorithm is called NofM because it explicitly searches for rules of the form:

If (N of the M antecedents are true) then ...

The NofM algorithm comprises six steps:

1. **Clustering.** The weights impinging on each hidden and output unit of the trained network are

grouped into clusters. Initially, each weight is treated as a cluster. The two nearest clusters are successively merged until no pair of clusters is closer than a preselected distance. The distance metric used for clustering is the difference in the means of the weight magnitudes for two clusters. Additionally, weights with small magnitudes are pruned from the network at this step.

2. **Averaging.** The magnitude of each weight is set to the average value of the weights in its cluster.
3. **Eliminating.** Weight clusters that are not needed in order to correctly activate a unit are eliminated. Two elimination procedures are applied: one algorithmic and one heuristic. The algorithmic elimination procedure identifies clusters that *cannot* have an effect on whether or not a unit's bias is exceeded. The heuristic elimination step eliminates clusters that do not have such an effect for any of the training examples.
4. **Optimizing.** The unit biases are retrained to adapt the network to the changes that been imparted by the previous steps.
5. **Extracting.** Each hidden and output unit is translated into a rule with weighted antecedents such that the consequent is true if the sum of the weighted antecedents exceeds the bias.
6. **Simplifying.** Weights and thresholds are eliminated and rules are expressed in the NOFM format.

Figure 2 illustrates the application of the NOFM to the unit shown in Figure 1. The weights have been grouped into two clusters, and each weight has been set to the average value of its cluster. One of the extracted rules is expressed in the NOFM format; the other two rules are trivial NOFM cases (1 of 1). The *eliminating* and *optimizing* steps are not depicted in this example.

3 EXTENDING NofM WITH SOFT WEIGHT-SHARING

An underlying assumption of the NOFM method is that the distribution of weights in the network will be conducive to forming a small number of clusters for each hidden and output unit. For knowledge-based neural networks, this is a reasonable assumption since the weights are clustered before training. For example, using the KBANN algorithm (Towell et al., 1990) to map a set of symbolic rules into a knowledge-based network, the weights that are specified by the domain theory have values of approximately 4 and -4, whereas the rest of the weights have values near 0. Experimental evidence indicates that the weights tend to be fairly well clustered after training as well (Towell, 1991).

The applicability of the NOFM method might seem to be limited to knowledge-based networks, since in con-

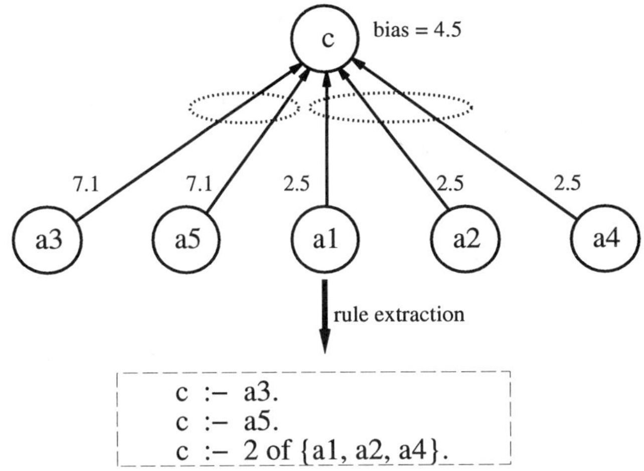

Figure 2: **Extracting Rules using the NOFM Method.** The dotted ovals illustrate how the weights have been grouped into clusters. Each weight has been set to the average value of its cluster.

ventional neural networks there is usually not a bias that leads weight values to be clustered after training. In fact, Towell (1991) reported that NOFM did not extract small sets of accurate rules from conventional networks. However, the approach that we explore in this paper does not rely on the network weights being initially clustered, but instead encourages clustering *during* network training. We use a method developed by Nowlan and Hinton (1992), termed *soft weight-sharing*, that encourages weights to form clusters during the training process. Although their method was motivated by the desire for better generalization, we explore it here as a means for facilitating rule extraction.

In the spirit of the minimum-description-length principle (Rissanen, 1978), soft weight-sharing uses a cost function that penalizes network complexity. Thus, during training the network tries to find an optimal tradeoff between data-misfit (i.e., the error rate on the training examples) and complexity. The complexity term in soft weight-sharing models the distribution of weights in the network as a mixture of multiple Gaussians. A set of weights is considered to be simple if the weights have high probability densities under the mixture model. Specifically, the cost function in soft weight sharing is the following:

$$C = \lambda E - \sum_{i \in wgts} \log \left[\sum_{j \in Gauss} \pi_j \, p_j(w_i) \right]$$

where E is the data-misfit term, λ is a parameter used to balance the tradeoff between data misfit and complexity, w_i is a weight in the network, $p_j(w_i)$ is the density value of w_i under the jth Gaussian, and π_j is the mixing proportion of the jth Gaussian. A mixing proportion is a weight that determines the influence of a particular Gaussian. The mixing proportions are constrained to sum to 1.

Neural learning algorithms perform gradient descent to locally minimize this cost function. The partial derivative of the cost function with respect to each weight is the sum of the usual error derivative plus a term due to the complexity cost of the weight:

$$\frac{\partial C}{\partial w_i} = \lambda \frac{\partial E}{\partial w_i} - \sum_{j \in Gauss} r_j(w_i) \frac{(\mu_j - w_i)}{\sigma_j^2}$$

Here μ_j and σ_j^2 are the mean and variance, respectively, of the jth Gaussian, and $r_j(w_i)$ is the conditional probability that w_i is being modelled by the jth Gaussian:

$$r_j(w_i) = \frac{\pi_j \; p_j(w_i)}{\sum_{k \in Gauss} \pi_k \; p_k(w_i)}$$

Thus, the effect of each Gaussian is to pull each weight toward the mean of the Gaussian with a force proportional to the density of the Gaussian at the value of the weight. When weights are pulled tightly around the means of the Gaussians, the network is similar to one that has fewer free parameters than connections (i.e., ordinary weight sharing). The parameter settings of each Gaussian – the mean μ_j, standard deviation σ_j, and mixing proportion π_j – are learned simultaneously with the weights during training.

Our approach to rule extraction involves training networks using a variant of soft weight-sharing and then applying the NOFM algorithm to the trained networks. Although the NOFM method was designed for knowledge-based neural networks, we hypothesized that it could be successfully applied to conventional networks, provided that the weights of the networks were grouped into clusters during training.

Whereas the NOFM algorithm works best when the weights impinging on *each unit* form clusters, standard soft weight-sharing tends to *globally* cluster network weights. Our implementation of soft weight-sharing hence assigns a local set of Gaussians to each unit. The complexity cost of a given weight is calculated with respect to only the Gaussians associated with the unit to which the weight connects.

4 DATA SETS

Our experiments address the hypothesis that soft weight-sharing is able to cluster the network weights during training such that NOFM is able to extract a small set of accurate rules. In order to evaluate the effectiveness of our approach, we use two problem domains to compare the accuracy and succinctness of our extracted rules against rules induced by the C4.5 system. Both problem domains involve predicting a class given a fixed-length "window" onto a string of interest. In the case of the *promoter* domain, the string is a DNA sequence, and in the NETTALK domain, the string is an English word (or part of one).

The *promoter* data set comprises 468 examples,[1] half of which are positive examples (i.e., promoters). Each example has 57 features which represent the DNA sequence. A single strand of DNA is a linear chain composed from the four nucleotides represented by the letters {A, G, C, T}. Thus all of the features for this problem are nominal features that can take on the values *A*, *G*, *C*, *T*, or *unknown*. Each example is a member of one of two classes: *promoter* or *non-promoter*. The positive examples for this data set are aligned such that the gene following each promoter begins in the seventh position from the right end of the window. Thus the leftmost 50 window positions are labelled `-50` to `-1`, and the rightmost seven are labelled `1` to `7`.

For the neural networks, a local representation is used for the *promoter* features. For each feature there are four input units – one corresponding to each of the nucleotides. When the value of a feature is known, the input unit corresponding to the value is given an activation of 1, and the other three units for the feature are given activations of 0. When a feature value is unknown, all four input units are given activations of 0.25.

Our simplified NETTALK data set consists of 5438 examples taken from the 1000 most common English words. Each example has seven features which represent the letters in the input window. Each feature can take on one of 27 values. There is a value corresponding to each letter of the alphabet, and a value to represent the absence of a letter. Since each example is formed from only a single word, when the window overhangs a word, the overhanging window positions are set to the "space" value. In the original NETTALK domain, the task involved predicting both a phoneme and a stress for each window position. In our experiments we have simplified the problem so that the classifiers are trained only to predict a stress (from five disjoint classes).

5 EXPERIMENTAL RESULTS

In this section we evaluate our approach to rule extraction by comparing the accuracy and comprehensibility of (1) rules extracted from neural networks, and (2) rules learned using the C4.5 system. The comprehensibility of a set of rules is difficult to measure. We measure the syntactic complexity of the rule sets and

[1] Note that this data set is larger and more biologically complicated than the one that was used by Towell et al. (1990). The latter data set is available by anonymous ftp from the UC-Irvine Repository of Machine Learning Databases and Domain Theories (ftp.ics.uci.edu).

use this as a crude proxy for comprehensibility. Specifically, we consider the number of rules and antecedents as measures of syntactic complexity.

5.1 THE PROMOTER DATA SET

For the *promoter* problem, we use a ten-fold cross-validation methodology[2] to assess the ability of our approach to extract accurate, comprehensible rules from trained networks. Our reported results represent averaged values for the ten runs.

The neural networks used for the *promoter* domain have fully-connected hidden units in a single layer. The number of hidden units used in each network is determined by cross-validation *within* the training set. That is, for each training set, networks with 20, 15, 10, 5, and no hidden units are trained, and cross-validation is used to pick the network that is to be trained on all of the data in the training set. After the number of hidden units is selected for each network, a similar cross-validation procedure is used to determine the λ parameter for soft weight-sharing. We use a conjugate-gradient learning algorithm (Kramer & Sangiovanni-Vincentelli, 1989) to train the weights and the Gaussian parameters of the networks. Each hidden and output unit has five local Gaussians which act on the weights feeding into the unit.

Decision trees are induced, and rules extracted from them, using Quinlan's (1993) C4.5 system. Cross-validation within each training set is used to determine the confidence levels for both tree pruning and rule pruning. The confidence level selected for tree pruning does not affect the rule-extraction results since the C4.5 rule-induction program operates on unpruned trees and performs its own pruning independently. Thus, the confidence level for tree pruning affects the generalization only of the decision trees. For each training set, we test confidence levels ranging from 5% to 95% and separately select tree-pruning and rule-pruning levels.

Table 1 shows the test set error rates on the *promoter* data set for the decision trees, rules extracted from the trees, neural networks, and rules extracted from the networks. As can be seen in the table, neural networks perform significantly better on this task than decision trees or the rules extracted from them. Additionally, the performance of the symbolic rules extracted from the neural networks is fairly close to the performance of the networks themselves, and better than the rules extracted from the decision trees. The difference in error rates between the rules extracted from networks and the C4.5 rules is significant at the 0.05 level using a paired, 1-tailed *t*-test.

[2]In ten-fold cross-validation, the available data is partitioned into ten sets. Classifiers are trained using examples from nine of the sets and tested on examples from the tenth set. This procedure is repeated ten times so that each set is used as the testing set once.

Table 1: **Generalization on the *Promoter* Data.**

approach		% test set error
C4.5	decision trees	16.9
	extracted rules	13.5
ANNs	networks	7.9
	extracted rules	11.1

Table 2: **Rule-set Sizes for the *Promoter* Data.**

approach	# rules	# antecedents
C4.5	23.2	47.3
ANNs	8.2	119.6

Table 2 shows the average number of rules and antecedents for the rules extracted from our networks and the rules induced by C4.5. The values for antecedents indicate the *total* number in a rule set. The rules extracted by the C4.5 algorithm are purely-conjunctive rules that tend to have few antecedents. Thus, the sets extracted from the decision trees contain more rules but fewer antecedents than those extracted from networks. The additional complexity of the rules extracted from networks, however, results in a significant gain in accuracy. Moreover, the rules extracted from networks have only 14.6 antecedents per rule on average, and these antecedents often refer to localized, contiguous parts of the DNA sequence. We feel, therefore, that their complexity is within the bounds of what biologists can readily understand.

Table 3 shows a set of rules extracted from one of the *promoter* networks. In addition to the NofM-style rules, this rule set has been expressed using a new predicate we call `more_than`. The `more_than` predicate has the following form:

$$N \texttt{ more\_than}(Pos\_Set,\ Neg\_Set)$$

where N is an integer, and *Pos_Set* and *Neg_Set* are sets of positive and negated antecedents, respectively. The predicate returns true if the number of satisfied antecedents in *Pos_Set* minus the number of satisfied antecedents in *Neg_Set* is greater than N. This predicate provides a succinct way of expressing rules that have many negated antecedents. Without such a predicate, negated antecedents tend to result in a large number of mostly-redundant rules. Since the knowledge-based networks to which the NofM algorithm was previously applied had very few negated antecedents, this predicate was not previously necessary.

The rule set shown in Table 3 exhibits several interesting characteristics. First, the rules abstract away

Table 3: **Rules Extracted from a *Promoter* Network.** The predicate `more_than` returns true if the number of satisfied antecedents in the first set minus the number of satisfied antecedents in the second set is greater than the supplied threshold. The notation `@-36` indicates the starting position of a given sequence; in this case the position is 36 nucleotides before the start of a putative gene. Dashes represent placeholders, so `{@-36 '--AG----A'}` has only three antecedents. The letter `S` is an ambiguity code that biologists use to represent `(C ∨ G)`.

```
promoter :-
    hidden2, not (hidden1), not (hidden4).

promoter :-
    hidden3, not (hidden1), not (hidden4).

promoter :-
    hidden2, hidden3,
    not 2 of {hidden1, hidden4}.

hidden1 :-
    5 more_than( {@-40 'C----C-G-C-G',
                  @-13 '-SG---', @-1'G'},
                 {@-40 'A---T--A----',
                  @-13 '-T---T'} ).

hidden1 :-
    not ({@-40 '-----T------'}),
    3 more_than( {@-40 'C----C-G-C-G',
                  @-13 '-SG---', @-1'G'},
                 {@-40 'A---T--A----',
                  @-13 '-T---T'} ).

hidden2 :-
    5 more_than( {@-40 'A---T-GA-A', @-13 '-T-'},
                 {@-40 'C----C-G--', @-13 '-SG'} ).

hidden2 :-
    {@-40 '-----T----'},
    3 more_than( {@-40 'A---T-GA-A', @-13 '-T-'},
                 {@-40 'C----C-G--', @-13 '-SG'} ).

hidden3 :-
    4 more_than( {@-40 'A---T-GA-AT',
                  @-13 '-T-A-T'},
                 {@-40 '-----C-G-C-', @-20 'G--G',
                  @-13 'GSGG'} ).

hidden3 :-
    {@-40 '-----T-----'},
    2 more_than( {@-40 'A---T-GA-AT',
                  @-13 '-T-A-T'},
                 {@-40 '-----C-G-C-', @-20 'G--G',
                  @-13 'GSGG'} ).

hidden4 :-
    4 of {@-44 'G', @-40 '----AC-G-C',
          @-24 'A--G', @-13 '-SG'}.
```

a significant amount of the complexity of the network from which they are extracted. There are only ten rules and a total of 106 antecedents. Six of the hidden units and more than 2400 of the weights that were present in the neural network are not represented in the rules. A second observation is that the rules focus on what are known by biologists to be the most significant regions of the DNA sequence. In particular, a domain theory developed by Michiel Noordewier (Towell et al., 1990) identifies the `-14` to `-7` and the `-37` to `-31` regions as containing the most important features of a promoter. These are termed the *contact* regions. The rules extracted from all of the hidden units specify antecedents primarily in these areas.

Although we have used the number of rules and antecedents as a basis for comparing the comprehensibility of extracted rule sets, it is important to note that this comparison does not take into account the semantic differences between the two types of rules. Whereas we have employed the *N*-`of`-*M* and `more_than` constructs in the network-extracted rules, C4.5 rules are purely conjunctive. A second difference is that the rules extracted from networks identify intermediate concepts between the input features and the output classes; these are the rules whose consequents correspond to hidden units. Although it is difficult to attach meaningful labels to the concepts represented by hidden units, we believe that in some cases, these intermediate terms might lead to rule sets that are more comprehensible than those which simply include the input and output terms. A third difference is that the network-extracted rules define only the positive (promoter) class, and employ the closed-world assumption to classify examples as negative.

5.2 THE NETTALK DATA SET

For the NETTALK domain, classifiers are trained on half of the example set and tested on the other half. Ten runs of this procedure are performed, and the reported results represent averaged values. As with the *promoter* domain, cross validation is used to determine the λ parameter and the number of hidden units for the networks, and the confidence levels for pruning C4.5 trees and rules. Five local Gaussians are used for each hidden and output unit, and a conjugate-gradient algorithm is used to learn all of the network parameters.

Since the NETTALK domain involves five classes, the rules extracted from trained networks are not necessarily mutually exclusive and exhaustive. In other words, a given input sequence may satisfy more than one of the class rules, or alternatively, it may satisfy none of the class rules. The C4.5 rule-extraction method also faces this complication when it prunes antecedents and rules from its rule set. C4.5 handles this problem in two ways: (1) rules are ordered by class, and the first rule to match a given instance determines the predicted class; (2) a default rule is used to classify in-

Table 4: **Generalization on the NETTALK Data.**

approach		% test set error
C4.5	decision trees	19.1
	rules	20.1
ANNs	networks	13.0
	rules	17.0

Table 5: **Rule-set Sizes for the NETTALK Data.**

approach	# rules	# antecedents
C4.5	233.5	466.5
ANNs	17.5	661.9

stances that do not satisfy any of the other rules. We employ the same policy in classifying instances using our network-extracted rules. The rules are ordered to minimize false-positive errors on the training set, and the default rule predicts the class which has the most training examples not covered by any rule.

Table 4 shows the test set error rates on the NETTALK data set for the decision trees, rules extracted from the trees, neural networks, and rules extracted from the networks. The results in this table indicate that the neural networks and the rules extracted from them outperform C4.5 decision trees and rules. The difference in error rates between the rules extracted from networks and the decision trees is significant at the 0.005 level using a paired, 1-tailed t-test.

Table 5 shows the average number of rules and antecedents in the extracted rule sets. The rule sets extracted from the neural networks contain far fewer rules than the rules generated from the decision trees, although the network rules have far more antecedents. This result points out an interesting tradeoff regarding comprehensibility: is it easier to understand a large body of simple rules or a small collection of complex rules?

5.3 THE EFFECT OF SOFT WEIGHT-SHARING

In order to evaluate the contribution of soft weight-sharing to the results presented in this section, we trained *promoter* and NETTALK networks using the same methodology as the previous experiments, except that soft weight-sharing was not employed. Surprisingly, the results we obtained for the *promoter* domain, in terms of rule generalization and comprehensibility, were essentially the same. The results for the NETTALK domain are presented in Table 6. Although soft weight-sharing does not seem to affect the generalization ability of the extracted rules, it has a significant impact on the concision of the rules. The rules extracted from the networks that employed soft weight-sharing had, on average, 108 fewer antecedents. This difference is significant at the 0.05 level using a paired, 1-tailed t-test.

Table 6: **The Effect of Soft Weight-Sharing (SWS) for the NETTALK Domain.**

approach	% error	# rules	# antes
ANNs w/ SWS	17.0	17.5	616.1
ordinary ANNs	16.9	16.0	724.5

In our experiments, we have evaluated our rule-extraction approach along two dimensions: generalization and comprehensibility. For neural networks, it is clearly more difficult to control the performance of a rule-extraction method along the dimension of comprehensibility. A rule set that generalizes as well as the network from which it was extracted can be obtained by simply replicating the network as a large set of rules. The results presented in Table 6 indicate that soft weight-sharing can act to significantly improve the performance of the NOFM algorithm along this dimension – comprehensibility – which is the most formidable dimension.

We are currently conducting experiments to evaluate the effectiveness of soft weight-sharing as we vary such parameters as network size, training-set size, number of Gaussians, output representation, etc.

6 CONCLUSIONS

We have demonstrated that small sets of accurate, reasonably concise symbolic rules can be extracted from ordinary artificial neural networks. Our approach to this problem involves exploiting the effectiveness of the NOFM algorithm by encouraging weight clustering during training. For two difficult problem domains, recognizing promoters in DNA, and mapping English text to stress patterns, our approach was able to induce rules that resulted in better generalization than rules learned using C4.5.

There are a number of issues regarding our approach that we plan to pursue in further research. One such issue is adapting the method so that it can extract concise rule sets from networks that have learned distributed representations. In a distributed representation, each concept at the hidden-unit level may be encoded by the activations of many hidden units, and each unit may play a part in representing many different concepts. Distributed representations tend to result in rule sets that are verbose and difficult to understand. The NOFM algorithm makes the assumption that each hidden unit corresponds to a meaningful concept, and thus it searches for rules by considering each hidden unit independently. Our proposed approach involves partitioning the space of hidden unit activations and then searching for rules that explain particular regions of this space.

A second area that we plan to investigate in future research is to employ a weight-pruning method, such as *Optimal Brain Damage* (LeCun et al., 1990), during learning. The effectiveness of the NofM algorithm is partly due to the weight pruning that it performs during its clustering step. The expected advantage of pruning weights *during* the learning process is that the remaining weights are able to adapt to the changes imparted by the pruning operation.

A third issue to be investigated is rule-pruning strategies. The C4.5 system, for example, incorporates clever techniques for pruning antecedents and for dropping entire rules. These methods improve both the generalization ability and the comprehensibility of the extracted rules. We plan to investigate the use of these methods in our system.

Extracting accurate, comprehensible rules from neural networks is an important problem in machine learning. We have described an approach that employs the NofM algorithm and soft weight-sharing, and demonstrated that it is able to extract accurate, comprehensible rules from networks trained on a difficult real-world problem. These promising results indicate that the problem of understanding representations learned by artificial neural networks may be tractable.

Acknowledgements

This work was partially supported by Department of Energy Grant DE-FG02-91ER61129 and National Science Foundation Grant IRI-9002413. Rich Maclin provided helpful comments on an earlier version of this paper.

References

Atlas, L., Cole, R., Connor, J., El-Sharkawi, M., Marks II, R. J., Muthusamy, Y., & Barnard, E. (1989). Performance comparisons between backpropagation networks and classification trees on three real-world applications. In Touretzky, D., editor, *Advances in Neural Information Processing Systems (volume 2)*. Morgan Kaufmann, San Mateo, CA.

Fisher, D. H. & McKusick, K. B. (1989). An empirical comparison of ID3 and back-propagation. In *Proc. of the 11th IJCAI*, (pp. 788–793), Detroit, MI.

Fu, L. M. (1991). Rule learning by searching on adapted nets. In *Proc. of the 9th Nat. Conf. on Artificial Intelligence*, (pp. 590–595), Anaheim, CA.

Kramer, A. H. & Sangiovanni-Vincentelli, A. (1989). Efficient parallel learning algorithms for neural networks. In Touretzky, D., editor, *Advances in Neural Information Processing Systems (volume 1)*. Morgan Kaufmann, San Mateo, CA.

LeCun, Y., Denker, J. S., & Solla, S. A. (1990). Optimal brain damage. In Touretzky, D., editor, *Advances in Neural Information Processing Systems (volume 2)*. Morgan Kaufmann, San Mateo, CA.

McMillan, C., Mozer, M., & Smolensky, P. (1991). The connectionist scientist game: Rule extraction and refinement in a neural network. In *Proc. of the 13th Conf. of the Cognitive Science Society*, Chicago, IL. Erlbaum.

Mooney, R., Shavlik, J., Towell, G., & Gove, A. (1989). An experimental comparison of symbolic and connectionist learning algorithms. In *Proc. of the 11th IJCAI*, (pp. 775–780), Detroit, MI. (A longer version appears in *Machine Learning*, 6).

Nowlan, S. J. & Hinton, G. E. (1992). Simplifying neural networks by soft weight-sharing. *Neural Computation*, 4:473–493.

Ourston, D. & Mooney, R. J. (1990). Changing the rules: A comprehensive approach to theory refinement. In *Proc. of the 8th Nat. Conf. on Artificial Intelligence*, (pp. 815–820), Boston, MA.

Pazzani, M. & Kibler, D. (1992). The utility of knowledge in inductive learning. *Machine Learning*, 9:57–94.

Pomerleau, D. A. (1991). Efficient training of artificial neural networks for autonomous navigation. *Neural Computation*, 3:88–97.

Quinlan, J. R. (1993). *C4.5: Programs for Machine Learning*. Morgan Kaufmann, San Mateo, CA.

Rissanen, J. (1978). Modeling by shortest data description. *Automatica*, 14:465–471.

Saito, K. & Nakano, R. (1988). Medical diagnostic expert system based on PDP model. In *Proc. of the IEEE International Conf. on Neural Networks*, (pp. 255–262), San Diego, CA. IEEE.

Sejnowski, T. & Rosenberg, C. (1987). Parallel networks that learn to pronounce English text. *Complex Systems*, 1:145–168.

Towell, G. G. (1991). *Symbolic Knowledge and Neural Networks: Insertion, Refinement and Extraction*. PhD thesis, University of Wisconsin – Madison.

Towell, G. G. & Shavlik, J. W. (1991). Interpretation of artificial neural networks: Mapping knowledge-based neural networks into rules. In Moody J., Hanson S. and Lippman, R., editors, *Advances in Neural Information Processing Systems (volume 4)*. Morgan Kaufmann, San Mateo, CA. (A longer version will appear in *Machine Learning*).

Towell, G. G., Shavlik, J. W., & Noordewier, M. O. (1990). Refinement of approximately correct domain theories by knowledge-based neural networks. In *Proc. of the 8th Nat. Conf. on Artificial Intelligence*, (pp. 861–866), Boston, MA. MIT Press.

Small Disjuncts in Action: Learning to Diagnose Errors in the Local Loop of the Telephone Network

Andrea Pohoreckyj Danyluk
NYNEX Science & Technology, Inc.
500 Westchester Avenue
White Plains, NY 10604
danyluk@nynexst.com

Foster John Provost
Computer Science Department
University of Pittsburgh
Pittsburgh, PA 15260
foster@cs.pitt.edu

Abstract

Learning *general* rules is a basic goal of many concept learning systems. In a 1989 paper, Holte, Acker, and Porter pointed out that this bias toward generality had resulted in a problem with small disjuncts. The problem they discussed was that small disjuncts had high rates of misclassification, and that it was difficult to eliminate the error-prone small disjuncts without affecting the performance of other disjuncts. We describe a real domain based on NYNEX MAX, an expert system that diagnoses the local loop in a telephone network. We demonstrate with two inductive learning systems that a range of disjunct sizes is important for this domain despite the relatively high error rates of the small disjuncts. We conclude that the need for smaller disjuncts is a major reason that it is difficult to learn from errorful data in this domain.

1 INTRODUCTION

Learning *general* rules is a basic goal of many learning systems [Mitchell, 1980]. Inductive learning systems often make use of a bias that prefers large disjuncts to small disjuncts, where a large (small) disjunct is one that correctly classifies many (few) training examples.[1] Many believe in the notion that it is better to capture generalities than to have a knowledge base of specific cases from which you cannot extrapolate.[2] There are a number of reasons for this belief. Large disjuncts tend to have fewer conditions on their applicability. They are therefore simpler and more comprehensible, which also makes them more acceptable to experts who might be required to evaluate them. A related reason is Occam's razor–that is, the belief that given two results with similar accuracies on training data, the description with fewer conditions is more elegant (and will be more predictive on future data). Complex small disjuncts could be overfitting the training data, which would make them less applicable to future unseen cases. More practical considerations include the fact that having many small disjuncts may decrease the efficiency of a system, both in terms of space and the time it takes to consider a disjunct for each new input. In dealing with real application domains where one must anticipate errors in the data, it is undesirable to capture specific "odd" cases, as they may be the random or systematic errors in the domain.

Holte, et al., pointed out that the bias toward large disjuncts focuses attention away from small disjuncts, which deserve equal attention for many reasons [Holte, et al., 1989]. Many concepts include rare or exceptional cases and it is desirable for induced definitions to cover these cases. Second, small disjuncts collectively may match a large percentage of the examples that satisfy a definition. The problem with small disjuncts, as pointed out by Holte, et al., is that they are much more error prone than large disjuncts. This work was followed up by Quinlan [Quinlan, 1991].

According to Holte, et al., "The net effect of eliminating all small disjuncts is hard to predict..." They assume that small disjuncts are necessary for high accuracy and discuss methods for decreasing their error rates. We provide support for their basic assumptions by showing that in one novel, real-world domain, small disjuncts are necessary for high accuracy. More generally, we will show that a range of disjunct sizes is necessary for this domain.[3] We demonstrate the need for a range of sizes using two very different learning systems: c4.5 and RL.

In the next section we introduce the MAX expert system, which performs diagnosis of telephone troubles.

[1] We will refer to large disjuncts as "general" and small disjuncts as "specific".

[2] A notable exception is case-based reasoning, where specific instances are stored. But there the general knowledge is in the matching function. Learning this is not a trivial problem.

[3] That is, it is necessary given the description language.

We then introduce the learning task for the MAX domain. In subsequent sections we give results of test runs with c4.5 and RL. We will demonstrate that a range of disjuncts are important for this domain despite the relatively high error rates of the small disjuncts. We will conclude with a brief discussion of the impact of noise in such a domain and posit that the need for smaller disjuncts is a major reason that it is difficult to learn from errorful data in this domain.

2 THE NYNEX MAX DOMAIN

MAX is an expert system that was developed by NYNEX Science and Technology, Inc.[4] for the high level diagnosis of customer-reported telephone problems. Specifically, MAX concentrates on the *local loop*, the final segment of the telephone network which connects the customer to the central office. The learning task for this domain is to create the knowledge base inductively from trouble cases and their resolutions. Section 2.1 describes the expert system in more detail[5], and Section 2.2 discusses the learning task.

2.1 THE MAX EXPERT SYSTEM

When customers have problems with their phone service, they call 611 to report the trouble. A phone company representative takes a report of the problem (the *trouble*) and also initiates electrical tests on the line (a *mechanized loop test*, or MLT).[6] The representative sends the information from the trouble report and the MLT to a maintenance administrator, who evaluates the trouble and determines how the company should take care of (how to *dispatch*) the trouble. The maintenance administrator also gets information from a screening decision unit, a primitive rule-based system for diagnosing problems based on a two-character *vercode*—a summary of the MLT results. In general, the vercode alone does not provide sufficient information for an optimal decision.

MAX (Maintenance Administrator eXpert) plays the role of a Maintenance Administrator, i.e., it uses the MLT test results, together with other information, to make a screening diagnosis. The only exception is that MAX has the option of referring certain problems to a human maintenance administrator. MAX diagnoses a problem based on the following information: results of the MLT, including the vercode, knowledge about the customer's line, and general knowledge about equipment.

MAX is currently running for over 55 maintenance centers. Some of its benefits are: minimal change to the maintenance center's work flow; consistency; speed; reduction of erroneous dispatches over the screening decision unit (see [Rabinowitz, et al., 1991] for details). Some of MAX's limitations are: it is running for many diverse sites, with parameters used to customize the knowledge base for a given site (and the parameters are difficult to set); and the knowledge base must be updated periodically due to changing conditions.

2.2 THE MAX LEARNING TASK

Due to the volume of troubles handled by MAX, even a small improvement in its accuracy is extremely valuable—each dispatch typically involves at least one hour of time by a highly trained worker. It is interesting to consider whether machine learning techniques can be useful to help in automating modifications to the knowledge base. The process of tuning and updating the MAX system is very tedious and time intensive, and must be done to account for differences that exist between sites, as well as for changes that occur over time. One direction we have been investigating is the possibility of creating inductively a MAX knowledge base from current data about troubles and resolutions.[7]

The features used by MAX for diagnosis are essentially the features used to describe the examples for learning, with only minor differences. The attributes are largely resistances and voltages. In all, there are 14 attributes, 12 of them numeric. In most (approximately 90%) cases, one or more features are missing from the examples.

The classes to be learned are the five possible dispatch diagnoses for MAX: (i) dispatch to the cable; (ii) dispatch to the customer premise; (iii) dispatch to the central office; (iv) request further testing; (v) send to a human. For the experiments described in this paper, the criterion used to evaluate the learned concept description was predictive accuracy. The relative cost of errors varies, however, and current work is addressing that issue. The classifications used in the following experiments are the diagnoses given by MAX. Training on MAX's classifications provides us with (a) a consistent data set; and (b) a data set that is analogous to a set of cases provided by a maintenance center expert. RL and c4.5 were trained on data from one maintenance center at a time as there may be variations in MAX's diagnoses from site to site. All results reported are from a single site. Comparable results have been obtained for other locations.

---

[4] NYNEX is the parent company of New York Telephone and New England Telephone.

[5] Some of the text in this section is paraphrased from [Rabinowitz, et al., 1991].

[6] MLT was developed by AT&T.

[7] Other approaches are also being investigated, including modification of the existing knowledge base [Pazzani, 1993].

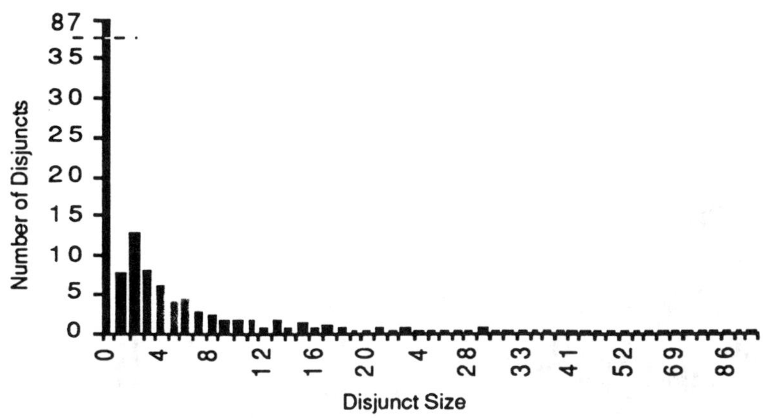

Figure 1: Number of Disjuncts for Varying Disjunct Sizes. Most disjuncts are small. Histogram plots number of disjuncts in concept description learned by c4.5 for varying disjunct sizes. The disjunct size is the number of examples covered, based on 500 training examples. Each bar is the average over ten runs with randomly selected training and test sets.

3 C4.5 RESULTS

Several experiments were performed using c4.5 [Quinlan, 1992]. In all cases, c4.5 was run with its default parameter settings. The gain ratio criterion was used to select tests. All results reported are before pruning, though the differences between the results before and after pruning are negligible.

For the first set of runs we used a set of 5845 examples. These were troubles that had been diagnosed by MAX in one maintenance center in one month. For each run of c4.5, a random subset of n examples was selected from this set as a training set. The maximum value of n in this set of runs was 5000. For each run, a randomly selected set of 845 examples was used as the test set. The training and test sets were non-overlapping. Accuracy on the test set was quite high when training with as few as 500 examples (89.05%, with s.d. 1.0), and after training on 5000 examples it reached 97% (s.d. .56). Results were averaged over ten sets of runs.

It is important to mention that we studied the examples that c4.5 was unable to classify correctly after training on 5000 examples. We found that in 60% of the cases c4.5's classification was actually better than MAX's. In this study, we presented to an expert the troubles that c4.5 had misclassified. We also gave the expert the MAX answer and the c4.5 answer, though we did not tell him which was which. The order of the two choices was also randomized. We asked the expert to select the diagnosis (dispatch) that he thought was better. In approximately 60% of the cases, he selected c4.5's dispatch.

We next performed a set of test runs to determine the occurrence of different-sized disjuncts in the decision trees learned for this domain. We trained c4.5 ten times on randomly selected sets of 500 examples. Figure 1 shows a histogram of our results, averaged over the 10 runs. The x-axis gives the size of a disjunct, i.e., the number of training examples covered by a leaf. The y-axis indicates the number of disjuncts, i.e., leaves, of that size. As shown in the figure, a wide range of disjuncts are learned by c4.5, and a significant number of those are small disjuncts.

We next performed a set of runs to evaluate the accuracy of different-sized disjuncts. We performed 10 runs in which we trained on 500 examples and tested on 2457. The training and test sets used in each run were randomly selected and disjoint. Figure 2a shows the number of test set examples classified by disjuncts of varying sizes, while Figure 2b shows the number of those that were classified erroneously.

The results of our experiments indicate that c4.5 is able to learn good decision trees for the MAX domain. Our analysis indicates that both large and small disjuncts appear in the trees learned, and that small disjuncts occur with relatively high frequency. Our analysis also confirms Holte, et al.'s conclusion that small disjuncts are more prone to errors than are large disjuncts. Experiments performed with RL indicate that small disjuncts cover such a large percentage of instances in this domain that they are necessary in spite of their error rates. Section 5 will discuss this in more

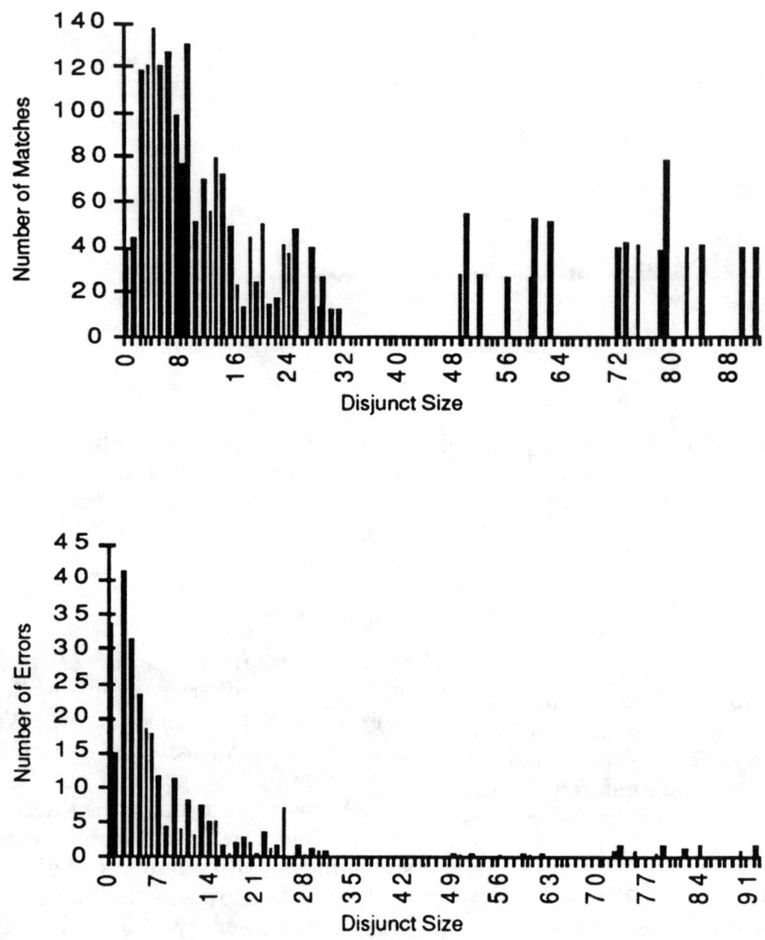

Figure 2: Number of Matches and Errors for Varying Disjunct Sizes. Smaller disjuncts are more error prone.

detail.

4 RL RESULTS

The RL learning system [Clearwater & Provost, 1990], a descendent of Meta-DENDRAL [Buchanan & Mitchell, 1978], searches for a disjunctive set of conjunctive rules. These rules are intended to form the knowledge base for an evidence-gathering performance system (a system which combines the evidence from several rules to make a classification). Below we describe RL briefly, show that RL can learn a set of rules that classifies troubles with high accuracy, and go on to study the contributions of large and small disjuncts.

RL structures its hypothesis space in a general-to-specific hierarchy rooted at the (syntactically) most general rule (every example is an element of the concept). Two types of specialization operators are used: (i) adding a conjunct, and (ii) specializing an existing conjunct. These operations are performed based on information provided in a partial domain model (PDM), which contains descriptions of the attributes, their types, and possible values and value hierarchies for each attribute. The PDM also contains other information used to determine when a rule is satisfactory/too general/too specific, and/or to restrict the hypothesis space.

The learning procedure keeps statistics on the various tentative rules and compares these with the criteria specified in the PDM. If a rule is too general, it is

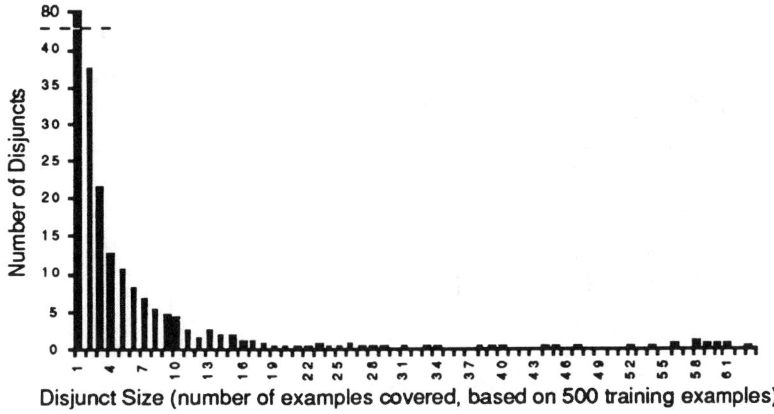

Figure 3: Number of Disjuncts for Varying Disjunct Sizes

specialized. If too specific, it is discarded along with the entire subtree rooted there. If satisfactory, it is saved. Several search methods are provided; a beam search was used for the results presented here. The evaluation function for the beam search is specified in the PDM; we used the default function, which rates node r_1 better than node r_2 if the ratio of true positives to false positives covered by r_1 is greater than that of r_2 (in a tie, the rule with the larger coverage wins). In summary, the search procedure is a beam search of the space of syntactically defined rules, in which sections of the rule space are pruned if they are guaranteed not to yield results that will prove satisfactory with respect to the criteria of the PDM. For this domain we used a multiclass version of RL. Throughout this section, a simple evidence-gathering system will be used for testing that classifies examples based on the rule with the highest certainty factor that matches the example (as in [Quinlan, 1987]).

Via the partial domain model, users can specify different biases in different domains. We were concerned with the effect of different disjunct sizes, which are represented in RL's partial domain model by coverage threshold levels (a rule is too general if it covers more negative examples than the negative threshold allows; a rule is too specific if it covers fewer examples than the positive threshold allows). In this domain, we knew that the data were very clean and that there existed special cases (that would appear infrequently). We therefore set RL's thresholds such that in order for a rule to be considered a "good" rule, it would have to cover at least one positive example, while covering no negative examples (a *perfect rules only* bias). With this bias, both large and small disjuncts would be learned.

Across ten runs with random subsets of 500 training examples and 2457 test examples, the rule sets learned by RL averaged 86.5% accuracy (with a s.d. of 1.0). On a separate set of ten runs, where the rule sets were pruned (in a manner similar to that in [Quinlan, 1987]), the average accuracy was 87.8% (with a s.d. of 1.4). These results are comparable with those of c4.5. In similar runs, c4.5 averaged 88.9% accuracy (with a s.d. of 0.9).

Figure 3 shows that in the concept descriptions learned by RL, small disjuncts are abundant (Figure 3 is analogous to Figure 1). As observed with c4.5, RL's smaller disjuncts are more error prone than its larger disjuncts (see Figure 4, analogous to Figure 2). Disjuncts' error rates generally decrease with increased size. (As in Figures 1 and 2, data indicate averages over ten runs with randomly selected training sets of 500 examples and test sets of 2457.)

5 GENERALITY VS. ACCURACY

In order to test the hypothesis that learning small disjuncts was necessary for learning high-accuracy concept descriptions, we conducted a series of RL runs with different minimum levels of generality. The minimum level of generality was enforced by the threshold on the positive coverage of learned rules. A positive threshold of p restricts RL from learning rules that cover less than p% of the positive examples of each class. In all cases, the rules were not allowed to cover any negative examples. Figure 5 depicts the relationship between the level of generality and the corresponding test-set accuracy. Each point in the figure is an average over ten runs with randomly selected train-

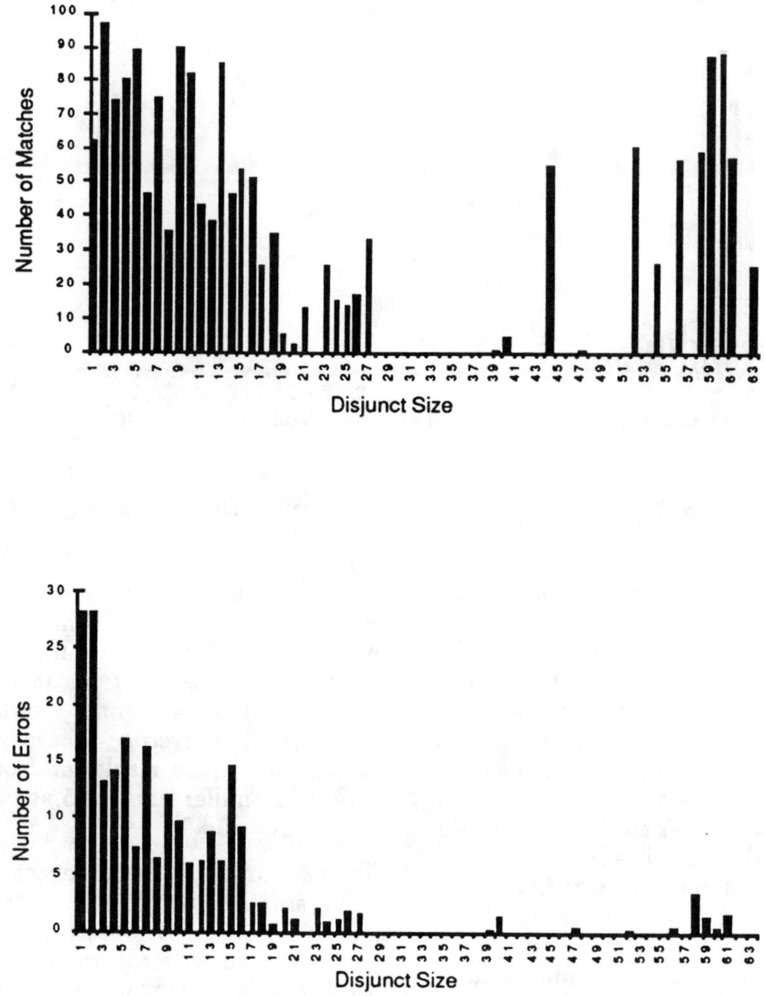

Figure 4: Number of Matches and Errors for Varying Disjunct Sizes

ing sets of 500 examples, and test sets of 2457. Error bars indicate 95% confidence intervals using Student's t.

Figure 5 shows a (decreasing) linear relationship between the minimum size of the learned disjuncts and the accuracy of the corresponding concept description (a line can be fit to the data with R=0.99). This indicates that (with respect to the rule-based description language) there are special cases in the MAX data that appear very infrequently, but are important parts of the concept description. This is consistent with our prior domain knowledge, and the assumptions of previous investigators. In fact, the linear relationship indicates that disjuncts of all sizes are integral parts of the learned concept descriptions.

6 DISCUSSION: DISJUNCT SIZES AND NOISE

The results of this study suggest that the incorporation of good mechanisms for learning small disjuncts is one reason for the widespread success of c4.5 (though the version we used did not include improvements outlined by Quinlan in [Quinlan, 1991]). Our initial success with c4.5, as well as our ability to choose different inductive biases in RL, led us to examine the features of our learning systems that allowed us to learn the knowledge base. It confirmed the need for a range of disjunct sizes, especially the important role played by small disjuncts.

Though c4.5 and RL were able to learn good knowl-

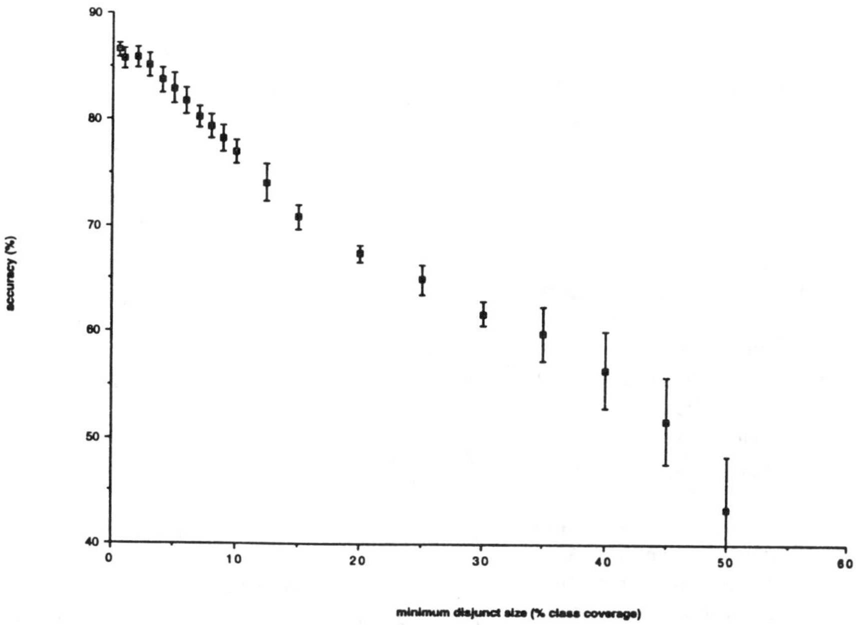

Figure 5: Minimum Disjunct Size Versus Accuracy. Increasing the generality required of rules learned by RL decreases the corresponding test-set accuracy. Graph plots the accuracy of concept descriptions leaned by RL when a minimum level of generality was enforced. The minimum level of generality is a requirement that a learned rule must cover at least a certain percentage of the examples of the corresponding concept. Each point is an average over ten runs, error bars are 95% confidence intervals based on Student's t.

edge bases for MAX, neither system was able to learn a good knowledge base when trained on noisy data. The difficulties stem from two major sources. First, it is difficult to distinguish between noise and true exceptions. In the MAX domain approximately half of the example coverage comes from small disjuncts (exception-type rules covering fewer than 10 training examples), all of which can be significantly affected by the presence of noise. Second, in the MAX domain, errors in measurement and classification often occur systematically rather than randomly. Thus it is difficult to distinguish between erroneous consistencies and correct ones.

We performed a set of runs in which we trained on troubles analyzed by MAX, but rather than using the MAX diagnosis as the classification for a trouble, we used the diagnosis as determined by the technician who actually solved the trouble in the field. We then tested on other troubles as diagnosed by the field techs. There are a number of sources of errors in this data, and many of the errors differ from the type of noise that one generally expects. They include electronic faults in data collection and reporting devices and noise in transmission lines. Additional sources of error include:

- Errors in repair: The trouble may not have been repaired correctly. Or a problem may have been solved, but there may in fact have been multiple troubles that should have been attended to.
- Errors in translation of codes: The people who solve the troubles indicate their diagnosis using a different set of codes than those used to dispatch the troubles. There is not an exact one-to-one correspondence between the two sets of classifications. Thus translating one coding scheme to another will introduce errors, some due to pure mistranslation and others due to inherent ambiguities.
- Errors in coding: The codes used to indicate the trouble found are complicated and errors in coding will occur naturally. A repair person might also deliberately miscode a diagnosis.

Many of these types of errors may occur systematically. This is especially true in the case of deliberate miscodings. We have no exact estimates of the number of errors occurring in the MAX data, where the trouble diagnoses are those actually given by the technicians. When trained and tested on this data, however, neither c4.5 nor RL was able to achieve accuracy above 60% even after training on 1000 examples.

Noise is a fundamental problem that has been addressed in many systems. The MAX domain has pointed out new issues to consider, however. In a domain where small disjuncts play a critical role in the overall performance of a system, it is imperative to find a mechanism to distinguish true exceptions from noise. Furthermore, in a domain such as ours, it is important to be able to distinguish between general rules that are correct, and erroneous trends. In order to achieve greater accuracy in MAX we will almost certainly require a good model of probable errors (more robust than the one we currently have) to perform intelligent instance selection.

7 CONCLUSIONS

Learning general rules is a fundamental goal of a number of learning systems. For a variety of reasons, ranging from comprehensibility to efficiency, many systems are biased to concentrate on general rules rather than on special cases. Holte, et al., first identified the fact that this bias drew attention away from another important problem, that of ensuring the accuracy of small disjuncts. We have described one domain, the NYNEX MAX domain, in which learning large disjuncts alone is not sufficient. However, learning a range of disjuncts is. Two learning systems, c4.5 and RL, were able to learn very accurate rules. c4.5 incorporated criteria for including both large and small disjuncts into its bias. The RL work showed that while learning a combination of large and small disjuncts was sufficient for learning concept descriptions with high accuracy, learning only large disjuncts was not. We have shown this to be true even though the error rate of disjuncts increases as the size decreases.

We agree with previous authors that the quality of both large and small disjuncts is important to the performance of a learning system. We show MAX to be a domain in which both are essential. We believe that there are other domains in the real world that require the ability to learn both generalities and special cases. This must be a capability of learning systems, if they are to succeed in these areas. Balancing the tradeoffs between true special cases and anomalies due to errors is still a great—and crucial—challenge. This is especially true since errors may be systematic as well as random.

References

Buchanan, B. & Mitchell, T. (1978). Model-directed Learning of Production Rules. In D. A. Waterman & F. Hayes-Roth (ed.), *Pattern Directed Inference Systems*, p. 297-312. New York: Academic Press.

Clearwater, S. & Provost, F. (1990). RL4: A Tool for Knowledge-Based Induction. In Proceedings of the Second International IEEE Conference on Tools for Artificial Intelligence, p. 24-30. IEEE C.S. Press.

Holte, R. C., Acker, L. E. & Porter, B. W. (1989). Concept Learning and the Problem of Small Disjuncts. In Proceedings of the Eleventh International Joint Conference on Artificial Intelligence, p. 813-818. San Mateo, CA: Morgan Kaufmann.

Mitchell, T. M. (1980). The Need for Biases in Learning Generalizations. Technical Report CBM-TR-117, Rutgers University.

Pazzani, M. J. (1993). Finding accurate frontiers: A new approach to analytic learning. In Proceedings of the National Conference of Artificial Intelligence. San Mateo, CA: Morgan Kaufmann.

Quinlan, J. (1987). Generating Production Rules from Decision Trees. In Proceedings of the Tenth International Joint Conference on Artificial Intelligence, p. 304-307. San Mateo, CA: Morgan Kaufmann.

Quinlan, J. R. (1991). Improved Estimates for the Accuracy of Small Disjuncts. *Machine Learning*, 6(1), p. 93-98.

Quinlan, J. R. (1992). *C4.5: Programs for Machine Learning.* San Mateo, CA: Morgan Kaufmann.

Rabinowitz, H., Flamholz, J., Wolin, E. & Euchner, J. (1991) NYNEX MAX: A Telephone Trouble Screening Expert. In R. Smith & C. Scott (ed.), *Innovative Applications of Artificial Intelligence 3*, p. 213-230. Menlo Park, CA: AAAI Press.

Concept Sharing: A Means to Improve Multi-Concept Learning

Piew Datta
Information and Computer Science Dept.
University of California, Irvine
Irvine, CA 92717-3425
pdatta@ics.uci.edu

Dennis Kibler
Information and Computer Science Dept.
University of California, Irvine
Irvine, CA 92717-3425
kibler@ics.uci.edu

Abstract

This paper describes several means for sharing between related concepts to improve learning in the same domain. The sharing comes in the form of substructures or possibly entire structures of previous concepts which may aid in learning other concepts. These substructures highlight useful information in the domain. Using two domains, we evaluate the effectiveness of concept sharing with respect to accuracy, concept size, search complexity, and noise resistance.

1 Introduction

Humans ability to learn is remarkable. One characteristic of human learning is that it employs multiple sources of knowledge, including examples, partial theories, and background knowledge. Markman (Markman, 1989) argues that human learning has a number of inherent biases which aid in the learning of natural concepts. We seek computational biases that can increase the accuracy of learned concepts.

We take a broader view of concept learning, namely that of learning multiple concepts instead of learning single concepts in a domain. A multi-class decision tree also learns multiple concepts, however, it does not employ our bias of concept sharing. When learning a set of concepts, concepts may share common substructures. Concept sharing allows partial or complete information from previously learned concepts to be shared for future learning. Our premise is that concepts from the same domain share some content, and therefore, substructures that are frequently used for learning concepts previously will be applicable for learning concepts subsequently. Concept sharing biases the representation of concepts to prefer sharing common substructures. We feel that sharing concept information is an additional form of knowledge that has not yet been exploited.

Various means for sharing structures and substructures among concepts exist. Sharing an entire concept structure among concepts is similar to systems that perform analogy and case-based reasoning. Their assumption about the similarity of cases and domains parallels our premise about sharing concept information. Sharing a substructure among concepts emphasizes useful pieces of information within a domain. This type of sharing is similar to constructive inductive systems that create substructures by applying operators on the primitive description elements (Schlimmer, 1987; Pagallo & Haussler, 1990).

Our goals for this paper are two-fold. First, we will introduce the problem of learning multiple concepts for inductive learning systems. Secondly, we demonstrate reuse of knowledge from prior concepts for learning subsequent concepts. An illustration of this information transference is implemented in Multiple concept FOCL (M-FOCL). M-FOCL is a relational concept learning algorithm that learns multiple concepts sequentially, while sharing knowledge among concepts. In Section 2, we review two relational learning algorithms FOIL and FOCL, on which an analysis of M-FOCL is based. Section 3 explains M-FOCL in greater detail and section 4 evaluates the effectiveness of the concept sharing by testing M-FOCL on two domains: chess and poker. We contrast our work with related work in learning multiple concepts in section 5. We conclude by summarizing our contributions and discussing future work.

2 Relational Horn clause learning algorithms

Before describing Multiple concept FOCL (M-FOCL) and FOCL (Pazzani & Kibler, 1990), we will describe FOIL (Quinlan, 1990) to explain the core learning method applied in these systems. Given a set of extensional predicates, positive examples, and negative examples, FOIL learns a relational Horn clause concept in terms of predefined predicates. This concept covers all of the positive examples and excludes all negative ones. FOIL constructs the concept by performing a hill-climbing search. It begins creating a clause by finding the predicate (including the choice of variables) that has the highest information gain. This predicate will cover some positive examples and possibly cover some negative examples. FOIL specializes the clause to exclude negative examples by conjoining additional predicates. After constructing a clause, FOIL discards all the covered examples and repeats the same process until no positive examples remain uncovered. The final concept is a disjunction of clauses.

FOCL follows FOIL's method for constructing concepts, but FOCL utilizes intensional predicates in the form of rules. These predicates are conjunctions or disjunctions of other predicates. They allow the user to define an existing domain theory for the relational learning system. FOCL's ability to use a domain theory allows it to reuse its own output, a Horn clause description, as input for learning another concept.

3 Multiple concept FOCL

The premise underlying the design of M-FOCL is that different concepts in the same domain share common content, and thus information gained from learning a concept is transferred when learning other concepts. When learning multiple concepts, M-FOCL adds the learned concepts to its domain knowledge. According to our premise these additional concepts should facilitate learning subsequent concepts. This allows M-FOCL to learn the concept and the types of information that are important in the domain. Thus by biasing the algorithm towards previously learned information, an increase in accuracy and efficiency may be possible.

The inputs to M-FOCL are positive and negative training examples, primitive predicates, and predicates of previously learned concepts. As output M-FOCL returns a relational Horn clause concept covering all positive examples and no negative examples, and adds the concept just learned to the predicates. The updated list of predicates is input back into M-FOCL when learning another concept, so that reuse of previous information is available. M-FOCL differs from FOCL in that it increases the available intensional predicates by creating predicates from concepts based on their past usefulness.

Currently M-FOCL takes advantage of the content of previously learned concepts in three different ways. Suppose that M-FOCL has learned the concept C, defined in pseudo-Prolog (Figure 1). We use C_i to represent clauses and P_{ij} to represent predicates. To simplify the description, we have not included the variables associated with C, C_i, or P_{ij}.

The first method, the *concept rule*, adds C as an intensional predicate to the domain knowledge. C is a

$$
\begin{gathered}
C:-P_{11},P_{12},\ldots,P_{1n_1}\equiv C_1\\
C:-P_{21},P_{22},\ldots,P_{2n_2}\equiv C_2\\
\vdots\\
C:-P_{k1},P_{k2},\ldots,P_{kn_k}\equiv C_k
\end{gathered}
$$

Figure 1: Concept C

disjunction of all clauses C_1 through C_k. The second method, the *clause rule*, adds a clause, C_i, for some i, to the language as an intensional predicate. The third method, the *conjunct rule*, adds a conjunction of predicates as an intensional predicate to the language. The conjunction consists of at least two predicates, P_{ix} and P_{iy}, that are also used in another clause C_j where $j \neq i$, and Cj can be from the concept just learned or from a background theory of past concepts. We only consider conjunctions that appear in more than one clause to reduce the number of new predicates introduced into the representation language. M-FOCL adds these predicates to its primitive predicate set when learning concepts. The applicability of these predicates for learning subsequent concepts will be determined by the information gain heuristic used in FOCL. The single difference between FOCL and M-FOCL is that M-FOCL uses these predicates during induction, whereas FOCL does not create these predicates and thus cannot use them. In a sense, M-FOCL is dynamically changing its representational bias by introducing new terms that have been found useful in the past.

The concept rule is useful in situations where the concept to be learned is a generalization of a previous concept. For example, when learning legal chess moves, a queen move subsumes a rook move, that is, by applying the concept rule, M-FOCL uses a rook move as part of the queen move definition. The clause rule creates a predicate from a clause that is useful when concepts share partial information or a concept is a specialization of a previous concept. For instance, if a queen move is already defined, when learning a rook move, M-FOCL uses one of the clauses defined in the queen concept that allows the queen to move vertically on the board, as part of the definition of the rook. Lastly, the conjunct rule is useful when concepts share some content, but do not share entire concepts or clauses. For example, since each piece must be on the board, each clause must represent this constraint. This constraint is not represented as an entire concept or a clause, but as a conjunction of some predicates. By using the conjunct rule, a predicate is created that is the conjunction of other predicates that form useful partial substructures.

An analogy can be drawn between learning new predicates in M-FOCL and learning macros in planning systems. Macros are learned from previous successful sequences of operators (Ruby & Kibler, 1991), whereas the concept, clause, and conjunct rules facilitate learning new predicates from previous concepts. In the same sense that macros aid the planning system to take larger steps in the hill-climbing search, creating new predicates helps M-FOCL take larger steps in its hill-climbing search, thereby changing the landscape of the hill-climbing search as well as potentially increasing the learning rate. By changing the landscape of the hill-climbing search, misleading local optima points may be avoided.

Using these three rules also allows M-FOCL to do less search for relevant predicates than FOCL. The effect of using previously learned substructures is to do selective lookahead in the hill-climbing search. If the selection is good, improved performance will result. Creating intensional predicates often reduces the depth of the search when a good selection is chosen, but it also increases the branching factor of the search. Therefore, the trade-offs for generating intensional predicates with these rules must be considered. This is analogous to the utility problem (Minton & Carbonell, 1987) while learning macros for planning.

In accordance with the idea of concept sharing, we developed the concept, clause, and conjunct rules. These rules facilitate M-FOCL's use of prior concepts to learn subsequent concepts. The examples that were used to create concepts are indirectly used to learn other concepts. When learning with noisy data, indirectly utilizing past examples has the effect of generating more examples to learn the concept and isolate noisy examples. They also may decrease search since M-FOCL uses previously learned information.

4 Evaluation

To empirically evaluate the usefulness of concept sharing, we tested FOCL against M-FOCL in two domains for our preliminary studies. The remainder of this section describes those domains in greater detail, describes the methodology used to run the experiments, and explains the experimental results.

4.1 The domains

The two domains used to evaluate M-FOCL are that of learning chess moves and learning poker hands. The learning problem in the chess domain is similar to those used in Vere (1977) and De Raedt & Bruynooghe (1992), however our experiments test a subset of the chess moves, specifically legal moves for the rook, bishop, knight, and queen. The moves are learned sequentially. Each example consists of the initial position of the piece and its final position described by the 4-tuple *(initial-rank,initial-file,final-rank,final-file)*. The moves are learned as if no other pieces are on the board.

The learning problem in the second domain consists of learning a subset of the possible five card poker hands. Specifically, the following concepts are learned: pair, three of a kind, four of a kind, two pair, and full house. For example, a *pair-in-hand* is defined as a hand with at least two cards of the same rank. The examples given to the system consist of the 5-tuple *(card1, card2, card3, card4, card5)* where the primitive predicates *rank(card,r)* and *suit(card,s)* describe the rank and suit of each of the cards.

Another representation we considered used the 1-tuple *(hand)* to describe the examples. The primitive predicates for this representation contained *card-in-hand(hand, card)*, *rank(card,r)*, and *suit(card,s)*. Thus the only difference between this representation and the former is that the former representation describes a relationship among the objects (cards), whereas in the latter representation, the concept is described using one object (hand) which consists of several objects (cards). The latter representation seems more intuitive, since it describes in detail the highly relational characteristics of the domain; however, FOCL and M-FOCL have space limitation problems when learning the concepts with this representation. For example, suppose FOCL is learning *pair-in-hand(?hand)* (where ? symbols preceding words denote variables) and it has already learned *card-in-hand(?hand, ?card1)* as the first literal in a clause. Since each hand contains five different cards, the number of possible bindings for the unbound variable *?card1* greatly increases the search space of possible horn clause theories (Quinlan, 1990). Indeed, the search space increases by a factor of 5, the number of cards in the hand. Next FOCL would add *card-in-hand(?hand,?card2)* which increases the search space by another factor of 5. In fact, each time FOCL adds the predicate *card-in-hand* the search space increases by a factor of 5. This representation may be reasonable when learning *pair-in-hand* since we need only two literals of the card-in-hand predicate, but FOCL quickly runs into space limitations when learning the other concepts such as three of a kind or full house, that require more instantiations of the *card-in-hand* predicate.

Although using the former representation with the 5-tuple *(card1, card2, card3, card4, card5)* avoids the extended tuple explosion, it suffers from a related search explosion. FOCL learns all of the concepts in the poker domain, but when M-FOCL learns one concept it uses the concept rule to change the concept into a rule for later use. The problem occurs when trying to evaluate the usefulness of the 5-arity concept rules. For example, suppose M-FOCL has already learned *pair-in-hand(?card1, ?card2, ?card3, ?card4, ?card5)* and will use that concept when learning *three-of-a-kind-in-hand*. When M-FOCL checks the information gain of *pair-in-hand* it must try the 120 combinations of the five variables when in reality the ordering of the variables does not affect the information gain. Our solution to this problem was to apply a commutative property on the variables in the predicate, allowing different orderings of the variables to be considered the same. We used the commutative constraint on the predicates (Pazzani & Kibler, 1992) and extended it from working only on 2-arity predicates to n-arity predicates. This constraint reduced the amount of search, but was only originally applied to pairs of variables. By extending this constraint to n-arity predicates, the search of each of the concept rules was reduced from 120 variable orderings to one ordering. This technique of using commutativity can be used whenever there is a relation among a set of objects where the ordering of the objects is irrelevant.

4.2 Methodology

To evaluate the usefulness of transferring information among concepts, we tested M-FOCL running in three different modes against FOCL. By running each of the modes separately, each of their effects on learning can be observed independently. In the first mode M-FOCL only used the concept rules (CNR) to create predicates; in the second mode, it uses only the clause rules (CLR) and in the last mode it only uses conjunct rules (CJR). FOCL was run without using any domain information. The tests were run in the following manner. When FOCL was used, a concept from the domain was learned, relevant information such as accuracy was recorded, and then the concept information was discarded. When M-FOCL was run in any mode, no initial theory was used. M-FOCL would first learn a concept. We then recorded the same information as that for FOCL; however, instead of discarding the concept, M-FOCL uses previously learned substructures for learning subsequent concepts.

We ran two experiments in the chess domain, one without any type of noise and the second with attribute noise. We also ran one experiment in the poker domain without noise. In all of the experiments we will report on the average accuracy and search complexity of the algorithms. Their accuracy is measured by using the final concept learned from each of the algorithms to classify randomly generated test examples. The percentage of these examples classified correctly is a measure of the accuracy of the algorithm. The search complexity of the algorithm is the number of predicates and variables tested to learn a concept.

In addition to accuracy and search complexity, we also measured the size of the learned concept. Since the M-FOCL methods create a 'background' theory by applying its three rules, we cannot just count the number of literals in each of the concepts. We took the sum of the literals needed to learn each of the concepts and divided by the number of concepts to get an average concept size. We used the method in Figure 2 to compute the concept size which measures concept and theory literals.

```
for each concept
  for each clause in concept
    for each literal in clause
      if primitive-literal
         or concept-rule
         or conjunct-rule
         or clause-rule then
          add 1 to total-literals
      if (conjunct-rule or clause-rule)
         and not used before then
          add number of rule body literals
              to total-literals
```

Figure 2: Measurement method for concept size

4.3 Experimental evidence

4.3.1 Learning noise-free chess moves

In this experiment we tested FOCL against M-FOCL running in three modes (CNR, CLR, CJR) in the chess domain. All of the chess examples were noise-free, but we varied the training size to see their effects on system search complexity, concept accuracy, and concept description size. According to our premise, M-FOCL should be able to use information from some concepts to aid learning other concepts. We used training sizes of 5, 15, 25, 35, and 45 of each positive and negative examples for each concept. We began with a set of five examples, used those to learn the concepts, and then added 10 more examples to create the training size of 15. Thus each example set was built on the previous set, resulting in a learning curve for the training set. For all training sizes, we evaluated the learned concept with 200 randomly generated positive and negative examples each. This experiment was run with 30 trials where one trial consists of learning all of the concepts in the domain using FOCL and the three M-FOCL methods on a random set of examples. We used the ordering for the M-FOCL methods, rook, bishop, queen, knight to demonstrate the advantage of concept sharing. Previously, we experimented with all orderings which when averaged together had similar results as with this ordering.

We averaged the accuracy over the 30 trials and each of the concepts. The M-FOCL methods were up to 3% more accurate on average than FOCL [1]. The CNR and CLR methods had the highest difference in accuracy from FOCL, whereas the CJR methods accuracy was the closest to FOCL's accuracy. The CJR method's behavior was close to FOCL's because there are only a few sets of substructures that are shared among con-

[1]M-FOCL using the CNR and CLR modes is statistically different than FOCL with 99% confidence for all training sizes. The CJR mode is statistically different than FOCL with 95% confidence for training size 35 and 99% confidence for training size 45. All significance tests use a one-sided t-test.

cepts in this domain, thus few conjunct rules were created. In terms of search complexity, the CNR method searched a space from .2% to 14% smaller than FOCL, and also had a higher accuracy than FOCL on all training sizes. However, some of the M-FOCL methods searched a larger space than FOCL. The CLR method searched a space 26% larger than FOCL for training size 5, but that difference was reduced to 4.2% as the training size increased to 45. The CJR method searched a space almost the same size as FOCL (Figure 3a).

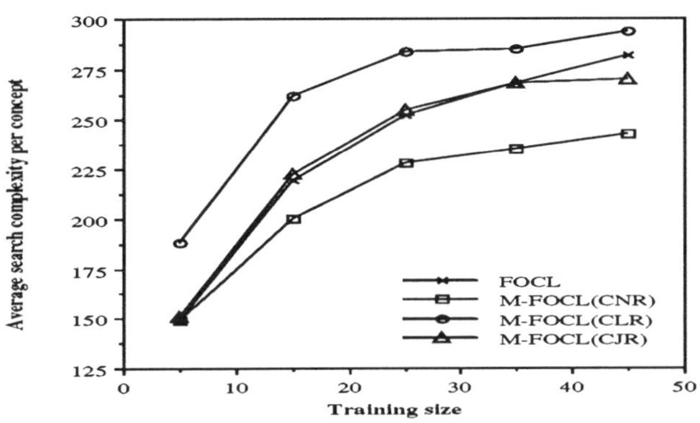

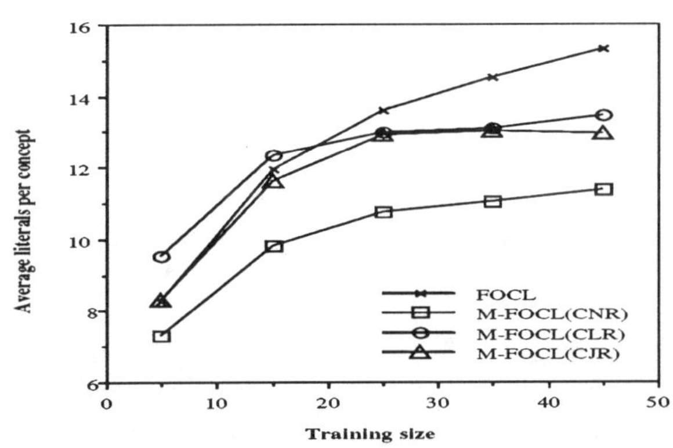

Figure 3: a). Search complexity versus training size. b). concept size versus training size.

Since the M-FOCL methods add background predicates to the description language, the description length of the concepts vary (Figure 3b.). The CNR method consistently used 12% to 25% fewer literals than FOCL to describe the concepts. When compared to FOCL, the CLR method uses 15% more literals for training size 5, and 3% more for training size 15, but uses 5% to 12% fewer for the remaining training sizes. Lastly, the CJR method uses about the same number of literals for training sizes 5 and 15, but then uses 5% to 15% fewer for the remaining training sizes. Thus for larger training sizes, the M-FOCL methods' concept description size decreases with relation to FOCL.

4.3.2 Learning chess moves with tuple noise

To test the robustness of our premise, we also experimented in the chess domain with attribute noise. We measure the amount of noise for a relation in the following manner. Associated with each relation is the set of tuples that satisfy the relation. Altering an element of the tuple is referred to as tuple or attribute noise. When creating attribute noise in the data, for each element in a tuple there is an n% chance that the element's value is assigned randomly, where n is the amount of attribute noise in the data (Quinlan, 1986).

In the noise test, we experimented in the chess domain with a training size of 25 examples and varied the amount of noise. We used noise levels of 10%, 20%, 30%, and 40%, and used a testing size of 200 examples. We ran 30 trials of each noise level and used the same ordering for the concepts as the previous chess experiments. Note that if an example attribute is noisy due to attribute noise, this does not necessarily misclassify the example.

The CLR and CJR methods had higher accuracy than FOCL for all training sizes[2]. Figure 4a. shows the accuracy for methods CLR, CJR, and FOCL. Although these methods have a higher accuracy, they also search a larger space. Method CLR searches a space approximately double the size of FOCL, while method CJR searches a space from 6% to 31% larger than FOCL's space. The size of CLR's description length was similar to that of FOCL's; however, CJR used from 11% to 13% fewer literals than FOCL to describe concepts (Figure 4b).

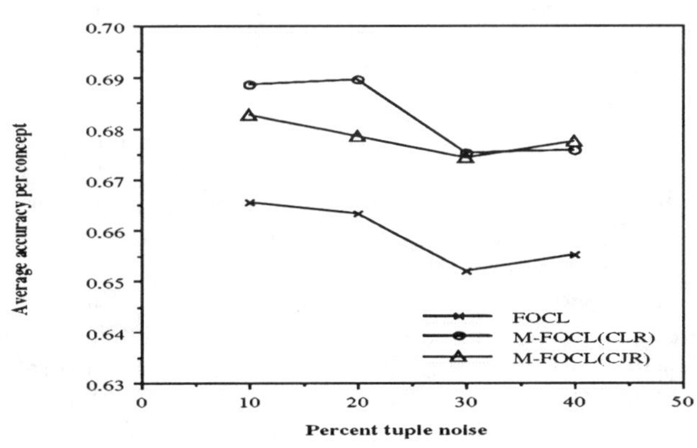

Figure 4: a.) Average accuracy vs. attribute noise.

[2]Method CLR is statistically significant from FOCL with a 97.5% confidence level for all training sizes. Method CJR is statistically significant from FOCL with a confidence level of 90% for 10% and 20% noise and 97.5% for 30% and 40% noise. Method CNR is not statistically significant than FOCL.

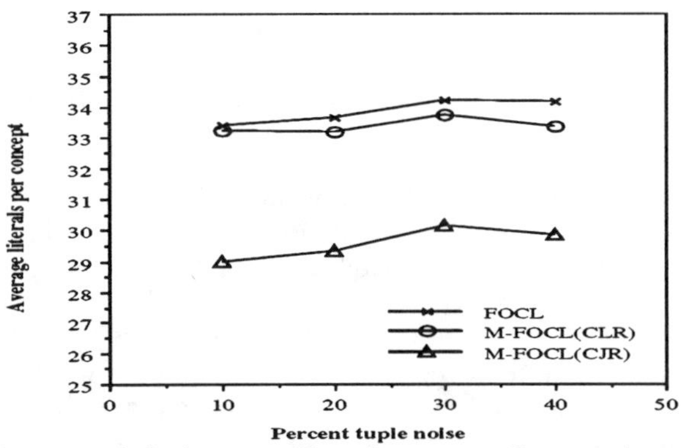

Figure 4: b.) Average literals vs. attribute noise.

4.3.3 Learning poker concepts

We also tested FOCL against M-FOCL in the poker domain. We ran 31 trials of training sizes of 25, 50, 75, and 100 each. We applied the same method used in the chess domain to create the training sizes, that is, we first created a training size of 25 and ran the systems on it, and then we added 25 more examples to create the 50 size training set. All training sets were tested using 500 positive and negative examples each. We used the following concept ordering for the three M-FOCL methods: pair, three-of-a-kind, four-of-a-kind, two-pair, and full-house.

Since the two domains tested have different characteristics, the results of the M-FOCL methods differ from the chess domain. The CLR and CJR methods were up to 5.5% more accurate than FOCL while the CNR method had a slightly lower accuracy than FOCL [3]. Figure 5a. shows the difference in accuracy for the M-FOCL methods. FOCL searched a smaller space than the M-FOCL methods. The CNR method searched a similar sized space to FOCL, while the other two methods searched a space 5 to 10 times greater than FOCL's search space. The CLR method searched the largest space because for each of the concepts, several clauses were being learned and made into clause rules, increasing the branching factor of the search. The learned concept size also varied for each of the systems. The CNR method used approximately the same number of literals to describe concepts as FOCL, while the other two methods used up to 48% fewer literals than FOCL (Figure 5b.). Methods CLR and CJR perform similarly judging from their accuracy and concept description size. In this domain the reoccurring conjuncts closely resemble the clauses learned, thus the subconcepts created by the two methods are very similar, explaining their similar performances.

[3] All of the M-FOCL methods are statistically different from FOCL with 99% confidence.

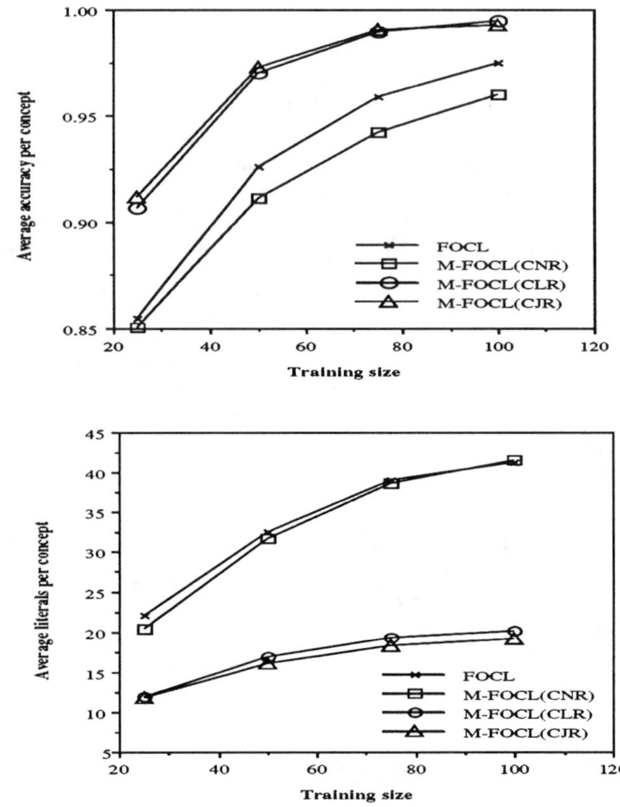

Figure 5: a.) Average accuracy vs. training size. b.) Average literals vs. training size.

Judging from the accuracy, search complexity, and concept size, the CNR method performs slightly worse than FOCL. This results mostly from the representation we used for this domain. The representation makes the card ordering important when in reality it is useless information. This information, however, was used when the concept rules were defined, making learning with the concept rules difficult. Although the commutative constraint was used to reduce the search space for the CNR method, it could not compensate for the irrelevant orderings of the cards in the concept rules. This ordering information also affected the other methods. The commutative constraint was not used for the clause and conjunct rules since the definition of any concept sharing rules were not known beforehand and therefore, we did not know if the commutative properties would be applicable. If the commutative constraint was available for the CLR and CJR methods, their search space would have been greatly reduced.

5 Related Work

Currently the idea of learning multiple concepts during classification, and biasing reuse of conceptual structures is a fairly unexplored area. Although there is not much work related to multiple concept learning in classification systems, we will describe related work in other areas of AI.

Systems using analogy (Falkenhainer, Forbus, & Gentner, 1986;De Raedt & Bruynooghe, 1992) and case-based reasoning systems (Branting, 1991; Kolodner, 1989) use additional sources of information either from another domain or from past cases. Since they are using different sources, the information must be generalized in some manner. Systems using analogy use a mapping from the source domain to the target domain. This global mapping defines the transformations from the old domain to the new domain. The mapping may generalize variables and predicates, keeping only the structure of the source domain. Cased-based reasoning retrieves cases from its past cases and generalizes by applying adaptation operators to locally modify the case. Thus for each new case, an old case must be retrieved and a local modification to the old case must be performed. Unlike these two methods of reasoning, concept sharing does not require generalizations for using past concepts to aid learning subsequent concepts. In addition, unlike case-based reasoning methods that require entire cases to be used for matching rather than partial cases, concept sharing emphases sharing any amount of information among concepts.

Learning multiple concepts allows the system to refine its representation language dynamically. Other systems that revise their language apply a variety of methods to create new predicates. STAGGER (Schlimmer, 1987) heuristically searches through the space of conjunctions, disjunctions, and negations of the primitive predicates, using a failure driven test and the examples to see if the new constructive predicates should be added. FRINGE (Pagallo & Haussler, 1990) revises its language by finding Boolean conjuncts of features at the fringe of its decision tree and creates new features from these conjuncts. By modifying the language dynamically, it avoids the replication problem (Pagallo & Haussler, 1990). Although M-FOCL has this self-transference ability, it has a broader scope since it also finds repetitions using other concepts in the domain rather than just within one concept. In addition, M-FOCL differs from these systems since it uses a more relaxed method of modifying the language, that is, it waits for regularities to occur before adding new descriptors to the language.

The theory revision system, EITHER (Mooney & Ourston, 1991) creates intermediate concepts using two operators, inter-construction and absorption, that are similar to the conjunct and concept rules used in M-FOCL. Although both systems use similar operators, they behave differently. EITHER uses a propositional language to describe its categories and ID3 as its inductive component, while M-FOCL uses a relational language and FOCL for its inductive learning. More importantly, M-FOCL does not use any theory initially, but, EITHER begins with an incomplete background theory. In addition, M-FOCL applies its rule operators during concept learning instead of afterwards as in EITHER. Lastly, EITHER performs a post analysis on the rules created to simplify its theory.

These and other systems dealing with predicate formation often generate predicates judged by their current usefulness, while M-FOCL uses past and current usefulness as a generation method. In addition M-FOCL uses information gain as an acceptance criteria for using new predicates in the learned concept description. Thus M-FOCL uses a two level filtering method for applying new predicates to learning.

6 Discussion

We have presented a broader perspective on classification that advocates learning concepts in the context of other concepts in the domain. We implemented this idea by transferring information from learning previous concepts to learning subsequent concepts in M-FOCL. In particular, by using the three rules for transferring knowledge from previously learned concepts, preliminary results show that M-FOCL can learn concepts more accurately, and under some circumstances, more efficiently than without concept sharing. Using M-FOCL to learn in the chess domain and the poker domain provides an illustration of the learning method and evidence for our premise that concepts in the same domain share information.

Concept sharing does have its limitations. If concepts do not share any subconcepts concept sharing will, in the best case, decrease efficiency, and in the worst case, could mislead the system into learning a less accurate description. For example, in the chess domain, the knight legal move did not use many subconcepts from the other concepts, and its subconcepts could not be used by other concepts. Learning the knight move in the context of the other chess concepts increased the search needed to find a concept since useless predicates were added to the language. Although the knight move did not share subconcepts with the other concepts, its presence did not decrease the accuracy of the learned concepts.

This paper concentrates on the sharing of substructures among concepts described relationally. We also intend to explore the usefulness of sharing when concepts are represented using an attributional or a neural network representation. We anticipate similar results; namely by enlarging the search space to include pieces of previously learned concepts, we expect that learning time will sometimes improve and other times degrade. However, we strongly expect that accuracy will always increase and concept description size will often decrease, as happened with these relational domains. In addition, we hope to characterize the usefulness of concept sharing to better predict situations where this technique would be beneficial for the learning process. The long term goal of this research is to merge concept learning and problem solving to enable systems to learn a domain. Learning a domain may include, among other aspects, learning multiple concepts, learning relationships among the concepts, and learning ways of problem solving using these concepts. We feel that concept learning is a method for defining a problem solving situation and naming the entities in the problem. By adding problem solving techniques, such as planning, we envision a more integrated system that has greater capabilities than either technique alone.

Acknowledgments

We would like to thank Kamal Ali, Cliff Brunk, and Mike Pazzani for their help with FOCL.

References

Branting, K. L. (1991). Exploiting the Complementarity of rules and precedents with reciprocity and fairness. In *Proceedings: Case-Based Reasoning Workshop.* San Mateo, CA: Morgan Kaufmann.

De Raedt, L., Bruynooghe, M. (1992). Interactive concept-learning and constructive induction by analogy. *Machine Learning,* volume 8, no. 2. Boston, MA: Kluwer Academic Publishers.

Falkenhainer, B., Forbus, K., Gentner D. (1986). *The structure-mapping engine.* (Technical Report no. UIUCDCS-R-86-1275). Urbana, Illinois: University of Illinois at Urbana-Champaign, Department of Computer Science.

Kolodner, J. L. (1989). Judging which is the "best" case for a case-based reasoner. *Proceedings: Case-Based Reasoning Workshop.* San Mateo, CA: Morgan Kaufmann.

Markman, E. (1989). *Categorization and naming in children.* Cambridge, Massachusetts: The MIT Press.

Minton, S., Carbonell, J. G. (1987). Strategies for learning search control rules: an explanation-based approach. In J. McDermott, ed.,*Proceedings of the Tenth International Joint Conference on Artificial Intelligence.* Los Altos, CA: Morgan Kaufmann.

Mooney, R. J., Ourston, D. (1991). Constructive induction in theory refinement. In Birnbaum, Collins, eds., *Proceedings of the Eighth International Workshop on Machine Learning.* San Mateo, CA: Morgan Kaufmann.

Pagallo, G., Haussler, D. (1990). Boolean feature discovery in empirical learning. *Machine Learning,* volume 5, no. 1. Boston, MA: Kluwer Academic Publishers.

Pazzani, M. J., Kibler, D. (1992). *The utility of knowledge in inductive learning. Machine Learning,* volume 9, no. 1. Boston, MA: Kluwer Academic Publishers.

Quinlan, J. R. (1986). The effect of noise on concept learning. *Machine Learning: An Artificial Intelligence Approach,* volume 2. Los Altos, CA: Morgan Kaufmann.

Quinlan, J. R. (1990). Learning logical definitions from relations. *Machine Learning,* volume 5 no. 3. Boston, MA: Kluwer Academic Publishers.

Ruby, D., Kibler, D. (1991). SteppingStone: An empirical and analytical evaluation. In *Proceedings of the Ninth National Conference on Artificial Intelligence.* Menlo Park, CA: AAAI Press/The Mit Press.

Schlimmer, J. C. (1987). "Incremental adjustment of representations." In P. Langley, ed., *Proceedings of the Fourth International Workshop on Machine Learning.* San Mateo, CA: Morgan Kaufmann.

Vere, S. A. (1977). Induction of relational productions in the presence of background information. In *Fifth International Joint Conference on Artificial Intelligence.* San Mateo, CA: Morgan Kaufmann.

Discovering Dynamics

Sašo Džeroski and Ljupčo Todorovski
Jožef Stefan Institute
Jamova 39, 61111 Ljubljana, Slovenia
Saso.Dzeroski@ijs.si Ljupco.Todorovski@ijs.si

Abstract

Machine discovery is concerned with the task of finding laws from experimental and/or observational data. Existing machine discovery systems have mostly generated laws describing static situations. The paper presents LAGRANGE, a system that constructs a set of differential and/or algebraic equations that describe an observed behavior of a dynamic system. As such, LAGRANGE extends the scope of machine discovery to dynamic systems. We show that LAGRANGE is able to generate appropriate sets of laws for several nonlinear dynamic systems from traces of their behavior.

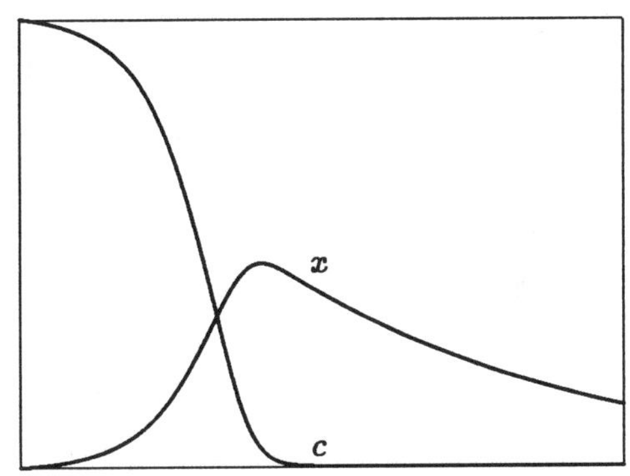

Figure 1: Behavior of a Simple Biological System.

1 Introduction

Consider a simple biological experiment. We place some nutrient and some bacteria in a jar of water. Having done this, we keep the water temperature constant and observe (at regular time intervals) how the concentrations of food and bacteria in the water change over time. Their behavior might look as shown in Figure 1, where c denotes the nutrient concentration and x denotes the bacteria concentration.

Typically, the task of a scientist would be to construct a model of the process that takes place in the jar. Various kinds of models may be constructed, but by far the most common are differential equations. The behavior of the above biological system can be described by the Monod equations [Jorgensen and Johnsen 1989] (p. 301):

$$\dot{c} = \frac{\mu_{max}}{y} \frac{c}{c + k_s} x$$
$$\dot{x} = (\mu_{max} \frac{c}{c + k_s} - k_d)\, x$$

The system variables of the dynamic system are c (nutrient concentration) and x (bacteria concentration). We define the constants to be $\mu_{max} = 0.1$, $k_d = 0.01$, $k_s = 100$, and $y = 0.6$. The above differential equations, combined with the initial state $c_0 = 300$ and $x_0 = 2$, predict the behavior shown in Figure 1.

One would expect a machine discovery system to help the scientist construct a model of the kind illustrated above, or even construct such a model itself from the observed behavior, and then present it to the scientist for inspection and evaluation. Unfortunately, a typical state-of-the-art machine discovery system is not capable of doing this kind of job. It might try to find a single formula relating c and x directly, disregarding their previous values. In addition, instead of being content with the data given to it and trying to make as much of it as possible, it might ask us to perform additional experiments. If more than two variables were measured, it might ask us to keep the values of all but two variables constant and vary the remaining two. This is inconvenient when we are dealing with dynamic systems, as we might not have experimental control over all the system variables.

The paper presents LAGRANGE, a system that extends the scope of machine discovery to dynamic systems. LAGRANGE is able to find a set of differential and/or algebraic equations, i.e. laws, governing the behavior of a dynamic system, such as the one described in the above example. The task of identification of dynamic systems and the LAGRANGE algorithm, designed to address this task, are described in Section 2. The results of several experiments with LAGRANGE are given in Section 3. Related work is briefly touched upon in Section 4. Finally, Section 5 concludes with a discussion and several directions for further work.

2 The LAGRANGE Algorithm

The task of identification of dynamic systems, addressed by LAGRANGE, can be defined as follows: Given an example behavior of a dynamic system, find a set of laws that describe the dynamics of the system. More precisely, a set of real-valued system variables is measured at regular intervals over a period of time, as illustrated in Table 1. The laws to be discovered (also called a model of the dynamic system) typically take the form of a set of differential equations.

Table 1: A Behavior Trace of a Dynamic System.

time	X_1	X_2	...	X_n
t_0	x_{10}	x_{20}		x_{n0}
t_0+h	x_{11}	x_{21}		x_{n1}
		...		
t_0+Nh	x_{1N}	x_{2N}		x_{nN}

The input to LAGRANGE is a behavior trace of a dynamic system, such as the one given in Table 1. In addition, the values of three parameters have to be specified. These include o, the order of the dynamic system (i.e. the order of the highest derivative appearing in the dynamics equations), d, the maximum depth of new terms introduced by combining old terms (variables), and r, the maximum number of independent regression variables used for generating equations.

Table 2 gives the LAGRANGE algorithm. Taking the set of system variables $S = \{X_1, \ldots, X_n\}$, LAGRANGE first introduces their time derivatives (up to order o). It then introduces new variables (terms) by repeatedly applying multiplication to variables from S and their time derivatives. Finally, given the set of all (old and new) variables, it generates and tests equations by using linear regression.

The time derivatives are introduced by numerical derivation in step 1. The following formula [Bohte 1991] (p. 73) is used to calculate time derivatives:

$$\dot{x}_i = \frac{1}{12 \cdot h}(x_{i-2} - 8 \cdot x_{i-1} + 8 \cdot x_{i+1} - x_{i+2})$$

where $x_i = X(t_0 + ih)$ and $\dot{x}_i = \dot{X}(t_0 + ih)$. If the measurement error for X is δ and $h < 1$, the error

Table 2: The LAGRANGE Algorithm.

1. Introduce time derivatives (up to order o) of the system variables
   $D := \emptyset$
   for all variables v in S **do**
     $v_0 := v$
     for $i := 1$ **to** o **do**
       $v_i := \frac{d}{dt}v_{i-1}$ (* $v_i = \dot{v}_{i-1}$ *)
       $D := D \cup \{v_i\}$
   $V := S \cup D$
2. Introduce new variables with multiplication
   $V_0 := V$
   for $l := 1$ **to** $d-1$ **do**
     $V_l := \emptyset$
     for all pairs of variables $(v, u) \in V_0 \times V_{l-1}$ **do**
       $n_{v,u} := v * u$
       $V_l := V_l \cup \{n_{v,u}\}$
       (* duplicate terms removed in this step *)
     $V := V \cup V_l$
3. Do linear regression (LR) on subsets of all variables
   $M := \emptyset$
   for $i := 1$ **to** $r+1$ **do**
     for all subsets $R \in \mathcal{P}(V)$, $|R| = i$ **do**
       choose dependent variable $y \in R$
       if $LR(y, R \setminus \{y\})$ is significant
       then $M := M \cup \{y = c_0 + \sum_{x \in R \setminus \{y\}} c_x x\}$
       (* add linear regression formula to M *)

of the numerical derivative calculated by the above formula is $\mathcal{O}(\delta/h)$. The error of the i-th derivative of X calculated in step 1 would then be $\mathcal{O}(\delta/h^i)$. Thus, due care should be exercised and derivatives should be measured whenever the measurement error is lower than the calculation error stated above.

Step 2 introduces as new variables all the terms of depth not greater than d, obtained from the system variables and their derivatives (variables from V_0). When introducing new variables, terms of depth l are gathered in V_{l-1}. A term $\prod_{i=1}^{n} X_i^{\alpha_i}$ is of depth l iff $l = \sum_{i=1}^{n} \alpha_i$. For example, X_1X_2 is of depth 2 and $X_1^3X_2^2$ is of depth 5. As V_0 contains $(o+1)\cdot n$ variables, V_l contains $\mathcal{O}(((o+1)n)^{l+1})$ variables. Consequently, at the end of step 2, $|V| = \mathcal{O}(((o+1)n)^d)$. The values of the new variables in all time points are also calculated in this step.

Equations are generated and tested in step 3. Roughly speaking, each subset of V sized at most $r+1$ is used to generate a linear equation, where one of the terms is expressed as a linear combination of the remaining ones. The constant coefficients in the linear equation are determined by applying linear regression to fit the corresponding values [Volk 1958] (pp. 260–278). The multiple correlation coefficient R [Volk 1958] (p. 275) is used to judge the significance of the equation. If $R > 1 - t_R$, where t_R is a prespecified threshold (a user definable parameter in LAGRANGE), the equation is considered significant and is retained in the model of the dynamic system. Note that LAGRANGE makes no explicit distinction between dependent and independent variables.

The total number of regressions tried is $\mathcal{O}(|V|^{r+1})$, that is $\mathcal{O}(((o+1)n)^{d(r+1)})$. While this number is exponential in the parameters d and r, we should note that small values of these parameters were sufficient for all the experiments we performed ($d = 2$, $r = 3$).

To illustrate the work of the algorithm, consider the biological experiment from the introduction, where the system variables are $S = \{c, x\}$. Assume that the values for o, d and r are one, two, and three respectively. The time derivatives $D = \{\dot{c}, \dot{x}\}$ are introduced in the first, and the new terms $V_1 = \{c^2, cx, c\dot{c}, c\dot{x}, x^2, x\dot{c}, x\dot{x}, \dot{c}^2, \dot{c}\dot{x}, \dot{x}^2\}$ in the second step. The third step considers all subsets of $V = S \cup D \cup V_1$ of cardinality one, two, three, and four during equation generation. These include the subsets $\{\dot{c}\}$, $\{\dot{c}, x, \dot{x}\}$ and $\{c\dot{x}, x, \dot{x}, cx\}$, the latter two generating the model equations.

The above description of the LAGRANGE algorithm is declarative. In practice, steps 2 and 3 are interleaved. First, linear equations are tried on the initial set of variables, determined in step 1. New terms are then introduced, layer by layer, and linear regressions for them are tried. This is repeated until the prespecified depth of new terms is reached. In addition, when a term is expressed as a linear combination of others, it is removed from the process of introducing new variables and testing regressions. This reduces the number of redundant equations generated and improves efficiency.

3 Experimental evaluation

The following procedure was used in the experimental evaluation of LAGRANGE: A set of differential equations modeling a real-life dynamic system was first chosen, as well as appropriate values for the parameters involved. The initial state for the system variables was next selected. The differential equations were then integrated for $N = 1000$ steps of $h = 0.01$ time units, using the the fourth-order Runge-Kutta method [Press et al. 1986] (pp. 550-554). The resulting behavior (a sequence of a thousand states) was then given to LAGRANGE, which generated a set of equations describing the behavior.

Models of several real-life dynamic systems were used to test LAGRANGE. These include the biological system described in the introduction, a cascaded tanks system [Kraan et al. 1991], a linear chemical reaction, a predator-prey system, and a nonlinear oscillatory chemical reaction (the Brusselator), the models for all three taken from [Babloyantz 1986]. All of these systems are first-order systems, i.e., the system variables and their first derivatives suffice for describing the dynamics of these systems.

The following parameter settings were used in LAGRANGE: For all test cases, the dynamic system order o was set to one, and r was set to three (at most three terms can appear on the right-hand side of a linear regression). Note that $r = 2$ suffices for all systems, except for the biological one. The maximum depth d of new terms was set to two and the significance threshold t_R was set to 0.00001. The only exception was made for the Brusselator example, where d was set to three (the term X^2Y that appears in the Brusselator equations is of depth three).

LAGRANGE is implemented in the C programming language. It was run on a Sun SPARC IPC workstation. For all models, the running times were of the order of seconds, except for the Brusselator, where the running time was one minute.

An equation might be re-discovered several times in similar forms. For example, the equation $X + Y = Z$ could be re-discovered as $X^2 + XY = XZ$. To simplify the implementation, we have removed such obvious redundancies manually. In future versions of LAGRANGE, this could be done automatically or care might be taken that such redundancies are not generated at all. More sophisticated redundancies have been left untouched, as in the chemical kinetics example.

Biological model

The differential equations given in the introduction were integrated for $N = 1000$ steps of $h = 0.1$ time units. A large integration step was chosen because the dynamics of this system is relatively slow as compared to the other systems considered. LAGRANGE generated the following model from the given behavior:

$$\begin{aligned} \dot{c} &= -\frac{1}{60}x - \frac{10}{6}\dot{x} \\ c\dot{x} &= -x - 100 \cdot \dot{x} + 0.09 \cdot cx \end{aligned}$$

This model is equivalent to the one given in the introduction if we take into account the particular values of the constants appearing there.

Cascaded tanks

A cascaded tanks system [Kraan et al. 1991] consists of two tanks (A and B), where water flows from the first into the second. The first tank has a constant inflow. The whole system can be described by the following model

$$\begin{array}{rclcrcl} i_A & = & c_1 & & & & \\ \dot{l_A} & = & i_A - o_A & & o_A & = & c_2\sqrt{l_A} \\ \dot{l_B} & = & o_A - o_B & & o_B & = & c_2\sqrt{l_B} \end{array}$$

where i_A is the inflow into tank A, o_A and o_B are the outflows from tanks A and B and l_A, l_B are the corresponding water levels. The values $c_1 = 200$ and $c_2 = 13$ were chosen for the constants and the behavior of the system was simulated from the initial state $l_{A0} = 10000, l_{B0} = 0$.

The following set of equations, equivalent to the above model, was generated by LAGRANGE:

$$\begin{array}{rclcrcl} i_A & = & 200 & & & & \\ \dot{l_A} & = & 200 - o_A & & 169 \cdot l_A & = & {o_A}^2 \\ \dot{l_B} & = & o_A - o_B & & 169 \cdot l_B & = & {o_B}^2 \end{array}$$

Taking into account that $i_A = c_1 = 200$, the equations for $i_A, \dot{l_A}$ and $\dot{l_B}$ are identical to the ones in the original model. The remaining two equations can be obtained by squaring their counterparts in the original model.

Chemical kinetics

The following is a simple chemical kinetics model of a two-step chemical reaction, where substance A is transformed into substance B, which is then transformed into substance C [Babloyantz 1986] (p. 37).

$$A \xrightarrow{k_1} B$$
$$B \xrightarrow{k_2} C$$

The constants k_1 and k_2 are the corresponding reaction rates. The evolution of the concentrations of the substances involved in the reaction is described by the following equations:

$$\begin{array}{rcl} \dot{A} & = & -k_1 A \\ \dot{B} & = & k_1 A - k_2 B \\ \dot{C} & = & k_2 B \end{array}$$

Only substance A was initially present ($A_0 = 100$, $B_0 = C_0 = 0$), and the reaction rates were $k_1 = 2$ and $k_2 = 3$. An equivalent model was generated by LAGRANGE:

$$\begin{array}{rrcl} & \dot{A} & = & -2 \cdot A \\ & \dot{B} & = & 2 \cdot A - 3 \cdot B \\ & \dot{C} & = & 3 \cdot B \\ (*) & C & = & 100 - A - B \end{array}$$

The equations for $\dot{A}, \dot{B}$ and $\dot{C}$ are obtained by filling in the values of the constants k_1 and k_2 in the original model. Equation (*), on the other hand, is not found in the original model. It expresses the law of mass conservation for the particular case at hand.

Population dynamics

A Volterra-Lotka model of periodic behavior can be used to model the coexistence of prey and predator populations [Babloyantz 1986] (p. 145). For example, take the populations of lynxes and hares. The latter is a vegetarian, the former a carnivore that hunts hares. The lynx population must behave in such a manner that it must not eat all the hares, or its own species will disappear. The dynamics of this system is described by the following model

$$\begin{array}{rcl} \dot{N_1} & = & k_1 N_1 - s N_1 N_2 \\ \dot{N_2} & = & s N_1 N_2 - k_2 N_2 \end{array}$$

where N_1 and N_2 represent the hare and lynx populations, respectively. We chose the initial hare and lynx populations to be $N_{10} = 10$ and $N_{20} = 140$, and the parameters $s = 0.01$, $k_1 = 1.6$, $k_2 = 0.2$. The following two equations were generated by LAGRANGE:

$$\begin{array}{rcl} N_1 N_2 & = & 160 \cdot N_1 - 100 \cdot \dot{N_1} \\ N_1 N_2 & = & 20 \cdot N_2 + 100 \cdot \dot{N_2} \end{array}$$

They can be obtained by substituting the values of the parameters in the original equations, then multiplying by $100 = 1/s$ and expressing $N_1 N_2$ from the resulting equations.

The Brusselator

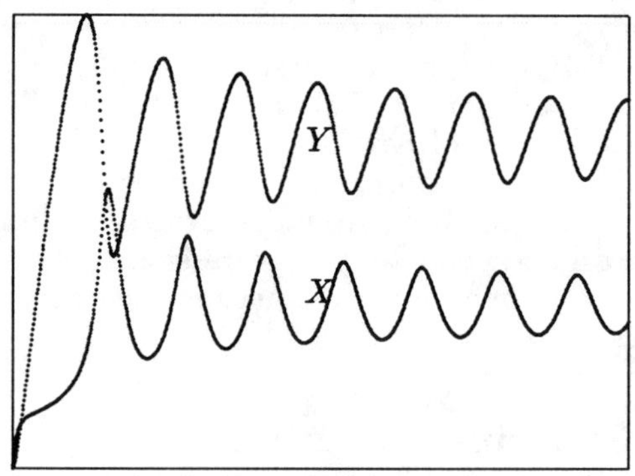

time

Figure 2: Behavior of the Brusselator.

The Brusselator is an oscillating chemical system [Babloyantz 1986] (pp. 175–177), in which the concentrations of two substances X and Y are trapped in an oscillatory time change, described by the following equations and illustrated in Figure 2.

$$\begin{array}{rcl} \dot{X} & = & A - (B+1)X + X^2 Y \\ \dot{Y} & = & BX - X^2 Y \end{array}$$

Substances A and B also take part in the reaction, but their concentrations are held constant through appropriate adjustments. The initial conditions were $X_0 = Y_0 = 0$, and the parameters were $A = 1$ and $B = 2$. From the behavior trace, LAGRANGE generated the following model:

$$\begin{aligned} X^2Y &= -1 + 3 \cdot X + \dot{X} \\ \dot{Y} &= 1 - X - \dot{X} \end{aligned}$$

Expressing the term X^2Y from the original equation for $\dot{X}$ yields the first equation generated by LAGRANGE. The second equation generated by LAGRANGE is obtained by adding the original equations and then expressing $\dot{Y}$ in terms of X and $\dot{X}$.

4 Related work

To relate our work to other work in the field of machine discovery and machine learning, let us briefly discuss the history of LAGRANGE. Although machine discovery has not paid much attention to dynamic systems (except for the recent recognition of the need for techniques that can handle such systems [Bielecki 1992]), there is a significant body of work devoted to learning qualitative models of dynamic systems [Coiera 1989], [Bratko et al. 1991], [Kraan et al. 1991], [Džeroski and Bratko 1992]. Some of this work relies on inductive logic programming [Lavrač and Džeroski 1993] systems to induce the models from example behaviors and background knowledge consisting of the definitions of the QSIM [Kuipers 1986] constraints.

The LINUS approach to inductive logic programming [Lavrač et al. 1991] is based on the idea of transforming an inductive logic programming problem to propositional form and then applying propositional learning systems. This is accomplished by using background knowledge predicates to introduce new variables and generate propositional features [Džeroski et al. 1992]. Our original idea for LAGRANGE was to use a similar approach in order to discover system dynamics: introduce new variables as the time derivatives of existing ones and then apply existing machine discovery systems. However, the latter did not meet our basic requirements for a machine discovery system to be used for discovering differential equations, which were:

- It must be able to find laws involving more than one variable from observational data only, i.e. without asking for additional experiments.
- It must be able to find a set of laws, rather than a single one, where all laws hold for the domain as a whole. It is not explicitly stated beforehand which system variables are dependent and which are independent.

Systems like BACON [Langley et al. 1987] and FAHRENHEIT [Żytkow and Zhu 1991] typically ask the scientist to perform experiments. While ABACUS [Falkenheiner and Michalski 1990] and FAHRENHEIT are able to discover more than one law in a domain, these laws usually hold in disjoint subspaces of the domain. There have been some ideas about discovering a set of simple laws from observational data with BACON, but they have not actually been incorporated into BACON. Thus, none of the above system meets both of the above criteria in a satisfactory way.

The Equation Finder [Zembowitz and Żytkow 1992], used as a module in FAHRENHEIT, comes closest to meeting the above requirements. Given a set of real-valued pairs (x_i, y_i), it tries to find a formula $Y = f(X)$, without asking for additional data. The main problem with Equation Finder is that it is looking for a function of one variable only. In dynamic systems, however, the value of a variable at time t_{i+1} can depend on the values of several variables at time t_i. This makes the ability to deal with functions of more than one variable a necessity.

One of the important features of Equation Finder is the ability to handle errors in the input data. Such a feature is necessary for handling real-life data. It is also important that the convergence of Equation Finder and its sensitivity to errors in the input data have been thoroughly analysed [Zembowitz and Żytkow 1992].

IDS [Nordhausen and Langley 1990] touches upon the problem of discovering dynamics. The qualitative schemata generated by IDS can be considered qualitative states of a system. The transitions between states (schemata) capture in a way the qualitative change of the system over time, i.e., its global dynamics. They are more of the phase transition type, rather than continuous state changes as described by differential equations. However, numeric laws within the qualitative states could, in principle, include time-dependent variables.

5 Discussion

The most important contribution of our work is the extension of the scope of machine discovery to dynamic systems. LAGRANGE is able to construct a set of differential and/or algebraic equations describing a given behavior of a dynamic system. In this way, it extends the scope of machine discovery systems from high-school physics ($F = ma$) to college physics ($F = m\ddot{x}$).

It is also important that LAGRANGE is able to generate a set of laws involving more than two variables from observational data only. This is in contrast with most machine discovery systems, which perform problem decomposition to find laws involving more than two variables. In practice, these systems keep some variables constant and ask the user (scientist) to vary the others. This may prove impossible in many cases, especially in the context of dynamic systems, as the scientist might not have full experimental control over all the system variables involved.

Our work is very much in the BACON tradition, showing that one can handle a large number of apparently complex laws with very simple discovery mechanisms. This is demonstrated by the successful use of LAGRANGE for generating models of several dynamic systems, including a biological system, a cascaded tanks system, two chemical reactions and a predator-prey population system. For these systems, LAGRANGE generates models correctly describing the given behaviors. Judging on the successful use of LAGRANGE in building models of dynamic systems, we conclude that LAGRANGE is a promising step towards the application of machine discovery to complex dynamic systems.

LAGRANGE can be improved in many ways, including handling of errors in the input data, taking into account multiple behavior traces, removing redundant laws in an intelligent way, introducing new terms by other transformations in addition to multiplication, and improving the search control.

The highest priority is the handling of measurement errors and noise in the input data, which is necessary for practical applications. At present, LAGRANGE does not take into account any errors in the input data, except through the t_R tolerance parameter (Section 2). Namely, if the data is less accurate, we may set t_R to a lower value and consider equations that are apparently less significant. However, a careful analysis of the sensitivity of LAGRANGE to changes in this parameter is needed. For applying LAGRANGE to real-life data, measurement errors should be taken into account more explicitly. The approach in Equation Finder [Zembowitz and Żytkow 1992] could be adapted for this purpose.

Although at present new terms are introduced by multiplication only, other transformations, such as those used in Equation Finder could be easily incorporated. The number of new terms would significantly increase in this case and would require reduction of the search complexity. Heuristics should thus be used to reduce the number of new terms introduced. In addition, the terms for linear regressions should be chosen in a more intelligent way.

Acknowledgements

This work is financially supported by the Slovenian Ministry of Science and Technology and in part by the ESPRIT III Basic Research Project No. 6020 on Inductive Logic Programming. Many thanks to Pat Langley and Jan Żytkow for their thorough and stimulating comments. Thanks also to Boris Kompare for suggesting the biological model as a test case.

References

[Babloyantz 1986]
Babloyantz, A. (1986). *Molecules, Dynamics, and Life.* John Wiley & Sons, Inc., New York.

[Bielecki 1992]
Bielecki, M. W. (1992). Machine discovery approach to dynamic systems in the real laboratory. In Żytkow, J. M., editor, *Proc. of the ML92 Workshop on Machine Discovery*, pages 58–62.

[Bohte 1991]
Bohte, Z. (1991). *Numerical Methods.* The Society of Mathematicians, Physicists and Astronomers of Slovenia, Ljubljana. In Slovenian.

[Bratko et al. 1991]
Bratko, I., Muggleton, S., and Varšek, A. (1991). Learning qualitative models of dynamic systems. In *Proc. Eighth International Workshop on Machine Learning*, pages 385–388. Morgan Kaufmann, San Mateo, CA.

[Coiera 1989]
Coiera, E. (1989). Learning qualitative models from example behaviours. In *Proc. Third International Workshop on Qualitative Physics.* Stanford, California.

[Džeroski and Bratko 1992]
Džeroski, S. and Bratko, I. (1992). Handling noise in inductive logic programming. In *Proc. Second International Workshop on Inductive Logic Programming.* Tokyo, Japan. ICOT TM-1182.

[Džeroski et al. 1992]
Džeroski, S., Muggleton, S., and Russell, S. (1992). PAC-learnability of determinate logic programs. In *Proc. Fifth ACM Workshop on Computational Learning Theory*, pages 128–135. ACM Press, New York, NY.

[Falkenheiner and Michalski 1990]
Falkenheiner, B. and Michalski, R. (1990). Integrating quantitative and qualitative discovery in the ABACUS system. In Kodratoff, Y. and Michalski, R., editors, *Machine Learning: An Artificial Intelligence Approach*, pages 153–190. Morgan Kaufmann, San Mateo, CA.

[Jorgensen and Johnsen 1989]
Jorgensen, S. and Johnsen, E. (1989). *Principles of Environmental Science and Technology.* Elsevier, Amsterdam.

[Kraan et al. 1991]
Kraan, I., Richards, B., and Kuipers, B. (1991). Automatic abduction of qualitative models. In *Proc. Fifth International Workshop on Qualitative Physics.* Austin, Texas.

[Kuipers 1986]
Kuipers, B. (1986). Qualitative simulation. *Artificial Intelligence*, 29(3):289–338.

[Langley et al. 1987]
Langley, P., Simon, H., and Bradshaw, G. (1987). Heuristics for empirical discovery. In Bolc, L., editor, *Computational Models of Learning.* Springer, Berlin.

[Lavrač and Džeroski 1993]
Lavrač, N. and Džeroski, S. (1993). *Inductive Logic Programming: Techniques and Applications.* Ellis Horwood, Chichester.

[Lavrač et al. 1991]
Lavrač, N., Džeroski, S., and Grobelnik, M. (1991). Learning nonrecursive definitions of relations with LINUS. In *Proc. Fifth European Working Session on Learning*, pages 265–281. Springer, Berlin.

[Nordhausen and Langley 1990]
Nordhausen, B. and Langley, P. (1990). A robust approach to numeric discovery. In *Proc. Seventh International Conference on Machine Learning*, pages 411–418. Morgan Kaufmann, San Mateo, CA.

[Press et al. 1986]
Press, W. H., Flannery, B. P., Teukolsky, S. A., and Vetterling, W. T. (1986). *Numerical Recipes.* Cambridge University Press, Cambridge, MA.

[Volk 1958]
Volk, W. (1958). *Applied Statistics for Engineers.* McGraw-Hill, New York, NY.

[Zembowitz and Żytkow 1992]
Zembowitz, R. and Żytkow, J. (1992). Discovery of equations: experimental evaluation of convergence. In *Proc. Tenth National Conference on Artificial Intelligence.* Morgan Kaufmann, San Mateo, CA.

[Żytkow and Zhu 1991]
Żytkow, J. and Zhu, J. (1991). Application of empirical discovery in knowledge acquisition. In *Proc. Fifth European Working Session on Learning*, pages 101–117. Springer, Berlin.

Synthesis of Abstraction Hierarchies for Constraint Satisfaction by Clustering Approximately Equivalent Objects

Thomas Ellman
Department of Computer Science
Hill Center for Mathematical Sciences
Rutgers University, New Brunswick, NJ 08903
ellman@cs.rutgers.edu

Abstract

Abstraction techniques are important for solving constraint satisfaction problems with global constraints and low solution density. In the presence of global constraints, backtracking search is unable to prune partial solutions. It therefore operates like pure generate-and-test. Abstraction improves on generate-and-test by enabling entire subsets of the solution space to be pruned early in a backtracking search process. Unfortunately, a suitable abstraction space may not be included in the problem description provided to a problem solving system. The benefits of abstraction will not be available unless the system can automatically construct an abstraction space. This paper describes how abstraction spaces can be generated by clustering the objects appearing in a problem into classes that contain approximately equivalent objects. It presents a program synthesis algorithm for automatically building abstraction spaces and hierarchic problem solvers that exploit approximate equivalence of objects. The fully implemented synthesis algorithm operates by analyzing declarative descriptions of classes of constraint satisfaction problems. The paper presents data from experimental tests of the synthesis algorithm and the resulting problem solvers on the NP-hard Partition and Minimum Flow Cut problems.

1 Introduction

Abstraction techniques are important for solving constraint satisfaction problems (CSPs) with global constraints and low solution density. Examples of such problems include the Partition problem and the Minimum Flow Cut problem, both of which are NP-hard [Garey and Johnson, 1979]. (See Figure 1). In the presence of global constraints, backtracking search is unable to prune partial solutions [Nadel, 1988]. It therefore operates like pure generate-and-test. When overall solution density is low, this approach is not effective, except when applied to small problems. Abstraction can improve the performance of backtracking by enabling entire subsets of the solution space to be pruned early in the search process. Unfortunately, a suitable abstraction space may not be included in the problem description provided to a problem solving system. The benefits of abstraction will not be available unless the system can automatically construct an abstraction space. This paper presents a method for automatically constructing abstraction spaces and hierarchic problem solvers for constraint satisfaction problems. Abstraction spaces are constructed by clustering objects appearing in the problem description into classes of approximately equivalent objects. The abstraction spaces can be utilized by a hierarchic problem solver that operates in two steps: (1) Find an abstract solution by ignoring differences between approximately equivalent objects. (2) Refine the abstract solution into a true solution that takes account of all differences between objects.

The strategy of approximate equivalence can be illustrated by considering the Partition problem: The problem specification includes a set E of elements and a weight $w(e)$ of each element e. The solution requires finding a subset M of E such that the weight of elements included in M equals the weight of elements excluded from M, i.e., the total weight is $W/2$, where W is the total weight of E. This constraint is global, since one cannot verify equality of the total weights without knowing the inclusion/exclusion status of each element. Backtracking algorithms therefore cannot easily use this constraint to prune partial solutions. The following procedure overcomes this limitation: First divide the elements of E into disjoint classes such that elements of roughly equal weight are grouped together. Now pretend that each element e of a given class actually has a whole interval range of weights, i.e., the range of weights spanned by the members of the class. Then select a *quota* for each class that represents the

- Partition: Given a set E and a weight $w(e)$ for each element e of E. Find a subset M of E such that the total weight of M equals the total weight of $E - M$.
- Minimum Flow Cut: Given a complete graph $G = (V, E)$, a function $w(v_1, v_2)$ assigning a weight to each edge, and an integer T. Find two equal sized subsets of V such that the total weight of edges crossing between subsets is no more than T.

Figure 1: Testbed Problems

number of elements of the class to be included in M. Given a quota for each class, compute upper and lower bounds on the total weight of elements included in M. If the goal weight $W/2$ does not lie within the bounds, then prune away this quota assignment and try another one. Otherwise, refine the quotas into an actual selection of elements to be included in the set M.

The behavior of a problem solver using a two level abstraction hierarchy is illustrated in Figure 2. The illustration shows how the search tree can be broken into two parts. The upper portion of the tree represents a space of "abstract states", (e.g., a space of quota assignments). Backtracking tests each complete abstract solution against an "abstract goal" (e.g., testing problem constraints against quota assignments). The problem solver will be complete provided that the abstract goal test is a *necessary* condition on refinability of abstract solutions, i.e., abstract states that fail to satisfy the abstract goal cannot be refined into concrete solutions. The lower portion of the tree represents a space of "concrete states", (e.g., a space of subset membership assignments). Backtracking tests each complete concrete solution against the original "concrete goal", (e.g., testing problem constraints against subset membership assignments). Search in the concrete space is also guided by "constrained variable range generators". These require each concrete state variable to assume only values that are consistent with the previously specified abstract solution, (e.g., obeying previously specified quota assignments).

A technique for constructing such hierarchic problem solvers is presented in this paper. It takes as input a declarative representation of a parameterized class of constraint satisfaction problems, called a PCSP. This input includes a description of a search space S and a boolean-valued goal function G defined on the elements of S. As output, it produces all of the remaining data needed to instantiate the hierarchic problem solver illustrated in Figure 2, including an abstraction space A; an abstract boolean-valued goal function $\ddot{G}$ defined on the elements of A; and a set of variable range generators that constrain concrete state variables to assume values consistent with a given abstract solution. A formal characterization of the abstraction space and goal function are given in Section 2. A description of the PSCP input problem representation is given in Section 3. The algorithm for synthesizing hierarchic problem solvers is given in Section 4. Results from testing the synthesized algorithms are presented in Section 5.

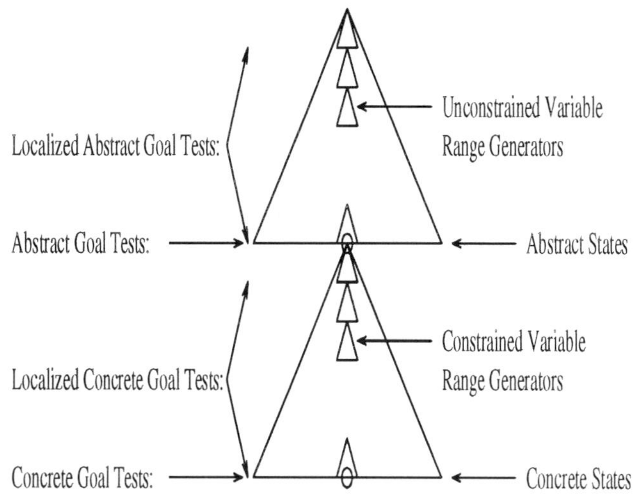

Figure 2: Hierarchic Problem Solver

2 Abstract Search Spaces

An "abstraction space" A may be defined formally as a partition of the states in the underlying "concrete space" S. Thus each abstract state $a \epsilon A$ is a set of concrete states $s \epsilon S$. Abstractions based on approximate equivalence can be defined by focusing on *function finding* problems, i.e., problems whose solution requires finding a function f that maps a given domain D into a given range R. Thus each state $s \epsilon S$ is a function that accepts some $d \epsilon D$ and returns a value $r \epsilon R$. An abstraction space may constructed by clustering the domain D into a collection $\hat{D}$ of disjoint sets. Each state $a \epsilon A$ will be a function $\ddot{f}$ which accepts a subset $\hat{d}$ in the collection $\hat{D}$ and returns a multiset of cardinality $|\hat{d}|$ of values drawn from the range R. An abstract solution thus specifies the multiset $\ddot{f}(\hat{d})$ of values assigned to a set $\hat{d}$ of objects; however it does not specify which value is assigned to which object. For example, in the Partition example described above, the domain D is the set E of elements and the range R is the set $\{True, False\}$ of boolean values. While a concrete solution $s \epsilon S$ assigns a value of $True$ or $False$ to each element $e \epsilon E$, an abstract solution $a \epsilon A$ assigns to each class $\hat{e} \epsilon \hat{E}$ a multiset of boolean values, or equivalently, a quota of $True$ values. Nevertheless, the abstract solution does not specify precisely which elements in $\hat{e}$ actually receive $True$ values. This type of abstraction is discussed more fully in [Ellman, 1993].

3 Parameterized CSPs

Classes of constraint satisfaction problems are represented using a notation called "parameterized constraint satisfaction problems" (PCSPs). A PCSP includes a *signature* S and a *goal-function* G. The signature is a declaration of the types of sets and functions that appear in problem instances, including: a list of names and data types (symbol or integer) of finite sets; a list of names of functions along with a declared domain and range for each; a list of names and data types of constants. The signature also declares each function to be either "known" or "unknown". The known functions are supplied as part of each problem instance specification. The unknown functions must be found by the problem solver in order to solve the problem. [1] [2] The goal function G serves to determine how the unknown functions may be specified in order to solve the problem. G is conceptually a map from the constants, known functions and unknown functions into the booleans. We use the notation $G(p, s)$ to indicate that G depends on the problem instance p (i.e., the known functions) and the solution s, (i.e., the unknown functions). A particular goal function G is represented by a boolean formula that may reference the known and unknown functions; primitive arithmetic $(+, -, *, /)$, relational $(<, \leq, >, \geq)$ and boolean $(\neg, \vee, \wedge)$ operations; as well as conditionals $If(c, x, y)$ and absolute values $Abs(x)$. G may also include universal $\forall$ or existential $\exists$ quantification and sums Σ or products Π of functions over sets declared in the signature. The signature and goal function for the Partition problem class are found in Figure 3.

- Signature:
  - Sets:
    - Elements E of type symbol.
    - Weights W of type integer.
  - Known: Weight $w : E \rightarrow W$
  - Unknown: Member $m : E \rightarrow \{True, False\}$
- Goal Function:

$$\begin{aligned} G(p,s) &= S_1(p,s) = S_2(p,s) \\ S_1(p,s) &= \textstyle\sum_{e \epsilon E(p)} if(m(e,s), w(e,p), 0) \\ S_2(p,s) &= \textstyle\sum_{e \epsilon E(p)} if(m(e,s), 0, w(e,p)) \end{aligned}$$

Figure 3: Partition Problem Class Specification

4 Synthesis of Problem Solvers

An algorithm for synthesizing a hierarchic problem solver is shown in Figure 4. The algorithm begins by clustering the domain D of the unknown function f into a collection $\hat{D}$ of equivalence classes. The clustering process divides D into classes based on similarity of values of some known function whose domain is D, and which is referenced by the goal function $G(p, s)$. Next, the original goal function $G(p, s)$ is transformed into an abstract goal $\ddot{G}(p, a)$ in order that it may operate on abstract states a. This transformation is achieved, in part, by a process of replacing each function f appearing in $G(p, s)$ with the corresponding "set operation" $\hat{f}$ or the corresponding "symmetric operation" $\bar{f}$, as defined in Figure 4. Finally, the revised goal is surrounded with a test for the appearance of $True$ in the returned set of boolean values. These transformations weaken the original goal so that it fails to distinguish between distinct members d and d' that occur the same class $\hat{d}$ of the collection $\hat{D}$ of equivalence classes. The resulting abstract goal is by construction a *necessary* condition on solvability of the abstract state a. The algorithm also constructs a refinement function R_d for each element d of the domain D. The function $R_d(p, a, s)$ takes the problem specification p, an abstract solution a, and a partially specified concrete solution s, and returns the set of possible values for $f(d)$ that are consistent with a and s.

When the synthesis algorithm is applied to the Partition problem description in Figure 3, it generates the abstract goal function shown in Figure 5. This goal function $G(p, a)$ begins by selecting an arbitrary candidate solution s consistent with the quotas described in a. It then applies to s an approximation $\tilde{G}(p, s)$ of the original goal function that is symmetric with respect to the collection $\hat{E}$ of equivalence classes. This symmetric goal function $\tilde{G}(p, s)$ treats each $e \epsilon E$ as if it has an interval $\bar{w}(e)$ of weights, rather than an actual weight $w(e)$. It performs interval arithmetic, interval comparisons, and boolean-set algebra to compute two intervals: $\hat{S}_1(p, a)$ represents a range of values for the sum of weights of *included* elements. $\hat{S}_2(p, a)$ represents a range of values for the sum of weights of *excluded* elements. Finally the abstract goal function checks whether these two intervals overlap. It thereby computes a necessary condition on the original goal.

The preceding discussion blurs the distinction between operations that happen at compile time (when the problem class is specified), and operations that happen

[1] Unknown functions are required to have symbolic domains. This requirement is necessary for the correctness of the algorithm for synthesizing abstract goal functions. No generality is lost since it could be enforced by mechanical translation.

[2] We use the notation $f(e,p)$ to indicate that the known function f depends on the problem instance p, as well as its argument e. We use the notation $f(e,s)$ to indicate that the unknown function f depends on the solution s, as well as its argument e. The problem instance p or solution s parameter will occasionally be omitted from $f(e,p)$ or $f(e,s)$ when its role is clear from the context.

Definitions:

- **Set Functions:** Given an arbitrary function $h : A \rightarrow B$, define the corresponding set function $\hat{h} : A \cup 2^A \rightarrow 2^B$, such that $\hat{h}(x) = \{h(x)\}$, if $x \epsilon A$, and $\hat{h}(x) = \{h(y) | y \epsilon x\}$ if $x \subseteq A$.
- **Symmetric Functions:** Given an arbitrary function $h : A \rightarrow B$, and a partition $\hat{A}$ of A, define the corresponding symmetric function $\bar{h} : A \cup 2^A \rightarrow 2^B$ such that $\bar{h}(x) = \{h(y) | y \epsilon Class(x)\}$, if $x \epsilon A$, and $\bar{h}(x) = \cup_{y \epsilon x} \{h(z) | z \epsilon Class(y)\}$, if $x \subseteq A$.

Algorithm: Given a search space S representing all functions f from D into R, and a goal function $G(p, s)$ defined on all $s \epsilon S$ and problem instances p:

1. Define an abstraction space A:
   (a) Define a partition $\hat{D}$ of D by clustering D based on similarity of values of D itself or some known function defined on D that is referenced by the goal function $G(p, s)$.
   (b) Let the abstraction space A represent all functions $\ddot{f}$ with domain $\hat{D}$ such that for all $\hat{d} \epsilon \hat{D}$, $\ddot{f}(\hat{d})$ returns a multiset over R of cardinality $|\hat{d}|$.
2. Synthesize an abstract goal $\ddot{G}(p, a)$ defined on all $a \epsilon A$ and problem instances p:
   (a) Construct an approximate goal function $\tilde{G}(p, s)$ that is exactly symmetric with respect to $\hat{D}$:
      i. Transform the original goal function $G(p, s)$ into a boolean set valued function $\hat{G}(p, s)$: Replace each reference to a known function h defined on domain D, with the corresponding symmetric function $\bar{h}$. Replace each primitive or known function h defined on $D' \neq D$, with the corresponding set function $\hat{h}$.
      ii. Let $\tilde{G}(p, s) = True \ \epsilon \ \hat{G}(p, s)$.
   (b) Define the abstract goal $\ddot{G}(p, a)$ to select an arbitrary $s \epsilon a$ and return $\tilde{G}(p, s)$.
3. Synthesize functions $R_d(p, a, s)$ that incorporate constraints between the abstract space A and the concrete space S. For each $d \epsilon D$, $R_d(p, a, s)$ is the set of values of $f(d)$ that are consistent with the abstract solution a and the partially specified concrete solution s. $R_d(p, a, s)$ is computed by taking the multiset difference between $\ddot{f}(\hat{d}, a)$, and the multiset of all $f(d, s)$ $(d \epsilon \hat{d})$ such that $f(d)$ is assigned a value in state s.

Figure 4: Synthesis Algorithm and Definitions

$$
\begin{aligned}
\ddot{G}(p, a) &= True \ \epsilon \ (\hat{S}_1(p, a) \hat{=} \hat{S}_2(p, a)) \\
\hat{S}_1(p, a) &= \hat{\sum}_{\hat{e} \epsilon \hat{E}(p)} \hat{\sum}_{(e,v) \epsilon (\hat{e}, \ddot{m}(\hat{e}, a))} if(v, \bar{w}(e, p), \{0\}) \\
\hat{S}_1(p, a) &= \hat{\sum}_{\hat{e} \epsilon \hat{E}(p)} \hat{\sum}_{(e,v) \epsilon (\hat{e}, \ddot{m}(\hat{e}, a))} if(v, \{0\}, \bar{w}(e, p))
\end{aligned}
$$

Figure 5: Abstract Partition Goal

at run time (when the problem instance is specified). In the current implementation, the abstract goal function and constrained variable range generators are synthesized at compile time. These operations are done only once for an entire class of constraint satisfaction problems. The costs of this compilation can therefore be amortized over many problem solving episodes. For this reason, the costs of constructing abstract goals and constrained variable range generators are not included in the CPU time measurements reported in Section 5. In contrast to this, the domain D is clustered into equivalence classes at run time, when the problem instance is known. Clustering must occur at run time whenever the domain or the features used to cluster the domain are expected to change from one problem instance to the next. Since clustering occurs at run time, and must be redone for each problem instance, the costs of clustering cannot be amortized over problem solving episodes. For this reason, clustering costs are included in the CPU time measurements reported in Section 5.

Several different algorithms are used for clustering the domain D into equivalence classes. [3] These algorithms are described in Figure 6. Random clustering ignores all features of the objects to be clustered. It is expected to be useful when the details of the resulting clusters are not as important as minimizing the cost of the clustering process itself. In contrast, bottom-up clustering does consider features of the objects to be clustered. It is expected to be useful when the value of good clusters outweighs the cost of finding them. Bottom-up clustering requires a user to specify at compile time which known function should be used to guide the clustering process. (In the Partition and Minimum Flow Cut problem classes, the user has only one choice.) Bottom-up clustering operates in three different versions depending on the data type of the feature f that guides the clustering process. The feature may be a scalar integer function (e.g., the weight function in the Partition problem); an integer vector function, (e.g., the rows of the weight matrix in the the Minimum Flow Cut problem); or a boolean vector function, (e.g., a bit vector representation of adjacency lists in an unweighted graph version of the Minimum Flow Cut problem). In each case, the bottom-up method at-

[3] The details of these clustering algorithms are not central to the claims of this paper. More sophisticated clustering algorithms are presented in [Kaufman and Rousseeuw, 1990].

Random Clustering: Form a list of singleton sets. Put the sets in random order. Repeatedly merge the first two sets on the list and put the merged set at the end of the list. Terminate when the abstract space induced by the clusters has the desired size.

Bottom-Up Clustering: Let f be the feature or feature vector selected to guide the clustering. First compute $f(d)$ for each d in the domain D. Let the initial clusters be a collection singleton sets of the elements of D. Repeatedly select two sets X and Y to be merged. At each step, choose the two sets X and Y such that the function f varies as little as possible over the set $X \cup Y$. Terminate when the abstract space induced by the clusters has the desired size:

- *Integer scalar features:* If f is an integer scalar valued function, then at each step we choose X and Y to minimize the difference between the largest and smallest values of f over $X \cup Y$:
- *Integer vector features:* If f is a integer vector valued function, then at each step we choose X and Y to minimize the average over all components f_i of the difference between the largest and smallest values of $f_i(z)$ for $z \epsilon (X \cup Y)$.
- *Boolean vector features:* If f is boolean vector valued function then at each step we choose X and Y to minimize the number of components of f in which members of $X \cup Y$ disagree.

Figure 6: Clustering Procedures

tempts to minimize the variation in the function f over elements that are placed in common clusters. Since the final clusters are used to induce the symmetric abstraction $\bar{f}$ of f that appears in the abstract goal $\ddot{G}$, pruning at the abstract level will be most successful when the value of f varies little over elements of a single cluster. Both clustering algorithms terminate when the induced abstraction space has a user-specified size. Random clustering takes $O(n)$ time, where n is the number of objects to be clustered. Bottom-up scalar clustering can be done in $O(nlog(n))$ time, by sorting the objects at the beginning of the process. Bottom-up vector clustering takes $O(n^2 l)$ time, where l is the length of the feature vector.

5 Experimental Results

A series of experiments was run to evaluate the performance of automatically synthesized problem solvers based on the idea of approximate equivalence. The experiments were performed on the NP-hard constraint satisfaction problems defined in Figure 1. Each experiment compared the performance of a "flat" problem solver, which uses no abstraction, to the performance of "hierarchic" problem solvers, which use abstraction based on approximate equivalence. The hierarchic and flat problem solvers use the same underlying backtracking code, but with different input specifications. In the first set of these experiments, the hierarchic solver used the bottom-up clustering strategy described in Figure 6. Clustering of elements $e \epsilon E$ in the Partition problem was guided by the integer scalar function giving the weight of each element. Clustering of vertices $v \epsilon V$ in the Minimum Flow Cut problem was guided by the integer vector function giving the weights of the edges from a given vertex to every other vertex. Two different methods were used to choose the size of the abstraction spaces. The "default" abstraction space has size $|S|^{1/2}$, where $|S|$ is the size of the concrete space. [4] The "optimized" abstraction space has size $|S|^k$. The exponent k was chosen manually, and separately for each problem class and clustering strategy, in order to minimize overall CPU time. The optimal values of k were experimentally found to be 0.74 for the Partition problem, and 0.83 for the Minimum Flow Cut problem. Thus the default abstraction spaces ($k = 0.5$) are smaller than the optimal size.

Results of these experiments are shown in Figures 7 and 8. Each graph plots problem size against performance measured in terms of CPU time. The Partition graph examines performance on randomly generated problems with the number of elements in the set E running from 4 to 16. The Minimum Flow Cut graph compares performance on randomly generated problems with the number of vertices in the graph G running from 4 to 16. In both graphs, each data point represents an average of 10 randomly generated problems. Notice that for large enough problems, both the default and optimized hierarchic problem solvers run more quickly than the flat problem solver, on both the Partition and Minimum Flow Cut problem classes. Furthermore, the difference becomes more dramatic as the problem size increases. A series of single-tailed paired t-tests was run to test the significance of these results. For both the Partition and Minimum Flow Cut problem classes, the default hierarchic solver is faster than the flat solver with significance above 99% on the largest problem size. Thus the default abstraction space improves performance in comparison to the ordinary flat problem solver. Furthermore, for both problem classes, the optimized hierarchic solver is faster than the default hierarchic solver with significance above 99% on the largest problem size. Thus a careful choice of the size of the abstraction space can significantly improve performance over the default size.

A series of experiments was also run to compare the "random" and "bottom-up" clustering methods shown in Figure 6. Comparisons based on the default size abstraction space are shown in Figure 9, for the Partition problem class, and Figure 10 for the Minimum

[4] The choice of the default abstraction space size is based on a rough analogy with Korf's result on the optimal size of abstraction spaces for state space search [Korf, 1987].

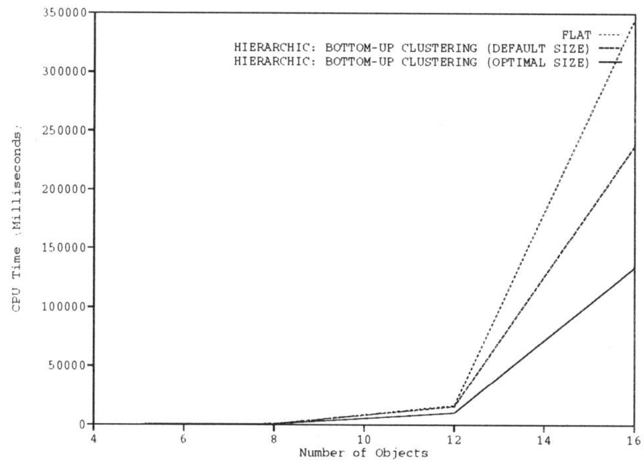

Figure 7: Partition CPU Time: Flat (Dotted) v. Hierarchic Bottom-Up Clustering Default Size (Dashed) v. Hierarchic Bottom-Up Clustering Optimal Size (Solid)

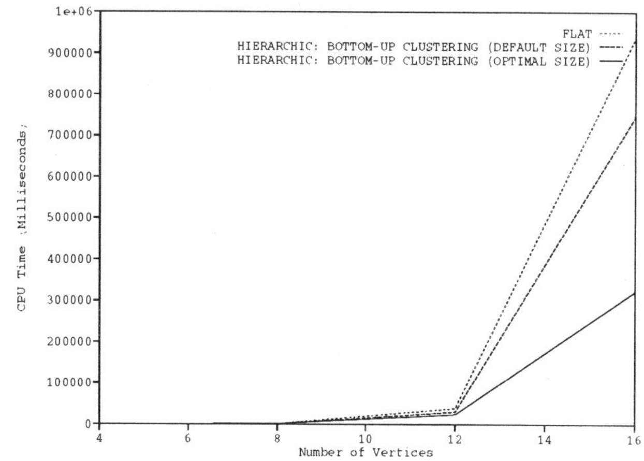

Figure 8: Min Flow Cut CPU Time: Flat (Dotted) v. Hierarchic Bottom-Up Clustering Default Size (Dashed) v. Hierarchic Bottom-Up Clustering Optimal Size (Solid)

Flow Cut problem class. Notice that bottom-up clustering leads to a faster problem solver than random clustering for the Partition problem class. (The single-tailed paired t-test significance level is above 99% on the largest problem size.) Notice also that bottom-up clustering does *not* lead to a faster problem solver than random clustering on the Minimum Flow Cut problem class. (The single-tailed paired t-test significance level is only 29% on the largest problem size.) Comparisons based on optimal size abstraction spaces are shown in Figure 11, for the Partition problem class, and Figure 12 for the Minimum Flow Cut problem class. These graphs show that for optimally sized spaces, bottom-up clustering leads to a faster problem solver than random clustering, when applied to both the Partition problem class and the Minimum Flow Cut problem class. (Single-tailed paired t-test significance levels for each problem class are above 99% on the largest problem size.)

The comparisons between "random" and "bottom-up" clustering can be explained by considering two factors that impact on the performance of a hierarchic problem solver: (1) The cost of the clustering that is needed to construct the abstract search space; (2) The effectiveness of pruning of abstract states. On the Partition problem, bottom-up (scalar) clustering is only marginally slower $O(nlog(n)$ than random clustering $O(n)$. In addition, bottom-up clustering leads to more effective pruning of abstract states than does random clustering. Therefore bottom-up clustering dominates random clustering for both the default and optimal abstraction spaces. In contrast to this, on the Minimum Flow Cut problem, bottom-up (vector) clustering is considerably slower $O(n^3)$ than random clustering $O(n)$. Thus bottom-up clustering will only be useful when the cost of clustering vertices is justified by an increase in the effectiveness of pruning of abstract states. This cost appears not to be justified when the abstract space is small, i.e., the default size. In this case, the clusters of vertices are so large that most information about the graph structure is lost, and pruning is relatively ineffective, even when clusters are chosen carefully. In contrast to this, the cost of clustering vertices is justified when the abstract space is larger, i.e., the optimal size. The smaller clusters of vertices preserve more of the graph structure and lead to more effective pruning of abstract states.

6 Future Work

Future work is planned to determine whether more sophisticated clustering algorithms, such as those discussed in [Kaufman and Rousseeuw, 1990], might yield more compact clusters and more effective pruning at the abstract level. More sophisticated clustering algorithms may also be necessary to handle more complex constraint satisfaction problems. In the test problems studied so far, only one function is the "unknown function". Thus only one domain is available to serve as the basis of abstraction. Likewise, in the test problems studied so far, only one feature function was available to guide clustering. More complex problems would likely include many unknown functions, defined on multiple domains, and many possible feature functions that can be used to guide clustering. For such complex problems, methods of automatically selecting the best domain(s) for abstraction, and the best features to guide clustering would likely be useful. Future work will investigate methods of automatically deter-

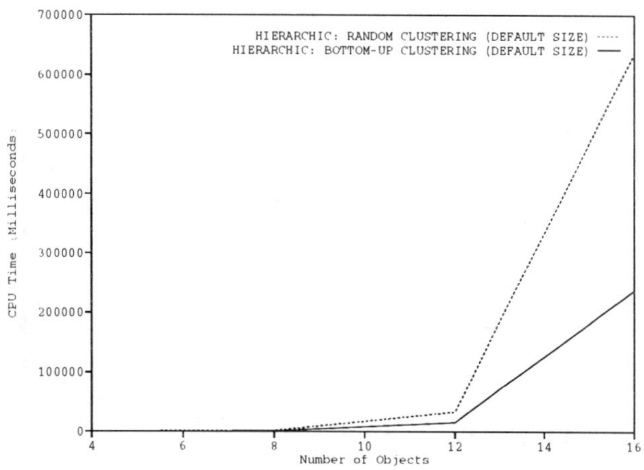

Figure 9: Partition CPU Time: Hierarchic Bottom-Up Clustering Default Size (Solid) v. Hierarchic Random Clustering Default Size (Dotted)

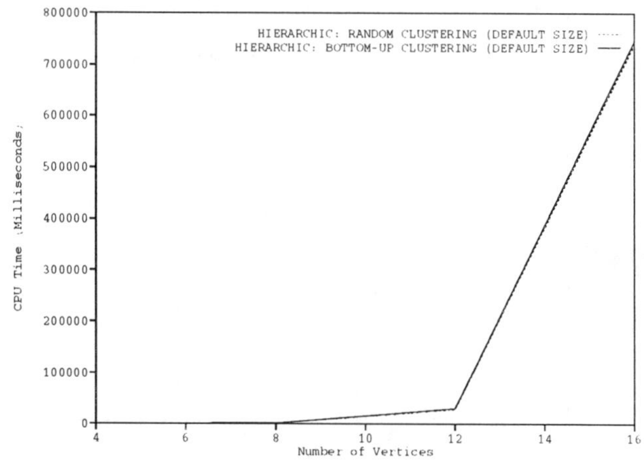

Figure 10: Min Flow Cut CPU Time: Hierarchic Bottom-Up Clustering Default Size (Solid) v. Hierarchic Random Clustering Default Size (Dotted)

mining how much abstraction is suitable for attacking a given constraint satisfaction problem. For example, in the current implementation, the size of the abstraction space is chosen arbitrarily. Our experiments suggest that the size of the abstraction space is a crucial parameter that must be chosen with care. A method of automatically determining the right size for a given problem would be useful. Finally, a natural extension of this work would synthesize a multi-level abstraction hierarchy. The sequence of abstraction spaces, from most concrete to most abstract, would correspond to the sequence of partitions generated by the bottom-up clustering algorithm. Use of such a multi-level hierarchy might eliminate the need for a means of automatically choosing an abstraction space of the best possible size, since many sizes would be available at once.

7 Related Work

Abstraction techniques have been studied previously in the context of planning [Knoblock *et al.*, 1991] and theorem proving [Giunchiglia and Walsh, 1992]. The research presented here is similar in spirit; however, it differs by focusing on constraint satisfaction problems, rather than planning or theorem proving. A program called "HiT" for automatically constructing abstraction spaces for CSPs is presented in [Mohan, 1991]. HiT differs from the method developed here by partitioning the range, rather than the domain, in function finding problems. HiT may therefore be seen as a complementary method of building abstraction spaces. Methods of attacking hierarchical CSPs are discussed in [Mackworth *et al.*, 1985]; however, the methods are aimed at exploiting an existing hierarchy rather than automatically constructing a new one. Abstractions based on quotas have been studied in the context of resource allocation problems [Lowry and Linden, 1992]. Approximate equivalence provides a rational reconstruction of the quota concept. Furthermore, approximate equivalence is more general, because it depends only on the algebraic form of the problem and not on semantic notions such as "resources". Approximations and abstractions have been used to construct heuristic evaluation functions in the context of constraint satisfaction [Dechter and Pearl, 1987] and state space search [Prieditis, 1991].

8 Summary

The research reported in this paper contributes to the field of Machine Learning in two distinct ways. To begin with, it has developed an *analytic learning* technique for improving the performance of problem solvers on constraint satisfaction problems. The technique is called "analytic" because in operates on a declarative description of a class of constraint problems (PCSP), rather than empirical data, or data obtained from problem solving experience. The analytic technique synthesizes the components of a hierarchic problem solver, i.e., an abstraction space, an abstract goal and a set of constrained variable range generators. Since these components can be used to solve many problem instances, the computational costs of analytic learning may be amortized over many problem solving episodes. In addition, this research has developed a novel way of utilizing clustering algorithms. In particular, it has showed how clustering algorithms can be used to construct hierarchies of abstraction spaces to speed the solution of constraint satisfaction problems.

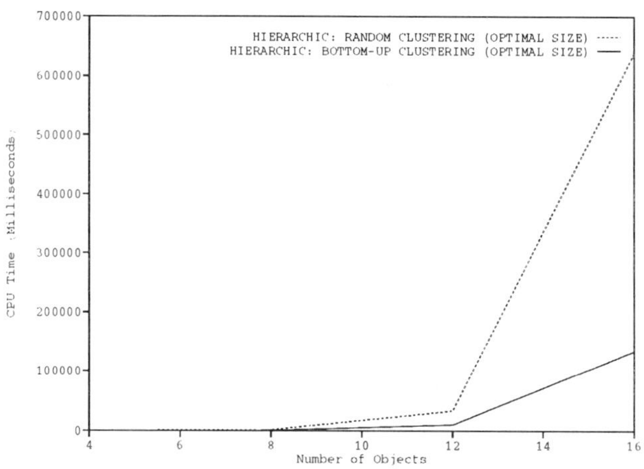

Figure 11: Partition CPU Time: Hierarchic Bottom-Up Clustering Optimal Size (Solid) v. Hierarchic Random Clustering Optimal Size (Dotted)

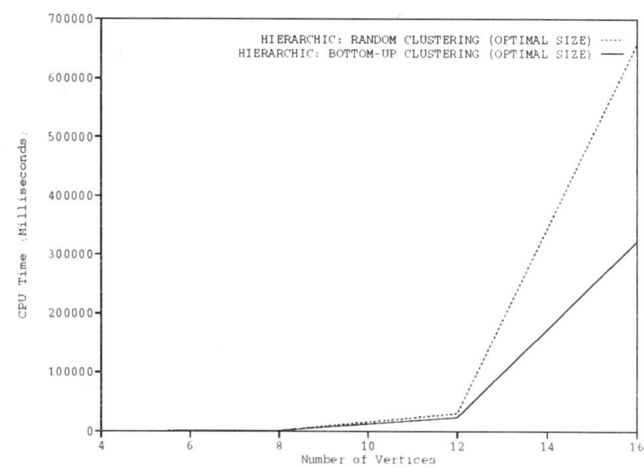

Figure 12: Min Flow Cut CPU Time: Hierarchic Bottom-Up Clustering Optimal Size (Solid) v. Hierarchic Random Clustering Optimal Size (Dotted)

Acknowledgments

The research reported in this paper is supported by the National Science Foundation under grants IRI-9017121 and IRI-9021607. This research has also benefited from discussions with Haym Hirsh and Christopher Tong. Thanks also to Saibal Patra for programming assistance.

References

[Dechter and Pearl, 1987] R. Dechter and J. Pearl. Network-based heuristics for constraint-satisfaction problems. *Artificial Intelligence*, 34:1–38, 1987.

[Ellman, 1993] T. Ellman. Abstraction via approximate symmetry. In *Proceedings of the Thirteenth International Joint Conference on Artificial Intelligence*, Chambery, France, August 1993.

[Garey and Johnson, 1979] M. R. Garey and D. S. Johnson. *Computers and Intractability: A Guide to the Theory of NP-Completeness.* W. H. Freeman and Company, New York, NY, 1979.

[Giunchiglia and Walsh, 1992] F. Giunchiglia and T. Walsh. A theory of abstraction. *Artificial Intelligence*, 57:323–389, 1992.

[Kaufman and Rousseeuw, 1990] L. Kaufman and P. Rousseeuw. *Finding Groups in Data: An Introduction to Cluster Analysis.* Wiley, New York, NY, 1990.

[Knoblock *et al.*, 1991] C. Knoblock, J. Tennenberg, and Q. Yang. Characterizing abstraction hierarchies for planning. In *Proceedings of the Ninth National Conference on Artificial Intelligence*, Anaheim, CA, 1991.

[Korf, 1987] R. E. Korf. Planning as search: A quantitative approach. *Artificial Intelligence*, 33(1):65 – 88, 1987.

[Lowry and Linden, 1992] M. Lowry and T. Linden. Generation and exploitation of aggregation abstractions for scheduling and resource allocation. Working Notes of the AAAI Workshop on Approximation and Abstraction of Computational Theories, San Jose, CA, 1992.

[Mackworth *et al.*, 1985] A. Mackworth, J. Mulder, and W. Havens. Hierarchical arc consistency: Exploiting structured domains in constraint satisfaction problems. *Computational Intelligence*, 1:118 – 126, 1985.

[Mohan, 1991] S. Mohan. Constructing hierarchical solvers for functional constraint satisfaction problems. Working notes of the AAAI Spring Symposium on Constraint-Based Reasoning, Stanford, CA, 1991.

[Nadel, 1988] B. Nadel. Tree search and arc consistency in constraint satisfaction algorithms. In L. Kanal and V. Kumar, editors, *Search in Artificial Intelligence*, pages 287 – 342. Springer Verlag, New York, NY, 1988.

[Prieditis, 1991] A. Prieditis. Machine discovery of effective admissable heuristics. In *Proceedings of the Twelfth International Joint Conference on Artificial Intelligence*, Sidney, Australia, 1991.

SKICAT: A Machine Learning System for Automated Cataloging of Large Scale Sky Surveys

Usama M. Fayyad
AI Group M/S 525-3660
Jet Propulsion Laboratory
California Institute of Technology
Pasadena, CA 91109
Fayyad@aig.jpl.nasa.gov

Nicholas Weir and **S. Djorgovski**
Palomar Observatory
M/S 105-24
California Institute of Technology
Pasadena, CA 91125
{weir,george}@deimos.caltech.edu

ABSTRACT

We describe the application of decision tree based classification techniques to the development of an automated tool for the reduction of a large scientific data set. The 2nd Palomar Observatory Sky Survey (POSS-II) will provide a comprehensive coverage of the northern celestial hemisphere in the form of digitized photographic plates containing on the order of 0.5 billion objects. It is necessary to classify the detected objects as stars, galaxies, or instrumental artifacts. The size of this data set precludes manual analysis. Image processing routines are used to identify sky objects and to extract a set of basic features for each object that are used to select a useful and robust set of attributes for classifying sky objects. The GID3* and O-BTree decision tree learning algorithms, in conjunction with the RULER system for statistically pruning and merging multiple trees, are used to classify the detected objects. The learning algorithms produced classifiers that can classify objects in the survey that are too faint for visual classification with an accuracy level of about 94%. This increases the number of classified objects in the final catalog by three-fold relative to the best techniques previously employed by extending at least one magnitude fainter than objects classified in photographic sky surveys to date. SKICAT represents a system in which machine learning played a powerful and enabling role, and solved a difficult, scientifically significant problem.

1. INTRODUCTION

In this paper we present an application of machine learning techniques to the automation of the task of cataloging sky objects in digitized sky images. The Sky Image Cataloging and Analysis Tool (SKICAT) is being developed for use on the images resulting from the 2nd Palomar Observatory Sky Survey (POSS-II) conducted by the California Institute of Technology (Caltech) [Reid91]. The photographic plates collected from the survey are being digitized at the Space Telescope Science Institute (STScI). This process will result in about 3,000 digitized images of roughly $23{,}040^2$ pixels each (16 bits per pixel). The survey consists of over 3 terabytes of data containing on the order of 5×10^7 galaxies, 5×10^8 stars, and over 10^5 quasars and represents a data set whose scope will probably not be surpassed in the next decade.

The first step in analyzing the results of a sky survey is to identify, measure, and catalog the detected objects in the image into their respective classes. Once the objects have been classified, further scientific analysis can proceed. For example, the resulting catalog may be used to test models of the formation of large-scale structure in the universe, probe Galactic structure from star counts, perform automatic identifications of radio or infrared sources, and so forth [Weir92]. Reducing the images to catalog entries is an overwhelming task which inherently requires an automated approach. The goal of our project is to automate this process, providing a consistent and uniform methodology for reducing the data sets. This will provide the means of objectively performing tasks that formerly required subjective and visually intensive manual analysis. Another goal of this work is to classify objects whose intensity (isophotal magnitude) is too faint for recognition by inspection, hence requiring an automated classification procedure. Faint objects constitute the majority of objects on any given plate. We target the classification of objects that are at least one magnitude fainter than objects classified in previous surveys using comparable photographic material.

The goals of this paper are to introduce the machine learning techniques we used, to give a general, high-level description of the application domain, and to report on the successful results which exceeded our initial goals. We therefore do not provide the details of either the learning algorithms or the technical aspects of the domain. We aim to point out an instance where learning algorithms proved to a be useful and powerful tool in the automation of scientific data analysis.

2. MACHINE LEARNING BACKGROUND

A familiar context in which machine learning classification techniques have been used is to overcome the "knowledge acquisition bottleneck" [Feig81] due to experts finding it difficult to express their knowledge in terms of concise situation-action rules. The growing number of large scientific databases provides another niche for machine learning applications. Problems include searching for and detecting patterns of interest, performing preprocessing necessary for subsequent analysis, as well as automating analysis subtasks. Sizes are now becoming too large for manual processing. Learning techniques can serve as effective tools for aiding in the analysis, reduction, and visualization of large scientific databases.

2.1. INDUCTION OF DECISION TREES

A particularly efficient method for extracting rules from data is to generate a decision tree [Brei84, Quin86]. A decision tree consists of nodes that are tests on the attributes. The outgoing branches of a node correspond to all the possible outcomes of the test at the node. The examples at a node in the tree are thus partitioned along the branches and each child node gets its corresponding subset of examples. A well-known algorithm for generating decision trees is Quinlan's ID3 [Quin86] with extended versions called C4 [Quin90].

ID3 starts by placing all the training examples at the root node of the tree. An attribute is selected to partition the data. For each value of the attribute, a branch is created and the corresponding subset of examples that have the attribute value specified by the branch are moved to the newly created child node. The algorithm is applied recursively to each child node until either all examples at a node are of one class, or all the examples at that node have the same values for all the attributes. Every leaf in the decision tree represents a classification rule.

Note that the critical decision in such a top-down decision tree generation algorithm is the choice of attribute at a node. Attribute selection in ID3 and C4 is based on minimizing an information entropy measure applied to the examples at a node. The measure favors attributes that result in partitioning the data into subsets that have low class entropy. A subset of data has low class entropy when the majority of examples in it belong to a single class. The algorithm basically chooses the attribute that provides the locally maximum degree of discrimination between classes. For a detailed discussion of the information entropy selection criterion see [Quin86, Fayy91,, Fayy92].

2.2. ALGORITHMS GID3* AND O-BTREE

The criterion for choosing the attribute clearly determines whether a "good" or "bad" tree is generated by the algorithm[1]. Since making the optimal attribute choice is computationally infeasible, ID3 utilizes a heuristic criterion which favors the attribute that results in the partition having the least information entropy with respect to the classes. This is generally a good criterion and often results in relatively good choices. However, there are weaknesses inherent in the ID3 algorithm that are due mainly to the fact that it creates a branch for each value of the attribute chosen for branching. The overbranching problem in ID3 leads to several problems, since in general it may be the case that only a subset of values of an attribute are of relevance to the classification task while the rest of the values may not have any special predictive value for the classes. These extra branches are harmful in three ways [Fayy91]:

1. They result in rules that are overspecialized (conditioned on particular irrelevant attribute values).
2. They unnecessarily partition the data, thus reducing the number of examples at each node. Subsequent attribute choices will be based on an unjustifiably reduced subset of data.
3. They increase the likelihood of occurrence of the missing branches problem (see [Chen88,Fayy91] for more details).

The GID3* algorithm was designed mainly to overcome this problem. It utilizes a vector distance measure applied to the class vectors of an example partition, in conjunction with the entropy measure, to create for each attribute a *phantom attribute* that has only a subset of the original attribute's values. We generalized the ID3 algorithm so that it does not necessarily branch on each value of the chosen attribute. GID3* can branch on arbitrary individual values of an attribute and "lump" the rest of the values in a single *default branch.* Unlike the other branches of the tree which represent a single value, the default branch represents a subset of values of an attribute. Unnecessary subdivision of the data may thus be reduced. See [Fayy91] for more details and for empirical evidence of improvement.

The O-Btree algorithm [Fayy92b] was designed to overcome problems with the information entropy selection measure itself. O-Btree creates strictly binary trees and utilizes a measure from a family of measures (C-SEP) that detects class separation rather than class impurity. Information entropy is a member of the class of impurity measures. O-Btree employs an orthogonality measure rather than entropy for branching. For details on problems with entropy measures and empirical evaluation of O-Btree, the reader is referred to [Fayy91,Fayy92b].

Both O-Btree and GID3* differ from ID3 and C4 along one additional aspect: the discretization algorithm used at each node to discretize continuous-valued attributes. Whereas ID3 and C4 utilize a binary interval discretization algorithm, we utilize a generalized version of that algorithm which derives multiple intervals rather than strictly two. For details and empirical tests showing that this algorithm does indeed produce better trees see [Fayy91,Fayy93]. We have found that this ability improves performance considerably in several domains.

2.3. THE RULER SYSTEM

There are limitations to decision tree generation algorithms that derive from the inherent fact that the classification rules they produce originate from a single tree. This fact was recognized by practitioners early on [Brei84,Quin87]. Tree pruning is used to overcome the fact that in any good tree there are always leaves that are overspecialized or predict the wrong class. The very reason which makes decision tree generation efficient: the fact that data is quickly partitioned into ever smaller

[1] See [Fayy90,Fayy91] for the details of what we formally mean by one decision tree being better than another.

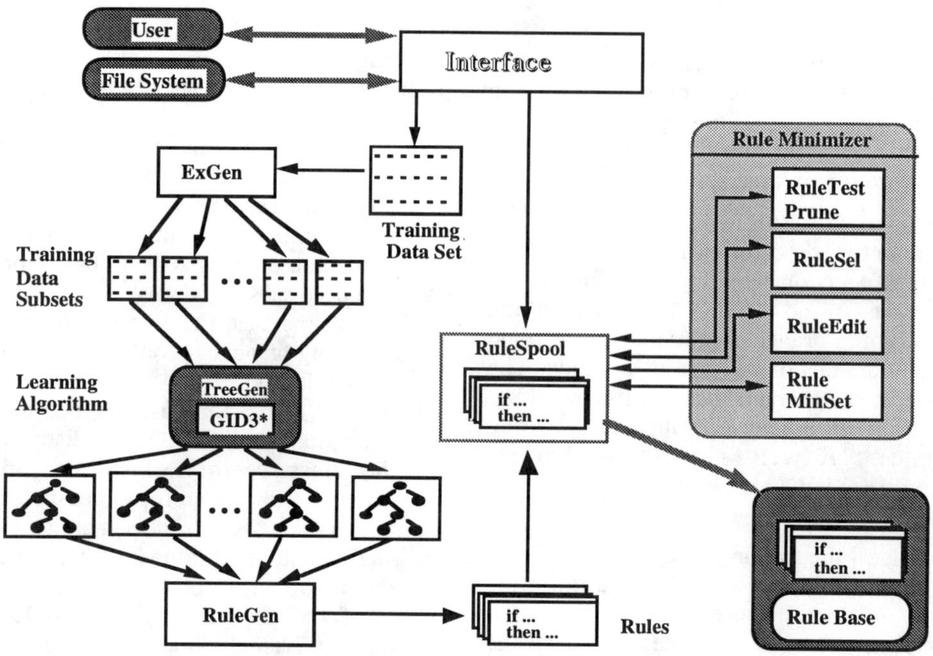

Figure 1. Architecture of the RULER Rule Induction System

subsets, is also the reason why overspecialization or incorrect classification occurs. It is our philosophy that once we have good, efficient, decision tree generators, they could be used to generate multiple trees and only the best rules in each tree are kept. We initially developed the RIST system [Chen90] which later evolved into the RULER system to implement such a scheme. Figure 1 gives an overview of the RULER system.

RULER starts with a data set, and randomly divides it into a training subset and test subset. A decision tree is generated from the training set and its rules are tested on the corresponding test set. Using Fisher's exact test [Finn63] (the exact hyper geometric distribution) RULER evaluates each condition in a given rule's preconditions for relevance to the class predicted by the rule. It computes the probability that the condition is correlated with the class by chance [2]. If this probability is higher than a small threshold (say 0.01), the condition is deemed irrelevant and is pruned. In addition, RULER also measures the merit of the entire rule by applying the test to the entire precondition as a unit. This process serves as a filter which passes only robust, general, and correct rules.

By gathering a large number of rules through iterating on randomly subsampled training sets, RULER builds a large rule base of robust rules that collectively cover the entire original data set of examples. A greedy covering algorithm is then employed to select a minimal subset of rules that covers the examples. The set is minimal in the sense that no rule could be removed without losing complete coverage of the original training set.

Using this method, we can typically produce a robust set of rules that has fewer rules than any of the original decision trees used to create it. Furthermore, any learning algorithm that produces rules can be used as the rule generating component. We use decision tree algorithms because they constitute a fast and efficient method for generating a set of rules from a training set. This allows us to iterate many times without requiring extensive amounts of time and computation.

3. CLASSIFYING SKY OBJECTS

Due to the large amounts of data being collected, a manual approach to classifying sky objects in the images is infeasible (it would require on the order of tens of man years). Existing computational methods for processing the images will preclude the identification of the majority of objects in each image since they are at levels too faint for traditional recognition algorithms or even manual inspection/analysis approaches. Our main goal is to provide an effective, objective, and examinable basis for classifying sky objects.

The photographic plates collected from the survey are being digitized at the Space Telescope Science Institute (STScI). This process will result in about 3,000 digital images of roughly $23{,}040^2$ pixels each. A digitized plate is subdivided into a set of partially overlapping frames. Each frame represents a small part of the plate that is small enough to be manipulated and processed conveniently. Figure 2 depicts the overall architecture of the SKICAT System. Low-level image processing and object separation is performed by a modified version of the FOCAS image processing software developed at Bell Labs [Jarv81,Vald82]. In addition to defining the objects in

[2] The Chi-square test is actually an approximation to Fisher's exact test when the number of test examples is large. We use Fisher's exact test because it is robust for small and large data sets.

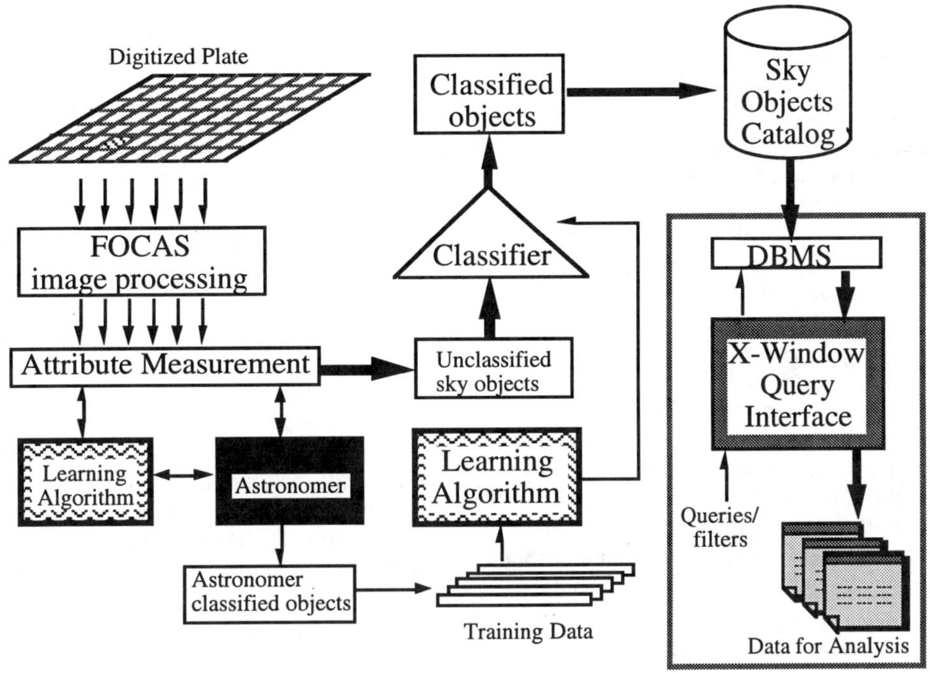

Figure 2. Architecture of the SKICAT System

each image, FOCAS also produces basic attributes describing each object. The discussion below will explain the loop in the bottom left-hand corner in which machine learning is employed in the attribute measurement process. The image processing steps detect contiguous pixels in the image that are to be grouped as one object. Attributes are then measured based on this segmentation.

An extra step in attribute measurement involves selecting a subset of the objects in the frame, designating them as being "sure-thing" stars, and fitting a point spread function (PSF) template to them by regression. The goal of this step is to define two normalized attributes called *resolution attributes*. These attributes are parameters of the PSF template and allow it to be fit to each sky object. The sure-thing stars are selected by the astronomer. They represent the "archetypal" stars in that image. Once the stars are selected, the template fitting and resolution parameter measurements are computed automatically. We refer to this problem as the *star selection subproblem.*

The total number of attributes measured for each object by SKICAT is 40. All steps are automated except for star selection and final sky object classification. The base-level attributes measured are generic quantities typically used in astronomical analyses [Vald82], they include:

isophotal magnitude	isophotal area
core magnitude	core luminosity
sky brightness	sky sigma (variance)
orientation	eccentricity (ellipticity)

Other quantities we measure include eight image moments: ir1, ir2, ir4, r1, r2, ixx, iyy, and ixy; the semi-major axis, and the semi-minor axis.

Once all attributes, including the resolution attributes, for each object are measured, final classification is performed for the purposes of the catalog. Our current goal is to classify objects into four major categories, following the original scheme in FOCAS: star (**s**), star with fuzz (**sf**), galaxy (**g**), and artifact (**long**). We may later refine the classification into more classes, however, classification into one of the four classes represents our initial goal.

3.1. CLASSIFYING FAINT OBJECTS AND THE USE OF CCD IMAGES

In addition to the scanned photographic plate, we have access to CCD images that span several small regions in some of the frames. CCD images are obtained from a separate telescope. The main advantage of a CCD image is higher resolution and signal-to-noise ratio at fainter levels. Hence, many of the objects that are too faint to be classified by inspection of a photographic plate, are easily classifiable in a CCD image. In addition to using these images for photometric calibration of the photographic plates, we make use of CCD images in two very important ways for the machine learning aspect:

1. CCD images enable us to obtain class labels for faint objects in the photographic plates.
2. CCD images provide us with the means to reliably evaluate the accuracy of the classifiers obtained from the decision tree learning algorithms.

Recall that the image processing package FOCAS provides the measurements for the base-level attributes (and the resolution attributes after star selection) for each object in the image. In order to produce a classifier that classifies faint objects correctly, the learning algorithm needs training data consisting of faint objects labeled with

Table 1. Summary of Results Using All Attributes

ID3		GID3*		O-Btree		RULER	
#rules	accuracy	#rules	accuracy	#rules	accuracy	#rules	accuracy
73	75.6%	58	90.1%	54	91.2%	45	94.2%

the appropriate class. The class label is therefore obtained by examining the CCD frames. Once trained on properly labeled objects, the learning algorithm produces a classifier that is capable of properly classifying objects based on the values of the attributes provided by FOCAS. Hence, in principle, the classifier will be able to classify objects in the photographic image that are simply too faint for an astronomer to classify by inspection. Using the class labels, the learning algorithms are basically being used to solve the more difficult problem of separating the classes in the multi-dimensional space defined by the set of attributes derived via image processing. This method is expected to allow us to classify objects that are at least one magnitude fainter than objects classified in photographic all-sky surveys to date.

3.2. CLASSIFICATION RESULTS

Starting with digitized frames obtained from a single digitized plate, we performed initial tests to evaluate the accuracy of the classifiers produced by the machine learning algorithms ID3, GID3*, and O-BTree. The data consisted of objects collected from four different plates from regions for which we had CCD image coverage (since this is data for which true accurate classifications are available). The learning algorithms are trained on a data set from 3 plates and tested on data from the remaining plate for cross validation. This estimates our accuracy in classifying objects across plates. Note that the plates cover different regions of the sky and that CCD frames cover multiple minute portions of each plate. The training data consisted of 1,688 objects that were classified manually by one of the authors (NW) by examining the corresponding CCD frames. It is noteworthy that for the majority of these objects, the astronomer would not be able to determine the classes by examining the corresponding survey (digitized photographic) images. All attributes used by the learning algorithms are derived from the survey images and not, of course, from the higher resolution CCD frames.

Using all the attributes, including the two resolution attributes derived after star selection, the classification results are shown in Table 1.

The results for RULER above are shown with O-Btree as the decision tree generation component and were obtained by cycling through tree generation and rule merging 10 times. Results Using GID3* as the tree generating component for RULER are similar. Using ID3 in the inner loop, however, the results were not as good: the accuracy in this case was only around 85%.

When the same experiments were conducted without using the *resolution scale* and *resolution fraction* attributes the results were significantly worse. The error rates jumped above 20% for O-BTree, above 25% for GID3*, and above 30% for ID3. The respective sizes of the trees grew significantly as well.

The initial results may be summarized as follows:

1. Algorithms GID3* and O-BTree produced significantly better trees than ID3.
2. Classification accuracy results of better than 90% were obtained when using two user-defined attributes: *resolution fraction* and *resolution scale*.
3. Classification results were not as reliable and stable if we exclude the two resolution attributes.

We took this as evidence that the resolution attributes are very important for the classification task. Hence we turned to addressing the star selection subproblem in order to automate step 6 above. Furthermore, the results point out that the GID3* and O-BTree learning algorithms are more appropriate than ID3 for the final classification task. As expected, the use of RULER resulted in improvement in performance.

3.3. AUTOMATING STAR SELECTION

Based on the initial results of the previous section, it was determined that using the resolution attributes is necessary since without them the error rates were significantly worse. We do not have the option of leaving star selection as a manual step in the process, since it is a time consuming task and will easily become the bottleneck in the system. We decided to use a machine learning approach to solve the star selection subproblem.

The star selection subproblem is a binary classification problem. Given a set of objects in an image, the goal is to classify them as sure-thing stars and non-sure-thing stars. Unlike the overall classification problem, the star selection problem turned out to be a much easier classification problem. The data objects from all three plates described above were classified manually by one of the authors (NW.) into *sure-stars*, *non-sure-stars*, and *unknowns*. The goal of the learning subproblem is to construct classifiers for selecting out sure-stars from any collection of sky objects. The results of applying the learning algorithms to the data sets described above, using only the basic set of attributes derived by FOCAS, gave the results shown in Table 2.

Table 2. Sure-star selection results.

ID3		GID3*		O-Btree	
#rules	accuracy	#rules	accuracy	#rules	accuracy
41	95%	35	97.3%	29	98.7%

In this case, using RULER with O-Btree did not change the results significantly. Note that a 98.7% accuracy rate on this subproblem is more than sufficient to indicate that this subproblem is essentially completely solved. Consequently, this allows us to automate all the steps in the plate processing and obtain an overall classification rate of better than 94% as shown in Table 1. One note about this learning subproblem: the results reflect the accuracy in selecting sure-thing stars and not the classification error rate. In other words, we only care about the performance in terms of sure-thing stars selected correctly. Sure-stars classified as galaxies or unknowns does not concern us since all we need is a subset of good stars to fit the PSF template to. Since this is not the main classification task, we only present the relevant performance aspects to avoid confusion.

In order to achieve stable classification accuracy results on classifying data from different plates, we had to spend some effort in defining normalized attributes that are less sensitive to plate-to-plate variation. It was determined that the base-level attributes such as area, background-sky-levels, and average intensity are image-dependent as well as object-dependent. It was also determined that a new set of user-defined attributes needed to be formulated. These attributes were to be computed automatically from the data, and are defined such that their values would be normalized across images and plates. A typical technique we used to derive such attributes is to derive non-linear curves in two dimensions defined by two of the base-level attributes and then define a new attribute to be the distance of each object in the 2-D plane to that curve. These quantities are ones that astronomers use, and many of them have physical interpretations.

It is beyond the scope of this paper to give the detailed definitions of these new attributes. As expected, defining the new "normalized" attributes raised our performance on both intra- and inter-plate classification to acceptable levels varying between 92% and 98% accuracy with an average of 94%. Note that without these derived attributes the cross-plate classification accuracy drops to 60%-80% levels when classifying data from different plates. Encoding of these attributes represents an implicit imparting of more domain knowledge to the learning algorithm.

3.4. Comparison with Neural Nets

In order to compare against other learning algorithms, and to preclude the possibility that a decision tree based approach is imposing *a priori* limitations on the achievable classification levels, we tested several neural network algorithms for comparison. The results indicate that neural network algorithms achieve similar, and sometimes worse performance than the decision trees. The neural net learning algorithms tested were:

1. traditional backpropagation,
2. conjugate gradient optimization, and
3. variable metric optimization.

Unlike backpropagation, the latter two training algorithms work in batch mode and use standard numerical optimization techniques in changing the network weights [Hert91]. They compute the weight adjustments simultaneously using matrix operations based on the total error of the network on the entire training set. Their main advantage over traditional backpropagation is the significant speed-up in training time.

The results can be summarized as follows: The performance of the neural networks was fairly unstable and produced accuracy levels varying between 30% (no convergence) and 95%. The most common range of accuracy on average was between 76% and 84%. Note that we had to perform multiple trials, each time varying:

1. the number of internal nodes in the hidden layer,
2. the initial network weight settings, and
3. the learning rate constant for backpropagation.

Upon examining the results of the empirical evaluation, we concluded that the neural net approach did not offer any clear advantages over the decision tree based learning algorithm. Although neural networks, with extensive training and several training restarts with different initial weights to avoid local minima, could match the performance of the decision tree classifier, the decision tree approach still holds several major advantages. The most important is that the tree is easy for domain experts to understand. In addition, unlike neural network learning algorithms, the decision tree learning algorithms GID3* and O-BTree do not require the specification of parameters such as the size of the neural net, the number of hidden layers, and random trials with different initial weight settings. Also, the required training time is orders of magnitude faster than the training time required for a neural network approach.

The stability of the performance of the decision tree algorithms, and the fact that a decision tree (or classification rule) is a lot easier to interpret and understand than a neural network, provided strong reasons for favouring the decision tree approach. We, therefore, decided to adopt the decision tree approach for our problem.

3.5. Verification & Reliability Estimates

As mentioned earlier, in addition to using the CCD frames to derive training data for the machine learning algorithms, we also use them to verify and estimate the performance of our classification technique. This is done by testing on data sets that are drawn independently from the training data. An additional source of internal consistency checks comes from the fact that the plates, and the frames within each plate are partially overlapping. Hence, objects inside the overlapping regions will be classified in more than one context. By measuring the rate of conflicting classifications, we can obtain further estimates of the statistical confidence in the accuracy of our classifier. For the purposes of the final catalog production, a method is being designed for resolving conflicts on objects within regions of overlap. We have not yet collected reportable results on this aspect of the problem.

In order to demonstrate the difficulty and significance of the classification results presented so far, consider the example shown in Figure 3. This figure shows four image patches each centered about a faint sky object that was classified by SKICAT. These images were obtained from a plate that was not provided to SKICAT in the

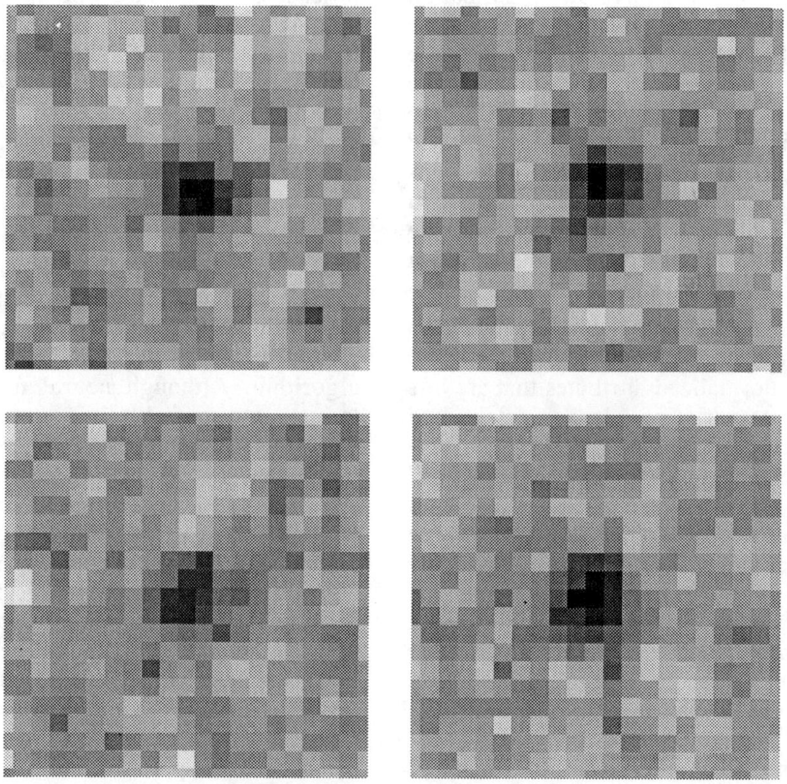

Figure 3. An illustrative example: four faint sky objects.

training cycle and the objects are part of a region in the sky containing the Abell 1551 cluster of galaxies near the North Galactic Pole. SKICAT classified the top two objects as stars and the bottom two as galaxies. According to astronomers (at least two of the authors), the objects shown in Figure 3 are too faint for reliable classification. As a matter of fact, an astronomer visually inspecting these images would be hard pressed to decide whether the object in the lower right hand corner is a star or galaxy. The object in the upper right hand corner appears as a galaxy based on visual inspection. Upon retrieving the corresponding higher resolution CCD images of these objects, it was clear that the SKICAT classification was indeed correct. Note that SKICAT produced the prediction based on the lower resolution survey images (shown in the figure). This example illustrates how the SKICAT classifier can correctly classify the majority of faint objects which even the astronomers cannot classify. Indeed, the results indicate that SKICAT performs this task with an accuracy better than 92% (for the faintest objects in the survey).

4. Conclusions and Future Work

In this paper, we gave a brief overview of the machine learning techniques we used for automating the sky object classification problem. SKICAT classifies objects that are at least one magnitude fainter than objects cataloged in previous surveys. This project represents a step towards the development of an objective, reliable automated sky object classification method.

The initial results of our effort to automate sky object classification in order to automatically reduce the images produced by POSS-II to sky catalogs are indeed very encouraging. We have exceeded our initial accuracy target of 90%. This level of accuracy is required for the data to be useful in testing or refuting theories on the formation of large structure in the universe and on other phenomena of interest to astronomers.

In addition to using machine learning techniques to automate classification, we used them to aid in the attribute measurement process. Since measurement of the resolution attributes requires interaction with the user in selecting sure-thing stars for template fitting, we used the same machine learning approach to automate the star selection process. By defining additional "normalized" image-independent attributes, we were able to obtain high accuracy classifiers for star selection within and across photographic plates. This in turn allows us to automate the computation of the powerful resolution attributes for each object in an image.

Final object classification will be, to some extent, also a matter of scientific choice. While objects in every catalog will contain a classification entry, all of the object attributes will be recorded as well. One could therefore reclassify any portion of the survey using alternative criteria better suited to a particular scientific goal (e.g. star catalogs vs. galaxy catalogs). The catalogs will also accommodate additional attribute entries, in the event other pixel-based measurements are deemed necessary. An important feature of the survey analysis system will be to facilitate such detailed interactions with the catalogs. The catalog generated by SKICAT will eventually contain about a billion entries representing hundreds of millions of sky objects. Unlike the traditional notion of a static printed catalog, we view our effort as targeting the development of a new generation of scientific analysis tools that render it possible to have a constantly evolving, improving, and growing catalog. Without the availability of these tools for the first survey (POSS-I) conducted over 4 decades ago, no objective and comprehensive analysis of the data was possible. In contrast, we are targeting a comprehensive sky catalog that will be available on-line for the use of the scientific community.

As part of our plans for the future we plan to begin investigation of the applicability of unsupervised learning (clustering) techniques such as AUTOCLASS [Chee88] to the problem of discovering clusters or groupings of interesting objects. The initial goals will be to answer the following two questions:

1. Are the classes of sky objects used currently by astronomers justified by the data: do they naturally arise in the data?
2. Are there other classes of objects that astronomers were not aware of because of the difficulty of dealing with high dimensional spaces defined by the various attributes?

The longer term goal is to evaluate the utility of unsupervised learning techniques as an aid for the types of analyses astronomers conduct after objects have been classified into known classes. Typically, astronomers examine the various distributions of different types of objects to test existing astrophysical models. Armed with prior knowledge about properties of interesting clusters of sky objects, a clustering system can search through catalog entries and point out potentially interesting object clusters to astronomers. This will help astronomers catch important patterns in the data that may otherwise go unnoticed due to the sheer size of the data volumes.

ACKNOWLEDGMENTS

We thank the Sky Survey team for their expertise and effort in acquiring the plate material. The POSS-II is funded by grants from Eastman Kodak Co., The National Geographic Society, The Samuel Oschin Foundation, NSF Grants AST 84-08225 and AST 87-19465, and NASA Grants NGL 05002140 and NAGW 1710. We thank Joe Roden of JPL for help on evaluating the performance of the learning algorithms. This work was supported by a NSF graduate fellowship (NW), Caltech President's Fund, NASA contract NAS5-31348 (SD& NW), and the NSF PYI Award AST-9157412 (SD).

The work described in this paper was carried out in part by the Jet Propulsion Laboratory, California Institute of Technology, under a contract with the National Aeronautics and Space Administration.

REFERENCES

[Brei84] Breiman, L., Friedman, J.H., Olshen, R.A., and Stone, C.J. (1984). Classification and Regression Trees. Monterey, CA: Wadsworth & Brooks.

[Chee88] Cheeseman, P. et al (1988) "Bayesian Classification." *Proc. of the 7th Nat. Conf. on Artificial Intelligence AAAI-88*, pp. 607-6611, Saint Paul, MN.

[Chen88] Cheng, J., Fayyad, U.M., Irani, K.B. and Qian, Z. (1999) "Improved Decision Trees: A gegneralized version of ID3" *Proc. of the 5th Int. Conf. on Machine Learning*. pp. 100-107. Morgan Kauffman.

[Chen90] Cheng, J., Fayyad, U.M., Irani, K.B. and Qian, Z. (1990) "Applications of machine learning techniques in semiconductor manufacturing." *Proceedings of the SPIE Conference on Applications of Artificial Intelligence VIII.* pp. 956-965, Orlando, Fl.

[Feig81] Feigenbaum, E.A. (1981) "Expert systems in the 1980s." In Bond, A. (Ed.) *State of The Art Report on Machine Intelligence.* Maidenhead: Pergamon-Infotech.

[Fayy90] Fayyad, U.M. and Irani, K.B. (1990). "What should be minimized in a decision tree?" *Proceedings of Eighth National Conference on Artificial Intelligence AAAI-90*, Boston, MA.

[Fayy91] Fayyad, U.M. (1991). *On the Induction of Decision Trees for Multiple Concpt Learning*. PhD Dissertation, EECS Dept. The University of Michigan.

[Fayy92a] Fayyad, U.M. and Irani, K.B. (1992) "On the handling of continuous-valued attributes in decision tree generation." *Machine Learning,* vol.8, no.2.

[Fayy92b] Fayyad, U.M. and Irani, K.B. (1992) "The attribute selection problem in decision tree generation." Proceeedings of the Tenth National Conference on Artificial Intelligence, AAAI-92. San Jose, CA.

[Fayy93] Fayyad, U.M. and Irani, K.B. "Multi-interval discretization of continuous-valued attributes for classification learning." *Proc. of the 13h International Joint Conference on Arificial Intelligence IJCAI-93.* Chambery, France: Morgan Kauffman.

[Finn63] Finney, D.J. , Latscha, R., Bennett, B.M., and Hsu, P. (1963). *Tables for Testing Significance in a 2x2 Contingency Table.* Cambridge: Cambridge University Press.

[Hert91] J. Hertz, A. Krogh, and R.G. Palmer (1991) *Introduction to the Theory of Neural Computation.* Reading, MA: Addison-Wesley.

[Jarv81] Jarvis, J. and Tyson, A. (1981) *Astronomical Journal* 86:41.

[Quin86] Quinlan, J.R. (1986) "The induction of decision trees." *Machine Learning* vol. 1, no. 1.

[Quin90] Quinlan, J.R. (1990) "Probabilistic decision trees." *Machine Learning: An Artificial Intelligence Approach vol. III.* Y. Kodratoff & R. Michalski (eds.) San Mateo, CA: Morgan Kaufmann.

[Reid91] Reid, I.N. et al (1991) "The scond Palomar sky survey" *Publications of the Astronomical Society of the Pacific*, vol. 103, no.665.

[Vald82] Valdes (1982) *Instrumentation in Astronomy IV*, SPIE vol. 331, no. 465.

[Weir92] Weir, N. Djorgovski, S.G., Fayyad, U. et al (1992) "SKICAT: A system for the scientific analysis of the Palomar-STScI Digital Sky Survey." *Proc. of Astronomy from Large databases II*, p. 509, Munich, Germany: European Southern Observatory.

Learning From Entailment: An Application to Propositional Horn Sentences

Michael Frazier
Department of Computer Science
University of Illinois
Urbana, IL 61801

Leonard Pitt
Department of Computer Science
University of Illinois
Urbana, IL 61801

Abstract

Let φ be an unknown theory. Can φ be efficiently inferred given examples of statements that φ entails and statements that φ does not entail? It is shown that if φ is a propositional Horn sentence, then φ can be efficiently learned in this model when the entailed statements are also Horn sentences. An application of the learning algorithm to the area of approximate entailment is discussed.

1 INTRODUCTION

A central goal in computational learning theory has been determining which types of boolean formulas may be efficiently inferred given only satisfying assignments (positive examples) and falsifying assignments (negative examples) of the unknown formula. A motivating viewpoint is that some unknown concept (for example, that of an elephant) may be expressed as a boolean formula of a particular form defined over variables which denote real-world attributes. For example, the formula *large* $\wedge$ *grey* $\wedge$ *has-trunk* $\wedge$ *eats-peanuts* might represent exactly the set of all elephants, to the extent that an assignment to the above boolean variables represents an elephant if and only if it satisfies the conjunction. In essence, the concept learning problem considers the denotation of a formula to be its set of satisfying instances, and the goal is to determine, from example instances, which unseen instances are in the denotation, and which are not. Call this type of learning *learning from examples.*

A related problem is obtained if we consider the denotation of a formula φ_* to be not its set of satisfying instances, but rather the set of formulas α such that φ_* entails α. Here an unknown formula ϕ_* may be viewed as a theory about the world, and positive examples α will be statements which follow from the theory. For example, if the theory contained the implications "large mobile things can crush you", "elephants are large things", and "elephants are mobile", then a positive example would be the entailed sentence "elephants can crush you", a fact one might wish to know if living near elephants.

The related learning problem is whether an unknown formula may be efficiently inferred from examples of statements that it entails and statements that it does not entail. Continuing with our example, we would hope to construct a theory about the world containing assertions such as "elephants are mobile" and "elephants are large things" given entailed assertions such as "elephants can crush you". Call this type of learning *learning from entailment.* This problem is central in a number of areas, including expert system design (build a knowledge base from example real-world facts) and logic programming (synthesize a Prolog program from example input/output behavior).

In recent years there have been numerous interesting results in the area of concept learning from examples (see annual proceedings from *Workshop on Computational Learning Theory*). These results were catalyzed by the introduction of reasonable formal definitions of efficient concept learning ([Valiant, 1984; Angluin, 1987]), and the development of techniques for constructing efficient learning algorithms and proving their correctness. In contrast, there has been relatively little work that applies these new definitions and techniques to the problem of learning from entailment (but see Section 2). In this paper we describe the problem of learning from entailment formally and present a polynomial-time algorithm that can learn an unknown propositional Horn sentence φ_* by posing certain natural queries to a teacher.

In particular, we consider the following learning protocol: Some propositional Horn sentence T_* is chosen and is unknown to the learner. The learning algorithm may ask two types of questions: An *equivalence query* is a Horn sentence H hypothesized by the learner. If H is logically equivalent to T_*, then the learner is told that he is correct, and the task is completed. Otherwise, a *counterexample* Horn clause C is returned, where C is entailed by either T_* or H but not both. A *membership query* is a Horn clause C proposed by the learner, and the answer is either "yes" or "no", depending on whether T_* entails C.

We prove the following:

Theorem 1 *Let T_* be any propositional Horn sentence over n variables. The algorithm LRN (figure 1), using equivalence queries and membership queries (of entailed clauses) answered with respect to the unknown formula T_*, halts in time polynomial in n and the size*[1] *of T_*, and outputs a Horn sentence H that is logically equivalent to T_*.*

More briefly, we'll say that LRN exactly learns the class of Horn sentences from entailment, using equivalence and membership queries. This learning model is, with one important exception, Angluin's standard, well-investigated model of exact learning from equivalence queries and membership queries ([Angluin, 1987]). The difference is that here the examples queried by the learner and the counterexamples to the learner's hypotheses are not assignments to the variables which may or may not satisfy T_*, but rather are Horn clauses which may or may not be entailed by T_*.

1.1 PAC–LEARNING

While it may seem unnatural to assume the learner has counterexamples to queried hypotheses available on demand, by applying standard transformations to a learning algorithm in the model of learning from examples (respectively, learning from entailment), we can obtain a learning algorithm (from examples (respectively, from entailment)) in Valiant's distribution-free, "probably approximately correct" (PAC), learning model ([Valiant, 1984]). Thus, as an immediate consequence of Theorem 1, there exists a PAC-variant of algorithm LRN (call it LRN-PAC), which asks membership queries, and receives clauses randomly chosen from an arbitrary unknown distribution, labeled as to whether they are entailed by an arbitrary unknown Horn sentence T_*. Further, LRN-PAC outputs a Horn sentence H that with high probability will accurately predict which clauses drawn from the same distribution are entailed by T_*. The running time of LRN-PAC is polynomial in the number of variables, the size of T_*, and other natural parameters.

1.2 ON–LINE LEARNING WITH BOUNDED MISTAKES

Algorithm LRN may also be used (with only minor modification) in an on-line learning setting, and will be guaranteed to make at most a polynomial number of predictive mistakes. As an illustration, consider an expert's apprentice trying to obtain the expert's knowledge which is representable as a propositional Horn sentence. The apprentice maintains some hypothesis, and uses it to predict facts (clauses) about the world. On occasion, the apprentice discovers an erroneous prediction. The apprentice discusses the error (counterexample) with the expert by making a number of membership queries about related clauses, and revises the hypothesis. Using algorithm LRN, the time to update each hypothesis is a polynomial in the number of variables and in the size of the smallest Horn sentence equivalent to the expert's theory. Further, the number of predictive errors that can ever occur *regardless of the sequence of presented clauses* is similarly bounded by such a polynomial.

1.3 MEMBERSHIP QUERIES ARE NECESSARY

We have shown[2] that in any of the above settings (exact learning with equivalence queries, PAC-learning, or on-line learning with bounded mistakes), that if the learner does not have access to membership queries, then the problem of learning Horn theories from entailment is as hard as that of learning arbitrary propositional conjunctive normal form formulas (CNF) (from examples) in the PAC setting without membership queries, which remains a central open problem in learning theory (even *with* membership queries). This suggests that the membership queries are necessary.

1.4 APPROXIMATE ENTAILMENT

Let T_* be a known theory. In general, we would like to answer questions of the sort "Is α entailed by T_*?" Depending on T_* and α, the general question can be undecidable, or at least computationally intractable. Consequently, several researchers have grappled recently with the notion of *approximate* entailment. Rather than answering questions of entailment about the actual theory T_* and query α, Dalal and Etherington propose answering questions of entailment about a variety of strengthenings and weakenings of T_* and α ([Dalal and Etherington, 1992]). They note that soundness or completeness or both can be lost under this protocol. Still, certain combinations of their strengthenings and weakenings do preserve either soundness or completeness and permit the question of entailment for queries to be answered efficiently.

Kautz and Selman construct a protocol in which soundness and completeness are preserved even at the expense of categoricity (i.e., some questions of entailment might be answered "I don't know") ([Selman and Kautz, 1991; Kautz and Selman, 1992]). Specifically, they consider the case where T_* is a propositional CNF theory and suggest approximating T_* by choosing as

[1] The size of a Horn sentence is the number of symbols needed to write the Horn sentence.

[2] The proof is available from the authors by email.

an upper bound the unique strongest Horn sentence entailed by T_* and choosing as a lower bound a weakest Horn sentence which entails T_*. Any Horn clause entailed by the upper bound is also entailed by T_*, and any Horn clause not entailed by the lower bound is not entailed by T_*. Further, since these bounds are Horn sentences, questions of entailment are efficiently answerable for a large class of formulas. They note that the upper bound, while unique, in some cases is exponentially larger than the actual CNF theory T_*. Similarly they note that the lower bound, while never much larger than T_*, is not necessarily unique.

Greiner and Schuurmans also use the idea of upper bounding and lower bounding a known CNF theory T_* with Horn sentences ([Greiner and Schuurmans, 1992]). They, however, demand that the upper bound be small. Rather than finding the unique Horn least upper bound (which may be large), they attempt to find, via hill-climbing, a small Horn upper bound that performs optimally at predicting questions about entailment among all Horn upper bounds that are "similar".

Current attempts to construct the Horn least upper bound have a "generate and test" flavor to them – Horn clauses are "generated", and are "tested" by determining (via resolution) whether or not the CNF theory entails the clause. If so, they are included in the Horn least upper bound.

One problem which arises is that even in cases where the Horn least upper bound is small, there seems to be no guarantee that the number of clauses tested is small.[3] Hence, the number of applications of a possibly exponential time resolution procedure might be much larger than the size of the smallest representation of the Horn least upper bound. Ideally, we would like to derive a Horn least upper bound from a CNF theory in time polynomial in the size of the Horn least upper bound. Although we cannot do this, in section 4 we show how algorithm LRN can be used to "lazily" construct a Horn least upper bound of a known CNF theory when queries about entailment are received in an on-line setting and periodically we are informed of some error in our entailment prediction. Further, the number of appeals to a potentially exponential-time resolution procedure is bounded by a polynomial in the size of the smallest representation of the Horn least upper bound, and the particular expression for the Horn least upper bound that is found is also at most polynomially larger than the best such expression.

[3]It is an easy task to construct a small CNF theory that has a small Horn least upper bound but has an exponential number of entailed Horn clauses.

2 RELATED WORK

This work is most closely related to the work of Angluin et al., that constructs an algorithm for learning Horn sentences from satisfying assignments ([Angluin et al., 1992]). The current algorithm is in fact an application of their algorithm, but with a number of twists. Though we do not show the formal transformation here, it is possible to decouple these twists from the current algorithm and learn using their algorithm as a black box[4]. The main ideas in the current algorithm and proof are the same as in their work, but some tricks were needed to overcome a few difficulties. The result is, in fact, a learning algorithm for a different learning problem. Their examples may be thought of as complete conjuncts (or fundamental products) that are labeled as entailing or not entailing the target. Here we do not care about such examples at all, rather our examples are Horn clauses that are labeled as being entailed or not being entailed *by* the target. As with their work, our algorithm learns propositional Horn sentences in time polynomial in the size of sentence to be learned.

Work in [Angluin, 1988] is also closely related to our work. There Angluin describes an algorithm for learning acyclic propositional Horn sentences (a proper subset of propositional Horn sentences) that uses *request for hint* queries. These queries are similar to our membership queries in that the learner presents a Horn clause and is told whether the clause is entailed. In the event the clause is entailed, the learner is either (1) told that the clause is subsumed by some clause in the target, or (2) given one of the variables (not in the learner's clause) that must be shown to be true on the way to showing that the variable in the consequent of the learner's clause is true. Thus, although related to our membership queries, her queries are stronger and therefore give a weaker result. Indeed, Angluin leaves

[4]The transformation involves constructing two polynomial time algorithms that use membership queries and equivalence queries to act as oracles for their algorithm HORN – one to answer the membership queries of the type asked by HORN and one to answer the equivalence queries of the type asked by HORN. The task accomplished by each algorithm is essentially converting between examples of the type available (which are clauses entailed by exactly one of the target and the current hypothesis) and the type used by HORN (which are variable assignments satisfying exactly one of the target and the current hypothesis). The technique is (1) set all variables in the antecedent of the counterexample clause to **true** then (2a) if the counterexample clause is entailed by the target, inspect the current hypothesis to compute the minimal model of the current hypothesis with these variables **true** (this will be a negative counterexample for HORN), otherwise (2b) the counterexample clause is entailed by the current hypothesis, so use membership queries to compute the minimal model of the target with these variables **true** (this will be a positive counterexample for HORN).

open the question that our work closes.

Other authors have looked at examples entailed by first-order formulas. For example, Page and Frisch look at atoms labeled according to whether they are entailed by a hidden first order formula ([Page and Frisch, 1992]). Their work examines more the effect of multiple occurrences of a variable in the hidden theory and less the effect of connectives in the hidden theory. Our work also uses entailment as the means of labeling examples. However, we use entailed examples to learn propositional formulas where the connectives play a significant role within the hidden formula as well as within the examples themselves.

There are some less closely related first-order results from the field of inductive logic programming where the target is a Prolog program. Shapiro describes a system for learning Prolog programs *in the limit* (ie, time is an unbounded resource) using atoms entailed by the program to be learned ([Shapiro, 1983]). Also, Džeroski et al. describe an algorithm that learns k-clause, determinate, function-free, first-order Horn clauses with bounded depth variables by transforming the target into a propositional monotone k-term DNF formula ([Džeroski et al., 1992]).

LRN()

1. **approxAnts** $= \emptyset$
2. **hypoth** $= \emptyset$
3. while **hypoth** is not equivalent to the target, let C be the counterexample returned by the equivalence oracle
   (a) $\tilde{\alpha} = \{\beta : \textbf{hypoth} \models (\text{ant}(C) \rightarrow \beta)\}$
   (b) if $\exists \alpha \in$ **approxAnts** such that
      - $\alpha \cap \tilde{\alpha} \subset \alpha$
      - $\text{RHS}(\alpha \cap \tilde{\alpha}) \neq \emptyset$

      i. then replace the first such α in **approxAnts** by $\alpha \cap \tilde{\alpha}$
      ii. else append $\tilde{\alpha}$ to **approxAnts**
   (c) **hypoth** $= \{\alpha \rightarrow \beta : \alpha \in \text{approxAnts}, \beta \in \text{RHS}(\alpha)\}$
4. return **hypoth**

RHS(α)

1. return $\{v : v \notin \alpha \text{ or } v = \textbf{false}, \boldsymbol{\in}(\alpha \rightarrow v)\}$

Figure 1: The algorithm LRN learns Horn sentences from entailment.

3 THE ALGORITHM

Throughout the paper, α (and any variation of α) is a (possibly empty) conjunction of propositional variables. We will frequently treat α as a set; in the case that α is empty, its conjunction represents the logical constant **true**. Throughout the paper, β (and any variation of β) represents a set of at most one propositional variable; in the case the β is empty, it is understood to represent the logical constant **false**. A *propositional Horn clause* is a formula of the form $\alpha \rightarrow \beta$; we refer to α as the *antecedent* of the clause and to β as the *consequent*. A *propositional Horn sentence* is a conjunction of propositional Horn clauses.

We use the boldface $\boldsymbol{\in}$ to denote a membership query and the non-boldface $\in$ for normal set membership. As is standard, we use $\models$ to denote logical entailment and use $\cap$ and $\subset$ for set intersection and *proper* subset, respectively. The algorithm LRN is shown in figure 1.

Two crucial properties of LRN are (1) that LRN keeps a monotonically growing sequence of antecedents **approxAnts** that provide clues about distinct clauses of the target and (2) that LRN provides increasingly better approximations as to the identity of these clauses. The current hypothesis **hypoth** is constructed from the antecedents comprising **approxAnts** by asking for each of these antecedents which consequents are supported by the target (line 3c). Upon receiving an equivalence query counterexample C (line 3), LRN computes the (unique) minimal model of **hypoth** satisfying the antecedent of C (line 3a) and tries to use this minimal model to chip away excess variables in some antecedent in **approxAnts** (line 3(b)i). If this attempt fails, LRN appends this minimal model to **approxAnts** as the initial approximation to the antecedent of some clause of the target for which no information (in the form of a counterexample) has yet been provided (line 3(b)ii).

Before arguing that LRN is correct and runs efficiently, we need the following supporting definition and lemma.

Definition 2 *If ϕ is a satisfiable formula, ψ is a falsifiable formula, and $\phi \models \psi$, then ϕ is said to entail ψ* non-trivially.

Lemma 3 *Let T be a Horn sentence. If $T \models (\alpha \rightarrow \beta)$ non-trivially, then α is a superset of the antecedent of some clause of T.*

Proof: If T contains some clause with an empty antecedent then the lemma holds vacuously.

For the case when T contains no clauses with empty antecedent, suppose by way of contradiction that the lemma does not hold. Make all variables in α **true** and all other variables **false**. (Since $\alpha \rightarrow \beta$ is falsifiable, this assignment falsifies it.) Now notice that since by supposition no antecedent in T is contained in α, at least one variable in each antecedent of T is **false**, thus every antecedent in T is **false**, and so T must be satisfied. Therefore $T \not\models \alpha \rightarrow \beta$, a contradiction.

□

Naming the hidden target Horn theory T_*, we will now argue correctness and efficiency.

Lemma 4 *At all times during the run of LRN,* $T_* \models$ **hypoth**.

Proof: The subroutine RHS is used to explicitly check that each clause of **hypoth** is entailed by T_*. A clause $\alpha \rightarrow \beta$ is placed in **hypoth** only if $\beta \in \text{RHS}(\alpha)$ (line 3c). This can only occur if $\in(\alpha \rightarrow \beta)$, hence $T* \models (\alpha \rightarrow \beta)$. Since T_* entails every clause of **hypoth**, $T_* \models$ **hypoth**. □

Corollary 5 *Any counterexample to* **hypoth** *with respect to* T_* *must be entailed by* T_* *but not by* **hypoth**.

Notice that we can easily determine whether the target is unsatisfiable by first making an equivalence query on an unsatisfiable Horn sentence, so for expository purposes we henceforth assume that the target is satisfiable. Also, if the target is a tautology then the first equivalence query made by LRN will be correct, so we henceforth also assume that the target is falsifiable. Finally, under these assumptions, since the counterexamples obtained by equivalence queries (line 3) are entailed by exactly one of two satisfiable Horn sentences, counterexample clauses are neither unfalsifiable nor unsatisfiable.

Lemma 6 *If* $\alpha \rightarrow \beta$ *is any counterexample of* **hypoth** *with respect to* T_**, then there is some clause* $\alpha_* \rightarrow \beta_*$ *of* T_* *such that* $\alpha_* \subseteq \alpha$ *and* $\beta_* \notin \alpha$.

Proof: By corollary 5, $T_* \models (\alpha \rightarrow \beta)$ and **hypoth** $\not\models (\alpha \rightarrow \beta)$. Because **hypoth** $\not\models (\alpha \rightarrow \beta)$, $\alpha \rightarrow \beta$ must be falsifiable. Consider the variable assignment that makes α **true** and makes all other variables **false**; this assignment falsifies $\alpha \rightarrow \beta$. Since $T_* \models \alpha \rightarrow \beta$ this assignment must falsify T_*. But T_* is falsified if and only if some clause $\alpha_* \rightarrow \beta_*$ of T_* is falsified. But this assignment falsifies $\alpha_* \rightarrow \beta_*$ if and only if $\alpha_* \subseteq \alpha$ and $\beta_* \notin \alpha$. □

The following lemma shows that no matter what counterexample LRN receives from the equivalence oracle, the antecedent that LRN actually uses to modify **approxAnts** is the antecedent of a (possibly different) counterexample.

Lemma 7 *If* $\alpha \rightarrow \beta$ *is a counterexample returned to LRN by the equivalence query oracle in line 3, then the* $\tilde{\alpha}$ *computed in line 3a is such that* $\tilde{\alpha} \rightarrow \beta$ *is also a counterexample.*

Proof: By corollary 5, $T_* \models (\alpha \rightarrow \beta)$ and **hypoth** $\not\models (\alpha \rightarrow \beta)$. Clearly $\tilde{\alpha}$ contains α, thus $T_* \models (\tilde{\alpha} \rightarrow \beta)$. We now show that if **hypoth** $\models (\tilde{\alpha} \rightarrow \beta)$, then **hypoth** $\models (\alpha \rightarrow \beta)$.

Suppose that **hypoth** $\models (\tilde{\alpha} \rightarrow \beta)$. Let e be any variable assignment that satisfies **hypoth**. If e does not satisfy α, then e satisfies $\alpha \rightarrow \beta$. On the other hand, if e does satisfy α then, since e satisfies **hypoth**, by construction e also satisfies $\tilde{\alpha}$. Since **hypoth** $\models (\tilde{\alpha} \rightarrow \beta)$ and since e satisfies **hypoth** and $\tilde{\alpha}$, e must satisfy β. But then e satisfies $\alpha \rightarrow \beta$. Thus **hypoth** $\models (\alpha \rightarrow \beta)$.

But **hypoth** $\not\models (\alpha \rightarrow \beta)$. Thus **hypoth** $\not\models (\tilde{\alpha} \rightarrow \beta)$. Therefore, $\tilde{\alpha} \rightarrow \beta$ is a counterexample to **hypoth** with respect to T_*. □

We want to show that **hypoth** is becoming increasingly closer to T_*; to do this we have the following definition which will help describe how far **hypoth** is from T_*.

Definition 8 *For* $\alpha \in$ **approxAnts**, *we say that* α properly covers *a clause* $\alpha_* \rightarrow \beta_*$ *if* $\alpha_* \subseteq \alpha$ *and* $\beta_* \notin \alpha$

We are now prepared to state and prove our main lemma.

Lemma 9 *If* α_1 *and* α_2 *are antecedents in distinct positions of the sequence* **approxAnts**, *then* α_1 *and* α_2 *each properly cover some clause of* T_**, but* α_1 *and* α_2 *do not properly cover the same clause of* T_*.

Proof: First observe that for every α in **approxAnts** there is some β such that $T_* \models (\alpha \rightarrow \beta)$. This is because line 3(b)i only replaces an element of **approxAnts** if the replacement, $\alpha \cap \tilde{\alpha}$, is such that $T_* \models (\alpha \cap \tilde{\alpha}) \rightarrow \beta$ for some β. On the other hand, line 3(b)ii simply appends the antecedent of the (possibly implicit (lemma 7)) counterexample constructed in line 3. But by corollary 5, this counterexample is entailed by T_*. Since every α, when placed in **approxAnts**, was a counterexample to **hypoth**, every α is the antecedent of some clause that is nontrivially entailed by T_*. Thus, by lemma 3, every α in **approxAnts** properly covers some clause of T_*. Hence α_1 properly covers some clause of T_* and α_2 properly covers some clause of T_*.

We now show that the clauses properly covered by α_1 and α_2 are different. Suppose not and consider the first iteration of the main loop in which this property fails to hold. Let α_1 and α_2 be two elements of **approxAnts** that properly cover the same clause $\alpha_* \rightarrow \beta_*$ of T_*. Without loss of generality, assume that this iteration of the main loop caused α_2 to appear in **approxAnts**. There are two ways in which this iteration could place α_2 in **approxAnts** – either α_2 was appended to **approxAnts** or α_2 was the result of intersecting $\tilde{\alpha}$ with some α_2' that was in **approxAnts** in the previous iteration of the loop.

In the former case, since α_1 and α_2 (which is actually $\tilde{\alpha}$) both properly cover $\alpha_* \rightarrow \beta_*$, $\alpha_1 \cap \tilde{\alpha}$ properly covers $\alpha_* \rightarrow \beta_*$, thus $\beta_* \in \text{RHS}(\alpha_1 \cap \tilde{\alpha})$ and so $\text{RHS}(\alpha_1 \cap \tilde{\alpha}) \neq \emptyset$. Thus, for LRN not to have used $\tilde{\alpha}$ to replace α_1 in **approxAnts**, it must be that $\alpha_1 \cap \tilde{\alpha} = \alpha_1$. But, since α_1 properly covers $\alpha_* \rightarrow \beta_*$, $\beta_* \in \text{RHS}(\alpha_1)$, and since α_1 was in **approxAnts** when **hypoth** was constructed for this iteration **hypoth** contains $\alpha_1 \rightarrow \beta_*$. Thus $\beta_* \in \tilde{\alpha}$, contradicting the assumption that $\tilde{\alpha}$ properly covers $\alpha_* \rightarrow \beta_*$. Thus, $\tilde{\alpha}$ could not have been appended to `approxAnts`.

In the latter case, where $\tilde{\alpha}$ was used to refine some antecedent already in `approxAnts`, we have that $\alpha_2 = \tilde{\alpha} \cap \alpha'_2$ where α'_2 is some element of `approxAnts` in the preceding iteration of the loop. Either α_1 precedes α_2 in `approxAnts`, or α_1 follows α_2 in `approxAnts`.

Consider the case in which α_1 precedes α_2 in `approxAnts`. If $\alpha'_2 \cap \tilde{\alpha}$ properly covers α_*, then either α'_2 properly covers $\alpha_* \rightarrow \beta_*$ or $\tilde{\alpha}$ properly covers $\alpha_* \rightarrow \beta_*$. But if α'_2 properly covered $\alpha_* \rightarrow \beta_*$, then the inductive hypothesis is violated because α_1 and α'_2 properly covered the same clause in the previous iteration. Thus, it must be the case that $\tilde{\alpha}$ properly covers $\alpha_* \rightarrow \beta_*$. Since LRN did not use $\tilde{\alpha}$ to refine α_1, it must be the case that $\tilde{\alpha} \cap \alpha_1 = \alpha_1$. But, in this case $\alpha_1 \subseteq \tilde{\alpha}$ and since α_1 properly covers $\alpha_* \rightarrow \beta_*$, then $\beta_* \in \text{RHS}(\alpha_1)$, and since α_1 was in S when **hypoth** was formed for this iteration, $\beta_* \in \tilde{\alpha}$, contradicting the assumption that $\tilde{\alpha}$ properly covers $\alpha_* \rightarrow \beta_*$.

Lastly consider the case where α_1 follows α_2 in `approxAnts`, in which case LRN did not try to refine α_1 with $\tilde{\alpha}$. If $\alpha'_2 \cap \tilde{\alpha}$ properly covers $\alpha_* \rightarrow \beta_*$ then either α'_2 properly covered $\alpha_* \rightarrow \beta_*$ or $\tilde{\alpha}$ properly covered $\alpha_* \rightarrow \beta_*$. If α'_2 properly covered $\alpha_* \rightarrow \beta_*$, then the inductive hypothesis is violated because in the previous iteration α_1 and α'_2 properly covered the same clause. Thus it must be the case that $\tilde{\alpha}$ properly covers $\alpha_* \rightarrow \beta_*$, that $\alpha_* \subseteq \alpha'_2$, and that $\beta_* \in \alpha'_2$; otherwise, $\alpha'_2 \cap \tilde{\alpha}$ could not properly cover $\alpha_* \rightarrow \beta_*$ and yet have α'_2 not properly cover $\alpha_* \rightarrow \beta_*$. Now by assumption α_1 properly covers $\alpha_* \rightarrow \beta_*$. Consider all antecedents used by LRN to create or refine (by intersection) the position in `approxAnts` currently occupied by α_1. Since $\alpha_* \subseteq \alpha_1$, every antecedent used by LRN in the position currently occupied by α_1 must have contained α_*. Further, since α_1 does not contain β_*, one of these antecedents must not have contained β_*. Call the first such antecedent $\tilde{\alpha}'$. Now observe that since α_2 contains both α_* and β_*, we know that every antecedent that has occupied the position currently occupied by α'_2 must have contained α_* and β_*. But then for every such predecessor, α''_2, of α'_2 we have that $\alpha''_2 \cap \tilde{\alpha}'$ is a proper subset of α''_2 because α''_2 contains β_* but $\tilde{\alpha}'$ does not. Further, because $\text{RHS}(\alpha''_2 \cap \tilde{\alpha}')$ properly covers $\alpha_* \rightarrow \beta$ we have that $\beta_* \in \text{RHS}(\alpha'_2 \cap \tilde{\alpha}')$, and therefore $\text{RHS}(\alpha'_2 \cap \tilde{\alpha}')$ is non-empty. This contradicts the assumption that $\tilde{\alpha}'$ was used to refine the position currently occupied by α_1.

Thus the antecedents in `approxAnts` properly cover distinct clauses of T_*. □

We now state our main theorem.

Theorem 10 *Let V be a finite set of propositional variables. The class of Horn formulas using only variables from V is polynomial time learnable from entailed examples using equivalence and membership queries.*

Proof: (Sketch) It is easily verified that each step in the `while` loop of LRN takes time at most polynomial in $|V|$ and size of the unknown Horn formula. We need only argue that there are only polynomially many iterations of the loop.

By lemma 9, every antecedent in `approxAnts` properly covers some antecedent in T_* and no two antecedents in `approxAnts` properly cover the same antecedent of T_*. Thus `approxAnts` never contains more elements than there are clauses in T_*. Furthermore, LRN never deletes any element of `approxAnts`, at worst it replaces some element of `approxAnts` by a proper subset of that element. This can happen at most as many times as there are variables in V. □

We immediately have the following corollaries.

Corollary 11 *Let V be a finite set of propositional variables. The class of Horn formulas using only variables from V is polynomial time learnable using examples and membership queries using Horn sentences as examples.*

Proof: (Sketch) At least one Horn clause of a counterexample Horn sentence must be suitable as counterexample for LRN. □

4 APPLICATION TO APPROXIMATE ENTAILMENT

We return to the problem of finding the Horn least upper bound of a known CNF theory, which was discussed in the introduction. Even when the Horn least upper bound for some theory is small, current methods do not guarantee that a small least upper bound will be found without post-processing the set of entailed Horn clauses found with an algorithm such as that in [Angluin et al., 1992]. Such an approach does not lessen the number of resolution proofs needed in the first place to obtain the set of entailed clauses.

By Lemma 9 algorithm LRN will never hypothesize a Horn sentence having more distinct antecedents than the target Horn sentence; it follows that LRN will never hypothesize, or output, a Horn sentence that has size more than n^2 times the size of the target, where n is the number of variables. This suggests we might use LRN in the context of approximate entailment in the following way: Given a known CNF theory φ, use LRN to learn the Horn least upper bound of the theory, using φ to answer membership and equivalence queries. However, although the final Horn sentence is guaranteed to be small, this approach too, could result in far too many resolution applications. Instead, we consider a setting in which φ is manipulated only when necessary (we consider running LRN in a "lazy" manner), and instead the environment is used to provide counterexamples to the correctness of the currently hypothesized Horn least upper bound. We consider two settings in which such an approach seems plausible.

Consider a setting in which an agent who happens to live near elephants is provided with some theory ϕ that describes the world. Our goal is to have the agent maneuver in the world without getting crushed. Among the ways in which our goal can be achieved are (1) have the agent cower in a corner predicting that everything will crush him, (2) in each situation determine from ϕ whether he will be crushed, or (3) tractably approximate ϕ by ϕ' and have him update ϕ' only when he observes (unpredicted by ϕ') something being crushed.

Clearly solution (1) is uninteresting. Solution (2) potentially suffers from the uninteresting features of solution (1) because in the cases where ϕ is intractable, the agent will, in effect, spend most of his time in a corner predicting that he will be crushed searching for a proof to the contrary. Solution (3) seems plausible in that the agent will spend much of his time exploring the world and only retreat to a corner to spend time manipulating ϕ when nature deems it necessary. We refer to the agent operating under solution (3) as a *lazy agent.* A bit more formally,

Definition 12 *Let ϕ be a (propositional) CNF theory, let $\Sigma = \{\sigma_1, \sigma_2, \ldots\}$ be a set of unlabeled clauses whose entailment by ϕ is to be predicted, and let $\Upsilon = \{\upsilon_1, \upsilon_2, \ldots\}$ be a set of* urgent *clauses labeled according to entailment by ϕ. Let $\xi_1, \xi_2, \ldots$ be a sequence defined over elements of $\Sigma \cup \Upsilon$. A* lazy *agent is an agent who uses a prediction strategy that*

1. *predicts the entailment of each ξ_i "quickly",*
2. *updates the prediction strategy only upon incorrectly predicting an element of Υ, and*
3. *predicts that ϕ entails ξ_i only if indeed $\phi \models \xi_i$*

Intuitively, the longer lived lazy agent is the one who predicts that more things are entailed. The scare quotes around the word "quickly" in the definition are intended to bias the agent toward using some ϕ' that is a tractable (yet small relative to ϕ) approximation to ϕ, if such a ϕ' exists. Updating ϕ' only upon seeing (labeled) elements of Υ is intended to capture the idea that only those predictions whose outcomes are observable in the world are important enough for the agent to spend time adjusting his prediction strategy to predict them correctly; it can be argued that the agent is concentrating on the facts that are relevant to the environment he is exploring.

Given this definition and discussion, an agent who uses LRN to acquire the Horn least upper bound to ϕ and uses intermediate hypotheses `hypoth` to predict the entailment of ξ_i seems a satisfactory lazy agent. Any clause entailed by the Horn least upper bound of ϕ must be entailed by some Horn clause entailed by the Horn least upper bound. It is an easy matter to test all of the (at most n) largest Horn clauses that entail the clause to see which ones are not entailed by `hypoth` and from among those use resolution on ϕ to find some new Horn clause to use as a counterexample for LRN to update `hypoth`. Further because LRN is an exact learning algorithm, we can treat it as an on-line algorithm with bounded mistakes. This means that on Horn clauses of Υ the agent will make at most a number of predictive errors polynomial in the size of the Horn least upper bound of ϕ. This is a quantitative means of measuring the amount of time spent on resolution over ϕ.

As a second setting, consider the work by Greiner and Schuurmans, which assumes an agent who receives a sequence of randomly generated clauses ([Greiner and Schuurmans, 1992]). For each clause, the agent determines (via resolution on ϕ) whether the clause is entailed, and if necessary, adjusts his approximation ϕ'' to the Horn least upper bound ϕ', to correct his prediction. However, the agent constrains ϕ'' to have size at most k, so that prediction remains efficient. To accomplish their goal, they define a set of transformations between Horn sentences of size at most k. In the end, they show that they find a ϕ'' that is locally optimal with respect to the neighborhood defined by the transformations. Hence, they may fail to find a global optimum, even if there is one of size at most k.

In contrast, we consider an agent who is given a set of randomly generated clauses, labeled by entailment according to ϕ. Since our algorithm produces a sequence of Horn sentences of monotonically increasing size, we can easily determine whether there is *any* Horn sentence of size k consistent with the sample. If the true Horn least upper bound has size at most k, or if the best size k Horn least upper bound approximation is consistent with the sample, then our algorithm will find a comparably performing Horn sentence having size at most kn^2. In this setting too, we are able to quantitatively specify the resolution work we must do by noting that resolution over ϕ is required only to answer membership queries, and our algorithm will make at most a number of membership queries that is polynomial in kn^2 and the size of the sample.

5 SUMMARY AND FUTURE WORK

Using techniques very similar to [Angluin et al., 1992], our work closes a question in computational learning theory left open by [Angluin, 1988]. The result is an algorithm that by asking natural questions is guaranteed to produce a Horn sentence logically equivalent to the unknown target being sought. Furthermore, the algorithm is guaranteed to take time at most polynomial in the size of the unknown Horn sentence.

This new algorithm is then applied to the problem of approximate entailment. Here, this work adds to the approaches found in the literature. Our approach differs from other approaches in that we confine the appeals to resolution to only those places where our polynomial time learning algorithm specifically asks about the entailment of a specific Horn clause. Our goal is to accelerate the construction of a tractable Horn upper bound of a known CNF theory by providing a sharp focus for the resolution machinery. A side effect of our learning algorithm is that it implicitly maintains a monotonically increasing lower bound on the size of the Horn least upper bound of the CNF theory. Extending this thought, can efficient learning algorithms further limit the number of appeals to, or further limit the focus of, resolution in constructing a tractable, useful approximation to a given CNF theory?

Treating clauses as examples for propositional formulas is a distinct contrast to virtually all the computational learning theory literature. As such, this work also provokes a number of questions in the realm of computational learning theory. For what other concept classes are entailment queries helpful? If clauses are useful examples for Horn sentences, what objects are reasonable examples for other concept classes? Certainly a good many of the theoretical tools (e.g. VC-dimension characterizations, prediction preserving reductions) used for handling variable assignments as examples are suitable for handling clauses as examples. A natural question to address, then, is how the richness of the theory concerning entailed clauses compares with the richness of the theory concerning satisfying assignments.

Acknowledgments

We thank Dana Angluin, Alan Frisch, and Michael Kearns for valuable discussions concerning this work. This work was supported in part by NASA Grant NAG 1-613 and by NSF Grant IRI-9014840.

References

[Angluin, 1987] Angluin, D. (1987). Learning regular sets from queries and counterexamples. *Information and Computation*, 75:87–106.

[Angluin, 1988] Angluin, D. (1988). Learning with hints. In *Proceedings of the First Annual Workshop on Computational Learning Theory*, pages 223–237.

[Angluin et al., 1992] Angluin, D., Frazier, M., and Pitt, L. (1992). Learning conjunctions of Horn clauses. *Machine Learning*, 9:147–164.

[Dalal and Etherington, 1992] Dalal, M. and Etherington, D. (1992). Tractable approximate deduction using limited vocabulary. In *CSCSI-92*, Vancouver.

[Džeroski et al., 1992] Džeroski, S., Muggleton, S., and Russell, S. (1992). Pac-learnability of logic programs. In *Proceedings of the 1992 Workshop on Computational Learning Theory*, pages 128–135, New York. The Association for Computing Machinery.

[Greiner and Schuurmans, 1992] Greiner, R. and Schuurmans, D. (1992). Learning useful Horn approximations. In *Proceedings of the Third International Joint Conference on Knowledge Representation*, Cambridge, MA.

[Kautz and Selman, 1992] Kautz, H. and Selman, B. (1992). Speeding inference by acquiring new concepts. In *Proceedings of AAAI-92*, San Jose.

[Page and Frisch, 1992] Page, C. D. and Frisch, A. M. (1992). Generalization and learnability: A study of constrained atoms. In Muggleton, S. H., editor, *Inductive Logic Programming*, chapter 2, pages 29–60. Academic Press, London.

[Selman and Kautz, 1991] Selman, B. and Kautz, H. (1991). Knowledge compilation using Horn approximations. In *Proceedings of AAAI-91*, Anaheim.

[Shapiro, 1983] Shapiro, E. Y. (1983). *Algorithmic Program Debugging*. MIT Press, Cambridge, MA.

[Valiant, 1984] Valiant, L. (1984). A theory of the learnable. *Communications of the ACM*, 27(11):1134–1142.

Efficient Domain-Independent Experimentation

Yolanda Gil
Information Sciences Institute, USC
4676 Admiralty Way
Marina del Rey, CA 90292
gil@isi.edu

Abstract

Planning systems often make the assumption that omniscient world knowledge is available. Our approach makes the more realistic assumption that the initial knowledge about the actions is incomplete, and uses experimentation as a learning mechanism when the missing knowledge causes an execution failure. Previous work on learning by experimentation has not addressed the issue of how to choose good experiments, and much research on learning from failure has relied on background knowledge to build explanations that pinpoint directly the causes of failures. We want to investigate the potential of a system for efficient learning by experimentation without such background knowledge. This paper describes domain-independent heuristics that compare possible hypotheses and choose the ones most likely to cause the failure. These heuristics extract information solely from the domain operators initially available for planning (incapable of producing such explanations) and the planner's experiences in interacting with the environment. Our approach has been implemented in EXPO, a system that uses PRODIGY as a baseline planner and improves its domain knowledge in several domains. The empirical results presented show that EXPO's heuristics dramatically reduce the number of experiments needed to refine incomplete operators.

1 Introduction

Learning from the environment is a vital capability for an autonomous agent. The lack of knowledge affects the planner's capabilities, and learning requires both detecting a failure and determining a correction of the knowledge base. Experimentation is a powerful tool for gathering additional information from the environment that helps determine the appropriate correction. Previous work on learning from the environment has not addressed the issue of how to choose good hypotheses for efficient experimentation [Shen, 1989, Hume and Sammut, 1991]. Others have tried to reduce or eliminate the need for experimentation by relying on causal theories or other types of background knowledge to build explanations for the failures that determine what is to be learned [Rajamoney, 1988, Kedar *et al.*, 1991, Hammond, 1986]. Learning only seems feasible when detailed knowledge of the domain at hand is available. The central issue of the acquisition and refinement of additional and necessarily complex background knowledge is still far from resolved. While explanations are powerful, it is not realistic to assume that they are always available to planners in any task domain and with enough detail to explain any possible failure. Our work was inspired by observation of human behavior upon failed expectations in absence of adequate domain understanding. For example, if we are presented with a new pen and we fail to write with it, we would most probably try to vary the writing action and try to make it work. We might tilt the point a little. We might try writing on a different type of paper. We might try to press harder. These small variations are what we call experiments, perhaps of a more mundane nature than those performed in a laboratory but nevertheless greatly responsible for our autonomy and adaptability. Do we reason about friction between felt tips and types of paper? Do we have knowledge about how ink flows through a cartridge? Humans learn through these experiments in many domains. Do we all have theories about everything in the world that we interact with? More importantly, are these theories necessary for building systems able to learn autonomously from the world? The work in this paper suggests that they are not. We claim that efficient experimentation is possible without any theory that supports our actions and explains our failures.

This paper presents an efficient experimentation strategy that does not have access to a theory that produces explanations for failures. Our approach is to use domain-independent heuristics that extract infor-

```
(GRIND-INCOMPLETE
 (preconditions
   (and
     (is-a <machine> GRINDER)
     (is-a <tool> GRINDING-WHEEL)
     (is-a <part> PART)
     (holding-tool <machine> <tool>)
     (side-up-for-machining <dim> <side>)
     (holding <machine> <device> <part> <side>)))
 (effects (
     (add (surface-finish <part> <side> SMOOTH))
     (add (size-of <part> <dim> <value>)))))
```

Figure 1: An incomplete model of grinding. Notice that, upon an execution failure, a great deal of background information would have been needed to explain that the presence of cutting fluid is important for grinding.

mation solely from the domain operators initially available for planning and the planner's experiences in interacting with the environment. The paper also shows the performance of these heuristics in their implementation in EXPO, a learning by experimentation capability within the PRODIGY system [Carbonell *et al.*, 1990] that improves the planner's knowledge in several domains. We begin with a brief description of our previous work.

2 Learning by Experimentation

Suppose that a planner is given a process planning domain with the incomplete operator shown in Figure 1. This operator models the process of grinding a metallic surface. A grinder holds a part with some holding device, and, using a grinding wheel as a tool, it changes the size of the part along a selected dimension. This operator may seem correct, but it is incomplete. For example, it is missing a precondition that states that the grinder must have cutting fluid. Any plans that use this operator for grinding will not be useful for grinding parts in the real world. These plans will include steps that set up the tool and the part correctly in the machine, but will not provide the grinder with cutting fluid. Grinding is an abrasive operation that generates heat as a result of the friction between the tool and the part. Cutting fluids cool both the cutting edges of the tool and the part, aid in chip clearance, and improve the surface finish. If no cutting fluid if present to absorb the heat, then the grinding process will not produce the desired size (the grinder and the part will overheat instead.) The focus of our research is to design learning systems that would correct the operator's preconditions and effects.

EXPO learns new preconditions through the Operator Refinement Method [Carbonell and Gil, 1990], that we summarize here briefly. Suppose that the system has build a plan to grind a part to make its length smaller. Before grinding the part, the system checks that the preconditions are true in the external world. After grinding it, the postcondition of GRIND is checked in the external state. The size of the part has changed to be of size k, but the surface finish is not as it was expected. This may be because the known effect that specifies the new surface finish is wrong, or because the operator is missing a necessary precondition. This method addresses the failure by considering the latter possibility as the working hypothesis first (see [Gil, 1992] for a discussion on the first possibility): that some unknown precondition is not true in the state and thus the grinding action is not working as the given operator specifies. To find out what the missing precondition is, EXPO considers conditions that were true in an earlier successful application of the operator that are not true now. To do so, EXPO retrieves the description of the past state when the action execution succeeded before, which contains all the facts that the planner believed to be true of the world at that point in time. Among the things that were true in that state, which may be many, is the fact that the grinder had fluid when the operation worked in the past[1]. Experimentation is needed to determine which one of the differences is relevant for this particular failure. The experiments will point out that the presence of cutting fluid is relevant for grinding, and EXPO corrects the operator to reflect this fact.

A typical set of hypotheses obtained by EXPO in its process planning domain has 50 to 100 elements, but for simplicity consider the following subset:

```
(size-of <part> WIDTH 3)
(size-of <part> LENGTH 7)
(size-of <part> HEIGHT 2.5)
(material-of <part> BRASS)
(has-fluid <machine>)
(surface-finish part26 <side> SAWCUT)
(holding drill1 vise2 part26 <side>)
(material-of part26 STEEL)
(is-a drill1 DRILL)
(is-a drill-bit1 DRILL-BIT)
(material-of part37 COPPER)
(has-hole part37 <side>)
```

As described in [Gil, 1992], it is important to minimize the number of experiments and their requirements. For each experiment the planner has to build a plan to set the environment in a state that satisfies that many predicates. Apart from the planning effort involved, the execution of those plans raises non-trivial issues. Plan execution may use up valuable resources (including time), produce non-desirable changes in the environment that are hard to undo, and interfere with the main goals of the system's task. If any information is available to identify a smaller subset of these candidates as more relevant, the experimentation effort may

[1] For a discussion on the case when the missing condition is not present, see [Gil, 1992].

be greatly reduced. In particular, if we can devise a way of ranking the candidates from most relevant to least, then each candidate can be tested individually. EXPO follows this strategy by ranking the candidate hypotheses heuristically.

3 Domain-independent Heuristics for Efficient Experimentation

EXPO's efficient experimentation is based on heuristics that exploit knowledge about the planning task to evaluate which predicates in a set of differences are more likely to have caused the failure. This section briefly describes these heuristics, summarized in Table 1. Their implementation in EXPO follows. For more details see [Gil, 1991, Gil, 1992].

One heuristic is locality of actions. The idea behind it is the following. The fact that there is a steel part lying somewhere else in the machine shop is not likely to affect our grinding operation. Facts about the machine and tool used and the part being ground are more likely to be relevant to the failure. This heuristic prefers predicates which contain some object that appears in the operator's bindings.

Structural similarity takes advantage of the fact a planning domain reflects the regularities of the actions needed to do a task. Consider the set of differences above as possible candidates for a new precondition of grinding. Many other operators change the size of a part. Many of them require the use of cutting fluid, which is in fact the relevant condition for this particular failure. Only some of them have conditions about the material of the part. And none of them has any conditions about the surface finish of a side of the part. This heuristic prefers predicates that are preconditions of operators that are similar to grinding according to some metric.

Generalization of experience takes advantage of the fact that the conditions needed for the action must have been present in all past successful executions of it. In fact, the precondition expression of an operator can be seen as a concept that represents the states in which the operator can be executed successfully, as in [Mitchell, 1978, Mitchell *et al.*, 1983, Langley, 1987, Langley *et al.*, In press]. Unlike these systems, EXPO takes the concept that reflects the LHS of the rule as a *heuristic* for learning, rather than as the sole basis for it. Thus, we can bias the generalization language without worrying about excluding the target concept. The generalization is used as a heuristic to guide the experiments, and it does not represent the precondition expression of the operator (although it is related). A summary of the planner's past experience of the action's behavior is useful to guide our search for the missing condition, because it highlights the conditions that were common to all the states when the action was executed before.

3.1 Implementation

To be able to generalize from experience, EXPO needs to keep track of the execution of actions. Each execution of an operator is either a success or a failure. A state in which a successful execution occurs corresponds to a positive instance of the concept, and a state in which a failure is obtained is a negative instance. EXPO keeps information about action executions in *situations*, which are composed of the operator whose action was executed, the result of the execution (success or failure), the list of bindings for the operator variables, and the list of predicates believed to be true immediately prior to the operator being executed (i.e., the state). The situations are used to maintain the current description of each operator's preconditions as a version space [Mitchell, 1978]. The algorithm is biased to produce conjunctive descriptions of the concept. This bias is appropriate for this application. The large majority of the precondition expressions in operators are conjunctions of predicates (or negations of predicates). This is because actions are easier to express if their effects under different conditions are described in separate operators. In this sense, even if the system aims to learn only conjunctive expressions of predicates it would be a great win. In fact, even though PRODIGY allows for a very expressive language in the preconditions, EXPO's generalization only contains the predicates in the preconditions that are part of the main conjunct. For example, if the precondition expression of an operator is `(and (A B C D (or E F)))`, E and F are never included in the generalization.

Version spaces implement the heuristic for selecting hypotheses based on its generalization of experience as follows. From the set of current candidate hypotheses, only the ones that appear in S (the ones that are common to all successful situations) and do not appear in G (since G contains the preconditions, they appear in the failure state) are selected.

The set of hypotheses selected by the generalization heuristic is then filtered by the locality heuristic. This heuristic selects only the hypotheses that contain constants and variables that appear in the bindings of the failure situation. This new subset of the hypotheses is then ranked by the heuristic of structural similarity as we explain now.

All the domain operators are organized by EXPO in a hierarchy using a simple clustering algorithm [Gil, 1992]. The root node contains all the operators in the hierarchy. For every node, the operators that are not in any of its children yet are examined to build a child node. The expression or expressions that appear in a larger number of operators[2] define the child node,

[2] in the preconditions, postconditions, or both. In our

heuristic	*description*
locality of actions	objects affected by the action are likely to be present in the operator's parameters
structural similarity	similar operators are likely to have similar preconditions
generalization of experience	necessary conditions have been present in all past successful executions of the action

Table 1: Domain-independent heuristics for suggesting better experiments.

and the operators that contain them are transferred to it. The algorithm works its way down in the tree until a node is reached that contains only one operator or all of its operators expressions are included in the node. When a new condition or effect for an operator is learned, the hierarchy is updated by recomputing the children of the node that contains the operator. Since this clustering algorithm is used as a heuristic, the emphasis is not so much in the accuracy of the result as long as it reflects to some extent the structural similarity behind the domain operators.

EXPO considers first the hypotheses that are selected by the three heuristics. Then, it considers the ones that the structural regularity heuristic rejected, then the ones rejected by the locality heuristic. Last, EXPO considers the rest of the hypotheses in the initial set.

Determining the missing precondition is done through iterative experimentation with the ranked list of candidate predicates. In EXPO, this process converges if the missing condition is an observable and non-inferred predicate that is within a conjunctive expression. If this is the case, the missing condition is included in the group of candidate hypotheses, and EXPO eventually encounters it and learns it through experimentation. If this is not the case, then the missing condition may be something else, e.g., a disjunction of some of those conditions, a quantified expression over some predicate, or an unobserved fact (see [Gil, 1992] for more details). EXPO does not learn these types of conditions.

Although the algorithms presented here can be made more sophisticated, we must keep in mind that they are used to implement heuristics and as such they are not required to be close to an optimal implementation of the idea behind them. In their simplicity, the results in the next section show that they are effective for this purpose.

4 Results

This section presents EXPO's performance with a robot planning domain in which 20% and 50% of the operator's preconditions were removed randomly. This means that from all the preconditions of all the operators a percentage was removed, so any operator can be missing any number of preconditions. We generated n problems randomly. All of the n problems were solvable within the time bound that PRODIGY was given. From the set of n solvable problems, we randomly chose m of them to be the training set. The rest constituted the test set. Notice that both sets are independent (they do not have any common instances). Initially, PRODIGY is given the incomplete domain and EXPO starts running the training problems. For each problem, EXPO obtains a plan from PRODIGY and tries to execute it in the external environment[3]. EXPO examines any expectation failures and applies the Operator Refinement Method together with the heuristics described in this paper for designing experiments. After the experiments determine the cause of the failure, EXPO corrects the operator and uses it for future plans.

Figures 2 and 3 present the number of experiments that are required to recover from the failures encountered by EXPO. The horizontal axis represents subsequent failures encountered by EXPO. The vertical axis shows the cumulative number of experiments needed until the missing condition is isolated. We show results with different combinations of the heuristics. We also plot the number of experiments needed when no heuristics are used, in which case EXPO tries in sequence the candidate predicates. The heuristics used are represented by a letter: g for generalization, s for structural similarity, and l for locality. A strategy that does less experiments in the absence of information is represented in the graph as *DC*. *DC* uses a divide-and-conquer strategy: it recursively splits the candidate set, using $log(n)$ experiments to isolate the correct hypothesis (n is the number of hypotheses).

Without any of the hypothesis-selection heuristics many experiments are needed, since the candidate hypotheses are tried one by one. Although DC does a smaller number of experiments than some of the heuristics used in isolation, we show below that there are other reasons why it is inefficient. The other curves show how effective each heuristic is individually and in combination with others. Each heuristic contributes in its own way to reducing the number of experiments.

experience with EXPO's domains, this does not make a difference in the effectiveness of the structural similarity heuristic.

[3]EXPO was not tested interacting with a physical environment, but with a software system that simulates one. The details of this simulation are described in [Gil, 1992].

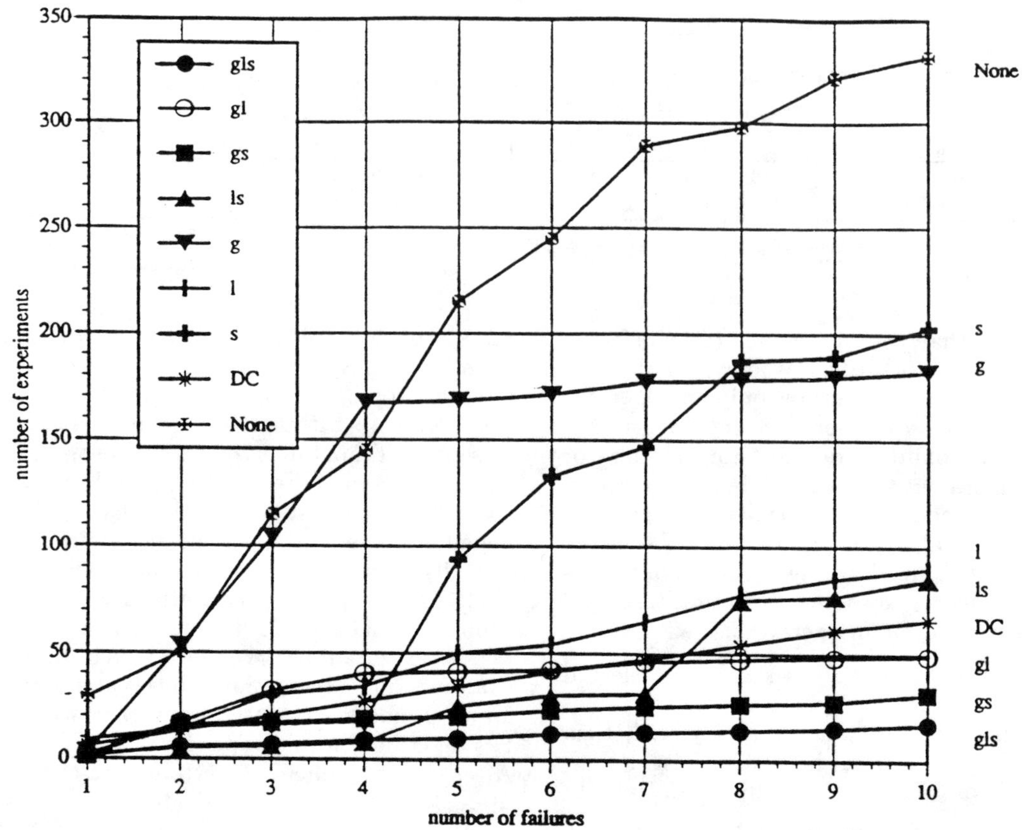

Figure 2: Given a domain missing 20% of its preconditions number of experiments that are necessary with all the combinations of the three hypotheses-selection heuristics: generalization of experience (g), locality (l), and structural similarity (s). The number of experiments needed is greatly reduced when the three of them are used. *DC* represents a divide-and-conquer strategy that does not use the heuristics.

For 20% incompleteness, the three heuristics combined yield the best results. For 50% incompleteness, gl is about as good as gls. This is because when the operators are very incomplete similar operators may be missing the same conditions, so s is not very helpful. The effectiveness of s improves as new knowledge is added to the domain.

As we mentioned above, even though *DC* needs few experiments, the planner must achieve $n-1$ additional goals for each failure (see [Gil, 1992] for more details). With 20% of the preconditions missing, the number of additional goals that are necessary to achieve for experimentation is as follows:

failure	*gls*	*g*	*l*	*s*	*none*	*DC*
5	10	168	50	94	215	341
10	17	172	90	110	332	652

Failure indicates the order of the failure in the sequence in which they are obtained. With 50% of the preconditions missing:

failure	*gls*	*g*	*l*	*s*	*none*	*DC*
5	40	172	27	118	205	377
10	71	276	102	177	460	691
17	89	370	201	325	728	1217

In summary, the combination of the three heuristics (generalization of experience, structural similarity, and locality) reduces dramatically the number of experiments required, and yields the best performance. A divide and conquer strategy over the set of candidates requires more experiments that also have much more complex setups.

5 Conclusion

The work presented in this paper shows that it is possible for a planner to recover from knowledge-level impasses autonomously without need of causal explanations. Our approach uses domain-independent heuristics for choosing good experiments that do not require any knowledge other than the operators defined for planning and the planner's experiences in interacting with the environment. EXPO's performance us-

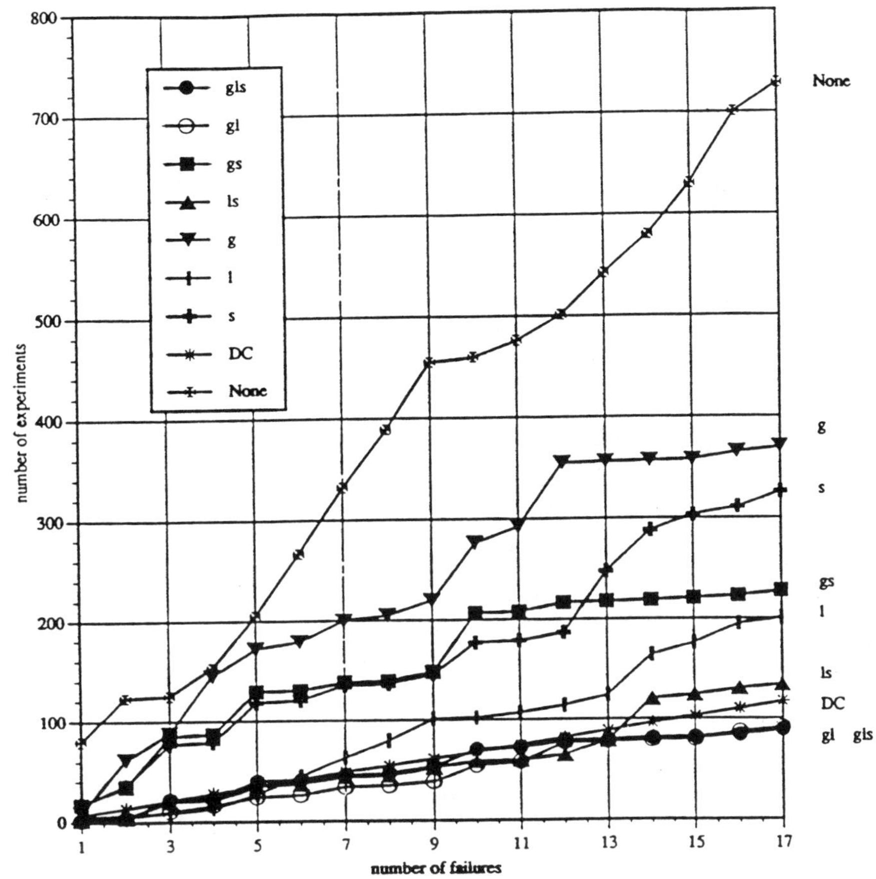

Figure 3: Given a domain missing 50% of its preconditions number of experiments that are necessary with all the combinations of the three hypotheses-selection heuristics: generalization of experience (g), locality (l), and structural similarity (s). The number of experiments needed is greatly reduced when the three of them are used. *DC* represents a divide-and-conquer strategy that does not use the heuristics.

ing all the heuristics combined shows that our method for experimentation is efficient. Additional domain-independent heuristics would improve this approach. The structural similarity heuristic can be extended to exploit other regularities in the domain, including inverse relations between operators. The knowledge intensive explanation-based methods would still outperform our system, but the problem of acquiring that additional knowledge remains. It would be interesting to combine the strengths of both approaches, relying on background domain knowledge when it exists and falling back on our heuristics otherwise.

Acknowledgments

This work was done while the author was at Carnegie Mellon University. I would like to thank Jaime Carbonell, Tom Mitchell, Herb Simon, and Nils Nilsson for their suggestions and support throughout my thesis work. The clarity of the paper and the work itself has also improved through comments from many people, including Kevin Knight, Eduardo Perez, and other members of the PRODIGY group. Thanks also to Ramesh Patil and Tom Russ for their comments on the paper.

This research was supported by the Avionics Laboratory, Wright Research and Development Center, Aeronautical Systems Division (AFSC), U.S. Air Force, Wright-Patterson AFB, Ohio 45433-6543 under Contract F33615-90-C-1465, ARPA Order No. 7597. The view and conclusions contained in this document are those of the author and should not be interpreted as representing the official policies, either expressed or implied, of DARPA or the U.S. government.

References

[Carbonell and Gil, 1990] Jaime G. Carbonell and Yolanda Gil. Learning by experimentation: The operator refinement method. In Y. Kodratoff and R. S. Michalski, editors, *Machine Learning, An Artificial Intelligence Approach, Volume III.* Morgan Kaufmann, San Mateo, CA, 1990.

[Carbonell *et al.*, 1990] J. G. Carbonell, Y. Gil, R. L. Joseph, C. A. Knoblock, S. Minton, and M. M. Veloso. Designing an integrated architecture: The PRODIGY view. In *Proceedings of the Twelfth Annual Conference of the Cognitive Science Society,* Boston, MA, 1990.

[Gil, 1991] Yolanda Gil. A domain-independent framework for effective experimentation in planning. In *Proceedings of the Eight International Workshop on Machine Leaning,* Evanston, IL, 1991. Morgan Kaufmann.

[Gil, 1992] Yolanda Gil. *Acquiring Domain Knowledge for Planning by Experimentation.* PhD thesis, Carnegie Mellon University, School of Computer Science, 1992.

[Hammond, 1986] Chris J. Hammond. *Case-based Planning: An Integrated Theory of Planning, Learning, and Memory.* PhD thesis, Yale University, New Haven, CN, 1986.

[Hume and Sammut, 1991] David Hume and Claude Sammut. Using inverse resolution to learn relations from experiments. In *Proceedings of the Eighth Machine Learning Workshop,* Evanston, IL, 1991.

[Kedar *et al.*, 1991] Smadar T. Kedar, John L. Bresina, and C. Lisa Dent. The blind leading the blind: Mutual refinement of approximate theories. In *Proceedings of the Eight Machine Learning Workshop,* Evanston, IL, 1991.

[Langley *et al.*, In press] Pat Langley, Ken Thompson, Wayne Iba, John H. Gennari, and John A. Allen. An integrated cognitive architecture for autonomous agents. In Walter Van De Velde, editor, *Representation and Learning in Autonomous Agents.* North Holland, Amsterdam, The Netherlands, In press.

[Langley, 1987] Pat Langley. A general theory of discrimination learning. In *Production System Models of Learning and Development.* MIT Press, Cambridge, MA, 1987.

[Mitchell *et al.*, 1983] Tom Mitchell, Paul Utgoff, and Ranan Banerji. Learning by experimentation: Acquiring and refining problem-solving heuristics. In *Machine Learning, An Artificial Intelligence Approach, Volume I.* Tioga Press, Palo Alto, CA, 1983.

[Mitchell, 1978] Tom M. Mitchell. *Version Spaces: An Approach to Concept Learning.* PhD thesis, Stanford University, Stanford, CA, 1978.

[Rajamoney, 1988] Shankar A. Rajamoney. *Explanation-Based Theory Revision: An Approach to the Problems of Incomplete and Incorrect Theories.* PhD thesis, University of Illinois at Urbana-Champaign, Urbana, IL, 1988.

[Shen, 1989] Wei-Min Shen. *Learning from the Environment Based on Percepts and Actions.* PhD thesis, School of Computer Science, Carnegie Mellon University, Pittsburgh, PA, 1989.

Learning Search Control Knowledge for Deep Space Network Scheduling

Jonathan Gratch*, Steve Chien+, and Gerald DeJong*

*Beckman Institute
University of Illinois
405 N. Mathews Av., Urbana, IL 61801
{gratch, dejong}@cs.uiuc.edu

+Jet Propulsion Laboratory
California Institute of Technology
4800 Oak Grove Drive, Pasadena, CA 91109-8099
chien@aig.jpl.nasa.gov

Abstract

While the general class of most scheduling problems is NP–hard in worst–case complexity, in practice, for specific distributions of problems and constraints, domain–specific solutions have been shown to perform in much better than exponential time. Unfortunately, constructing such techniques is a knowledge–intensive and time–consuming process that requires a deep understanding of the domain and the scheduler. The goal of our work is to develop techniques to allow for automated learning of an effective domain–specific search strategy given a general problem solver with a flexible control architecture. In this approach, a learning system searches a space of possible control strategies, using statistics to evaluate performance over the expected problem distribution. We discuss an application of the approach to scheduling satellite communications. Using problem distributions based on actual mission requirements, our approach identified strategies that both decrease the amount of CPU time required to produce schedules, and increase the percentage of problems that are solvable within computational resource limitations.

1 INTRODUCTION

General problem solving tasks like planning and scheduling are inherently complex. Nevertheless, in many practical situations these complex problems have reasonable solutions (e.g. traveling salesman problem [Held70]). Often we can take advantage of the structure of a domain or the distribution of problems to formulate effective solutions to complex problems. Unfortunately, a system designer must devote considerable expense to the performance aspects of an algorithm.

In this article we investigate the use of a machine learning approach to automatically improve a performance element with respect to a specific domain and distribution of problems. The performance element must be flexible, meaning there are control decisions that effect search that may be resolved in alternative ways. The overall learning problem we are addressing can be specified as follows. Given a flexible performance element *PE* with control points $CP_1 \ldots CP_n$, where each control point CP_i corresponds to a particular control decision and for which there is a set of alternative decision methods $M_{i,1} \ldots M_{i,k}$,[1] a ***control strategy*** is a selection of a specific method for every control point (e.g, $STRAT = \langle M_{1,3}, M_{2,6}, M_{3,1}, \ldots \rangle$). A control strategy determines the overall behavior of the scheduler. It may effect properties like computational efficiency or the quality of its solutions. Let *PE(STRAT)* be the problem solver operating under a particular control strategy. The function *U(PE(STRAT), d)* is a real valued *utility function* that is a measure of the goodness of the behavior of the scheduler over problem *d*. The goal of learning can be expressed as: given a problem distribution *D*, find *STRAT* so as to maximize the *expected utility* of *PE*. Expected utility is defined formally as:

$$\sum_{d \in D} U(PE(STRAT), d) \times probability(d)$$

For example, in a planning system such as PRODIGY [Minton88], when planning to achieve a goal, control points would be: how to select an operator to use to achieve the goal; how to select variable bindings to instantiate the operator; etc. A method for the operator choice control point might be a set of control rules to determine which operators to use to achieve various goals plus a default operator choice method. A strategy would be a set of control rules and default methods for every control point (e.g., one for operator choice, one for binding choice, etc.). Utility might be defined as a function of the time to construct a plan.

Our proposed solution to this learning problem, sometimes called the *utility problem* [Minton88], is embodied in the COMPOSER system. COMPOSER can be characterized as a hill-climbing search in the space of possible strategies. The learning system alternately conjectures changes to the current control strategy and statistically evaluates them to determine how well they enhance expected utility.

1. Note that a method may consist of smaller elements so that a method may be a set of control rules or a combination of heuristics.

In this paper we describe an application of the COMPOSER framework to learning search strategies for an automated scheduling technique in a NASA domain of space-craft communication scheduling. Two important aspects of this evaluation are that the task and problem distribution are based on a real-world situation, and the scheduling approach was developed independently of our learning work [Bell92]. The implementation includes a novel approach for improving learning efficiency. The performance of the system, along with previous results in artificial planning domains [Gratch91, Gratch92], demonstrates COMPOSER's flexibility and its potential to identify beneficial knowledge in practical learning problems.

2 COMPOSER

COMPOSER is a statistical approach to improving the expected utility of problem solving. The overall approach is one of generate and test hill-climbing. Given an initial problem solver, a *transformation generator* constructs a set of possible transformations to the control strategy. Each of these changes is evaluated statistically over the expected distribution of problems. A transformation is adopted if it increases the expected utility of solving problems over that distribution. The generator then constructs a set of transformations to this new strategy and so on. For a complete description of the method see [Gratch92]. The algorithm is summarized in the Appendix.

COMPOSER's solution is applicable in cases where the following conditions apply.

1. The control strategy space can be structured to facilitate hill-climbing search. In general, the space of such strategies is so large as to make exhaustive search intractable. COMPOSER requires a transformation generator that structures this space into a sequence search steps, with relatively few transformations at each step. In Section 3.4 we discuss some techniques for incorporating domain specific information into the structuring of the control strategy space.

2. There is a large supply of representative training problems so that an adequate sampling of problems can be used to estimate expected utility for various control strategies.

3. Problems can be solved with a sufficiently low cost in resources so that estimating expected utility is feasible.

4. There is sufficient regularity in the domain such that the cost of learning a good strategy can be amortized over the gains in solving many problems.

COMPOSER can be seen as one of a class of statistical approaches to improving the expected utility of problem solving (see also [Greiner92, Laird92, Subramanian92]. The principle drawback of these techniques is that they find only local maxima, they may require many examples, and examples can be expensive to process. Furthermore, their statistical properties rest upon assumptions that may not hold in practice. Greiner and Jurisica demonstrate that, under very weak assumptions, the number of examples, or *sample complexity,* can be bounded by a polynomial function of the allowable statistical error [Greiner92]. Weak assumptions are a way of ensuring wide applicability. Unfortunately, the resulting bounds prove too large for most practical applications (see [Buntine89, Gratch92]). COMPOSER embodies stronger statistical assumptions suggested by the Central Limit Theorem [Hogg78 pp. 192–195]. These stronger assumptions drastically reduce the number of examples required to make statistical decisions, but they limit the applicability of the approach. In previous evaluations these stronger assumptions have proved reasonable: COMPOSER's assumptions produced sample complexities two to three order of magnitudes less than the weak assumptions adopted by Greiner and Jurisica, *without* compromising the statistical error [Gratch92]. However these promising results have the drawback that they are based on artificial domains and problem distributions. The ultimate usefulness of our approach depends on its behavior on real-world domains, which this paper addresses.

3 THE DEEP SPACE NETWORK

We applied the COMPOSER approach to improving the performance of a scheduler operating in the domain of spacecraft communication scheduling. The resulting system is called DSN-COMPOSER. The scheduling problem is a complicated real world task that has proved challenging to state-of-the-art scheduling techniques. The problem is to allocate communication requests between earth-orbiting satellites and the three 26-meter antennas at Goldstone, Canberra, and Madrid. These antennas make up part of the Deep Space Network (DSN) that is responsible for communication with earth-orbiting and inter-planetary spacecraft. Each satellite has a set of constraints, called project requirements, that define its communication needs. For example, the Nimbus-7 satellite must have at least four 15-minute communication slots per day, and these slots cannot be greater than five hours apart. Two factors complicate the problem. First, antennas are a limited resource – two satellites cannot communicate with the same antenna at the same time. Second, satellites can only communicate with certain antennas at certain times, depending on their orbits.

Scheduling is done on a weekly basis. A weekly scheduling problem is defined by three elements: (1) the set of satellites to be scheduled, (2) the constraints associated with each satellite, and (3) a set of time periods specifying all temporal intervals when a satellite can legally communicate with an antenna. Two time periods conflict if they use the same antenna and overlap in temporal extent. A valid schedule specifies a non-conflicting subset of all possible time periods where each project's requirements are satisfied.

3.1 THE SCHEDULER SYSTEM

LR-26 is a heuristic approach to the scheduling problem [Bell92] developed at the Jet Propulsion Laboratory. It provides a good platform for learning as it can be modified easily to incorporate alternative heuristic strategies. Furthermore, it uses an expert crafted control strategy that provide a challenging base-line to judge learned knowledge. There is also significant motivation to improve the effectiveness of the default control strategy. If LR-26 is chosen to replace the human scheduler, it will serve as one module in a larger interactive system. This system must make many repeated calls to the scheduler to compare variants of each weekly schedule. For this reason, LR-26 must provided solutions in a timely fashion.

Scheduling is formulated as a 0-1 integer programming problem [Taha82]. This is a methodology for finding an assignment to integer variables that maximizes the value of an *objective function*, subject to a set of linear constraints. The objective function characterizes the "value" of the solution. Many constraint satisfaction problems (CSP) are easily cast as integer programming problems [Mackworth92]. In the DSN domain, time periods are treated as 0-1 integer variables (0 if the time period is excluded from the schedule or 1 if it is included), the objective is to maximize the number of time periods in the schedule subject to the project requirements and temporal conflict constraints which are expressed as sets of linear inequalities. Integer programming is NP-hard, and the size of our scheduling problems makes the conventional approach impractical: a typical problem has approximately 650 variables and 1300 constraints. LR-26 embodies a heuristic approach called *lagrangian relaxation* [Fisher81]. Lagrangian relaxation requires identifying a set of constraints that, if removed, make the problem computationally easy. These constraints are "relaxed," meaning they no longer act as constraints but instead modify the objective function. A relaxed objective function is automatically generated such that satisfying relaxed constraints increases the value of the relaxed solution. The relaxed problem is by definition easy to solve and often finding the highest value relaxed solution solves the original problem. Furthermore, each relaxed constraint has a weight associated with it when it is added to the objective function. By systematically adjusting these weights and re-solving the relaxed problem, a solution to the unrelaxed problem is often efficiently discovered. Even if the unrelaxed problem cannot be solved in this manner, this weight adjustment cycle can move the scheduler closer to a solution, allowing the unrelaxed solution to be discovered with less search. LR-26 relaxes inter-antenna constraints. This representation facilitates an efficient implicit representation of temporal conflict constraints, which make up more than half of all constraints in a typical problem.

LR-26 combines lagrangian relaxation with standard constraint satisfaction search techniques. The scheduler performs depth-first search through a space of partial schedules. A variable is assigned a value of *in* if the associated time period is included in the partial schedule, *out* if it is excluded from the partial schedule. The scheduler constructs a complete schedule by incrementally extending the partial schedule. First it attempts to completely extend the schedule using the lagrangian relaxation method. If the relaxed solution satisfies all constraints it is returned. Otherwise, a set of possible extensions to the partial schedule is created and these are recursive explored. Extensions are created by choosing an unsatisfied constraint, identifying a set of uncommitted variables in the constraint, and assigning possible values to these variables. The set of extensions are placed on a stack to implement the depth-first search. The search continues until a solution is uncovered or a time-bound is reached. Currently the scheduler implements a time-bound of five CPU minutes. Any problem not solved within this bound is deemed unsolvable.

LR-26 can be viewed as a recursive application of four control decisions: (1) decide on a lagrangian weight adjustment scheme, terminating if a viable solution is found; otherwise (2) choose an unsatisfied constraint, (3) determine a set of extensions to the partial schedule that satisfy the constraint, and (4) determine an order to explore these extensions. The scheduler embodies a heuristic method for each of these control operations. These operations provide natural points at which to insert alternative learned methods.

3.2 PROBLEM DISTRIBUTION

We constructed a distribution of scheduling problems using the requirements and time periods of satellites using the deep space network. Ideally, we would use the identical problem distribution faced by the human experts in this domain. Unfortunately, not all of this information is in electronic form and thus is difficult to present to the LR-26 scheduler. There does, however, exist a large electronic database of information for many of the projects in the deep space network. We used this database to construct a large body of scheduling problems that are representative of, if not identical to, the type of problems faced by the human schedulers. Problems are generated by randomly choosing combinations of projects from the available data. The requirements and time periods represent the requirements and time periods of actual projects. The primary difference between these and actual problems lies in the particular combinations of projects that appear in the schedule.

We performed some initial evaluations of the LR-26 scheduler on these generated problems. We observed that some problems could not be solved by the scheduler using any of several search control strategies even with large resource bounds. This is consistent with the observation that the scheduling problem is inherently NP-Hard – there will be some problems that cannot be efficiently solved, even with good heuristics. These problems tend to dilute any performance improvement that we might gain through learning. For our experiments we eliminated this complicating factor by constructing our problem distribution without these unsolved problems. These problems were identified by solving each randomly generated problem multiple times using about twenty different search strategies (the strategies were identified during our pilot investigations). If a problem could not be solved by any of the strategies within the time bound, it was not added to the experimental distribution. For comparative purposes we include a secondary set of experiments that incorporate these unsolved problems. For a complete description of how training examples are generated, see [Gratch93].

3.3 EXPECTED UTILITY

In the DSN application a chief concern is with the computational efficiency of the scheduler. There is a strong need that the scheduler return quickly on average. This behavioral preference can be expressed by a utility function related to the computational effort required to solve a problem. As the effort to solve a problem increases, the utility of the problem solver on that problem should decrease. In this paper we characterize this preference by making utility the negative of the CPU time required by the scheduler on a problem.

3.4 HEURISTICS FOR LR-26

LR-26 combines lagrangian relaxation and constraint satisfaction search techniques to increase scheduling efficiency. Nevertheless, scheduling is still quite expensive. While the problems are of sufficient complexity that some search is unavoidable, alternate search control methods can drastically impact the amount of search required, especially as there is substantial repetition in this domain. Many projects use the antennas for many years, and their project requirements vary little across weeks. Because possible slots for specific antennas communicating with spacecraft are dictated by spacecraft orbits, the space of potential communication slots also contains significant regularity. This suggests that heuristics can be crafted to exploit this regularity to improve performance.

Many heuristics have been suggested to improve scheduling efficiency. Often these heuristics are stated as general principles (e.g. "first instantiate variables that maximally constraint the rest of the search space" [Dechter92]) and there may be many ways to realize them in a particular scheduler and domain. Furthermore, there are almost certainly interactions between methods used at different control points that makes it difficult to construct a good overall strategy. These factors conspire to make manual developing and evaluation of heuristics a tedious, time consuming task that requires significant knowledge about the domain and scheduler. As a result, only a limited set of alternate heuristics were considered in LR–26's development. We formalized a much larger set for automatic consideration.

As described previously, there are four basic control points in LR–26: a weight adjustment method, constraint selection method, a method for constructing alternative solutions for the constraint, and method for ordering these alternatives. We allow for both a primary and secondary sort function to order candidate constraints, so there are effectively five control points. A control strategy consists of a particular heuristic method for each of the five control points. For LR–26 there are 4 alternative methods for the lagrangian weight adjustment control point, 9 alternative methods for each constraint selection sort (9 for the primary sort and 9 for the secondary sort – excluding the primary sort but including the possibility of no secondary sort), 2 alternative methods for constructing alternative solutions to a constraint, and 4 alternative methods for ordering alternative solutions to a constraint. Exhaustively searching the space of possible control strategies is in general computationally infeasible. As there are roughly 4×9×9×2×4=2592 possible strategies in the LR-26 control strategy search space, to exhaustively search the control strategy space, taking a significant number of examples per strategy (fifty) at a cost of 5 CPU minutes per problem would require approximately 450 CPU days.

Some example methods are as follows. For the weight adjustment, methods perform adjustments at every search node, perform only at root node, never perform adjustments. Methods for selecting constraints involve features of the constraints and constraint graph. Prefer the shortest constraint (e.g. the one that mentions the fewest unbound variables) and prefer the constraint that mentions the variables that temporally conflicts with the most other variables are examples of constraint selection methods (recall variables correspond to time-periods). For constructing alternative solutions, there were 2 methods: force the first variable in the constraint into the schedule for one child and out for the second child; and construct a child for each variable in the constraint, forcing that variable into the schedule. Examples of alternative ordering methods include preferring high conflict variables and preferring low conflict variables[2]. These heuristics can be viewed as variable ordering heuristics from the CSP literature [Dechter92].

COMPOSER requires this search to be structured for hill-climbing search. A simple way to organize the search through this strategy space would be to treat all control points a equal and consider all single method changes to a given control strategy. This was the strategy in our PRODIGY implementation of COMPOSER [Gratch92]. Here, we used our knowledge of the scheduler to take advantage of interactions (or lack thereof) between control points to help structure the search. The intent of this organization is to reduce the branching factor in the control strategy search and improve the expected utility of locally optimal solutions. This approach led to a transformation generator that implements a layered search through the strategy space. Each control point is assigned to a level. The control strategy space is search by evaluating all combinations of methods at a single level, adopting the best combinations, and then

2. This is a prime example of the difficulty of determining good heuristics. Selecting high conflict variable has the benefit of rapidly forcing many time-periods to be in or out of the schedule (e.g. reducing the number of steps to solution). Selecting low conflict intervals advocates adding those time-periods which cost little, and thus may satisfy constraints without causing conflicts [Dechter92].

moving onto the next level. The organization is shown below:

Level 0: weight adjustment
Level 1: constructing alternatives
Level 2: secondary constraint sort, child sort
Level 3: primary constraint sort

The weight adjustment and alternative construction control points were separated because they are relatively independent from the other control points. While there is clearly some interaction between weight search, alternative construction, and the other control points, a good selection of methods for pricing and alternative construction should perform well across all constraint and child sorts. The primary constraint sort was separated into another level because it was the sole control point that the implementor of LR–26 had spent time experimenting and optimizing. Thus, we believed that it was unlikely the default strategy could be improved upon, and hence relegated to a separate level.

Given this transformation generator, DSN-COMPOSER hill-climbs across levels. It first entertains weight adjustment methods, then alternative construction methods, then combinations of secondary constraint sort and child sort methods, and finally primary constraint sort methods. Each choice is made given the previously adopted methods. Searching the structured space involves evaluating at most 4+2+9×4+9=51 strategies.

This leveled search can be viewed as the consequence of asserting certain types of relations between control points. Independence relations indicate cases in which the utility of methods for one control point is roughly independent of the methods used at other control points. Dominance relations indicate that the changes in utility from changing methods for one control point are much larger than the changes in utility for another control point. Finally, inconsistency relations indicate when a method M_1 for control point X is inconsistent with method M_2 for control point Y. This means that any strategy using these methods for these control points need not be considered.

3.5 EXTRACTING UTILITY INFORMATION

To perform its evaluations, COMPOSER must be able to determine, given a current control strategy, a transformation, and a problem, what improvement the transformations provides over the current strategy on that problem. How we can extract this information depends intimately on the utility function, the form of the transformations, and the extent to which we can model the behavior of the problem solver. In the best case we possess a detailed cost model of the problem solver that efficiently derives the ramification of proposed modifications without actually solving the problem (e.g. [Greiner89, Subramanian90]). In the worst case we can resort to brute-force simulation: solve the problem with and without the proposed modification and observe the difference in utility between the two solution attempts. In the former case the cost of processing an example is tied to the efficiency of manipulating the model. In the later case the cost is tied to the efficiency of the problem solver and grows linearly with the number of transformations we consider.

In the current context we found it necessary to use the later, more costly, alternative. Given m candidate transformations, DSN-COMPOSER solves each problem $m+1$ times; once with the current control strategy and once using each of the m transformations. This allows us to generate the m incremental utility values. There are several issues that lead us to this particular solution. In particular we found that other more efficient proposals for gathering statistics (see [Gratch92, Greiner92]) were not appropriate to this problem. We elaborate on this issue in Section 5.

4 EXPERIMENT AND RESULTS

DSN-COMPOSER should, with high probability, improve the expected utility of the scheduler over the distribution of problems. This can be seen as two basic claims that can be tested empirically. First, DSN-COMPOSER should identify transformations that improve the expert strategy. Second, it should identify these transformations with the confidence predicted by the statistical theory. Besides testing these claims, we are also interested in two secondary questions. How quickly does the technique improves expected utility (e.g., how many examples are required to make statistical inferences?). Also, many problems are unsolvable within five minutes with the expert strategy. Can DSN-COMPOSER improve the number of solvable problems?

When DSN-COMPOSER learns a strategy, its behavior is guided by a random selection of training examples according to the problem distribution. As a result of this random factor, the system will exhibit different behavior on different runs of the system. On some runs the system may learn high utility strategies. On other runs the random examples may poorly represent the distribution and the system may adopt transformations with negative utility. The typical behavior can be estimated from several runs of the system.

For the experiments a learning run consists of 300 randomly selected training examples. The expected utility of all learned strategies is assessed on an independent test set of 1000 test examples. A measurement of learning rate is determined by recording the strategy learned by DSN-COMPOSER after every 20 examples. Thus we can see the result of learning with only twenty examples, only forty examples, etc. To assess statistical error, we perform twenty runs of the system on twenty distinct training sets.

COMPOSER has two parameters. The parameter δ specifies the acceptable level of statistical error. This is the chance that the technique will adopt a bad transformation or reject a good one. In DSN-COMPOSER this is set to a standard value of 5%. COMPOSER bases each statistical inferences on at least n_0 examples. In DSN-COMPOSER n_0 is set to the empirically determined value of fifteen.

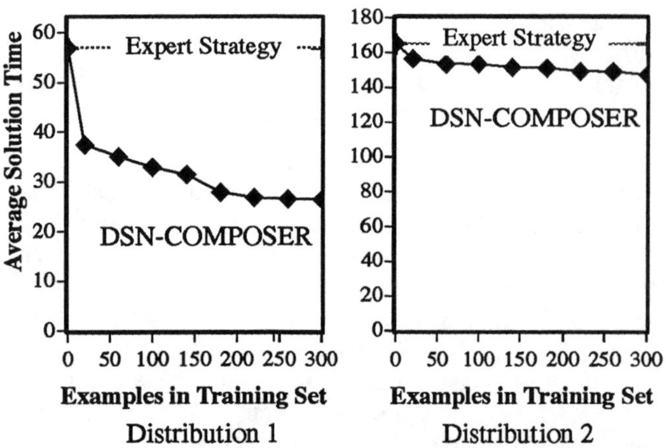

Summary of Results			Dist. 1	Dist. 2
Avg. Solution Time (seconds per prob.)	Expert Strategy		57	165
	Learned Strategies	avg. across trials	27	147
		best strategy	12	140
		worst strategy	36	160
Statistical Error Rate		predicted	5%	5%
		observed	3%	6%
Solution Rate (% of solvable probs.)	Expert Strategy		93%	51%
	Learned Strategies	avg. across trials	95%	54%
		best strategy	97%	59%
		worst strategy	92%	50%

Figure 1. Learning curves showing performance as a function of the number of training examples and table of experimental results. Results are provided for original distribution (Distribution 1) and the distribution including unsolved problems (Distribution 2).

Recall that we purposely excluded several inherently difficult scheduling problems from the problem distribution. These problems, if added to the problem distribution, should make learning more difficult as no strategy is likely to provide a noticeable improvement within the five minute resource bound. Nevertheless, it is important to show that DSN-COMPOSER does not require the elimination of these problems. To test this we created a new distribution by incorporating these problems into the original distribution and repeated the experiments. Results for both sets of experiments are shown in Figure 1. The original distribution is called Distribution 1 while the second is referred to as Distribution 2.

The results support the two primary claims. For Distribution 1, the system learned search control strategies that yielded a significant improvement in performance. It reduced the average time to solve a problem from 57 to 27 seconds (a 53% improvement). There is modest variance in the expected utility of the strategies learned in the twenty trials. The best of these strategies required only 12 seconds on average to solve a problem (an improvement of 78%). The observed statistical accuracy remained well within the theoretically predicted bound: of 93 transformations adopted across the twenty trials, only 3% decreased expected utility. It took an average of 58 examples to adopt each transformation. The human expert strategy was unable to solve 7% of the scheduling problems within the resource bound. One strategy learned by the system reduced this number to 3%.

For Distribution 2, learned strategies reduced the average solution time from 165 to 147 seconds (an 11% improvement). The best learned strategies required 160 seconds on average to solve a problem (an improvement of 15%). The observed statistical accuracy did not significantly differ from the theoretically predicted bound: of 107 transformations were adopted across the trials, only 6% decreased expected utility. The introduction of the difficult problems resulted in higher variance in the distribution of incremental utility values and this is reflected in a higher sample complexity: an average of 108 examples to adopt each transformation. Some improvement was noted on the supposedly unsolvable problems. One strategy learned by DSN-COMPOSER increased the number of solvable problems from 51% to 59% (a 16% improvement).

Most of the learned improvement came from improved methods for lagrangian weight adjustment, secondary constraint sorting, and child ordering. The best learned strategy performed no weight adjustment, preferred constraints that contained time periods with high levels of temporal conflicts, and, among child nodes, prefer alternatives with few temporal conflicts. By avoiding the weight adjustment, DSN-COMPOSER implies that there is no utility in using lagrangian weights to improve the first relaxed solution. One interpretation of the constraint and child methods is that search should proceed by first identifying a highly constrained constraint, and then choose the least constrained way of satisfying it. It is interesting that this is consistent with the general recommendations in the CSP literature [Dechter92].

5 DISCUSSION

This paper evaluates COMPOSER on a real-world domain. COMPOSER is grounded in a mathematical framework. While the framework embodies statistical assumptions, there is a theoretical support for these (the Central Limit Theorem) and they enjoy wide acceptance in the statistical community. Admittedly, these statistical approaches have not seen wide use within machine learning systems, so there is some reason to be cautious about their applicability. However, the current scheduling results and previous demonstrations in artificial planning domains [Gratch92] provide growing support for the effectiveness and generality of the COMPOSER framework.

An important aspect of statistical frameworks like COMPOSER is their flexibility. In our research we have applied the technique to scheduling and planning tasks, in both cases improving the average time to produce solutions. Cohen and Greiner illustrate how such statistical frameworks can apply to a wide variety of utility functions. For example, by choosing another utility function we could guide DSN-COMPOSER towards influencing other aspects of LR-26's behavior such as increasing the amount of flexibility in the generated schedules.

Our experience in the scheduling domain uncovered several aspects of COMPOSER that can be improved. Its performance is tied to the transformations it is given and the expense of processing examples. Just as an inductive learning technique relies on good attributes, if COMPOSER is to be effective, there must exist good methods for the control points that make up a strategy. Because of the nature of hill-climbing, even if a good strategy exists, there is no guarantee that COMPOSER can find it. One may have to consider carefully how to explore the transformation space.

When it is available, knowledge such as dominance and independence can improve learning efficiency and mitigate the effects of local maxima. An important question is to what extent this information influenced the expected utility of the learned knowledge in the DSN domain. We are currently performing a series of experiments to address this question. We are also interested in whether this type of information could assist learning in our earlier PRODIGY implementation. An obvious question is if such information can be acquired automatically. Another could help overcome the problem of local maxima. One strategy we are investigating is to perform several learning trials, starting the system at a differing random locations in the strategy space. This is similar to the training strategy for neural network systems.

In the LR-26 domain the cost of processing each training example grows linearly with the number of candidates at each hill-climbing step. While this is not bad from a complexity standpoint, it is a pragmatic concern. There have been a few proposals to reduce the expense in gathering statistics. In [Gratch92] we exploited properties of the transformations to gather statistics from a single solution attempt. That system relied on so-called "rejection rules" [Minton88] that only avoid backtracking. The same technique could not be applied to "preference rules" that suggest novel search directions. Greiner and Jurisica [Greiner92] propose one method for evaluating preference rules from a single solution attempt by maintaining upper and lower bounds on the utility of the novel search paths. In the LR-26 domain these bounds are too weak to discriminate between alternative search strategies because there is very little overlap between the search spaces explored by alternative control strategies. Presumably this could also occur in other domains.

Finally, an important issue is the notion of a shifting problem distribution. COMPOSER assumes a stable distribution of problems. In many domains this may not be an appropriate assumption. For example, there are properties in the deep space network that produce distribution shifts: old satellites are deactivated, new satellites are launched, and orbits change in a predictable pattern. We ignored these factors in our experiments by combining all problems into a single batch and choosing a random ordering. One solution to shifting distributions is to use a moving window of problems, periodically retraining the system with new problems added to the front of the window and old problems removed from the end. Alternatively, it might be possible to predict and exploit predictable shifts to guide its behavior.

Acknowledgements

Portions of research was performed at the University of Illinois under National Science Foundation grant NSF-IRI-92-09394 and portions at the Jet Propulsion Laboratory, California Institute of Technology under a contract with the National Atmospheric and Space Administration. We thank Colin Bell and Eric Biefeld for many helpful comments and discussions.

References

[Bell92] C. E. Bell, "Scheduling Deep Space Network Data Transmissions: A Lagrangian Relaxation Approach," ***Internal JPL report***, July 1992.

[Buntine89] W. Buntine, "A Critique of the Valiant Model," ***Proceedings of the Eleventh International Joint Conference on Artificial Intelligence***, Detroit, MI, August 1989, pp. 837–842.

[Dechter92] R. Dechter, "Constraint Networks," in ***Encyclopedia of Artificial Intelligence***, Stuart C Shapiro (ed.), John Wiley and Sons, Inc., 1992.

[Fisher81] M. Fisher, "The Lagrangian Relaxation Method for Solving Integer Programming Problems," ***Management Science 27***, 1 (1981), pp. 1–18.

[Gratch91] J. Gratch and G. DeJong, "A Hybrid Approach to Guaranteed Effective Control Strategies," ***Proceedings of the Eighth International Workshop on Machine Learning***, Evanston, IL, June 1991.

[Gratch92] J. Gratch and G. DeJong, "COMPOSER: A Probabilistic Solution to the Utility Problem in Speed–up Learning," ***Proceedings of the National Conference on Artificial Intelligence***, San Jose, CA, July 1992, pp. 235–240.

[Gratch93] J. Gratch and S. Chien, "Learning Search Control Knowledge for the Deep Space Network Scheduling Problem: Extended Report and Guide to Software," Technical Report UIUCDCS–R–93–1789, Department of Computer Science, University of Illinois, Urbana, IL, January 1993.

[Greiner89] R. Greiner and J. Likuski, "Incorporating Redundant Learned Rules: A Preliminary Formal Analysis of EBL," ***Proceedings of the Eleventh International Joint Conference on Artificial Intelligence***, Detroit, MI, August 1989, pp. 744–749.

[Greiner92] R. Greiner and I. Jurisica, "A Statistical Approach to Solving the EBL Utility Problem," ***Proceedings of the Na-***

tional Conference on Artificial Intelligence, San Jose, CA, July 1992, pp. 241–248.

[Held70] M. Held and R. M. Karp," "The Traveling Salesman Problem and Minimum Spanning Trees"," ***Operations Research 18***, (1970), pp. 1138–1162.

[Hogg78] R. V. Hogg and A. T. Craig, ***Introduction to Mathematical Statistics***, Macmillan Publishing Co., Inc., London, 1978.

[Laird92] P. Laird, "Dynamic Optimization," ***Proceedings of the Ninth International Conference on Machine Learning***, Aberdeen, Scotland, July 1992, pp. 263–272.

[Mackworth92] A. K. Mackworth, "Constraint Satisfaction,"in ***Encyclopedia of Artificial Intelligence***, Stuart C Shapiro (ed.), John Wiley and Sons, Inc., 1992.

[Minton88] S. Minton,in ***Learning Search Control Knowledge: An Explanation–Based Approach***, Kluwer Academic Publishers, Norwell, MA, 1988.

[Subramanian90] D. Subramanian and R. Feldman, "The Utility of EBL in Recursive Domain Theories," ***Proceedings of the National Conference on Artificial Intelligence***, Boston, MA, August 1990, pp. 942–949.

[Subramanian92] D. Subramanian and S. Hunter, "Measuring Utility and the Design of Provably Good EBL Algorithms," ***Proceedings of the Ninth International Conference on Machine Learning***, Aberdeen, Scotland, July 1992, pp. 426–435.

[Taha82] H. A. Taha, ***Operations Research, an Introduction***, Macmillan Publishing Co., INC., 1982.

Appendix: COMPOSER Algorithm

Let *PE* denote a performance element. COMPOSER takes an initial element, PE_0, and identifies a sequence, PE_0, PE_1, ... where each subsequent *PE* has, with probability 1 - δ, higher expected utility. *TRANSFORMS(PE)* is a function that takes a *PE* and returns a set of candidate changes. *APPLY(t, PE)* is a function that takes a transformation, $t \in TRANSFORMS(PE)$, and a *PE* and returns a new *PE'* that is the result of transforming *PE* with *t*. Let $U_j(PE)$ denote the utility of *PE* on problem *j*. The change in utility that a transformation provides for the *j*th problem, called the *incremental utility* of a transformation, is denoted by $\Delta U_j(t|PE)$. This is the difference in utility between solving the problem with and without the transformation: $\Delta U_j(t|PE) = U_j(APPLY(t, PE)) - U_j(PE)$. COMPOSER finds a *PE* with high expected utility by identifying transformations with positive expected incremental utility. The expected incremental utility is estimated by averaging a sample of randomly drawn incremental utility values. Given a sample of *n* values, the average of that sample is denoted by $\overline{\Delta U}_n(t|PE)$. The likely difference between the average and the true expected incremental utility depends on the variance of the distribution, estimated from a sample by the *sample variance* $S_n^2(t|PE)$, and the size of the sample, *n*. COMPOSER provides a statistical technique for determining when sufficient examples have been gathered to decide, with error δ, that the expected incremental utility of a transformation is positive or negative. The algorithm is summarized in Figure 2.[3]

3. This reflects three differences from [Gratch92]. The first is the correction of a typo in the definition of Φ(a) that appeared in that paper. The second is superficial – TRANSFORM introduces all transformations at the beginning of a step, instead of incrementally. While we still allow the later, the former reflects the current implementation. Finally, we adopt the δ^* term, recommended by [Greiner92]. The error at each step is dependent on the cardinality of T. While δ^* is overly conservative for most applications, we feel this is more reasonable than the overly liberal previous approach of ignoring the cardinality of T.

Let $PE = PE_0$ T = TRANSFORMS(PE) $j = 0$ $\delta^* = \delta/(2|T|)$

While more examples and T ≠ ∅ do

$j = j + 1$

∀t∈T: Get $\Delta U_j(t|PE)$ /* Gather statistics and find transformations that have reached significance */

$$significant = \left\{ t \in \mathbf{T} : j \geq n_0 \text{ and } \frac{S_j^2(t|PE)}{(\overline{\Delta U}_j(t|PE))^2} < \frac{j}{a^2} \right\} \quad \text{where } \Phi(a) = \int_{-\infty}^{a} \left(1/\sqrt{2\pi}\right) exp\left[-0.5y^2\right] dy = \delta^*$$

$\mathbf{T} = \mathbf{T} - \{t \in significant : \overline{\Delta U}_j(t|PE) < 0\}$ /* Discard transformations that decrease expeced utility */

If $\exists t \in stopped : \overline{\Delta U}_j(t|PE) > 0$ Then /* Adopt transformation that most increases expected utility */

$PE = Apply(x \in significant : \forall y \in significant\left[\overline{\Delta U}_j(x|PE) > \overline{\Delta U}_j(y|PE)\right], PE)$

T = TRANSFORMS(PE) $j = 0$ $\delta^* = \delta/(2|T|)$

Return (PE)

Figure 2: The COMPOSER algorithm

Learning procedures from interactive natural language instructions

Scott B. Huffman
Artificial Intelligence Laboratory
The University of Michigan
1101 Beal Ave.
Ann Arbor, Michigan 48109–2110
huffman@umich.edu

John E. Laird
Artificial Intelligence Laboratory
The University of Michigan
1101 Beal Ave.
Ann Arbor, Michigan 48109–2110
laird@umich.edu

Abstract

Despite its ubiquity in human learning, very little work has been done in artificial intelligence on agents that learn from interactive natural language instructions. In this paper, we examine the problem of learning procedures from interactive, situated instruction, in which the student is attempting to perform tasks within the instructional domain, and asks for instruction when it is needed. We present Instructo-Soar, a system that behaves and learns in response to interactive natural language instructions. Instructo-Soar learns completely new procedures from sequences of instruction, and also learns how to extend its knowledge of previously known procedures to new situations. These learning tasks require both inductive and analytic learning. Instructo-Soar exhibits a multiple execution learning process in which initial learning has a rote, episodic flavor, and later executions allow the initially learned knowledge to be generalized properly.

1 INTRODUCTION

The hallmark of universal computation systems is their ability to take instructions. This ability separates computers from other machines, which can perform only a limited number of tasks. Instructability allows computers to perform any of an infinite number of tasks. However, computers take instructions in a way that is radically different from the way humans do. Computers receive instructions in the form of programs. This method of communication from instructor (programmer) to computer is characterized by the following properties.

- **Artificial language.** Programmers must translate knowledge into a language that requires precise artificial terminology and syntax.
- **Unsituated instruction.** The instruction does not occur within the context of the computer attempting to solve a specific problem.
- **Non-interactive instruction.** The instructor determines when and what to instruct without any feedback from the computer.

These properties have a number of implications for the instructor:

1. The instructor must know what procedures are already encoded in the computer, to avoid redundancy and conflicts.
2. The instructor must understand the effects of long sequences of instruction, because a complete instructional sequence must be generated.
3. The instructor must create a procedure that applies in every situation it will be exposed to.
4. The instructor must specify the procedures in complete detail; no steps may be omitted or abstracted.

In contrast, humans can engage in apprenticeship instruction, in which the student actively tries to acquire knowledge to aid in problem solving. This type of instruction has the following properties:

- **Natural language.** Instructor and student speak the same language, and the language is highly flexible.
- **Situated instruction.** The instructor and student are situated within a specific task. The instructor does not need to predict the effects of long instruction sequences because the student performs the task in response to individual instructions. The instructor needs to produce instructions for only the situation at hand, not for all possible situations. The student can use the situation to disambiguate instruction, and cue the recall of relevant domain knowledge.
- **Interactive instruction.** The student can request help during a task. This frees the instructor from specifying the procedure in full detail;

instructions are given when needed. The instructor need not know exactly what the student knows about the task. If the student is unable to fill in missing steps or details, more instruction can be requested.

In this paper, we describe Instructo-Soar, a system that learns procedures from interactive natural language instructions. Instructo-Soar attempts to solve problems within a task domain, and requests instruction when it does not know how to make progress on a problem. The instructions are simple English imperative sentences. They can include commands for primitive or known operators, for complex operators that the system does not know how to apply in the current situation, and for completely new complex operators that the system must learn from scratch. These latter cases lead to a recursive use of instruction where the system learns a hierarchy of operators. Both analytic and empirical learning methods are employed so that after instruction, the system can perform similar tasks (and subtasks) without instruction. Learning of a new procedure is initially by rote, using an episodic memory acquired as a side-effect of natural language comprehension. During later executions of the task, analytic techniques generalize the procedure.

2 RELATED WORK

This work is most closely tied to work on learning from external guidance and advice taking [McCarthy, 1968; Carbonell *et al.*, 1983]. Prior research in these areas has usually emphasized one of the following: natural language instruction, situated instruction, or interactive instruction.

SHRDLU [Winograd, 1972] learned new goal specifications by directly transforming sentences into state descriptions, but did not learn how to perform procedures. Others have learned declarative knowledge bases from natural language (e.g., [Haas and Hendrix, 1983]). A number of recent systems perform in response to natural language input, but do no learning [Vere and Bickmore, 1990; Chapman, 1990; DiEugenio and White, 1992]. Lewis *et al.* [1989] present a system that learns operator sequences from natural language instructions taken in batch form (unsituated and non-interactive). Alterman *et al.* [1991] and Martin and Firby [1991] describe situated systems that recover from execution errors by learning from instruction.

There have been a variety of systems that learn from observation [Redmond, 1989; Segre, 1987; Wilkins, 1988; VanLehn, 1987]. These systems take traces of expert behavior on a specific problem and learn general procedures using analytic techniques such as explanation-based learning [Mitchell *et al.*, 1986]. However, these system do not support interaction with the instructor.

Learning apprentice systems (LAS's) [Mitchell *et al.*, 1990; Kodratoff and Tecuci, 1987; Golding *et al.*, 1987; Laird *et al.*, 1990] extend the work on learning from observation by providing some interactivity: typically, the system suggests steps to the instructor. However, the instructor can only select actions that are directly performable at the current problem state. LAS's cannot take instructions specifying new, unknown actions (that thus must be learned) or actions with unmet preconditions (which the agent may or may not know how to achieve). For example, LEAP's [Mitchell *et al.*, 1990] instructor inputs a complete circuit implementing a desired function, but cannot instruct the system to perform some new, unknown circuit transformation. Since whole circuits are learned for each function, LEAP avoids the problem of an instructor "skipping steps" by specifying operations with unmet preconditions. In addition, learning apprentice systems require that either the termination conditions of the procedure being taught (the goal concept [Mitchell *et al.*, 1986]) are already known, or that the instructor provide a complete description of termination conditions. Finally, these systems typically have no natural language capability.

3 INSTRUCTION WITHIN AN AUTONOMOUS AGENT

One factor that most previous work on instruction has ignored is the integration of learning from instruction within an autonomous agent. To learn from interactive instruction, an autonomous agent must have general reasoning capabilities, and be able to recognize when its knowledge is insufficient and instruction is needed. Instructions must be assimilated into a possibly large body of existing knowledge, and instructional learning must be smoothly integrated with the agent's other learning and problem solving methods. An agent must maintain its ability to respond to its environment even while accepting instructions, and must be able to apply learning from instruction to a wide variety of tasks.

Supporting these capabilities is dependent in part upon the architecture in which the agent in constructed. We use Soar [Laird *et al.*, 1987] as our underlying architecture. Soar's basic structure provides a framework in which these capabilities can be approached.

In Soar, all activity occurs by applying operators to states within problem spaces, supporting general problem solving and planning. Our instruction learning techniques learn and extend operators, and thus have the potential to be applicable to any problem encoded in Soar. When a Soar agent cannot make progress within a problem space, an impasse arises, and a subgoal is generated to resolve the impasse. Any type of knowledge might be applied within the subgoal, so learning from instruction can co-exist with learning from other knowledge sources, such as experimentation, analogy, etc. Learning occurs through chunking, a form of explanation-based learning, which summarizes the results of subgoal processing, avoiding the impasse in the future. Chunking occurs over all subgoals, so instructional learning can be performed as part of the ongoing activity of the agent, rather than using a separate mechanism that interrupts the normal course of activity.

Instructo-Soar's problem spaces implement an agent with three main categories of knowledge: natural language processing knowledge, originally developed for NL-Soar [Lehman *et al.*, 1991]; knowledge about obtaining and using instruction; and knowledge of the task domain itself. This task knowledge is extended through learning from instruction. Assumed characteristics of the Instructo-Soar agent include:

1. **Relevant relationships.** The agent has knowledge of all of the relevant task relationships, and can derive them from perception.
2. **Primitive operators.** The agent knows a set of primitive operators that it can execute, internally simulate, and map natural language to.
3. **Reading ability.** The agent can read the instructions, even if it has no knowledge of an operation within the current task domain that corresponds to the instruction.
4. **Locality of instruction.** The agent assumes that an instruction applies to the *most recent* unachieved operation.

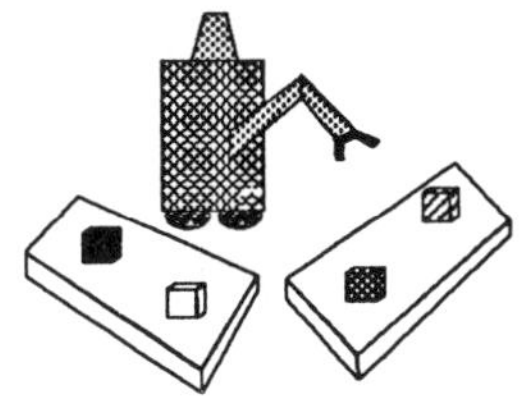

(a)

Pick up the red block.
  Move to the yellow table.
  Move the arm above the red block.
    Move up.
  Move down.
  Close the hand.
  Move up.
  The operator is finished.

(b)

Figure 1: (a). Initial situation of agent; (b) Instructions to teach operator.

4 LEARNING FROM INSTRUCTION

Consider the agent and situation shown in Figure 1(a). The agent has primitive operators for moving to tables, opening and closing its hand, and moving its arm up, down, and into relationships with objects (e.g., above blocks). This is the primary domain Instructo-Soar has been applied to; the techniques have also been applied in a more limited way to a flight domain, in which Soar controls a flight simulator and instructions are given for simple maneuvers like taking off [Pearson *et al.*, 1993]. To explain Instructo-Soar's performance, we will use the example of teaching the agent in Figure 1(a) to pick up blocks. Since picking up blocks is not a known operator, when told "Pick up the red block," the agent must learn a new operator.

To learn a new operator, an agent must learn each of the following:

1. **Mapping from natural language:** What instruction(s) map onto the new operator. The mapping allows the agent to select the operator when commanded in the future.
2. **Operator template**: Knowledge of the operator's arguments and how they can be instantiated. For picking up blocks, the agent acquires a new operator with a single argument, which may be instantiated with any block that isn't currently picked up.
3. **Implementation:** How to perform the operator. New operators are built from primitive and/or previously learned operators, so implementation takes the form of a series of sub-operators (e.g., move to the proper table, grasp the block, etc.)
4. **Termination:** Knowledge of when the new operator is achieved. This is the goal concept of the new operator. For "pick up", the termination conditions include holding the desired block, with the arm up.

Instructo-Soar handles simple imperative sentences, and learns a straightforward mapping of an instruction's semantic argument structure to a newly generated operator template. In general, mapping from instructions to task operators and objects can be difficult, as it can require complex natural language comprehension, and possibly reasoning about the task itself [Huffman and Laird, 1992; DiEugenio, 1992].

To learn a general operator implementation from instructions, an agent must determine the proper scope of applicability of each instruction. Some features of the current task and situation are important conditions, while others may be ignored. For example, when told to pick up a red block, does it matter that the block is red? Perhaps, if building a stoplight. But if trying to block open a door, the key feature may be the block's weight. Thus, learning from instruction can involve both generalization (that "red" doesn't matter, although explicitly mentioned) and specialization (that the weight matters, although not mentioned).

To learn general implementations, Instructo-Soar uses explanation-based learning (EBL) as realized by chunking in Soar. Proper generalization requires understanding how each instruction contributes to achieving the goal. However, during the initial execution of the instructions for a new operator, the agent does not know the termination conditions (goal concept) of the operator; therefore, generalization on this basis is impossible. Thus, initial learning is based on a weak inductive step: believing what the instructor says. This learning is rote and overspecific, with an "episodic" flavor. At the end of the initial execution, the termination conditions, or goal concept, of the new operator can be induced. On later executions, the agent *can* form an understanding of how the instructions, recalled from its episodic memory, allow the goal to be reached, using its knowledge of primitive operator effects (domain theory). This allows the implementation sequence to be learned deductively (and generally), based on achievement of the induced goal concept. We will describe the details of the technique using an example.

5 EXAMPLE

Consider the agent shown in Figure 1(a) being instructed to pick up blocks. The agent is given the instructions shown in Figure 1(b) during the course of performing the task.

5.1 FIRST EXECUTION

The agent begins with knowledge of the primitive operators, but no knowledge of the new operator it will be instructed to perform. Following the first execution, the agent must be able to perform at least the exact same task without being re-instructed. Thus, the agent must learn, in some form, *all* of the parts of the new operator, as described in the previous section.

The first instruction given is "Pick up the red block." It is comprehended using Soar's natural language capability, NL-Soar [Lehman *et al.*, 1991], which produces a semantic structure and resolves "the red block" to a block in the agent's environment. However, the semantic structure produced does not correspond to any known operator, indicating that the agent must learn a new operator. Thus, a new, empty operator is generated (e.g., `new-op14`), with an argument structure that directly corresponds to the semantic structure's arguments (here, one argument, `object`). The system learns a mapping from the semantic structure to the new operator, heuristically restricting arguments to be of the same type (e.g., `isa block`) as in the current instruction.

Next, the new operator is selected for execution. Since the agent doesn't know any implementation for the operator, it immediately impasses and asks for further instructions. Each instruction in Figure 1(b) is given, comprehended and executed in turn. For instance, "Move to the yellow table" is comprehended, mapped to a known operator, and executed. These instructions provide the implementation for the new operator.

The instruction "Move the arm above the red block" provides an example of learning to achieve the preconditions of a known operator. This operation is known, and the agent can perform it when its hand is in the upper plane. However, here the hand is in the lower plane, so the operation cannot be performed directly. Thus, the agent asks for instruction about this operator, and is told to move the arm up. This achieves the precondition, and after moving up the agent has sufficient knowledge to complete the move above operation without further instruction. As a result, a rule is learned that will propose moving up to achieve this precondition in the future. Thus, a known operation has been extended to apply in a new situation; further instruction could extend it even further, for instance allowing the agent to "move above" starting from a state where it's not even next to the table. Note that the interactive nature of instruction means that the instructor *need not know* beforehand whether the agent knows how to apply an operation from the current situation. This recursive instruction of sub-operations could be multiple levels deep, allowing for a great flexibility of instruction sequences, depending what the agent already knows. A simple mathematical analysis shows that for a sequence of only six primitive actions, with preconditions for each action, over 100 possible sequences of interactive instruction are possible [Huffman, 1992]. This contrasts with learning from observation, in which systems learn from observing only the sequence of primitive operations performed to carry out the task.

After completing the "move above" action, the agent continues receiving and executing instructions for the new "pick up" operator. Ultimately, the implementation sequence for "pick up" will be learned at the proper level of generality, based on understanding how each instructed operator leads to successful execution of the new operator. During the initial execution, however, this is impossible, because the goal of this new operator is not yet known. Thus, the agent resorts to *rote learning*, recording exactly what it was told to do, in exactly what situation.

This recording process is not an explicit memorization step; rather, it occurs as a side effect of language comprehension. While reading each sentence, the agent learns a set of rules that encode the sentence's semantic features. The rules help NL-Soar to resolve referents in later sentences (implementing a simple version of Grosz's focus space mechanism [Grosz, 1977]). The rules record each instruction, indexed by the goal it applies to and its place in the instruction sequence. This episodic "case" corresponds to a lock-step, overspecific sequencing of the instructions given to perform the new operator. For instance, the agent encodes that "to pick-up (that is, new-op14) the red block, rb1, I was first told to move to the yellow table, yt1." One issue that arises here is whether and when to generalize the index and information contained within the case. However, at this point any generalization would be purely heuristic, since the agent was unable to explain the various steps of the episode.

Finally, the agent is told "The operator is finished," indicating that the goal of the new operator has been achieved. This triggers the agent to learn termination conditions for the new operator. Learning termination conditions is an inductive concept formation problem. Standard concept learning approaches may be used here; however, typically, an instructor will expect learning within a small number of examples. Currently, the system uses a simple heuristic: it compares the current state to the initial state the agent was in when commanded to perform the new operator. Everything that has *changed* is considered a part of the termination conditions of the new operator. In this case, the changes are that the robot is standing at a table, holding a block, and the block and gripper are both up in the air.

This heuristic forms the system's inductive bias for learning termination conditions. It allows learning from a single example, but is clearly too simple. Conditions that changed may not matter; e.g., perhaps it doesn't matter to picking up blocks that the robot ends up at a table. Unchanged conditions may matter; e.g., if learning to build a "stoplight", block colors are important.

Instructo-Soar performs this induction by EBL over an overgeneral theory (as, e.g., [Miller and Laird, 1991; VanLehn *et al.*, 1990; Rosenbloom and Aasman, 1990]). Although not sophisticated here, this type of inductive learning has the advantage that the agent can alter the bias to reflect other available knowledge. This might include more instruction (e.g., simply asking which features are relevant [Laird *et al.*, 1990]); analogy to other known operators (e.g., pick up actions in related domains), domain heuristics, etc.

On the first pass, then, the agent:

- Carries out a sequence of instructions achieving a new operator.
- Learns a new operator template.
- Learns the mapping from natural language to the new operator.
- Learns a rote execution sequence for the new operator.
- Induces the termination conditions of the new operator.

Since the agent has learned all of the necessary parts of an operator, it will be able to perform the same task again without instruction. However, since the implementation of the operator is rote, it can only perform the *exact* same task. It has not learned generally how to pick up blocks yet.

Since the goal is now known, the system could explain and generalize the instruction sequence directly after the first execution. This is a reasonable possibility, but the multi-step simulation required has two disadvantages:

1. The agent's ongoing performance of the tasks at hand (either by acting or by taking more instruction) is temporarily suspended. This could be awkward if instruction of the new procedure being simulated is nested within the instructions for larger tasks that must still be completed, or if these tasks have temporal constraints.
2. The multiple step simulation is susceptible to compounding of domain theory errors. That is, a significant error in simulating any step of the procedure (or the interaction of multiple small errors) can lead to an incomplete or incorrect explanation of goal achievement. Simulating to explain each *individual* instruction, as described below, avoids this problem because each successive simulation begins from the current external state, which reflects the true effects of the previous instructions.

Thus, we have opted for generalizing on future executions.

5.2 LATER EXECUTIONS

Later, in the same situation the agent is again asked to pick up the red block. The agent selects the newly learned operator, and then reaches an impasse because it does not yet know the general implementation sequence for the operator (how to pick up blocks in the general case). Here, the agent attempts to recall instructions it was given during the first execution. It retrieves, instruction by instruction, the rote case it learned previously.

After each retrieval, before carrying out the instruction in the external world, the agent attempts to explain to itself *why* the instructed operator leads to achievement of the higher-level goal of picking up the block. This explanation attempt takes the form of an internal simulation. Starting from the current world state, the agent internally simulates the recalled operator. Thus, the *situatedness* of the instruction plays a key role in the learning process, because the current situation grounds the explanation. The agent continues to simulate operators until it either reaches its higher-level goal (internally) or does not know what to do next. If the goal is reached, the path taken to the goal comprises an explanation of how the recalled operator leads to goal achievement.

From this explanation, the system learns a general rule that proposes the recalled operator under the right conditions. The rule both generalizes and specializes the original instruction. In "move to the yellow table"'s case, the color of the table is generalized away, because it was not critical for achievement of the goal, while the fact that the table has the block to be picked up on it is included in the proposal rule's conditions.

After learning the complete general implementation, the agent will perform the task without reference to the rote case. If asked to "Pick up the green block," `new-op14` is selected and instantiated with the green block as its argument. Then, the general sub-operator proposal rules for `new-op14` fire one by one, implementing the operator, until finally the termination conditions are recognized and the operator is terminated. Since the general proposal rules test state conditions directly, the agent can perform the task starting from any state along the implementation path, and can react to unexpected conditions (e.g., another robot stealing the block). In contrast, the rote implementation had to be performed from the same initial state each time, and its steps were not conditional on the state.

6 RESULTS

In the robotic domain described earlier, Instructo-Soar has been applied to learn a hierarchy of task operators, shown in Figure 2. The system read 24 natural language instructions (14 unique sentences) and learned 1357 chunks broken down as shown in the figure. It learned four completely new operators (shown in bold), how to achieve preconditions for a known operator (`move above`), and the extension of a new operator (extending "pick up" to work if the robot already is holding a block after initially learning "pick up" when the gripper was empty). This hierarchy can be taught using many different instruction orderings. For instance, new operators that appear as sub-operators (e.g., `grasp`) can be taught either before teaching higher operators (e.g., `pick up`), or during teaching of them. If during, the agent recursively requests instruction for the lower new operator. Thus the instructor need not know whether the agent knows a procedure before commanding it. This is an important advantage of interactive instruction for autonomous agents, which may have large amounts of knowledge. Similarly, the instructor may suggest an action that has unmet preconditions (thus skipping steps in the instruction sequence), assuming the agent knows how to achieve them before performing the action. If the agent does not, it can request more instruction, and learn how to achieve the preconditions.

Instructo-Soar exhibits a number of interesting learning characteristics:

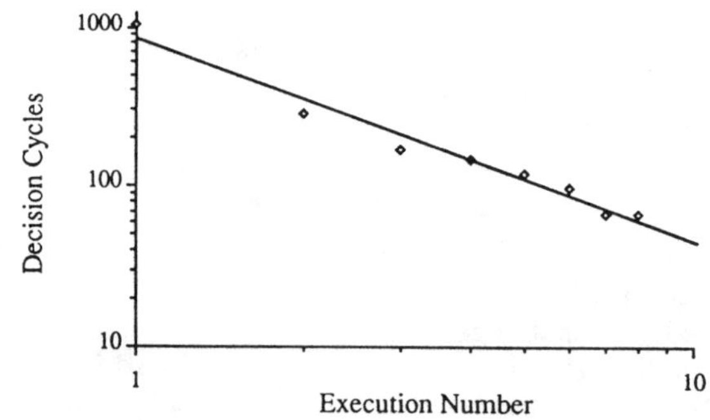

Figure 3: Decision cycles vs. learning trial for executing "pick up".

- **Multiple recall strategies.** Instructo-Soar has two strategies it can use in recalling past instructions. After recalling and internally simulating an instructed operator, the agent still may not know how that operator leads to the goal. At this point, the agent may terminate its internal simulation, and carry out the recalled operator in the external world. This is a *single recall* strategy, which is appropriate when the agent is under pressure to act quickly. Alternatively, the agent may attempt to recall further instructions, simulating each in turn, until the higher-level goal is reached. This is a *multiple recall* strategy, which leads to faster learning, but is more susceptible to errors in the agent's domain theory (primitive operator knowledge), as described above.
- **Bottom-up learning** (single recall strategy). Limiting recall to a single step allows only a single sub-operator per execution to be generalized. Generalized learning begins at the end of the implementation sequence and moves towards the beginning. As Figure 3 shows for learning "pick up", the resulting learning curve closely approximates the power law of practice [Rosenbloom and Newell, 1986] ($r = 0.98$).
- **Effectiveness of hierarchical instruction** (single recall strategy). Due to the bottom-up effect, the system learns more quickly when taught hierarchical organizations than flat sequences. General learning for an N step operator takes N executions using a flat instruction sequence. Taught hierarchically as $\sqrt{N}$ sub-operators with $\sqrt{N}$ steps each, only $\sqrt{N}$ executions are required for full general learning. Hierarchical organization has the additional advantage that more operators are learned that can be used in future instruction.
- **Degradation without domain theory.** If the agent does not have knowledge of the primitive operators' effects, learning degrades to rote learning. This appears to be consistent with psychological research showing that subjects given procedural instructions learn and perform better when they have a domain model [Kieras and Bovair, 1984].

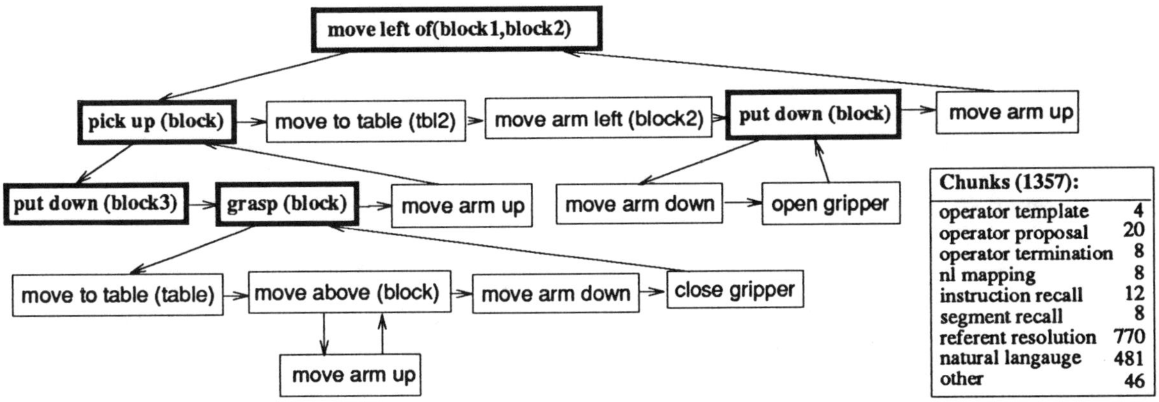

Figure 2: A hierarchy of operators learned by Instructo-Soar. Primitive operators are shown in light print; learned operators are in boldface.

7 CONCLUSION

We have described Instructo-Soar, an agent that learns and extends procedures by receiving interactive, situated natural language instructions. The agent learns completely new operators: preconditions, implementation, and termination conditions (goal concept), in contrast to learning apprentice systems, which learn only implementations, and preconditions of those implementations, for known operators. New operators learned by Instructo-Soar may be specified in later instructions for other operators, leading to learning of operator hierarchies. From the initial execution of a new operator, the agent learns a rote, overspecific execution sequence, and induces termination conditions. On later executions, the execution sequence is generalized by using internal simulation to explain each instruction.

Instructo-Soar can be extended in a number of directions. In addition to positive imperative sentences, we are currently investigating learning from other types of instructions, such as positive and negative constraints, conditionals, and actions with monitoring conditions [Huffman and Laird, 1992]. The difference-of-states method used to induce operator termination conditions is being extended to allow instructor feedback about the induced conditions. Finally, allowing weaker forms of explanation, such as analogy and heuristic causality theories (e.g., [Pazzani, 1991; VanLehn *et al.*, 1992; Schank and Leake, 1989]), would lead to more graded degradation of learning with domain theory incompleteness. These types of explanation might also lead the agent to alter its basic domain theory, for instance by inferring previously unknown affects of primitive actions.

Acknowledgments

This research was sponsored by NASA/ONR under contract NCC 2-517. The authors wish to thank Paul Rosenbloom, Jill Lehman, Rick Lewis, and Randy Jones for valuable comments on earlier drafts.

References

[Alterman *et al.*, 1991] R. Alterman, R. Zito-Wolf, and T. Carpenter. Interaction, comprehension, and instruction usage. Tech. Report CS-91-161, Computer Science Dept., Brandeis Univ., 1991.

[Carbonell *et al.*, 1983] J. G. Carbonell, R. S. Michalski, and T. M. Mitchell. An overview of machine learning. In R. S. Michalski, J. G. Carbonell, and T. M. Mitchell, editors, *Machine Learning: An artificial intelligence approach.* Morgan Kaufmann, 1983.

[Chapman, 1990] D. Chapman. *Vision, Instruction, and Action.* PhD thesis, Massachusetts Institute of Technology, 1990.

[DiEugenio and White, 1992] B. DiEugenio and M. White. On the interpretation of natural language instructions. In *Proceedings COLING 92*, July 1992.

[DiEugenio, 1992] B. DiEugenio. Understanding natural language instructions: The case of purpose clauses. In *Proceedings of Annual Meeting of the ACL*, July 1992.

[Golding *et al.*, 1987] A. Golding, P. S. Rosenbloom, and J. E. Laird. Learning search control from outside guidance. In *Proceedings of the Tenth International Joint Conference on Artificial Intelligence*, pages 334–337, August 1987.

[Grosz, 1977] B. J. Grosz. *The Representation and use of focus in dialogue understanding.* PhD thesis, University of California, Berkeley, 1977.

[Haas and Hendrix, 1983] N. Haas and G. G. Hendrix. Learning by being told: Acquiring knowledge for information management. In R. S. Michalski, J. G. Carbonell, and T. M. Mitchell, editors, *Machine*

Learning: An artificial intelligence approach. Morgan Kaufmann, 1983.

[Huffman and Laird, 1992] S. B. Huffman and J. E. Laird. Dimensions of complexity in learning from interactive instruction. In Jon Erikson, editor, *Proceedings of Cooperative Intelligent Robotics in Space III, SPIE Volume 1829*, November 1992.

[Huffman, 1992] S. B. Huffman. An analysis of instruction sequences. Artificial Intelligence Laboratory, University of Michigan, 1992.

[Kieras and Bovair, 1984] D. E. Kieras and S. Bovair. The role of a mental model in learning to operate a device. *Cognitive Science*, 8:255–273, 1984.

[Kodratoff and Tecuci, 1987] Y. Kodratoff and G. Tecuci. DISCIPLE-1: Interactive apprentice system in weak theory fields. In *Proceedings of the Tenth International Joint Conference on Artificial Intelligence*, pages 271–273, August 1987.

[Laird *et al.*, 1987] J. E. Laird, A. Newell, and P. S. Rosenbloom. Soar: An architecture for general intelligence. *Artificial Intelligence*, 33(1):1–64, 1987.

[Laird *et al.*, 1990] J. E. Laird, M. Hucka, E. S. Yager, and C. M. Tuck. Correcting and extending domain knowledge using outside guidance. In *Proceedings of the Seventh International Conference on Machine Learning*, 1990.

[Lehman *et al.*, 1991] J. Lehman, R. L. Lewis, and A. Newell. Natural language comprehension in Soar: Spring 1991. Tech. Report CMU-CS-91-117, School of Computer Science, Carnegie Mellon Univ., 1991.

[Lewis *et al.*, 1989] R. L. Lewis, A. Newell, and T. A. Polk. Toward a Soar theory of taking instructions for immediate reasoning tasks. In *Proceedings of the Annual Conference of the Cognitive Science Society*, August 1989.

[Martin and Firby, 1991] C. E. Martin and R. J. Firby. Generating natural language expectations from a reactive execution system. In *Proceedings of the Thirteenth Annual Conference of the Cognitive Science Society*, pages 811–815, August 1991.

[McCarthy, 1968] J. McCarthy. The advice taker. In M. Minsky, editor, *Semantic Information Processing*, pages 403–410. MIT Press, 1968.

[Miller and Laird, 1991] C. Miller and J. E. Laird. A constraint-motivated lexical acquisition model. In *Proceedings of the 13th Annual Conference on the Cognitive Science Society*, pages 827–831, Boston, 1991.

[Mitchell *et al.*, 1986] T. M. Mitchell, R. M. Keller, and S. T. Kedar-Cabelli. Explanation-based generalization: A unifying view. *Machine Learning*, 1, 1986.

[Mitchell *et al.*, 1990] T. M. Mitchell, S. Mahadevan, and L. I. Steinberg. LEAP: A learning apprentice system for VLSI design. In Yves Kodratoff and R. S. Michalski, editors, *Machine Learning: An artificial intelligence approach, Vol. III.* Morgan Kaufmann, 1990.

[Pazzani, 1991] M. Pazzani. Learning to predict and explain: An integration of similarity-based, theory driven, and explanation-based learning. *Journal of the Learning Sciences*, 1(2):153–199, 1991.

[Pearson *et al.*, 1993] D. J. Pearson, S. B. Huffman, M. B. Willis, J. E. Laird, and R. M. Jones. Intelligent multi-level control in a highly reactive domain. In *Proceedings of the International Conference on Intelligent Autonomous Systems*, Pgh., PA., 1993.

[Redmond, 1989] M. Redmond. Combining case-based reasoning, explanation-based learning and learning from instruction. In *Proceedings of the International Workshop on Machine Learning*, pages 20–22, 1989.

[Rosenbloom and Aasman, 1990] P. S. Rosenbloom and J. Aasman. Knowledge level and inductive uses of chunking (ebl). In *Proceedings of the National Conference on Artificial Intelligence*, 1990.

[Rosenbloom and Newell, 1986] P. S. Rosenbloom and A. Newell. The chunking of goal hierarchies: A generalized model of practice. In R. S. Michalski, J. G. Carbonell, and T. M. Mitchell, editors, *Machine Learning: An artificial intelligence approach, Volume II.* Morgan Kaufmann, 1986.

[Schank and Leake, 1989] R. C. Schank and D. B. Leake. Creativity and learning in a case-based explainer. *Artificial Intelligence*, 40:353–385, 1989.

[Segre, 1987] A. M. Segre. A learning apprentice system for mechanical assembly. In *Third IEEE Conference on Artificial Intelligence for Applications*, pages 112–117, 1987.

[VanLehn *et al.*, 1990] K. VanLehn, W. Ball, and B. Kowalski. Explanation-based learning of correctness: Towards a model of the self-explanation effect. In *Proceedings of the 12th Annual Conference of the Cognitive Science Society*, pages 717–724, 1990.

[VanLehn *et al.*, 1992] K. VanLehn, R. M. Jones, and M. T. H. Chi. A model of the self-explanation effect. *Journal of the learning sciences*, 2(1):1–59, 1992.

[VanLehn, 1987] K. VanLehn. Learning one subprocedure per lesson. *Artificial Intelligence*, 31(1):1–40, 1987.

[Vere and Bickmore, 1990] S. Vere and T. Bickmore. A basic agent. *Computational Intelligence*, 6:41–60, 1990.

[Wilkins, 1988] D. C. Wilkins. Knowledge base refinement using apprenticeship learning techniques. In *Proceedings of the National Conference on Artificial Intelligence*, pages 646–651, 1988.

[Winograd, 1972] T. Winograd. *Understanding Natural Language.* Academic Press, New York, 1972.

Generalization under Implication by Recursive Anti-unification

Peter Idestam-Almquist
Department of Computer and Systems Sciences
Stockholm University and the Royal Institute of Technology
Electrum 230, 164 40 Kista, Sweden
pi@dsv.su.se

Abstract

In the area of inductive learning, generalization is a main operation, and the usual definition of induction is based on logical implication. Recently there has been a rising interest in clausal representation of knowledge in machine learning. Almost all inductive learners that use clausal representation perform generalization under θ-subsumption rather than generalization under implication. The main reason is that there is a well-known and reasonably efficient technique to compute least general generalizations under θ-subsumption, but not under implication. Generalization under θ-subsumption is incomplete with respect to implication, and this incompleteness only occurs for recursive clauses. For recursive clauses there is a type of generalizations, called indirect roots, which are not possible to find under θ-subsumption. We will describe a technique, called recursive anti-unification, to compute indirect roots. By this technique we can also compute minimally general common indirect roots of clauses, which are guaranteed to be minimally general generalizations under implication.

1 INTRODUCTION

In the area of inductive learning, generalization is a main operation, and the usual definition of induction is based on logical implication [2]. Least general generalizations are of special interest since they are known to be correct whenever there exist correct generalizations. In recent years there has been a rising interest in clausal representation of knowledge in machine learning. Plotkin has already in the early 1970's described a technique for computation of least general generalizations of clauses under θ-subsumption [12]. Unfortunately, the results obtained by this technique sometimes are over-generalizations with respect to implication.

The difference between θ-subsumption and logical implication is important since almost all inductive learners that use clausal representation, for example CIGOL [10], GOLEM [7], LFP2 [14], ITOU [13], and CLINT [1], perform generalization under θ-subsumption rather than generalization under implication. The main reason is that there is a well-known and reasonably efficient technique to compute least general generalizations under θ-subsumption, but not under implication.

Already Plotkin realized that generalization under θ-subsumption is incomplete for recursive clauses [12]. Recursion is an important program structure in logic programming. The ability to learn recursive clauses is therefore crucial when using clausal representation. In [9] Muggleton shows that the incompleteness of generalization under θ-subsumption only concerns one type of generalizations of recursive clauses, which we call indirect roots. For example, the following clause C is an indirect root of the clause E:

$$C = (p(x) \leftarrow p(f(x))),$$
$$D = (p(x) \leftarrow p(f(f(x)))),$$
$$E = (p(a) \leftarrow p(f(f(a)))).$$

The clause C implies E since D is a resolvent of C resolved with itself, and E is an instance of D. The generalization C of E can not be found by any generalization procedure based on θ-subsumption on clauses, since the variable x in C replaces the term a in the head and another term $f(a)$ in the body of clause E.

Recently some other approaches to the problem of generalization under implication have been presented, one by Lapointe and Matwin [5], one by Muggleton [9], and one by Idestam-Almquist [4]. In [5] and [9] they deal with the problem of finding some typical root from only one example. We on the other hand are concerned about finding minimally general common indirect roots of two or more examples. The technique descibed in [5] is restricted to only two particular types of recursive clauses. The algorithm presented in [9] can find almost all roots of single recursive clauses, but it is non-deterministic. In [4] a technique to reduce generalization under implication to generalization under θ-subsumption is described. Unfortunately the technique is most of theoretical interest since it is computationally intractable.

In this paper a technique to compute indirect roots, called recursive anti-unification, will be presented. For example, the pair of terms $(x, f(x))$ is a recursive anti-unification of the pair of terms $(a, f(f(a)))$, which indicates how the generalization C can be obtained from the clause E (see above). By recursive anti-unification, we can compute minimally general common indirect roots of clauses, which are guaranteed to be minimally general generalizations under implication. We will also show how recursive anti-unification can be used to find indirect roots of single recursive clauses, in the two typical cases where generalization under θ-subsumption is incomplete. Recursive anti-unification in that way extends the framework of inductive generalization developed by Plotkin [12]. The computation of a recursive anti-unification is also very efficient. Our technique can be seen as a development and a generalization of the ideas presented in [5].

In this work we will only consider Horn clauses. We refer to [6] for the basic definitions and notations in logic programming, and to [8] for an introduction to inductive logic programming. In section 2 a necessary background for our learning problem, generalization of clauses, is given. In section 3 our generalization technique, recursive anti-unification, is presented, and in section 4 we compare it with related work. Finally in section 5 we give some concluding remarks.

2 PRELIMINARIES

The basic definitions and terminology of generalization of clauses will be given in this section. It includes anti-unification, least general generalizations under θ-subsumption, minimally generalizations under implication, and powers and roots of clauses.

2.1 ANTI-UNIFICATION

For least general generalizations of simple expressions (terms and literals) we prefer the term anti-unification to separate it from our terminology of generalization of clauses. The anti-unification of two simple expressions is the least general simple expression which is an anti-instance of both given simple expressions. We also infer the notion of term substitution to describe how an anti-unification has been achieved.

Definition A finite set of the form $\{(s_1, t_1)/x_1, \ldots, (s_n, t_n)/x_n\}$ is a *term substitution* if and only if $\{x_1/s_1, \ldots, x_n/s_n\}$ and $\{x_1/t_1, \ldots, x_n/t_n\}$ are substitutions, and the pairs $(s_1, t_1), \ldots, (s_n, t_n)$ are distinct.

Definition A simple expression G is an *anti-instance* of a simple expression E if and only if there exists a substitution θ such that $G\theta = E$, that is E is an instance of G. A simple expression G is an *anti-unification* of two simple expressions E and F, described by a term substitution $\{(s_1, t_1)/x_1, \ldots, (s_n, t_n)/x_n\}$, if and only if:
a) G is an anti-instance of E and F, such that $G\{x_1/s_1, \ldots, x_n/s_n\} = E$ and $G\{x_1/t_1, \ldots, x_n/t_n\} = F$, and
b) each anti-instance of E and F, is also an anti-instance of G.

The anti-unification of the terms $f(a, g(a, a), b, c)$ and $f(b, g(a, b), a, a)$ is the term $f(x, g(a, x), y, z)$, and it is described by the term substitution $\{(a, b)/x, (b, a)/y, (c, a)/z\}$. The anti-unification of the terms $f(a)$ and $g(a)$ is x, while the anti-unification of the literals $p(a)$ and $q(a)$ is undefined.

2.2 GENERALIZATION UNDER θ-SUBSUMPTION

As already mentioned in the introduction, least general generalization under θ-subsumption is the most common form of generalization of clauses. The following definitions are taken from [12], but the terminology is adapted to inductive logic programming.

Definition A clause C θ-subsumes a clause D, denoted $C \preceq D$, if and only if there exists a substitution θ such that $C\theta \subseteq D$.

Definition A clause C is a *least general generalization under θ-subsumption* (LGGθ) of two clauses D and E, denoted $C = lgg(D, E)$, if and only if:
a) $C \preceq D$ and $C \preceq E$, and
b) for each clause F, such that $F \preceq D$ and $F \preceq E$, then also $F \preceq C$.

Consider the following clauses:

$$C = (p(a) \leftarrow q(a), q(f(a))),$$
$$D = (p(b) \leftarrow q(f(b))), \text{ and}$$
$$E = (p(x) \leftarrow q(f(x))).$$

Then the clause E is an LGGθ of C and D. An LGGθ of two clauses can be computed by collecting all anti-unifications of one literal in the first and one literal of the second input clause. Thus, we have

$$lgg(C_1, C_2) = \{L \mid L_1 \in C_1,\ L_2 \in C_2 \text{ and } L \text{ is an anti-unification of } L_1 \text{ and } L_2\},$$

where the same pair of terms are replaced by the same variable throughout. For the above clauses C and D, by this method, we obtain the generalization:

$$F = lgg(C, D) = (p(x) \leftarrow q(y), q(f(x))).$$

The term substitution $\{(a, b)/x, (a, f(b))/y\}$ describes how the generalization F has been achieved from C and D. The clause F is equivalent under θ-subsumption to the clause E, since $E \preceq F$ and $F \preceq E$.

2.3 GENERALIZATION UNDER IMPLICATION

We agree with Niblett [11] that there is no reason why the straight forward notion of implication, instead of θ-subsumption, should not be used as a basis for generalization.

Definition A clause C *implies* a clause D, denoted $C \Rightarrow D$, if and only if every model of C is a model of D ($C \models D$).

It is easy to see that if a clause C θ-subsumes a clause D then C implies D. But the converse does not hold which is shown by the following clauses:

$$C = (p(x) \leftarrow p(f(x))), \text{ and}$$
$$D = (p(x) \leftarrow p(f(f(x)))).$$

Then $C \Rightarrow D$, but C does not θ-subsume D.

For Horn-clauses there are no least general generalizations under implication, which is shown in [11] by the following example. Let

$$E = (p(x) \leftarrow p(f(f(y)))), \text{ and}$$
$$F = (p(x) \leftarrow p(f(f(f(x))))).$$

Then both C and E implies both D and F, but neither C implies E nor E implies C. Since there are no least general generalizations of Horn-clauses under implication, we instead put our interest to minimally general generalizations under implication.

Definition A Horn-clause C is a *minimally general generalization under implication* (MinGGI) of two Horn-clauses D and E if and only if:
a) $C \Rightarrow D$ and $C \Rightarrow E$, and
b) for each Horn-clause F such that $F \Rightarrow D$, $F \Rightarrow E$ and $C \Rightarrow F$, then also $F \Rightarrow C$.

In the example above, both clause C and clause E are MinGGIs of D and F.

2.4 POWERS AND ROOTS OF CLAUSES

In [9] Muggleton introduces the notions of powers and roots of clauses, for a type of specialization and generalization of recursive clauses, where the clauses are resolved with themselves. The definitions of nth powers and nth roots of clauses are based on a function $\mathcal{L}$.

Definition Let T be a clausal theory. Then, the *function* $\mathcal{L}$ is recursively defined as:
a) $\mathcal{L}^1(T) = T$, and
b) $\mathcal{L}^n(T) = \{R \mid C \in T, D \in \mathcal{L}^{n-1}(T)$ and R is a resolvent of C and $D\}$ ($n > 1$).

Definition A clause D is an *nth power* of a clause C if and only if D is a variant of a clause in $\mathcal{L}^n(\{C\})$ ($n \geq 1$). We also say that C is an *nth root* of D.

Reconsider the clauses from section 2.3. The clause D is a second power of the clause C, and the clause F is a third power of C.

It might be the case that a clause implies another clause, but neither θ-subsume it nor is a root of it. For this relationship we define indirect powers and indirect roots. The notion of indirect roots gives us a clear picture of the two generalization steps involved in a generalization under implication, namely to find an anti-instance and to find a root of the anti-instance.

Definition A clause D is an *indirect nth power* of a clause C if and only if there exists a clause E such that $E \preceq D$ and E is an nth power of C. We also say that C is an *indirect nth root* of D.

Let C and D be clauses as above, and

$$G = (p(a) \leftarrow p(f(f(a))), q(b)).$$

Then C is an indirect second root of G, since C is a second root of D and D θ-subsumes G.

Note that a root of a clause is also, by definition, an indirect root of that clause. In [9] it is shown that all generalizations of clauses under implication are indirect roots of these clauses. MinGGIs of clauses may consequently also be called minimally general common indirect roots of these clauses.

3 GENERALIZATION BY RECURSIVE ANTI-UNIFICATION

The difference between θ-subsumption and implication causes an incompleteness of generalization under θ-subsumption, which sometimes causes inductive learners to give over-general results. In this section, we will describe two different cases when such over-generalizations occur. We will also present a technique, called recursive anti-unification, to handle these cases. By recursive anti-unification we can compute indirect roots and MinGGIs of clauses.

3.1 INTERNAL CONNECTIONS

In this subsection we will describe the first case where LGGθs are over-generalizations w.r.t. implication. Consider the following clauses:

$$C = (p(a) \leftarrow p(f(f(f(f(a)))))),$$
$$D = (p(b) \leftarrow p(f(b))),$$
$$E = (p(x) \leftarrow p(f(y))), \text{ and}$$
$$F = (p(x) \leftarrow p(f(x))).$$

Then the clause E is an LGGθ of C and D. But E is overly general, since there is a clause F which implies both C and D, and is strictly more specific than E.

Let us analyze the cause of the over-generalization in this example. There is a hidden connection between the constant a in the head and in the body of clause C. There is also a similar connection between the constant b in the head and in the body of clause D. This connection is lost in the generalization E, but is kept in the generalization F. Since the anti-unification of the atoms in the heads of C and D is done separated from the anti-unification of the atoms in their bodies, and only identical pair of terms are replaced by the same variable, such connections are usually lost in the computation of an LGGθ. We call this kind of connections, internal connections, because they are found within the atoms $p(a)$ and $p(f(f(f(f(a)))))$, and $p(b)$ and $p(f(b))$. Before we give the formal definition of internal connections we need a precise notation of positions.

Definition A *position* p of a term s in a term or atom t is defined as follows:
a) if $s = t$ then $p = \langle\rangle$,
b) if $t = f(t_1, \ldots, t_n)$ and $q = \langle q_1, \ldots, q_m\rangle$ is a position of s in t_i for some $1 \leq i \leq n$ then $p = \langle (f, i), q_1, \ldots, q_m\rangle$, and
c) if q is a position of t in s then $p = -q$.

We will particularly be interested in pairs of terms (s, t) such that s is found in the same position in the atom in the head of a clause as t is found in an atom in the body of the same clause.

Definition Let $C = (A \leftarrow B_1, \ldots, B_n)$ be a clause. Then (s, t) is a *recursive pair of terms* of C in position p in (A, B_k) if and only if s is a term found in position p in A and t is a term found in position p in B_k $(1 \leq k \leq n)$.

There is one recursive pair of terms of clause C (see above). It is $(a, f(f(f(f(a)))))$, where the term a is found in position $\langle (p, 1)\rangle$ in $p(a)$ and $f(f(f(f(a))))$ is found in the same position in $p(f(f(f(f(a)))))$. For recursive pairs of terms, we look for internal connections.

Definition Let (s, t) be a recursive pair of terms. Then a pair (S, p) is an *internal connection* from s to t if and only if:
a) $S = [s_0, \ldots, s_n]$ is an ordered set of terms such that $s_0 = s$ and $s_n = t$, and either
b) $p = \langle p_1, \ldots, p_n\rangle$ is a position such that s_i is found in s_{i+1} in position $\langle p_{n-i}\rangle$ for every $0 \leq i \leq n-1$, or
c) $p = -\langle p_1, \ldots, p_n\rangle$ is a position such that s_i is found in s_{i-1} in position $\langle p_i\rangle$ for every $1 \leq i \leq n$.

The internal connection from the term a to the term $f(f(f(f(a))))$ is

$$(S, p) = ([a, f(a), f(f(a)), f(f(f(a))), f(f(f(f(a))))],\\ \langle (f, 1), (f, 1), (f, 1), (f, 1)\rangle).$$

Note that S is an ordered set of terms where each term is a subterm of the succeeding term, and that p is the position where the term a is found in $f(f(f(f(a))))$. The reason why we include function symbols in the position description, is because they must be taken into consideration when we compute indirect roots of clauses.

3.2 EXTERNAL CONNECTIONS

In this subsection we will describe another case where LGGθs are over-generalizations. Consider the following clauses:

$$\begin{aligned} C &= (p(a) \leftarrow q(a, b), p(b)),\\ D &= (p(c) \leftarrow q(c, d), q(d, e), p(e)),\\ E &= (p(x) \leftarrow q(x, y), q(z, w), p(w)), \text{ and}\\ F &= (p(u) \leftarrow q(u, v), p(v)). \end{aligned}$$

Then the clause E is an LGGθ of C and D. But E is overly general since F implies both C and D, and is more specific than E. To see that F is more specific than E, note that $E\{x/u, y/v, z/u, w/v\} = F$. That E is an over-generalization in this example is due to that the connection from the term c to the term e, via the term d, in clause D is lost. This connection is found outside the atoms $p(c)$ and $p(e)$, and we therefore call it an external connection.

Definition Let (s, t) be a recursive pair of terms of a clause $C = (A \leftarrow B_1, \ldots, B_m)$. Then a pair (S, P) is an *external connection* from s to t if and only if:
a) $S = [s_0, \ldots, s_n]$ is an ordered set of terms such that $s_0 = s$ and $s_n = t$, and
b) $P = [(p_1, q_1), \ldots, (p_n, q_n)]$ is an ordered set of pairs of positions such that s_i is found in position p_{i+1} in B_j and s_{i+1} is found in position q_{i+1} in B_j for some $1 \leq j \leq m$ for every $0 \leq i \leq n-1$.

The external connection from the term c to the term e in the clause D is

$$(S, P) = ([c, d, e], [(\langle (q, 1)\rangle, \langle (q, 2)\rangle), (\langle (q, 1)\rangle, \langle (q, 2)\rangle)]).$$

The ordered set of terms S describes which terms that are involved in the connection from c to e, and the ordered set of pairs of positions describes where they are found. The term d for example is found both in position $\langle (q, 2)\rangle$ in the atom $q(c, d)$ and in position $\langle (q, 1)\rangle$ in the atom $q(d, e)$, and thus constitutes a link in the connection from c to e. All the information included in an external connection is needed for the computation of indirect roots.

3.3 FACTORS AND DIVISORS OF CONNECTIONS

In this subsection we will describe a way to caracterize similarities between connections. For that purpose we introduce the notions of factors and divisors, both of internal and of external connections. Factors will be used in the computation of indirect roots of clauses, and divisors will be used in the computation of common indirect roots of two or more clauses.

Definition The *concatenation* of two positions $p = \langle p_1, \ldots, p_k\rangle$ and $q = \langle q_1, \ldots, q_m\rangle$ is the position $pq = \langle p_1, \ldots, p_k, q_1, \ldots, q_m\rangle$. A position q *times* a positive integer n is the position $q \cdot n = q_1 \ldots q_n$, where each $q_i = q$ $(1 \leq i \leq n)$. Let p be a position and (S, p)

an internal connection such that $p = q \cdot n$. Then q is a *divisor* of p and n is a *factor* of p, and we will also say that q is a *divisor* and n is a *factor* of the internal connection (S, p).

For the internal connection

$$(S,p) = ([a, f(a), f(f(a)), f(f(f(a))), f(f(f(f(a))))], \langle (f,1),(f,1),(f,1),(f,1)\rangle),$$

there are three different divisors and factors since

$$\begin{aligned}\langle (f,1),(f,1),(f,1),(f,1)\rangle &= \\ &= \langle (f,1),(f,1),(f,1),(f,1)\rangle \cdot 1 \\ &= \langle (f,1),(f,1)\rangle \cdot 2 \\ &= \langle (f,1)\rangle \cdot 4.\end{aligned}$$

In a similar way we also define divisors and factors of external connections.

Definition Let $P = [(p_1, p'_1), \ldots, (p_n, p'_n)]$ and $Q = [(q_1, q'_1), \ldots, (q_n, q'_n)]$ be ordered sets of pairs of positions. Then the *concatenation* of P and Q is $PQ = [(p_1, p'_1), \ldots, (p_n, p'_n), (q_1, q'_1), \ldots, (q_n, q'_n)]$, and Q *times* a positive integer n is $Q \cdot n = Q_1 \ldots Q_n$, where each $Q_i = Q$ $(1 \le i \le n)$. Let P be an ordered set of pair of positions and (S, P) an external connection such that $P = Q \cdot n$. Then Q is a *divisor* of P and n is a *factor* of P, and we will also say that Q is a *divisor* n is a *factor* of the external connection (S, P).

For the external connection

$$(T,P) = ([b,c,d], [(\langle (q,1)\rangle, \langle (q,2)\rangle), (\langle (q,1)\rangle, \langle (q,2)\rangle)]),$$

there are two different divisors and factors, since

$$\begin{aligned}[(\langle (q,1)\rangle, \langle (q,2)\rangle), (\langle (q,1)\rangle, \langle (q,2)\rangle)] &= \\ &= [(\langle (q,1)\rangle, \langle (q,2)\rangle), (\langle (q,1)\rangle, \langle (q,2)\rangle)] \cdot 1 \\ &= [(\langle (q,1)\rangle, \langle (q,2)\rangle)] \cdot 2.\end{aligned}$$

As we have seen there are two common factors of the connections (S, p) and (T, P), namely 1 and 2.

3.4 RECURSIVE ANTI-UNIFICATION

Recursive anti-unification is a generalization technique for pairs of terms, which can be used to compute indirect roots and MinGGIs of clauses. In this subsection we will present the technique, and in the following subsections we will describe how it can be used. Recursive anti-unification uses connections between the terms and factors of these connections.

Definition Let (s, t) be a recursive pair of terms, $(S, P) = ([s_0, \ldots, s_m], Q \cdot n)$ a connection from s to t. Then a pair of terms (u, v) is a *recursive anti-unification* of (s, t) w.r.t. (S, P) and n, described by the term substitution τ, if and only if either:
a) $n = 1$, $(u, v) = (s, t)$, and $\tau = \emptyset$, or
b) $n > 1$, (u', v') is a recursive anti-unification of $(s_{m/n}, s_m)$ w.r.t. $([s_{m/n}, \ldots, s_m], Q \cdot (n-1))$ and $n-1$ described by τ_1, (u, v) is an anti-unification of $(s_0, s_{m/n})$ and (u', v') described by τ_2, and $\tau = \tau_1 \cup \tau_2$.

Recursive anti-unification is essentially a sequence of anti-unifications, where the current factor determines the number of anti-unifications involved. The recursive anti-unification of any pair of terms w.r.t. any connection and the factor 1, is equal to the given pair of terms. In other words, no generalization is done when the factor is 1.

The recursive anti-unification of the pair of terms $(a, f(f(f(f(a)))))$ w.r.t. the connection

$$(S,p) = ([a, f(a), f(f(a)), f(f(f(a))), f(f(f(f(a))))], \langle (f,1),(f,1),(f,1),(f,1)\rangle)$$

and the factor 2 is $(x, f(f(x)))$. It is achieved by anti-unification of the pairs of terms $(a, f(f(a)))$ and $(f(f(a)), f(f(f(f(a)))))$, which is described by the term substitution $\{(a, f(f(a))/x\}$.

Let us also see how the recursive anti-unification of the pair of terms $(a, f(f(f(f(a)))))$ w.r.t. the connection (S, p) and the factor 4 is obtained. First the two pair of terms $(f(f(a)), f(f(f(a))))$ and $(f(f(f(a))), f(f(f(f(a)))))$ are anti-unified, which gives the anti-unification

$$\alpha_1 = (f(f(x)), f(f(f(x)))).$$

Then the pair of terms $(f(a), f(f(a)))$ is anti-unified with α_1, which gives the new anti-unification

$$\alpha_2 = (f(y), f(f(y))).$$

Then finally the pair of terms $(a, f(a))$ is anti-unified with α_2. This gives us the final anti-unification

$$\alpha_3 = (z, f(z)),$$

which also is the desired recursive anti-unification. This whole process is described by the term substitution $\{(a, f(a))/x, (a, f(x))/y, (a, f(y))/z\}$.

The recursive anti-unification of the pair of terms (c, e) w.r.t. the external connection

$$(T,P) = ([c,d,e], [(\langle (q,1)\rangle, \langle (q,2)\rangle), (\langle (q,1)\rangle, \langle (q,2)\rangle)])$$

and the factor 2, is (y, z). It is achieved by anti-unification of the pairs of terms (c, d) and (d, e), and the corresponding term substitution is $\{(c, d)/y, (d, e)/z\}$. It may seem uninteresting that the pair of variables (y, z) is a recursive anti-unification of (c, e), but for external connections the important information lies within the term substitution. How this information is used in the computation of an indirect root will be described in the next subsection.

3.5 COMPUTATION OF INDIRECT ROOTS

In this subsection we will describe how indirect roots of clauses can be computed by using recursive anti-unification. The first thing we do when to compute an indirect root of a clause, is to collect all recursive pairs of terms. Consider the clause

$$C = (p(a,c) \leftarrow q(c,d), q(d,e), p(f(f(f(f(a)))), e)).$$

For this clause we have two recursive pairs of terms: $(a, f(f(f(f(a)))))$ and (c, e). For the first pair of terms there is the internal connection

$$(S,p) = ([a, f(a), f(f(a)), f(f(f(a))), f(f(f(f(a))))], \langle(f,1),(f,1),(f,1),(f,1)\rangle).$$

For the second pair there is the external connection

$$(T,P) = ([b,c,d], [(\langle(q,1)\rangle, \langle(q,2)\rangle), (\langle(q,1)\rangle, \langle(q,2)\rangle)]).$$

As mentioned in section 3.3, there are two common factors of (S,p) and (T,P), namely 1 and 2. These common factors give us the important information that there is an indirect first root and an indirect second root of clause C. The indirect first root of C is trivial since every clause is a first root of itself, but the indirect second root of C is of interest. An indirect second root of C can be constructed by computing the recursive anti-unifications of the pair of terms $(a, f(f(f(f(a)))))$ and (c,d) w.r.t. the connections (S,p) and (T,P), and the factor 2.

As shown in section 3.4, $(x, f(f(x)))$ is the recursive anti-unification of $(a, f(f(f(f(a)))))$ w.r.t. (S,p) and the factor 2. It was also shown that (y,z) is the recursive anti-unification of (c,e) w.r.t. (T,P) and the factor 2, described by the term substitution

$$\tau = \{(c,d)/y, (d,e)/z\}.$$

Having these two recursive anti-unifications, it is easy to construct an indirect second root of C. It is done by replacing the recursive pair of terms by their respective recursive anti-unifications. Thus we obtain the clause

$$D = (p(x,y) \leftarrow q(c,d), q(d,e), p(f(f(x)), z)).$$

Since there is an external connection from c to e in clause C, there should be an external connection from y to z in clause D. As mentioned in the previous subsection, the important information of the external connection lies within the term substitution τ. To achieve a connection from y to z, we should anti-unify $q(c,d)$ and $q(d,e)$ using the term substitution τ, and thus obtain the atom $q(y,z)$. In this way we obtain the indirect root

$$E = (p(x,y) \leftarrow q(y,z), p(f(f(x)), z)),$$

which includes all found connections between terms in the clause C.

However, E is not a minimally general indirect second root of the clause C. If we seek such a root of C, then we should keep all atoms in the body of clause C in our generalization, and thus obtain

$$F = (p(x,y) \leftarrow q(y,z), p(f(f(x)), z), q(c,d), q(d,e), p(f(f(f(f(a)))), e)).$$

3.6 COMPUTATION OF MinGGIs

In this subsection we will describe a technique to find minimally general common indirect roots of clauses, or in other words minimally general generalizations under implication (MinGGIs) of clauses. As noted in the previous subsection, when to compute an indirect root of a clause we should find a common factor of all connections in the clause. When to compute a common indirect root of two or more clauses, we have some extra conditions. Firstly, the recursive pairs of terms of each clause must be found in the same positions. Secondly, the divisors of the corresponding connections in each clause must be equal.

Consider the clauses

$$C = (p(a,c) \leftarrow p(f(f(f(f(a)))), c)), \text{ and}$$
$$D = (p(b,d) \leftarrow p(f(f(b)), d)).$$

In clause C there is the recursive pair of terms $(a, f(f(f(f(a)))))$ and in clause D there is the recursive pair of terms $(b, f(f(b)))$. Both these recursive pair of terms are found in position $\langle(p,1)\rangle$, and for them we have the internal connections

$$(S,p) = ([a, f(a), f(f(a)), f(f(f(a))), f(f(f(f(a))))], \langle(f,1),(f,1),(f,1),(f,1)\rangle), \text{ and}$$
$$(T,q) = ([b, f(b), f(f(b))], \langle(f,1),(f,1)\rangle).$$

Now, to compute a common indirect root of C and D, we must find a common divisor of (S,p) and (T,q). There are two such divisors, namely

$$q_1 = \langle(f,1),(f,1)\rangle \text{ and}$$
$$q_2 = \langle(f,1)\rangle,$$

which tell us that there are two common indirect roots of C and D. The indirect roots of clause C w.r.t. the divisors q_1 and q_2 are

$$C_1 = (p(x,c) \leftarrow p(f(f(x)), c)), \text{ and}$$
$$C_2 = (p(x,c) \leftarrow p(f(x), c)),$$

and the indirect roots of clause D w.r.t. the divisors q_1 and q_2 are

$$D_1 = (p(b,d) \leftarrow p(f(f(b)), d)), \text{ and}$$
$$D_2 = (p(x,d) \leftarrow p(f(x), d)).$$

The common indirect roots E and F of C and D are then found by computing the LGGθs of C_1 and C_2, respectively D_1 and D_2. In this way we obtain

$$E_1 = (p(x) \leftarrow p(f(f(x)))) \text{ w.r.t. the divisor } q_1, \text{ and}$$
$$E_2 = (p(x) \leftarrow p(f(x))) \text{ w.r.t. the divisor } q_2.$$

Note that E_1 is strictly more specific than E_2 under implication, and that q_1 is greater than q_2. Thus E_1 is an MinGGI of C and D, and it is found by choosing the *greatest common divisor* of the connections (S,p) and (T,q).

4 RELATED WORK

In this paper we have considered the problem of generalization under implication. Recently some other approaches to this problem have been presented by Lapointe and Matwin [5], Muggleton [9] and Idestam-Almquist [4]. Both in [5] and in [9] the computation of a root of a clause is done from only one example, and the nth root with maximum n is preferred. As a consequence of that the resulting clause can easily become over-general. For example the clause

$$C = (even(s(s(s(s(x))))) \leftarrow even(x))$$

will be generalized to

$$D = (even(s(x)) \leftarrow even(x)),$$

which says that every natural number is even. Remember that our purpose for considering indirect roots of clauses is to avoid over-generalizations. In this paper we have instaed considered the problem of finding minimally general generalizations of two or more clauses. For example given the clause C and the clause

$$E = (even(s(s(s(s(s(s(0))))))) \leftarrow even(0))$$

we will find the following clause by recursive anti-unification:

$$F = (even(s(s(x))) \leftarrow even(x)),$$

which is an MinGGI of C and E.

The algorithm described in [9] can find almost all roots of single recursive clauses, but it is non-deterministic. It is based on canonical flattening of clauses and inversion of renaming substitutions, and these techniques require the input clauses to be uninstantiated. Hence, the algorithm can only find (direct) roots of clauses.

A system described in [5], called LOPSTER, can efficiently find some indirect roots of clauses. It is based on sub-unification, which is a generalization of unification. Although we have a different basis for recursive anti-unification, the underlying ideas are similar to those of sub-unification. In [5] the class of learnable clauses is restricted to two particular types of recursive clauses, which are called purely recursive and left recursive. A *purely recursive clause* is a clause of the form

$$(p(t_1, \ldots, t_n) \leftarrow p(x_1, \ldots, x_n)),$$

where each x_i is a variable occurring in t_i $(1 \leq i \leq n)$. A *left recursive clause* is a clause of the form

$$(p(t_1, \ldots, t_m, y_1, \ldots, y_n) \leftarrow p(x_1, \ldots, x_m, z_1, \ldots, z_n), B_1, \ldots, B_k),$$

where each x_i is a variable occurring in t_i $(1 \leq i \leq n), y_1, \ldots, y_n, z_1, \ldots, z_n$ are variables and $B_1, \ldots, B_k$ are atoms. It is clear that these two types of clauses only cover a fraction of all possible recursive clauses. For example quite simple clauses such as the following are not covered:

$$G = (reverse([x|y], z, w) \leftarrow reverse(y, [x|z], w)) \text{ and}$$
$$H = (ancestor(x, z) \leftarrow parent(x, y), ancestor(y, z)).$$

In [4] a technique to reduce generalization under implication to generalization under θ-subsumption is described. The technique is proved to be complete, in the very wide sense that any clause can be learned and every generalization under implication be found. Unfortunately this is most of theoretical interest since the technique is computationally intractable. The time complexity of the technique is double-exponential, and it is unrealistic to expect the technique to have any practical applicability.

5 CONCLUDING REMARKS

For recursive clauses there is a type of generalizations under implication, called indirect roots, which are not possible to find by generalization under θ-subsumption. We have presented a technique, called recursive anti-unification, to compute indirect roots of clauses. We have also introduced the notions of divisors and factors of connections, which make it possible to compute minimally general common indirect roots of clauses, which are guaranteed to be minimally general generalizations under implication (MinGGIs). Recursive anti-unification is a generalization of anti-unification, which is the usual technique to compute least general generalizations under θ-subsumption (LGGθs).

The main difference between recursive anti-unification and the approaches taken by others, is that we are concerned about finding minimally general generalization under implication, while others are concerned about finding typical generalizations under implication. A more thoroughly description of recursive anti-unification can be found in [3].

We have described two cases for which generalization under θ-subsumption of single-recursive clauses are incomplete, namely when there exist an internal or external connection. We have also described how recursive anti-unification can eliminate the incompleteness in these two cases. However there exist cases for which recursive anti-unification does not work. Consider the following clauses

$$C = (p(x, a) \leftarrow p(b, x)) \text{ and}$$
$$D = (p(a, a) \leftarrow p(b, b)).$$

The clause C implies D, since D is a second power of C, but the generalization C of D can not be found by recursive anti-unification. There exists no recursive pair of terms of C such that the connection between x in $p(x, a)$ and x in $p(b, x)$ is included. We call this type of connections, *cross connections*, because neither the position of x in $p(x, a)$ is a subposition of the position of x in $p(b, x)$, nor vice versa. Cross connections disappear when a clause is resolved with itself, and recursive anti-unification can not be used to find such connections. Fortunately clauses with cross connections are very rare and often even undesirable. For example clauses such as

$$E = (marriedto(x, y) \leftarrow marriedto(y, x))$$

are only intended to be used once in a derivation. In logic programming, clauses of this kind may easily give rise to infinitely many derivations of the same answer, which is undesirable.

Recursive anti-unification is implemented in SICStus Prolog, and it is efficient. To compute a recursive anti-unification of a pair of terms w.r.t. a connection and a factor n, only requires $n - 1$ applications of anti-unification. However, the generalization technique we have described also includes finding internal and external connections between terms, and computation of LGGθs. To find an internal connection is computationally simple since it only involves a control if a term is a subterm in another term. Unfortunately, to find an external connection is much more complicated, which is due to that the atoms in a clause by definition are not ordered. To find an external connection therefore involves a search in the space of possible orders of the atoms.

If we only consider clauses of the form $(A \leftarrow B)$ then there can not be any external connections. Hence, to compute indirect roots and MinGGIs of clauses of that form is not computationally costly. The time complexity is polynomial. If we consider arbitrary Horn clauses, for which there may exist external connections, then the time complexity grows exponentially with the size of the input clauses.

Jörg-Uwe Kietz has noted (personal communication) that there exist clauses for which there exist infinitely many external connections. We do not think this causes any problem for recursive anti-unification. However the consequences need to be examined, which is a question for future research.

In inductive learning a generalization is often carried out in relation to a theory (background knowledge). That problem has not been considered in this paper, but recursive anti-unification can also be used to compute generalizations relative a theory, by extending Plotkin's framework of relative least general generalization [12] and its improvements w.r.t. efficiency [7]. A description of how it can be done is however a question for future work.

Acknowledgement

This work was partially supported by NUTEK, the Swedish National Board for Technical and Industrial Development under the contract 9001734, and is a part of the work in the ESPRIT BRA ILP project 6020.

References

[1] L. De Readt. *Interactive Concept Learning.* PhD thesis, Department of Computer Science, Katholieke Universiteit Leuven, 1991.

[2] Michael R. Genesereth and Nils J. Nilsson. *Logic Foundations of Artificial Intelligence.* Morgan Kaufmann, 1987.

[3] P. Idestam-Almquist. *Generalization of Horn Clauses.* PhD thesis, Department of Computer and Systems Sciences, Stockholm University and the Royal Institute of Technology, 1993. Forthcoming.

[4] P. Idestam-Almquist. Generalization under implication by using or-introduction. In *Proceedings of the European Conference on Machine Learning.* Springer-Verlag, 1993.

[5] Stéphane Lapointe and Stan Matwin. Sub-unification: A tool for efficient induction of recursive programs. In *Proceedings of the Ninth International Conference on Machine Learning.* Morgan Kaufmann, 1992.

[6] J. W. Lloyd. *Foundations of Logic Programming.* Springer-Verlag, 1987. Second edition.

[7] S. Muggleton and C. Feng. Efficient induction of logic programs. In *Proceedings of the First Conference on Algorithmic Learning Theory.* Ohmsha Publishers, Tokyo, 1990.

[8] Stephen Muggleton. Inductive logic programming. *New Generation Computing,* 8(4):295–318, 1991.

[9] Stephen Muggleton. Inverting implication. *Artificial Intelligence Journal,* 1993. To appear.

[10] Stephen Muggleton and Wray Buntine. Machine invention of first-order predicates by inverting resolution. In *Proceedings of the Fifth International Conference on Machine Learning.* Morgan Kaufmann, 1988.

[11] Tim Niblett. A study of generalization in logic programs. In *Proceedings of the Third European Working Session on Learning.* Pitman, 1988.

[12] G. D. Plotkin. *Automatic Methods of Inductive Inference.* PhD thesis, Edinburgh University, 1971.

[13] Céline Rouveirol. Extensions of inversion of resolution applied to theory completion. In S. Muggleton, editor, *Inductive Logic Programming.* Academic Press, San Diego, California, 1992.

[14] Ruediger Wirth. Completing logic programs by inverse resolution. In *Proceedings of the Fourth European Working Session on Learning.* Pitman, 1989.

Supervised learning and divide-and-conquer: A statistical approach

Michael I. Jordan
Department of Brain and Cognitive Sciences
MIT
Cambridge, MA 02139
jordan@psyche.mit.edu

Robert A. Jacobs
Department of Psychology
University of Rochester
Rochester, NY 14627
robbie@psych.rochester.edu

Abstract

We present a novel statistical model for supervised learning. The model is based on the principle of divide-and-conquer, and is similar in spirit to models such as CART, ID3 and MARS. We formulate the problem of learning the parameters of the model as a maximum likelihood estimation problem and develop an Expectation-Maximization (EM) algorithm for the model. Comparative simulation results are presented in the robot dynamics domain.

1 INTRODUCTION

The principle of divide-and-conquer is a principle with wide applicability throughout applied mathematics. In this paper we explore a particular application of the divide-and-conquer principle to the problem of supervised learning. We describe a statistical approach to supervised learning that makes use of generalized linear model (GLIM) theory both for the "divide" component and the "conquer" component of a recursively-defined learning system.

In the statistical literature and the machine learning literature, divide-and-conquer approaches have become increasingly popular. The CART algorithm of Breiman, et al. (1984), the MARS algorithm of Friedman (1991), and the ID3 algorithm of Quinlan (1986) are well-known examples. These algorithms fit surfaces to data by explicitly dividing the input space into a nested sequence of regions, and by fitting simple surfaces (e.g., constant functions) within these regions.

Although divide-and-conquer algorithms have much to recommend them, one should be concerned about the statistical consequences of dividing the input space. Dividing the data can have favorable consequences for the bias of an estimator, but it generally increases the variance of the estimator, as can be seen by considering linear regression, in which the variance of the estimates of the slope and intercept depend quadratically on the spread of data on the x-axis. The points that are the most peripheral in the input space are those that have the maximal effect in decreasing the variance of the parameter estimates.

The foregoing considerations suggest that divide-and-conquer algorithms generally tend to be variance-increasing algorithms. This is indeed the case and is particularly problematic in high-dimensional spaces where data become exceedingly sparse (Scott, 1992). Our response to this dilemma is to make use of a variance-decreasing familiar in the neural network literature—we make use of "soft" splits of data (Bridle, 1989; Nowlan, 1991; Wahba, et al., 1993), allowing data points to lie simultaneously in multiple regions. This allows the parameters in one region to be influenced by data in neighboring regions, ameliorating the severe effects on variance of lopping off distant data. We also address the issue of bias, allowing the splits to be formed along hyperplanes at arbitrary orientations in the input space. This lessens the bias due to high-order interactions among the inputs and allows the algorithm to be insensitive to the particular choice of coordinates used to encode the data (an improvement over methods such as ID3 and MARS, which are coordinate-dependent).

The work that we describe here makes contact with a number of branches of statistical theory. First, as in our earlier work on modular neural networks (Jacobs, et al., 1991), we formulate the learning problem as a mixture estimation problem. We show that the algorithm that is generally employed for the *unsupervised* learning of mixture parameters (Cheeseman, et al., 1988; Titterington, et al., 1985)—the Expectation-Maximization (EM) algorithm of Dempster, Laird and Rubin (1977)—can also be exploited for the *supervised* learning problem. Second, we utilize generalized linear model (GLIM) theory (McCullagh & Nelder, 1983) to provide the basic statistical structure for the components of the architecture. In particular, the "soft splits" referred to above are modeled as *log-linear* models—a specific form of GLIM.

We also show that the algorithm developed for the efficient fitting of GLIM's—the iteratively reweighted least squares (IRLS) algorithm—can be usefully employed in our model, in particular as the M step of the EM algorithm. Finally, we show that these ideas can be developed in a recursive manner, yielding a tree-structured approach to estimation that is reminiscent of CART, ID3 and MARS.

2 HIERARCHICAL MIXTURES OF EXPERTS

The algorithms that we discuss in this paper are supervised learning algorithms. We explicitly address the case of regression, in which the input vectors are elements of $\Re^m$ and the output vectors are elements of $\Re^n$. Our model also handles classification problems and counting problems in which the outputs are integer-valued. The data are assumed to form a countable set of paired observations $\mathcal{X} = \{(\mathbf{x}^{(t)}, \mathbf{y}^{(t)})\}$. In the case of the *batch* algorithm discussed below, this set is assumed to be finite; in the case of the *on-line* algorithm, the set may be infinite.

We propose to solve nonlinear supervised learning problems by dividing the input space into a nested set of regions and fitting simple surfaces to the data that fall in these regions. The regions have "soft" boundaries, meaning that data points may lie simultaneously in multiple regions. The boundaries between regions are themselves simple parameterized surfaces that are adjusted by the learning algorithm.

The hierarchical mixture-of-experts (HME) architecture is shown in Figure 1.[1] The architecture is a tree in which the *gating networks* sit at the nonterminals of the tree. These networks receive the vector $\mathbf{x}$ as input and produce scalar outputs that are a partition of unity at each point in the input space. The *expert networks* sit at the leaves of the tree. Each expert produces an output vector $\boldsymbol{\mu}_{ij}$ for each input vector. These output vectors proceed up the tree, being multiplied by the gating network outputs and summed at the nonterminals.

All of the expert networks in the tree are linear with a single output nonlinearity. We will refer to such a network as "generalized linear," borrowing the terminology from statistics (McCullagh & Nelder, 1983). Expert network (i, j) produces its output $\boldsymbol{\mu}_{ij}$ as a generalized linear function of the input $\mathbf{x}$:

$$\boldsymbol{\mu}_{ij} = f(U_{ij}\mathbf{x}), \tag{1}$$

where U_{ij} is a weight matrix and f is a fixed continuous

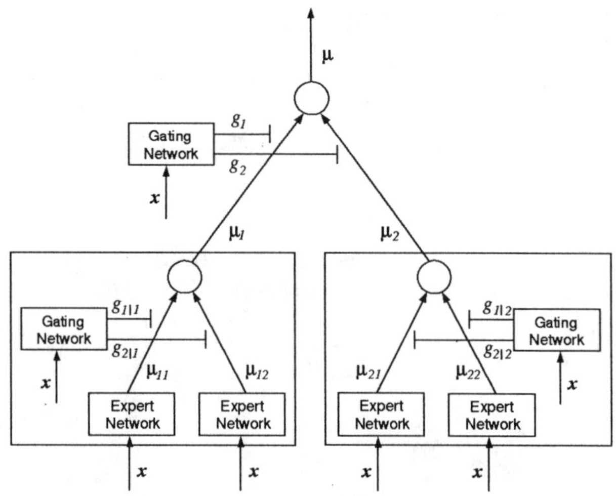

Figure 1: A two-level hierarchical mixture of experts.

nonlinearity. The vector $\mathbf{x}$ is assumed to include a fixed component of one to allow for an intercept term.

For regression problems, $f(\cdot)$ is the identity function (i.e., the experts are linear). For binary classification problems, $f(\cdot)$ is generally taken to be the logistic function, in which case the expert outputs are interpreted as the log odds of "success" under a Bernoulli probability model (see below). Other models (e.g., multiway classification, counting, rate estimation and survival estimation) are handled readily by making other choices for $f(\cdot)$. These models are smoothed piecewise analogs of the corresponding GLIM models (cf. McCullagh & Nelder, 1983).

The gating networks are also generalized linear. At the top level, define linear predictors ξ_i as follows:

$$\xi_i = \mathbf{v}_i^T \mathbf{x}, \tag{2}$$

where $\mathbf{v}_i$ is a weight vector. Then the ith output of the top-level gating network is the "softmax" function of the ξ_i (Bridle, 1989; McCullagh & Nelder, 1983):

$$g_i = \frac{e^{\xi_i}}{\sum_k e^{\xi_k}}. \tag{3}$$

Note that the g_i are positive and sum to one for each $\mathbf{x}$. The gating networks at the lower level are defined similarly, yielding outputs $g_{j|i}$ that are obtained by taking the softmax function of linear predictors $\xi_{ij} = \mathbf{v}_{ij}^T \mathbf{x}$.

The output vector at each nonterminal of the tree is the weighted output of the experts below that nonterminal. That is, the output at the ith nonterminal in the second layer of the two-level tree is:

$$\boldsymbol{\mu}_i = \sum_j g_{j|i} \boldsymbol{\mu}_{ij}$$

[1] To simplify the presentation, we restrict ourselves to a two-level hierarchy throughout the paper. All of the algorithms that we describe, however, generalize readily to hierarchies of arbitrary depth. See Jordan and Xu (1993) for a recursive formalism that handles arbitrary trees.

and the output at the top level of the tree is:

$$\boldsymbol{\mu} = \sum_i g_i \boldsymbol{\mu}_i.$$

Note that both the g's and the $\boldsymbol{\mu}$'s depend on the input $\mathbf{x}$, thus the total output is a nonlinear function of the input.

2.1 REGRESSION SURFACE

Given the definitions of the expert networks and the gating networks, the regression surface defined by the hierarchy is essentially a smoothed piecewise function. The gating networks provide a nested partitioning of the input space and the expert networks provide generalized-linear maps within the regions defined by the partition. To understand the nature of the smoothing, consider a one-level hierarchy with two expert networks. In this case, the gating network has two outputs, g_1 and g_2. The gating output g_1 is given by:

$$g_1 = \frac{e^{\xi_1}}{e^{\xi_1} + e^{\xi_2}} \quad (4)$$

$$= \frac{1}{1 + e^{-(\mathbf{v}_1 - \mathbf{v}_2)^T \mathbf{x}}}, \quad (5)$$

which is a logistic ridge function whose orientation is determined by the direction of the vector $\mathbf{v}_1 - \mathbf{v}_2$. The gating output g_2 is equal to $1 - g_1$. For a given $\mathbf{x}$, the total output $\boldsymbol{\mu}$ is the convex combination: $\boldsymbol{\mu} = g_1\boldsymbol{\mu}_1 + g_2\boldsymbol{\mu}_2$. This is a weighted average of the experts, where the weights are determined by the ridge function. Along the ridge, $g_1 = g_2 = \frac{1}{2}$, and both experts contribute equally. Away from the ridge, one expert or the other dominates. The amount of smoothing across the ridge is determined by the magnitude of the vector $\mathbf{v}_2 - \mathbf{v}_1$. If $\mathbf{v}_2 - \mathbf{v}_1$ is large, then the ridge function becomes a sharp split and the weighted output of the experts becomes piecewise generalized-linear. If $\mathbf{v}_2 - \mathbf{v}_1$ is small, then each expert contributes to a significant degree on each side of the ridge, thereby smoothing the piecewise map. The smoothing is exponential. In the limit of a zero difference vector, $g_1 = g_2 = \frac{1}{2}$ for all $\mathbf{x}$, and the total output is the same fixed function of $\mathbf{x}$ on both sides of the fictitious "split."

In general, the partitioning induced by a given gating network is a smoothed tesselation of the input space. Lower-level gating networks induce a partition within the partition induced by higher-level gating networks. The weights in a given gating network determine the amount of smoothing across the partition at that particular level of resolution: large weight vectors imply sharp changes in the regression surface across a ridge and small weights imply a smoother surface. In the limit of zero weights in all gating networks, the entire hierarchy reduces to a fixed average (a linear system in the case of regression).

2.2 A PROBABILITY MODEL

The hierarchy can be given a probabilistic interpretation. We suppose that the mechanism by which data are generated by the environment involves a nested sequence of decisions that terminates in a regressive process that maps $\mathbf{x}$ to $\mathbf{y}$. The decisions are modeled as multinomial random variables. That is, for each $\mathbf{x}$, we interpret the values $g_i(\mathbf{x}, \mathbf{v}_i^0)$ as the multinomial probabilities associated with the first decision and the $g_{j|i}(\mathbf{x}, \mathbf{v}_{ij}^0)$ as the (conditional) multinomial probabilities associated with the second decision. We use a statistical model to model these probabilities; in particular, our choice of parameterization (cf. Equations 2 and 3) corresponds to a *log-linear* probability model (see Jordan & Jacobs, 1993). A log-linear model is a special case of a GLIM that is commonly used for "soft" multiway classification (McCullagh & Nelder, 1983). Under the log-linear model, we interpret the gating networks as modeling the input-dependent, multinomial probabilities of making particular nested sequences of decisions.

Once a particular sequence of decisions has been made, output $\mathbf{y}$ is assumed to be generated according to the following generalized linear statistical model. First, a linear predictor η_{ij} is formed:

$$\boldsymbol{\eta}_{ij}^0 = U_{ij}^0 \mathbf{x},$$

where the superscript refers to the "true" values of the parameters. The expected value of $\mathbf{y}$ is obtained by passing the linear predictor through the *link function* f:

$$\boldsymbol{\mu}_{ij}^0 = f(\boldsymbol{\eta}_{ij}^0).$$

The output $\mathbf{y}$ is then chosen from a probability density P, with mean $\boldsymbol{\mu}_{ij}^0$ and "dispersion" parameter $\boldsymbol{\phi}_{ij}^0$. We denote the density of $\mathbf{y}$ as:

$$P(\mathbf{y}|\mathbf{x}, \boldsymbol{\theta}_{ij}^0),$$

where the parameter vector $\boldsymbol{\theta}_{ij}^0$ includes the weights U_{ij}^0 and the dispersion parameter $\boldsymbol{\phi}_{ij}^0$. We assume the density P to be a member of the exponential family of densities (McCullagh & Nelder, 1983). The interpretation of the dispersion parameter depends on the particular choice of density. For example, in the case of the n-dimensional Gaussian, the dispersion parameter is the covariance matrix Σ_{ij}^0.[2]

Given these assumptions, the total probability of generating $\mathbf{y}$ from $\mathbf{x}$ is the mixture of the probabilities of generating $\mathbf{y}$ from each of the component densities, where the mixture components are multinomial probabilities:

$$P(\mathbf{y}|\mathbf{x}, \boldsymbol{\theta}^0) = \sum_i g_i(\mathbf{x}, \mathbf{v}_i^0) \sum_j g_{j|i}(\mathbf{x}, \mathbf{v}_{ij}^0) P(\mathbf{y}|\mathbf{x}, \boldsymbol{\theta}_{ij}^0). \quad (6)$$

[2]Not all exponential family densities have a dispersion parameter; in particular, the Bernoulli density discussed below has no dispersion parameter.

Note that $\boldsymbol{\theta}^0$ includes the expert network parameters $\boldsymbol{\theta}_{ij}{}^0$ as well as the gating network parameters $\mathbf{v}_i^0$ and $\mathbf{v}_{ij}^0$. Note also that we can utilize Equation 6 without the superscripts to refer to the probability model defined by a particular HME architecture, irrespective of any reference to a "true" model.

Example (regression)
In the case of regression the probabilistic component of the model is generally assumed to be Gaussian. Assuming identical covariance matrices of the form $\sigma^2 I$ for each of the experts yields the following hierarchical probability model:

$$P(\mathbf{y}|\mathbf{x}, \boldsymbol{\theta}) = \frac{1}{(2\pi)^{n/2}\sigma} \sum_i g_i \sum_j g_{j|i} e^{-\frac{1}{2\sigma^2}\|\mathbf{y}-\boldsymbol{\mu}_{ij}\|^2}.$$

Example (binary classification)
In binary classification problems the output y is a discrete random variable having possible outcomes of "failure" and "success." The probabilistic component of the model is generally assumed to be the Bernouilli distribution (McCullagh & Nelder, 1983). In this case, the mean μ_{ij} is the conditional probability of classifying the input as "success." The resulting hierarchical probability model is a mixture of Bernoulli densities:

$$P(y|\mathbf{x}, \boldsymbol{\theta}) = \sum_i g_i \sum_j g_{j|i} \mu_{ij}^y (1 - \mu_{ij})^{1-y}.$$

2.3 POSTERIOR PROBABILITIES

In developing the learning algorithms to be presented in the remainder of the paper, it will prove useful to define posterior probabilities associated with the nodes of the tree. The terms "posterior" and "prior" have meaning in this context during the training of the system. We refer to the probabilities g_i and $g_{j|i}$ as *prior* probabilities, because they are computed based only on the input $\mathbf{x}$, without knowledge of the corresponding target output $\mathbf{y}$. A *posterior* probability is defined once both the input and the target output are known. Using Bayes' rule, we define the posterior probabilities at the nodes of the tree as follows:

$$h_i = \frac{g_i \sum_j g_{j|i} P_{ij}(\mathbf{y})}{\sum_i g_i \sum_j g_{j|i} P_{ij}(\mathbf{y})} \tag{7}$$

and

$$h_{j|i} = \frac{g_{j|i} P_{ij}(\mathbf{y})}{\sum_j g_{j|i} P_{ij}(\mathbf{y})}, \tag{8}$$

where we have dropped the dependence on the input and the parameters to simplify the notation.

We will also find it useful to define the joint posterior probability h_{ij}, the product of h_i and $h_{j|i}$:

$$h_{ij} = \frac{g_i g_{j|i} P_{ij}(\mathbf{y})}{\sum_i g_i \sum_j g_{j|i} P_{ij}(\mathbf{y})} \tag{9}$$

This quantity is the probability that expert network (i, j) can be considered to have generated the data, based on knowledge of both the input and the output. Once again, we emphasize that all of these quantities are conditional on the input $\mathbf{x}$.

In deeper trees, the posterior probability associated with an expert network is simply the product of the conditional posterior probabilities along the path from the root of the tree to that expert.

2.4 THE LIKELIHOOD

We treat the problem of learning in the HME architecture as a maximum likelihood estimation problem. The log likelihood of a data set $\mathcal{X} = \{(\mathbf{x}^{(t)}, \mathbf{y}^{(t)})\}_1^N$ is obtained by taking the log of the product of N densities of the form of Equation 6, which yields the following log likelihood:

$$l(\boldsymbol{\theta}; \mathcal{X}) = \sum_t \ln \sum_i g_i^{(t)} \sum_j g_{j|i}^{(t)} P_{ij}(\mathbf{y}^{(t)}). \tag{10}$$

We wish to maximize this function with respect to the parameters $\boldsymbol{\theta}$.

2.5 THE EM ALGORITHM

In the following sections we develop a learning algorithm for the HME architecture based on the Expectation-Maximization (EM) framework of Dempster, Laird, and Rubin (1977). We derive an EM algorithm for the architecture that consists of the iterative solution of a coupled set of iteratively-reweighted least-squares problems.

The EM algorithm is a general technique for maximum likelihood estimation. In practice EM has been applied almost exclusively to unsupervised learning problems. This is true of the neural network and machine learning literature, in which EM has appeared in the context of clustering (Cheeseman, et al., 1988; Nowlan, 1991), as well as the statistics literature, in which applications include missing data problems, mixture density estimation, and factor analysis (Dempster, Laird, & Rubin, 1977). Another unsupervised learning application is the learning problem for Hidden Markov Models, for which the Baum-Welch reestimation formulas are a special case of EM. There is nothing in the EM framework that precludes its application to regression or classification problems; however, such applications have been few.

EM is an iterative approach to maximum likelihood estimation. Each iteration of an EM algorithm is composed of two steps: an Estimation (E) step and a Maximization (M) step. The M step involves the maximization of a likelihood function that is redefined in each iteration by the E step. An application of EM generally begins with the observation that the optimization of the likelihood function $l(\boldsymbol{\theta}; \mathcal{X})$ would be simplified if only a set of additional variables, called "missing" or "hidden" variables, were known. In this context, we refer to the observable data $\mathcal{X}$ as the "incomplete data" and posit a "complete data" set $\mathcal{Y}$ that includes the missing variables $\mathcal{Z}$. We specify a probability model that links the fictive missing variables to the actual data: $P(\mathbf{y}, \mathbf{z}|\mathbf{x}, \boldsymbol{\theta})$. The logarithm of the density P defines the "complete-data likelihood," $l_c(\boldsymbol{\theta}; \mathcal{Y})$. The original likelihood, $l(\boldsymbol{\theta}; \mathcal{X})$, is referred to in this context as the "incomplete-data likelihood." It is the relationship between these two likelihood functions that motivates the EM algorithm. Note that the complete-data likelihood is a random variable, because the missing variables $\mathcal{Z}$ are in fact unknown. An EM algorithm first finds the expected value of the complete-data likelihood, given the observed data and the current model. This is the E step:

$$Q(\boldsymbol{\theta}, \boldsymbol{\theta}^{(p)}) = E[l_c(\boldsymbol{\theta}; \mathcal{Y})],$$

where $\boldsymbol{\theta}^{(p)}$ is the value of the parameters at the pth iteration and the expectation is taken with respect to $\boldsymbol{\theta}^{(p)}$. This step yields a deterministic function Q. The M step maximizes this function with respect to $\boldsymbol{\theta}$ to find the new parameter estimates $\boldsymbol{\theta}^{(p+1)}$:

$$\boldsymbol{\theta}^{(p+1)} = \arg\max_{\boldsymbol{\theta}} Q(\boldsymbol{\theta}, \boldsymbol{\theta}^{(p)}).$$

The E step is then repeated to yield an improved estimate of the complete likelihood and the process iterates.

An iterative step of EM chooses a parameter value that increases the value of Q, the expectation of the complete likelihood. What is the effect of such a step on the incomplete likelihood? Dempster, et al. proved that an increase in Q implies an increase in the incomplete likelihood:

$$l(\boldsymbol{\theta}^{(p+1)}; \mathcal{X}) \geq l(\boldsymbol{\theta}^{(p)}; \mathcal{X}).$$

with equality obtaining only at the stationary points of l. Thus the likelihood l increases monotonically along the sequence of parameter estimates generated by an EM algorithm. In practice this implies convergence to a local maximum.

2.6 APPLYING EM TO THE HME ARCHITECTURE

To develop an EM algorithm for the HME architecture, we must define appropriate "missing data" so as to simplify the likelihood function. We define indicator variables z_{ij} such that one and only one of the z_{ij} is one for any given data point. These indicator variables have the interpretation as labels that specify which expert in the probability model generated the data point. This choice of missing data yields the following complete-data likelihood:

$$l_c(\boldsymbol{\theta}; \mathcal{X}) = \sum_t \sum_i \sum_j z_{ij}^{(t)} \ln\{g_i^{(t)} g_{j|i}^{(t)} P_{ij}(\mathbf{y}^{(t)})\}. \quad (11)$$

Note the relationship of the complete-data likelihood in Equation 11 to the incomplete-data likelihood in Equation 10. The use of the indicator variables z_{ij} has allowed the logarithm to be brought inside the summation signs, substantially simplifying the maximization problem. We now define the E step of the EM algorithm by taking the expectation of the complete-data likelihood:

$$Q(\boldsymbol{\theta}, \boldsymbol{\theta}^{(p)}) = \sum_t \sum_i \sum_j h_{ij}^{(t)} \ln\{g_i^{(t)} g_{j|i}^{(t)} P_{ij}(\mathbf{y}^{(t)})\}, \quad (12)$$

where we have used the fact that:

$$\begin{aligned} E[z_{ij}^{(t)}] &= P(z_{ij}^{(t)} = 1|\mathbf{y}^{(t)}, \mathbf{x}^{(t)}, \boldsymbol{\theta}^{(p)}) \\ &= \frac{P(\mathbf{y}^{(t)}|z_{ij}^{(t)} = 1, \mathbf{x}^{(t)}, \boldsymbol{\theta}^{(p)}) P(z_{ij}^{(t)} = 1|\mathbf{x}^{(t)}, \boldsymbol{\theta}^{(p)})}{P(\mathbf{y}^{(t)}|\mathbf{x}^{(t)}, \boldsymbol{\theta}^{(p)})} \\ &= \frac{P(\mathbf{y}^{(t)}|\mathbf{x}^{(t)}, \boldsymbol{\theta}_{ij}{}^{(p)}) g_i^{(t)} g_{j|i}^{(t)}}{\sum_i g_i^{(t)} \sum_j g_{j|i}^{(t)} P(\mathbf{y}^{(t)}|\mathbf{x}^{(t)}, \boldsymbol{\theta}_{ij}{}^{(p)})} \\ &= h_{ij}^{(t)}. \end{aligned}$$

The M step requires maximizing $Q(\boldsymbol{\theta}, \boldsymbol{\theta}^{(p)})$ with respect to the expert network parameters and the gating network parameters. Examining Equation 12, we see that the expert network parameters influence the Q function only through the terms $h_{ij}^{(t)} \ln P_{ij}(\mathbf{y}^{(t)})$, and the gating network parameters influence the Q function only through the terms $h_{ij}^{(t)} \ln g_i^{(t)}$ and $h_{ij}^{(t)} \ln g_{j|i}^{(t)}$. Thus the M step involves the following separate maximizations:

$$\boldsymbol{\theta}_{ij}^{(p+1)} = \arg\max_{\boldsymbol{\theta}_{ij}} \sum_t h_{ij}^{(t)} \ln P_{ij}(\mathbf{y}^{(t)}),$$

$$\mathbf{v}_i^{(p+1)} = \arg\max_{\mathbf{v}_i} \sum_t \sum_k h_k^{(t)} \ln g_k^{(t)},$$

and

$$\mathbf{v}_{ij}^{(p+1)} = \arg\max_{\mathbf{v}_{ij}} \sum_t \sum_k h_k^{(t)} \sum_l h_{l|k}^{(t)} \ln g_{l|k}^{(t)}.$$

Note that each of these maximization problems are themselves maximum likelihood problems, given that P_{ij}, g_i and $g_{j|i}$ are probability densities. Moreover, given our parameterization of these densities, the log likelihoods that we have obtained are weighted log likelihoods for generalized linear models (GLIM's). An efficient algorithm known as iteratively reweighted least-squares (IRLS) is available to solve the maximum likelihood problem for such models (McCullagh & Nelder, 1983). We discuss IRLS briefly in the Appendix; see Jordan and Jacobs (1993) for more details.

In summary, the EM algorithm that we have obtained involves a calculation of posterior probabilities in the outer loop (the E step), and the solution of a set of weighted IRLS problems in the inner loop (the M step). We summarize the algorithm as follows:

HME Algorithm 1

1. For each data pair $(\mathbf{x}^{(t)}, \mathbf{y}^{(t)})$, compute the posterior probabilities $h_i^{(t)}$ and $h_{j|i}^{(t)}$ using the current values of the parameters.
2. For each expert (i, j), solve an IRLS problem with observations $\{(\mathbf{x}^{(t)}, \mathbf{y}^{(t)})\}_1^N$ and observation weights $\{h_{ij}^{(t)}\}_1^N$.
3. For each top-level gating network, solve an IRLS problem with observations $\{(\mathbf{x}^{(t)}, h_k^{(t)})\}_1^N$.
4. For each lower-level gating network, solve an IRLS problem with observations $\{(\mathbf{x}^{(t)}, h_{l|k}^{(t)})\}_1^N$ and observation weights $\{h_k^{(t)}\}_1^N$.
5. Iterate using the updated parameter values.

Jordan and Jacobs (1993) also present an approximation to this algorithm in which the gating networks are fit by least-squares rather than maximum likelihood. In this case, the IRLS inner loop reduces to a weighted least-squares problem that can be solved without iteration.

2.6.1 Simulation Results

We tested the algorithm on a difficult nonlinear system identification problem. The data were obtained from a simulation of a four-joint robot arm moving in three-dimensional space. The network must learn the *forward dynamics* of the arm; a mapping from twelve coupled input variables to four output variables. This mapping is highly nonlinear due to the rotating coordinate systems and the interaction torques between the links of the arm.

We generated 15,000 data points for training and 5,000 points for testing. For each epoch (i.e., each pass through the training set), we computed the relative error on the test set.[3]

We compared the performance of a binary hierarchy to that of the best linear approximation, a backpropagation network, the CART algorithm and the MARS algorithm. The hierarchy was a four-level hierarchy with 16 expert networks and 15 gating networks. Each expert network had 4 output units and each gating network had 1 output unit. The backpropagation network had 60 hidden units, which yields approximately the same number of parameters in the network as in the hierarchy. The MARS algorithm was run with a maximum of 16 basis functions, based on the fact that each such function corresponds roughly to a single expert in the HME architecture.

Architecture	Relative Error	# Epochs
linear	.31	NA
backprop	.09	5,500
HME	.10	35
CART	.17	NA
CART (oblique)	.13	NA
MARS	.16	NA

Table 1: Average Values of Relative Error and Number of Epochs Required for Convergence for the Batch Algorithms.

Table 1 reports the average values of minimum relative error for all architectures. (For backprop and the HME algorithm, the minima were defined by a sequence of three successive increases in the relative error.) Both CART and MARS were run four times, once for each of the output variables. We combined the results from these four computations to compute the total relative error. Two versions of CART were run; one in which the splits were restricted to be parallel to the axes and one in which oblique splits of the input space were allowed.

All of the architectures that we studied performed significantly better than the best linear approximation. The CART architecture with oblique splits performed better than CART with axis-parallel splits. The HME architecture yielded a significant improvement over MARS and CART. Backpropagation produced the lowest relative error of the algorithms tested; however, five of the backpropagation runs had to be thrown out because they failed to converge within the allotted time.

These differences in relative error should be treated with some caution. The need to set free parameters for some of the architectures (e.g., backpropagation) and the need to make structural choices (e.g., number of hidden units, number of basis functions, number of experts) makes it difficult to match architectures. The HME architecture, for example, involves parameter dependencies that are not present in a backpropagation network. A gating network at a high level in the tree can "pinch off" a branch of the tree, rendering useless the parameters in that branch of the tree. Raw parameter count is therefore only a very rough guide to architecture capacity; more precise measures are needed (e.g., VC dimension) before definitive quantitative comparisons can be made.

The differences between backpropagation and HME in terms of convergence time are more definitive. HME reliably converges approximately two orders of magni-

[3] Relative error is computed as a ratio between the mean squared error and the mean squared error that would be obtained if the learner were to output the mean value of the outputs for all data points.

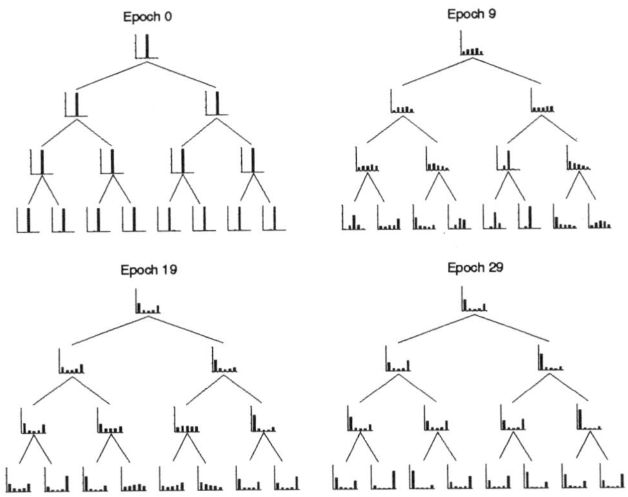

Figure 2: A sequence of histogram trees for the HME architecture. Each histogram displays the distribution of posterior probabilities across the training set at each node in the tree.

tude faster than backpropagation.

As shown in Figure 2, the HME architecture lends itself well to graphical investigation. This figure displays the time sequence of the distributions of posterior probabilities across the training set at each node of the tree. At Epoch 0, before any learning has taken place, most of the posterior probabilities at each node are approximately 0.5 across the training set. As the training proceeds, the histograms flatten out, eventually approaching bimodal distributions in which the posterior probabilities are either one or zero for most of the training patterns. This evolution is indicative of increasingly sharp splits being fit by the gating networks. Note that there is a tendency for the splits to be formed more rapidly at higher levels in the tree than at lower levels.

2.7 AN ON-LINE ALGORITHM

Jordan and Jacobs (1993) derive an on-line algorithm for the HME architecture using techniques from recursive estimation theory (Ljung & Söderström, 1986).

The on-line update rule for the parameters of the expert networks is given by the following recursive equation:

$$U_{ij}^{(t+1)} = U_{ij}^{(t)} + h_i^{(t)} h_{j|i}^{(t)} (\mathbf{y}^{(t)} - \boldsymbol{\mu}_{ij}^{(t)}) \mathbf{x}^{(t)T} R_{ij}^{(t)}, \quad (13)$$

where R_{ij} is the inverse covariance matrix for expert network (i, j). This matrix is updated via the equation:

$$R_{ij}^{(t)} = R_{ij}^{(t-1)} - \lambda^{-1} \frac{R_{ij}^{(t-1)} \mathbf{x}^{(t)} \mathbf{x}^{(t)T} R_{ij}^{(t-1)}}{\lambda [h_{ij}^{(t)}]^{-1} + \mathbf{x}^{(t)T} R_{ij}^{(t-1)} \mathbf{x}^{(t)}}, \quad (14)$$

Architecture	Relative Error	# Epochs
backprop (on-line)	.07	63
HME	.11	2

Table 2: Average values of relative error and number of epochs required for convergence for the on-line algorithms.

where λ is a decay parameter.

Similar update rules are obtained for the parameters of the gating networks. See Jordan and Jacobs (1993) for further details.

2.7.1 Simulation Results

The on-line algorithm was tested on the robot dynamics problem described in the previous section. The performance of the algorithm was compared to an on-line backpropagation network. Parameter settings for the backpropagation network were obtained by a coarse search through the parameter space, yielding a value of 0.15 for the learning rate and 0.20 for the momentum.

The minimum values of relative error and the convergence times for both architectures are provided in Table 2.

The on-line algorithm for backpropagation is significantly faster than the corresponding batch algorithm (cf. Table 1). This is also true of the on-line HME algorithm, which converges in two passes through the data.

3 CONCLUSIONS

We have presented a novel tree-structured architecture for supervised learning. This architecture is based on a statistical model, and makes contact with a number of branches of statistical theory, including mixture model estimation and generalized linear model theory. The learning algorithm for the architecture is an EM algorithm.

There are other tree-structured learning algorithms in the machine learning literature that share features of the HME approach, including the use of oblique splits of the input space and incremental update procedures (e.g., Utgoff & Brodley, 1990). The major advantage of the HME approach is the use of a statistical framework. The statistical framework motivates some of the variance-decreasing features of the HME approach, such as the use of "soft" splits. The statistical approach also provides a unified framework for handling a variety of data types, including binary variables, ordered and unordered categorical variables, and real variables, both at the input and the output. The use of maximum likelihood allows standard tools from statistical theory to be brought to bear in developing inference procedures, fitting procedures, and measures of uncertainty for the architecture. It also opens the door to the Bayesian approaches that have been found to be useful in the context of unsupervised mixture model estimation (Cheeseman, et al., 1988).

4 APPENDIX

We briefly describe the IRLS algorithm for the case of a scalar output (see Jordan and Jacobs, 1993, for a derivation of the algorithm and more details).

Let $\mathbf{x}$ be an input vector, $\boldsymbol{\beta}$ a parameter vector, $\eta = \mathbf{x}^T\boldsymbol{\beta}$ a linear predictor, and $\mu = f(\eta)$ an output. For a data set $\mathcal{X} = \{(\mathbf{x}^{(t)}, y^{(t)})\}$, let X denote the matrix whose rows are the $\mathbf{x}^{(t)}$. IRLS updates the parameter vector by repeatedly solving the following weighted least-squares equations:

$$\boldsymbol{\beta}_{r+1} = (X^T W X)^{-1} X^T W \mathbf{z}, \tag{15}$$

where W is a diagonal weight matrix having elements $w^{(t)} = f'(\eta^{(t)})^2/\mathrm{Var}[y^{(t)}]$ and $\mathbf{z}$ is defined as follows: $\mathbf{z} = X\boldsymbol{\beta}_r + \mathbf{e}$, where $\mathbf{e}$ is the vector whose components are:

$$e^{(t)} = (y^{(t)} - \mu^{(t)})/f'(\eta^{(t)}).$$

The algorithm must iterate because W depends on the parameters.

IRLS can be shown to be a Fisher scoring algorithm for the maximum likelihood estimation of a GLIM model (McCullagh & Nelder, 1983). Its convergence properties are therefore similar to those of Newton-Raphson.

Acknowledgements

This project was supported by grants from the McDonnell-Pew Foundation, ATR Auditory and Visual Perception Research Laboratories, Siemens Corporation, by grant IRI-9013991 from the National Science Foundation, and by grant N00014-90-J-1942 from the Office of Naval Research. The project was also supported by NSF grant ASC-9217041 and NSF grant ECS-9216531. Michael I. Jordan is a NSF Presidential Young Investigator.

References

Breiman, L., Friedman, J. H., Olshen, R. A., & Stone, C. J. (1984). *Classification and Regression Trees.* Belmont, CA: Wadsworth International Group.

Bridle, J. (1989). Probabilistic interpretation of feedforward classification network outputs, with relationships to statistical pattern recognition. In F. Fogelman–Soulie & J. Hérault (Eds.), *Neurocomputing: Algorithms, Architectures, and Applications.* New York: Springer-Verlag.

Cheeseman, P., Kelly, J., Self, M., Stutz, J., Taylor, W., & Freeman, D. (1988). Autoclass: A Bayesian classification system. In *Proceedings of the Fifth International Conference on Machine Learning,* Ann Arbor, MI.

Dempster, A. P., Laird, N. M., & Rubin, D. B. (1977). Maximum likelihood from incomplete data via the EM algorithm. *Journal of the Royal Statistical Society, B, 39,* 1-38.

Friedman, J. H. (1991). Multivariate adaptive regression splines. *The Annals of Statistics, 19,* 1-141.

Golub, G. H. & Van Loan, G. F. (1989). *Matrix Computations.* Baltimore, MD: The Johns Hopkins University Press.

Jacobs, R. A, Jordan, M. I., Nowlan, S. J., & Hinton, G. E. (1991). Adaptive mixtures of local experts. *Neural Computation, 3,* 79-87.

Jordan, M. I. & Jacobs, R. A. (1993). *Hierarchical mixtures of experts and the EM algorithm.* Computational Cognitive Science Tech. Rep. 9301, MIT, Cambridge, MA.

Jordan, M. I. & Xu, L. (1993). *Convergence results for the EM approach to mixtures-of-experts architectures.* Computational Cognitive Science Tech. Rep. 9303, MIT, Cambridge, MA.

Ljung, L. & Söderström, T. (1986). *Theory and practice of recursive identification.* Cambridge: MIT Press.

McCullagh, P. & Nelder, J.A. (1983). *Generalized Linear Models.* London: Chapman and Hall.

Nowlan, S.J. (1991). *Soft competitive adaptation: Neural network learning algorithms based on fitting statistical mixtures.* Tech. Rep. CMU-CS-91-126, CMU, Pittsburgh, PA.

Quinlan, R. (1986). Induction of decision trees. *Machine Learning, 1,* 81-106.

Scott, D. W. (1992). *Multivariate Density Estimation.* New York: John Wiley.

Titterington, D. M., Smith, A. F. M., & Makov, U. E. (1985). *Statistical Analysis of Finite Mixture Distributions.* New York: John Wiley.

Utgoff, P. E. & Brodley, C. E. (1990). An incremental method for finding multivariate splits for decision trees. In *Proceedings of the Seventh International Conference on Machine Learning,* Los Altos, CA.

Wahba, G., Gu, C., Wang, Y., & Chappell, R. (1993). *Soft classification, a.k.a. risk estimation, via penalized log likelihood and smoothing spline analysis of variance.* Tech. Rep. 899, University of Wisconsin, Madison.

Hierarchical Learning in Stochastic Domains: Preliminary Results

Leslie Pack Kaelbling
Computer Science Department
Box 1910
Brown University
Providence, RI, USA 02912-1910
lpk@cs.brown.edu

Abstract

This paper presents the HDG learning algorithm, which uses a hierarchical decomposition of the state space to make learning to achieve goals more efficient with a small penalty in path quality. Special care must be taken when performing hierarchical planning and learning in stochastic domains, because macro-operators cannot be executed ballistically. The HDG algorithm, which is a descendent of Watkins' Q-learning algorithm, is described here and preliminary empirical results are presented.

1 INTRODUCTION

Reinforcement learning is a general tool for deriving strategies that optimize a fixed reinforcement function in a stochastic environment. A crucial problem in reinforcement learning is *temporal credit assignment*: how to choose actions based on good results that happen after (perhaps long after) the action is taken. This problem is solved well in the general case by *temporal difference* methods, such as Watkins' Q learning [Barto *et al.*, 1989, Watkins, 1989] and Sutton's TD algorithm [Sutton, 1988].

In much of the work on reinforcement learning, however, researchers have studied a restriction of the problem to cases of "goals of achievement." Rather than having an arbitrary mapping of states of the world to reinforcements for the agent, there is a single "goal" situation at which the agent must arrive as soon as possible. Goals of achievement can be modeled in the general reinforcement-learning framework by having the goal situation generate a positive reinforcement and all other situations a zero reinforcement. Because there is a discounting factor built into the temporal-difference methods, actions that lead to the goal sooner rather than later will be preferred.

Domains with goals of achievement can be learned more efficiently by methods that are tailored to this special case. In previous work [Kaelbling, 1993b], we discussed the *DG learning* algorithm, which is analogous to Q learning, but directly suited to goals of achievement. In the basic single-goal case, DG learning is somewhat more effective than Q learning. The real importance of DG learning is shown when we consider the case of goals of achievement that change over time; the common scenario of a taskable delivery robot is an instance of this sort of problem. A simple extension to DG learning allows a large amount of between-task transfer, making it greatly preferable to Q learning for this sort of problem, without requiring any complex mechanisms.

Unfortunately, the DG learning algorithm is expensive, both in terms of the number of learning instances required to achieve good performance and in computational time and space per instance. In this paper, we consider learning to achieve goals in a two-level hierarchy. The new algorithm, HDG, is more efficient than DG in both time and space; preliminary empirical results show that it learns more quickly initially, but has a somewhat sub-optimal asymptotic performance. As state spaces become huge, we can use multiple levels of hierarchy to achieve great performance improvements that will, in general, offset a degree of sub-optimality in performance.

In the following sections we present background material on Q and DG learning, discuss the nature of our hierarchies, define the HDG learning algorithm, and give some preliminary experimental results. We conclude by comparing this to related work and by considering directions for future work.

2 Q AND DG LEARNING

We assume that a learning agent is embedded in an environment in such a way that it can discriminate the set S of distinct world situations and can take the set A of actions on the world. The world is modeled as a Markov process, making stochastic transitions based on its current situation and the actions taken by the agent. We let $T(s, a, s')$ be the probability that the world will make a transition to situation s' given that it was in situation s and the agent executed action a. In addition, for each situation s and action a, $r(s, a)$ is the *reinforcement value* of taking action a in situation s.

In general, this value is a scalar random variable; it must have a stationary distribution, but the same situation-action pair may have different results on different trials.

2.1 Q Learning

The general reinforcement-learning problem is typically stated as finding a policy that maximizes expected discounted future reinforcement. A policy π is a mapping from S to A. The expected discounted future reinforcement of a policy π in a situation s is defined as

$$\sum_{t=0}^{\infty} \gamma^t er(t) \ ,$$

where $er(t)$ is the expected value of the reinforcement obtained at step t, given that the agent started in situation s and executed policy π. The variable γ is the *discounting factor*; it controls the degree to which rewards in the distant future affect the total value of a policy and is usually just slightly less than 1.

Given definitions of the transition probabilities and the expected reinforcements, it is possible to solve for the optimal policy, using methods from dynamic programming. A more interesting case occurs when we wish simultaneously to learn the dynamics of the world and to construct the policy. Watkins' Q learning algorithm gives us an elegant and efficient method for doing this.

Let $Q^*(s, a)$ be the expected discounted reinforcement for taking action a in situation s and continuing thereafter with the optimal policy. It can be recursively defined by

$$Q^*(s,a) = er(s,a) + \gamma \sum_{s' \in S} T(s,a,s') \max_{a' \in A} Q^*(s',a') \ .$$

Because we do not know T and er initially, we construct incremental estimates of the Q values on line. Starting with $Q(s, a)$ at any value (but typically 0), every time an action is taken, we update the Q values as follows:

$$Q(s,a) := (1-\alpha)Q(s,a) + \alpha(r + \gamma \max_{a' \in A} Q(s',a')) \ ,$$

where r is the actual reinforcement value received for taking action a in situation s, s' is the next situation, and α is a learning rate (between 0 and 1).

Given the Q values, there is a policy defined by taking, in any situation s, the action a that maximizes $Q(s, a)$. Watkins showed [Watkins, 1989] that, given some assumptions, including that every situation-action pair is tried infinitely often on an infinite run, the Q values will converge to the true Q^* values, and hence the induced policy will converge to the optimal one.

Of course, in any practical situation, as the learned Q values converge to the true Q^* values, we will have to use the policy to control action. But in doing so, we are in danger of violating the requirement that every situation-action pair be tried infinitely often. This is an instance of the exploration versus exploitation trade-off; it has been treated extensively elsewhere [Kaelbling, 1993a, Thrun, 1992]. In the interest of simplicity in this paper, we generate actions probabilistically based on the Q values using a Boltzmann distribution. Given a situation s, we choose action a with probability

$$\frac{e^{Q(a,s)/T}}{\sum_{a \in A} e^{Q(a,s)/T}} \ .$$

This serves to choose actions whose values are much better than the others with much greater likelihood. The *temperature* parameter T controls the amount of exploration (the degree to which actions other than the one with the best Q value are taken).

2.2 DG Learning

The DG learning method applies only to domains in which the aim of the agent is to arrive at some goal situation in the least number of steps. We still assume that the world makes stochastic transitions, but the goal is explicitly named and there is no reinforcement function. The aim of DG learning, at its simplest, is to arrive at the policy that minimizes the expected number of steps to the goal. The method is applicable without change to the case where the goal varies on line: now a policy is a mapping from $S \times S$ to A, specifying an action to take based on the current situation and the goal situation.

We define $DG^*(s, a, g)$ to be the expected number of steps required to get to situation g from situation s by starting with action a and continuing with the optimal policy. It is conveniently described recursively as

$$DG^*(s,a,g) = 0$$

if $s = g$ and

$$DG^*(s,a,g) = 1 + \sum_{s' \in S} T(s,a,s') \min_{a' \in A} DG^*(s',a',g)$$

otherwise.

Rather than learning T then calculating DG, we estimate DG directly on line. Starting with $DG(s, a, g)$ at any value (but typically 0), every time an action is taken, we update the DG values as follows:

$$\begin{aligned} DG(s,a,g) \ := \ & (1-\alpha)DG(s,a,g) \\ & + \alpha(1 + \min_{a' \in A} DG(s',a',g)) \ , \end{aligned}$$

where α is the learning rate and s' is the next situation.

A policy can be directly constructed from the DG values by choosing, for every current situation s and goal situation g, the action a that minimizes $DG(s, a, g)$. Although no theoretical results have yet been developed with respect to this learning procedure, we conjecture that it can be shown to converge under restrictions similar to those for the Q-learning result.

The trade-off between exploration and exploitation is important in DG learning as well; we use the Boltzmann distribution to construct action probabilities, though interval estimation techniques [Kaelbling, 1993a] could be employed for more careful exploration.

2.3 Updating all Goals in DG Learning

A very simple kind of extra learning step can be directly added to DG learning. Whenever an action a is taken as a step from situation s to a goal g, we update the value of $DG(s, a, g)$ by looking ahead one step at the value of $DG(s', a', g)$ for the maximizing a'. This look-ahead process hinges on the relationship between s, a, and s'; the goal is relevant only for bookkeeping purposes.

We define *all-goals* updating mode for DG learning to update $DG(s, a, g')$ for all $g' \in S$, independent of what goal was being sought when the action was taken. This updating mode requires an amount of work linear in the size of the set of situations; if this cost is prohibitive, a random or systematically-chosen subset of goals could be updated on each iteration.

The work that is done in updating all goals will not speed learning or performance for the particular goal that is being achieved; but it *will* result in an extremely efficient transfer of knowledge to the achievement of other goals. Singh [Singh, 1992c] has also addressed this issue, but in a more complex network architecture and for a different class of goals. We have found that DG learning with all-goals updating performs very well, learning to achieve changing goals with an order of magnitude less data than is required by conventional Q learning [Kaelbling, 1993b].

2.4 Computational Complexity of DG Learning

We are interested in three complexity measures of the learning algorithms: execution time without learning, execution time with learning, and space. Each step, without learning, requires finding the action with the maximum DG value for the given start and goal situations; assuming that array indexing is constant time, this requires $O(|A|)$ time, where A is the set of possible basic actions. If we perform all-goals updating, it requires an additional $O(|S||A|)$ time per instance. The DG values require $O(|S|^2|A|)$ space.

3 LANDMARK NETWORKS

When we plan a route for driving a long distance, we don't even attempt to find the optimal path; rather, we take advantage of an existing path hierarchy. We plan a route from our current location to the nearest freeway on-ramp, plan a series of legs on freeway segments, then plan a route from the freeway off-ramp to our destination. The hierarchical DG learning algorithm presented in this paper will use a related hierarchical structure known as a *landmark network*.

Given a set, S, of situations, a landmark network is specified by the tuple $\langle L, NL, N\rangle$, where $L \subset S$ is a distinguished set of *landmark* situations, $NL : S \rightarrow L$ is a mapping from each situation to its nearest landmark, and $N : L \rightarrow 2^L$ is a mapping from each landmark to a set of neighbor landmarks. For such a structure to make sense, we need a distance metric on S; the most useful one would be expected

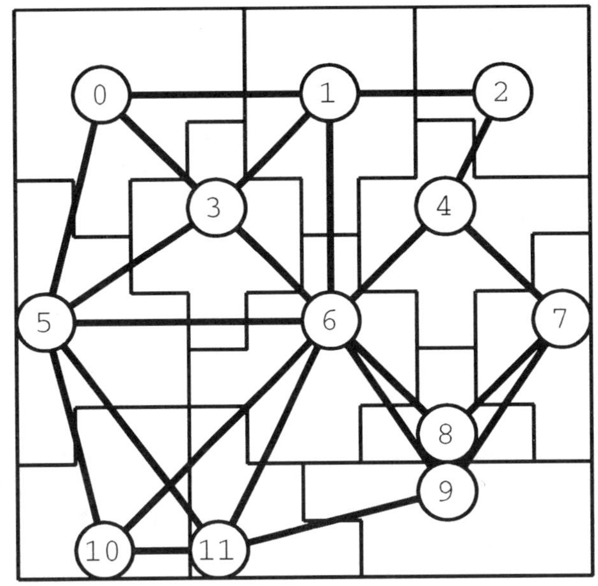

Figure 1: Landmark network constructed on a discrete space

number of steps needed to get from situation to situation using the optimal strategy. We will not have that information available to us initially, however, so any approximation that allows us to partition S into subsets that contain situations relatively near each other will do. At the end of the paper, we speculate on how to learn a good landmark structure.

The N function defines a connectivity graph among the landmarks; it provides an abstract level at which to plan paths. From a landmark, l, we can choose to move toward any landmark in $N(l)$. If the graph is highly connected, then there are lots of alternatives and the routes will be very efficient. But high connectivity increases the branching factor of our search, potentially making planning and learning less efficient.

A landmark network can be constructed for any space of situations, but navigation in cartesian space is a good illustrative example because we have a great deal of intuitive experience with such spaces. One way to construct plausible landmark networks in cartesian space is to use the Delaunay triangulation [Preparata and Shamos, 1985]. The landmark situations can be distributed in any way over the space. Then, a Voronoi diagram is constructed on those landmarks, partitioning the space into regions of situations that share the same closest landmark. Finally, any two landmarks whose Voronoi regions touch are connected. Even in discrete spaces that do not satisfy the triangle inequality, it is possible to perform an analogous partition. Figure 1 shows a landmark network constructed in this way on a discrete space. Each square in the grid is a situation; the ones with circles are landmarks. The light rectilinear lines indicate the neighborhood boundaries, and the heavy lines indicate the neighbor relation among landmarks.

4 HDG LEARNING ALGORITHM

Given a landmark network, we can modify the DG learning algorithm to work in the hierarchical space; we will call this algorithm HDG for *hierarchical distance to goal* learning. We first describe the internal structures of the algorithm and how they can be used to select actions, then provide a method for learning them.

4.1 Acting hierarchically

In a deterministic domain, it is easy to construct hierarchical navigation algorithms. First you move to the nearest landmark, then you move along the edges in the landmark network until you're at the landmark nearest the goal, then you move to the goal. In stochastic domains, it is more difficult, because there is no nominal path between landmarks that can be followed ballistically (using the previous analogy, it is possible to mistakenly drive off the freeway at any moment). Therefore, rather than using landmarks as way-points, we use them as locations to aim for, reducing the number of possible goals for DG learning. This kind of navigation more closely resembles the navigation done in sailing or flying rather than navigation on freeways.

The basic operation of the HDG algorithm is as follows: given a current situation s and a goal situation g,

1. Find nearest landmark to s, $NL(s)$, and nearest landmark to g, $NL(g)$.
2. If $NL(s) = NL(g)$, then execute the best local action for getting from s to g.
3. Otherwise, let l_i be the second landmark on the shortest path from $NL(s)$ to $NL(g)$.
4. Choose the best local action for getting from s to l_i and execute it.

In order to support this algorithm we need two data structures. At the low level, we need to store DG values from every situation s to every other situation s' such that $NL(s) = NL(s')$. These values will allow us to choose the best actions to take in final phase of getting to the goal once in the correct region (step 2 above). In addition, we need DG values from every situation s to every landmark in $N(NL(s))$; that is, to every landmark that is a neighbor of the nearest landmark (step 4 above). At the next level of abstraction, we need to be able to find shortest paths between landmarks. We define $\Gamma(l_1, l_2, l_3)$ to be the shortest distance from landmark l_1 to l_3 on a path between landmarks that starts by going to landmark l_2, where l_2 is a neighbor of l_1. Let

$$D(l_1, l_2) = \min_a DG(l_1, a, l_2)$$

for any $l_2 \in N(l_1)$. Then,

$$\Gamma(l_1, l_2, l_3) = D(l_1, l_2) + \min_{l_i} \Gamma(l_2, l_i, l_3)$$

and step 3 above can be accomplished by finding the $l_i \in N(NL(s))$ that minimizes

$$\Gamma(NL(s), l_i, NL(g)) \ .$$

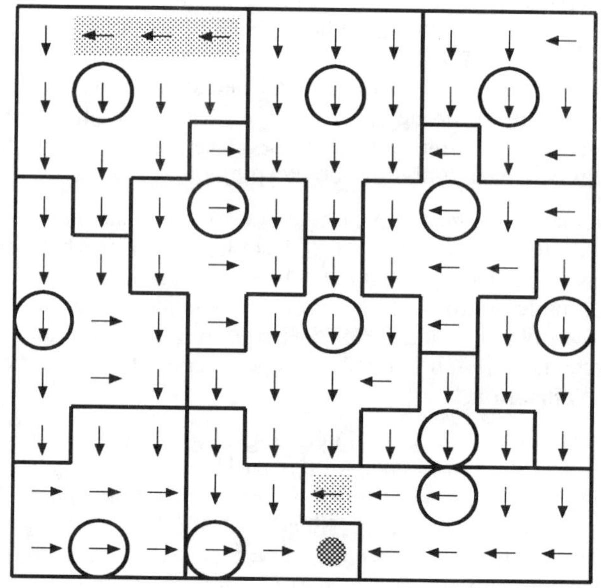

Figure 2: Policy for achieving goal in bottom center of the space.

We can rewrite the algorithm more precisely as:

- If $NL(s) = NL(g)$, then execute the basic action a that minimizes $DG(s, a, g)$.
- Otherwise, let l_i be the landmark that minimizes $\Gamma(NL(s), l_i, NL(g))$ and execute the basic action a that minimizes $DG(s, a, l_i)$.

This algorithm results in a behavior of aiming toward the next appropriate landmark; it is rarely the case that the agent actually goes through the landmark situations, though, because as soon as a new region is entered, the landmark toward which it is aiming is changed. Figure 2 shows the policy derived from the hierarchical action algorithm for the goal indicated by a dark circle in the middle of the bottom row. The squares highlighted in grey indicate situations in which this policy disagrees with the optimal low-level policy. In the upper left corner, the error arises because the shortest path via landmarks includes the landmark in the middle at the far left; rather than aiming straight for the goal, the policy is aiming for that next landmark, resulting in a perturbation of the path to the left. Similarly, in the situation just above the goal situation, the policy is aiming at the landmark in the next region, rather than straight at the goal. The policy for this goal has more of these deviations than those for other goals. This may be an artifact of the simplicity of the domain. Note that these policies are not explicitly stored, but are computed as needed by the method given above.

4.2 Learning

The DG values are learned just as they are in the basic DG algorithm. We perform all-goals updating, but notice that the space of target goals is much smaller; it encompasses only the other situations in the same partition as well as the neighboring landmarks.

The Γ values are defined as a function of the DG values. It is difficult to learning them using a standard incremental technique, however, because the landmarks are so rarely actually encountered. Instead, we simply periodically recompute the Γ values. We start by setting

$$\Gamma(l_1, l_2, l_2) = D(l_1, l_2)$$

for all $l_2 \in N(l_1)$ and setting

$$\Gamma(l_1, l_2, l_1) = 0$$

for all l_1, l_2, then use a modified version of the Floyd-Warshall all-sources shortest-paths algorithm [Cormen *et al.*, 1990] to compute the rest of the Γ values. Early in a run, the DG values change very rapidly, so the Γ values should be recomputed frequently; as the run progresses, the frequency of recomputation can be decreased.

4.3 Computational Complexity

Let $|L|$ be the number of landmarks, $|D|$ be an upper bound on the number of neighbors a landmark can have (the degree of the landmark graph), and $|P|$ be an upper bound on the size of a neighborhood. To execute a single step, without learning, we need time $O(1)+O(|D|)+O(|A|)$; it requires constant time to look up the two nearest landmarks in a table, then time on the order of the degree of the landmark graph to find the best next landmark, then time on the order of the number of primitive actions to select the best action. When we add all-goals updating for the DG values, it requires time $O(|A|(|P| + |D|))$, because we have to find the best action for every other situation in the same partition as well as for every neighboring landmark. To compute Γ values at constant-time intervals requires time $O(|D||L|^3)$, so every execution step takes time $O(|D||L|^3 + |A|(|P| + |D|))$. The cost of computing Γ will tend to be the leading factor, but its effect can be limited in two ways. In the following work, the values are recomputed quite rarely, so the cost is amortized over a large number of steps. If $|L|$ gets quite large, then it would be appropriate to construct a further level of hierarchy to reduce this complexity; the final section discusses possibilities for doing this.

It requires space $O(|S|)$ to store a table for NL, space $O(|D||L|)$ to store a table for N, space $O(|S||A|(|P| + |D|))$ to store the DG values, and space $O(|D||L|^2)$ to store the Γ values. So the total space complexity is $O(|S||A|(|P| + |D|) + |D||L|^2)$.

Compared to the DG algorithm, we trade a factor of $|P| + |D|$ for a factor of $|S|$ in both time and space and incur some extra overhead for the abstraction level. In general, $|P|$ will be approximately equal to $|S|/|L|$, and we can see the tension that arises about the number of landmarks. The more landmarks, the more expense we incur at the abstract level, but the smaller the partitions, and hence, the smaller the DG array and the less work required to update it. In addition, the more landmarks there are, the better the paths will be. We can easily limit $|D|$ to a small constant, then consider how to choose $|L|$ optimally. In order to minimize space, we can choose $|L| = |S|^{2/3}|A|^{1/3}$, giving space complexity of $O(|S|^{4/3}|A|)$. To minimize time, we can choose $|L| = |S|^{1/4}|A|^{1/4}$, giving time complexity of $O(|S|^{3/4}|A|)$.

5 PRELIMINARY EXPERIMENTAL RESULTS

In this section we present some preliminary experimental results comparing the DG and HDG learning algorithms. We use the domain shown in figure 1 above. Each location on the grid is a single situation, and the actions available to the agent are to move north, south, east, and west. If the agent tries to move through a boundary, it stays where it was. The domain is stochastic, with the agent landing in the nominal square (that is, the square to the north if the north action is taken) with probability .2; it lands in each of the squares neighboring the nominal square with probability .2, as well. This error distribution was chosen arbitrarily; informal testing with other error distributions seemed to yield similar results.

The domain has dynamic goals; as soon as the agent reaches the current goal, the goal is moved to a new location chosen uniformly at random. Both algorithms were tested on runs of length 20,000. For both of them, parameter values α (learning rate) of 0.4 and T (temperature) of 0.1 were determined through experimentation to be best. The algorithms were compared with these parameter settings on 10 runs of length 20,000. The averaged learning curves for each algorithm are shown together in figure 3. The HDG algorithm performs better earlier in the run, but has lower asymptotic performance. This lower performance is due, in part, to the fact that paths are constrained by the landmark network. It may also be due to the fact that there is experimentation taking place at two levels in the HG algorithm; the Boltzmann distribution is used both to choose the best next landmark and to choose the best low-level action. Once the domain is well learned, this extra experimentation contributes to slightly degraded performance. We expect that in larger domains with multiple levels of hierarchy, the difference between the early performance of DG and HDG will be considerably greater.

Both algorithms were implemented quite naively and straightforwardly. In the HDG algorithm, the Γ values are recomputed every 1000 ticks. The HDG algorithm runs over 3 times as fast as the DG algorithm.

The HDG algorithm was also tested on randomly-generated landmark networks; the results did not vary widely, which suggests that the method is relatively insensitive to the de-

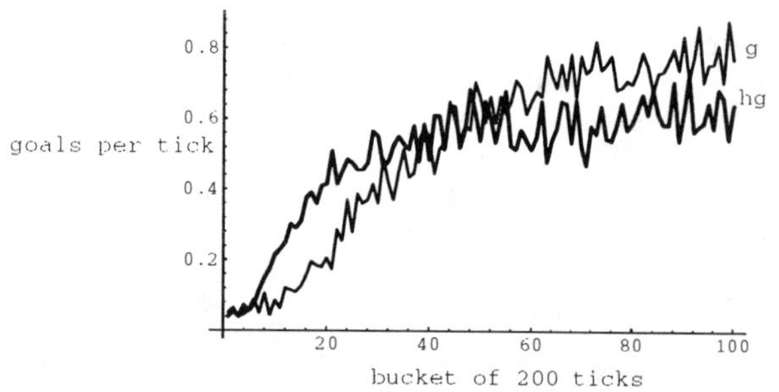

Figure 3: Learning curves of DG and HDG algorithms on stochastic grid world; average of 10 runs of length 20,000

tails of the landmark network.

6 RELATED WORK

The most closely related work, using hierarchies in the context of reinforcement learning, is that of Singh [Singh, 1992a, Singh, 1992b]. Singh addresses the slightly different learning problem of *sequential tasks*, in which each of a sequence of subgoals must be achieved in turn. This task structure induces a natural temporal abstraction hierarchy consisting of *macro operations*. This domain has the especially nice property that planning at higher levels of abstraction does not result in sub-optimal solutions. Singh's algorithm learns forward models (transition probabilities and expected reinforcements) at different levels of abstraction, then uses Sutton's Dyna [Sutton, 1990] technique (also used by Whitehead and Ballard [Whitehead and Ballard, 1989]) of simulating experience using the models. He finds that learning is much more efficient when updates are performed using models at a higher level of abstraction. The HDG method applies to a different class of tasks, in which the goal varies over time and is a particular low level situation. In addition, the DG and HDG methods learn without constructing forward models, with the all-goals updating on the DG values and the Floyd-Warshall computation of the Γ values performing the similar function of propagation information throughout the entire policy.

In his thesis, Lin [Lin, 1993] explores a model of hierarchical learning in which the system first learns elementary "skills" from pre-specified reinforcement functions, then learns how to compose them in order to maximize reinforcement at some higher level of abstraction. This work assumes that the environment is deterministic and that it is possible to "reset" the agent by instantaneously moving it to another part of the state space. This work is difficult to compare to standard Q learning, because some initial training on the basic skills must take place. Lin argues, plausibly, that such training is done in a variety of biological agents, and might be necessary for artificial agents, as well.

Finally, Dayan and Hinton [Dayan and Hinton, 1993] have developed *feudal reinforcement learning*. It has a strict hierarchy of "managers," each of whom can dictate subgoals to managers below them. At every level, the actions are executed until they terminate, and control is given away to the lower level as in a subroutine call. This method works very well in the deterministic domain in which it was tested. However, in stochastic domains, giving control away may mean that an entirely inappropriate low-level behavior is taking place. In addition, as Lin points out, it can be difficult to find termination conditions for low-level actions. The feudal learning method is more generally applicable than HDG, in that it does not rely on having goals of achievement; however, the general reinforcement function is not allowed to change dynamically. The feudal learning algorithm, as it stands, has potential difficulty with the higher levels of abstraction being non-Markovian; however, the authors conjecture that there are techniques available to address this problem.

7 FUTURE WORK

Much remains to be done in the exploration of this hierarchical approach to learning to achieve goals, both on the experimental and theoretical levels.

Experimentally, the most convicing validation of the method will be to apply it to a real-world domain. Two domains from different levels of robotics suggest themselves. One would be an extension of the pole-balancing domain, in which the posture of the pole is specified explicitly as a goal; we could ask the system to keep the pole leaning to the left, or to stay on the right third of its track. A more useful problem would be realistic navigation in an outdoor or hallway environment in which exact locations cannot be sensed reliably.

There has been some recent work on approximation algorithms for shortest path problems in cartesian space [Klein and Sairam, 1992]. It may be possible to use these or related results to show that, in certain kinds of domains, the optimal paths in the hierarchical models are within a constant factor in length of the optimal paths in the lowest-level model.

We have only explored a single level of hierarchy in this paper. It is clear how to continue this process: a set of level 2 landmarks can be chosen, inducing a clustering on the level 1 landmarks. Rather than having to learn Γ values for every pair of level 1 landmarks, the algorithm can learn them only within neighborhoods, as is done currently with DG values. Multiple levels of hierarchy will have to be introduced as state spaces get extremely large.

Finally, we have a bootstrapping problem surrounding the partitioning of the space; getting a useful partition presupposes much of the knowledge required to generate a good strategy. As the DG values are learned, the algorithm can revise its partition of the space and the neighborhood relation. In addition, it might be possible to move landmarks dynamically or to add and delete them. One suggestion, due to Chris Watkins, would be to notice landmarks that are rarely chosen as next steps and delete them, adding new landmarks in more useful places.

In order to make learning to achieve goals more practical, we must understand how to do it hierarchically. This paper has presented an initial practical step in that direction.

Acknowledgements

This work was supported in part by a National Science Foundation National Young Investigator Award IRI-9257592 and in part by ONR Contract N00014-91-4052, ARPA Order 8225.

References

[Barto *et al.*, 1989] Barto, A. G.; Sutton, R. S.; and Watkins, C. J. C. H. 1989. Learning and sequential decision making. Technical Report 89-95, Department of Computer and Information Science, University of Massachusetts, Amherst, Massachusetts. Also published in *Learning and Computational Neuroscience: Foundations of Adaptive Networks*, Michael Gabriel and John Moore, editors. The MIT Press, Cambridge, Massachusetts, 1991.

[Cormen *et al.*, 1990] Cormen, Thomas H.; Leiserson, Charles E.; and Rivest, Ronals L. 1990. *Introduction to Algorithms.* The MIT Press / McGraw Hill, Cambridge, Massachusetts.

[Dayan and Hinton, 1993] Dayan, Peter and Hinton, Geoffrey E. 1993. Feudal reinforcement learning. In *Advances in Neural Information Processing Systems 5*, San Mateo, California. Morgan Kaufmann.

[Kaelbling, 1993a] Kaelbling, Leslie Pack 1993a. *Learning in Embedded Systems.* The MIT Press, Cambridge, Massachusetts. Also available as a PhD Thesis from Stanford University, 1990.

[Kaelbling, 1993b] Kaelbling, Leslie Pack 1993b. Learning to achieve goals. In *Proceedings of the Thirteenth International Joint Conference on Artificial Intelligence*, Chambéry, France. Morgan Kaufmann.

[Klein and Sairam, 1992] Klein, Philip N. and Sairam, S. 1992. Parallel and dynamic approximation schemes for planar shortest paths. Technical Report 92-61, Computer Science Department, Brown University, Providence, Rhode Island.

[Lin, 1993] Lin, Long-Ji 1993. *Reinforcement Learning for Robots Using Neural Networks.* Ph.D. Dissertation, Carnegie Mellon University, Pittsburgh, Pennsylvania.

[Preparata and Shamos, 1985] Preparata, Franco P. and Shamos, Michael Ian 1985. *Computational Geometry: An Introduction.* Springer-Verlag, New York.

[Singh, 1992a] Singh, Satinder Pal 1992a. Reinforcement learning with a hierarchy of abstract models. In *Proceedings of the Tenth National Conference on Artificial Intelligence*, San Jose, California. AAAI Press. 202–207.

[Singh, 1992b] Singh, Satinder Pal 1992b. Scaling reinforcement learning algorithms by learning variable temporal resolution models. In *Proceedings of the Ninth International Conference on Machine Learning*, Aberdeen, Scotland. Morgan Kaufmann. 406–415.

[Singh, 1992c] Singh, Satinder Pal 1992c. Transfer of learning by composing solutions of elemental sequential tasks. *Machine Learning* 8(3):323–340.

[Sutton, 1988] Sutton, Richard S. 1988. Learning to predict by the method of temporal differences. *Machine Learning* 3(1):9–44.

[Sutton, 1990] Sutton, Richard S. 1990. Integrated architectures for learning, planning, and reacting based on approximating dynamic programming. In *Proceedings of the Seventh International Conference on Machine Learning*, Austin, Texas. Morgan Kaufmann.

[Thrun, 1992] Thrun, Sebastian B. 1992. The role of exploration in learning control. In White, David A. and Sofge, Donald A., editors 1992, *Handbook of Intelligent Control: Neural, Fuzzy, and Adaptive Approaches.* Van Nostrand Reinhold, New York.

[Watkins, 1989] Watkins, C. J. C. H. 1989. *Learning from Delayed Rewards.* Ph.D. Dissertation, King's College, Cambridge.

[Whitehead and Ballard, 1989] Whitehead, Steven D. and Ballard, Dana H. 1989. A role for anticipation in reactive systems that learn. In *Proceedings of the Sixth International Workshop on Machine Learning*, Ithaca, New York. Morgan Kaufmann. 354–357.

Constraining Learning with Search Control

Jihie Kim and Paul S. Rosenbloom
Information Sciences Institute and Computer Science Department
University of Southern California
4676 Admiralty Way
Marina del Rey, CA 90292, U.S.A.
jihie@isi.edu, rosenbloom@isi.edu

Abstract

Many learning systems must confront the problem of run time after learning being greater than run time before learning. This utility problem has been a particular focus of research in explanation-based learning. In past work we have examined an approach to the utility problem that is based on restricting the expressiveness of the rule language so as to guarantee polynomial bounds on the cost of using learned rules. In this article we propose a new approach that limits the cost of learned rules without guaranteeing an a priori bound on the match process or restricting the expressibility of rule conditions. By making the learning mechanism sensitive to the control knowledge utilized during the problem solving that led to the creation of the new rule — i.e., by incorporating such control knowledge into the explanation — the cost of using the learned rule becomes bounded by the cost of the problem solving from which it was learned.

1 Introduction

The identification of the utility problem in explanation-based learning (Minton 1988), has prompted considerable research on how to assure — or at least to improve the chances — that learned knowledge which is intended to speed up system performance will in fact do so, rather than slow it down. Our own efforts on the utility problem have focused on two subissues with respect to Soar, an architecture that combines general problem solving abilities with a chunking mechanism that is a variant of explanation-based learning (Rosenbloom, Laird, Newell, and McCarl 1991). The first subissue is the problem of *expensive chunks* (Tambe, Newell, and Rosenbloom, 1990; Tambe and Rosenbloom 1990), in which individual learned rules are so expensive to use that the system suffers a slow down from learning. The second subissue is the *average growth effect* (Doorenbos, Tambe, and Newell 1992; Doorenbos 1993), in which the system learns so many rules — none of which individually need be all that expensive — that a slow down results.

In this article we focus on expensive chunks. The prior work on expensive chunks demonstrated their existence in a number of tasks, identified their origins in the exponential (in the number of rule conditions) upper-bound on the cost of matching individual rules, and investigated a range of possible restrictions on the expressibility of the rules that permit polynomial upper-bounds on match cost. The most successful of these restrictions is *unique-attributes*, in which match cost is bounded by a linear function of the number of conditions. Imposition of the unique-attributes restriction disallows object attributes from having more than one value. Values can be structured objects with many parts, but they cannot be unstructured sets of objects. Figure 1-a shows an unrestricted encoding for part of a state in the blocks world. The attribute *block* of object S1 is not a unique attribute because it has three distinct values. Figures 1-b and 1-c show two different unique-attribute encodings of the same structure.

(S1 ^type state)	(S1 ^type state)	(S1 ^type state)
(S1 ^block B1)	(S1 ^block B1)	(S1 ^focus B2)
(S1 ^block B2)	(B1 ^next B2)	(B1 ^left B1)
(S1 ^block B3)	(B2 ^next B3)	(B1 ^right B3)
(a)	(b)	(c)

Figure 1: Unrestricted (a) and unique-attribute (b-c) encodings in the blocks world.

Although a number of systems have been successfully recoded into unique-attributes, and reaped significant time savings as a result, there are still some outstanding problems with it. In particular, the encoding radically increases the number of rules used in specifying some tasks, and may also require many more rules to be learned to achieve the same level of coverage (that is, generality) as was previously attainable by a small number rules.

In this article, we propose an alternative diagnosis for the cause of expensive chunks, along with a new approach for eliminating expensive chunks that is derived from this new diagnosis. The core idea is to focus on the relationship between the problem-space search upon which the learning is based and the search performed, during match, by the rule learned from this problem-space search. In the search of the problem space, some path — that is, some sequence of operators — is followed that eventually leads to a result. The actual path followed usually depends on meta-level control rules that determine which operators are selected for which states. These control rules should affect only the efficiency with which the result is found, and not its correctness. As a result, when a new rule is acquired from a trace of this problem solving, the control rules are not included as part of the explanation of the result. This omission, which turns out to also be the approach taken in PRODIGY (Minton 1993)[1], increases the generality of the learned rules, while it should not affect their correctness.[2]

The problem with this approach, however, is that the learned rules are not now constrained by the path actually taken in the problem space, and thus can perform an exponential amount of search even when the original problem-space search was highly directed (by the control rules). For example, with suitable control knowledge in the Grid Task (Tambe, Newell, and Rosenbloom 1990) it is possible to solve the problem of finding a path between two nodes in time that is linear in the length of the path. However, the rule learned from this search may be so general that, when it matches, it searches over all paths of that length. This rule is quite general, as it can solve any problem that has a solution of that length; however, this generality is only obtained at an enormous cost (i.e., the cost is exponential in the length of the path).

The solution suggested by this diagnosis is to incorporate traces of the control rules utilized in the problem-space search into the explanation of the result. This should enable the match process for learned rules to focus on just the precursors for the path that was actually followed, and thus ensure that the match process for a learned rule is bounded in complexity by the problem-space search from which it was learned. Because the match process runs at a faster rate than the problem solving process, this should solve the expensive chunks problem by ensuring that using the learned rule takes no more time than was taken by the original search.

This approach is closest in spirit to that taken in (Shell and Carbonell, 1991). In that work, iterative paths found during problem-space search resulted in the addition of iterative constructs to the macro-operators acquired from the search. These iterative macro-operators are then used in a way that guarantees that they take the same path followed in the problem space. Shell and Carbonell claim that their approach solves the expensive chunks problem. However, it doesn't completely because not all expensive chunks arise from iteration. Our approach captures the same basic intuition, but in a manner that it is both more general and simpler. It is more general because it captures the factors that determined the entire path, rather than just the iterative portions, and thus handles all of the causes of expensive chunks. It is simpler because it does not require an enhanced macro-language or special purpose mechanisms for detecting iteration. Instead, it simply expands by a small amount the content of the explanation used during learning.

In contrast to our earlier approaches to expensive chunks, this new approach *imposes no expressibility limitations on the encoding of tasks.* On the positive side, this means that the problem of expensive chunks can be solved without increasing the difficulty of task encoding. On the negative side, this means that no sub-exponential bound is being imposed on the match process — if the original rules encoded into the system require exponential matches, then so may the learned rules. We have thus effectively split off the goal of removing expensive chunks from the related goal of guaranteeing bounds on the match, and in the process found a weaker approach that solves the former but not the latter, but with no limit on task expressibility.

Despite this result, this new approach is not free of problems. One significant problem is that it doesn't specify what to do when decisions in a search are based on *lack of knowledge.* In such circumstances, the learning process has no explanation for why a choice was made, and therefore can acquire rules that are just as expensive as those learned by the unaltered learning mechanism. The other significant problem is that, as with unique-attributes, this approach can lead to learned rules that are less general than would be acquired by the unaltered learning mechanism. This comes about here, not because of limitations on the representation, but because additional conditions are incorporated into learned rules based on control rules that are now part of the explanation. These conditions provide efficiency, but at the cost of eliminating search that otherwise would allow the rules to apply in more circumstances.

[1]In Prodigy, selection and rejection rules are included in the explanation, but preference rules are not. Likewise, Soar currently also includes require and prohibit preferences, but not desirability preferences.

[2]In Soar, this actually can at times affect correctness, but the discussion of this will be postponed to the final section.

In the next section we look at this first, lack-of-knowledge problem in more detail, and identify two possible solutions. In the subsequent section we present experimental results from using the new approach to expensive chunks in combination with one of the proposed solutions to the lack-of-knowledge problem; in particular, a solution that depends on a novel restriction on the expressiveness of the resulting system. In the process we will discuss the impact of the second, specialization-of-learned rules problem. The final section summarizes and discusses issues for future work.

2 Decisions Based on Lack of Knowledge

In Soar, a real lack of knowledge — as reflected in an insufficient set of *preferences* about a decision — leads to an impasse rather than to a decision. Thus it might seem that Soar wouldn't suffer from this problem. However, it does have a construct — an *indifferent* preference — that allows the explicit statement of indifference among a set of choices. The decision procedure is then free to select randomly among the indifferent choices. The resulting choice is thus made in such a way that no explanation of the selection among the indifferent alternatives is possible based just on the initial situation.

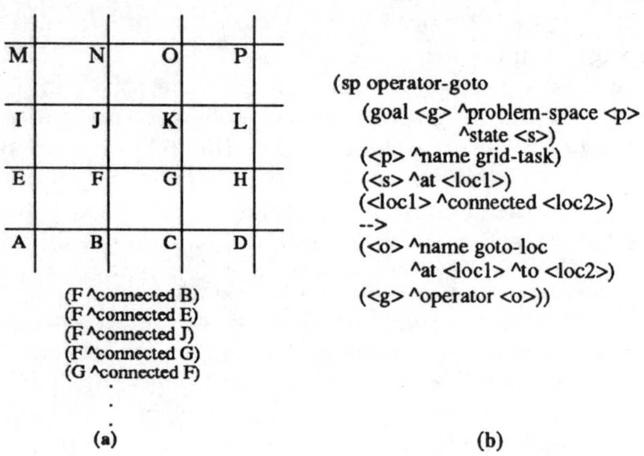

Figure 2: The Grid Task.

Consider an example from the Grid Task — a problem known to lead to expensive chunks (Tambe, Newell, and Rosenbloom 1990) — shown in Figure 2-a. The problem is to go from point F to point P, a path of length four. Because point F is connected to four adjacent points, four operators are suggested by rule *operator-goto* (Figure 2-b)[3]. Since the knowledge required to choose among them is not directly available in productions, an impasse occurs on operator selection. In the subgoal created for this impasse, Soar

[3]Symbols enclosed in angle brackets are variables.

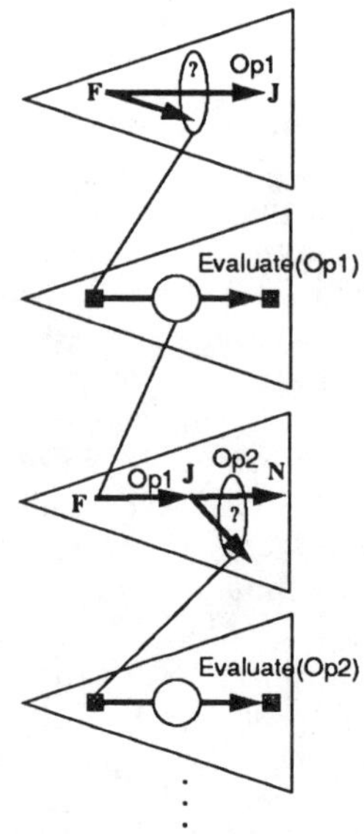

Figure 3: Problem solving in the Grid Task.

normally employs the *selection* problem space, which contains *evaluate* operators that can be applied to the competing task operators. Once generated, these evaluations will be turned into preferences that allow one of the task operators to be selected. However, the system has no direct knowledge about which of the four operators it ought to evaluate first, so without further assistance it would impasse again, and possibly continue this recursive subgoaling indefinitely. To avoid this, one of Soar's general background rules generates indifferent preferences for the set of evaluate operators. This lets it pick one at random, and begin to make progress.

If, as is often the case, the information about how to evaluate an operator is not directly available, an evaluation subgoal (to implement the evaluate operator) is created. The task in this third-level subgoal is to determine the utility of the operator. To do this, it performs a bit of lookahead search, trying out the task operator (possibly in simulation) on the original task state. If the resulting state can be evaluated, then the subgoal terminates, otherwise the process continues, recurring on the question of what task operator to apply to this new state. Figure 3 shows this search process in the Grid Task which continues until the point P is reached.

In this overall lookahead search, indifferent preferences indirectly determine which path the system moves down, by directly determining which of the operators are evaluated at each point. However, the rules learned from this search can gather no explanation from the indifferent preferences as to why one path was taken rather than another. Figure 4 shows such a learned rule. This rule says that if you are at location <l1>

```
(sp chunk-example
    :chunk
    (goal <g> ^problem-space <p> ^state <s>
              ^operator <o> + ^desired <d>)
    (<o> ^name goto-loc ^at <l1> ^to <l2>)
    (<p> ^name grid-path)
    (<s> ^at <l1>) (<d> ^at <l5>)
    (<l2> ^connected <l3>) (<l3> ^connected <l4>)
                           (<l4> ^connected <l5>)
    -->
    (<g> ^operator <o> >))
```

Figure 4: An expensive chunk learned from indifferent choices.

and want to get to location <l5>, and there is an operator that takes you from <l1> to <l2>, and there is a connected path from <l2> to <l5> (via two intermediate points, <l3> and <l4>), then the operator is the best choice. This rule is expensive because it may need to search an exponential number of paths of length four to find one that has this property. Even if the original problem-space search happened to locate the correct path by accident on its first try, or if outside guidance was provided to lead it down the correct path, the resulting rule would still incorporate this exponential search.

There are (at least) two possible ways of solving this problem. The first is to alter the learning and match processes so that they more appropriately reflect the semantics of indifferent preferences. Use of an indifferent preference means that a random selection of a single path should be made. However, the match algorithm always follows all paths. So, reflecting the semantics of indifference should involve altering the learning and match processes so that use of indifferent preferences during problem-space search yields the random choice of a single alternative during the corresponding part of the match of the learned rule. If, in fact, the indifferent preference meant that the system really didn't care which of the paths was taken, then any random selection made by the matcher should be as good as any other. If, however, the indifferent preference actually signified lack of knowledge about the correct path, and not all paths actually do lead to success, then the match will follow one path randomly, and thus will succeed only stochastically.

This first direction looks pretty interesting. It solves the problem without introducing an expressibility limitation, while at the same time introducing a stochasticity into the use of learned rules, and a resulting gradualness in performance improvement that may be quite useful in modeling human cognition. However, it requires a significant enough alteration in the basic architecture of Soar, that we have decided to first investigate a simpler alternative, and leave this one for future work.

The second way of solving the problem, and the one underlying the results reported here, is to disallow the use of indifferent preferences. Their ability to select randomly among alternatives is then replaced by explicit default orderings on the alternatives. If there are any substantive reasons why one alternative should be selected ahead of another, they can be incorporated into this ordering. To the extent that there are no substantive reasons, an arbitrary ordering can be imposed. The key, though, is that these orderings are generated explicitly by rules that distinguish among the alternatives, and therefore leave behind a trace that can be used in explaining why one alternative is picked over the others. This may not provide a "good" explanation, in the sense of capturing a suitable level of generality to support transfer to related situations; however, it will at least be sufficient to distinguish the one selected alternative from the others during the match, and thus to make the resulting learned rules cheap.

For the Grid Task, an arbitrary ordering of the operators can be assigned according to the direction of movement. For example, first *up*, then *down*, then *left*, and finally *right*. It is important to note that this ordering is just used in place of the indifferent preferences on the evaluate operators in the selection space. Thus it determines the order in which the operators are evaluated, but does not dictate an ordering on the task operators. This latter ordering is still to be learned, as a new set of control rules, from the lookahead search.

The elimination of indifferent preferences amounts to a limitation on the system's expressibility, though of a form quite different from those previously investigated. It also clearly may impact the generality of the resulting rules, at least to the extent that arbitrary orderings are imposed. As such, it needs to be evaluated, just as was the unique-attributes restriction, in terms of the trade-offs it provides among expressibility, speed, and generality.

3 Experimental Results

In this section we look at how well the incorporation of search control into learned rules, in combination with the elimination of indifferent preferences, compares with both an unaltered version of Soar and a unique-attributes version. The results are all from Soar6 (version 6.0.3), the latest C-based release of Soar (Doorenbos 1992), which is approximately 10-40 times faster than Soar5 (the previous Lisp-based release). The experimental version is just like the standard system, except that the explanations upon which new rules are based incorporate traces of the control rules that determined the choices made in problem solving. In particular, the system computes the minimum set of preferences sufficient to determine each choice that was made, so that if the set of preferences overdetermines the choices, the redundant preferences (and their rule traces) are pruned from the explanation to make the created rule as general as possible.

Grid Task	Average CPU Time (sec)	
	Before Learning	After Learning
Original	5.38	24.79
Search control	6.83	1.18
Unique-attribute	6.82	0.95

Table 1: Average CPU time in the Grid Task.

```
(sp chunk-search control
   :chunk
   (goal <g> ^operator <r> + ^operator <u> +
      ^operator <d> + ^desired <d1> ^state <s>
   (<r> ^priority 4 ^at <l1> ^to <l2>)
   (<u> ^priority 3) (<d> ^priority 1)
   (<s> ^at <l1>) (<d1> ^at <l8>)
   (<l2> ^right <l3> ^connected <l3>
        ^down <l4> ^connected <l4>
        ^up <l5> ^connected <l5>)
   (<l3> ^up <l6> ^connected <l6>
        ^down <l7> ^connected <l7>)
   (<l6> ^connected <l8> ^up <l8>)
   -->
   (<g> ^operator <r> >))
```

(a)

```
(sp chunk-unique-attribute
   :chunk
   (goal <g> ^operator-right <r> +
      ^desired <d> ^state <s>
   (<r> ^at <l1> ^to <l2>)
   (<s> ^at <l1>) (<d> ^at <l5>)
   (<l2> ^right <l3>)
   (<l3> ^up <l4>)
   (<l4> ^up <l5>)
   -->
   (<g> ^operator <r> >))
```

(b)

Figure 5: Chunks from search-control and unique-attribute versions.

Table 1 shows the average CPU time per problem (in seconds) for the three versions, across seven different problems in the Grid Task, both before and after learning. All of the grid problems used here are searches for paths of length six; for example, in Figure 2-a, a problem to go from point A to point P is a length-six problem. For experimental efficiency, the results shown here also assume a 10x10 bounded grid instead of the unbounded grid in Figure 2-a. The first row in Table 1 shows the times before and after learning for the unaltered version of Soar. Without including search control in chunking, or restricting the task representation, the time after learning is greater than the time before learning for all these problems (by an average factor of 4.61), and for one of the problems it is more than a factor of nine greater. This is true even though the number of problem solving steps (i.e., decisions) is decreased via learning from 133 to 8. This extra cost is directly attributable to the large amount of time spent matching expensive chunks.

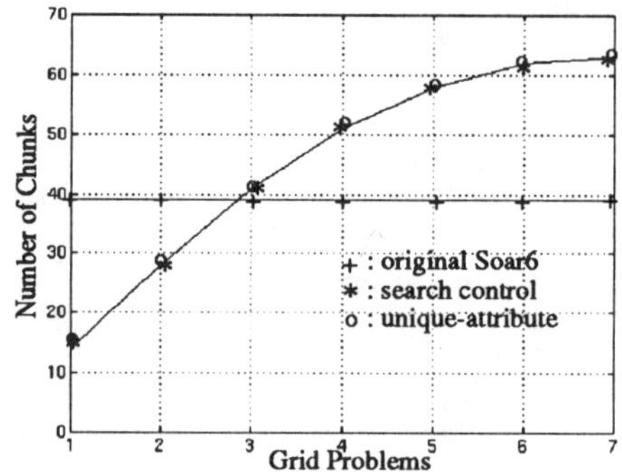

Figure 6: Number of accumulated chunks in the Grid Task.

The second and third rows in Table 1 show the corresponding CPU times for the search-control and unique-attributes versions of the Grid Task.[4] Both show more than a factor of five reduction in execution time after learning. In each problem, they show essentially the same pattern: the time after learning is a small constant value that is uniformly less than the time before learning. This implies that both have solved the expensive chunks problem for this task.

The extra time before learning in the search-control and unique-attribute versions stems from the increase in tokens brought about the additional rule conditions that discriminate among moving directions, as shown in the conditions of the chunks in Figure 5. These two chunks correspond to the expensive chunk in Figure 4. The difference in run times after learning between the search-control version and the unique-attribute version in Table 1 is also due to the extra conditions in the search-control-version chunks. However, this yields only a minor effect, as analyzed in (Tambe 1991).

Figure 6 shows the cumulative number of chunks acquired while solving the eight Grid-Task problems. The unmodified version of Soar learned general enough chunks from the first problem to cover all of the other length-six problems. The other two approaches needed to learn additional chunks for each new problem. In these problems, both learned the same number of rules with the same generality. Although there are additional contraints induced by the extra conditions in Figure 5-(a), both chunks in Figure 5 have the same generality in that they describe the same grid path followed by the lookahead search to reach the desired point, and nothing more than that.

[4]The unique-attribute representation replaces the multi-attribute $^{\wedge}$*connected* with four distinct attributes $^{\wedge}$*up*, $^{\wedge}$*down*, $^{\wedge}$*left* and $^{\wedge}$*right*.

Eight-puzzle Task	Average CPU Time (sec)	
	Before Learning	After Learning
Original	5.31	9.75
Search control	5.30	1.55
Unique-attribute	5.72	1.21

Table 2: Average CPU time in the Eight-puzzle Task.

Table 2 compares these three methods on the Eight-puzzle Task — another task known to produce expensive chunks (Tambe, Newell and Rosenbloom 1990). In the multi-attribute representation, a state points to nine bindings (using attribute ^binding), each of which connects a cell from the static 3x3 structure of the board to a tile. For example, in (B1 ^cell C1) (B1 ^tile T1), binding B1 connects cell C1 to tile T1. A cell points to all of its neighboring cells. For example, (C1 ^next C2),(C1 ^next C3), and so on.

The search-control version used here distinguishes operators by the direction that they move the blank cell: down, up, left and right. The unique-attribute representation removes the multi-attribute ^*binding* by numbering it, ^*binding1*, ^*binding2*,. . ., ^*binding9*, and replaces ^*next* with 4 attributes ^*down*, ^*up*, ^*left* and ^*right*. As shown in Table 2, the time after learning is less than the time before learning in the search-control and unique-attribute versions, while the original Soar requires more CPU time after learning. As in the Grid Task, both the search-control and unique-attribute versions have eliminated the expensive chunks that occur in the unmodified version. The difference in run times between the search-control version and the unique-attribute version stems from the same reason as in the Grid Task.

The number of rules used to encode the Eight Puzzle in the three versions tells an interesting story. The original version of Soar uses 13 rules, the search-control version uses 16 rules, and the unique-attributes version uses 93 rules. The small growth in going from Soar to the search-control version stems from the need to differentiate and provide a default order on the domain operators. If there are n possible operators, n-1 additional rules are required. The large growth in the unique-attributes version stems from the need to create rules for each specialization of a generic attribute into a more specialized unique-attribute. In general, if there are n tests of multi-attributes in a rule, each with m possible specializations, then the unique-attributes version will need to substitute m^n specialized rules.[5]

Figure 7 shows the cumulative number of chunks learned while solving the nine Eight-puzzle problems.

[5]There are ways to reduce this number by splitting these tests across a sequence of rules, but that approach also has its own problems.

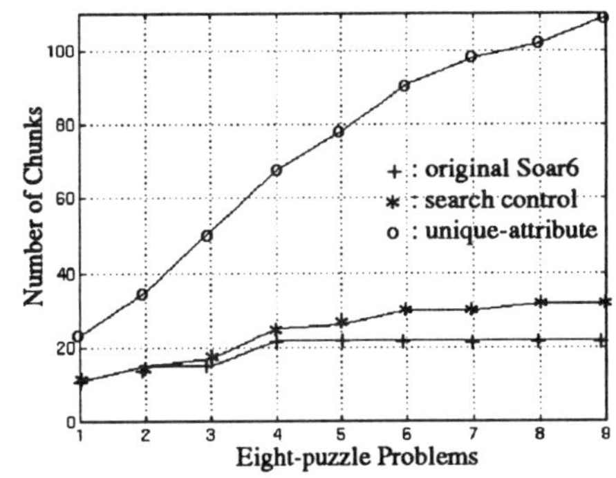

Figure 7: Number of accumulated chunks in the Eight-puzzle Task.

The search-control version required 32 new rules, as compared to 109 new rules for the unique-attribute version, and 22 new rules for the original version. Thus, for this task, the search-control version is quite close to the original Soar version, and both show a distinct advantage over unique-attributes.

Unique-attributes' need here for many new rules stems from the same source as its large number of initial rules, plus the following fact. The search-control version need not distinguish between values of a multi-attribute as long as it doesn't affect the decision that is based on lack of knowldge, while the unique-attribute version must replace the muti-attribute anyhow. Attribute ^*binding* in the above Eight-puzzle task is an example of a multi-attribute that doesn't affect the decision based on lack of knowledge.

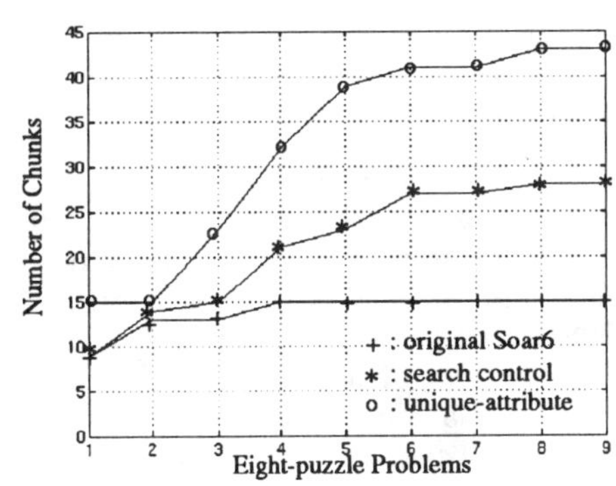

Figure 8: Number of chunks in different Eight-puzzle representation.

The Eight Puzzle can also be expressed via a different set of rules, without the multi-attribute ^*binding*. Although there is considerable reduction in the number of rules, Figure 8 shows that the unique-attribute version still needs more rules because of the former effect.

4 Summary and Discussion

Unique-attributes solve the expensive chunks problem by restricting the expressiveness of rules down to where the match can be guaranteed to run in polynomial (in particular, linear) time. This provides strong assurances about system performance, but also negatively impacts task creation and learned-rule generality. Here we have proposed and investigated a new approach — based on including search-control in the explanations upon which new rules are based — that solves the expensive chunks problem, but not by enforcing a fixed computational bound on the match process. Instead, the complexity of the match of a learned rule is bounded by the complexity of the search from which it was learned. This gives up an overall guarantee on system performance, but given an initially encoded system, learning will not make it worse. In exchange for this weakening of the guarantee, this new approach shows potential for ameliorating both of the negative side effects introduced by unique-attributes.

One additional positive side-effect of the search-control approach is that it removes one possible source of overgeneralization in Soar (Laird, Rosenbloom, and Newell 1986). Though search control is not supposed to affect the correctness of results generated in problem spaces, it sometimes unavoidably does. In situations in which results are returned from a problem space before the goal test succeeds, or where the goal test is itself overgeneral, search control may play an influential role in determining the correctness of the result. Under such circumstances, the current approach — not including this search control in the explanation process — can yield overgeneral learned rules. However, by including this search control into the explanation of the result, the proposed approach removes this potential source of overgenerality.

A possible negative side-effect of the search-control approach is that it increases the difficulty of directing the reconstruction process that underlies Soar's approach to knowledge-level learning (Rosenbloom, Laird, and Newell 1987; Rosenbloom and Aasman 1990). There we took advantage of search control's absence from explanations in learning a rule whose actions mirrored some perceived object structure, but whose conditions did not test the perceived object. With this option no longer available, a new approach must be employed. One possibility that was actually already under investigation independently of this work, is a form of *situated reconstruction*, in which reconstruction is guided by features of the immediate situation other than those to be reconstructed (Vera, Lewis and Lerch 1993).

In addition to investigating options for knowledge-level learning, several other issues need near-term attention. At the top of the list is extending the experimental results to a wider range of tasks — both those that traditionally yield expensive chunks and those that don't — and to quantitative analyses of speed ups and (losses of) generality. Also useful would be a theoretical analysis of the method, and of its potential to avoid (or lead to) slow downs with learning. There is also a subtle issue that needs to be addressed that only occurs when there are more options available at performance than at learning time; in particular, if the conditions learned to discriminate among the options available at learning time are not sufficient to discriminate among these new options, additional match search may be introduced. Finally, altering the architecture so as to permit the appropriate use of indifferent preferences would enable the removal of the one expressibility limitation that it was found necessary to impose.

Acknowledgments

This research was supported under subcontract to the University of Southern California Information Sciences Institute from the University of Michigan as part of contract N00014-92-K-2015 from the Defense Advanced Research Projects Agency (DARPA) and the Naval Research Laboratory (NRL).

Thanks to Milind Tambe and Soar group in USC-ISI for valuable comments on earlier draft of this paper, and to Bob Doorenbos for useful hints on Soar6 source code.

References

Doorenbos, B., Tambe, M., & Newell, A. (1992). Learning 10,000 chunks: What's it like out there? *Proceedings of the Tenth National Conference on Artificial Intelligence.* (pp. 830-836).

Doorenbos, B. (1992). Soar6 release notes.

Doorenbos, B. (1993). Matching 100,000 learned rules. *Proceedings of the Eleventh National Conference on Artificial Intelligence.* (to appear).

Laird, J., Rosenbloom, P., & Newell, A. (1986). Overgeneralization during knowledge compilation in Soar. *Proceedings of the Workshop on Knowledge Compilation.* (pp. 46-57).

Minton, S. (1988). Quantitative results concerning the utility of explanation-based learning. *Proceedings of the Seventh National Conference on Artificial Intelligence.* (pp. 564-569).

Minton, S. (1993). Personal Communication.

Rosenbloom, P. S., Laird, J. E., & Newell, A. (1987). Knowlege level learning in Soar. *Proceedings of the Sixth National Conference on Artificial Intelligence.* (pp. 499-504).

Rosenbloom, P. S. & Aasman, J. (1990). Knowledge level and inductive uses of chunking (EBL). *Proceedings of the Eighth National Conference on Artificial Intelligence.* (pp. 821-827).

Rosenbloom, P. S., Laird, J. E., Newell, A., & McCarl, R. (1991). A preliminary analysis of the Soar architecture as a basis for general intelligence. *Artificial Intelligence 47.* (pp. 289-325).

Shell, P. & Carbonell, J. (1991). Empirical and analytic performance of iterative operators. *The 13th Annual Conference of The Cognitive Science Society.* (pp. 898-902).

Tambe, M. (1991). Eliminating combinatorics from production match. PhD thesis, Computer Science Department, Carnegie Mellon University

Tambe, M., Newell, A., & Rosenbloom, P. (1990). The problem of expensive chunks and its solution by restricting expressiveness. *Machine Learning,* Vol. *5.* (pp. 299-348)

Tambe, M., & Rosenbloom, P. (1990). A framework for investigating production system formulations with polynomially bounded match. *Proceedings of the Eighth National Conference on Artificial Intelligence.* (pp. 693-700).

Vera, A., Lewis R. L., & Lerch F. J. (1993). Situated decision-making and recognition-based learning: Applying symbolic theories to interactive tasks. *Proceedings of the Fifteenth Annual Conference of the Cognitive Science Society.* (to appear).

Scaling Up Reinforcement Learning for Robot Control

Long-Ji Lin*
School of Computer Science
Carnegie Mellon University
Pittsburgh, Pennsylvania 15213

Abstract

The aim of this research is to extend the state of the art of reinforcement learning and enable its applications to complex robot-learning problems. This paper presents a series of scaling-up extensions to reinforcement learning, including: *generalization by neural networks*, *using action models*, *teaching*, *hierarchical learning*, and *having a short-term memory*. These extensions have been tested in a physically-realistic robot simulator, and combined to solve a complex robot-learning problem. Simulation results indicate that each of the extensions could result in either significant learning speedup or new capabilities. This research concludes that it is possible to build artificial agents that can acquire complex control policies effectively by reinforcement learning.

1 Introduction

Reinforcement learning is an attractive technique for adaptive control; in general it involves much less human effort than many other learning techniques. The main problem, however, is that the existing reinforcement learning methods (such as Q-learning [14]) typically converge very slowly. Moreover, most (if not all) of them assume that the world is a Markov decision process. For many robot problems of interest, this assumption does not hold, however.

This paper describes four ways to speed up reinforcement learning: *generalization by neural networks*, *using action models*, *teaching*, and *hierarchical learning*. This paper also discusses approaches to reinforcement learning in non-Markovian environments— by having a memory of its past, an agent can deal with a wide range of non-Markovian tasks. This paper discusses these extensions, describes a mobile robot task in a physically-realistic simulator, presents simulation results, and finally summarizes the lessons learned from this research.

*Currently at Siemens Corporate Research, Inc., 755 College Road East, Princeton, NJ 08540 (email: ljl@learning.scr.siemens.com).

2 The Learning Algorithm

In the reinforcement learning paradigm, the learning agent receives a scalar performance feedback called *reinforcement* or *payoff* after each action execution. The objective of learning is to construct a *control policy* so as to maximize its performance. The performance measure used here is the *discounted cumulative reinforcement* or, for short, *utility*.

Q-learning is a widely-used reinforcement learning method [14, 3, 5]. The idea of Q-learning is to construct an evaluation function called *Q-function*:

$$Q(state, action) \rightarrow utility$$

The Q-function is used to predict the discounted cumulative reinforcement (i.e., utility) for each state-action pair given that the agent is in that state and executes that action. Given the Q-function, the control policy is simply to choose the action having the highest utility.

2.1 Generalization and Using Action Models

For generalization, the Q-function can be represented by multi-layer neural networks called *Q-nets*, and incrementally trained by a combination of the error back-propagation algorithm and *temporal difference* methods, TD(λ) [12]. Figure 1 shows the learning algorithm used in this research, which is briefly discussed below.

Two terms are defined here. An *experience* is a quadruple, (x_t, a_t, x_{t+1}, r_t), meaning that at time t, action a_t in response to state x_t results in the next state x_{t+1} and reinforcement r_t. During learning, the agent records its experiences. The sequence of experiences collected in a learning trial is called a *lesson*. After the

Algorithm for Q-learning agents to replay $\{(x_0, a_0, x_1, r_0) \cdots (x_n, a_n, x_{n+1}, r_n)\}$:
1. $t \leftarrow n$;
2. $e_t \leftarrow Q(x_t, a_t)$;
3. $u_{t+1} \leftarrow Max\{Q(x_{t+1}, k) \mid k \in actions\}$;
4. $e'_t \leftarrow r_t + \gamma[(1-\lambda)u_{t+1} + \lambda e'_{t+1}]$;
5. Adjust the Q-net for action a_t by back-propagating the error $(e'_t - e_t)$ through it with input x_t;
6. If $t = 0$ exit; else $t \leftarrow t - 1$; go to 2;

Figure 1: The learning algorithm— experience replay

trial, the lesson is *replayed* by the learning algorithm (Figure 1) to train the Q-nets. In fact, many lessons can be stored and repeatedly replayed as if the agent experienced again and again what it had experienced before. The experiences within a lesson is replayed in temporally *backward* order; in this order, credit/blame at the end of a lesson can be propagated to the preceding states effectively. What the algorithm does is basically the following: Step 2 computes the current estimate of the utility of the state-action pair (x_t, a_t). Steps 3 and 4 compute a new estimate of the same utility based on a new experience. Ideally the two estimates should be equal, so we want to minimize the difference between the two estimates, which can be done by the connectionist error back-propagation algorithm.

This way of using experiences is called *experience replay*, which can be related to Sutton's DYNA architecture [13]. In DYNA, the learning agent incrementally constructs an action model during learning. When the model is good enough, it allows the agent to mentally experience the effects of its actions without actually executing them. In this way, the agent often can save many action executions required to learn a good control policy [13, 3]. Experience replay is in fact a simple technique that implements this idea. By sampling experiences in the past, experience replay in effect uses a model. In essence, the collection of experiences is a model; it represents not only explicitly the environment's input-output patterns but also implicitly the probability distribution of multiple outcomes of actions (if the world is stochastic).

Experience replay is important in dealing with a *re-learning problem*, which may occur in training neural networks. During training a network, if an input pattern has not been presented for quite a while, the network typically will forget what it has learned for that pattern and thus need to re-learn it when that pattern is seen again later. This problem is called the re-learning problem. Consider the following scenario: The state space consists of two parts, A and B. The agent is now exploring part A, and has not visited part B for a long period of time. The agent may thus forget what it has learned for part B. By experience replay, the agent can mentally re-experience part B and refresh what it has learned.

The experience replay algorithm can be used in batch mode or in incremental mode. In incremental mode the networks are adjusted after replaying each experience, while in batch mode the networks are adjusted only after replaying a whole lesson. The algorithm will do exactly what TD(λ) does only when it is used in batch mode. However, the advantage of backward replay is greatest when the incremental mode is used.

To be efficient in terms of computational time and memory space, the agent may keep and replay only recent experiences, because experiences in the far past typically involve many bad action choices and are thus less worth keeping than recent experiences. Note that the correctness of Q-learning relies on the assumption that *next states are visited in proportion to their probabilities of happening.* Improper experience replay (e.g., replaying a particular experience many times consecutively) may invalidate this assumption, causing an *over-replay problem.* One way to minimize this problem is to replay each experience roughly the same number of times.

This learning algorithm has worked quite well for a few nontrivial problems. For example, in [3] I described an agent managing to avoid predators and reach food in a simulated environment. In that work, TD($\lambda = 0$) was used. In this research, TD($\lambda = 0.7$) was usually used, and found to result in a few times of speedup over TD($\lambda = 0$). See [5] for further discussions.

3 The Domain: A Mobile Robot Simulator

The most complex domain used in this research was a mobile robot simulator (Figure 2), which was intended to mimic a real robot called Hero and an office environment. The environment consists of three rooms, two narrow doorways, and a battery charger. A light is placed on top of the charger so that the robot can distinguish the charger from other obstacles. The robot has 6 actions: turn $\pm 15^o$, turn $\pm 60^o$, and move ± 12 inches. It has a sonar sensor and a light intensity sensor mounted on its top. Both sensors can rotate and collect 24 readings (separated by 15 degrees) per rotation. In addition, the robot has a compass and four collision sensors placed around its body. To be realistic, about 8% control error is added to the robot's actuators and about 10% sensing error added to the sensors.

The robot's task is to learn a control policy for finding the battery charger and electrically connecting to it. It may start from any location with any orientation. The

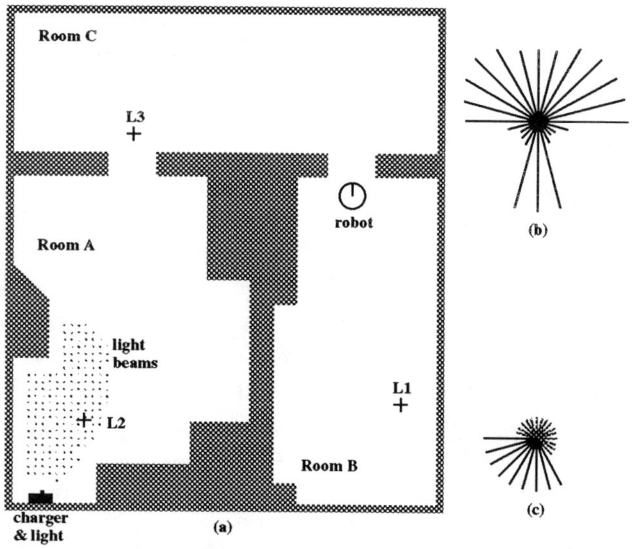

Figure 2: (a) A simulated robot and its environment. The radius of the robot is 12 inches. The size of the environment is 360 inches by 420 inches. (b) Sonar readings received at L3. (c) Light readings at L2.

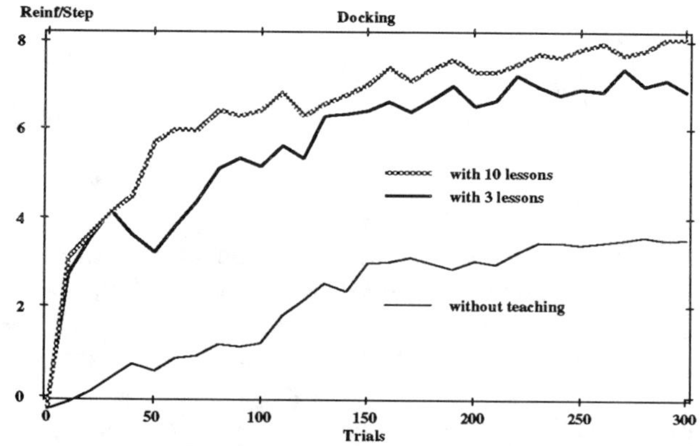

Figure 3: Learning curves for docking. The Y axis indicates the average reinforcement per step, and the X axis indicates the number of trials attempted so far. Each trail ended when the goal was achieved or else after 30 steps. The curves show the mean perform over 7 runs.

robot begins with no knowledge about its effectors, sensors, and the environment. The reinforcement for the task is 100 when the robot successfully connects to the charger and 0 otherwise. This learning task is hard for several reasons:

- the state space is continuous and large,
- the optimal control policy is complex,
- the reward delay is long— it takes the robot approximately 100 steps to reach the charger from Location L1 (Figure 2), and
- the robot faces a *hidden state* problem— when the robot is in Room C, it cannot make good distinctions between the two doorways from its immediate sensory information, thus the robot cannot decide whether to enter a door or not based on its current inputs.

4 A Docking Task and Teaching

Because the battery recharging task is hard, this research began with an easier task called docking. The goal of this task is also to connect to the charger, but this time the robot always starts from places in the light area where the light is visible (Figure 2). The reinforcement signal for the docking task is -10 if collision occurs, 100 if the robot succeeds, and 0 otherwise. The state inputs include 24 sonar readings, 24 light readings, and 4 collision readings. The learning process consists of many learning trials. In each trial, the robot starts from a random position in the light area. For exploration, the robot chooses actions randomly, but prefers actions having high utilities. Each trial ends when the goal is achieved or else after 30 steps. As mentioned previously, the Q-function is represented by multi-layer feed-forward neural networks; single-layer perceptrons worked poorly for all of the tasks described in this paper.

In the first attempt, the robot's performance was found very poor. One of the reasons is that docking and obstacle avoidance are sort of contradictory. Once the robot learns to avoid obstacles, it may never dare to bump into the charger— learning is stuck in local optima. In the second attempt, a technique called *teaching* was employed. By teaching, I took control over the robot and demonstrated how the target task could be solved from some initial states. The demonstrated solutions were recorded as lessons, and replayed by the experience replay algorithm (Figure 1). Teaching is useful in three ways:

- Partial solutions can be readily available from teachers.
- Teaching can direct the learner to first explore the promising part of the search space which contains the goal states. This is important when the search space is large and thorough search is impractical.
- Teaching can help the learner avoid being stuck in local optima during the search for optimal control.

Figure 3 shows the robot's performance with and without teaching involved. As we can see, significant improvement was obtained with as few as three taught lessons.

As mentioned in Section 2.1, improper experience replay may cause an over-replay problem. Similarly, if a taught lesson is replayed many times in a short period of time, it is possible that the Q-nets become too specific to the particular situations involved in that taught lesson. Thus, it is important for agents not to be over-trained on teaching examples.

It is instructive to compare the teaching technique presented here with supervised learning techniques (such as the one used by Pomerleau [10] to train neural networks for driving a vehicle). In supervised learning, the agent requires many state-action patterns generated by a human teacher, and in general we don't expect the agent to become better than the teacher. In reinforcement learning, the agent does not require a lot of teaching examples, because it can also learn from trial-and-error. In general, reinforcement learning agents can learn and become better than the teacher, if the teacher is not an expert.

5 Hierarchical Learning

After solving the simple docking problem, this research went on to apply the same learning technique to the battery recharging task and see what would happen. In order to avoid the hidden state problem (mentioned in Section 3) for the moment, it is assumed that the robot's sensory inputs include the robot's global X-Y position in the environment. (See [5] for the input representations used in this work.)

In one experiment, the robot, which was provided with 10 taught lessons, performed the recharging task poorly. Roughly speaking, the robot could accomplish the recharging task only when it started from Room A even after 300 learning trials. Perhaps given sufficient time, it would learn a good policy, but the needed time may be impractically long.

This poor performance can be explained by the fact that the optimal policy for choosing primitive actions is so complex that it can hardly be represented by a single neural network, let alone be learned efficiently. One way to deal with complex learning tasks is *hierarchical learning*. The essential idea is based on *task decomposition* and the use of *abstraction* [2, 7, 11, 4]. To efficiently solve a complex learning problem, humans often decompose the problem into simpler subproblems. Once we have learned skills to solve each subproblem, solving the original problem becomes easier, because we now can concentrate on the high-level features of the problem and ignore the low-level details, which presumably will be filled in when the previously learned skills are actually applied.

Basically three steps are involved in doing hierarchical learning:

1. **Task Decomposition.** A complex task is decomposed into multiple elementary tasks. The original task is thus reduced to the task of integrating the solutions to the elementary tasks to form the solution to the original task.
2. **Learning elementary skills.** An elementary skill needs to be learned to solve each elementary task. A skill is equivalent to a control policy. Here Q-learning can be used, and each elementary skill corresponds to a Q-function: $Q(state, action) \rightarrow utility$.
3. **Learning a high-level skill.** A high-level skill for coordinating the elementary skills needs to be learned in order to solve the original task. Learning a high-level skill is conceptually similar to learning an elementary skill. Again, Q-learning can be used, and the high-level skill corresponds to a Q-function: $Q(state, skill) \rightarrow utility$.

A formal model of hierarchical reinforcement learning is proposed in [5], in which a complexity analysis for some deterministic and discrete domains is also presented. The analysis shows a theoretical complexity reduction by hierarchical learning (from n^2 to n, where n is the number of states).

5.1 Task Decomposition

The recharging task can be decomposed into four elementary tasks:

- following walls while keeping them on the robot's right/left hand side (WFR/WFL),
- passing a door starting from places near the door (DP), and
- docking on the charger starting from the light area (DK).

For instance, to connect to the battery charger from Location L1 (Figure 2), the robot simply executes WFR to get to the vicinity of the right door, executes DP to get out of Room B, executes WFL to reach the left door, executes DP again to get into Room A, executes WFR again to get close to the charger, and finally executes DK to get connected to the battery charger.

To define an elementary task, we need to specify two things:

- a reinforcement function specifying the goal of the task, and
- an *application space* specifying the portion of the state space for which a skill will be trained.

The application space of a skill can be thought of as the *precondition* of the skill. For example, here I want to train a docking skill for getting the robot connected to the charger as long as the robot can detect the light source on top of the charger, therefore I define the application space of docking to roughly correspond to the light area. Similarly, I define the application space of door passing to roughly correspond to the locations where a door opening can be detected. The application space for wall following is simply the whole state space.

Since a skill is only trained for its own application space, if a skill is executed when the agent is not in the application space, the agent may never achieve the goal of the skill. For instance, a door passing skill is not expected to achieve its goal, if there is no door nearby.

5.2 Learning High-level Skills

Section 4 has described how the docking skill can be learned effectively by a combination of reinforcement learning and teaching. The other elementary skills can be learned similarly. High-level skills can also be learned in a similar manner, although there may be complications. For example, we typically assume that primitive actions terminate automatically, but an elementary skill (such as wall following) may have no termination conditions and last forever once it is activated. Consequently, the high-level policy is responsible for deciding not only which is the optimal elementary skill but also when to terminate the active elementary skill.

In this work, the decision about which skill to choose is made by the robot on *each primitive step*. In other words, the robot checks to see which skill is most appropriate; applies it for one single step; determines the next appropriate skill; applies that skill for another step; and so on. In this way, the robot can react to new situations promptly. An important question, however, is the following: The robot needs to learn a high-level policy for deciding the optimal skill for each state. In other words, it needs to learn $Q(state, skill)$. If hierarchical learning is not used, the robot has to learn $Q(state, action)$. Is learning $Q(state, skill)$ much easier than learning $Q(state, action)$? The answer is positive, because the former Q-function is less complex than the latter, which is easily seen by noting that the robot need switch actions much more frequently than switch skills.

The robot requires good exploration strategies to learn $Q(state, skill)$ effectively, because the state space here is large. Because the robot already has some knowledge (i.e., Q-functions) about the elementary skills it has learned previously, it can use this knowledge for effective exploration. For further details, see [4, 5].

In one experiment, the robot learned the elementary skills (i.e., wall following, door passing, and docking) separately, and completed the learning before starting to learn a high-level skill for battery recharging. The robot typically learned a good high-level skill within 60 trials. This learning scheme— learning elementary and high-level skills separately and independently— may be desired to prevent potential instability; it is hard to imagine what may happen if all the high-level and elementary skills are trained simultaneously. It is possible that the learning of each skill would become unstable or easily fall into a poor local optimum due to unexpected interactions among changing skills. On the other hand, in this scheme it may be hard to determine when the elementary skills need no further training and allow the high-level skill to be learned.

In another experiment, each elementary skill was trained separately for about 10 trials. The performance of those skills was quite poor at this point, but the robot went on to learn the high-level recharging skill, anyway. As it was learning the high-level skill, the elementary skills were further polished. This learning scheme provides a compromise between the tradeoffs mentioned in the above paragraph. After 150 trials, the robot obtained good performance. Although this performance was about 10% worse than that obtained in the previous experiment, it need not wait for the elementary skills to be trained completely before learning the recharging skill.

5.3 Related Work

Mahadevan and Connell [7] presented a robot that learned to find and push boxes. They first found that their robot, based on Q-learning, could not solve the learning problem as a monolithic task. In contrast, the robot was able to solve the problem after they decomposed it into subtasks that could be solved effectively. Coordination of the subtasks was pre-wired in their case. Lewis et al. [2] studied a six legged insect robot, which successfully learned to walk based on genetic algorithms and neural networks. The robot developed its walking skill in two stages: It first learned an oscillation behavior for each leg, and then learned a complete walking behavior that coordinates the six oscillation behaviors.

However, the advantage of hierarchical learning over non-hierarchical learning is gained at the cost of *a prior* domain-specific knowledge, which often comes from human designers. For example, to enable the robot here to do hierarchical learning, I have provided it with domain knowledge, such as a proper decomposition of the recharging task, and a proper selection of reward functions and application spaces for the elementary tasks. A challenge is to have the robot learn this kind of domain knowledge on its own.

Singh [11] also addressed the issue of hierarchical learning within the reinforcement learning paradigm. He described an efficient way to construct the Q-function of a composite task from the Q-functions of elementary tasks. Singh has demonstrated for a simple case that his architecture could learn a new elementary skill that was not explicitly specified. This suggests a possible way for robots to discover on their own a proper way to decompose a task. However, his technique could not handle elementary skills that do not have termination conditions (e.g., wall following). He also assumed that a high-level module can make optimal decisions without knowing the world state, which is quite a strong assumption.

6 Hidden State

Recall that in the previous section, the robot was provided with its X-Y coordinate location. With this X-Y information, the robot is able to make a distinction between the two door openings, or else the robot will face the hidden state problem mentioned in Section 3.

The hidden state problem, which is also known as *perceptual aliasing* [15], can be explained by the following example. Consider a gift-packing task, which involves four steps: open a closed box, put a gift in it, close the box, and seal it. When facing a closed box, the robot cannot see whether there is a gift in the box or not, and therefore cannot decide whether to open the box or to seal it, unless the robot has some sort of memory of its past.

But, facing a large volume of information in the past, how can an agent encode and use history information efficiently and effectively? There are basically two possible approaches. One is to allow the agent to access a limited amount of history information through a sliding window. The other approach is more complicated; it requires the agent to somehow come up with a (small) set of history features that summarizes the agent's past. The first approach can be realized by time-delay neural networks, while the second one by recurrent networks. The type of recurrent networks used in this research is the Elman network [1]. The Elman network is like a standard network, but has in its input layer a set of *context units*, which holds feedback activations coming from the network state at a previous clock time. The context units function as short-term memory, and because of them, the output of the network depends on the past as well as on the current input.

Figure 4 shows three possible memory architectures that allow Q-learning agents to deal with hidden states. In the *window-Q* architecture, the Q-net is implemented by a time-delay network. The inputs to the Q-net include the current input as well as recent inputs. In the *recurrent-Q* architecture, the Q-net is a recurrent network. Both architectures are straightforward extensions to the basic Q-learning architecture. In the *recurrent-model* architecture, the Q-net is a simple feed-forward network, but its state inputs include a set of history features, which comes from learning a recurrent action model (represented by Elman networks). The idea behind this architecture is as follows: If the agent can discover a set of history features useful for predicting the behavior of the external world, then this set of features should be sufficient for optimal control. See [6] for details.

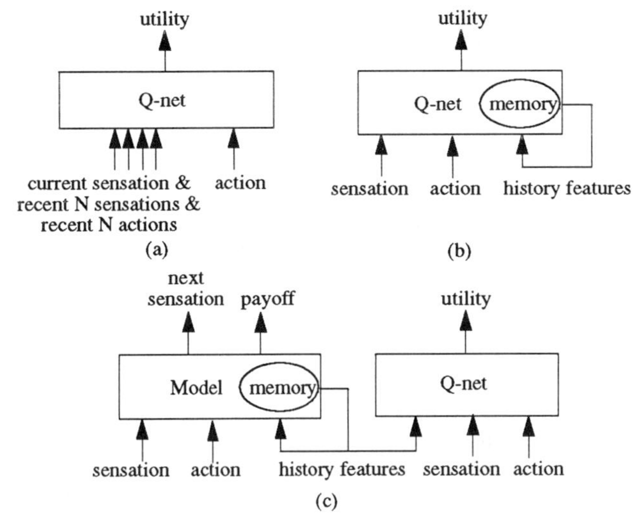

Figure 4: Three memory architectures for reinforcement learning with hidden states: (a) window-Q, (b) recurrent-Q, and (c) recurrent-model.

6.1 Network Structures and Training

Both the Q-function and action model take two kinds of inputs: sensation and action. There are two alternative network structures to realize them. One is a monolithic network whose input units encode both the sensation and the action. For domains with discrete actions, this structure is often undesirable, because the monolithic network is to be trained to model a highly nonlinear function— given the same sensation (and same history features), different actions may demand very different outputs of the network. An alternative is what I call the OAON (*One Action One Network*) architecture, which uses multiple networks (one for each action, assuming actions are discrete) to represent the Q-function and the model. In this work, I always used the OAON network structure, and found it much superior to the first alternative, the monolithic structure.

Time-delay networks can be trained by the back-propagation algorithm, while recurrent networks can be trained by a recurrent version of the back-propagation algorithm called *back-propagation through time* or BPTT. BPTT is based on the observation that a recurrent network spanning multiple steps can be converted to an equivalent feed-forward network by duplicating the network over time. Once a conversion is done, back-propagation can be applied.

6.2 Performance

The three architectures all worked fine for several simple learning tasks [6]. But they all have shortcomings. The window-Q can only capture a bounded history, which is a strong limitation for control. A potential problem with the recurrent-Q is that this architecture attempts to solve three difficult problems at the same time and within a single component— the three problems are credit assignment, generalization, and hidden states. In comparison, recurrent-model attempts to solve the hidden state problem by learning an action model, and the other two problems by connectionist Q-learning. However, the recurrent model approach may be too expensive to apply, because the action model will attempt to model every aspect of the environment, no matter whether it is relevant or irrelevant [6].

For example, in a simulation experiment, a learning agent was provided with two random sensory bits, which simulated two difficult-to-predict and irrelevant features in the agent's state representation. The addition of these two bits had little impact on the performance of the window-Q and recurrent-Q architectures, but gave a noticeable negative impact on the recurrent-model architecture, because the action model was unable to reduce the prediction errors on the two random bits. As a result, the recurrent-model could not obtain a stable representation of the history features (i.e., context units), which in turn destabilized a well-trained Q-net.

Considering those shortcomings, the recurrent-Q approach appeared more appropriate than the other two in dealing with the hidden state problem faced by the simulated robot. The hidden state problem involved in this task is in fact not serious. The history features the robot needs to learn are mainly the features that can help make distinctions between the two doorways. Therefore, it does not seem worthwhile to learn a complex recurrent model, which will inevitably attempt to model many detailed but unimportant aspects of the environment, such as where obstacles are located. The window-Q architecture was tried (although not extensively); it seemed that a large window size would be needed for this task.

Simulation results indicate that the robot (using recurrent-Q) generally developed a good recharging skill after 150 trials. This indicates that the robot had developed some useful history features for making distinctions between the two doors. (Unfortunately, it is hard to understand what history features were actually learned.)

7 Unexpected Environmental Changes

In a final experiment, the robot's environment was modified (Figure 5). The modifications (see Figure 5) included two new obstacles (one in Room A and one in Room B), movement of two existing obstacles (both in Room A), small movement of the battery charger, and small movement of both door openings. Without additional training, the control policies that the robot had learned were able to adapt to those environmental

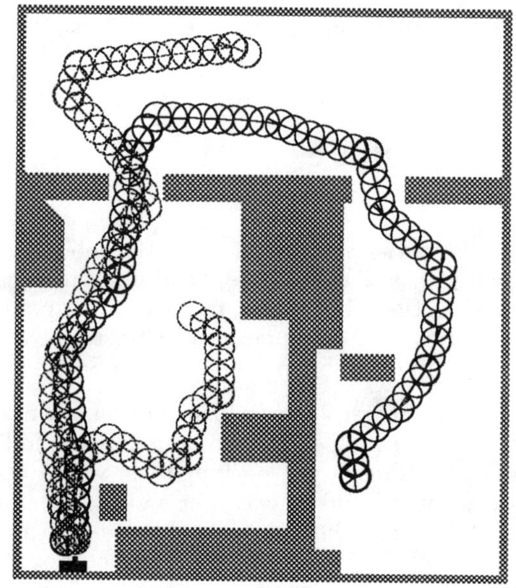

Figure 5: Three found solution paths in the presence of unexpected environmental changes.

changes quite successfully. This success demonstrated the good generalization achieved by neural networks.

8 Summary

This section summarizes the lessons learned from this research:

- Reinforcement learning can be naturally integrated with artificial neural networks to obtain high-quality generalization. For example, a simulated robot has successfully trained neural networks to approximate *nonlinear* Q-functions for several nontrivial tasks. Neural networks were found to handle control errors and sensing errors quite well in this research. They also achieved good generalization, which can be seen by noting that the robot described here could adapt to small environmental changes without additional training (Section 7). On the other hand, neural networks seemed very computationally expensive. They typically require many presentations of training data before they converge. Neural networks can be highly parallelized, however.
- Reinforcement learning agents can save many learning trials by using an action model, which can be learned on-line. Experience replay is a simple technique that implements this idea. The technique is simple and has been found effective in reducing learning trials, but did not seem to be an efficient way of reusing experiences— in this research, each experience was typically replayed 60 times to obtain good performance. To be efficient, experience replay should be performed se-

lectively. For example, we may estimate the information gain from replaying an experience, and allow only experiences with high information gain to be replayed (for example, see [9, 8]).

- TD(λ) methods were found to converge a few times faster with $\lambda > 0$ (typically $\lambda = 0.7$ in this work) than with $\lambda = 0$.

- Reinforcement learning agents can take advantage of instructive training instances provided by human teachers, resulting in a significant learning speedup. Teaching can also help learning agents avoid local optima during the search for optimal control. Simulation experiments indicate that even a small amount of teaching may save agents many learning trials.

- Reinforcement learning agents can significantly reduce learning time by hierarchical learning. Simulation experiments indicate that a robot with hierarchical learning can solve a complex problem, which otherwise is hardly solvable within a reasonable time. Though not presented here, a complexity analysis for deterministic and discrete domains has shown that learning complexity can be greatly reduced by hierarchical learning [5].

- Learning agents can deal with a wide range of non-Markovian environments by having a memory of their past. Three memory architectures were discussed. They worked reasonably well for a variety of simple problems, and one of them was also successfully applied to solving a complex robot problem.

This paper concludes that it is possible to build artificial agents that can acquire complex control policies effectively by reinforcement learning.

Acknowledgements

I thank Tom Mitchell, Rich Sutton, Sebastian Thrun, Lonnie Chrisman, Rich Caruana, Sven Koenig, Nils Nilsson, Chuck Thorpe and two anonymous reviewers of this paper for providing valuable comments on this work. This work was supported by Fujitsu Laboratories Ltd.

References

[1] J.L. Elman. Finding structure in time. *Cognitive Science*, 14:179–211, 1990.

[2] M.A. Lewis, A.H. Fagg, and A. Solidum. Genetic programming approach to the construction of a neural network for control of a walking robot. In *Proceedings of the 1992 IEEE International Conference on Robotics and Automation*, pages 2618–2623, Nice, France, 1992.

[3] Long-Ji Lin. Self-improving reactive agents based on reinforcement learning, planning and teaching. *Machine Learning*, 8:293–321, 1992.

[4] Long-Ji Lin. Hierarchical learning of robot skills by reinforcement. In *Proceedings of the 1993 IEEE International Conference on Neural Networks*, 1993. (To appear).

[5] Long-Ji Lin. *Reinforcement Learning for Robots Using Neural Networks.* PhD thesis, Carnegie Mellon University, School of Computer Science, 1993. Technical Report CMU-CS-93-103.

[6] Long-Ji Lin and T.M. Mitchell. Reinforcement learning with hidden states. In *Proceedings of the Second International Conference on Simulation of Adaptive Behavior: From Animals to Animats.* The MIT Press, 1993. (To appear).

[7] S. Mahadevan and J. Connell. Scaling reinforcement learning to robotics by exploiting the subsumption architecture. In *Proceedings of the Eighth International Workshop on Machine Learning*, pages 328–332, Evanston, Illinois, 1991. Morgan Kaufmann.

[8] A.W. Moore and C.G. Atkeson. Prioritized sweeping: Reinforcement learning with less data and less real time. *Machine Learning.* (To appear).

[9] Jing Peng and R.J. Williams. Efficient learning and planning within the Dyna framework. In *Proceedings of the Second International Conference on Simulation of Adaptive Behavior: From Animals to Animats.* The MIT Press, 1993. (To appear).

[10] D.A. Pomerleau. *Neural Network Perception for Mobile Robot Guidance.* PhD thesis, Carnegie Mellon University, School of Computer Science, 1992. Technical Report CMU-CS-92-115.

[11] S.P. Singh. Transfer of learning by composing solutions of elemental sequential tasks. *Machine Learning*, 8:323–339, 1992.

[12] R.S. Sutton. Learning to predict by the methods of temporal differences. *Machine Learning*, 3:9–44, 1988.

[13] R.S. Sutton. Integrated architectures for learning, planning, and reacting based on approximating dynamic programming. In *Proceedings of the Seventh International Conference on Machine Learning*, pages 216–224, Austin, Texas, 1990. Morgan Kaufmann.

[14] C.J.C.H. Watkins. *Learning from Delayed Rewards.* PhD thesis, University of Cambridge, England, 1989.

[15] S.D. Whitehead and D.H. Ballard. Learning to perceive and act by trial and error. *Machine Learning*, 7:45–83, 1991.

Overcoming Incomplete Perception with Utile Distinction Memory

R. Andrew McCallum
Department of Computer Science
University of Rochester
Rochester, NY 14627
mccallum@cs.rochester.edu

Abstract

This paper presents a method by which a reinforcement learning agent can solve the incomplete perception problem using memory. The agent uses a hidden Markov model (HMM) to represent its internal state space and creates memory capacity by splitting states of the HMM. The key idea is a test to determine when and how a state should be split: the agent only splits a state when doing so will help the agent predict utility. Thus the agent can create only as much memory as needed to perform the task at hand—not as much as would be required to model all the perceivable world. I call the technique UDM, for Utile Distinction Memory.

1 INTRODUCTION

As researchers explore the problem of learning situated behaviors for robotic tasks, they face the dual blessing and curse of *perceptual aliasing* [Whitehead and Ballard, 1990]. Perceptual aliasing occurs when there is not a one-to-one mapping between the agent's perception of the world and different world situations. It is a blessing because it can represent as equivalent different world states in which the same action is required. It is a curse because it can also confound different world states in which *different* actions are required. Ideally one would like to keep the good generalization and get rid of the bad.

The task of making desirable distinctions between perceptually aliased states is made more difficult when the agent also suffers from *incomplete perception* [Chrisman *et al.*, 1991]. If, at any time, no redirection of the perceptual system can produce immediate percepts that distinguish two significantly different world states, then the agent has incomplete perception. World states are significantly different if the agent's best action is not the same in each. Thus incomplete perception is a function of the perceptual system, the world and the task. For example, in a maze constructed of identical-looking barriers, two hallways in different locations may appear the same no matter how carefully one examines the current surroundings. In such situations the agent will require some additional information to disambiguate the aliased states. One way to do this is by introducing some kind of memory of past percepts and actions. The agent could then distinguish its current location from identical-looking maze locations by "remembering how it got there." (For instance, even if I were walking around our department blindfolded, I might know that I'm in the north hallway instead of the south hallway because I remember that I turned right after exiting the elevator.)

Chrisman has presented a technique, called the Perceptual Distinctions Approach, to solve the incomplete perception problem [Chrisman, 1992]. The agent builds a hidden Markov model [Rabiner, 1989] that acts as a predictive model of the environment. The states of the HMM are the internal states of the agent, and estimated future discounted reward values for each action, or *state-action values*, are stored in each of the HMM states. The agent uses Watkins' Q-learning [Watkins, 1989], except that the agent retrieves and adjusts Q-values using the state-action values from all the HMM states proportionally according to the HMM state occupation probabilities. The technique increases the number of HMM states based on statistical significances in the agent's ability to predict perception.

Because the new state occupation probabilities of a HMM depend not only on the current percept, but also on the previous state probabilities and the previous action, a HMM state can represent memory. For instance, it is possible to set the transition probabilities in a HMM such that it is extremely unlikely that the agent has arrived in a particular state unless the agent has come from some other particular previous state. By building chains of such states with exclusive transition probabilities, the occupation of a state can represent an arbitrary amount of memory about past percepts and actions.

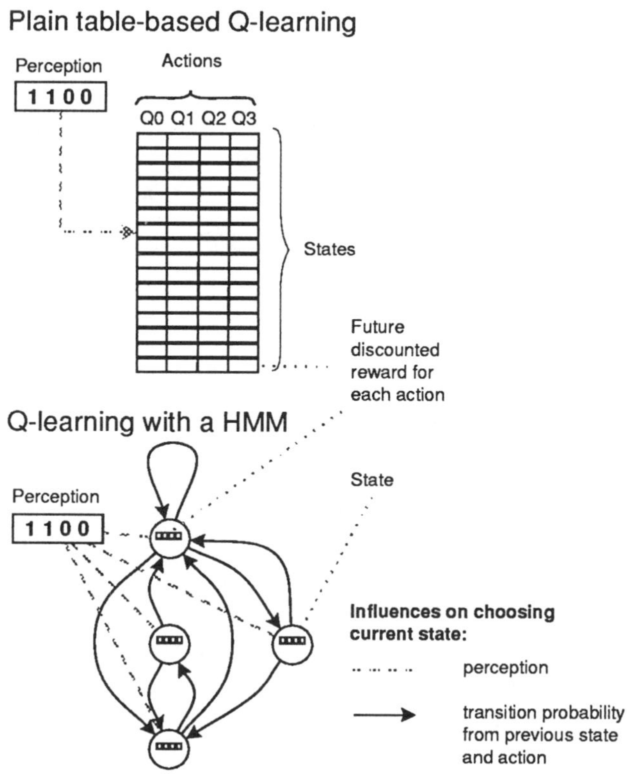

Figure 1: In plain table-based Q-learning the current state is determined entirely by the current percept. Using a HMM, the agent can determine its current state using the current percept, *and* the previous action and previous state. Plain Q-learning internal states correspond to rows of the Q-table. The internal states of an agent using HMM's correspond to states of the HMM. In each case an internal state holds a collection of future discounted reward estimates, one for each action.

The Utile Distinction Memory (UDM) method presented in this report shares the HMM foundation with Chrisman's technique. It uses a HMM to represent the agent's internal state space; it keeps state-action values in the states of the HMM, and it retrieves and adjusts the state-action values according to state occupation probabilities. The chief difference lies in the way that the size of the HMM state space is increased. Instead of creating new states based on predicting perception, UDM creates new states only when it can show statistically significant increases in the agent's ability to predict *reward*.

This difference causes a fundamental shift in the agent's representational approach. Utility-based distinctions will build an agent internal state space only as large as needed to perform the task at hand[1], whereas perception-based distinctions will build a state space large enough to represent all the world as the agent perceives it. If the agent's task is simple, but the world is complex and the agent can perceive manifestations of the world complexity, we would still like the agent's internal state space to be simple. The difficulty of learning should be proportional to the difficulty of the task, not the complexity of the world.

2 UTILITY-BASED DISTINCTIONS FOR MEMORY

How can the agent know when splitting a state will help it predict utility? Often a perceptually aliased state that affects utility will have wildly fluctuating reward values, however, we cannot base a state splitting test solely on reward variance; some changes in reward are caused by the stochastic nature of the world, and splitting the state will not help the agent more consistently get high reward. The agent must be able to distinguish between changes in reward caused by a stochastic world, and changes that could be predicted after performing a split. What new information does splitting a state give the agent? After splitting a state the agent has the ability to distinguish between two previously aliased states based on knowledge about which state it came from.

The key idea behind Utile Distinction Memory is as follows: UDM keeps future discounted reward information associated with the incoming transitions to a state. If the state satisfies the Markov property then all the reward values should be similar; however, if there are statistically significant differences in the rewards, then the identity of the state the agent comes from *is* significant to predicting reward, the state must be non-Markovian, and splitting this state would help the agent more consistently predict reward.

One split may allow further distinctions because it will create new separate transitions into other states. In that UDM can recursively build a tree of distinctions it is similar to Chapman and Kaelbling's G algorithm [Chapman and Kaelbling, 1991], except that it builds distinctions in memory space instead of perception space.

3 DETAILS OF THE ALGORITHM

A slightly longer description of UDM can be found in [McCallum, 1992]. A hidden Markov model is comprised of a finite set of states, $\mathcal{S} = \{s_1, s_2, ..., s_N\}$ and a finite number of observations (percepts), $\mathcal{O} = \{o_1, o_2, ..., o_M\}$. We also include a finite set of actions $\mathcal{A} = \{a_1, a_2, ..., a_K\}$.[2] For each state there is a vector of observation probabilities—we write $B(o_i|s_j)$ for the probability of seeing observation o_i while in

[1] In reinforcement learning good task performance is *defined* by the reward the agent receives.

[2] The inclusion of actions actually makes this a *Partially Observable Markov Decision Process.*

state s_j. For each state-action pair there is a vector of transition probabilities—the notation $A(s_k|s_i, a_j)$ signifies the probability that executing action a_j from state s_i will result in state s_k. The agent's belief about the state of the world is maintained in a vector of its state occupation probabilities, written $\vec{\pi}(t) = \langle \pi_1(t), \pi_2(t), ..., \pi_N(t)\rangle$, where $\pi_i(t)$ is the agent's belief that the world state is represented by s_i at time t.

To calculate the state occupation probabilities at time $t+1$, the agent uses the "forward" part of the Baum forward-backward procedure [Rabiner, 1989],

$$\pi_j(t+1) = k \cdot B(o_{t+1}|s_j) \sum_i A(s_j|s_i, a_t)\, \pi_i(t) \quad (1)$$

where k is whatever constant is needed to make $\sum_i \pi_i(t+1) = 1$, and o_{t+1} is the agent's observation at time $t+1$, and a_t is the action executed by the agent at time t.

While choosing actions and altering state-action values with the reward from actions, UDM uses Q-learning superimposed on hidden Markov models, just as in [Chrisman, 1992]. We write $q(s_i, a_j)$ for the state-action value of action a_j in state s_i. The agent obtains Q-values representative of the agent's current belief about the world state from the state-action values kept in the HMM states by letting all the HMM states "vote" in proportion to their occupation probability:

$$Q(\vec{\pi}(t), a_j) = \sum_i \pi_i(t)\, q(s_i, a_j) \quad (2)$$

The agent then chooses the action, a^*, with the largest Q-value, (*i.e.*, $a^* = \text{argmax}_a Q(\vec{\pi}, a)$. The state-action values are updated according to the standard Q-learning rule, again modified to use the state occupation probabilities:

$$\begin{aligned} \forall s_i\ q(s_i, a_t) &= (1 - \beta\pi_i(t))q(s_i, a_t) + \\ &\quad \beta\pi_i(t)(r_t + \gamma U(\vec{\pi}(t+1)) \quad (3) \\ U(\vec{\pi}(t+1)) &= \max_a Q(\vec{\pi}(t+1), a) \quad (4) \end{aligned}$$

where $\beta, 0 < \beta < 1$, is the learning rate, $\gamma, 0 < \gamma < 1$, is the temporal discount factor, and $U(\vec{\pi}(t+1))$ is the expected utility of the current state given the agent's beliefs about which states it may be in. Effectively the state occupation probability, $\pi_i(t)$, becomes part of the learning rate. Thus far we have not diverged from [Rabiner, 1989] and [Chrisman, 1992]. Next I describe the part of the algorithm specific to UDM.

With the incoming transitions to a state, UDM keeps statistics on the future discounted reward received after leaving the state in question. Future discounted reward is also called *return*. If the state is Markovian with respect to return, then the return values on all the incoming transitions should be similar. However if there are statistically significant differences between any of the incoming transitions, splitting the state and appropriately dividing the transitions between the split states will help the agent predict return.

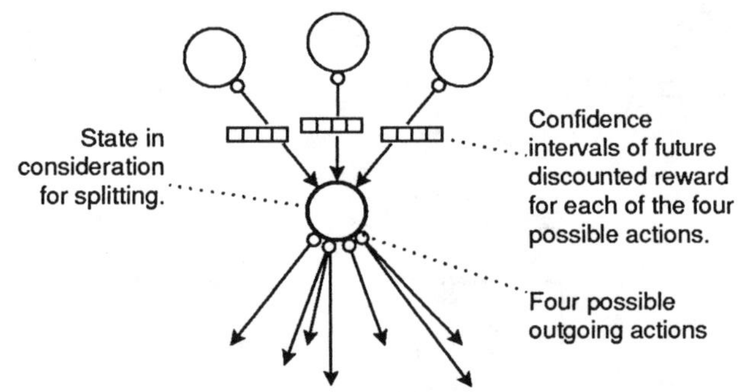

Figure 2: A state in consideration for splitting. Associated with incoming transitions UDM keeps confidence intervals of future discounted reward for each action executed from the state in question.

Since two perceptually aliased states in the world may have the same utility, but require different actions, UDM actually keeps separate statistics for the different actions executed from the HMM state.

Statistical significance is tested using confidence intervals, which we calculate with the same method described in [Kaelbling, 1990]. For each interval we keep a running count, n, a sum of values, $\sum x$, and a sum of the squares of the values, $\sum x^2$. The upper and lower bounds are then calculated by

$$\bar{x} \pm t_{\alpha/2}^{(n-1)} \frac{s}{\sqrt{n}} \quad (5)$$

where $\bar{x} = (\sum x)/n$ is the sample mean, and

$$s = \sqrt{\frac{n\sum x^2 - (\sum x)^2}{n(n-1)}} \quad (6)$$

is the sample standard deviation, and $t_{\alpha/2}^{(n-1)}$ is the Student's t function with $n-1$ degrees of freedom. The parameter α, determines the confidence with which values will fall inside the interval.

These return statistics kept with transitions are never used to change the agent's state-action values, $q(i, A)$; they are only used to determine when and how to split a state.

The agent begins with a fully connected hidden Markov model containing a state for each percept. The observation probabilities, $B(o_i|s_j)$, are preset such that each percept is biased toward a different state.[3] The transition probabilities, $A(s_k|s_i, a_j)$, are all made equal. The agent then executes a series of m-step trials. During each trial it updates the $q(s_i, a_j)$ values according the equations above, and also keeps a record

[3]Currently UDM has the ability to discover beneficial memory distinctions, but not perceptual distinctions, thus the model is initialized to distinguish between all percepts.

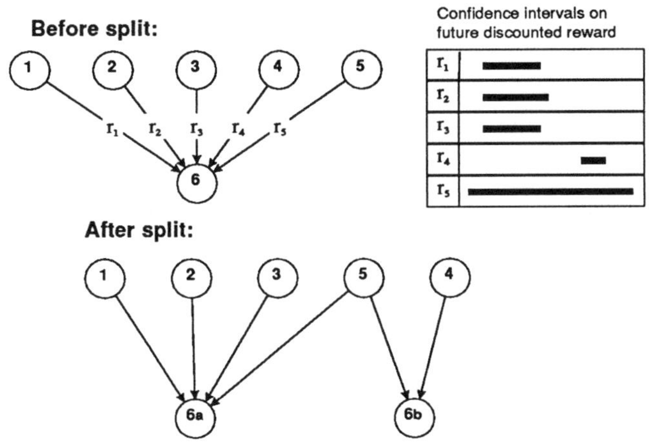

Figure 3: Determining when and how a state should be split by using confidence intervals on future discounted reward. Consider all incoming transitions to state 6, and compare the set of confidence intervals corresponding to each action executed from state 6. If any of the intervals do not overlap, then the agent has determined that by treating state 6 differently depending on which state it came from it can get a statistically significant increase in its ability to predict reward. The set of intervals is divided into clusters of overlapping intervals, and each cluster is assigned to a different copy of state 6. The confidence interval table in the upper right only shows the intervals for one outgoing action.

of the actions, percepts, and rewards in history arrays A[t], P[t] and r[t].

At the end of each m-length trial the agent runs the tests for determining what states, if any, should be split. This begins by performing the Baum-Welch procedure for updating the model parameters. The procedure improves the model's ability to use percepts and actions to distinguish the agent's current state, but since the test used for splitting states is separate from Baum-Welch, the agent will not create new memory capacity in order to predict perception. In the process of the Baum-Welch procedure the agent calculates improved estimates of the state occupation probabilities over time, $\pi_i(t)$, and estimates of the transition occupation probabilities over time, $\xi(s_i, a_j, s_k|t)$, (the probability that at time t the agent passed from state s_i to state s_k using action a_j). See [Rabiner, 1989] for details. Then the agent calculates return values over time, return[t], using the reward history, r[t]:

$$\begin{array}{l} \texttt{return}[m] = \texttt{r}[m] \\ \text{for } t = m-1 \text{ to } 0 \\ \quad \texttt{return}[t] = \texttt{r}[t] + \gamma \cdot \texttt{return}[t+1] \end{array} \tag{7}$$

where γ is the temporal discount factor. Because any state could be aliased and could have state-action values resulting from a meaningless combination rewards from different world states, the state-action values (and state utilities defined as the maximum over the state-action values) cannot be trusted, and only reward directly from the world is used to calculate return.

Now the agent has all the information necessary to assign return values to specific transitions. The agent considers the value of return[t] at each time step and includes this value in the statistics for each transition in proportion to the transition occupation probability at the previous time step:

$$\begin{array}{l} \text{for } t = 1 \text{ to } m-1 \\ \quad \text{for all transitions, } \texttt{trans}\text{, that use action } \texttt{A}[t-1] \\ \quad\quad \texttt{lr} = \beta \cdot \xi_{\texttt{trans}}[t-1] \\ \quad\quad \texttt{trans.count}_{\texttt{A}[t]} \mathrel{+}= \texttt{lr} \\ \quad\quad \texttt{trans.sum}_{\texttt{A}[t]} \mathrel{+}= \texttt{lr} \cdot \texttt{return}[t] \\ \quad\quad \texttt{trans.sumsquares}_{\texttt{A}[t]} \mathrel{+}= \texttt{lr} \cdot (\texttt{return}[t])^2 \end{array} \tag{8}$$

where β is the agent's learning rate, lr is the learning rate for a particular transition at a particular time, and $\xi_{\texttt{trans}}[t-1]$ is the transition occupation probability $\xi(s_i, a_j, s_k|t-1)$ at time $t-1$ of the particular transition, trans, belonging to source state s_i, action a_j and destination state s_k. The trans-dot quantities in the last three lines refer to the three statistics necessary for computing the upper and lower bounds; trans.count is the count, n, trans.sum is the sum, $\sum x$, and trans.sumsquares is the sum of squares, $\sum(x^2)$. The A subscripts indicate that they are indexed by the different actions executed in the destination state of the transition.

Using the count, sum, and sum of squares the agent can obtain upper and lower bounds of the return value confidence intervals for each transition. The agent determines if the returns on two incoming transitions are statistically significant by measuring whether or not their confidence intervals overlap. When any two of the confidence intervals with the same outgoing action fail to overlap the state is split.

The agent divides the set of incoming transitions into disjoint subsets, such that all transitions in a subset overlap with each other and each subset is as large as possible. To perform this clustering optimally is actually an NP-complete problem (Minimum Cover, [Garey and Johnson, 1979]), but in practice, greedy solutions are adequate. After the clustering, the state is duplicated (including incoming and outgoing transitions) enough times so that there is one copy per cluster. Then, any incoming transitions that are not elements of a duplicate state's assigned cluster are removed.

States may also be joined if the union of their incoming transitions all overlap with each other, and if one set of incoming transitions is a subset of the other. If the analysis at the end of any m-length trial results in any splits or joins, the trans-dot statistics are reinitialized.

Figure 4: One of several mazes successfully solved by UDM. The agent's perception is defined by a bit vector of length four in which the bits specify whether or not there is a barrier to the agent's immediate north, east, south, west. The numbers in the squares are the decimal equivalents of the bit vectors interpreted in binary. Although the three state 5's are all perceptually equivalent, the agent must learn to go south in the 5 in the center, and go north in the 5's on the right and left. The hidden Markov model built by UDM has two states with high probabilities of observing 5—one representing the 5 in the center and the other combining the two 5's on the right and left. Percept 10 is also aliased, and is split in two since different actions are required in the two world states. See Figure 5 for diagrams of the HMM built to solve this maze.

4 EXPERIMENTAL RESULTS

I have demonstrated UDM working in a grid world where perception is defined by immediately adjacent barriers. The Local Perception Grid World (LPGW) is based on simulated worlds used by [Sutton, 1990], [Whitehead, 1992], [Thrun, 1992] and others. The agent moves about a discrete grid by executing the actions `North`, `East`, `South`, and `West`. Whenever the agent attempts to move into a grid occupied by a barrier, the agent remains where it is and receives a reward of -1.0. Whenever the agent moves into any of the one or more "goal" squares, it receives a reward of 1.0. For all other actions the agent receives a reward of -0.1. After reaching the goal square the agent is randomly transported to another location in the maze.

The difference between the LPGW and the other grid worlds is that instead of defining perception as the unique row and column numbers of the agent's position (a perception that does not cause perceptual aliasing), LPGW defines perception to be a bit vector of length four in which the bits specify whether or not there is a barrier to the agent's immediate north, east, south and west. This perception is rich with perceptual aliasing possibilities (and is also a bit more realistic for a navigating robot one might build).

In some experiments I also added noise to the Grid World. With probability 0.1 the agent perceives some other perception vector than its current world position would have specified. Also with probability 0.1 the agent's chosen actions are randomly changed to one of the other four.

One maze solved by UDM appears in Figure 4. Without noise, UDM consistently learned the optimal policy for this maze in five trials of 500 steps each. The agent used a learning rate of $\beta = 0.6$, a temporal discount factor of $\gamma = 0.7$, a confidence on the upper and lower bounds of $(1-\alpha) = 0.95$, and a random action probability (exploration rate) of 0.1. The sequence of HMM's created appear in Figure 5. Notice that percept 5 is represented by only two states even though there are three world states that produce percept 5. On the sides, where the same action is required, UDM keeps the two world state 5's aliased to the same internal state. With noise, UDM learned the same optimal policy, but the agent required 15 trials of 500 steps each.

5 CONCLUSIONS

The Utile Distinction Memory technique provides a refutation to the "Utile-Distinction Conjecture" [Chrisman, 1992], which stated that is was impossible to introduce only memory distinctions that impact utility. As such, UDM acts as a starting point from which to design improved learners that use memory to create selective, task-specific representations of their environment.

There are other mechanisms for creating memory besides hidden Markov models. Lin and Mitchell present successful results with agents that use a fixed-size window of past percepts and actions, and also agents that use recurrent neural networks with context units [Lin and Mitchell, 1992]. These methods do not split or add nodes to the network during learning and thus the memory capacity must be known and fixed before learning begins.

We could also say [Tan, 1991] deals with incomplete perception in that his robot remembers the results of several perceptual actions to determine its internal state. However, it has no mechanism for memory that spans across an overt action and the algorithm only works in deterministic worlds. The first point prevents Tan's agent from solving tasks like the Local Perception Grid World where perceptual information is limited to only the immediately adjacent squares. The first point also makes the memory problem much simpler—the agent no longer has to determine what to remember and when to forget: it remembers the results of all its perceptual actions, then throws all its memory away when it does an overt action.

UDM is not without limitations and problems. The computational requirements for the state splitting test are significant, both in terms of storage and calculation. Any method that uses the Baum-Welch procedure requires $O(KN^2m)$ time and storage. As long as $K < m$, UDM does not increase these requirements, however, the increased constants are not insignificant. Hopefully UDM's minimal, task-specific state splitting will allow small enough state spaces to at least partially make up for this.

UDM splits states in order to increase memory-based distinctions, but it currently has no method for splitting states to increase perceptual distinctions that predict future reward. For this reason UDM begins with one state per percept, a strategy that will obviously not work for large perception spaces. Some method for making perceptual distinctions will be necessary, and it seems plausible that Chapman and Kaelbling's G algorithm [Chapman and Kaelbling, 1991] or even some technique based on confidence intervals for the unused perception bits in a state should work in conjunction with UDM.

Although UDM can build memory chains of arbitrary length, it does require that some statistically significant benefit be detectable for each split individually in sequence. UDM has solved mazes with multi-step paths between the reward-predicting percepts and the reward, however, it would not be able to solve problems in which a conjunction of percepts in sequence predicted reward, but each of the percepts on its own was independent of future reward. This assumption about the detectable relevance of pieces of information in isolation is also made by [Chapman and Kaelbling, 1991] and [Maes and Brooks, 1990]; additionally, it is a key factor in Genetic Algorithms.

My primary goal in working with memory for learning agents is to use memory to disambiguate the ubiquitous perceptual aliasing that occurs with *active perception* [McCallum, 1993]. In fact, the use of memory with active perception has the potential to solve UDM's lack of splitting for perceptual distinctions quite nicely. Imagine an agent that chooses from among overt and perceptual actions that each return one bit, and this one bit makes up the agent's entire immediate perception space, (*one*-bit perception being the extreme case). We can think of the different perceptual actions as each returning a different bit of the total perception vector available from the current world state. The agent can generalize in perception space by only executing the actions necessary to get the bits that are currently relevant. This scheme is even better than generalizing by using "don't cares" as a mask on the perception vector because the agent's policy can effectively act as a decision tree that specifies which bits are needed—depending on the result of a bit gathered early in the process the agent can decide whether or not it needs to gather more bits before it executes an overt action. This scheme will also allow the agent to execute open-loop sequences of actions. Taking this route, however, will require addressing the assumption about the detectable relevance of individual spilts because perceptual bits that provide useful information only in conjunction violate the assumption. For example, a student driver learning to pass should pull into the passing lane when the car in front is close, and the rearview mirror is clear, and the blind-spot is clear. Verifying this conjunction requires remembering results from three eye movements. When true, this conjunction is highly correlated with reward, however, any of the bits individually is not.

Acknowledgments

This work has benefited from discussions with many colleagues, including: Dana Ballard, Mary Hayhoe, Jeff Schneider, Jonas Karlsson and Polly Pook. I am grateful to Dana Ballard, Jeff Schneider and Virginia de Sa for making helpful comments on an earlier draft.

This material is based on work supported by NSF research grant no. IRI-8903582, NIH/PHS research grant no. 1 R24 RRO6853, and a grant from the Human Science Frontiers Program.

References

[Chapman and Kaelbling, 1991] David Chapman and Leslie Pack Kaelbling. Learning from delayed reinforcement in a complex domain. In *Proceedings of IJCAI*, 1991.

[Chrisman *et al.*, 1991] Lonnie Chrisman, Rich Caruana, and Wayne Carriker. Intelligent agent design issues: Internal agent state and incomplete perception. *Working Notes of the AAAI Fall Symposium: Sensory Aspects of Robotic Intelligence*, 1991.

[Chrisman, 1992] Lonnie Chrisman. Reinforcement learning with perceptual aliasing: The perceptual distinctions approach. In *AAAI-92*, 1992.

[Garey and Johnson, 1979] Michael R. Garey and David S. Johnson. *Computers and Intractability, A Guide to the Theory of NP-Completeness.* W. H. Freeman and Company, 1979.

[Kaelbling, 1990] Leslie Pack Kaelbling. *Learning in Embedded Systems.* PhD thesis, Stanford University, 1990.

[Lin and Mitchell, 1992] Long-Ji Lin and Tom M. Mitchell. Reinforcement learning with hidden states. In *Proceedings of the Second International Conference on Simulation of Adaptive Behavior: From Animals to Animats*, 1992.

[Maes and Brooks, 1990] Pattie Maes and Rodney A. Brooks. Learning to coordinate behaviors. In *Proceedings of AAAI-90*, pages 796–802, 1990.

[McCallum, 1992] R. Andrew McCallum. First results with utile distinction memory for reinforcement learning. Technical Report 446, University of Rochester Computer Science Dept., 1992.

[McCallum, 1993] R. Andrew McCallum. Learning with incomplete selective perception. Technical Report 453, University of Rochester Computer Science Dept., April 1993. PhD thesis proposal.

[Rabiner, 1989] Lawrence R. Rabiner. A tutorial on hidden Markov models and selected applications in speech recognition. *Proceedings of the IEEE*, 77(2), February 1989.

[Sutton, 1990] Richard S. Sutton. Integrating architectures for learning, planning, and reacting based on approximating dynamic programming. In *Proceedings of the Seventh International Conference on Machine Learning*, Austin, Texas, 1990. Morgan Kaufmann.

[Tan, 1991] Ming Tan. Cost sensitive reinforcement learning for adaptive classification and control. In *AAAI*, 1991.

[Thrun, 1992] Sebastian B. Thrun. Efficient exploration in reinforcement learning. Technical Report CMU-CS-92-102, CMU Comp. Sci. Dept., January 1992.

[Watkins, 1989] C.J.C.H. Watkins. *Learning from Delayed Rewards.* PhD thesis, Cambridge University Psychology Dept., 1989.

[Whitehead and Ballard, 1990] Steven D. Whitehead and Dana H. Ballard. Learning to perceive and act. Technical Report 331, University of Rochester Computer Science Dept., June 1990.

[Whitehead, 1992] Steven Whitehead. *Reinforcement Learning for the Adaptive Control of Perception and Action.* PhD thesis, Department of Computer Science, University of Rochester, 1992.

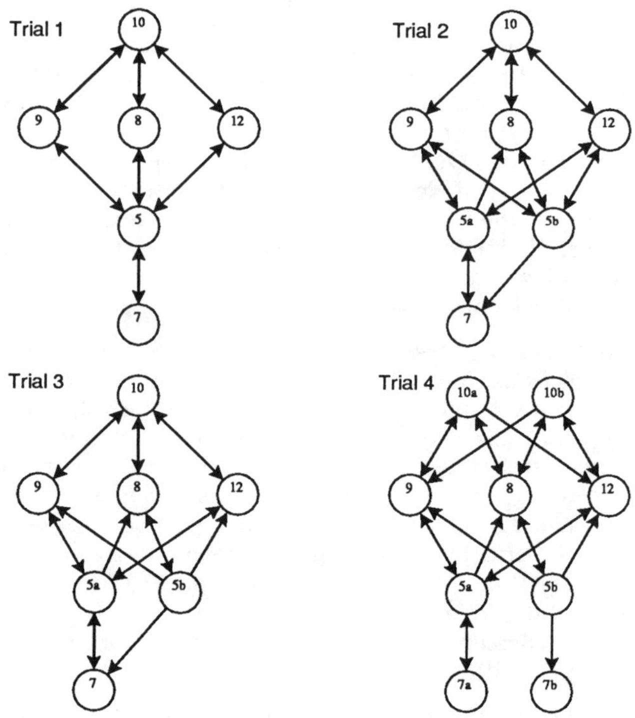

Figure 5: The sequence of hidden Markov models created by UDM as it learns the task shown in Figure 4. The HMM states are fully connected, but the diagrams only show transitions with probability greater than 0.3. Also not shown here are the different actions that cause the transitions. **Trial 1:** The agent has learned some transition probabilities, but it has not yet gathered enough statistics to split any states. **Trial 2:** The agent has discovered that the future discounted reward received after leaving state 5 is significantly different when it arrives from state 8 than it is when it arrives from state 7. UDM has duplicated state 5, creating 5a and 5b, then removed the state 8 incoming transition from 5a and removed the state 7 incoming transition from 5b. **Trial 3:** The agent has found non-overlapping confidence intervals on the transitions into 5b—arriving from state 8 is significantly different than arriving from states 9 or 12. UDM temporarily splits 5b into 5b and 5c, but then 5c is joined with 5a. **Trial 4:** Two splits occur at the end of this trial. Average future reward after leaving the center state 7 is greater than after leaving the side state 7's because from the center state 7 the agent is teleported to locations that are are often closer to the goal. UDM splits state 7 recognizing that arriving from 5a is different than arriving from 5b. State 10 is also split because the confidence intervals for leaving 10 by going east and leaving 10 by going west don't overlap in the transitions coming from states 9 and 12. The agent will now arrive in state 10a from state 9 and arrive in state 10b from state 12. There are no more changes to the HMM after trial 5.

Explanation Based Learning: A Comparison of Symbolic and Neural Network Approaches

Tom M. Mitchell
School of Computer Science
Carnegie Mellon University
Pittsburgh, PA 15213
Tom.Mitchell@cs.cmu.edu

Sebastian B. Thrun
University of Bonn
Institut für Informatik III
Römerstr. 164, D-5300 Bonn, Germany
Thrun@uran.informatik.uni-bonn.de

Abstract

Explanation based learning has typically been considered a symbolic learning method. An explanation based learning method that utilizes purely neural network representations (called EBNN) has recently been developed, and has been shown to have several desirable properties, including robustness to errors in the domain theory. This paper briefly summarizes the EBNN algorithm, then explores the correspondence between this neural network based EBL method and EBL methods based on symbolic representations.

1 Introduction

Explanation based learning (EBL) is an important paradigm for machine learning because it offers a means of using prior knowledge to generalize more correctly from fewer training examples. EBL was originally conceived as a symbolic learning method ([DeJong and Mooney1986], [Mitchell *et al.*1986]), based on creating and analyzing explanations derived from symbolic rules. While it has been used successfully to learn control knowledge to speed up search ([Laird *et al.*1988], [Minton1988]), the chief limit to its usefulness lies in the requirement that its prior knowledge, or domain theory, be complete and correct. Recent research has produced a number of proposals for extending EBL approaches to accommodate imperfect domain theories (e.g., for several dozen, see the Workshop of Combining Inductive and Analytical Learning [Machine Learning Workshop1989]). Despite progress in this area, we still have not found the final answer to the question of how to best unify EBL and inductive learning.

An explanation based learning method based purely on neural network representations has recently been proposed [Mitchell and Thrun1993], [Thrun and Mitchell1993], which provides a means of combining an inductive learning component (neural network Backpropagation) with an explanation based learning component. In preliminary experiments, this algorithm (called EBNN) has been demonstrated to successfully use approximate, previously learned, domain knowledge of widely varying quality to guide generalization. EBNN is a direct analog to symbolic EBL methods in that it maintains separate representations of the domain theory and the target function, and uses the domain theory to explain and generalize each individual training example.

The goal of this paper is to examine the correspondence between EBL methods based on symbolic and neural network representations. To ground the comparison, we consider two specific algorithms: a prototypical pure symbolic EBL algorithm, Prolog-EBG [Kedar-Cabelli and McCarty1987], and explanation based neural network learning, EBNN. We first present an overview of the EBNN algorithm. Following this we define the abstract EBL problem and EBL method that is common to both symbolic and neural network approaches. Finally, we examine key differences in detailed representations and algorithms, that lead to different capabilities and convergence properties for these two approaches. The main result revealed by this analysis is a fundamental difference in the types of information that can be extracted from symbolic versus neural network explanations, and a fundamental difference in convergence characteristics when learning a target function represented by sets of rules versus a single neural network.

2 An Overview of EBNN

This section summarizes the EBNN learning algorithm and presents preliminary experimental results illustrating its robustness to errors in the domain theory. Additional details regarding the algorithm and the experimental results are available in [Thrun and Mitchell1993] and [Mitchell and Thrun1993]. Note this section is a summary extracted from those papers.

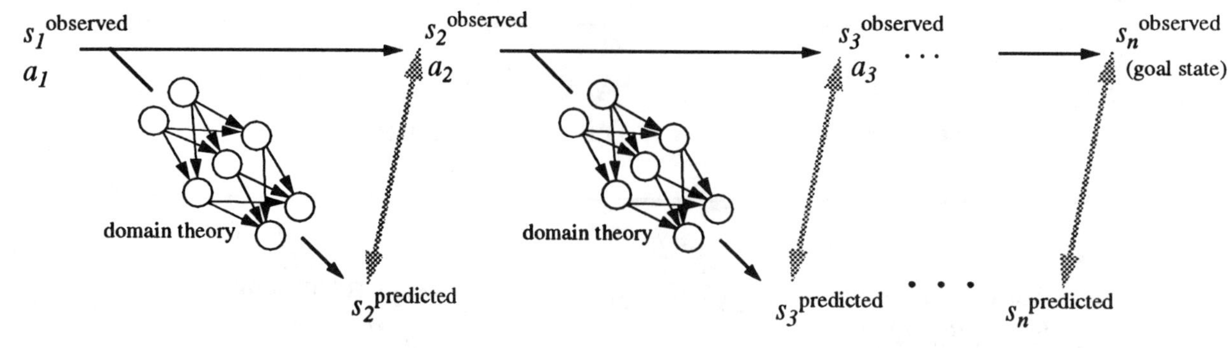

Figure 1: **Training Episode:** Starting from the initial state s_1, the action sequence $a_1, a_2, \ldots, a_{n-1}$ was observed to produce the final state s_n, a goal state. The domain knowledge represented by neural networks can be used to *explain* how the observed state-action sequence resulted in achieving the goal. EBNN extracts slopes of the target function (i.e., the derivative of the goal feature of the final state with respect all features of the initial state) from this explanation.

2.1 Neural Network Domain Theories

In EBNN, the domain theory is represented by artificial neural networks. By using neural network learning algorithms such as the Backpropagation procedure [Rumelhart *et al.*1986], the domain theory can be learned from scratch and does not require the availability of a priori knowledge from a human trainer. As in symbolic EBL, EBNN uses the domain theory to guide learning of the target concept by explaining and analyzing observed training examples.

To illustrate EBNN, consider an agent (perhaps a robot) which must learn a strategy for choosing which of its actions to apply in any given state in order to (eventually) achieve its goal. Consider, for example, the episode shown in figure 1. Starting from an initial state s_1, the sequence of actions $a_1, a_2, \ldots, a_{n-1}$ is observed to produce the goal state s_n. The learning task is this case is to learn the concept "the class of states, s for which the action a will lead eventually to a goal state." This concept will be represented by a boolean function from states and actions to $\{0,1\}$. Once learned, this evaluation function allows the agent to select actions that achieve its goal.

2.2 Explaining and Analyzing Observed Episodes

One could apply standard explanation-based learning methods to this problem, provided the agent initially possessed a perfect domain theory describing the effects of its actions on the world state. Instead, we consider the case where the robot has only an approximate, previously learned theory of the effects of its actions. This domain theory is represented by a collection of neural networks, one for each action. The network characterizing action a_i takes as input the description of an arbitrary state, and produces as output a description of the predicted resulting state (i.e., each network represents the same type of information as typically represented by symbolic precondition-postcondition action descriptions). EBNN applies these action model networks to explain and learn from each observed episode in which it achieves its goal. More precisely, EBNN applies the following three step process to each observed episode in which the agent successfully achieves its goal:

1. Explain: An *explanation* is a post-facto prediction of the observed episode using the domain knowledge. Explanations are constructed by using the neural network domain theory to post-facto predict, and thus explain, why action a_1 applied at state s_1 led to the observed state s_2, why a_2 led to s_3, and so on. Note that predicted states usually deviate from the observed ones, since inductively learned domain theories are only approximately correct.

2. Analyze: The role of the explanation is to elucidate how achieving the final goal *depends on* the various features of the observed initial state, s_1. In symbolic EBL, this dependency is used to extract the *weakest precondition* under which the same explanation would have produced the same outcome. Since EBNN represents its domain theory by neural networks, it is difficult to extract weakest preconditions. However, since neural networks are real-valued differentiable functions, one can use the dependencies in the explanation to extract the *derivatives (i.e., slopes)* of the final goal feature with respect to each feature of the initial state, s_1. EBNN examines the specific chain of neural net activations and weights in the explanation, to analytically extract these derivatives.

More specifically, consider the last state-action pair $\langle s_{n-1}, a_{n-1}\rangle$ shown in figure 1, which led to the goal state s_n. Neural networks correspond to differentiable functions. Using the last step of the explanation for this episode, the slopes of the goal features of the predicted final state s_n with respect to s_{n-1} and a_{n-1} can be extracted by computing the derivative of the neural network function. These slopes describe the dependence of the final state s_n on the previous state s_{n-1}, and action a_{n-1}. In particular, they measure how infinitesimally small changes applied to s_{n-1} or a_{n-1} will change the final state s_n. The extraction of

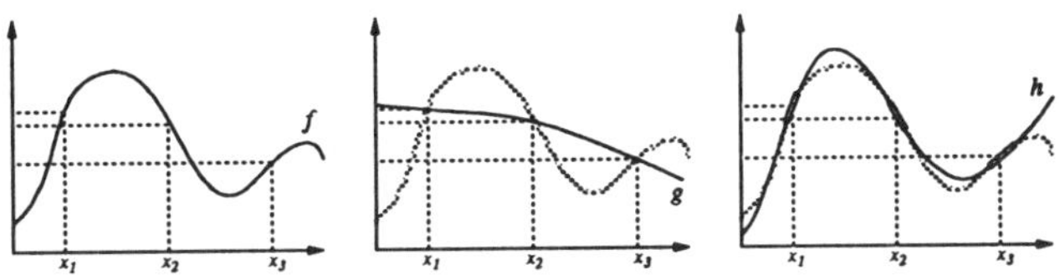

Figure 2: **Fitting slopes:** Let f be a target function for which three examples $\langle x_1, f(x_1)\rangle$, $\langle x_2, f(x_2)\rangle$, and $\langle x_3, f(x_3)\rangle$ are known. Based on these points the learner might generate the hypothesis g. If the slopes are also known, the learner can do much better: h.

slopes can be chained back through the entire episode by applying the chain rule of differentiation to the entire explanation. The result of this analysis is the set of derivatives (slopes) of the target concept (goal state) with respect to each state-action pair in the observed episode. As stated above, these slopes measure the pointwise *dependence* of the target concept on the features of the states and actions in the observed episode.

3. Refine: The slopes extracted from the explanation, along with the observed training example itself, are used to refine the learner's hypothesis regarding the target function. The target function in EBNN is represented by a separate neural network (or any other representation appropriate for approximating real-valued functions from sample values and sample slopes). This is analogous to symbolic EBL, in which the learned target function is also represented separately from the initial domain theory. However, whereas symbolic EBL produces a new rule for each explained example, EBNN uses just a single network[1] to represent the target function. This single target function network is incrementally updated with each new training example, both inductively and analytically, to iteratively approximate the true target function. In the episode from our example, each state-action pair in the episode, $\langle s_i, a_i\rangle$ becomes a training example for inductively and analytically refining the target network. The **inductive component of learning** corresponds to updating the target network to produce the target output *value* (e.g., 1 if the example leads to achieving the goal). Inductive learning is crucial for compensating for errors in the domain theory. The **analytical component of learning** corresponds to updating the network to fit the target output *slopes*, extracted analytically from the explanation. As shown in figure 2, these slopes influence the learned network by overriding the default bias of interpolating between observed points. Therefore the analytical component in EBNN enables faster generalization from less training data, if slopes are sufficiently accurate. In the case that the target function is represented by a neural network, the Backpropagation algorithm can be extended to fit slopes as well as values, as may be found in [Simard *et al.*1992].

To summarize, the target concept is iteratively approximated by updating it (a) inductively, to fit the empirically observed *training values* of the target function, and (b) analytically, to fit the analytically derived *training slopes* obtained by explaining the observed example in terms of a previously learned domain theory.

2.3 Accommodating Imperfect Domain Theories

Since the domain theory is learned inductively from training instances[2], its accuracy might thus be arbitrarily poor, resulting in arbitrarily poor explanations and extracted slopes. How can the learner avoid the damaging effects of such incorrect slopes arising from a poor domain theory?

EBNN reduces the undesired influence of incorrect domain theory predictions by estimating the *accuracy* of the extracted slopes, based on the fit between the observed sequence of states and those predicted by the explanation (this heuristic is called LOB*). More specifically, each time the domain theory is used for post-facto predicting a state s_{k+1}, its prediction $s_{k+1}^{\text{predicted}}$ may deviate from the observed state $s_{k+1}^{\text{observed}}$. We define the 1-step prediction accuracy at state s_k, denoted by $c_1(i)$, as 1 minus the normalized prediction error:

$$c_1(i) \quad := \quad 1 - \frac{\| s_{i+1}^{\text{predicted}} - s_{i+1}^{\text{observed}} \|}{\text{max\_prediction\_error}}$$

For a given episode we define the n-step accuracy $c_n(i)$ as the product of the 1-step accuracies in the next n steps. For states n steps away from the end of the episode, the analytically derived training information (slopes) is weighted by the n-step accuracy times the weight of the inductive component (values). Although the experimental results reported in Section 2.4 are promising, the generality of this approach is an open question, due to the heuristic nature of the assumption LOB*.

2.4 Experimental Results in a Simulated Robot Learning Domain

EBNN was evaluated in a simulated robot navigation domain. The world and the action space are depicted in Figure 3a&b. The learning task is to find an evaluation function Q, for which the greedy policy navigates

[1] In our experiments we used 5 networks, one for each action. The important point is that the target function is represented in a fixed (set of) networks, rather than a growing number of rules. We also experimented with a nearest neighbor representation of the target function.

[2] This process is not to be confused with the inductive learning of the target function.

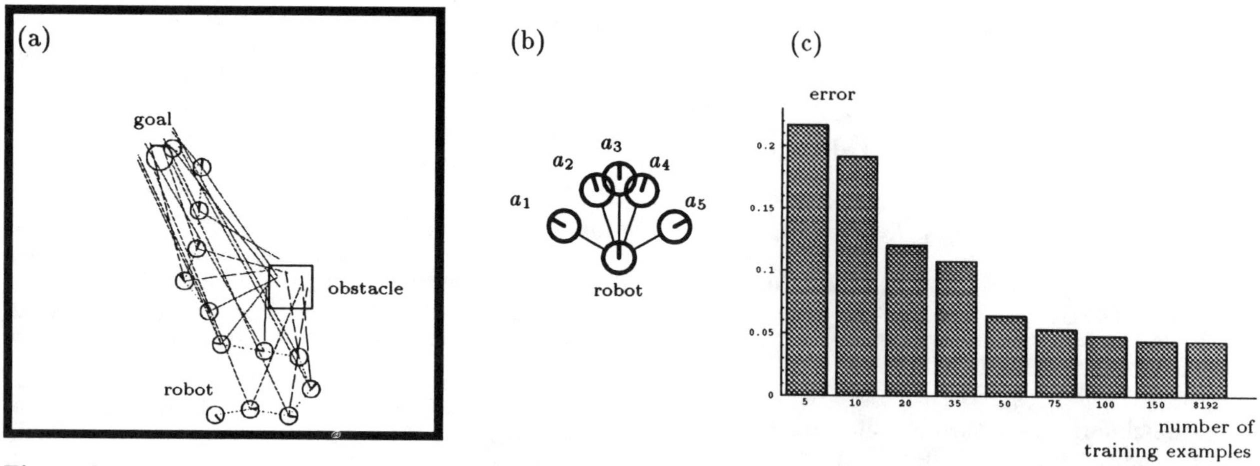

Figure 3: a. The simulated robot world. b. Actions. c. The squared generalization error for each of nine domain theories trained on different numbers of training examples.

the agent to its goal location (circle) from arbitrary starting locations, while avoiding collisions with the walls or the obstacle (square). States are described by the local view of the agent, in terms of distances and angles to the center of the goal and to the center of the obstacle. Note that the world is deterministic in these experiments, and there is no sensor noise.

In order to allow exploration of the robot environment and to compensate for the necessary non-optimal action choices, we applied EBNN to Watkins' Q-Learning [Watkins1989] together with Sutton's *temporal difference learning* $TD(\lambda)$ [Sutton1988] (with $\lambda = 0.7$ and a reward *discount* $\gamma = 0.8$)[3]. Each discrete action was modeled by a separate neural network. We used neural network Backpropagation learning for learning action models. The evaluation functions Q were approximated by an instance-based local approximation technique, modeling the Q separately for each action. In this instance-based technique, each training instance, together with its slopes, was explicitly memorized. Given a new point as a query, generalization was achieved by fitting a local second order polynomial over the three nearest neighbors in the instance memory. This polynomial fit both the values and the slopes. In our initial experiments, this instance-based technique outperformed neural networks for representing the target functions.

Experiment 1: "What is the impact of the analytical component of EBNN, given a strong domain theory?" In this experiment we first allowed the agent to train each of the action modeling networks that form its domain theory using 8192 randomly generated training examples. This results in a fairly accurate, but still imperfect, domain theory, which was then used by EBNN. The results of EBNN are shown by the thick black line in Figure 4. In contrast, the results of applying standard inductive learning (Backpropagation) are shown by the line marked "without analytical learning". EBNN required significantly less training data than inductive learning in order to reach the same level of performance.

Experiment 2: "How does EBNN degrade with progressively weaker domain theories?" We repeated Experiment 1 using weaker domain theories, trained with 5, 10, 20, 35, 50, 75, 100, 150, and 8192 training examples per action network. The additional curves in Figure 4 show the results of using EBNN with these weaker domain theories. These curves demonstrate that EBNN degrades gracefully to the performance of pure induction, as the accuracy of the domain theory decreases.

3 Correspondence between Symbolic and Neural Network EBL

As described above, EBNN is the neural network analog of symbolic explanation-based learning methods. In this section we describe the common abstraction of symbolic EBL and EBNN. We then explore the specific differences between these two algorithms, and the significant impact that these algorithmic differences have on their relative capabilities. While there are many variants of symbolic EBL, for the purposes of grounding the discussion we will consider only one prototypical algorithm: Prolog-EBG, as described in [Kedar-Cabelli and McCarty1987]. Furthermore, while both neural networks and nearest-neighbor schemes have been used to represent the target function in EBNN, in this discussion we assume the target function is represented by a neural network.

It is also important to note that a variety of techniques have been proposed for combining analytical and in-

[3]We will omit the somewhat lengthy details here, since they are not essential for the understanding of EBNN. See [Thrun and Mitchell1993] and [Mitchell and Thrun1993] for a detailed description.

(a)

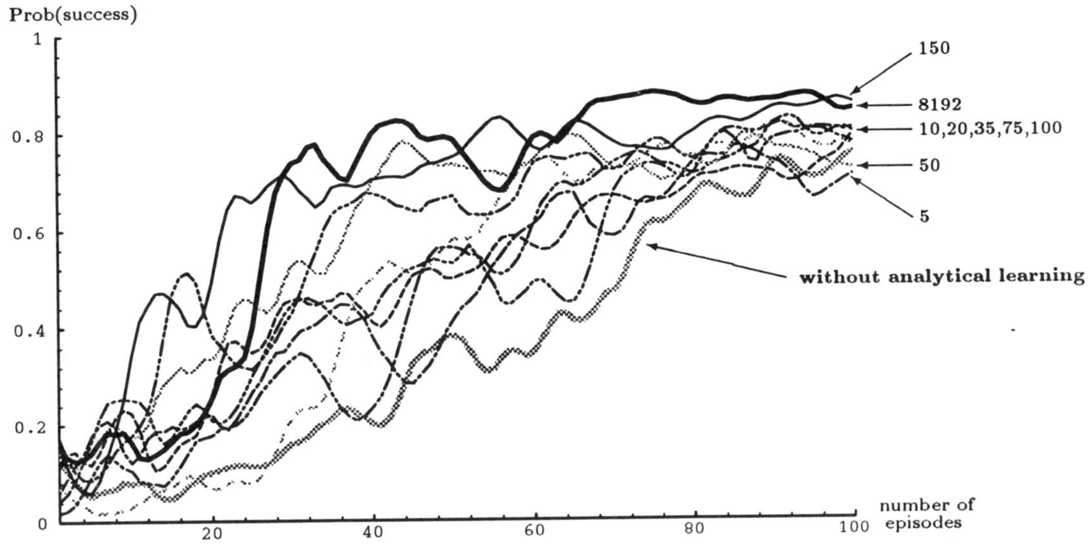

Figure 4: EBNN using various domain theories, compared against pure induction. The bold grey line is the learning curve for pure inductive learning, i.e., Q-Learning and TD(λ). Other curves show the performance of EBNN, using domain theories of differing accuracies, pre-trained with from 5 to 8192 training examples for each action model network. The performance (vertical axis) is measured on an independent test set of 20 starting positions. All curves are averaged over 3 learning runs and are also locally window-averaged.

ductive learning, which do not involve explaining individual training examples, and which are therefore outside the scope of this discussion. These include, for example, Shavlik's [Shavlik and Towell1989] and Fu's [Fu1989]) methods for using symbolically encoded domain knowledge to initialize the topology and weights of neural networks which are then inductively refined.

3.1 The Explanation-Based Learning Problem

The common problem addressed by the symbolic Prolog-EBG method and the neural network EBNN method can be characterized as follows:

Given:

- **Target function:** the function to be learned.
- **Domain theory:** prior knowledge capable of predicting/explaining the output of the target function given its input
- **Training instances:** examples of input, output pairs of the target function
- **Operationality criterion:** constraints on how the learned function must be described

Determine:

An operational representation of the target function that best fits both the observed training instances and the given domain theory

Note that while both Prolog-EBG and EBNN make use of a domain theory, it is represented in very different forms in the two cases. In Prolog-EBG, the domain theory is described by a collection of horn clauses, whereas in EBNN it is a collection of neural networks. Note that each neural network in the domain theory can be interpreted as a complex inference rule, capable of concluding an output assertion (represented by its output activations) from the input assertion (represented by its input activations).

The operationality criterion, which specifies the acceptable form for the learned target function, is similar in Prolog-EBG and EBNN. In both cases, the target function value is computed directly from the observable attributes of the example. In Prolog-EBG this target function is represented by horn clauses, while in EBNN it is represented by a neural network or some other approximator for real-valued functions.

Notice that the above problem definition requires that the learned function be a best fit to both the training instances and the domain theory. Strictly speaking, Prolog-EBG is used only when the training examples are consistent with the domain theory, and it therefore produces learned rules that constitute a *perfect* fit to both the domain theory and observed examples. However, much current work on symbolic EBL (e.g., [Machine Learning Workshop1989], [Mooney and Ourston1989], [Pazzani1989]) deals with the same class of situations as EBNN: situations in which the observed training examples are not strictly entailed by the domain theory, and for which the goal is therefore to learn a function that best fits both the imperfect domain theory and the observed training examples.

3.2 The Explanation-Based Learning Method

The common abstraction of the Prolog-EBG and EBNN algorithms is to perform, for each observed training example, i, the following steps:

1. *Explain* i, by showing how the domain theory predicts the value of the target function for input i
2. *Analyze* this explanation to determine the relevance of different features of i with respect to the target function
3. *Refine* the current representation of the target function to take into account this new training example and the information about feature relevance extracted from the explanation.

Both Prolog-EBG and EBNN construct similar explanations: chains of inferences based on the domain theory, predicting the observed target function value from attributes of the examples. However, they differ significantly in the ways in which they use their explanations to refine the hypothesized target function.

The key difference in the use of explanations stems from the difference in representing dependencies using symbolic versus neural network domain theories: symbolic rules typically refer to (i.e., match) only a *subset* of the training example attributes, whereas neural networks compute their output based on weighted combinations of *all* example attributes. Therefore, symbolic explanations typically indicate that the target function value depends on only *some subset of the training example attributes*, whereas neural network explanations indicate that the explained value depends to some degree on *every training example attribute.*

In Prolog-EBL, the features of the training example that are mentioned in the symbolic explanation are easily distinguished from those that are not, and the regression of the target concept expression through the explanation yields the weakest preconditions under which that explanation will hold. A new rule is then created using these weakest preconditions for its antecedent, and the explained target function value as its consequent.

With explanations based on neural networks, the process of regressing logical expressions in order to extract weakest preconditions cannot be applied. Instead, the dependency of the target function value on example features is extracted in the form of partial derivatives of the target function with respect to the example attributes, evaluated at the training example point. These partial derivatives, or slopes, summarize the knowledge implicit in the domain theory as it applies to the current explanation. These analytically derived slopes are then used to update the neural network that defines the target function. In particular, the weights of the target function network are adjusted to make its slope closer to the slope suggested by the explanation.

The key differences between symbolic and neural network EBL methods include the following:

Difference in dependencies extracted from explanations. As discussed above, symbolic EBL extracts weakest preconditions from explanations, whereas neural network EBL extracts partial derivatives of the target function with respect to example attributes.

Difference in target function coverage and correctness. As new training examples are encountered, symbolic EBL methods acquire an increasing number of rules that allow it to predict the target function value for an increasing proportion of the space of examples. In contrast, neural network EBL begins with a (very poor) description of the target function that covers the entire space of examples. As it acquires examples, its improvement lies in improving the quality of its approximation to the target function, rather than its coverage. In brief, symbolic EBL learns a function that is always correct and increasingly complete in its coverage, whereas neural net EBL learns a function that is always complete and increasingly correct.

Difference in mechanisms for learning new features. Symbolic EBL procedures have been demonstrated to acquire new features analytically, as a side-effect of extracting weakest preconditions (e.g., [Utgoff1986]). In contrast, Backpropagation neural net learning has been demonstrated to acquire useful new features inductively, in the hidden layer units of the network (e.g., [Rumelhart *et al.*1986]). In EBNN, both analytical and inductive components have an influence on the features that are acquired in the hidden layer of the target function. While we have not explored this issue, it seems an interesting opportunity for combining the analytical derivation of useful features based on prior knowledge with the statistical approaches associated with inductive neural network learning.

Difference in permanence of memory. Symbolic methods that learn rules update the target function by adding new rules which are usually assumed to be permanent. EBNN, however, has no corresponding notion of permanent memory. Instead, all new information, whether empirically or analytically derived, can at most cause an incremental change to the weights of the learned network. Furthermore, the influence of that new information will eventually be forgotten as it is incrementally overridden by subsequent data. This difference in memory permanence is primarily a result of the difference between bounded memory representations (e.g., fixed-size neural networks) and unbounded (e.g., arbitrarily large rule sets). If EBNN is used with a nearest neighbor (unbounded memory) representation of the target function, then the situation changes significantly. The difference in permanence of memory appears to have important implications for recovering from incorrect learning, for learning performance in cases where certain rare experiences are very important, and for maintaining consistency when the domain theory and target function are being simultaneously learned.

3.3 Differences in Capabilities

The above sections have described the EBL problems addressed by symbolic and neural network EBL methods, as well as the correspondence between the representations and algorithms they employ. These differences in algorithms have a number of implications for the relative capabilities of these two approaches:

Robustness to errors in domain theory and training data. One central motivation for developing the EBNN algorithm was to provide an explanation-based learning mechanism capable of using imperfect training data and domain theories which were themselves learned from scratch and of unknown reliability. As shown in the experimental results, EBNN is able to successfully learn from very weak or very strong domain theories. Its robustness follows from two characteristics: First, for each individual training example it uses both inductive and analytical methods for updating the target function. Second, it relies more strongly on the analytical learning component for examples that are explained accurately, and more strongly on the inductive component for poorly explained examples. While a variety of symbolic EBL methods have been developed that address imperfect domain theories none has yet been demonstrated to operate over the broad spectrum of learned domain theories of varying quality illustrated for EBNN.

Scaling issues. One well-known scaling problem associated with EBL (and other rule learning methods) is that the more rules learned, the longer it can require to match them to a new example. Because neural nets have a fixed response time regardless of how much they are trained, they have an advantage along this dimension. However, an offsetting issue has to do with the ability to represent arbitrarily complex functions. Because symbolic methods create collections of rules, each of which may cover some particular part of the domain, they can represent arbitrarily complex target functions by arbitrarily large rule sets. Here neural networks are at a disadvantage, since for any fixed-size network there will be complex functions that cannot be accurately represented. Put briefly, neural networks provide fixed response time but sacrifice fidelity in approximating the target function, whereas symbolic rules can provide better fidelity but sacrifice response time.

Ability to learn real-valued functions. Symbolic EBL is typically applied to problems where the target function can take on only a finite number of possible values. In part this is because a distinct learned rule is typically required for each observed output value of the target function. Neural net EBL offers the opportunity to apply explanation based methods to learning real-valued functions, such as the Q function learned in the robot control example. One potential advantage of learning real-valued functions is that it provides a way of applying EBL to learning about optimizing search (again, as illustrated by the robot learning example in which the goal is to maximize the robot's total reward). For example, consider the task of learning rules to control search. Symbolic EBL has been applied with great success to learning rules that recommend actions leading to a goal state, but has been remarkably unsuccessful at learning rules that lead along the minimum cost solution path. The reason is that explaining why one action has lower cost than another involves explanations regarding real-valued quantities, typically leading to very detailed explanations and very specific rules. The robot Q-Learning example above demonstrates that EBNN can be practically applied to learning such optimizing search control.

Human understandability. Symbolic rule-based representations are without doubt more understandable to humans than neural network representations. While there is work on extracting symbolic summaries of the knowledge implicit in neural network weights, an acceptable general-purpose method is still not available.

4 Summary and Conclusions

We have examined the correspondence between EBL methods using symbolic and neural network representations. The main points following from this discussion may be summarized as follows:

1. Explanation-based learning which has previously been considered a symbolic learning method can naturally be extended to neural network representations. The EBNN algorithm represents both the domain theory and the target function as neural networks, and successfully uses explanations of individual examples to guide generalization of the target function.
2. There is a qualitative difference between the information that can naturally be extracted from explanations based on symbolic rules and explanations based on neural networks: symbolic explanations yield *weakest preconditions* under which the explanation holds, whereas neural net explanations yield *partial derivatives of the target function* with respect to each of its inputs, evaluated at the training example point. These constitute two different ways of characterizing the relevance of training example attributes with respect to the target function.

3. There is a qualitative difference between the convergence properties stemming from neural net versus rule based representations for the target function. Neural net learning involves incrementally approximating the complete target function, whereas learning sets of rules involves incrementally extending the piecewise coverage of the target function's domain. This leads to significant differences in the cost of applying the learned function, the ability to learn very complex functions, the trustworthiness of the learned function before convergence, and the ease of interleaving learning of the domain theory and target function.

The analysis in this paper sheds some light on the tradeoffs between symbolic and neural net EBL methods. In particular, it shows that there are advantages to both: Neural net EBL offers a robust means of blending inductive and analytical learning, a natural method for learning real-valued functions that are especially relevant to learning optimal search control, and avoids the slow-down effect often associated with learning too many symbolic rules. Symbolic EBL offers advantages in scaling to more complex functions (due to its modular, multi-rule representation of the target function), in human comprehensibility, and in supporting first-order representations. Methods that combine the advantages of both these approaches are an excellent target for further research.

Acknowledgments

We thank Ryusuke Masuoka for his invaluable help in refining the EBNN algorithm and code. Jude Shavlik and Paul Rosenbloom and the CMU Robot Learning Group have contributed useful ideas during discussions of the correspondence between symbolic and neural network EBL methods. This research was sponsored in part by the Avionics Lab, Wright Research and Development Center, Aeronautical Systems Division (AFSC), U.S. Air Force, Wright-Patterson AFB, OH 45433-6543 under Contract F33615-90-C-1465, Arpa Order No. 7597, and by a grant from Fujitsu Laboratories Ltd.

References

[DeJong and Mooney1986] Gerald DeJong and Raymond Mooney. Explanation-based learning: An alternative view. *Machine Learning*, 1(2):145–176, 1986.

[Fu1989] Li-Min Fu. Integration of neural heuristics into knowledge-based inference. *Connection Science*, 1(3):325–339, 1989.

[Kedar-Cabelli and McCarty1987] Smadar Kedar-Cabelli and Thorne McCarty. Explanation based learning as resolution theorem proving. In *Proceedings of the fourth international workshop on machine learning*, pages 383–389, Irvine, CA, 1987. Morgan Kaufmann.

[Laird *et al.*1988] John Laird, Paul Rosenbloom, and Allen Newell. Chunking in SOAR: The anatomy of a general learning mechanism. *Machine Learning*, 1(1):11–46, 1988.

[Machine Learning Workshop1989] Workshop on combining empirical and explanation-based learning. In Alberto M. Segre, editor, *Proceedings of the sixth international workshop on machine learning*, pages 1–93, San Mateo, CA, 1989. Morgan Kaufmann.

[Minton1988] Steven Minton. *Learning Search Control Knowledge: An Explanation-Based Approach.* Kluwer Academic Publishers, 1988.

[Mitchell and Thrun1993] Tom M. Mitchell and Sebastian B. Thrun. Explanation-based neural network learning for robot control. In J. E. Moody, S. J. Hanson, and R. P. Lippmann, editors, *Advances in Neural Information Processing Systems 5*, San Mateo, CA, 1993. Morgan Kaufmann. (to appear).

[Mitchell *et al.*1986] Tom M. Mitchell, Rich Keller, and Smadar Kedar-Cabelli. Explanation-based generalization: A unifying view. *Machine Learning*, 1(1):47–80, 1986.

[Mooney and Ourston1989] Raymond Mooney and Dirk Ourston. Induction over the unexplained: Integrated learning of concepts with both explainable and conventional aspects. In Alberto M. Segre, editor, *Proceedings of the sixth international workshop on machine learning*, pages 5–7, San Mateo, CA, 1989. Morgan Kaufmann.

[Pazzani1989] Michael J. Pazzani. Detecting and correcting errors of omission after explanation-based learning. In *Proceedings of IJCAI-89*, pages 713–718, 1989.

[Rumelhart *et al.*1986] David E. Rumelhart, Geoffrey E. Hinton, and Ronald J. Williams. Learning internal representations by error propagation. In D. E. Rumelhart and J. L. McClelland, editors, *Parallel Distributed Processing. Vol. I + II.* MIT Press, 1986.

[Shavlik and Towell1989] Jude W. Shavlik and G.G. Towell. An approach to combining explanation-based and neural learning algorithms. *Connection Science*, 1(3):231–253, 1989.

[Simard *et al.*1992] Patrice Simard, Bernard Victorri, Yann LeCun, and John Denker. Tangent prop – a formalism for specifying selected invariances in an adaptive network. In J. E. Moody, S. J. Hanson, and R. P. Lippmann, editors, *Advances in Neural Information Processing Systems 4*, pages 895–903, San Mateo, CA, 1992. Morgan Kaufmann.

[Sutton1988] Richard S. Sutton. Learning to predict by the methods of temporal differences. *Machine Learning*, 3, 1988.

[Thrun and Mitchell1993] Sebastian B. Thrun and Tom M. Mitchell. Integrating inductive neural network learning and explanation-based learning. *Proceedings of the IJCAI*, to appear, 1993.

[Utgoff1986] Paul E. Utgoff. *Machine Learning of Inductive Bias.* Kluwer Academic Publishers, 1986.

[Watkins1989] Chris J. C. H. Watkins. *Learning from Delayed Rewards.* PhD thesis, King's College, Cambridge, England, 1989.

Combinatorial optimization in inductive concept learning

Dunja Mladenić
Artificial Intelligence Laboratory
Computer Science Department
J. Stefan Institute, Jamova 39
61000 Ljubljana, Slovenia
dunja.mladenic@ijs.si

Abstract

Local optimization algorithms, standardly used in combinatorial optimization, can be applied in inductive concept learning. Learning can be defined as search of the space of concept descriptions, guided by some heuristic function. The paper presents learning with stochastic local optimization algorithms (based on *Simulated annealing*) and deterministic local optimization algorithms (*k-opt* known from solving the 'travelling salesman' problem). These algorithms and some of their combinations have been tested within the ATRIS shell, and their performance compared on different real-world machine learning problems. The rule induction shell ATRIS was developed to enable simple use of existing and adding of new optimization algorithms and noise-handling mechanisms, to enable simple 'cross validation' experiments, experiments with different attributes considered as class and different attribute subsets used for learning. The main objective of this paper is an empirical analysis of different optimization algorithms and some of their combinations in comparison with a decision tree learning algorithm.

1 INTRODUCTION

Inductive concept learning can be viewed as search of the space of concept descriptions. The choice of the description language of concepts L_C determines the search space, called the ***hypothesis space***. Depending on the choice of the hypothesis language, ***inductive learning systems*** can learn either attribute descriptions or first-order relational descriptions. We will only relate to ***attribute-value learning***, in which training examples and induced hypotheses are described in terms of a fixed collection of attribute values.

In inductive learning systems, the structure of the search space is determined by generalisation/specialisation operators. Usually locally optimal search is performed by using a hill-climbing and/or a beam-search strategy. For example, the decision tree induction system ASSISTANT (Cestnik, Kononenko and Bratko 1987) performs hill-climbing, and the rule induction systems AQ15 (Michalski et al. 1986) and CN2 (Clark and Niblett 1989, Clark and Boswell 1991) perform beam-search. Their success in dealing with real-world problems lies also in the choice of ***heuristics*** used to guide the search and to stop the construction of trees/rules.

Local optimization algorithms, standardly used in combinatorial optimization, can be applied in inductive concept learning. In general, local combinatorial optimization (Papadimitriou and Steiglitz 1982) is based on: (1) a ***set of candidate solutions*** of a given problem Φ, (2) a ***cost function*** $P : \Phi \rightarrow \Re$ used to guide the search for an optimal solution and (3) the ***transformations*** used for 'moving' from one solution to another. To apply known local optimization algorithms in inductive concept learning, three above mentioned categories must be defined: (1) is the hypothesis space; (2) is some heuristic function; (3) are the transformations that depend on the internal concept description representation .

The paper presents the use of stochastic local optimization algorithms (based on *Simulated annealing*) (Press et al. 1987) and deterministic local optimization algorithms (***k-opt***, known from solving the 'travelling salesman' problem) (Syslo, Deo and Kowalik 1983). Algorithms and some of their combinations have been tested and compared on different real-world machine learning problems. Section 2 introduces the concept learning problem and the concept description language. Section 3 describes each of the combinatorial optimization algorithms used in our experiments. Section 4 presents the rule induction shell ATRIS inside which the combinatorial optimization algorithms were used. The results of the experiments are given in Section 5. Section 6 concludes with some ideas for the further work.

2 PROBLEM DEFINITION

In learning from examples, the *target concept* C is a subset of the given *example space* of objects, labelled $\oplus$ if they are elements of the target concept (*positive examples*), and $\ominus$ (*negative examples*) otherwise. Instead of being classified into one of the two *classes* ($\oplus$ or $\ominus$), an object can be classified into one of the mutually exclusive classes C_k, $k = 1, \ldots, n$. The learning task is defined as follows: Given is the description language of examples L_E, the hypothesis language L_C, the coverage relation between L_C and L_E and the quality criterion defined on elements of L_C. The task is to find a *concept description*, expressible in L_C, satisfying the quality criterion. Usually, the quality criterion requires the induced hypothesis to be complete and consistent with respect to the examples, i.e., that it covers all the positive examples and no negative example. When learning from imperfect data, the consistency and completeness criteria need to be relaxed in order to avoid overly specific hypotheses (see stopping criteria in the Section 4.2.1).

Let L_E be the language of attribute value tuples, and L_C a language of *if-then* rules. In an attribute-value hypothesis language, a *selector* relates an attribute to a value or a disjunction (so-called *internal disjunction*) of values. As an example from a simple 'Saturday morning' domain (Quinlan 1986), [*Outlook* = *sunny* ∨ *rainy*] is a selector. A conjunction of selectors forms a *complex*:

$$R_i = \bigwedge_j \left[A_j = \bigvee_k V_{jk} \right]$$

R_i stands for the i-th *complex*, A_j for the j-th attribute and V_{jk} for the k-th value of the j-th attribute. A hypothesis is a set of *if-then* rules of the form **if** *Complex* **then** *Class*. An example rule is the following:
if [*Outlook* = *sunny*] ⋀ [*Humidity* = *normal*] **then** *Suitable* = *yes*.

In the ATRIS rule induction shell, briefly described in Section 4, an internal bit representation is used, similar to the one used by De Jong and Spears (De Jong and Spears 1991). For example, the previously mentioned Quinlan's 'Saturday morning' domain has four attributes:
A1 - Outlook ∈ {*sunny, overcast, rainy*}, *A2 - Temperature* ∈ {*hot, mild, cool*}, *A3 - Humidity* ∈ {*high, normal*}, *A4 - Windy* ∈ {*no, yes*} . An example complex

$$[Outlook = sunny] \bigwedge [Humidity = normal]$$

is represented with the following binary vector:

A_1			A_2			A_3		A_4	
1	0	0	0	0	0	0	1	0	0

3 COMBINATORIAL OPTIMIZATION ALGORITHMS USED FOR RULE INDUCTION

In ATRIS, inside the covering algorithm (described in Section 4.2.1) for a single rule induction, some local combinatorial optimization algorithm is used. The two stochastic search algorithms, *Simulated annealing* (Press et al. 1987) and *'Markovian neural networks'* (Kovačič 1991), are described in Section 3.1. Deterministic search algorithms *k-opt* are described in Section 3.2. Notice that for each algorithm at least one *transformation* used for 'moving' from one candidate solution to another should be defined. With the transformations, the neighbourhood for each candidate solution (concept description) is defined. In all used local combinatorial optimization algorithms the start position has been randomly chosen.

3.1 STOCHASTIC LOCAL SEARCH ALGORITHMS

The method of *Simulated annealing* is based on the analogy with thermodynamics, (for slowly cooled systems, nature is able to find the minimum energy state). For a selected evaluation function, which is to be minimized, the method performs stochastic search in a discrete state space. To apply this algorithm to the optimization of a rule represented as a binary vector, the modification (negation) of a randomly chosen bit in the rule binary vector, is taken as the *transformation*. For example, neighbour of the rule (1 0 0 0 0 0 0 1 0 0) from Section 2 is the rule (0 0 0 0 0 0 0 1 0 0) if the first value was selected for modification, or the rule (1 1 0 0 0 0 0 1 0 0) if the second value was chosen, etc.

Simulated annealing algorithm applied to rule optimization is as follows:

```
T := StartTemperature;
current_rule := random rule; {random binary
   vector}
repeat
   Randomly select value in the current_rule bi-
   nary vector;
   if modification of the selected value improves
    the current_rule then
      current_rule := modified_rule;
   else {modified rule is of lower quality}
      With probability exp((qmr − qr)/T) exe-
    cute:
        current_rule := modified_rule;
   end if
   T := T * factor; {factor < 1}
until T < EndTemperature;
output current_rule;
```

Parameter T (temperature) is used in the probability function[1] and to control the **repeat-until** loop. Probability function, used in the above algorithm, is calculated from the quality of a modified rule (qmr), the quality of the current rule (qr) and the parameter temperature (T).

The other stochastic search method is an extension of simulated annealing based on 'Markovian neural networks' (Kovačič 1991) which perform 'Markovian' simulated annealing. The difference is that we randomly select more than one value in the binary vector and probabilisticaly choose one to modify the rule; better modifications (in terms of rule quality) are more likely to be chosen.

3.2 DETERMINISTIC LOCAL SEARCH ALGORITHMS

Deterministic search algorithms named *k-Opt*, can be modified for the purpose of a single rule optimization as listed below. The *transformation* used in these algorithms for 'moving' in the candidate solution space is the modification (negation) of *1, 2, ..., k*, randomly chosen bits in a binary vector representing a rule.

```
current_rule := random rule; {random binary
   vector}
repeat
   Find one (two, or three) values in the rule bi-
     nary vector, modification of which maximizes
     the quality of the rule (i.e., no other modifi-
     cation of one (two, or three) values provides
     a rule with better quality);
   if modified_rule is of better quality than
     current_rule then
       current_rule := modified_rule;
   end if
until no modification to better rule quality is
   possible;
output current_rule;
```

The above algorithm is called *1-Opt* if (in the first step of **repeat-until** loop) it checks only rules with one modified value, *2-Opt* if it checks rules with one or two modified values, *3-Opt* if it checks rules with one, two or three modified values. In general *k-Opt* can be preformed by checking rules with up to *k* values modified. The 'faster' variant of algorithm (*2-OptF*, *3-OptF*) searches for the first modification that provides rule with better quality and not the modification which maximizes quality of the rule.

In the ATRIS shell, currently *2-Opt*, *3-Opt*, *2-OptF* or *3-OptF* can be used for learning and *1-Opt*, *2-Opt*, *3-Opt*, *2-OptF* or *3-OptF* for post-processing.

[1] The lower the temperature, the more unlikely the significant change to lower quality rule.

4 ATRIS: A SHELL FOR RULE INDUCTION

The idea of the ATRIS shell is to enable simple design of experiments, usage of existing (and simple adding of new) optimization algorithms and heuristic functions. When different algorithms are integrated in a single system (shell), the idea of combining them comes naturally. The ATRIS rule induction shell supports three main parts: pre-processing of data, construction of a hypothesis and its post-processing.

4.1 PRE-PROCESSING

The input to ATRIS is designed to enable a simple design of experiment with different parameters (selected heuristic, learning algorithm, post-processing algorithm, example validation). Additionally, different experiments can be performed on the same set of examples by selecting an attribute to be treated as the class and the attributes to be used in the induced hypothesis. The pre-processor of ATRIS allows for undefined attribute values in examples (in the current implementation these are simply replaced by the majority attribute value) and the use of built-in background knowledge. For example, the pre-processor can check for the equality of attribute values on pairs of attributes of the same type (having the same set of possible values). Using this idea, originating from the LINUS relation learning system (Lavrač, Dzeroski and Grobelnik 1991), an extended set of tuples is generated and used in learning.

Pre-processed data are converted into an internal representation described in Section 2.

4.2 THE HYPOTHESIS CONSTRUCTION

4.2.1 The basic covering algorithm

The construction of a hypothesis is performed by combinatorial optimization algorithms used within the classical covering algorithm as follows:

```
Hypothesis := ∅;
for each class do
   PExs := positive training examples;
   NExs := negative training examples;
   repeat
      Rule := new rule induced from PExs and
     NExs; {where induction is perfomed by a
     combinatorial optimization algorithm}
      Hypothesis := Hypothesis ⋃ Rule;
      From PExs delete examples covered by
     Rule;
   until PExs = ∅ (or some other stopping cri-
     terion is satisfied);
end for
output Hypothesis;
```

The covering algorithm loop is controlled by a *stopping*

criterion, used to decide when to stop the induction of rules for the current class. This criterion can be referred to as the *sufficiency criterion.* Combinatorial optimization algorithms contain a *stopping criterion,* usually referred to as the *necessity criterion,* if it is part of the heuristic function that is used to guide the search. In domains with exact and non-noisy data, the sufficiency criterion requires completeness (coverage of all positive examples) and the necessity criterion requires consistency (no covered negative example). In domains with imperfect data, the two criteria are implemented as heuristics for evaluating the expected classification accuracy, aimed at avoiding overly specific hypotheses.

4.2.2 Heuristic function

Several probability estimates can be applied to evaluate the quality (the classification accuracy) of a rule. In the ATRIS shell, four heuristic functions are implemented, the *relative frequency* being the simplest, but also unreliable when estimating probabilities from a small training set. To alleviate this problem, the *Laplace estimate* can be used. This estimate, however, relies on the assumption that the prior probability of the classes is uniformly distributed (Mingers 1989), which is rarely true in practice. To avoid this assumption, Cestnik (Cestnik 1990) proposed the *m-estimate* which was successfully used in the 'naive' Bayesian classifier (Cestnik 1990) and in tree pruning (Cestnik and Bratko 1991). The parameter m used in the m-estimate is set subjectively and expresses our confidence in the experimental evidence (training examples). In practical use, it was found that setting the value for parameter m is not a trivial problem. Quinlan (Quinlan 1991) uses an *adapted form of the Bayes-Laplace* formula, with the aim to improve the estimate for the accuracy of small disjuncts. Namely, Quinlan offers a formula that uses the prior probability of the target class in the 'context' of the rule (and no other parameter like m); "although no theoretical justification for this choice can be given" (Quinlan 1991).

Since the aim of this paper is to analyse different local optimization algorithms and their possible combinations, the simplest heuristic function (*relative frequency*) was used in the experiments.

4.3 POST-PROCESSING

The main post-processing mechanism in ATRIS uses deterministic local optimization algorithms (described in Section 3.2) to refine each induced rule. This mechanism is briefly described below. Another mechanism is a variant of *reduced error pruning* (Quinlan 1987) which enables deletion of redundant rules.

The deterministic local optimization post-processing mechanism can be applied to improve the results of both stochastic and deterministic optimization algorithms as follows.

- The stochastic search algorithm typically finds a solution which can still be locally optimized, since search is stopped by the value of the parameter called 'temperature' (see Section 3.1). For example, the results of learning with Simulated annealing can be optimized by post-processing with *3-Opt* (see Section 5).
- The deterministic search algorithm finds locally optimal solution (see Section 3.2) and post-processing has to be performed by some 'wider' (lager neighbourhood) deterministic optimization algorithm. For example, learning with *2-Opt* algorithm and post-processing with *3-Opt* algorithm give typically better results than just learning with *2-Opt*, and uses less time than just learning with *3-Opt* (see Section 5).

5 EXPERIMENTS AND RESULTS

To investigate the combinations of local optimization algorithms implemented in ATRIS, an empirical analysis of implemented algorithms was performed. All experiments were performed on a SUN-4. Experiments were carried out on three machine learning domains. For each domain, 10 validations on the 70% training—30% testing split were used; for each validation, four experiments were performed with a different initial value for the random number generator (Park and Miller 1988).

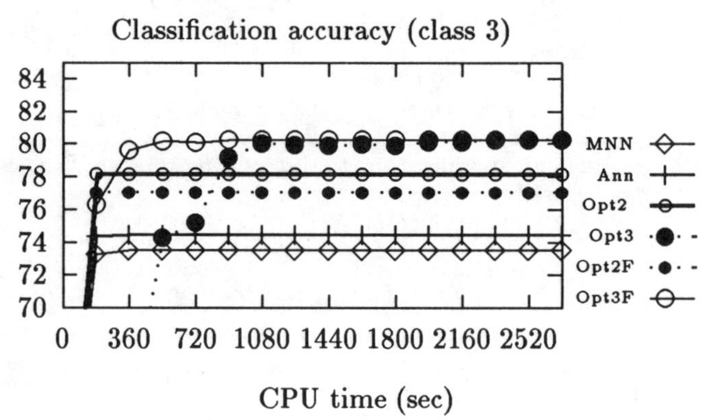

Figure 1: Classification accuracy on testing examples when focusing rules for class 3, domain 'lymphography'.

Domain used for the first experiments is the 'lymphography' medical domain, consisting of 148 examples describing lymphographic symptoms with 18 attributes and classified into one of 4 diagnostic classes (Cestnik, Kononenko and Bratko 1987, Clark and Boswell 1991). Figure 1 presents classification accuracy for the third class (on testing examples) of six local optimization algorithms: *Simulated annealing*, *Markovian*

neural networks, ***2-Opt***, ***3-Opt***, ***2-OptF***, ***3-OptF***.

When calculating the classification accuracy, some examples can be covered by different rules describing different classes. In such case, ATRIS uses the voting method (Kononenko 1991) to predict the class of the example. On the other hand, some of the examples may not be covered by the induced rules. ATRIS uses a very simple method to overcome this problem; to each uncovered example the majority class is assigned.

For the purpose of the algorithm analysis, classification accuracy was calculated at different *CPU time limits* (e.g. 180 sec, 360 sec, ...).[2] When classifying testing examples for a specific *time limit* a *focused* class (e.g. class 3 in the Figure 1) is selected. For the focused class, only the rules induced in the time up to *time limit* (e.g. in the first 360 sec) were used in the classification. For each other class, all the induced rules were used (induced in any time limit). For example, in Figure 1 for the *time limit* 360 sec *Markovian neural networks* achieved 73.5 % accuracy and *3-OptF* achieved 80.2 % accuracy.

From Figure 1 one is inclined to divide the used algorithms, according to the achieved accuracy, into three groups: (1) stochastic algorithms (the lowest accuracy), (2) *2-Opt* and *2-OptF*, and *3-Opt* and *3-OptF* (the highest accuracy). Furthermore, an analysis of the (increasing) number of induced rules and the (decreasing) number of uncovered positive training examples in CPU time was performed. The result was the idea to combine stochastic algorithms (for searching rules) and deterministic algorithms (to perform locally optimal search in post-processing of rules) and to combine two deterministic algorithms (the faster for searching rules and the slower but wider for post-processing)[3]. Stochastic algorithms, *Simulated annealing* (Ann) and *Markovian neural networks* (MNN), were combined with deterministic algorithms, *1-Opt*(Opt1), *3-Opt*(Opt3), *3-OptF*(Opt3F). *Opt-1* was used for post-processing as the simplest and *3-Opt* and *3-OptF* as the most accurate ones. Deterministic algorithms were tested with and without post-processing.

For the analysis of 12 algorithm combinations (see Figure 2), three machine learning domains were used: 'lymphography' already described above; 'primary tumor', also a medical domain consisting of 339 examples and describing location of primary tumor with 17 attributes and 22 diagnostic classes; 'KRK' (chess endgame positions) domain consisting of 1000 examples describing engame positions with 6 attributes and 2 classes (whether win for black). The number of induced rules grows linearly with the CPU time and is similar for different algorithms except in domain 'lymphography', where *Simulated annealing* in

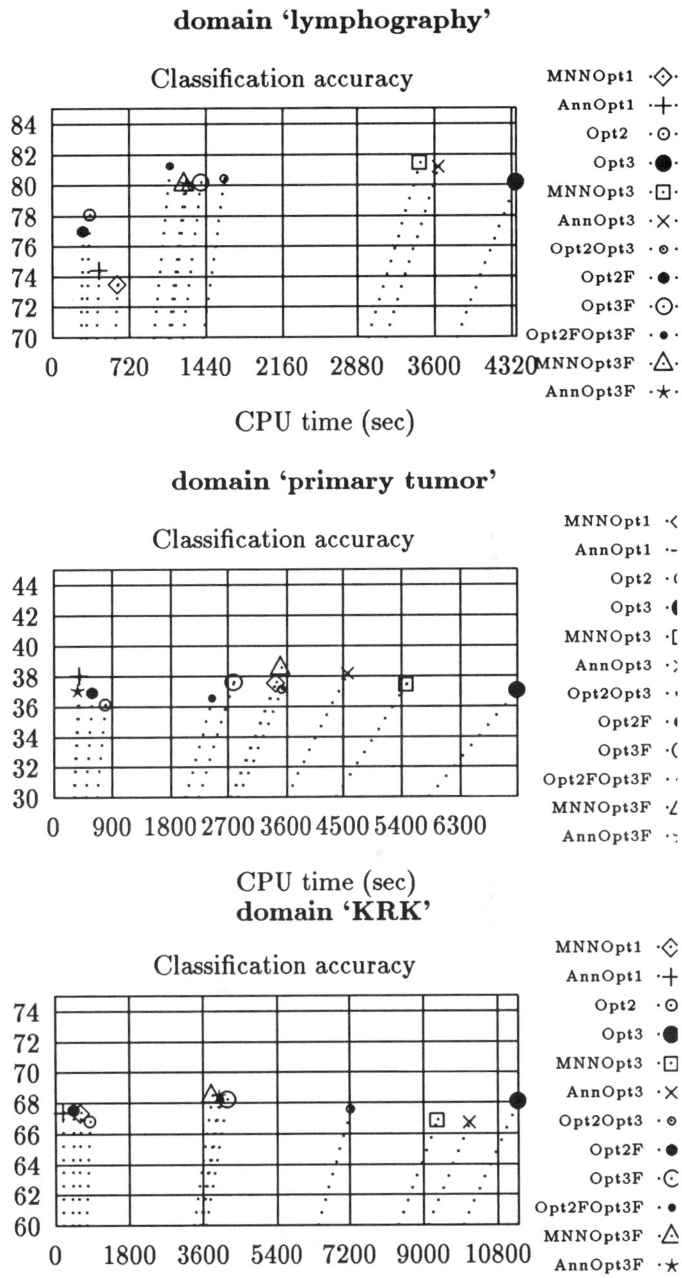

Figure 2: The analysis of optimization algorithms for three domains (classification of test examples).

[2]For each class, time was measured separately. Each rule is then labelled with the time used for its induction.

[3]Notice that *2-Opt* is in some way a subset of *3-Opt*.

combination with *1-Opt* (AnnOpt1) induced twice as many rules as the most of the other methods, but also achieved a very low accuracy (see Figure 2). Classification accuracy is presented at Figure 2. For all domains, algorithms 'group' with respect to CPU time used. The fastest were *Simulated annealing* (AnnOpt1), *2-Opt* (Opt2), *2-OptF* (Opt2F) and the slowest *3-Opt* (OPt3). The highest classification accuracy was achieved by combinations of algorithms using *3-Opt* or *3-OptF* in post-processing, e.g., by MNNOpt3 and Opt2FOpt3F, MNNOpt3F, MNNOpt3F and AnnOpt3F in the three domains respectively.

To get an idea about accuracy of the analysed algorithms, experiments with theASSISTANT algorithm were performed on the same training/testing data. ASSISTANT, using no pruning mechanisms, achieved 77.24% accuracy on 'lymphography', 39.95% on 'primary tumor' and 64.35% on 'KRK'. Most of the analysed optimization algorithms achieved as good or even better accuracy than ASSISTANT[4].

6 CONCLUSION AND FURTHER WORK

Stochastic and deterministic local optimization algorithms, standardly used in combinatorial optimization, have been applied in inductive concept learning. Analysis of these optimization algorithms was performed on three well known machine learning domains. To enable simple testing of different optimization algorithms and simple design of experiments, the rule induction shell ATRIS was developed. At the moment it has six optimization algorithms and four heuristic estimates. Results of the experiments inspired the idea of combining the optimization algorithms to achieve an efficiency/accuracy tradeoff. Some algorithm combinations were tested by means of learning with one and post-processing with the other, while rule induction with two (or more) different optimization algorithms is left for further work.

In further work we plan to improve the noise-handling and classification methods, such as dealing with undefined attribute values, prediction of the class for an uncovered example, combining of rules covering the same classification example. It shoud be noted that in the experiments the simplest heuristic for estimating the expected classification accuracy was used. Certainly, better accuracy could have been achieved by using the other three heuristics already implemented . Some further improvement of results could be achieved by adding new optimization algorithms in the ATRIS shell (as *Tabu search* (Glover 1990)), as well as by using existing and adding new built-in background knowledge. The main idea which was provided by the experiments is that learning should be performed with some accurate and quite fast algorithm (e.g. *Markovian neural networks* post-processed with *3-OptF*) using an appropriate heuristic estimate considering noise in the specific domain. At the moment, using the ATRIS capability of choosing the attribute to be treated as the class and the attributes to be used in the hypothesis, learning of rules describing functional dependencies among attributes is being investigated (Savnik 1993).

[4]Notice that slightly lower accuracy achieved on 'primary tumor' could be a consequence of the fact that ATRIS assigns the majority attribute value to examples with unknown values and does not use the more sophisticate 'naive' Bayesian formula as ASSISTANT does.

Acknowledgements

This work was supported by the Slovenian Ministry of research and Technology. Medical data sets were obtained from the University Medical Center in Ljubljana, provided by Milan Sokolič ('lymphography') and Matjaž Zwitter ('primary tumor'). Chess endgame ('KRK') data set was originaly provided by Michael Bain. I wish to thank Marko Grobelnik, Nada Lavrač and Darko Zupanič for their contribution in the first phase of development of the ATRIS shell (Mladenić et al. 1992) and Ivan Bratko, Nada Lavrač, Ross Quinlan and Irma Sutlič for their comments to the paper.

References

Cestnik, B. (1990) Estimating probabilities: A crucial task in machine learning. *Proc. of ECAI'90*, pp. 147-149, Stockholm, Sweden.

Cestnik, B., Kononenko, I. and Bratko, I. (1987) ASSISTANT 86: A knowledge elicitation tool for sophisticated users. In Bratko, I. and Lavrač, N. (eds.) *Progress in machine learning*, pp. 31-45. Wilmslow, Sigma Press.

Cestnik, B. and Bratko, I. (1991) On estimating probabilities in tree pruning. *Fifth European Working Session on Learning, EWSL 91*, pp. 138-150. Porto, Portugal, Springer-Verlag.

Clark, P. and Niblett, T. (1989) The CN2 induction algorithm. *Machine Learning 3 (4)*, pp. 261-283. Kluwer Academic Publishers.

Clark, P. and Boswell, R. (1991) Rule induction with CN2: Some recent improvements. *Proc. of EWSL 91*, pp. 151-163. Porto, Portugal, Springer-Verlag.

De Jong, K.A. and Spears, W.M. (1991) Learning concept classification rules using genetic algorithms. *Proc. IJCAI-91*, pp. 651-656. Sydney, Australia. Morgan Kaufmann.

Glover, F. (1990) Tabu search – part I/II. *ORSA Journal on Computing 2, 3 (1)*, pp. (I) 190-206, (II) 4-32.

Kononenko, I. (1991) An experiment in machine learning of redundant knowledge. *Proc. of Intern. Conf.*

MELCON 1991, pp. 1146-1149. Ljubljana, Slovenia.

Kovačič, M. (1991) Markovian neural networks. *Biological Cybernetics 64*, pp. 337-342. Springer-Verlag.

Lavrač, N., Džeroski, S. and Grobelnik, M. (1991) Learning nonrecursive definitions of relations with LINUS. *Proc. of EWSL 91*, pp. 265-281. Porto, Portugal, Springer-Verlag.

Michalski, R.S., Mozetič, I., Hong, J. and Lavrač. N. (1986) The multipurpose incremental learning system AQ15 and its testing application to three medical domains. *Proc. of AAAI-86*, pp. 1041-1045. PA: Philadelphia. Morgan Kaufmann.

Mingers, J. (1989) An empirical comparison of pruning methods for decision tree induction. *Machine Learning 4 (2)*, pp. 319-342. Kluwer Academic Publishers.

Grobelnik, M. and Lavrač, N. (1992) Stochastic search in inductive concept learning. *Proc. of ISSEK Workshop'92*. Bled, Slovenia.

Papadimitriou, C.H. and Steiglitz, K. (1982) Optimization problems. In *Combinatorial optimization: Algorithms and complexity*, pp. 1-24. Prentice-Hall, Inc. Englewood Cliffs

Park, S.K. and Miller, K.W. (1988) Random number generators: good ones are hard to find. *Comm. ACM 31, 10*, pp. 1192-1201.

Press, W.H., Flannery, B.P., Teukolsky, S.A. and Vetterling, W.T. (1987) Combinatorial minimization: Method of simulated annealing. In *Numerical Recipes: The art of scientific computing*, pp. 326-334. Cambridge University Press.

Quinlan, J.R. (1986) Induction of decision trees. *Machine Learning 1*, pp. 81-106. Kluwer Academic Publishers.

Quinlan, J.R. (1987) Simplifying decision trees. *International Journal of Man-Machine Studies 27*, pp. 221-234. Academic Press.

Quinlan, J.R. (1991) Improved estimate for the accuracy of small disjuncts, Technical note. *Machine Learning 6*, pp. 93-98. Kluwer Academic Publishers.

Savnik, I. (1993) Induction of functional dependencies from relations. *Technical report*, J.Stefan Institute, Ljubljana, Slovenia.

Syslo, M.M., Deo, N. and Kowalik, J.S. (1983) Local search heuristics. In *Discrete optimization algorithms*, pp. 368-380. Prentice-Hall. Inc. Englewood Cliffs

Decision Theoretic Subsampling for Induction on Large Databases

Ron Musick
Computer Science Division
University of California
Berkeley, CA 94720
musick@cs.Berkeley.EDU

Jason Catlett
Room 6H-524, AT&T Bell Laboratories
600 Mountain Avenue (P.O. Box 636)
Murray Hill, NJ 07974-0636, USA
catlett@ulysses.att.com

Stuart Russell
Computer Science Division
University of California
Berkeley, CA 94720
russell@cs.Berkeley.EDU

Abstract

Standard methods of constructing decision trees can be prohibitively expensive when induction algorithms are given very large training sets on which to compare attributes. This expense can often be avoided. By using a subsample for this calculation, we can get an approximation to the information gain used to assess each attribute. Selecting an attribute on this basis involves a certain risk, which depends on the subsample size and the information gain values observed. This paper addresses the questions of assessing when the choice may be made with a given expected error, and determining a sampling strategy that minimizes the computation cost of making it. The theory is entirely analogous to that used for decision-theoretic control of search. An empirical evaluation shows that an implementation performs well over an appropriately wide range of inputs on two fundamental tasks: deciding whether a choice of attribute can be safely made on a given sample, and if not, estimating how large a subsample is likely to be required to do so.

1 INTRODUCTION

Decision tree learning has been perhaps the most successful machine learning technique in real-world applications. Unfortunately, several problems of scale arise when using the standard algorithms on the huge training sets offered by very large corporate and scientific databases. Extracting, handling, and learning from a large training set can represent a very considerable effort (sometimes days or more of both human and machine time). In some applications the benefit of increased accuracy obtained from the additional data justifies this expense, but often the economically rational decision is to use only a subset of the available training instances, discarding attributes that are not likely to be useful. The current state of the art lacks a sound and principled way to do this. There has been little theoretical machinery available to address the following very fundamental questions:

- How likely is it that a better choice of attribute at a node of a decision tree might be found if more training instances were used?
- How many training instances would be needed to confidently state that one attribute is at least as good as another?
- What sequence of subsamples from a large data set will be the most economical way to choose the best attribute to within a specified expected error?

This paper develops the machinery to answer such questions. Its most immediate application is to speed up the basic decision tree induction algorithm. An earlier approach to this problem [Catlett, 1992] shows that the algorithm can be reduced from roughly quadratic to linear time (in the number of training examples) without significant loss of accuracy by using sequential samples called peepholes. Two ad-hoc components of that method can now be placed on a sound analytical basis: the determination of whether an attribute should be discarded from consideration on larger peepholes, and the choice of the sizes for the peepholes.

Other uses can be made of these methods. For example, they can be applied to the task of deciding whether an attribute should be discarded completely from the induction process by monitoring how it compares to alternatives in situations of interest. This allows comparatively ineffective or redundant attributes to be weeded out, thus reducing learning time as training set sizes are scaled up. This can be done automatically, or interactively with a human expert. Despite this paper's focus on decision trees, these methods are also applicable to other selective induction algorithms where attributes are chosen based on similar information theoretic criteria.

Ultimately, we wish to control the tradeoff between the cost of induction from larger training sets and the increased accuracy they provide. This work makes significant progress towards that goal, providing both an analytical framework within which to consider these questions and an application of the concepts that is successful in empirical tests.

Section 2 recapitulates some technical background on the use of the information gain criterion for choosing attributes. Section 3 shows how the variance of the information gain can be estimated. Section 4 shows how to calculate the expected loss in information gain associated with making a choice from a given subsample. Section 5 turns this into a sampling strategy. Section 6 is an empirical evaluation of the first two parts of the method.

2 OVERVIEW

A top down decision tree learning algorithm [Quinlan, 1986] builds a decision tree classifier from a data set $\mathcal{S} = \{s_1 \ldots s_s\}$ using attributes $\mathcal{A} = \{A_1 \ldots A_m\}$. It operates by first selecting an attribute to form the root of the tree, then splitting the data set according to the attribute value and applying itself recursively to each subset thus formed. For large training sets, the major costs arise in selecting an attribute for the root of the current subtree, and in choosing appropriate threshold values for numeric attributes.

Attributes are normally selected using information gain calculations. The information gain of an attribute A_i given a sample $\mathcal{S}$ of size S is

$$g(A_i) = I(p, n) - e_i$$

where p, n are the numbers of positive and negative examples in the sample; $I(p, n)$ is the total information (in bits) required to classify a random example, given by

$$I(p,n) = -\frac{p}{p+n}\log_2\frac{p}{p+n} - \frac{n}{p+n}\log_2\frac{n}{p+n};$$

and e_i is the expected amount of information needed to classify a random example (the information content), given information about the value of A_i. Note that over the set of attributes, $I(p, n)$ is constant; thus for a relative measure of the information gain of the attributes, we need only consider e_i. If we assume, for the sake of simplicity of exposition, that the attribute is binary with values + and −, we then have (with $S = p_i^+ + n_i^+ + p_i^- + n_i^-$)

$$\begin{aligned} e_i &= \frac{p_i^+ + n_i^+}{S} I(p_i^+, n_i^+) + \frac{p_i^- + n_i^-}{S} I(p_i^-, n_i^-) \\ &= -\frac{p_i^+}{S}\log_2\left(\frac{p_i^+}{p_i^+ + n_i^+}\right) - \frac{n_i^+}{S}\log_2\left(\frac{n_i^+}{p_i^+ + n_i^+}\right) - \\ & \quad \frac{p_i^-}{S}\log_2\left(\frac{p_i^-}{p_i^- + n_i^-}\right) - \frac{n_i^-}{S}\log_2\left(\frac{n_i^-}{p_i^- + n_i^-}\right) \qquad (1) \end{aligned}$$

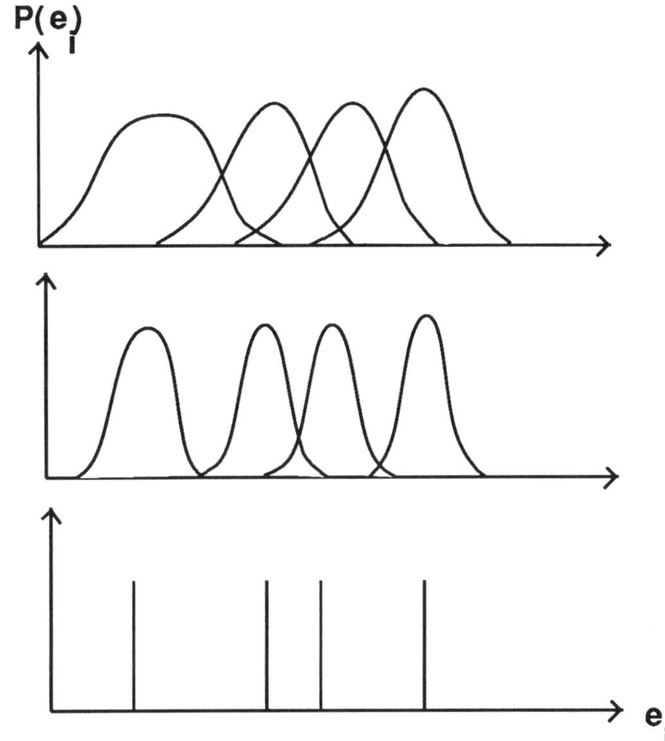

Figure 1: **Attribute Gain Distributions**
Probability distributions of attribute gains for small, medium and complete samples.

Our method works by considering subsamples of the entire data set. Given a subsample, we estimate the actual information content of each attribute with Equation 1. From this, we can derive the conditional probability distribution for the true information content given the estimated version. It turns out that the conditional probability distribution is in fact approximately normal.

Figure 1 illustrates these distributions for four attributes. The top figure shows a typical situation with a small sample, where the gain is plotted on the x-axis and its probability on the y-axis. The second shows the situation after more examples have been examined, and the third shows the situation after the database has been exhausted. When trying to pick the best attribute, it is clear that a choice made using the small sample is quite likely to be wrong, whereas we probably don't need to wait until the database is exhausted to be reasonably sure of the right choice. This shows a strong analogy to the problem of picking the best move in game-playing, when only the estimates of move values are available to work with. The techniques used here are thus similar in concept to those in [Russell and Wefald, 1991]. The following sections show how to calculate both the distributions and the expected information loss associated with selecting an attribute on the basis of a subsample. Given this information, we can calculate the expected increase in the quality of the selected attribute from further sampling, compare it to the cost of sampling, and thus derive an optimal stopping point.

3 INFORMATION CONTENT DISTRIBUTIONS

Let $f_i^S(x_i)$ be the distribution of the random variable x_i, representing the true information content of A_i, given a subsample $\mathcal{S}$ of size S. Like many sample statistics, e_i is approximately normally distributed around the information content $\hat{e}_i$ estimated from the subsample:[1]

$$f_i^S(x_i) \approx N[\hat{e}_i, \sigma_i].$$

The variance σ_i for the sample can be determined exactly. Let r_1 be the random variable that represents the true fraction of positive instances that attribute A_i classifies as +, given $\mathcal{S}$ (so $\frac{p_i^+}{S}$ is the current best estimate of r_1). Also, let r_2, r_3 and r_4 be defined similarly, with estimates $\frac{n_i^+}{S}, \frac{p_i^-}{S}$, and $\frac{n_i^-}{S}$. Then, from Equation 1, the variance is given as

$$\begin{aligned} \sigma_i^2 &= var(r_1 \log_2(\frac{r_1}{r_1+r_2}) + r_2 \log_2(\frac{r_2}{r_1+r_2}) + \\ &\quad r_3 \log_2(\frac{r_3}{r_3+r_4}) + r_4 \log_2(\frac{r_4}{r_3+r_4})). \quad (2) \end{aligned}$$

Under sampling with replacement, the joint distribution $f(r_1, r_2, r_3, r_4)$ is a dirichlet, and the marginal distribution of each variable is a beta (for example, r_1 is distributed as a beta with the parameters p_i^+ and $S - p_i^+$). We can solve for σ_i^2 exactly with the use of the digamma function (Ψ) and its derivative. Keeping in mind that

$$var(x) = E(x^2) - E(x)^2,$$

the trick is to find an exact expression for $E(\log_2 r_1)$ and $E(r_1 \log_2 r_1)$, then manipulate these expressions to find σ_i^2. We will sketch the derivation of these quantities.

First, for $E(\log_2 r_1)$, we know that:

$$E(\log_2 r_1) = \frac{E(\ln r_1)}{\log_2 e} = \frac{\int \ln(r_1) r_1^{p_i^+-1}(1-r_1)^{S-p_i^+-1}dr_1}{\beta(p_i^+, S-p_i^+)log_2 e}.$$

The next critical piece of information is:

$$\begin{aligned} \frac{\partial}{\partial a_1} \ln \beta(a_1, a_2) &= \frac{\partial}{\partial \beta(a_1,a_2)} \ln \beta(a_1, a_2) \frac{\partial}{\partial a_1} \beta(a_1, a_2) \\ &= \frac{\int \frac{\partial}{\partial a_1} r_1^{a_1-1}(1-r_1)^{S-a_1-1}dr_1}{\beta(a_1, S-a_1)} \\ &= \frac{\int \ln(r_1) r_1^{a_1-1}(1-r_1)^{S-a_1-1}dr_1}{\beta(a_1, S-a_1)}. \end{aligned}$$

[1]Empirical tests on the goodness of fit of the normal to the actual distribution show that though not exact, the fit is reasonably good.

It follows that

$$E(log_2 r_1) = \frac{1}{log_2 e} \frac{\partial}{\partial p_i^+} \ln \beta(p_i^+, S-p_i^+).$$

Finally,

$$\begin{aligned} \frac{\partial}{\partial a_1} \ln \beta(a_1, a_2) &= \frac{\partial}{\partial a_1} \ln \frac{\Gamma(a_1)\Gamma(a_2)}{\Gamma(a_1+a_2)} \\ &= \Psi(a_1) - \Psi(a_1+a_2), \end{aligned}$$

giving

$$E(log_2 r_1) = \frac{1}{log_2 e}(\Psi(p_i^+) - \Psi(S)). \quad (3)$$

The derivation of $E(r_1 \log_2 r_1)$ follows in a similar manner:

$$E(r_1 \log_2 r_1) = \frac{\int r_1 \ln(r_1) r_1^{p_i^+-1}(1-r_1)^{S-p_i^+-1}dr_1}{\beta(p_i^+, S-p_i^+)log_2 e},$$

$$\begin{aligned} \frac{\partial}{\partial a_1} \ln \beta(a_1+1, a_2) &= \frac{\int r_1 \ln(r_1) r_1^{a_1-1}(1-r_1)^{S-a_1-1}dr_1}{\beta(a_1+1, S-a_1)} \\ &= \Psi(a_1+1) - \Psi(a_1+a_2+1), \end{aligned}$$

resulting in

$$E(r_1 \log_2 r_1) = \frac{1}{log_2 e} \frac{p_i^+}{S}(\Psi(p_i^+ + 1) - \Psi(S+1)). \quad (4)$$

The $\frac{p_i^+}{S}$ term comes from $\frac{\beta(p_i^+ + 1, S-p_i^+)}{\beta(p_i^+, S-p_i^+)}$.

Simple extensions can made to Equations 3 and 4 to complete the solution for σ_i^2. The main advantage of this formulation of the variance is that the digamma function and its derivative (which shows up for terms like $E(r^2(log_2 r)^2)$) has several quick and accurate approximations [Abramowitz and Stegun, 1972], which lead to fast computation of variances that are as precise as desired.

4 EXPECTED LOSS

Consider choosing between just two attributes A_1 and A_2, where we assume without loss of generality that the estimated gain of A_1 is currently higher than that of A_2 (Figure 2). What is the expected loss in information gain associated with choosing A_1?

If A_1 has true gain x_1, and A_2 has true gain x_2, then if $x_2 > x_1$, the loss is $x_2 - x_1$. Otherwise, there is no loss. Hence the expected loss is given by[2]

$$L(S) = \int_{x_1=0}^{1} \int_{x_2=x_1}^{1} (x_2 - x_1) f_2^S(x_2) f_1^S(x_1) dx_2 dx_1. \quad (5)$$

[2]This assumes independence of the attribute gains; that is to say that knowledge of the gain of one attribute does not affect the prediction of the gain of the second attribute.

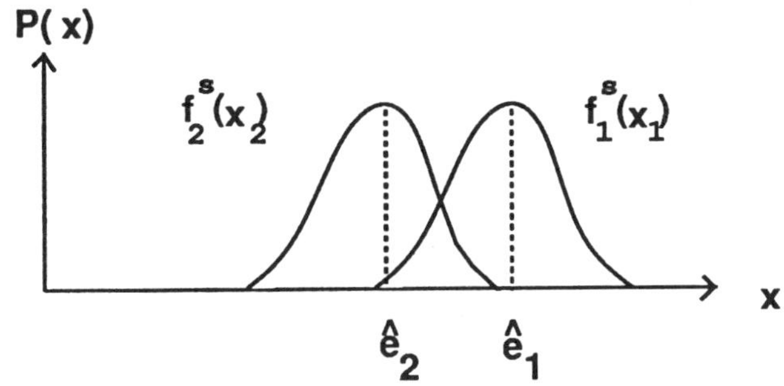

Figure 2: **Expected Loss**
Choosing A_1 may incur a loss if A_2 is actually better.

Inserting the normal approximations for $f_1^S(x_1)$ and $f_2^S(x_2)$ obtained above, and realizing that $y = x_2 - x_1$ is the normal $N(\hat{e} = \hat{e_2} - \hat{e_1}, \sigma = \sqrt{\sigma_1^2 + \sigma_2^2})$, we get

$$\hat{L}(S) = \frac{1}{\sigma\sqrt{2\pi}} \int_{y=0}^{1} y e^{-\frac{(y-\hat{e})^2}{2\sigma^2}} dy. \quad (6)$$

This is an approximation because it is possible for x_1 or x_2 to be greater than 1 (which is not a valid information content), but for $y = x2 - x1 \in [0, 1]$, and thus be counted in Equation 6. The integral is easy to solve, and the approximation begins to degrade only when the information content comes to within a standard deviation or two of 1, at which point $\hat{L}(S)$ provides an upper bound on $L(S)$. Because $\hat{L}(S) \geq L(S)$, the solution proposed here will tend to be somewhat conservative, and thus tend to take larger samples than required. However, the empirical results in Section 6 show that this effect is barely noticeable.

5 SAMPLING STRATEGY

To find the optimal stopping point, we need information on the expected quality of the tree, the cost of sampling, and a utility measure specifying what the user is willing to pay for different quality trees. As a preliminary cut, we use the expected loss $\hat{L}(S)$ as the quality measure (the smaller the loss, the higher the quality), and allow only the simplest form of a utility measure, a single point, the *loss tolerance*. This measure is such that a decision made with a quality worse than the loss tolerance has no value, and a decision made with quality greater than or equal to the loss tolerance has full value.

Given this information, a simple approach to reach the optimal stopping point (the one-shot approach) is to calculate the expected required sample size (ERSS) needed to reach the loss tolerance, and then to take a sample of that size. This approach has drawbacks, but the calculation of ERSS is useful both in itself, and for the next section.

The first step is to find the variance σ_{lt}^2 required to satisfy the equation

$$\hat{L}(S) - \textit{loss tolerance} = 0. \quad (7)$$

Then, any sample of sufficient size to produce a variance less than or equal to σ_{lt}^2 is acceptable in that it will be likely to produce a tree with full utility. The ERSS is the smallest such sample size. To solve Equation 7, take a small initial sample of a few hundred instances, calculate the parameters $\hat{e}$, and σ^2, then solve by iteration for the σ that satisfies Equation 7. We only vary σ in $\hat{L}(S)$ because it is the sole parameter that changes in a fairly predictable manner as the sample size increases. The other parameter, $\hat{e}$, is determined by the ratios $\frac{p_i^+}{S}, \frac{n_i^+}{S}, \frac{p_i^-}{S}$ and $\frac{n_i^-}{S}$. The most informed choice that can be made here is to assume that as S increases, the ratios, and therefore $\hat{e}$ will remain constant. In empirical trials, we used a bisection iteration to solve for σ_{lt}, which turned out to be efficient. To date, it has required no more than 12 iterations to reach a solution.

The last step is to relate the sample size S with the variance. To do this, we compute a second order polynomial from two points: (σ^2, S) from the original sample, and $(\sigma'^2, 2S)$. The ERSS is the sample size along this curve that corresponds to σ_{lt}^2. The empirical results show that this calculation of the ERSS meets with good success.

However, the one-shot sampling approach is not adequate; what is needed is a sampling *strategy* that determines an entire sequence of samples to take. ERSS is an estimate of I^*, the optimal number of random samples required to reach the loss tolerance. The argument against the one-shot strategy is that once an ERSS is produced, we have an estimate for I^* based on some incomplete information (information that currently can not support a decision that meets the loss tolerance). If the next sample size is simply the ERSS, the risk is run that ERSS $\gg I^*$ (in fact, we occasionally saw ERSSs of up to 42 million instances, from initial sample sizes of 250). The opposite approach is to increase each sample size by one instance, until the expected loss matches the loss tolerance; but this approach is likely to be very expensive. Somewhere in the middle of these two extremes lies a more rational strategy.

5.1 SIZE OF THE NEXT SAMPLE

The goal is to find a large enough sample $\mathcal{S}$ so that Equation 7 is satisfied, but to do this with minimal cost (in this case, time). The generic algorithm for this problem has the form:

On iteration k, $k \in 1..n$

1. Grab or generate a random sample $\mathcal{S}_k$.
2. Compute $\hat{L}(S)$
3. If $\hat{L}(S) \leq$ *loss tolerance* then stop; else
4. Determine the size $\mathcal{S}_{k+1}$ for the next step, Goto 1.

The cost of this operation is dependent on the size S_k of the sample[3]. The cost can be modeled as a linear function of two factors: the overhead time required to process a sample of any size, and the additional time required for each instance in the sample (c and i, respectively). Therefore the cost of one operation (one sample) is $c + S_k i$, and the total cost of the algorithm is $nc + \sum_{k=1}^{n} S_k i$. Since the minimal cost is $c + I^* i$, we want to find the variables n and S_k (for $k \in 1..n$) that minimize[4]

$$nc + \sum_{k=1}^{n} S_k i - (c + I^* i).$$

At this point we restrict the general form of the algorithm. The restriction is to force $S_j = S_k = S$ on each iteration, and furthermore to add each sample $\mathcal{S}_k$ to the previous samples $\mathcal{S}_1 \ldots \mathcal{S}_{k-1}$ when computing $\hat{L}(S)$. By combining subsequent samples like this, we are essentially building up the final sample $\mathcal{S}$ one chunk at a time. The new form of the minimization is to find the n and S that minimize

$$nc + nSi - (c + I^* i). \tag{8}$$

With this restricted algorithm, the stopping condition tells us that the sample on the last iteration will be at most $S - 1$ instances larger than I^*. To solve the minimization, set $nS - I^* = S - 1$, giving $n = \frac{S-1+I^*}{S}$. Substitute this into Equation 8, and minimize by setting the derivative to 0. Since I^* is unknown, estimate it with the ERSS.

The result is that the suggested size of the next sample to take is

$$S = \sqrt{(ERSS - 1)\frac{c}{i}}. \tag{9}$$

Note that $\frac{c}{i}$ is a machine/algorithm specific constant which can be estimated for any system.

The end result is to choose the next size of the sample as a function of the square root of the ERSS, as opposed to immediately generating a sample of size ERSS. In the implementation, we calculate the next sample size based on Equation 8, but allow ERSS to change with each iteration (the additional information gives a better estimate of I^*).

[3]Note that cost of steps 2, 3 and 4 of the operation are independent of the sample size, they just depend on summary statistics of the sample.

[4]The trivial solution $n = 1$, $S_1 = I^*$ is not acceptable, it is the one-shot approach.

6 EVALUATION

There are two hypotheses that could be tested in an empirical evaluation of these methods:

1. the algorithm's answers (decision whether to defer the choice and if so, the estimated sample size required to commit) are sensible on an appropriately wide range of inputs, and
2. when the algorithm is used in the construction of decision trees, the resulting speedup and any loss of accuracy are appropriate to the parameters used.

This paper tests the first, more fundamental hypothesis only. The fact that faster choices of attribute (using similar but ad hoc techniques) can lead to speedups of at least an order of magnitude on practical tasks has already been established in previous work [Catlett, 1992]. This section describes the evaluation method used to test the first hypothesis, and presents and discusses the results.

6.1 METHOD OF EVALUATION

The evaluation uses synthetic data rather than data from real domains, because we need to know the value of a parameter which is not obtainable on real data: the true difference in information gain (DIG) between two attributes. The information gain (IG) for an attribute computed from some finite set of examples is only an estimate of the "true" IG. As the sample size increases, the relative frequencies of each combination of class and attribute value converge towards the true joint distribution, so the estimates for IG converge towards the attribute's "true" IG. With synthetic data, we start with the occult knowledge of the true distribution and use it to generate the counts for class and attribute values according to the desired sample size. But it can also be used to calculate the attribute's true IG, along with the DIG between a pair of attributes following two possibly different distributions. The DIG provides a measure of both the difficulty of choosing between the attributes and of the gravity of making the wrong choice. Choosing between a pair of attributes with a large DIG such as 0.1 bits will typically be easy even on a small sample of a hundred examples; but making the wrong choice is likely to yield a less accurate tree.

As a concrete illustration of what could for practical purposes be considered a small value for DIG, we duplicated Quinlan's [Quinlan, 1986] 14 element weather data 512 times and compared the original attribute "outlook" (gain of 0.24675 bits) with an almost identical copy where one of the 7168 examples had been corrupted so as to disadvantage it most (the first example's value was changed from "sunny" to "overcast"). The DIG between the original and the corrupted attribute was 0.00163 bits. In consideration of this, we usually quote figures for DIGs in millibits.

Our experiments present the algorithm with millions of choices between attributes, following a wide variety of sample sizes, distributions (hence DIGs) and loss tolerances. For the sake of anyone who wishes to reproduce the evaluation or to investigate the nature of the set of the distributions used, this paragraph specifies the parameterized procedure that generates the set. Taking the simplest case of two attributes (A and B) with two values each (a^+, a^-, b^+, b^-) and two classes (p and n), a complete joint distribution on these three variables can be specified with the probabilities of eight mutually exclusive and exhaustive events. Each joint distribution is computed from seven numbers representing the following conditional probabilities: $P(p), P(a^+|p), P(b^+|p, a^+)$, $P(b^+|p, a^-), P(a^+|n)$, $P(b^+|n, a^+)$, and $P(b^+|n, a^-)$. The specific values taken for probabilities were $1/2, 1/4, ... 1/2^{ndv}$, where the positive integer ndv is the parameter given to the procedure. These values are taken in every combination by the seven conditional probabilities, so the number of distributions it produces is ndv^7. These experiments used $ndv = 4$, generating 16384 distributions. For each combination of 13 values for sample size and 3 for loss tolerance, only a single set of class and attribute value counts was generated; ideally many should be used.

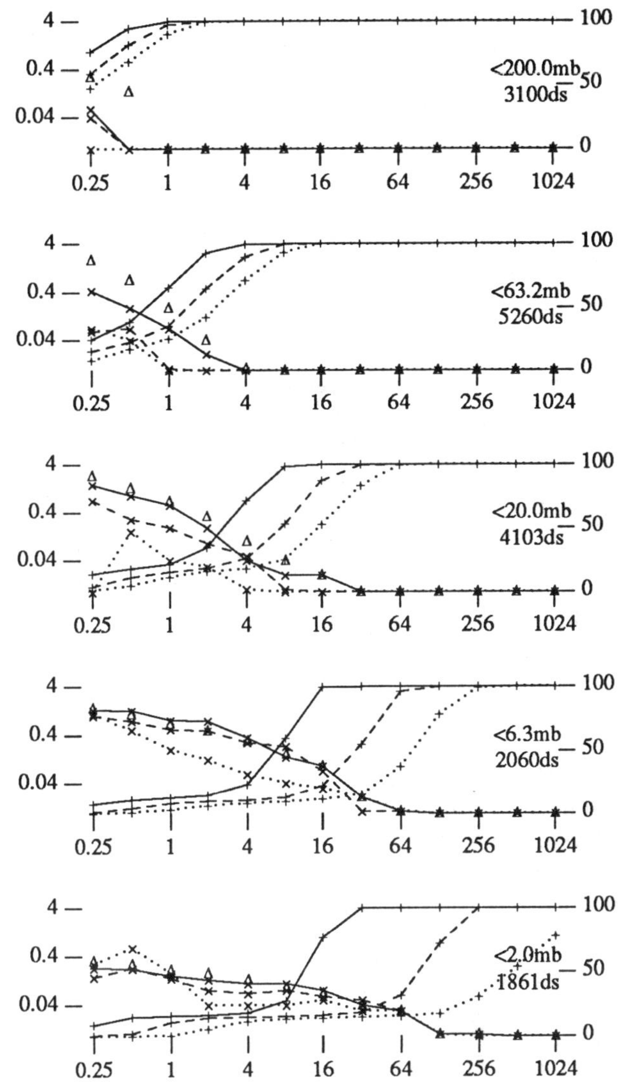

Figure 3: **Commit Rates and Average Loss**
For legend, see Section 6.2

6.2 CHOICE OF COMMIT OR DEFER

The two dependent variables measured in this experiment are the commit rate (the percentage of cases on which the algorithm committed to a choice between the two attributes), and the average loss (the sum of the DIGS for those cases where the attribute with the smaller gain was chosen, divided by the number of cases with a committed decision, whether right or wrong). The distributions are separated into five "buckets," each containing all those with the DIGS within a certain range, as indicated in the graphs of Figure 3. The upper number with one place after the decimal point at the center right of each graph gives the upper limit on DIGs in millibits (mb) appearing in the bucket; the lower limit is implicitly the upper limit of the next bucket. The integer below it gives the number of distributions in each bucket. The lowest graph covers distributions where the DIGs are so low that the attributes are identical or practically indistinguishable; its lower limit is zero.

The graphs share the following format. The log scale x-axis shows the size of the samples generated in units of thousands of examples. The linear scale y-axis on the right side of the graph refers to the percentage of samples on which a decision was made (the commit rate). The log scale y-axis on the left indicates the average loss on those samples where a decision was made, in millibits. Values less than 0.01mb are are lumped together as zero. Curves for both commit rate (marked by a "+") and average loss (marked by an "×") are provided for three values of loss tolerance: 4mb (solid), 0.4mb (dashed), and 0.04mb (dotted). Triangles mark the average losses that are sustained by the "strawman" alternative of always committing to the attribute with the larger information gain on the sample.

The broad trends in the graph are as one would expect. The strawman loss curves tend steadily towards zero as sample size is increased. The steeper slope of these curves for the larger DIGs is due to two factors. The average losses tend to be larger on small samples, because the individual losses (DIGs) being averaged are larger, and because the decision is more often wrong on the small sample than on a larger sample. Every commit curve has an S-shape; the "knee" where it ramps up is pushed to the right as DIG decreases (lower buckets) and as loss tolerance decreases (from solid to dashed to dotted curves). Intuitively, this means more examples are required as the alternatives become more similar and as higher accuracy is requested.

The loss curve for a lower loss tolerance is generally lower; a few exceptions occur for very small commit rates where the figure given as average loss may consist of a single case. The solid curve (greatest tolerance, hence least conservative) sustains losses below the strawman's only on the upper three buckets. The dashed curve is more conservative: on the upper buckets, it maintains losses that are roughly an order of magnitude below the strawman losses. Its knee consistently sits around the point where the strawman losses drop below 0.04. The dotted loss curve is the most conservative: its losses are so low on all buckets that they are only occasionally distinguishable from zero. Giving the algorithm a loss tolerance of 40mb or more yielded a 100% commit rate across the board.

It is unreasonable to expect the commit rate to jump to 100% as soon as the average loss in one of the buckets drops below the loss tolerance. The algorithm has the task of keeping the average loss below the loss tolerance over all the distributions given to it that could have produced a given sample (weighted by the probability of that distribution given the sample), not just over distributions with true DIGs within a certain specified range.

6.3 RESULTS FOR THE ERSS

The second experiment assesses the accuracy of the algorithm's forecasts for the expected required sample size (ERSS) to commit. To do this we create a new pair of cases from each case on which the algorithm defers, generating more examples[5] from the same distribution as the original case: the number of examples in one of the pair is slightly larger (25%) than the size indicated by the ERSS; in the other it is slightly smaller. Both of these enlarged samples are then given to the algorithm to see whether it commits. We deem the ERSS accurate on the case if the algorithm commits on the larger sample but defers on the smaller one. If it defers on both we deem the ERSS underestimated. If it commits on both we deem it overestimated. The unhappy last combination, where it commits on the smaller sample and defers on the larger one, can never be eradicated because of the stochastic way the cases are generated; we call these results "reversed." Table 1 shows the percentages for each of these four combinations, over a variety of loss tolerances and sample sizes. The third column gives the number of cases on which the algorithm deferred.

LT mbits	SS 1000's	NC	Under %	Hit %	Over %	Rev %
4	0.25	11857	36.9	24.5	34.5	4.1
4	0.5	10153	33.0	30.0	32.8	4.2
4	1	8351	27.6	37.7	30.0	4.8
4	2	6362	23.7	44.7	26.8	4.8
4	4	4270	19.0	52.5	23.2	5.3
4	8	2225	15.0	61.8	18.8	4.4
4	16	439	9.6	77.2	10.3	3.0
4	32	0	-	-	-	-
0.4	0.25	14427	41.9	17.2	38.1	2.8
0.4	0.5	13141	39.9	20.0	37.6	2.6
0.4	1	11706	37.1	24.2	35.8	2.9
0.4	2	10179	34.6	28.2	34.5	2.7
0.4	4	8375	32.2	34.6	30.9	2.4
0.4	8	6894	29.2	39.7	28.4	2.7
0.4	16	5358	25.8	47.3	24.7	2.1
0.4	32	4014	21.9	53.9	22.0	2.1
0.4	64	2880	18.0	63.3	16.8	1.9
0.4	128	1973	14.8	68.7	14.8	1.7
0.4	256	1303	12.6	74.0	11.4	2.0
0.4	512	854	8.0	81.4	8.7	2.0
0.4	1024	412	11.2	76.5	10.9	1.5

Table 1: **ERSS Accuracy**
Accuracy of estimated required sample size for the algorithm to commit.

Hit rates rise monotonically: the greater the sample size, the more accurate the figure for ERSS. For a given sample size, greater accuracy is obtained where loss tolerance is greater. This is very plausible because small loss tolerances require larger samples to commit on, so the correct figure for ERSS becomes a more distant target. At all times the percentages for under- and over-estimates are approximately equal, as we would want.

For practical purposes, the important conclusion to be drawn from this table is that after a few thousand examples, the majority of the estimates of the required sample size are fairly accurate (+/-25%), and that the algorithm behaves sensibly and smoothly over the relevant range of parameters. For a wider tolerance (+/-50%), the majority is reached at 500 examples for 4mbits and 2000 for 0.4 mbits.

7 CONCLUSION

This paper raised four questions important to large-scale induction: how to decide whether the better attribute can be confidently chosen on a given subsample, how to estimate the size of the subsample required to do so, how much is this choice likely to cost in terms information gain, and how to choose the sequence of

[5] Both the new cases included all the counts from the original cases, as this is consistent with the algorithm's approach. The evaluation could also be done with the new cases generated from independent samples, which may better suit other methods.

subsamples to achieve this most efficiently. The theory and detailed methods to address these issues were presented, along with an empirical evaluation of most of them.

Future work includes an evaluation of the sampling strategy, and in the longer term, adding the capacity to relate information gain to accuracy during the construction of the tree, which would allow the induction process to be tailored to the economics of the particular application being built.

Acknowledgements

We thank Wray Buntine for the variance derivation, Kenji Yamanishi of NEC Research Institute for early discussions, and the anonymous reviewers for their comments. The second author's contribution was based largely on work at the University of Sydney that was supported in part by the Australian Research Council. The third author was supported in part by NSF PYI Award IRI-9058427.

References

[Abramowitz and Stegun, 1972] M. Abramowitz and I. Stegun. *Handbook of Mathematical Functions.* Dover Publications, New York, 1972.

[Catlett, 1992] J. Catlett. Peepholing: choosing attributes efficiently for megainduction. In *Proceedings of the Ninth International Conference in Machine Learning*, pages 49–54, 1992.

[Quinlan, 1986] J. R. Quinlan. Induction of decision trees. *Machine Learning*, 1:81–106, 1986.

[Russell and Wefald, 1991] S. J. Russell and E.H. Wefald. *Do the Right Thing: Studies in Limited Rationality.* MIT Press, Cambridge, MA, 1991.

Learning DNF Via Probabilistic Evidence Combination

Steven W. Norton and Haym Hirsh
Department of Computer Science
Hill Center for the Mathematical Sciences
Busch Campus
Rutgers University
New Brunswick, NJ 08903
norton@cs.rutgers.edu, hirsh@cs.rutgers.edu

Abstract

One approach to learning DNF expressions from examples is to use a conjunctive learner to separately form each of the disjuncts. This paper describes a learning algorithm that follows this approach, extending our earlier work on learning conjunctive classifiers from noisy data to learning DNF classifiers from noisy data. Because every disjunct does not cover every positive example, such learners must decide which positive examples to cover with each disjunct being learned. The central idea here is to model as *representational noise* the uncertainty as to whether a positive example should be treated as positive for a particular disjunct, in addition to whatever other noise may be imposed on the data by the environment. In experiments with synthetic data our learning method exhibits statistically significantly lower error rates during early learning when compared to the C4.5 algorithm, and on seven out of eight real-world datasets the error rates of classifiers learned by the new algorithm meet or exceed those of the classifiers learned by C4.5.

1 INTRODUCTION

The classifier learning problem is to use a set of labeled training data to induce a concept description that will accurately classify as yet unseen testing data. In past work [Norton and Hirsh, 1992] we introduced an approach to this problem based on incremental probabilistic evidence combination, and showed that it exhibits superior early-learning error rates when used to learn conjunctive classifiers from noisy data. One important feature of the conjunctive learner is that it allows knowledge about the training data to be brought to bear during learning, such as models of label and attribute noise, as well as hybrid models that combine multiple noise models.

However, learning conjunctions is a problem of somewhat limited scope, and more practical learning systems must be able to learn in more expressive languages. This paper extends our earlier work to the problem of learning DNF classifiers from noisy data. The basic idea is to apply the conjunctive learner iteratively to learn a term at a time until the entire DNF classifier is formed. In doing so we are using a separate-and-conquer strategy similar to that of the AQ system and its successors [Michalski, 1983, Michalski *et al.*, 1986]. Two notable features that distinguish this approach from AQ are its ability to use knowledge about the nature of the training data (such as models of noise) and its ability to form multiple terms on each iteration.

Underlying our approach is a solution to a problem facing all separate-and-conquer learners [Clark and Niblett, 1989, Michalski *et al.*, 1986, Pagallo and Haussler, 1990, Quinlan, 1990], namely that not all positive examples of the full disjunctive expression are actually classified as positive by all disjuncts. Thus some of the positive examples should effectively be treated as *negative* examples for some disjuncts. The difficulty is knowing which positive examples to treat as negative for which disjuncts.

Our solution is to exploit the conjunctive learner's ability to use a model of noise and to model the uncertainty as to whether an example should truly be treated as positive as a case of *representational noise.* The problem of finding a single term is viewed as one of finding a conjunctive "approximation" to the desired DNF expression, where the overall learner returns the disjunction of these conjunctive approximations. The result is that the learning algorithm reasons about all the training data when learning each disjunct, and based on its representational-noise model decides automatically how each example should be treated. The learner is furthermore able to take into account other domain-specific knowledge characterizing the underlying noise process.

This approach has been implemented in the IPEC-

DNF learning system (Induction as Probabilistic Evidence Combination—DNF). On synthetic data, IPEC-DNF exhibits statistically significantly lower error rates early in learning and asymptotically equivalent error rates later in learning when compared to the C4.5 algorithm [Quinlan, 1987]. Since in real-world learning problems one is constrained to use whatever amount of data is provided, and in many cases this quantity is limited, an advantage early in learning is important. In fact, on seven of the eight real-world databases tested, IPEC-DNF learns classifiers that meet or exceed the accuracy of those learned by C4.5 as determined by 10-fold cross-validation.

The paper is structured as follows. Section 2 describes the conjunctive term learner. Section 3 then gives examples of four noise models that can be used by the conjunctive term learner: noiseless data, label noise, representational noise, and finally the combination of label and representational noise that is used by the conjunctive learner in its role as part of IPEC-DNF. Section 4 describes the overall approach for learning DNF from noisy data, and is followed by experimental results in Section 5. A discussion of future work and a final summary conclude the paper in Sections 6 and 7.

2 LEARNING CONJUNCTIONS AS INCREMENTAL PROBABILISTIC EVIDENCE COMBINATION

Learning can be formulated as a problem of reasoning under uncertainty [Duda and Hart, 1973, Buntine, 1990, Norton and Hirsh, 1992]. Initially the concept description language delimits the set of legal classifiers and the learner is uncertain as to the identity of the correct one. As training data are processed, some classifiers become more likely as others become less likely. The learner converges to a final result as uncertainty is gradually reduced.

In MAP learning, maximum *a posteriori* probability is used as the criterion for selecting a concept description as the final result of learning. In particular, the *a posteriori* probability of a hypothesis is the probability of the hypothesis given all available evidence. The MAP approach says to choose the hypothesis with greatest *a posteriori* probability. In the context of inductive classifier learning, if H_i is a possible classifier and S^* the set of correct training data, the MAP approach dictates that the most desirable hypothesis is whichever H_i maximizes $P(H_i|S^*)$.

However, data are often subject to noise, and thus S^* is usually unavailable to the learning algorithm. Learning must therefore make do with the actual observed data O, which may (and often will) differ from the true data S^* due to whatever noise processes are at work in the domain. In general, such noise processes can induce both label noise and attribute noise. In the specific context of MAP learning, noise processes are described probabilistically by a distribution $P(o|s)$ relating single observations to single true examples. When noise is present it is impossible to maximize $P(H_i|S^*)$ since S^* is unknown, and thus the MAP learning approach instead maximizes $P(H_i|O)$, since it is O, rather than S^*, that is actually available to the learner.

In more detail, the MAP approach taken in our past work involves making informed speculations about the nature of the true but unseen data S^* based on the observed data O and on knowledge of the noise process. These speculations give rise to multiple "supposed" sequences of data, each of which may be the actual, but unobserved, training data. Let $VS(S_j)$ denote the set (i.e. version space) of classifiers that correctly classify each example in a sequence S_j. Furthermore, let $P(O|S_j)$ represent the probability that sequence O is observed if S_j is in fact the true data sequence. Our earlier paper showed that for any classifier H_i, $P(H_i|O)$ is proportional to

$$\sum_{\substack{j \\ H_i \in VS(S_j)}} P(O|S_j) \tag{1}$$

Our approach is to maintain during learning a list of *evidence tuples* of the form $\langle VS(S_j), P(O|S_j)\rangle$, each representing the set of classifiers consistent with a supposed sequence together with the probability that the sequence accounts for the observations.[1] No further information is required to evaluate posterior probabilities $P(H_i|O)$.

To implement this approach, the preceding reformulation of the basic MAP objective function can itself be reformulated into a form particularly suitable for *incrementally* processing data, and leads to the following pair of update equations, one for the set of classifiers consistent with a supposed sequence and another for the probability that the supposed sequence accounts for the observed data:

$$VS(S_j^{m+1}) = VS(S_j^m) \cap VS(s_j^{m+1}) \tag{2}$$
$$P(O^{m+1}|S_j^{m+1}) = P(O^m|S_j^m)P(o^{m+1}|s_j^{m+1}) \tag{3}$$

(s_j^i represents the i-th element of data sequence S_j, S_j^i represents the first i elements of data sequence S_j, o^i represents the i-th observation, and $VS(s)$ represents the version space of classifiers consistent with the single example s). In English, according to Equation (2) the set of classifiers consistent with a sequence of $m+1$ supposed examples can be computed by intersecting

[1]Note that the set of classifiers consistent with a sequence is maintained rather than the sequence itself. This way the learner can recognize inconsistent sequences, identifiable when their version spaces collapse, and prune such sequences or tuples as they arise.

the set consistent with the first m examples and the set consistent with the last example [Hirsh, 1990]. According to Equation (3) the conditional probability of the observed data sequence given a supposed sequence can be computed by multiplying the conditional probabilities of each of the sequence's component examples.

To learn, each example is converted into and represented as a set of evidence tuples representing the supposed examples that may have given rise to the observed example, together with the probability of that happening. A complete learning session begins with complete uncertainty; this is represented by the single evidence tuple $\langle VS(\emptyset), 1.0\rangle$ where $VS(\emptyset)$ denotes the set of all legal conjunctive classifiers. Each individual observation results in a set of evidence tuples (whose particulars depend of course on the given model of noise). This set of evidence tuples is combined with the tuples for past evidence using Equations (2) and (3). If n evidence tuples $\langle VS_i, P_i\rangle$ result from learning on past data, and k new tuples $\langle VS_j, P_j\rangle$ express the evidence of the new example, learning computes kn updated tuples $\langle VS_i \cap VS_j, P_i \times P_j\rangle$ and then removes all tuples having empty version spaces (which correspond to inconsistent supposed sequences).

One practical issue this approach faces when implemented is that learning can potentially generate an exponential number of evidence tuples: if every example generates two evidence tuples, and no version space collapses, then processing each example doubles the number of evidence tuples maintained by the learner. The implementation of this MAP approach therefore trades off correctness for efficiency and simply removes version spaces associated with sufficiently unlikely supposed sequences (i.e., those with low posterior probabilities). This controls the complexity and does not seem to sacrifice accuracy.[2]

Finally, each tuple contains a *set* of classifiers, and it is necessary to specify how a single final classifier is returned as the result of learning. When the evidence representation method for a given model always coverts data into tuples with disjoint sets of classifiers the evidence representation is said to be *disjoint.* Disjoint evidence representations are fairly common, and they include all the evidence representations considered in this paper. Disjoint evidence schemes are particularly convenient since they imply that all evidence tuples at each step of learning will be disjoint, and therefore any hypothesis H_i will be in at most one tuple. The result is that all classifiers with highest posterior probability appear only in a single tuple, the one with highest probability, and some element from this version space should be returned as the result of learning. The implementation described here simply selects the most specific classifier from this highest-rated set (i.e., it selects the singleton S-set element from the highest-rated tuple's version space).

[2]The implementation furthermore uses the $[S, N]$ representation for version spaces [Hirsh, 1992] to avoid the potential for exponentially large boundary-set representations for the version spaces [Mitchell, 1982, Haussler, 1988]. The key operations of updating version spaces and checking for collapse are efficient in the $[S, N]$ representation.

3 EXAMPLES OF NOISE MODELS

The preceding section described our conjunctive learner somewhat abstractly, where a given model of the noise process forms the basis for converting a training example into a collection of evidence tuples for use by update equations (2) and (3). This section presents a number of examples of noise models and the resulting evidence tuples generated for observed examples. It begins with the simple case of noiseless data, and builds up through a number of other examples to the noise model used in our approach to learning DNF from noisy data.

3.1 EXAMPLE 1: NOISELESS DATA

As the first example, consider learning conjunctions from noiseless data. To specify the evidence tuples for a given example it is necessary to specify what examples could have given rise to the observed example, and for each what the probability is that the relevant noise processes actually would give rise to the observed example. In the case of noiseless data this is particularly easy. Since every observation o will be correct as given, there will always be only one supposed example it could be. o will always be the true example s with $P(o|s) = 1.0$. For each example o a single evidence tuple $\langle VS(o), 1.0\rangle$ is therefore generated.

As learning progresses, the learner combines each new (singleton) evidence tuple with the single tuple summarizing past data, yielding singleton evidence tuples throughout learning (with the probability component perpetually set to 1.0). The net result is that learning from noiseless data with this incremental evidence combination strategy is equivalent to the incremental version-space merging emulation of the candidate-elimination algorithm [Hirsh, 1990].

3.2 EXAMPLE 2: LABEL NOISE

A second, more sophisticated example of a noise model is a generalization of the label-noise model described in our earlier paper. Consider learning from data subject to uniform label noise with a noise rate for positive data of $\eta_p < 0.5$ and for negative data $\eta_n < 0.5$. In a two-class problem each example yields two supposed examples—and thus two evidence tuples—one labeling the example + and the other labeling the example −. If $VS(\neg o)$ denotes the set of concept descriptions inconsistent with o (i.e., the version space of classifiers consistent with o if its classification were flipped), the resulting tuples for observed positive examples are $\langle VS(o), 1-\eta_p\rangle$ and $\langle VS(\neg o), \eta_p\rangle$ and for negative examples $\langle VS(o), 1-\eta_n\rangle$ and $\langle VS(\neg o), \eta_n\rangle$.

This approach to learning from data with label noise has the attractive property that when $\eta_p = \eta_n = \eta$ the evidence tuple with highest posterior probability simply contains the classifiers that make the fewest mistakes on the training data (regardless of the actual value of η, as long as it is less that 0.5). Similarly, if either η_p or η_n is zero the highest-rated version space contains the classifier that makes the fewest mistakes on the class (positive or negative) that is subject to noise.

3.3 EXAMPLE 3: REPRESENTATIONAL NOISE

The preceding subsection presented a model of label noise for use by our MAP-based conjunctive learner. Such noise models might best be called *environmental noise models*, since they model noise processes operating in the actual training-data environment. One can also consider the case where data appear noisy due to representational issues, such as when the concept description language and the actual target concept that generated the training data are mismatched. A typical example of this is when the target classifier represents some linear relationship among two or more variables, whereas the learner is constrained to use axis-parallel hyperplanes.

Our approach to learning DNF is to view the problem of forming a single disjunctive term as one of learning in the presence of *representational noise*, where the task is one of approximating a DNF expression with a single conjunctive term. The approach to finding such a conjunction is to consider all the data and find a conjunction that covers some positive data and no negative data. The positive data that are not covered by the given approximation are treated as being noisy with respect to the given term being learned.

Note that there is an asymmetry between positive and negative data, and thus positive and negative data must be converted into somewhat different evidence tuples. Assuming the data are correct, and that the only source of uncertainty is the so-called representational noise, a given conjunction should exclude all negative examples. Therefore each negative example is treated as correct and gives rise to a single evidence tuple assigning probability 1.0 to the version space of classifiers that excludes the example. On the other hand, for each positive example we associate a fixed probability α that it is positive for a given term, where $0.5 < \alpha \leq 1$ so that treating positive examples as positive is preferred. The resulting evidence tuples for positive and negative data are as follows:

$$\text{If } o = \langle x,+\rangle \quad \{\langle VS(o),\alpha\rangle, \langle VS(\neg o), 1-\alpha\rangle\}$$
$$\text{If } o = \langle x,-\rangle \quad \{\langle VS(o),1\rangle\}$$

3.4 EXAMPLE 4: COMBINING REPRESENTATIONAL AND LABEL NOISE

Suppose that in addition to the representational-noise scenario of the previous section data are subject to a uniform label-noise process that alters class labels with probability $0 \leq \eta < 0.5$.[3] The problem is still to learn a single conjunction, but converting each example into a set of evidence tuples is now a bit more complicated, since learning must resolve both representational noise and environmental noise.

The basic idea is that a positive observation coincides with a positive true example with probability $1-\eta$. The probability that a given disjunct covers it calls for another factor of α yielding a probability of $\alpha(1-\eta)$ for $VS(o)$ and the rest for $VS(\neg o)$. Similarly, a negative observation corresponds to a positive true example only for noise events (probability η). The probability that a given disjunct covers it calls for an additional factor α, yielding $\alpha\eta$ for the inconsistent classifiers in $VS(\neg o)$ and the rest for $VS(o)$. These arguments result in the following evidence tuples for a given example o.

$$\begin{array}{ll} \text{If } o = \langle x,+\rangle & \{\,\langle VS(o),\alpha(1-\eta)\rangle\,, \\ & \;\;\langle VS(\neg o)), 1-\alpha(1-\eta)\rangle\,\} \\ \text{If } o = \langle x,-\rangle & \{\,\langle VS(o), 1-\alpha\eta\rangle\,, \langle VS(\neg o), \alpha\eta\rangle\,\} \end{array}$$

Note that while the α parameter was constrained earlier to $0.5 < \alpha \leq 1.0$, here it must lie in the more limited range $\frac{1}{2(1-\eta)} < \alpha \leq 1.0$, so that the probability of treating a positive example as positive is greater than the probability of treating a positive example as negative.

4 LEARNING DNF FROM NOISY DATA

The preceding two sections have described our basic conjunctive learner and noise models that together form the core of our overall DNF learner. The key idea is that DNF data can be viewed as the union of sets of data, each corresponding to a single term in the DNF expression. Thus the strategy is to learn each term of the DNF expression with our conjunctive learner and an appropriate noise model, such as the representational-noise model of Section 3.3, the representational and label model of Section 3.4, or some other model that combines the representational-noise model with whatever model of environmental noise is appropriate for the given problem, with learning returning a disjunction of such terms.

[3] Unlike Subsection 3.2, for expository purposes we will assume positive and negative data have the same noise rate η. The change to two different noise rates is straightforward.

This basic approach to learning DNF expressions follows that of more traditional separate-and-conquer algorithms. The basic loop for such learners is to form a single term that covers as much of the positive data as possible while covering little negative data. On each loop the covered data are removed and the process repeats until all the positive examples have been covered by some term.

One way in which our separate-and-conquer approach differs from others in the literature in that each pass of the conjunctive learner can end with multiple evidence tuples having non-negligible posterior probabilities. Thus, rather than learning a single term on each pass, IPEC-DNF forms multiple conjunctive terms on each pass whenever possible. If, after processing the training data on some iteration, S is the most specific classifier (i.e., it is in the S set) of the highest-rated version space, IPEC-DNF first returns S as a new term of the growing DNF and then discards every tuple whose own S-set element covers some example covered by S. If tuples remain, it means they cover data disjoint from the data covered by S, so IPEC-DNF returns as a new term the S-set element of the highest-rated remaining tuple. This process repeats until all tuples have been removed, and the net effect is that several disjoint terms can be added to the evolving DNF expression on each application of the conjunctive learner.

To use IPEC-DNF for noisy data the two parameters η (the label noise rate) and α (the representational noise rate) must be set by the user. While in many realistic contexts the former may be known, α is more an artifact of our formalization of representational noise and must be set on a more subjective basis. More generally, when neither value is known a priori, the parameters enable a user to express information about tradeoffs between the two types of noise. For example, η can be selected based on how clean the data seems to be, perhaps based on an exploratory evaluation of the data. An analysis of the uniform label noise evidence representation shows that choosing a large α value expresses a bias for generality, making learning prefer terms covering larger amounts of data, whereas choosing a smaller α value has the opposite effect. α can be chosen accordingly. One could even use cross-validation methods to find appropriate values for these parameters for a given learning session [Weiss and Kulikowski, 1991].

One potential difficulty if our separate-and-conquer approach is naively implemented is the pruning of unlikely evidence tuples by the conjunctive term learner. It is possible for "bad" orderings of data to cause a set of classifiers to look unlikely at the start of learning and be pruned, whereas the resulting evidence tuples would actually have appeared better later in learning or under a different ordering of the training data. The conjunctive learner will actually fail in such situations, since the removal of the correct terms only leaves tuples whose version spaces collapse later in learning.

IPEC-DNF handles this difficulty in two ways. One is to process all "unambiguous" evidence first. Unambiguous evidence refers to examples converted into singleton evidence tuples with associated probability 1.0, such as from noiseless negative examples (Section 3.3). When this is impossible IPEC-DNF simply tries several randomized orderings of the data. Our limited investigation of this second approach using synthetic data finds that attempting even just four orderings yields a statistically significant performance improvement.[4]

5 EXPERIMENTAL RESULTS

This section describes our initial experimental evaluations of IPEC-DNF. The two-part evaluation compared IPEC-DNF to C4.5 [Quinlan, 1987] using both synthetic and real-world datasets. C4.5 was used because it is widely available, well-known, and generally performs well across a wide range of problems. Since C4.5 gives results both for pruned and unpruned trees, our results reflect whichever attributed a lower error rate to C4.5. In every experiment C4.5 was run with windowing disabled and with discrete attribute subsetting enabled.

The synthetic portion of the evaluation involved approximately 125,000 paired runs of C4.5 and IPEC-DNF in an instance space defined by 10 binary attributes. Each experiment consisted of at least 50 trials. Experiments were parameterized by the number of terms in the given target classifier and the average number of attributes fixed per term [Pagallo and Haussler, 1990]. The number of terms was allowed to vary from 2 to 6, and the average number of non-"don't-care" attributes per term was allowed to vary from 4 to 8 with a standard deviation of 1.3. A stratified random sample of 50% positive and 50% negative examples was generated from each DNF. 2000 samples were used for training, and 5000 for testing. Error rates were gathered periodically throughout training.

Figure 1—which is typical of our other experimental runs—gives the average results for 50 runs of 3-term DNF with 5 attributes fixed per term. In this plot a score of 1.0 represents perfect generalization. The scores for IPEC-DNF are indicated by the vertical lines, and the scores for C4.5 without pruning by the curve. Prior to about 50 examples the two algorithms are indistinguishable. After that IPEC-DNF outperforms C4.5, though with diminishing advantage. As with our earlier conjunctive learning results [Norton and Hirsh, 1992], the observed differences between

[4] In some respects this can be viewed as an alternative to intelligent selection of "seed" examples in AQ[Michalski and Larson, 1978], in that the goal of both techniques is minimize the effects of poor data orderings.

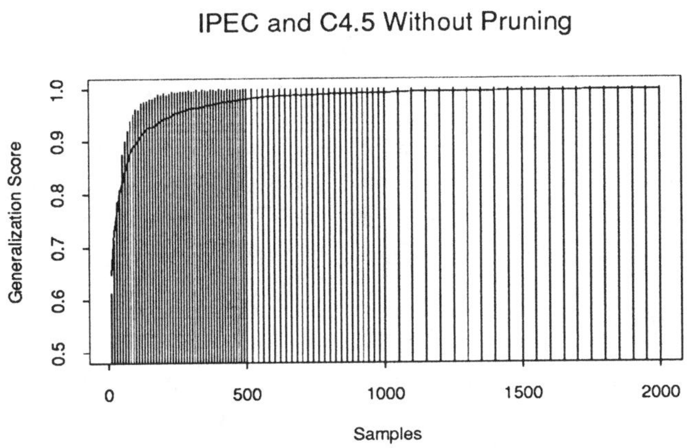

Figure 1. Comparing the Performance of IPEC-DNF and C4.5

Table 1. Error Rates Comparison

Dataset	IPEC	C4.5	Majority
Mushrooms	0.0%	0.0%	48.2%
Breast Cancer	4.8%	5.4%	34.5%
Hepatitis	9.9%	13.4%	20.6%
Liver Disorders	33.9%	35.6%	42.0%
Credit Screening	22.4%	15.3%	44.5%
Thyroid Data	8.4%	8.7%	30.2%
Party Affiliation	3.1%	3.1%	45.2%
Crime Bill Vote	14.1%	15.2%	40.8%

C4.5 and IPEC-DNF are statistically significant.

The performance of the two programs was also studied on real data obtained from the UCI Repository of Machine Learning Databases and Domain Theories. The error-rate estimates given for IPEC-DNF and C4.5 in Table 1 are based on 10-fold cross-validation. The last column indicates the error rate of a rule that always uses the majority classification. Many of the databases include examples with missing attribute values. These were used for training but were excluded from testing. The mushroom database was treated as noiseless. For each data set IPEC-DNF was run twice, once assuming no environmental noise ($\eta = 0$) and once assuming a small amount of environmental noise ($\eta = 0.05$). In each case $\alpha = 0.8$ was used to reflect a slight preference for generality. Whichever was better was reported as the results of learning. (In other words, our results do not represent the result of a search for the "best" values of these parameters, but rather the results of an initial "guess" for the parameter values that was unchanged once learning began.)

The mushrooms dataset consists of 8124 examples describing poisonous and edible mushrooms with 22 nominally valued attributes. For this problem both IPEC-DNF and C4.5 (without pruning, which was the better performer in this case) converge to a correct classifier, with IPEC-DNF finding a 2-term DNF expression.

The Wisconsin Breast Cancer Database consists of 699 examples describing benign and malignant tumors. Removing a sample code number leaves 9 attributes, each in the range 1 to 10. The best performance of C4.5 was 5.4%, obtained with pruning enabled. A 9-term DNF expression with 4.8% error rate was found using the evidence representation for noiseless data.

The hepatitis database consists of 155 examples described by 6 continuous and 13 nominal attributes. The learning task is to predict patient survival. C4.5 using pruning achieves a 13.4% error rate on this database. A 3-term DNF with a 9.9% error rate was found using the evidence representation for noisy data.

The fourth database contains descriptions of 345 patients with and without liver disorders. Six continuous attributes describe blood and liver chemistry as well as daily average alcoholic beverage consumption. C4.5 using pruning achieves a 35.6% error rate. IPEC-DNF achieves a 33.9% rate with an 18-term DNF by using the noiseless data model.

The credit screening database is the only one tested on which C4.5 outperformed IPEC-DNF. Its 690 entries are described by 15 attributes, both continuous and nominal. C4.5 scored 15.3% error versus 22.4% for IPEC-DNF. 26 terms characterize the positive class versus 15 positive branches in the final decision tree. A closer examination of the DNF error rate shows 13.8% false negatives and 8.6% false positives, despite the large number of terms. In this case it seems likely that IPEC-DNF learned a sufficient number of terms, but that they were too specific.

The thyroid database consists of 215 instances, originally of a 3-class problem. All five attributes are continuous. For this experiment the hyperthyroid and hypothyroid examples were combined into a single class. Using a five-term DNF, IPEC-DNF achieves an 8.4% error rate. C4.5's unpruned decision tree achieves an error rate of 8.7%.

The remaining experiments are based on Congressional voting record data for 1984. The original data consists of 435 examples, each recording the vote on 16 key bills (y, n, or unknown), plus the Congressmen's party affiliation, Republican or Democrat. One problem is to predict the party affiliation from the full voting record. The two learning algorithms do equally well, achieving a 3.1% error rate. The other problem is derived by using 15 votes plus party affiliation to learn to predict the vote on the crime bill. Examples without a y or n crime-bill vote are not used. IPEC-DNF learns to predict the outcome with a single conjunctive rule (1-term DNF with the label-noise model) having just 14.1% error. The better of the decision trees has a 15.2% error rate.

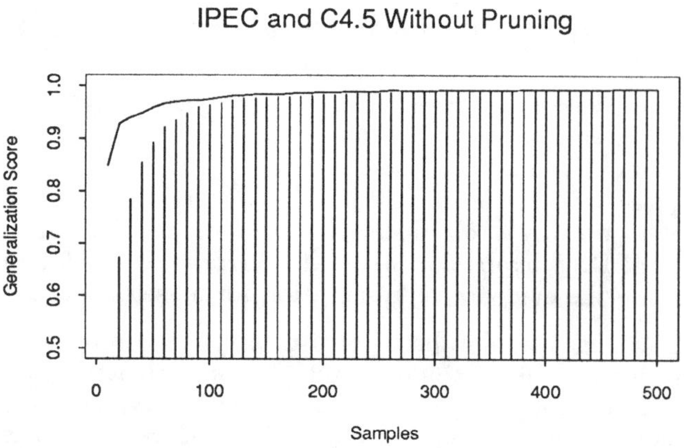

Figure 2. Comparing Early Learning on the Mushroom Data

Finally, since both algorithms converged to a correct mushroom classifier, we performed an additional experiment to determine which learned faster. Learning curves were generated much as before. 500 mushrooms were randomly selected for training. Of the remaining 7624 examples, only those without missing values were used for testing. Error rates were gathered periodically during each of 50 trials. The average generalization scores are given in Figure 2, where the solid curve denotes C4.5 and the vertical lines IPEC-DNF. Even though both learning algorithms converge to a correct classifier after the same number of examples, C4.5 enjoys statistically significantly better error rates through the first 80 examples, after which the two learning algorithms are equivalent. Re-examination of the error rates showed that the errors attributed to IPEC-DNF in early learning were almost entirely false negatives.

In summary, based on the results of the synthetic trials, it was no surprise that IPEC-DNF and C4.5 converged to correct mushroom classifiers given so many examples. We also felt that IPEC-DNF had a good chance to give improved results for the smaller datasets, as was born out in five out of seven of the remaining domains. In learning from the credit-screening data and early-learning from the mushroom data, false negatives constitute the majority of the errors of the IPEC-DNF classifiers. It is unlikely that this is the result of learning too few terms. In the credit-screening case, the number of IPEC terms is almost 75% larger than the number of corresponding branches in the C4.5 tree. Instead, the learned terms seem too specific. We hypothesize that the most-specific term-selection strategy accounts for this effect.

6 FUTURE WORK

IPEC-DNF represents on-going work, and there are a number of future directions that we are exploring. There is still much to be done experimentally, including comparing IPEC-DNF to other disjunctive concept learners as well as more distant approaches such as neural networks or regression-based methods. These studies should help to clarify the conditions under which IPEC-DNF performs better or worse than other learners, for instance in the credit-screening domain.

Understanding the sensitivity of IPEC-DNF to its various parameters is also important. In particular, we would like to develop a principled method for setting η and α. Angluin and Laird [1988] have a procedure for estimating η for k-DNF learning from noisy data. That procedure might be adopted or adapted for use in IPEC-DNF. Cross-validation [Weiss and Kulikowski, 1991] might also be appropriate for setting α.

In addition, we are investigating other methods for selecting final results from the highest-rated version space(s) during each application of the core term-learning system, such as choosing more general terms depending on coverage [Holte *et al.*, 1989], or choosing terms probabilistically in the fashion of the Gibbs classifier [Haussler *et al.*, 1991]. Other possibilities are suggested by Buntine's [1990] option-tree work on integrating multiple probabilistic models in classifier learning.

Thus far we have explored only a limited number of environmental-noise models for use by the conjunctive MAP learner. In addition to the noise models described in this paper, we are exploring other noise models including problem-specific attribute noise models, such as for learning sequence-identification rules in molecular biology. Finally, we plan to investigate the use of our conjunctive learner with other representational-noise models as the core element of other separate-and-conquer learning methods, such as for learning decision lists [Rivest, 1987].

7 SUMMARY

This paper describes an iterative-disjunct-formation approach to learning DNF expressions from noisy data, implemented in the IPEC-DNF learning system. Under this approach a learner can be viewed as repeatedly attempting to form a single, conjunctive approximation to the DNF expression, returning a disjunction of the learned "approximations" as the result of learning. The key idea in this work is to model as *representational noise* the uncertainty as to whether a positive example should be treated as positive for a particular conjunctive "approximation." The result is a learning algorithm that allows a user to specify both environmental and representational noise models appropriate for a given learning task.

Acknowledgments

This work was partially supported by NSF grant IRI-9209795. The Wisconsin breast cancer database was contributed to the UCI Repository by Dr. William H. Wolberg of the University of Wisconsin Hospitals [Mangasarian and Wolberg, 1990]. Once again we thank William Cohen for helpful comments on an earlier draft.

References

[Angluin and Laird, 1988] D. Angluin and P. Laird. Learning from noisy examples. *Machine Learning*, 2(4):343–370, 1988.

[Buntine, 1990] W. Buntine. *A Theory of Learning Classification Rules.* PhD thesis, University of Technology, Sydney, 1990.

[Clark and Niblett, 1989] P. Clark and T. Niblett. The CN2 induction algorithm. *Machine Learning*, 3:261–284, 1989.

[Duda and Hart, 1973] R. Duda and P. Hart. *Pattern Classification and Scene Analysis.* John Wiley and Sons, 1973.

[Haussler *et al.*, 1991] D. Haussler, M. Kearns, and R. Schapire. Bounds on the sample complexity of Bayesian learning using information theory and the VC dimension. In *Computational Learning Theory: Proceedings of the Fourth Annual Workshop.* Morgan Kaufmann, 1991.

[Haussler, 1988] D. Haussler. Quantifying inductive bias: AI learning algorithms and Valiant's learning framework. *Artificial Intelligence*, 36(2):177–222, 1988.

[Hirsh, 1990] H. Hirsh. *Incremental Version-Space Merging: A General Framework for Concept Learning.* Kluwer, Boston, MA, 1990.

[Hirsh, 1992] H. Hirsh. Polynomial-time learning with version spaces. In *Proceedings of the Tenth National Conference on Artificial Intelligence (AAAI-92).* AAAI Press, 1992.

[Holte *et al.*, 1989] R. C. Holte, L. E. Acker, and B. W. Porter. Concept learning and the problem of small disjuncts. In *IJCAI89: Proceedings of the Eleventh International Joint Conference on Artificial Intelligence*, pages 813–818. Morgan Kaufmann Publishers, 1989.

[Mangasarian and Wolberg, 1990] O. L. Mangasarian and W. H. Wolberg. Cancer diagnosis via linear programming. *SIAM News*, 23(5):1–18, 1990.

[Michalski and Larson, 1978] R. S. Michalski and J. B. Larson. Selection of most representative training examples and incremental generation of vl1 hypotheses: The underlying methodology and description of programs ESEL and AQ11. Report 867, University of Illinois, 1978.

[Michalski *et al.*, 1986] R. S. Michalski, I. Mozetic, J. Hong, and N. Lavrac. The multi-purpose incremental learning system AQ15 and its application to three medical domains. In *Proceedings of the National Conference on Artificial Intelligence*, pages 1041–1045, Philadelphia, PA, August 1986.

[Michalski, 1983] R. S. Michalski. A theory and methodology of inductive learning. In R. S. Michalski, J. G. Carbonell, and T. M. Mitchell, editors, *Machine Learning: An Artificial Intelligence Approach*, pages 83–134. Morgan Kaufmann Publishers, Los Altos, CA, 1983.

[Mitchell, 1982] T. M. Mitchell. Generalization as search. *Artificial Intelligence*, 18(2):203–226, 1982.

[Norton and Hirsh, 1992] S. W. Norton and H. Hirsh. Classifier learning from noisy data as probabilistic evidence combination. In *AAAI92: Proceedings of the Tenth National Conference on Artificial Intelligence*, pages 141–146. AAAI Press / MIT Press, 1992.

[Pagallo and Haussler, 1990] G. Pagallo and D. Haussler. Boolean feature discovery in empirical learning. *Machine Learning*, 5(1):71–99, 1990.

[Quinlan, 1987] J. R. Quinlan. Inductive knowledge acquisition: A case study. In J. R. Quinlan, editor, *Application of Expert Systems*, pages 157–173. Turing Institute Press, 1987.

[Quinlan, 1990] J. R. Quinlan. Learning logical definitions from relations. *Machine Learning*, 5(3):239–266, 1990.

[Rivest, 1987] R. L. Rivest. Learning decision lists. *Machine Learning*, 2:229–246, 1987.

[Weiss and Kulikowski, 1991] S. M. Weiss and C. A. Kulikowski. *Computer Systems That Learn.* Morgan Kaufmann, Los Altos, CA, 1991.

Explaining and Generalizing Diagnostic Decisions

Paul O'Rorke
Yousri El Fattah
Margaret Elliott
Dept. of Info. and Comp. Sci.
University of California, Irvine
Irvine, CA 92717-3425, U.S.A.
{ororke,fattah,melliott}@ics.uci.edu

Abstract

We present methods for explaining, generalizing, and learning from diagnostic decisions involving tradeoffs. The methods combine decision theory with extensions of explanation-based learning and qualitative reasoning. The explanation methods search for comprehensible justifications of diagnostic decisions. "Qualitative logics of decision" are used to provide generalizations that enable users to understand individual decisions as members of classes of similar decisions. Generalization supports automated knowledge acquisition using abduction and explanation-based macro learning. We illustrate the methods using detailed examples of two prototypical diagnostic decisions involving tradeoffs, deciding whether or not to operate and whether to test or treat. We provide evaluation metrics and the results of empirical measurements. Empirical results indicate that rules learned using a coarse form of qualitative reasoning provide correct decisions on more important tradeoffs.

1 EXPLAINING AND GENERALIZING DECISIONS

Diagnostic decision-making involves tradeoffs. For example, technicians often must decide whether to verify that a suspected fault is actually present. Sometimes it is more cost-effective to replace potentially faulty components because confirmation is expensive but repair is relatively cheap. We have developed the methods described in this paper for diagnostic applications involving this sort of decision-making.

The methods described here provide explanations of diagnostic decisions. Explanation has long been recognized as an important topic in AI, including AI work on diagnosis (e.g., see Swartout, 1983). A new class of normative diagnostic expert systems that use decision theory[1] is emerging (Heckerman, Horvitz, & Nathwani, 1992). The decisions of these systems are based on Bayesian calculations that are difficult for users to comprehend. An important question is how to provide comprehensible explanations of such decisions.

The explanation methods given here generalize examples so that they can be seen as members of large classes of similar situations that warrant the same decisions. The generalizations enable explanation-based (DeJong & Mooney, 1986; Mitchell, Keller, & Kedar-Cabelli, 1986) and abductive (O'Rorke, 1990) learning.

We present a method that learns information relevant to decision-making from examples. The examples may involve uncertainty about whether one or another disorder is present. Values or utilities are associated with the outcomes of the sequences of actions and events that can occur. There may be costs associated with diagnostic tests and with repair procedures. The method employs an abduction engine capable of macro-learning and learning at the knowledge level. It is implemented in a PROLOG meta-interpreter called AMAL (Abductive MAcro Learner). AMAL is a superset of EBG systems such as (Kedar-Cabelli & McCarty, 1987). A full description of the method, its implementation, its application in four domains, and a description of how abduction enables the acquisition of information about the user's subjective estimates of probabilities and values is given in (O'Rorke, 1992).

This paper focuses on how we have extended traditional EBG methods so as to enable AMAL to explain and learn about diagnostic decisions. We describe the use of "qualitative logics of decision" to transform decision-theoretic constraints on expected utilities into qualitative constraints on the relevant costs, probabilities, and utilities. We introduce two systems for qualitative reasoning about decisions, an initial coarse but simple system and a relatively refined but complex system.

[1] The initial chapters of (Raiffa, 1968) and (North, 1968) provide background information about decision-theory.

Table 1: Fragments of a Qualitative Logic of Decision

DECISION THEORY

$$op \leftarrow \delta_d \times odds > -\delta_{\bar{d}}$$

QUANTITY THEORY

$$X > Z \leftarrow X \geq Y \wedge Y > Z$$
$$AX > AY \leftarrow X > Y \wedge A > 0$$
$$AX \geq AY \leftarrow X \geq Y \wedge A \geq 0$$

OPERATIONALITY CRITERION

$$\langle cond \rangle \rightarrow \langle term \rangle \langle relation \rangle \langle term \rangle$$
$$\langle term \rangle \rightarrow \delta_d \mid -\delta_{\bar{d}} \mid odds \mid 0 \mid 1$$
$$\langle relation \rangle \rightarrow > \mid \geq$$

1.1 AN EXPLANATION-BASED LEARNING METHOD

Explanation-based learning simultaneously specializes a given theory while generalizing examples. In order to learn decision rules that will enable intelligent trade-offs, we provide a "qualitative logic of decision." This is a first order logical theory with the following major components: a decision theory, a theory of quantities, and an operationality criterion. The decision theory specifies when actions are reasonable. Knowledge of quantities is used to transform decision-theoretic constraints on expected utilities into relatively simple constraints on costs, probabilities, and utilities. The operationality criterion determines the assertions that are allowed to appear in the foundations of explanations. The use of constraints on quantities and the representational bias provided by the operationality criterion contribute to the qualitative character of the logics of decision.

A coarse but simple qualitative logic of decision is shown in Table 1. The first rule specifies when the expected utility of an operation will be higher than that of the alternative. Note that this rule is the result of implicit assumptions that there are only two actions under consideration (*op* or its negation), there is one predicate of interest (*d* for "disorder"), and the action does not affect the probability of this predicate.[2]

In the notation used here, δ_d corresponds to the relative advantage of *op* as opposed to $\overline{op}$ when the disorder is present. This is the difference in utility of the outcome of doing *op* vs. the utility of the alternative $(U_{op,d} - U_{\overline{op},d})$. Similarly, $\delta_{\bar{d}}$ is the relative advantage of *op* when the disorder is absent $(U_{op,\bar{d}} - U_{\overline{op},\bar{d}})$.

A collection of rules about inequalities is shown next. These rules express knowledge about quantities. The backward-chaining abduction engine uses them to transform complex constraints specified by the decision theory into operational constraints that are more comprehensible.

The remaining rules provide a grammar defining an operationality criterion. The definition of operationality in Table 1 requires explanations to be in terms of direct comparisons between relevant quantities. In this case, only comparisons between gains δ_d, losses $-\delta_{\bar{d}}$, *odds*, and the qualitative landmarks 0 and 1 are allowed.

We give AMAL concrete decision problems specified as queries about whether it makes sense to do a given operation under given conditions. AMAL constructs proofs that the actions should be taken in the given situations. AMAL generalizes the particular decision problems by specializing the general decision theory and theory of quantities. Irrelevant details of the case are discarded. The underlying abstract explanation can be used to justify the current decision and to decide similar cases in the future.

1.2 AN EXAMPLE: DECIDING WHETHER TO OPERATE

We illustrate the method with an example based on a medical diagnosis exercise in (Charniak & McDermott, 1986). It involves a patient diagnosed to be suffering from an "enlarged thymus." The diagnosis is uncertain. The probability p_d that the thymus is enlarged is given as .75; there is a .25 probability $p_{\bar{d}}$ that the thymus is not enlarged. The goal of the exercise is to decide whether to operate to remove the thymus.

Assume that removing an enlarged thymus costs 100 utility points but it results in a good situation with utility 850 and failing to operate on an enlarged thymus results in an extremely bad situation with utility -1000. Assume that operating on an ordinary thymus results in a situation with utility -150 and doing nothing on an ordinary thymus results in a slightly better situation with utility -100.

In terms of odds, losses, and gains, *odds* $= 3$, $\delta_d = 1850$, and $\delta_{\bar{d}} = -50$; where *odds* is $p_d/p_{\bar{d}}$, δ_d is the difference in utility of operating versus not operating given that the thymus is enlarged and $\delta_{\bar{d}}$ is the difference in utility of operating versus not operating given that the thymus is not enlarged. It is better to operate than to do nothing in this example.

Figure 1 shows a proof (computed by AMAL) that one should do the operation. While the proof grounds out in statements involving the exact values of δ_d, $\delta_{\bar{d}}$, and *odds*, AMAL generalizes the proof, thus learning more general conditions such that *op* is a reasonable action. This is done by throwing away the irrelevant details of the example (shown in the oval in figure 1). The exact numbers involved are irrelevant. If the conditions shown in boxes in figure 1 hold, then one should do

[2]These assumptions are relaxed in Section 3.1.

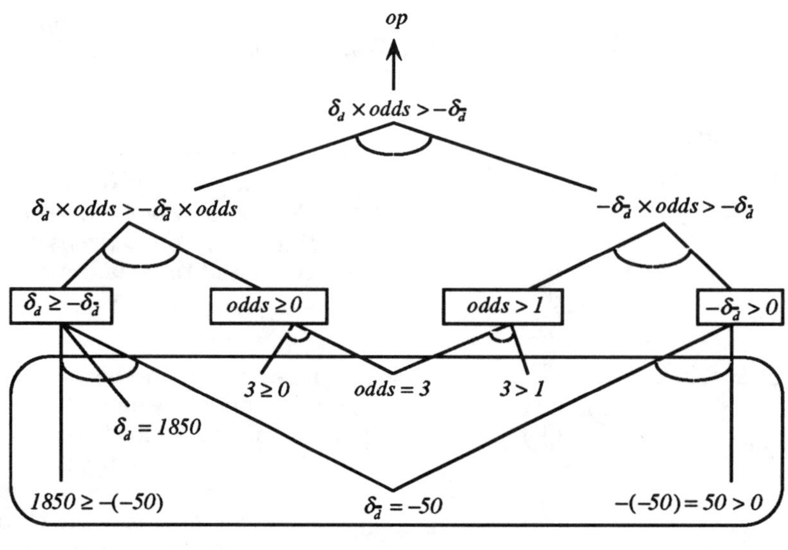

Figure 1: Reasons Supporting the Operation in the Thymus Example

op. In other words, $op \leftarrow \delta_d \geq -\delta_{\bar{d}} \geq 0 \wedge odds > 1$. This qualitative decision rule says that one should do an operation whenever the potential gain is at least as large as the potential loss and the odds favor success.

2 EMPIRICAL EVALUATION

AMAL learns from sequences of examples. It checks new rules against previous rules to see if one is a substitution instance of the other. AMAL discards new rules that are subsumed by old ones in this sense. This section presents results of learning on sequences of examples like the thymus example. Metrics that can be used to evaluate one aspect of the quality of the learned rules are also introduced and applied to the results of learning.

2.1 LEARNING FROM MULTIPLE EXAMPLES

We gave AMAL two sets of decision problems spanning all four quadrants in the decision space. AMAL learned the decision rules shown in Table 2.

The first set of problems was artificially generated so as to ensure that landmark values were included in the data. This set was restricted to three quadrants including only one of the two tradeoff quadrants. The second set of problems randomly sampled all four quadrants using rectangular distributions on three independent parameters: $p_d \in [0, 1]$, $\delta_d \in [-1000, 1000]$, and $\delta_{\bar{d}} \in [-1000, 1000]$.

The learned rules specify intuitively plausible and valuable sets of conditions under which an operation is rational. The *WinWin* rule covers situations where doing *op* is advantageous regardless of the *odds*. The *LoseLose* rule covers situations where *op* leads to losses regardless of *odds*. The remaining rules cover tradeoff regions. Rule Y_1 deals with situations where there is no prospect of loss. Rule N_1 covers situations where there is no chance of gain. N_4 indicates that one should not do *op* when one is certain to lose. Rules Y_2 and Y_3 say that one should do *op* if the potential gain outweighs the potential loss and the odds of the gain are better than even. One should not do *op* when it has a less then even chance of success and the downside outweighs the potential gain (rules N_2 and N_3).

The first two rules were learned in both experiments. The remaining rules differ because the initial sample set was designed to hit landmark values. This results in specific rules or conditions that take care of special cases like $odds = 0$. When the classes of decision problems are randomly generated, these landmarks are almost always missed. The resulting rules are less complete but they are simpler and more compact, and their performance is effectively identical on randomized tests such as the evaluation in the next section.

2.2 EVALUATION METRICS AND RESULTS

The explanation and learning method is inherently incomplete. Some decisions cannot be explained or generalized or decided by learned rules. One such decision similar to the thymus example is: $\delta_d = 50$, $\delta_{\bar{d}} = -1850$, $odds = 3$. In this tradeoff, the odds are 3:1. This is greater than the loss to gain ratio of $1850/50 = 37$ so $\overline{op}$ is the preferred action according to decision theory. But the coarse logic of decision (Table 1) cannot explain this recommendation, nor does it support learning from this example so the rules of Table 2 do not apply. Although it is possible to fall back upon quantitative decision-theoretic calculations when

Table 2: Rules Learned From Multiple Examples

EXAMPLES INCLUDING LANDMARKS	RANDOM EXAMPLES
$WinWin : op \leftarrow$	$\delta_d > 0 \wedge \delta_{\bar{d}} > 0$
$LoseLose : \overline{op} \leftarrow$	$0 > \delta_d \wedge 0 > \delta_{\bar{d}}$
$Y_1 : op \leftarrow \delta_d > 0 \wedge \delta_{\bar{d}} = 0 \wedge odds > 0$	
$Y_2 : op \leftarrow \delta_d \geq -\delta_{\bar{d}} \wedge odds > 1$	$op \leftarrow \delta_d \geq -\delta_{\bar{d}} > 0 \wedge odds > 1$
$Y_3 : op \leftarrow \delta_d > -\delta_{\bar{d}} \wedge odds \geq 1$	$op \leftarrow \delta_d \geq -\delta_{\bar{d}} \wedge 0 > -\delta_{\bar{d}} \wedge 1 > odds$
$N_1 : \overline{op} \leftarrow \delta_d = 0 \wedge -\delta_{\bar{d}} > 0$	$\overline{op} \leftarrow -\delta_{\bar{d}} \geq \delta_d > 0 \wedge 1 > odds > 0$
$N_2 : \overline{op} \leftarrow -\delta_{\bar{d}} \geq \delta_d \wedge 1 > odds > 0$	$\overline{op} \leftarrow -\delta_{\bar{d}} \geq \delta_d \wedge 0 > \delta_d \wedge odds > 1$
$N_3 : \overline{op} \leftarrow -\delta_{\bar{d}} > \delta_d \wedge 1 \geq odds > 0$	
$N_4 : \overline{op} \leftarrow -\delta_{\bar{d}} > 0 \wedge odds = 0$	

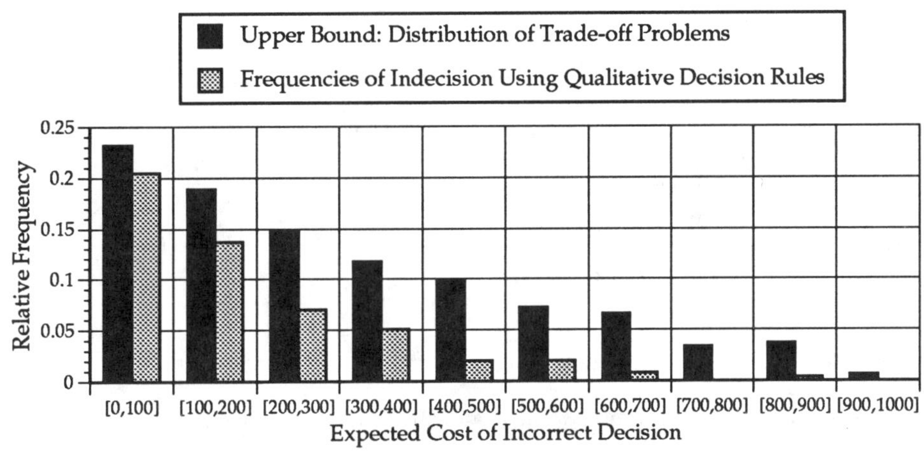

Figure 2: Relative Frequencies as a Function of Expected Costs of Errors

our qualitative approximation fails us, it is useful to measure how often this can be expected to occur. In this section, we provide a measure that takes into account the importance of the problems. We show how the measure can be applied to assess the quality of sets of learned qualitative decision rules.[3]

We randomly generated 1000 tradeoffs using rectangular distributions on δ_d, $\delta_{\bar{d}}$, and p_d. Figure 2 shows two bar charts. The horizontal axis corresponds to the absolute value of the difference between the expected value of doing an operation and the expected value of not doing it. The bars correspond to sets of problems such that the relative advantage of making the correct decision — or, equivalently, the expected cost of an error — has a value in the corresponding interval. The vertical axis shows the percentages of the problems that fall in the intervals shown on the horizontal axis.

The first set of bars shows the distribution of the test problems. Most problems are unimportant in the sense that little is lost if they are decided incorrectly; few problems are important in the sense that errors lead to large losses. Over 20% of the problems are in the lowest value bin. As the cost of errors increases, the number of problems declines. Only 6 of the 1000 problems (.6%) fall in the top value bin. These bars, together with the axis $y = 0$, serve to bound the quality of the rules. The upper bound corresponds to making the wrong decision in every case so that the maximum possible losses are incurred. The axis $y = 0$ corresponds to making the correct decisions so that no losses are incurred.

The second set of bars corresponds to the test problems that are not covered by the qualitative decision rules. (Recall the example: $\delta_d = 50$, $\delta_{\bar{d}} = -1850$, $odds = 3$.) Slightly more than half (512) of the 1000 randomly generated tradeoff problems are not decided by the rules. However, the bar chart indicates that the qualitative rules are biased towards covering more important cases. Looking at the least important and the most important problems, the qualitative rules do not cover 84% of the cases involving expected losses under 100 but they cover all of the problems with expected losses over 900. Only 15% of the most important problems (those in the top 5 bins) are not covered.

Intuitively, the reason is that the qualitative rules ap-

[3]The same measure can also be used to evaluate qualitative methods for decision-making and for explaining decisions.

proximate two regions separated by a surface defined by decision theory. The most important decision problems correspond to points far from the decision surface and relatively unimportant problems correspond to points near the surface. Distant points are captured by the approximation more often than points near the surface. In cases like the one discussed here, it is possible to visualize the decision surface and the approximations. Three dimensional plots show the gap between the actual decision surface and the qualitative approximations (O'Rorke, El Fattah, & Elliott, 1993). A mathematical analysis based on the geometry of the decision regions verifies the quantitative values of the empirical measurements in Figure 2 to within a few percentage points.

The metric and experimental method introduced in this section provide quantitative information about an important aspect of the quality of qualitative approximations. They verify that we get the behavior we desire and expect from qualitative decision rules, namely that they provide decisions on more important cases, missing less important cases. In addition, the metrics and methods support comparisons of alternatives. Here we compare three alternatives: a coarse qualitative logic of decision vs. perfectly good and abysmally bad decision-making. We plan to apply the metrics to more refined qualitative logics of decision. More expressive logics are capable of explaining and generalizing additional decisions at the cost of additional computation and representational complexity. The metrics and methods discussed here provide information bearing on the question of what might be gained in going to a more complete system.

A more sophisticated qualitative logic of decision that includes a form of order of magnitude reasoning (Raiman, 1991) is introduced in the next section. The new system covers additional tradeoffs and handles more complex problems including "test or treat" decisions.

3 ORDER OF MAGNITUDE REASONING

We have developed a logic supporting order of magnitude reasoning about decisions. (Some important parts of the logic are shown in Table 3.) It is based on a generalized "greater than" relationship defined, assuming $0 < \epsilon < 1$ and $n \in \{1, 2, \ldots\}$, as follows:

$$X \underset{n}{>} Y \stackrel{\text{def}}{\equiv} X\epsilon^{n-1} > Y.$$

Let the negation of this relationship be defined:

$$X \underset{n}{\not>} Y \stackrel{\text{def}}{\equiv} X\epsilon^{n-1} \not> Y.$$

Define generalized "greater than or equal to" relationships in a similar fashion.

Table 3: A Logic of Decision with O(M) Reasoning

DECISION THEORY

$$EU(test\ldots[yes \rightarrow op, no \rightarrow \overline{op}]) > EU(\overline{op}[\,]) \leftarrow$$
$$\delta_d p(y|d)p_d > cost(test) + cost(op)p_y - \delta_{\bar{d}} p(y|\bar{d})p_{\bar{d}}.$$
$$EU(test\ldots[yes \rightarrow op, no \rightarrow \overline{op}]) > EU(op[\,]) \leftarrow$$
$$cost(op)p_n - \delta_{\bar{d}} p(n|\bar{d})p_{\bar{d}} > cost(test) + \delta_d p(n|d)p_d.$$

O(M) QUANTITY THEORY

$$\begin{array}{rcl}
X \underset{m+n-1}{>} Z & \leftarrow & X \underset{m}{>} Y \underset{n}{>} Z \\
X \underset{n-m+1}{>} Z & \leftarrow & Y \underset{m}{\not>} X \wedge Y \underset{n}{>} Z \\
U \underset{m}{>} \sum_{i=1}^{n} X_i & \leftarrow & \forall i[U \underset{m+1}{>} X_i] \wedge \frac{1}{n} \geq \epsilon \\
X + Y \underset{n+1}{\not>} Y & \leftarrow & X \underset{n}{\not>} Y \wedge \frac{1}{2} \geq \epsilon \\
U_1U_2 \underset{m+n-1}{>} L_1L_2 & \leftarrow & U_1 \underset{m}{>} L_1 \wedge U_2 \underset{n}{>} L_2 \\
XY \underset{m-n+1}{>} L & \leftarrow & X \underset{m}{>} L \wedge 1 \underset{n}{\not>} Y \\
XY \underset{m-n+1}{>} L & \leftarrow & X \underset{m}{>} 1 \wedge L \underset{n}{\not>} Y \\
\frac{A}{B} \underset{n}{>} 1 \equiv 1 & \underset{n}{>} & \frac{B}{A} \equiv A \underset{n}{>} B
\end{array}$$

OPERATIONALITY CRITERION

$$\begin{array}{rcl}
\langle relation \rangle & \rightarrow & \underset{n}{>} \mid \underset{n}{\geq} \mid \underset{n}{\not>} \mid \underset{n}{\not\geq} \\
\langle term \rangle & \rightarrow & 0 \mid 1 \mid cost(op) \mid cost(test) \mid \\
& & \delta_d \mid -\delta_{\bar{d}} \mid p_d \mid p_{\bar{d}} \mid \\
& & p(y|d) \mid p(n|d) \mid p(y|\bar{d}) \mid p(n|\bar{d})
\end{array}$$

We usually confine ourselves to $n \in \{1, 2, 3\}$. When $n = 1$ we have the usual inequality $X > Y$. When $n = 2$ we have the usual "much greater than" relationship $X \gg Y$ (Mavrovouniotis & Stephanopoulos, 1988). When $n = 3$ we write $X \ggg Y$ and we say "X is much *much* greater than Y."

The rules shown in the center of Table 3 are representative examples that are useful in qualitative order-of-magnitude reasoning about decisions. These rules are immediate consequences of the definitions. The rules include two transitivity rules, two rules bounding sums, three rules bounding products, and quotient rules. The sum rules generally apply to sums with few terms. The first product rule remains true upon replacement of all "greater than" ($>$) relationships with "not much greater than" ($\not>$) relationships. It yields shrinkage and magnification rules as special cases when factors are set to 1. Shrinkage rules bound the size of products involving factors smaller than one. Magnification rules bound the size of products involving factors larger than one. An important special case that may help the reader's intuition is:

$$XY > 1 \leftarrow X \gg 1 \not\gg Y. \tag{1}$$

The equivalences provide quotient rules that can be

used to translate a constraint on one and a quotient into a constraint on the numerator and denominator of the quotient. Note that the corresponding negations are equivalent to $A \underset{n}{\not>} B$.

3.1 AN EXAMPLE OF TEST OR TREAT

Consider the following medical diagnosis example of a test or treat scenario. Let the cost of the test be 900, and let the operation cost 10,000. Let the test be symmetric and such that the false positive ratio $p(y|\bar{d}) = .001$ Assume that the odds of the patient having the disease are 1:3 so $p_d = .25$. Let the utility of doing nothing when the disease is absent $U_{\bar{d},\overline{op}}$ be zero. Let the utility of doing the operation when the disease is absent be the same as the utility of not doing the operation when the disease is present and let both be: $U_{\bar{d},op} = U_{d,\overline{op}} = -1,000,000$. Let the utility of doing the operation when the disease is present be: $U_{d,op} = 50,000$.

The correct decision in this case is to do the test and then do the operation if it is called for by the result of the test. The alternatives yield disastrous results. This conclusion is not particularly sensitive to the exact numbers involved. In the remainder of this section, we show how order of magnitude reasoning helps generate an explanation and generalization of the example that can be summarized:

> It is better to test and then operate if and only if the test indicates the disorder when
>
> 1. the potential gain is much *much* larger than the cost of the operation and this is much larger than the cost of the test,
> 2. the gain is larger (but not much larger) than the potential loss,
> 3. the probability of the disorder is significant but it is more likely the disorder is absent,
> 4. the test's true positive rate is significant and much *much* larger than the false positive rate,
> 5. the true negative rate is much larger than the false negative rate, and
> 6. epsilon is sufficiently small ($1/4 \geq \epsilon$).

The first rule in Table 3 specifies when testing is superior to doing nothing. The inequality on expected utilities is true by a sum rule if $\boxed{\frac{1}{3} \geq \epsilon}$ and if the potential gains are much greater than each of the costs:

$$\begin{aligned} \delta_d p(y|d)p_d &\gg cost(test), && (2)\\ &\gg cost(op)p_y, && (3)\\ &\gg -\delta_{\bar{d}} p(y|\bar{d})p_{\bar{d}}. && (4) \end{aligned}$$

The inequality (2) follows from an instance of a shrinkage rule:

$$\delta_d p(y|d)p_d \gg cost(test) \leftarrow \delta_d \underset{4}{>} cost(test) \wedge 1 \not\ggg p(y|d)p_d$$

if the conjunction holds. The first conjunct follows from

$$\boxed{\delta_d \ggg cost(op) \gg cost(test)}$$

by a transitivity rule. The second conjunct $1 \not\ggg p(y|d)p_d$ is true by a product rule since $\boxed{1 \not\gg p_d}$ and $\boxed{1 \not\gg p(y|d)}$.

The inequality (3) follows by an instance of a shrinkage rule if

$$\boxed{\delta_d \ggg cost(op)} \wedge p_y \not\gg p(y|d)p_d.$$

Expanding p_y in the second conjunct yields:

$$p(y|d)p_d + p(y|\bar{d})p_{\bar{d}} \not\gg p(y|d)p_d.$$

By a sum rule, this follows if $p(y|\bar{d})p_{\bar{d}} \not> p(y|d)p_d$. This is equivalent by the quotient rules to $L^+ odds \geq 1$ (the posterior odds after accounting for positive evidence are better than even).[4] This follows from rule 1 since

$$L^+ \gg 1 \not\gg odds, \text{ or, alternatively, } \boxed{p(y|d) \gg p(y|\bar{d})}$$
$$\text{and } \boxed{p_{\bar{d}} \not\gg p_d}$$

The inequality (4) is equivalent to the following according to the quotient rules.

$$L^+ odds \gg \frac{-\delta_{\bar{d}}}{\delta_d}$$

This inequality states that the posterior odds after positive evidence should be much greater than the loss to gain ratio. This follows by transitivity if $L^+ odds \gg 1 \geq -\delta_{\bar{d}}/\delta_d$. The posterior odds are much greater than one by a magnification rule if

$$L^+ \ggg 1 \not\gg odds, \text{ or in other words,}$$
$$\boxed{p(y|d) \ggg p(y|\bar{d})} \text{ and } \boxed{p_{\bar{d}} \not\gg p_d}$$

The loss to gain ratio is less than one since, in the example, $\boxed{\delta_d > -\delta_{\bar{d}}}$. This completes the proof that testing is superior to doing nothing in this case.

Using some additional rules of order of magnitude reasoning similar to those presented in Table 3, the inferiority of doing the operation without testing can be explained and generalized. The second rule on expected utilities in Table 3 applies. The conditions of this rule follow if the operation costs much more than the test ($cost(op) \gg cost(test)$), the potential gain is not much greater than the potential loss ($\delta_d \not\gg -\delta_{\bar{d}}$), the disorder is less likely to be present than absent ($p_{\bar{d}} > p_d$),

[4] L^+ is short for $p(y|d)/p(y|\bar{d})$

the test's true negative rate is larger than its false positive rate ($p(n|\bar{d}) > p(y|\bar{d})$) and much larger than its false negative rate ($p(n|\bar{d}) \gg p(n|d)$), and epsilon is sufficiently small ($1/4 \geq \epsilon$).

Collecting the operational constraints that were found to hold in the example and eliminating duplications and redundancies yields the following general conditions favoring testing over both alternatives:

1. $\delta_d \ggg cost(op) \gg cost(test)$,
2. $\delta_d > -\delta_{\bar{d}} > 0$ but $\delta_d \not\gg -\delta_{\bar{d}}$,
3. $p_{\bar{d}} > p_d$ but $1 \not\gg p_d$,
4. $1 \not\gg p(y|d) \ggg p(y|\bar{d})$,
5. $p(n|\bar{d}) \gg p(n|d)$, and
6. $1/4 \geq \epsilon$.

The English interpretations of these constraints given earlier were derived by manually interpreting $X \gg Y$ as "X is much greater than Y," "$1 \not\gg X$" as "X is significant," and so on.

4 RELATED WORK

This continues our earlier work on abductive explanation-based learning. In (O'Rorke & Morris, 1992) we showed how to use abduction to generate hypotheses in diagnostic signal interpretation. Abduction also generates interesting hypotheses in explaining diagnostic decisions. For a more complete description of the abductive aspects of AMAL and an example of abduction in the context of a diagnostic decision drawn from the expert systems literature, see (O'Rorke, 1992).

This work also follows upon our earlier work on explanation-based learning for diagnosis. Our earlier work investigated methods for integrating macro-learning and model-based diagnosis to obtain speedup (El Fattah & O'Rorke, in press). This work was based on a logical theory of diagnosis (Reiter, 1987) and (unlike our current work) it did not consider probabilities, costs, and utilities.

Although this paper focused on decision-making in the context of diagnosis and troubleshooting, it is possible to generalize this work to other kinds of decisions. In (O'Rorke, et al., 1993) we discuss this generalization and describe current limitations and future directions.

It has been shown that diagnostic decision models can be compiled to advantage under some circumstances (Heckerman, Breese, & Horvitz, 1989). We expect similar improvements in computational efficiency to result from our methods (although the methods and tasks involved are different). The qualitative decision rules learned here could eliminate the need to generate explanations from scratch and could reduce the duplication of decision analyses.

The work reported here is inspired by work in the field of qualitative reasoning (Weld & de Kleer, 1990). Most work in this area focuses on physical reasoning. Decision-making and explaining decisions are relatively new tasks for work on qualitative reasoning. Early work on a qualitative approach to decision-making involved a computer program called VOTE that implements a case-based cognitive model of how members of congress decide whether to vote for or against bills (Slade, 1991a, 1991b).

Methods based on subjective Bayesian probability theory are among the most successful AI techniques for dealing with uncertainty. Unfortunately, most Bayesian techniques involve numeric computations that do not support abstract explanations. Techniques described in (Wellman, 1990) integrate symbolic and probabilistic reasoning but only support planning "up to tradeoffs." Our work breaks through the tradeoff barrier.

The closest related work is by (Langlotz, Shortliffe, & Fagan, 1988). Our work differs from this earlier work in that we use abduction and backward chaining to generate explanations rather than deductive forward chaining. Another difference is that we use new order of magnitude methods in support of qualitative reasoning about decisions. A more recent system called DETES also generates explanations of diagnostic decisions using a set of axioms based on decision theory (Kim & Kim, 1991). Our approach differs in that we identify abstract classes of similar situations warranting the same decision.

5 CONCLUSION

This paper provides methods for explaining, generalizing, and learning from diagnostic decisions. The methods are based on qualitative logics of decision that use knowledge about quantities to transform constraints on expected utilities into constraints on probabilities of disorders, test accuracies, and so on. The paper describes a basic coarse but simple approach and a more refined but more complex approach using order of magnitude reasoning. The order of magnitude system improves completeness at a reasonable cost in terms of comprehensibility and tractability. The order of magnitude reasoning methods are novel in that they include new rules that help resolve tradeoffs and the "grain size" ϵ is chosen dynamically during explanatory reasoning.

Explanations generated by the methods justify decisions rendered in specific examples in general terms. Qualitative decision rules generated by the methods specify general conditions supporting decisions. Evaluations using metrics that consider the importance of decision problems show that the methods are biased towards explaining and learning the more important classes of decisions.

Acknowledgements

The LPA MacPROLOG program AMAL was written by Paul O'Rorke, David Aha, Margaret Elliott, Mei-Fan Chou, and Patricia Tang. *Mathematica* (Wolfram Research, 1991) was used in experiments and for visualization. Reviewers made constructive critical remarks on a previous draft. This paper is a result of research supported in part by National Science Foundation Grant Number IRI-8813048, Douglas Aircraft Company, and the University of California Microelectronics Innovation and Computer Research Opportunities Program.

References

Charniak, E., & McDermott, D. (1986). Planning exercise. In *Introduction to Artificial Intelligence* (pp. 519–524). Reading, MA: Addison-Wesley Publishing Company.

DeJong, G. F., & Mooney, R. (1986). Explanation-based learning: An alternative view. *Machine Learning, 1*(2), 145-176.

El Fattah, Y., & O'Rorke, P. (in press). Explanation-based learning for diagnosis. *Machine Learning.*

Heckerman, D. E., Breese, J. S., & Horvitz, E. J. (1989). The compilation of decision models. *Proceedings of the Fifth Workshop on Uncertainty in Artificial Intelligence* (pp. 162–173). Windsor, Ontario: Association for Uncertainty in Artificial Intelligence, Mountain View, CA.

Heckerman, D. E., Horvitz, E. J., & Nathwani, B. N. (1992). Towards normative expert systems: Part I The Pathfinder project. *Methods of Information in Medicine, 31*, 90–105.

Kedar-Cabelli, S. T., & McCarty, L. T. (1987). Explanation-based generalization as resolution theorem proving. In P. Langley (Ed.), *Proceedings of the Fourth International Workshop on Machine Learning* (pp. 383–389). Irvine, CA: Morgan Kaufmann.

Kim, S. H., & Kim, J. K. (1991). Explanation in a decision-theoretic consulting system: An axiomatic approach. *Applied Artificial Intelligence, 5*, 393–409.

Langlotz, C. P., Shortliffe, E. H., & Fagan, L. M. (1988). A methodology for generating computer-based explanations of decision-theoretic advice. *Medical Decision Making, 8*, 290–303.

Mavrovouniotis, M. L., & Stephanopoulos, G. (1988). Formal Order-of-Magnitude Reasoning in Process Engineering. *Computer Chemical Engineering, 12*, 867–880.

Mitchell, T. M., Keller, R. M., & Kedar-Cabelli, S. T. (1986). Explanation-based generalization: A unifying view. *Machine Learning, 1*(1), 47–80.

North, D. W. (1968). A tutorial introduction to decision theory. *IEEE Transactions on Systems Science and Cybernetics, SSC-4*(3).

O'Rorke, P. (1990). Integrating abduction and learning. *Working Notes of the AAAI Spring 1990 Symposium on Automated Abduction.* Palo Alto, CA: AAAI.

O'Rorke, P. (1992). *Abduction and learning: Case studies in diverse domains* (Technical report 92-98. Submitted for publication.). Department of Information and Computer Science, University of California, Irvine.

O'Rorke, P., El Fattah, Y., & Elliott, M. (1993). Explanation-based learning for qualitative decision-making. In N. Piera-Carrete (Ed.), *Proceedings of the Third IMACS International Workshop on Qualitative Reasoning and Decision Technologies* (pp. *to appear*). Barcelona, Spain.

O'Rorke, P., & Morris, S. (1992). Abductive signal interpretation for nondestructive evaluation. In G. Biswas (Ed.), *Conference on Applications of Artificial Intelligence X: Knowledge-Based Systems* (pp. 68–75). Orlando, FL: SPIE — The International Society for Optical Engineering.

Raiffa, H. (1968). *Decision analysis: Introductory lectures on choices under uncertainty* (first ed.). New York, NY: Random House.

Raiman, O. (1991). Order of magnitude reasoning. *Artificial Intelligence, 51*(1–3), 11–38.

Reiter, R. (1987). A theory of diagnosis from first principles. *Artificial Intelligence, 32*, 57–95.

Slade, S. (1991a). Goal-based decision strategies. *Proceedings of the Thirteenth Annual Conference of the Cognitive Science Society.* : Lawrence Erlbaum Associates.

Slade, S. (1991b). Qualitative decision theory. *Proceedings of the Case-Based Reasoning Workshop.* San Diego, CA: DARPA-ISTO.

Swartout, W. R. (1983). XPLAIN: a system for creating and explaining expert consulting programs. *Artificial Intelligence, 21*, 285–325.

Weld, D. S., & de Kleer, J. (Ed.). (1990). *Readings in qualitative reasoning about physical systems.* San Mateo, CA: Morgan Kaufmann.

Wellman, M. P. (1990). *Formulation of tradeoffs in planning under uncertainty.* San Mateo, CA: Morgan Kaufmann.

Wolfram Research, I. (1991). *Mathematica* Version 2.03 Enhanced. Champaign, IL: Wolfram Research, Inc.,

Combining Instance-Based and Model-Based Learning

J. R. Quinlan
Basser Department of Computer Science
University of Sydney
Sydney Australia 2006
quinlan@cs.su.oz.au

Abstract

This paper concerns learning tasks that require the prediction of a continuous value rather than a discrete class. A general method is presented that allows predictions to use both instance-based and model-based learning. Results with three approaches to constructing models and with eight datasets demonstrate improvements due to the composite method.

Keywords: learning with continuous classes, instance-based learning, model-based learning, empirical evaluation.

1 INTRODUCTION

Among the many approaches to supervised learning, instance-based and model-based methods belong to two extremes. Instance-based approaches represent what has been learned as a collection of *prototypes* couched in the same language as that used to describe training data. A prototype might be just one of the training cases, or some hypothetical case computed from one or more of them (such as the weighted average of a set of cases). An unseen case is classified by finding similar prototypes and using their classes in some way to form a prediction. Different instance-based systems vary in how they assess the similarity of two cases, specify the number of similar prototypes to be used, and combine predictions from individual prototypes. Stanfill and Waltz [1986] and Aha, Kibler, and Albert [1991] provide examples of these mechanisms and discussions of the merits of instance-based learning.

Model-based approaches, on the other hand, represent what has been learned in some theory language that is richer than the language used to describe data. Learning methods of this kind construct explicit generalizations of the training cases, rather than allowing generalization to flow implicitly from the similarity measure above. When a task domain has many irrelevant attributes, an explicit generalization expressed by some model can be more intelligible than a set of prototype cases and can also lead to better predictions. Breiman, Friedman, Olshen and Stone [1984] and Quinlan [1993a] present arguments in favor of learning by constructing symbolic models.

This paper considers tasks of learning to predict numerical values, a form of supervised learning in which the classes are continuous rather than discrete. A general method for combining instance-based and model-based learning for such tasks is proposed. This method, which can be used with any form of model, is illustrated here using three of them – familiar *linear regression* [Press, Flannery, Teukolsky, and Vetterling, 1988], *model trees* [Quinlan, 1992], and *neural networks* [Hinton, 1986; McClelland and Rumelhart, 1988; Hinton, 1992]. Over a representative collection of datasets, the composite methods often produce better predictions than either instance-based or model-based approaches.

2 USING MODELS AND INSTANCES

We assume some set of training cases T. Each case consists of an attribute-value vector and a known class value, here a number rather than a category. Using T, some instance-based method assembles a set of prototypes P and a model-based method constructs a predictive model M. For a case or prototype C, we will write $V(C)$ to represent the class value of C and $M(C)$ to represent the value predicted for C by M. (Note that, since prototypes are expressed in the same language as cases, we can apply the model to both cases and prototypes.)

Suppose now that we are to predict the class value for some unseen case U. Using the model-based approach we would get $M(U)$. If the instance-based approach were employed, a subset $\{P_1, P_2, ..., P_k\}$ of the prototype points would first be identified as being similar to U; the values $\{V(P_1), V(P_2), ..., V(P_k)\}$ would then be combined in some way to give the predicted value of U.

Consider one of the selected prototypes, P_i say. The rationale for making use of $V(P_i)$ in computing a predicted value for U is that P_i is similar to U, so $V(P_i)$ should be similar to $V(U)$. Prototype P_i will not generally be identical to U, but the nature of the difference between them is not taken into account, even if some measure of their similarity is used to determine the weight of $V(P_i)$ in the combined prediction.

The model M, however, provides a way of taking explicit account of the difference between the unseen case and the prototype. Specifically, the model M predicts the difference between the class values of P_i and U to be

$$M(P_i) - M(U).$$

If the model is correct, the adjusted value

$$V(P_i) - (M(P_i) - M(U))$$

should be a better predictor of the class value of U than the quantity $V(P_i)$ alone. The composite method differs from the instance-based method only in carrying out this adjustment to the class values of selected prototypes before they are combined to give a prediction.

3 EMPIRICAL EVALUATION

This straightforward idea for combining instance-based and model-based learning has been evaluated using a simple instance-based paradigm, three different forms of model-based learning, and eight learning tasks. Short descriptions of each follow.

3.1 INSTANCE-BASED LEARNING

The instance-based approach used here is based on IBL [Kibler, Aha, and Albert, 1988]. Prototypes consist of all training cases without any modification. The dissimilarity of two cases is computed by summing their normalized differences over each attribute, defined as

- for discrete attributes: 0 if the attribute values are the same, 1 otherwise; and
- for continuous-valued attributes: the ratio of the absolute difference between the values divided by value range of the attribute.

To classify an unknown case, the three most similar prototypes are found and their associated class values averaged. (When the instance-based approach is combined with a model-based approach, the class values are adjusted before their mean is computed.)

3.2 REGRESSION

The first of the methods for constructing predictive models is the ubiquitous multivariate linear regression [Press *et al*, 1988] that is often used as the starting point for statistical data analysis. Let C_i denote the value of the ith attribute for case C, or the rank of this value if the ith attribute is discrete (nominal). We assume a model of the form

$$M(C) = \alpha_0 + \sum_i \alpha_i \times C_i$$

and find the coefficients $\{\alpha_i\}$ to minimize the sum of the squares of the differences between the actual and predicted values for the training cases. These coefficients can be found by inverting a matrix, with some minor complications when the matrix is singular.

3.3 MODEL TREES

The second is a system called M5 that uses recursive partitioning to build a piecewise linear model in the form of a model tree [Quinlan, 1992]. The idea is to split the training cases in much the same way as when growing a decision tree, using a criterion of minimizing intra-subset variation of class values rather than maximizing information gain. Whereas a leaf of a decision tree contains just a class name, the corresponding leaf of a model tree is a linear model relating the class values of the training cases to their attribute values. *Regression trees* [Breiman *et al*, 1984] are based on a similar divide-and-conquer strategy, but have values rather than linear models at the leaves.

Consider a set T of training cases for which a model tree is to be constructed. Unless T contains few cases or their values vary only slightly, it is split according to the outcomes of a test. Every potential test is evaluated by determining the subset of cases associated with each outcome; let T_i denote the subset of cases that have the ith outcome of the potential test. If we treat the standard deviation $sd(T_i)$ of the target values of cases in T_i as a measure of error, the expected reduction in error as a result of this test can be written

$$\Delta error = sd(T) - \sum_i \frac{|T_i|}{|T|} \times sd(T_i).$$

After examining all possible tests, M5 chooses one that maximizes this expected error reduction. (For comparison, CART [Breiman *et al*, 1984] chooses a test to give the greatest expected reduction in either variance or absolute deviation.)

The major innovations of M5 come into play after the initial tree has been grown:

Error estimates: M5 often needs to estimate the accuracy of a model on unseen cases. First, the *residual* of a model on a case is just the absolute difference between the actual target value of the case and the value predicted by the model. To estimate the error of a model, M5 first determines the average residual of the model on the training cases used to construct it. This will generally underestimate the error on unseen cases, so M5 multiplies the value by $(n+\nu)/(n-\nu)$, where n is the number of training cases and ν is the number of parameters in the model. The effect is to increase the estimated error of models with many parameters constructed from small numbers of cases.

Linear models: A linear model is constructed for the cases at each node of the model tree using standard regression techniques. This model, however, is restricted to the attributes that are referenced by some test or linear model in the subtree at this node. As M5 will compare the accuracy of a linear model with the accuracy of a subtree, this ensures a level playing field in which the two types of models use the same information.

Simplification of linear models: Each linear model is then simplified by eliminating parameters so as to minimize its estimated error. Even though the elimination of parameters generally causes the average residual to increase, it also reduces the multiplicative factor above, so the estimated error can decrease. M5 uses a greedy search to remove variables that contribute little to the model; in some cases, M5 removes all variables, leaving only a constant.

Pruning: Each internal node of the tree now has both a simplified model and a model subtree. The one of these with lower estimate error is chosen; if this is the linear model, the subtree at this node has been pruned to a leaf.

Smoothing: Pregibon [private communications, 1989, 1992] observes that the prediction accuracy of tree-based models can be improved by a smoothing process. When the value of a case is predicted by a model tree, the value returned by the model at the appropriate leaf is adjusted to take account of models at nodes along the path from the root to that leaf. The form of smoothing used by M5 differs from that developed by Pregibon, but the motivation is similar. The predicted value is backed up from the leaf to the root as follows:

- The predicted value at the leaf is unchanged.
- If the case follows branch S_i of subtree S, let n_i be the number of training cases at S_i, $PV(S_i)$ the predicted value at S_i, and $M(S)$ the value given by the model at S. The predicted value backed up to S is

$$PV(S) = \frac{n_i \times PV(S_i) + k \times M(S)}{n_i + k}$$

where k is a smoothing constant[1].

[1]The default value of 15 was used in all experiments.

Smoothing has most effect when leaf models are constructed from few training cases and do not agree with models higher in the tree.

3.4 NEURAL NETS

The third form of model is the neural network. Geoffrey Hinton very kindly agreed to develop the network models used in these experiments, as described below:

"The neural networks all contained one layer of hidden units that used the logistic function to convert their combined input into their output. The single output unit of each network was linear and the error function was the sum of the squared differences between the actual and desired outputs. All input and output values for each training set were normalized to have zero mean and unit variance and the same normalization (based on the training set) was used for the test set.

"To reduce overfitting, the number of hidden units was kept small and, in addition, a penalty was imposed on the squared values of the weights. So the overall cost function that was minimized during training was the sum of the error function and a penalty coefficient times the sum of the squared weights.

"The precise number of hidden units and the coefficient of the penalty term were different for each task. To decide the values of these two parameters, one third of one of the training sets was held-out as a validation set. The remaining two thirds of the training set was then used to train many different networks containing different numbers of hidden units and different penalty coefficients. For each task, the largest number of hidden units explored was the number that gave about 2 training cases per connection, and the smallest number explored was the one that gave about 5 training cases per connection. Within this range, up to 6 different numbers of hidden units were tried. The penalty coefficients explored were 0, 0.01, 0.02, 0.03, 0.04, 0.05, 0.06, 0.08, 0.1, 0.12, 0.16, and 0.2. For each setting of these two parameters, the network was trained 3 times starting with different random weights uniformly distributed in the range -0.3 to +0.3. The parameters that gave the smallest average error on the validation set were selected. Ideally, this whole procedure should have been repeated for each of the 10 training sets used for each task, but to save time, the parameters were determined from the first training set of each task.

"The training was performed using the default conjugate gradient method of the Xerion neural network simulator developed at the University of Toronto. The user does not need to specify any parameters for this method. Training is terminated when the error decreases by less than 10^{-6}." [Hinton, private communication, 1993]

3.5 DATASETS

The four "pure" methods and three composites were tested on eight datasets drawn from seven domains that were selected to provide a range of learning challenges:

- *pw-linear:* (200 cases)
  This is a piecewise linear function defined by Breiman *et al* [1984]. There are 10 attributes, X_1 having equiprobable values -1 and 1, and X_2 to X_{10} having equiprobable values -1, 0, and 1. The generating function is

  $$V(X) = \begin{cases} 3X_2 + 2X_3 + X_4 + 3 + Z & \text{if } X_1{=}1 \\ 3X_5 + 2X_6 + X_7 - 3 + Z & \text{if } X_1{=}{-1} \end{cases}$$

  where Z is a random Gaussian noise term with variance 2. Attributes X_8, X_9 and X_{10} have no bearing on the class value.
- *housing:* (506 cases)
  This dataset, obtained from the Statistics library maintained by Carnegie Mellon University, concerns housing values in suburbs of Boston. There are 12 continuous attributes and one binary-valued attribute.
- *cpu:* (209 cases)
  Ein-Dor and Feldmesser [1987] published this dataset that relates the measured performance of CPUs to six continuous-valued and one multi-valued discrete attribute (the vendor). Although the paper also develops a new set of derived features, the attributes used in these experiments are the original parameters of the cpu such as minimum and maximum memory size.
- *auto-price:* (159 cases)
  The class value for this dataset is the 1985 list price of common automobiles. There are 16 continuous attributes covering quantities such as the automobile's size, weight and engine capacity.
- *auto-mpg:* (398 cases)
  This is another dataset from the CMU Statistics library. The data concern city-cycle fuel consumption in miles per gallon, to be predicted in terms of 3 multi-valued discrete and 5 continuous attributes. (The dataset was used as the testbed for graphical analysis packages at the 1983 American Statistical Association Exposition.)
- *servo:* (167 cases)
  This interesting collection of data, provided by Karl Ulrich, refers to an extremely non-linear phenomenon – predicting the rise time of a servomechanism in terms of two (continuous) gain settings and two (discrete) choices of mechanical linkages.
- *lhrh:* (526 cases)
  This final domain concerns a very difficult task – predicting the biomedical activity of LHRH peptides that are chains of exactly 10 amino acids. The information was obtained from Arris Pharmaceutical Corporation of San Francisco, who used an extensive table compiled by Dr Marvin Karten of the U.S. National Institutes of Health. This domain supplies two datasets:
  - *lhrh-att:* Each peptide is described in terms of 48 binary and 80 continuous attributes that measure properties of the individual amino acids and properties of the peptide as a whole. This dataset provides a very high-dimensional test of all the methods.
  - *lhrh-def:* Each peptide is described only by the names of its constituent amino acids. There are thus 10 discrete-valued attributes, all of which have very many values – about 400 amino acids occur at one or more places in the 526 peptides. Recall that linear models and neural networks use the rank of discrete attribute values. Since the amino acid names are ordered randomly, this dataset provides little joy to model-based learning systems!

Results have previously been reported for at least four of these domains. Breiman *et al* [1984] give performance figures for CART on *pw-linear* and *housing*; Ein-Dor and Feldmesser [1987] and Kibler *et al* [1988] describe experiments with *cpu*; and the latter paper also discusses *auto-price*.

3.6 EXPERIMENTS AND RESULTS

Each dataset was analysed by each method using the same 10-way cross-validation. The dataset was divided into ten blocks of near-equal size and distribution of class values. For every block in turn, each method was trained on the remaining blocks and tested on the hold-out block. Results, averaged over all test blocks, thus reflect predictive performance on unseen cases.

The first measure of performance is average error magnitude (or residual) on unseen cases, summarized in Table 1. Each column is associated with one dataset, each row with one method. The first row refers to the simple *default* method that always predicts the average value of the training set; this serves as a reference point for the underlying difficulty of the prediction tasks. The next rows show the results for instances alone and then for pairs of pure models and composite methods.

The same information is presented graphically in Figure 1, where the average error magnitudes have been normalized by dividing by the corresponding magnitude given by the default procedure.

Because all methods were evaluated with the same cross-validation partitions, each trial using exactly the same training and test cases, the sensitive one-tailed paired test of significance can be used. For every dataset, we are interested in seeing how each composite

Table 1: Average error on unseen cases

	pw-linear	housing	cpu	auto-price	auto-mpg	servo	lhrh-att	lhrh-def
default procedure	3.77	6.65	96.0	4578	6.53	1.15	2.28	2.28
instances alone	1.73	2.90	34.0	1689	2.72	0.52	0.91	0.85
regression	2.13	3.29	35.5	1848	2.61	0.86	1.10	2.01
regression + instances	1.56	2.45	30.0	1430	2.37	0.48	0.97	1.22
model trees	1.10	2.45	28.9	1562	2.11	0.45	0.96	1.29
model trees + instances	1.21	2.32	28.1	1386	2.18	0.30	0.88	0.97
neural nets	1.14	2.29	28.7	1833	2.02	0.30	1.07	1.16
neural nets + instances	1.29	2.23	29.0	1677	2.06	0.29	0.99	1.04

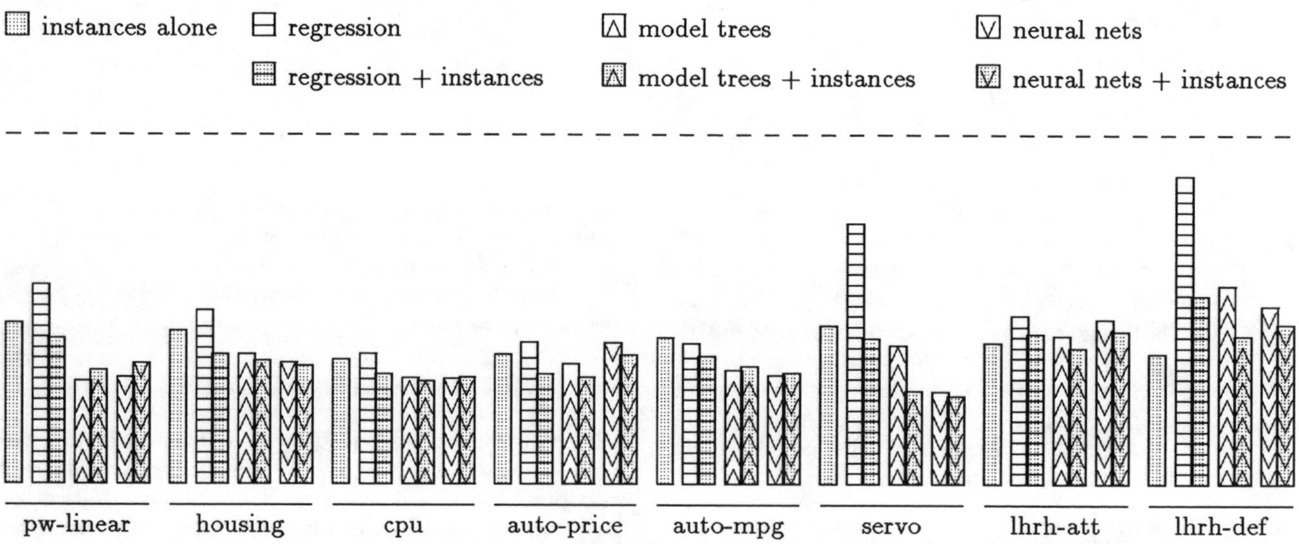

Figure 1: Average error on unseen cases

method compares to the two pure methods from which it is constituted, e.g. how *model trees + instances* compares with *instances* alone and with *model trees* alone. This gives six comparisons for each dataset, or 48 comparisons in all.

At the 5% significance level, the composite methods are significantly better than the constituent pure methods in 31 comparisons, about the same in twelve comparisons, and significantly worse in only five comparisons. The five cases in which composite models are significantly worse are:

- In the *pw-linear* task, model trees are superior to *model trees + instances* and neural networks are superior to *neural nets + instances.* Both the model trees and neural nets find close approximations to the true underlying function (minus the noise term). The use of prototypes with a near-perfect model causes a slight increase in error, since the noise is absent from the model but present in the prototype cases.
- The other three cases all concern the *lhrh-def* task, instances alone being superior to all three composite methods. For this dataset, where attribute values are just the names of amino acids, all models are (understandably) very weak and their use to adjust prototype estimators introduces substantial errors.

On the positive side, the composite methods often score big wins. The improved accuracy of the *regression + instances* composite over simple regression is uniformly (and dramatically) apparent on all datasets. The *servo* dataset also highlights the effectiveness of

Table 2: Relative error (%) on unseen cases

	pw-linear	housing	cpu	auto-price	auto-mpg	servo	lhrh-att	lhrh-def
instances alone	21.7	22.7	20.0	26.0	23.0	25.6	20.7	17.5
regression	33.5	29.4	19.7	20.1	19.4	49.2	31.5	84.5
regression + instances	18.3	16.8	11.8	14.8	17.3	19.7	26.9	37.8
model trees	9.5	18.6	17.2	16.2	14.7	28.7	23.6	39.6
model trees + instances	11.7	16.5	12.0	12.8	16.0	16.5	21.0	25.4
neural nets	10.1	13.6	11.0	28.5	12.5	11.4	28.3	32.4
neural nets + instances	12.6	12.9	11.1	25.7	13.4	10.6	25.4	27.5

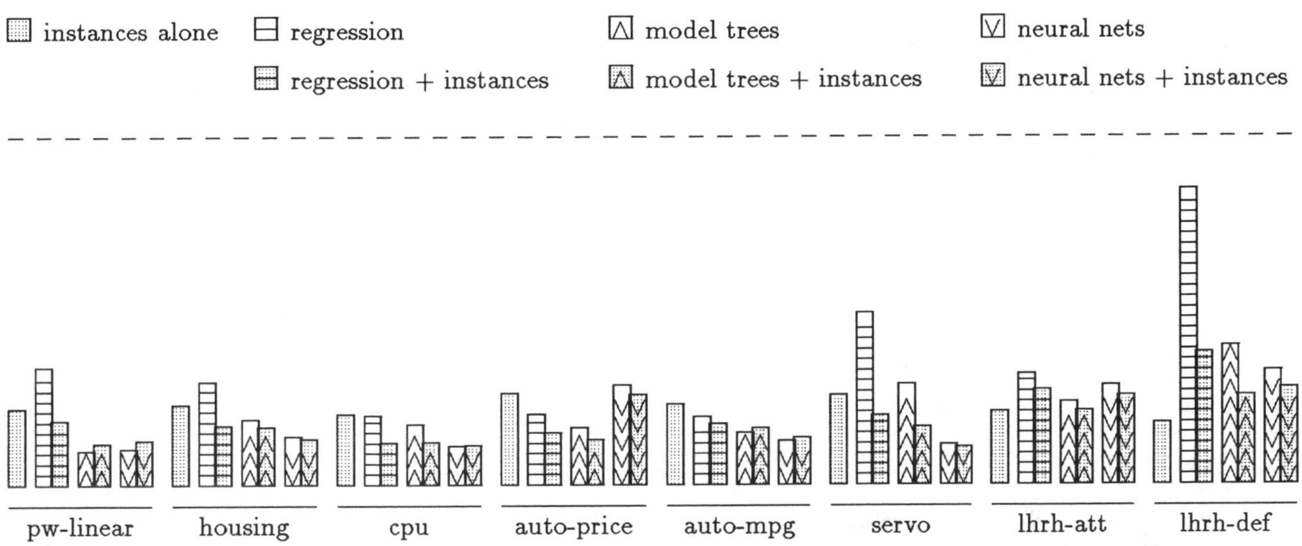

Figure 2: Relative error on unseen cases

the composite methods: average error is nearly halved in the case of regression, is reduced by 33% for model trees, and is reduced slightly even for networks (where the pure method is already doing extremely well). In the few cases for which the composite models are inferior to one or other of their constituent models, the difference in accuracy is usually small.

The second performance measure investigated is *relative error* [Breiman *et al*, 1984], defined as the variance of the residuals on unseen cases, divided by the variance of the class values themselves. (Dispite its name, this statistic thus measures squared error.) As with the normalized metric used in Figure 1, the value is 100% for any method that always predicts the mean value. Relative errors are presented in Table 2 and repeated in graph form in Figure 2. The results show a similar pattern, although the error-squared measure accentuates differences in some domains.

Table 3: Average relative error (%) across tasks

instances alone	22.2
regression	35.9
regression + instances	20.4
model trees	21.0
model trees + instances	16.5
neural nets	18.5
neural nets + instances	17.4

As a rough indicator of overall performance, the relative errors for each method were averaged over all eight tasks (Table 3).

Finally, there might be some concern that the use of an unsophisticated instance-based paradigm could have distorted these rather positive results. However, per-

Table 4: Comparison of relative error

	model trees + instances	CART	IBL
pw-linear	12%	17%	
housing	16%	22%	
cpu	11%		23%
auto-price	11%		19%

formance of the various methods compares favorably with results from other systems. For example, Table 4 shows relative error of the *model trees + instances* composite compared with published results from CART on the first two domains and with computed results from IBL on the next two. The composite fares well on this comparison, and might achieve even better accuracy if it were changed to incorporate more advanced instance-based methods such as those described by Aha *et al* [1991].

4 CONCLUSION

This paper has described a simple method for combining instance-based and model-based learning for tasks that involve the prediction of values. The advantages of the approach have been illustrated using three disparate model-learning methods and a variety of domains. The approach is quite general and should be applicable to any instance-based method and any form of learned model.

The method achieves its power through using the same training data to provide local information (in the form of prototypes) and a global model. Both kinds of knowledge are brought to bear when the class value of an unseen case is predicted. The method seems to provide robust improvement, with two exceptions:

- If the model is extremely weak, as was the case with the *lhrh-def* dataset, it is advisable to use the instances alone.
- If the model is near-perfect but there is unavoidable noise, as with model trees for the *pw-linear* domain, the use of local information might introduce additional error.

I have also experimented with a similar composite approach in which the model attempts to predict differences directly [Quinlan, 1993b]. For domains in which such a difference model can be found, including *servo* and *lhrh-def* among the present datasets, this approach produces predictors that are better still.

Acknowledgements

This research has been made possible by grants from the Australian Research Council and assisted by a research agreement with Digital Equipment Corporation. I am extremely grateful to Geoff Hinton, who designed, trained, and evaluated the 80 neural nets used in these experiments. Donald Michie made several helpful suggestions, especially the idea of trying composite regression models. The paper was improved as a result of comments by Mike Cameron-Jones.

Thanks to Dr Marvin Karten, National Institutes of Health, Bethesda MD, and to Arris Pharmaceutical Corporation, San Francisco, for access to the LHRH peptide data, and to Karl Ulrich for the servomechanism dataset. I also gratefully acknowledge using datasets from the UCI Data Repository and StatLib at CMU.

References

Aha, D.W., Kibler, D., and Albert, M.K. (1991), Instance-based learning algorithms, *Machine Learning 6*, 1, 37-66.

Breiman, L., Friedman, J.H., Olshen, R.A., and Stone, C.J. (1984), *Classification and regression trees*, Belmont, California: Wadsworth.

Ein-Dor, P. and Feldmesser, J. (1987), Attributes of the performance of central processing units: a relative performance prediction model, *Communications of the ACM 30*, 4, 308-317.

Hinton, G.E. (1986), Learning distributed representations of concepts, *Proceedings Eighth Annual Conference of the Cognitive Science Society*, Amherst. Reprinted in R.G.M. Morris (Ed), *Parallel Distributed Processing: Implications for Psychology and Neurobiology*, Oxford University Press.

Hinton, G.E. (1992), How neural networks learn from experience, *Scientific American 267*, 3, (September 1992), 144-151.

Kibler, D., Aha, D.W., and Albert, M.K. (1988), Instance-based prediction of real-valued attributes, Technical Report 88-07, ICS, University of California, Irvine.

McClelland, J.L., and Rumelhart, D.E. (1988), *Explorations in Parallel Distributed Processing*, Cambridge: MIT Press.

Press, W.H., Flannery, B.P., Teukolsky, S.A., and Vetterling, W.T. (1988), *Numerical Recipes in C*, Cambridge University Press.

Quinlan, J.R. (1992), Learning with continuous classes, *Proceedings 5th Australian Joint Conference on Artificial Intelligence*, Singapore: World Scientific, 343-348.

Quinlan, J.R. (1993a), *C4.5: Programs for Machine Learning*, San Mateo, California: Morgan Kaufmann.

Quinlan, J.R. (1993b), A case study in machine learning, *Proceedings 16th Australian Computer Science Conference*, Brisbane, 731-737.

Stanfill, C. and Waltz, D. (1986), Toward memory-based reasoning, *Communications of the ACM 29*, 12, 1213-1228.

Data Mining of Subjective Agricultural Data

R. Bharat Rao
Learning Systems Department
Siemens Corporate Research
755 College Road East
Princeton, NJ 08541
bharat@learning.scr.siemens.com

Thomas B. Voigt
Dept. of Horticulture
Knowledge-Based Modeling Lab.
Univ. of Illinois at UrbanaChampaign
1201 S. Dorner
Urbana, IL 61801
voigt@kbml.plant.uiuc.edu

Thomas W. Fermanian
Dept. of Horticulture
Knowledge-Based Modeling Lab.
fermo@kbml.plant.uiuc.edu

Abstract

The National Turfgrass Evaluation Program was established to collect data on the performance of cultivars of different turfgrass species. This data is highly subjective, consisting of visual ratings of turfplots by evaluators of varying experience at sites throughout the U.S. In this paper we describe a methodology for mining this large database through learning models to make recommendations about specific cultivars depending upon maintenance and environmental conditions. Our experiments show that learned models outperform human experts in a number of areas. Our studies also indicate that the many of human experts lack the necessary experience to discriminate between specific cultivars. This knowledge is of great commercial and environmental importance in the turfgrass industry.

1 INTRODUCTION

With the improvement of data collection, transmission, and storage methods, many organizations have amassed large quantities of data relating to different aspects of their business. This data is a gold mine of valuable information and there is tremendous potential for developing machine learning techniques for *data mining* applications. These applications show no greater promise than in a number of agricultural domains. Their implementation is not easy, however, due to the variety and nature of the collected biological data.

The National Turfgrass Evaluation Program (NTEP[1]) was formed in 1980 to standardize the evaluation of turfgrasses produced in various breeding programs. Over the last 13 years, NTEP has collected data about the performance of many different species of turfgrass at sites over the United States. For the purposes of this paper, we have focussed on a single species, *Poa pratensis* L. (Kentucky bluegrass), one of the most commonly used turf species in the country. There are currently more than 150 different types or *cultivars*[2] of Kentucky bluegrass. The initial NTEP database contains evaluations taken for 84 cultivars at 45 sites, every month, for 4 years. Each monthly evaluation for a cultivar plot consists of recording the *management regime* (i.e., the values of turf management parameters such as irrigation level, quantity/type of fertilizer, etc.) and assigning a single *quality* rating for cultivar performance. The quality rating is made by an evaluator who *visually* inspects the cultivar plot and assigns an integer value between 1 (worst) and 9 (best). This rating is based on factors such as the turf color, uniformity of leaf width, and the number of shoots.

While the database is quite large, the more serious problem is the *subjective* nature of the data. Quality ratings at differing sites are made by evaluators with widely differing experiences. Even at a single site cultivar performance may be estimated by an experienced turfgrass scientist one month, and by a graduate student or technical staff the next month. Statistical analysis of quality ratings (Horst, et al., 1984) have shown that when turfgrass evaluators rated the same cultivar plot at the same site, at the same time, the assigned ratings varied greatly (i.e., one evaluator's '7' may be another's '4'). When one considers that in addition to the varying experience of the data collectors, the NTEP ratings were also affected by factors such as weather, time of evaluation, and the sites being spread throughout the country, it is clear that the ratings are highly subjective.

In many domains, it is possible to interview human experts to acquire the knowledge for expert systems. However, traditional turfgrass practice has been to classify cultivars into two groups, *low* or *high* maintenance cultivars. Based on the level of maintenance at a site and a few

[1]NTEP is a non-profit, self-supporting program jointly sponsored by the National Turfgrass Federation, Inc., and the United States Department of Agriculture (USDA).

[2]Cultivar —"An assemblage of cultivated plants distinguished by any characters which, when reproduced sexually or asexually, retain their distinguishing features" (Turgeon, 1991).

other conditions, the expert typically suggests a small set of cultivars from one of these two groups. While this may have been satisfactory several decades ago, the last 30 years have seen the number of cultivars increase tremendously as research centers produce new genotypes every year. Selecting the appropriate cultivar for a new site or optimizing the management regimes for an existing cultivar can have vast commercial implications in the multi-*billion* dollar golf course and lawn-care industries. For instance, precise determination of appropriate cultivars for given management and environmental conditions can result in drastically reduced pesticide use. This is because a turfgrass that is properly matched to its growing situation is less susceptible to pest invasion.

The primary goal of this research is to learn relationships from the subjective NTEP database to make recommendations about selection and management for specific cultivars. We begin by statistically processing the data to remove some of the effects of shifts in rating ranges by different evaluators from the subjective quality ratings and merging it with a weather database in an effort to gather the relevant *environment* parameters. Machine learning and statistical techniques are applied to acquire models. We present studies comparing the performance of the models with human experts and then use the learned models to make recommendations in typical turf situations. The learned models will eventually be incorporated into the TURFPLAN (Liu, et al., 1991) expert system for selection of turfgrass species and their cultivars.

2 OVERVIEW

Traditional database technology has been geared towards processing business data. In the recent past, the application of *database mining* (Brice & Alexander, 1990; Krishnamurthy & Imielinski, 1991; Tsur, 1990) has acquired considerable significance. Researchers have developed and applied machine learning and statistical techniques to automatically acquire knowledge from large databases (Agrawal, et al., 1992; Ginsberg, et al., 1988; Hunter, 1990; Piatetsky-Shapiro & Frawley, 1991) and to learn rules for expert systems (Shapiro, 1987; Shaw & Gentry, 1988; Spur, et al., 1991).

While expert systems for agriculture (Whittaker, et al., 1987) have achieved success in several different domains (Benson, et al., 1992; Huirne, et al., 1992; Schueller, et al., 1986; Yamoah, et al., 1990), evaluation methods commonly used in crop science have limited application to turf science as turfgrass specialists are concerned with different growth objectives, mainly, the visual quality of the vegetation. For example, while the harvested yield per acre is an excellent measure of the performance of a variety of wheat, the primary function of turfgrass is ornamental. Therefore, *visual evaluation* is the most important way of measuring turfgrass performance. An earlier statistical study assessing visual evaluation techniques in the turfgrass domain (Horst, et al., 1984) concluded that the results of regional and national cultivar trials needed to be considered with caution and that techniques for visually assessing turfgrass were inadequate due to the subjectivity of this data.

The NTEP data, however, is the main source from which this knowledge can be derived as human turf experts lack the detailed information needed to distinguish between individual cultivars (see Section 5). Statistical researchers have worked on modeling probabilistic opinion (Kosko, 1991; Krishnan & Nandy, 1990; Smyth, 1993; West, 1992; West & Crosse, 1992), but much of it is focussed on the single expert case. In our methodology we statistically analyze the data to try to separate out some objective features. We use our knowledge about the data collection methods to obtain relative measures of cultivar performance for each individual turfgrass evaluator. The individual opinions are then re-combined to obtain a more objective database "**E**" (see Section 3).

The next step is to determine if we can acquire useful knowledge from **E**. In the studies described in Section 4, we apply several different modeling algorithms to classify the performance of cultivars under different management regimes. Using the IND (Buntine, 1989) package we are able to easily implement several well-known tree classifier algorithms, namely C4 (Quinlan, 1986), CART (Breiman, et al., 1984), and Bayesian decision trees (see Buntine, 1991 for an evaluation of different classifiers). We also apply AQ (Michalski, et al., 1986) and logistic regression to a selected subset of **E**, and compared the performance of all these algorithms with an expert panel. Based on these experiments, we apply C4 to learn models from the entire data segment. These models were used to make recommendations for a number of different situations for two of the most common types of tasks faced by turfgrass experts. The performance of the C4 models is compared with a large expert panel in Section 5.

3 STATISTICAL PROCESSING OF THE NTEP DATA

As a first step, raw NTEP data was first separated into blocks of data from a single testing site and single months' quality ratings. This assured that the data in each block was evaluated by the same person. The mean quality ratings were then statistically analyzed using a standard mean separation test, Fishers LSD at $\alpha = 0.05$ (Steel & Torrie, 1980).

Based on its mean separation position in each block, the cultivars were then separated into three performance categories: top; medium; and bottom, as shown in Figure 1. For example, if there were three distinct mean separations, a, b, and c, each mean group was assigned to one category. In situations where there were more than three LSD assignments, the total number of assignments was divided by 3 and assigned a performance category. In cases where the total number of LSD letter assignments was not evenly

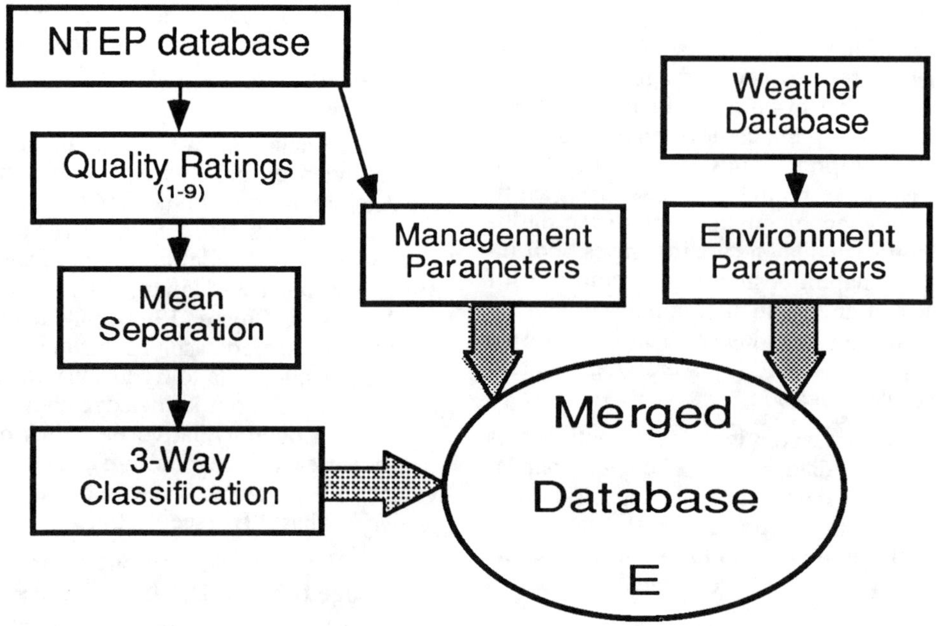

Figure 1: Developing the Example Database from NTEP Data

divisible by 3, the remnant letter assignments were placed in the lower performance categories.

This attempt to standardize the quality ratings in a smaller range of values was prompted by the method in which the data was originally collected. Previous studies (Horst, et al., 1984; Lush, 1990) have shown an inconsistency in the rating ranges used by different evaluators. We wished to minimize the impact of these rating range shifts on any selected learning approach. Upon completion of this step, each of the 84 Kentucky bluegrass cultivars was assigned a performance category (top, medium, or bottom) for each month and site combination.

The cultivar performance data was then merged with site management information obtained from the raw NTEP data. Finally, this merged data file was combined with monthly precipitation, average temperature, and degree day (base 65°F) data obtained from National Oceanic and Atmospheric Administration publications. The final data set was then separated by cultivar into examples consisting of a string of 12 integers corresponding to performance category, soil texture, pH, phosphorus, potassium, nitrogen fertilization level, light quantity, mowing height, irrigation practices, monthly precipitation, average monthly temperature, and monthly degree days.

4 INITIAL STUDY: PREDICTING CULTIVAR PERFORMANCE

The primary source of expertise in the turfgrass domain is the human experts. Turfgrass specialists are routinely called upon to choose cultivars for establishing new turfs and to determine management regimes for existing turfs. While some superintendents at golf courses or other turf sites are very knowledgeable about turf management, their expertise is typically limited to the handful of cultivars they regularly use at their sites. The experts most qualified to make recommendations about the selection and use of cultivars are experienced turfgrass scientists and breeders. For the initial study described in this section, we used two experts from the University of Illinois as an expert panel.

The goal of this initial study was to evaluate the effectiveness of different model-building techniques for mining the subjective data. The performance of the human experts served as a benchmark. Given the paucity of experts in this domain, it was decided that if the learned models were comparable in accuracy to the human experts, their performance would be deemed satisfactory. For this initial study, we used only one year's data (1983) from the transformed database **E**, for 4 relatively well-established Kentucky bluegrass cultivars ('Haga', 'South Dakota Common', 'Midnight', and 'Sydsport'). For each of the four cultivars, 201 examples were available for testing. Of the data, 90% was used as a training set to learn the model, and 10% as a test set. The human experts were provided with the training and test sets, with the performance data removed from the test set. They were required to classify the test examples as top, medium, or bottom performers based on the training set and their intimate knowledge of the cultivars. The predictive accuracy was determined by tracking the number of times the expert predicted the actual performance for the test set.

We also learned models from the training set using some well known decision tree building algorithms: C4, CART (with two different Standard errors), and a Bayesian tree building algorithm. In addition, the AQ algorithm was also used. Logistic regression was used in place of standard regression because there were 3 performance category assignments as opposed to a continuous string of assignments. The learned models were used to predict the quality of the events in the test set. The predictive accuracies for a *10-way cross-validation* as suggested in Breiman, 1984, are displayed in Table 1 (averaged over all 4 cultivars).

Table 1: Comparative Performance of Human and Machine Learning Strategies

Learning strategy	Percent predictive accuracy (10-way)	Model complexity	Model formation time
C4	59.4	low	short
Cart (SE=1)	59.3	low	short
Bayes	60.1	low	short
Cart (SE=0)	58.6	low	short
AQ15	62.7	med	med
Regression	59.2	high	med
Human	43.1	high	long

While the accuracies of the ML algorithms are not especially high, they represent a significant increase in accuracy compared to the human experts. The relatively low accuracies (around 60%) are not surprising, given that the database **E** still has a large subjective component in spite of the statistical pre-processing. In general, the decision-tree algorithms were the fastest at building models (taking between a few seconds and 2 minutes on a SUN4 to learn a model for a single cultivar), followed by logistic regression and AQ which took about 15-20 minutes for model formation.

As we plan to eventually use the learned models in a turfgrass expert system, it is essential for human experts to evaluate and validate the data. Therefore, the comprehensibility of the models is crucial (this is why we did not include neural networks in our study). The algorithms are ranked in Table 1 in increasing order of complexity. The logistic regression models were not as quickly comprehended by other turf experts and AQ produced a large number of very specialized rules from the database **E**. The decision tree algorithms were the most readable. Michie, 1987, argues strongly that the AI goal of producing concepts that are comprehensible to humans dictates that the size of decision trees must be kept within a small "human window".

All the learning algorithms produced models of similar accuracy. As C4 consistently produced the most compact trees compared with the other algorithms (using number of nodes as a complexity criterion), it was the algorithm of choice for the more detailed study described in the next section. The choice of C4 was perhaps appropriate, in light of C4 being successfully applied to learn trees from large databases (Carter & Catlett, 1987; Catlett, 1991).

It should be noted that the credentials of the experts we used were among the best possible (perhaps a handful of turf breeders may have been better qualified, at least for the cultivar strains developed and sold by their companies). Despite both experts being very familiar with the 4 cultivars that had been in wide use for the last 12 years, their predictive accuracy was very low. Part of the problem was undoubtedly due to the database still having a large subjective component even after the statistical processing. Also, humans are typically not very good at these kinds of classification tasks involving a large number of numerical variables. Finally, it could be argued that this was an artificial task for the human experts, whose expertise was geared towards improving rather than predicting cultivar performance. Even then, this initial study seemed to indicate that human expertise in distinguishing between different cultivars is fairly poor. This was confirmed by the studies described in the next section.

5 LEARNING MODELS FROM THE NTEP DATA

Turfgrass experts make two types of turf selection decisions. In turf *establishment* situations, the expert is given an environment and management regime and must recommend a small group of cultivars that will flourish under the conditions. In turf *management* situations, the expert is presented with established cultivars under an environment regime and must recommend a management regime. Nine turfgrass experts from the Midwest formed an expert panel for the two studies described in this section.

5.1 STUDY 1: TURF ESTABLISHMENT SITUATIONS

An expert from the panel chose a subset of 16 Kentucky bluegrass cultivars from the 84 in **E**. The expert was requested to pick among the best known cultivars, so that the panel would be very familiar with the choices. Another expert was requested to devise a few turf establishment situations typical of those faced by human experts. Neither expert referred to the data or had access to any models while making up the questionnaire shown in Figure 2.

The four situations in the questionnaire represent a broad spectrum of management regimes, with the golf course fairway representing a most intense maintenance situation and the highway right-of-way is an example of very limited maintenance. Each expert was requested to recom-

Please check the Kentucky bluegrass cultivar boxes that would be top performers for an establishment situation. You may check as many boxes as you wish for each situation. A culivar may be selected for more than one situation.

Situation	Adelphi	Glade	Ram-1
New York state golf course fairway soil=loam, pH=6.8, soil potassium=350 lbs/acre, soil phosphorus=200 lbs/acre; automatic irrigation	❑	❑	❑
Kansas football field soil=modified sandy loam, pH=7.2, potassium=250 lbs/acre, soil phosphorus=100 lbs/acre; manual irrigation	❑	❑	❑
Illinois airport turf soil=silty-clay loam, pH=6.2, potassium=150 lbs/acre, soil phosphorus=65 lbs/acre; less than 2 lbs. nitrogen /year; no irrigation	❑	❑	❑
Virginia highway right of way clay soil, pH = 5.5, potassium =275 lbs/acre, soil phosphorus = 100 lbs/acre; no fertilization; no irrigation	❑	❑	❑

Figure 2: Questionnaire for Turf Establishment Situations

mend a group of cultivars (from the set of 16) that they deemed to be top performers for the situations.

Based on the results of the previous section, the C4 algorithm was used to learn a model for each of the 16 cultivars using the data for the remaining 3 years (1982, 1984, and 1985) for that cultivar in the entire database **E**. The accuracy of the models (based on learning from 2 years data and testing on the third, for 3 repetitions) for the 16 cultivars was slightly lower than that reported in the previous section. This was probably due to the wide variation in climatic conditions from year to year. The aim of this study was to determine if the learned models were able to discriminate between cultivars in typical turf establishment situations.

The questionnaire described the management regime for each situation. From the weather database we were able to determine the average monthly weather conditions at the sites for 3 years. We were thus able to create a test set by replicating the management regime 36 times and using the weather conditions for each month to fill in the environment parameters. The 16 models learned by C4 were used to predict the quality for each event in the test set. From this we calculated the *top-fraction*, T_f, as shown below

$$T_f = \frac{\text{number of events predicted as top performers}}{\text{number of test events}} \begin{cases} \text{if } T_f \geq 0.8 & \text{TOP} \\ \textit{else} & \text{not TOP} \end{cases}$$

A threshold of 0.8 seemed a natural choice because with only one exception, no value of T_f fell between 0.5 and 0.8. In Table 2, we indicate the cultivars that were rated as top performers by C4 for each situation.

According to our experts, for some of the situations as many as 10 cultivars could be recommended. However, typically most experts selected fewer cultivars, especially for the last two situations. It was decided that a cultivar would be "recommended" if it was chosen by 2 or more experts on the panel (marked with an "x" in Table 2). In a few occasions, there was a high degree of consensus with 5-6 experts picking the same cultivar. These situations were indicated with a bold "**X**" in Table 2. The table shows that for all situations where a cultivar was chosen by 5 or more experts the C4 models recommended the cultivar as well.

The final row in Table 2 shows the *relative* match between C4 and the human experts. For example, for the first situation C4 recommended 8 of the 10 cultivars (80% match) that the experts chose, and the human panel recommended 8 of the 9 cultivars (82%) the C4 models recommended as top performers. The relative match between the choices was quite high for the first two situations. However, for the last two (low maintenance) situations, the experts picked far fewer cultivars than C4. One reason for this is that turfgrass experts are infrequently called upon to make recommendations in low maintenance situations. Also, most of the sites in the database used a high maintenance regime, and therefore, the models may have been less accurate for other regimes. This could be remedied by recommending that NTEP require more variation in management regimes at sites for future data collection.

Table 2: Top Performers for Turf Establishment Situations

Cultivar	Situation							
	NY golf fairway		Kansas ftball field		Illinois airport turf		Virginia right of way	
	Human	C4	Human	C4	Human	C4	Human	C4
Adelphi	x		x	x				
Glade	x	x		x				
Ram-I		x	x	x				
Nugget								
S-21	x				x		x	x
Baron	x	x	X	x		x		x
Parade		x	x					
Rugby	x	x	X	x		x		x
Touchdown	X	x	X	x		x		x
Haga	x	x		x		x		
Kenblue					X	x	x	x
Midnight	X	x	x	x				
A-34	x	x	x	x	x			
Sydsport	x	x	X	x				
S. D. Cmn					X	x	X	x
Merion		x		x				
Rel. match	80	82	89	73	50	33	100	50

However, when the experts were queried about why they picked (or did not pick) a specific cultivar for a situation, it came to light that experts used some external factors in arriving at their decisions. For instance, according to the model, 'Touchdown' would be a top performing cultivar in the low maintenance situation for the highway right-of-way (Situation 4). However, the experts did not pick 'Touchdown' because it is an expensive strain and would never be used in such a situation. Similarly, an expert's reason for not choosing 'Merion' in Situation 4, was due to past studies indicating its susceptibility to disease. As disease and cost data were not included in **E**, it is not surprising that the model disagreed with the experts in these situations. It also appeared that factors such as commercial advertising by companies was also a factor. It was not surprising that 'Touchdown' which has long been marketed as a turf for athletic fields (Situation 2) was the only unanimous choice in our survey. Also, 'Midnight', which has been the focus of a heavy advertising campaign over the last year, ranked second highest, being picked by 6 experts.

This study showed that even with the subjective data, C4 was able to learn models that matched human performance. The performance of the models relative to the expert panel was better than the performance of a single expert when compared against the rest of the panel.

5.2 STUDY 2: TURF MANAGEMENT SITUATIONS

It was decided that the simplest (and probably the best) way to test human performance in a management situation would be to isolate a single management parameter that would have to be set. In fact, rather than set a value for the parameter (as in real life) the expert was asked to choose between "high" and "low" management levels for the parameter. Future studies could use combinations of cultivars.

A computer scientist with no expertise in the turfgrass domain examined the 16 decision trees created by C4. From these he selected 5 situations consisting of a cultivar, a management parameter, and a value that seemed to be indicative of a top performance classification for that cultivar. One of the experts in the panel then suggested an alternate setting for that management variable representing the other end of the scale (low versus high management). An additional "dummy" situation where the decision tree did not choose the variable, was also included. The 6 situations in the second evaluation were sent to the 8 other experts, with instructions to choose the parameter setting that was most conducive to top performance. The experts could leave the question unanswered if they were unsure about the influence of that parameter, and could select both columns to indicate equal (or no) influence.

Table 3 shows the results of the expert evaluation. Of the 5 situations where the models seemed to indicate a definite choice, the experts agreed with the model on 2, disagreed on 2 more, and were evenly divided on the last one. In the "dummy" situation (row 4 in Table 3) the experts were equally divided as well, with one expert choosing both values to indicate equal influence (the only such choice in the entire survey).

Unlike the turf establishment study, there was not much of a match between the human experts and C4. However, the most telling aspect of this study was that every expert expressed a lack of confidence in his/her ability to answer detailed questions about the individual cultivars. In many cases, the experts did not even make a recommendation. It was clear that the expertise required to answer these kinds of questions was not available.

Table 3: Human and Model Performance in Turf Management Situations

Cultivar	Value 1	no. of experts[a]	Value2	no. of experts
Kenblue[b]	soil texture= loamy sand	4	**soil texture= clay**[c]	2
S-21	soil pH=5	0	**soil pH=7.5**	5
Midnight	mowed at=3 inches	5	**mowed at=1 inch**	3
S. D. Common	soil pH=5	2	soil pH=8	2
Midnight	P=150 lbs/acre	3	**P=300 lbs/acre**	3
Kenblue	**little irrigation**	5	automatic irrigation	2

[a] Number of experts (out of 8) selecting this value as most likely to promote top quality turf.
[b] Presented to experts with maintenance restriction of little or no irrigation.
[c] **Bold** values chosen by examining C4 model, as most likely to promote top quality turf.

6 CONCLUSIONS

This research has several useful outcomes. The methodology presented in this paper provides a way to acquire domain expertise by using machine learning for data mining applications on the NTEP database. The results of this study also bear out our contention that even highly-qualified human turfgrass experts do not possess the detailed level of information necessary to match cultivar performance with a set of environmental situations. In the past, the small number of available turfgrass cultivars made knowledge of specific cultivar attributes unnecessary. However, experts have not been able to keep up with with the recent influx of several new and different cultivars. With increased pressure from the public to maintain turfs at lower cost with less pesticides, this cultivar-selection expertise will become vital in the near future.

This research also supplies information that can improve our knowledge about turfgrass cultivars. Many of the newly discovered relationships between the cultivar performance and the environment/management parameters have never been investigated in field experiments. These discovered relationships provide turfgrass researchers with testable hypotheses for future studies.

In addition to applying this methodology to the other species in the NTEP database, we hope that it will be applicable to several other agricultural domains. There are large amounts of unprocessed vegetable, fruit, and dairy data that can be profitably mined using these procedures.

Finally, based on our studies, we are able to make recommendations to NTEP about modifying the data collection procedures to facilitate data mining activities. To better evaluate future cultivar performance, we are recommending that NTEP select more varied test sites, impose different management regimes at the various sites, and collect more complete environmental data. Modification in the format of collected data is also recommended to reduce some of the subjective differences which have existed in the past.

Acknowledgments

This study was conducted when R. Bharat Rao was a student at the University of Illinois. We thank the National Turfgrass Evaluation Program (Grant no. SRA-166), University of Illinois Agricultural Experiment Station, and the Illinois Turfgrass Foundation for their support of this project. The authors also wish to acknowledge Kevin Morris, NTEP National Director, Beltsville, and Zeyad Najem, Computer Science, University of Illinois, for their assistance in data transfer and preparation. We are grateful to Wray Buntine, NASA Ames Research Center, and R.S. Michalski, George Mason University, for providing us with the code for the IND and AQ systems respectively. We also thank Jean Haley, Randy Kane, Zac Reicher, Clark Throssell, David Ward, David Wehner, and Dan Weissenberg for serving on our expert panel. We thank the reviewers for their insightful comments.

References

Agrawal, R., Ghosh, S., Imielinski, T., Iyer, B., & Swami, A. (1992). An interval classifier for database mining applications. In *VLDB 92*.

Benson, V. W., Harris, B. L., & Richardson, C. W. (1992). Using expert systems and process models to enhance u.s. agriculture (commentary). *Journal of Soil & Water Conservation*, *47*:234-235.

Breiman, L., Friedman, J. H., Olshen, R. A., & Stone, C. J. (1984). *Classification and Regression Trees*. Wadsworth.

Brice, R., & Alexander, W. (1990). Finding interesting things in lots of data. In *23rd Hawaii International Conference on System Sciences*.

Buntine, W. L. (1989). Learning classification rules using bayes. In *Sixth International Workshop on Machine Learning*.

Buntine, W. L. (1991). Classifiers: A theoretical and empiricial study.

Carter, C., & Catlett, J. (1987). Assessing credit card applications using machine learning. *IEEE Expert*, *2*(3):71-79.

Catlett, J. (1991). Megainduction: a test flight. In *The Eighth International Workshop on Machine Learning*, (pp. 596-599).

Ginsberg, A., Weiss, S. M., & Politakis, P. (1988). Automatic knowledge base refinement for classification systems. *Artificial Intelligence*, *35*(2):197-226.

Horst, G., L. , Engelke, M. C., & Meyers, W. (1984). Assessment of visual evaluation techniques. *Agronomy Journal*, *76*:619-622.

Huirne, R. B. M., Dijkhuizen, A. A., & Renkema, J. A. (1992). Computerized analysis of individual sowherd performance (chess, computerized herd evaluation system for sows). *American Journal of Agricultural Economics*, *74*:388-399.

Hunter, L. (1990). Knowledge acquisition planning for inference from large databases. In *23rd Annual Hawaii International conference on System Sciences*, 2 (pp. 35-44).

Kosko, B. (1991). Stochastic competitive learning. *2*:522-529.

Krishnamurthy, R., & Imielinski, T. (1991). Practitioner problems in need of database research: Research directions in knowledge discovery. *Sigmod Record*, *20*(3):76-78.

Krishnan, T., & Nandy, S. C. (1990). Efflciency of discriminant analysis when initial analysis are classified stochastically. *Pattern Recognition*, *23*(5):529-537.

Liu, H., Fermanian, T. W., & Carmer, S., A. (1991). Expert system for planning the establishment of turfs. *Agronomy Journal*, *83*:140-143.

Lush, W. M. (1990). Turf growth and performance evaluation based on turf biomass and tiller density. *Agronomy Journal*, *82*:505-511.

Michalski, R. S., Mozetic, I., Hong, J., & Lavrac, N. (1986). The multi-purpose incremental learning system AQ15 and its testing application in three medical domains. In *Fifth National Conference on Artificial Intelligence*, (pp. 1041-1047).

Michie, D. (1987). Current developments in expert systems. In J. R. Quinlan (Eds.), *Applications of Expert Systems* Turing Institute Press.

Piatetsky-Shapiro, G., & Frawley, W., J. (Ed.). (1991). *Knowledge Discovery in Databases*. AAAI Press.

Quinlan, J., R. (1986). Induction of decision trees. *Machine Learning*, *1*(1):81-106.

Schueller, J., K. , Slusher, R. M., & Morgan, S. M. (1986). An expert system with speech synthesis for troubleshooting grain combine performance. *Transactions of the ASAE*, *29*.

Shapiro, A. D. (1987). *Structured Induction in Expert Systems*. Turing Institute Press.

Shaw, M. J., & Gentry, J. A. (1988). Using an expert system with inductive learning to evaluate business loans. *Financial Management*, *17*:45-56.

Smyth, P. (1993). Learning with stochastic supervision. In Petsche, Hanson, Kearns, & Rivest (Eds.), *Computational learning Theory and Natural Learning Systems*

Spur, G., Specht, D., & Weiss, S. (1991). Integration of learning approaches for maintenance tasks. *Computers in Industry*, *17*:269-277.

Steel, R. G., & Torrie, J. H. (1980). *Principles and Procedures of Statistics: A Biometrical Approach*. McGraw Hill.

Tsur, S. (1990). Data dredging. , *13*(4):58-63.

Turgeon, A. J. (1991). *Turfgrass managment*. Prentice Hall.

West, M. (1992). Modeling agent forecast distributions. *Journal of the Royal Statistical Society*, *54*(2):553-567.

West, M., & Crosse, J. (1992). Modeling probabilistic agent opinion. *Journal of the Royal Statistical Society*, *54*(1):285-299.

Whittaker, A. D., Thieme, R. H., & Jones, D. D. (1987). Guidelines for getting started with expert systems. *Agricultural Engineering*, *68*:24-27.

Yamoah, C. F., Burleigh, J. R., & Malcolm, M. R. (1990). Application of expert systems to study of acid soils in rwanda. *Agriculture, Ecosystems & Environment*, *30*:203-218.

Lookahead Feature Construction for Learning Hard Concepts

Harish Ragavan
NCR Corporation
3325 Platt Springs Road
West Columbia, SC 29169
ragavan@cs.uiuc.edu

Larry Rendell
Beckman Institute & Computer Science Dept.
University of Illinois at Urbana-Champaign
405 N. Mathews Avenue, Urbana, IL 61801
rendell@cs.uiuc.edu

Abstract

Difficult real-world concepts occur when a domain is poorly understood. The relationship of such a concept to its *primitive* attributes is complex and obscure. The resulting difficulty for learning algorithms can been quantified in terms of attribute interaction, concept complexity, or function variation. One measure of attribute interaction is entropy or *blurring,* which ranks synthetic boolean and real-world concepts in the same order as typical induction algorithms' decreasing accuracy. Empirical results show that high blurring degrades the accuracy of decision tree builders, extensions of basic methods, alternative symbolic approaches, backpropagation, and multi-variate adaptive regression splines. Greedy decision tree learners become inaccurate because they assess one attribute at each node. A new global search algorithm, *LFC,* for decision tree learning uses directed lookahead to address feature interaction, improving accuracy at reasonable cost. *LFC* also addresses the general verbosity problem in decision trees. The algorithm caches search information as newly constructed features. Its hypothesis representation is variable, from decision trees at one extreme to decision lists on the other. The combination of lookahead search and feature construction markedly improves performance, giving accuracies unobtained by any other algorithms, including those that do global search alone or feature construction alone.

1 Introduction

Although the phrase "hard concept" could mean various things, our use of the term is specific to a representation problem in attribute-based learning. The difficulty of concept learning depends on representation; representation rests on knowledge. Problems that have had the benefit of expert knowledge to hone good attributes are relatively easy to solve [Holte, 1993; Rendell & Seshu, 1990].

Representations differ in abstraction. A good, abstract representation for chess involves piece advantage and center control, while primitive attributes are the contents of board squares. A high-level representation for symbol recognition might include definitions of lines and circles, whereas a low-level representation gives pixel gray-levels. No satisfactory abstract representation is yet known for protein structure prediction, but a hard starting point is the primary sequence of amino acids.[1]

To reflect these differences, the quality of a representation has been measured using various formalisms, which generally quantify attribute interaction. Rendell and Ragavan [1993] examine several simplifications and select an entropy measure that they call *blurring.* The blurring of a concept is the average entropy in the concept over all relevant attributes, conditioned on each attribute in turn. This measures attribute interaction because each term in the conditional expression corresponds to a one-dimensional projection in instance space. Singly, attributes provide little information about the concept class when interaction is high. For difficult concepts (e.g., parity), any one-dimensional projection is a "blur" comprising many highs and lows of concept class-membership (positive and negative examples). Consequently, such a projection shows a high degree of uncertainty about the concept. The greater the difficulty of the concept, the more blurred the projections become.

[1] Although a concept may be hard when the representation is primitive, adequate data are often available. No extant algorithm can handle very hard concepts, but the role of an ultimate empirical method is to find (a theory that defines) appropriate abstract features from the primitive attributes, with or without the help of knowledge other than the data.

Since extreme blurring occurs in important real-world problems, and since standard algorithms perform badly on hard concepts with high attribute interaction [Devijver and Kittler, 1982; Rendell and Seshu, 1990], induction methods should be improved along these lines. Some algorithms have been designed to address interaction, such as backpropagation [Rumelhart *et al.*, 1986] and *MARS* [Friedman, 1991]. In Section 2 we present a new algorithm called *LFC*, for *lookahead feature construction*. Section 3 reports experiments comparing *LFC* with several other methods, including symbolic, statistical, and connectionist algorithms. We use several domains, including controlled synthetic data and a few of the Irvine data bases. The experiments show that *LFC* induces more accurate descriptions than other methods. Our analysis explains why.

2 The *LFC* Algorithm

The *LFC* algorithm, outlined in Figure 1, is a recursive splitter that uses the *ID3* [Quinlan, 1983] information gain function Φ. To overcome problems associated with greedyness, *LFC* incorporates cached lookahead controlled by beam search with branch-and-bound in a geometric representation; we explain this in more detail below. *LFC* accepts discrete-valued representations such as integers, booleans, and nominals. Continuous-valued attributes are intervalized by minimizing the class entropy in each interval.

LFC first selects a subset of α attributes from the n original attributes for the beam. The beam features are initially selected from the original attributes, and subsequently from both the original attributes and the constructed features. *LFC* uses the $\alpha \ll n$ beam features as operands for the feature construction (caching) algorithm *FC* (Fig. 1). The feature construction operators are negation and conjunction, although disjunction may also be used. If all three operators are given, *FC* chooses either conjunction or disjunction, whichever is better, to avoid repeating semantically equivalent features. After a maximum search depth of l levels, the "best" (highest Φ) feature is selected for the decision node.

This constructed feature is then pruned back by evaluating the number of misclassifications by the feature on an independent test sample [Breiman *et al.*, 1984]. The last (usually least significant) attribute in the feature (a conjunction of attribute literals) is iteratively dropped, until the error is minimized, or until a single attribute remains.

After constructing a new feature for a decision-tree node, *LFC* splits the data and iterates on each partition block, until either a specified mix of positive and negative examples or a minimum sample size for splitting is reached (stopping criterion).

Constrained Feature Formation Algorithm *FC*

Given: A set of original attributes $F_{original}$, beam features F_{beam}, window width λ, and training examples D_{train}.

Returns: A set of new features, F_{new}.

1. Select the best feature f_{best} from F_{beam}. Remove original attributes lying at a distance greater than λ from f_{best} in S, retaining only $F'_{original} \subseteq F_{original}$.
2. Select an attribute x from $F'_{original}$ that is not already present in F_{beam}. Let $f_{original}$ = either x or $\neg x$, whichever maps closer to $(P_{max}, 0)$.
3. Try to construct a new feature $f_{new} = f_{best} \wedge f_{original}$.
   IF f_{new} is worse than either f_{best} or $f_{original}$ then discard f_{new} ELSE $F_{new} := F_{new} \cup f_{new}$.
4. Remove f_{best} from F_{beam} and repeat steps 1-4 until $F_{beam} = \emptyset$.

Main Learning Algorithm *LFC*

Given: A set of original attributes $F_{original}$, beam size α, maximum search depth l, stopping sample size β, and training examples D_{train}.

Returns: A decision tree with new features.

IF $|D_{train}| < \beta$ or all the examples in D_{train} are of the same class, create a leaf node. If the majority of examples in D_{train} is positive, label the leaf as positive, otherwise negative.

ELSE

1. $F_{new} := F_{original}$.
2. Select the α best features for the beam, $F_{beam} \subseteq F_{new}$. Call *FC* to construct new features F_{new} from F_{beam} and $F_{original}$.
3. IF no feature in F_{new} is better than any feature in F_{beam}, or if the limit l is reached, then stop the beam search
   ELSE Repeat steps 2 and 3.
4. Select the feature with the lowest Ψ from F_{beam} and prune it. Call this f^*_{best}.
5. Create a new decision-tree node corresponding to f^*_{best}.
6. For each partition block Π from splitting D_{train} using f^*_{best}, set $D_{train} := \Pi$ and recursively call LFC.

Figure 1: Pseudo-code for the Algorithm: *LFC* (bottom) and *FC* (top).

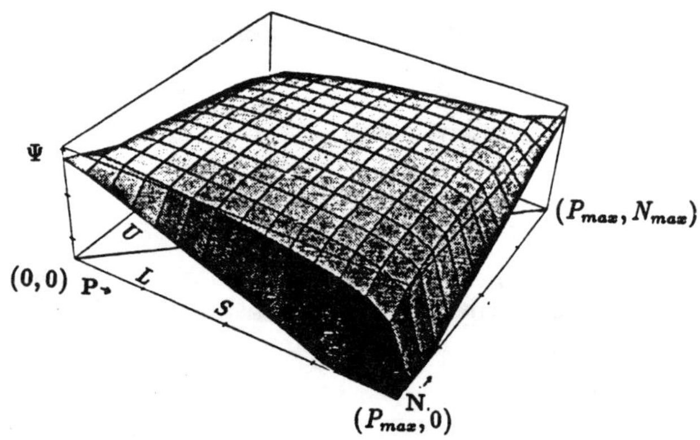

Figure 2: Geometric Representation for Feature Construction.

2.1 Constraining Construction Geometrically

The most novel aspect of *LFC* is its geometric search. Mehlsam [1989] did related work, but his contribution differs in several ways. Mehlsam proved that his algorithm *FEACON* finds optimal solutions, where optimality is defined with respect to constructions using disjunction ∨. *LFC* differs from *FEACON* in several ways: First, *FEACON* searches feature space by moving objects with different class labels to different partition blocks, whereas *LFC* does feature construction using operators. Second, *FEACON* used greedy search, whereas *LFC* uses directed lookahead search and branch-and-bound, eliminating large portions of the search space for feature construction. Finally, and most important, Mehlsam used a geometric representation for analysis, but did not take advantage of this representation to have *FEACON* construct features. In contrast, our technique incorporates an analytic method directly into the algorithm to constrain feature construction drastically. *LFC* constructs new features by utilizing their coordinates in the geometric representation to estimate their quality and screen them dynamically, before any construction.

Let P_{max} and N_{max} be the total number of positive and negative examples in the training data. Consider the rectangular plane S bounded by $(0,0)$ and (P_{max}, N_{max}), with axes **P** and **N** as shown in Figure 2. The line **B** given by $((0,0),(P_{max}, N_{max}))$ bisects S into a lower half-plane L and an upper half-plane U. We use $\rho(x)$ to indicate the point (p,n) on S corresponding to x, where x is an original attribute or a new feature.

In Figure 2, the *conditional entropy* [Ragavan *et al.*, 1993] $\Psi(x)$ is expressed as a function of the number of positive and negative examples covered by x, p, and n respectively. Ψ is maximum at points along **B**; these points correspond to (original or new) features with low discriminatory power. In L, Ψ decreases monotonically along any line parallel to **P** and increases monotonically along any line parallel to **N**. Ψ has the minimum value 0 at $(P_{max}, 0)$.

The surface Ψ is convex, with no interior minima [Mehlsam, 1989]. For different training data and concepts, the values of P_{max} and N_{max} vary with the number of positive examples in the sample, but the surface retains its convexity and stretches or shrinks along either of the axes, depending on the data. The points $(P_{max}, 0)$ and $(0, N_{max})$ correspond to perfect covers for the positive and negative examples, respectively. A hypothesis covering all the positive examples and excluding all the negative examples maps to the extremity of S given by $(P_{max}, 0)$. Features corresponding to conjunctive terms of the concept C map to points on **P**, whereas terms of its complement $\bar{C}$ map to points on **N**.

Initially, every original attribute-value x is mapped to a point (p,n) on S, where p and n are the number of positive and negative examples covered by this attribute-value. In subsequent steps of the beam search, the beam features are also mapped to S. A point on Ψ corresponding to an original attribute moves when the attribute is conjoined with another attribute or feature: the new point corresponding to the new feature differs from either of the original points corresponding to the component attributes. *LFC*'s construction process tends to move the new points toward the **P** axis, with non-increasing values for the new **P** coordinates. When the new point reaches the **P** axis, a cover for some of the positive examples (and no negative examples) is found and the search terminates.

2.2 Constraining without Information Loss

Of all possible new features, most have high Ψ values, because the frequency of feature occurrence diminishes exponentially with Ψ. Thus the vast majority of features contain little information about the concept, and may be filtered out. Suppose an original attribute lies in the Ψ range 0.2 to 0.3. It is then sufficient to search for features with Ψ values lower than the value for this attribute, since we know the worst we can do is 0.3. This is the basic idea behind focusing feature construction search in *LFC*.

This task is fairly easy if we look at where the features map in Figure 2. High Ψ features lie along **B** or close to it. Ψ decreases as we move away from **B** toward **P** (or **N**) (see [Ragavan *et al.*, 1993]). If we focus search on features lying in a neighborhood around the original attribute and between the **P** (or **N**) axis, we can eliminate most or all of the high entropy features lying close to **B**. The remaining neighborhood contains far fewer features than the space of all possible features, making it is easier to find ones that lie in the Ψ range

Table 1: Algorithm Accuracy Dependent on Two Capacities

Concept to Learn	Blurring measure Δ	*ID3* (basic algorithm	*FRINGE*-like with feature construction	Basic algorithm with lookahead	*LFC* (lookahead & construction)
f_1	0.63	92.6	95.2	95.6	98.0
f_2	0.70	86.6	90.8	93.1	95.0
f_3	0.82	76.0	78.8	82.5	92.3
f_4	0.87	71.8	75.6	82.2	88.1

0 to 0.2. In contrast, a generate-and-test paradigm would waste computation by producing many high entropy features, evaluating them, then discarding them later.

The geometric relationships lets *LFC* constrain its search without loss of information. By using the representation of Figure 2 directly for feature construction, *LFC* relates a given construction operator to particular natural constraints in the representation, and uses the result to prune search. As detailed below, the conjunction of two attributes maps to a point within the intersection of the two rectangles defined by each of the original attribute coordinates and the origin. This constraint can be used to bound the best possible values of the conjunction of these two attributes.

2.3 Constraint using Branch-and-Bound

LFC limits its lookahead search for new features in two ways: by using geometric constraints as just explained, and by limiting the breadth and depth of search. These two constraints are combined to order features by their quality. The search width (maximum beam size) is chosen parametrically. Search deepens by one level at a time, progressively constructing a new feature. The construction stops automatically when some feature reaches the **P** axis in Figure 2.

Before doing any construction, *FC* applies a "window" filter around an operand x, to filter points lying too far away from $\rho(x)$ or **P**. A parameter λ (between 0 and 1) specifies the relative width of the window. When an operand is selected from the beam for constructing a new feature, the original attributes mapping outside this window are filtered out, and only those inside the window are used for construction. This technique filters several attributes lying near **B**, drastically reducing the number of constructed features.

As one of its two operands, *FC* chooses a feature from the beam; for its second operand, *FC* selects an original attribute value closest to $(P_{max}, 0)$. For boolean attributes, this corresponds to choosing either a literal (e.g., x_1) or its negation ($\bar{x}_1$), whichever maps closer to $(P_{max}, 0)$. These operands are conjoined to give a new feature, if the branch-and-bound technique does not eliminate it. Starting from a point $\rho(x)$ on S corresponding to an original attribute x, *FC* produces new features mapping to points that progress towards **P**. As new features are built, their points on S move closer to **P**, eventually stopping at **P**, even if the maximum search depth l is not reached by this time.

3 Empirical Results

We selected several learning algorithms that might differ in their behavior on harder concepts. The algorithms we tested included a standard decision-tree method *ID3* [Quinlan, 1983]), a feature construction extension *FRINGE* and the decision list program *GREEDY3* [Pagallo, 1990], lookahead feature construction *LFC* [Ragavan *et al.*, 1993], the common connectionist method of backpropagation (*BackProp*) [Rumelhart, 1986], and multi-variate adaptive regression splines (*MARS*) [Friedman, 1991].

The main performance criterion we report on here is predictive accuracy, with some attention to speed. Ragavan et al. [1993] examine other criteria, such as decision tree consistency and comprehensibility, which promote expert-system interaction. We ran the algorithms with various data.

3.1 The Importance of Combining Construction and Lookahead

For a preliminary assessment of *LFC* on varying amounts of blurring, we first used synthetic data to control attribute interaction. We generated several random synthetic boolean concepts, selecting four and ordering them by their blurring (entropy) values Δ. The boolean concepts were: $f_1 = x_1x_2x_3 + x_1x_2x_4 + x_1x_2x_5$; $f_2 = \bar{x}_1\bar{x}_2\bar{x}_3 + \bar{x}_2x_4\bar{x}_3 + \bar{x}_3\bar{x}_4\bar{x}_1$; $f_3 = \bar{x}_5\bar{x}_3x_6 + \bar{x}_6x_8\bar{x}_5 + x_8\bar{x}_3\bar{x}_2$; $f_4 = \bar{x}_6x_1x_8 + x_8x_4\bar{x}_1 + \bar{x}_9\bar{x}_8x_1$. Table 1 shows their blurring values.

The blurring measure codes three aspects of concept difficulty [Rendell and Ragavan, 1993]. One is attribute interaction or inherent concept complexity. Another cause of blurring is noise; attribute and class noise produce false positives and negatives, which increase entropy. The third cause of blurring is fundamental representational inadequacy, which improperly maps different objects (having varied class values) to

Table 2: Algorithm Accuracy Comparison using Various Domains

Concept	Blurring	*ID3*	*FRINGE*	*GREEDY3*	*BackProp*	*MARS*	*LFC*
Iris versicolor	0.56	100	100	86.7	-	98.8	100
f1	0.63	92.6	94.0	86.2	95.0	68.8	98.0
f2	0.70	86.6	85.4	77.9	88.5	86.0	95.0
f3	0.82	76.0	77.0	72.5	82.5	69.1	92.3
f4	0.87	71.8	71.8	60.5	82.0	50.3	88.1
Pima Diabetes	0.88	53.7	53.7	57.9	*	56.0	78.8
Bankruptcy	0.91	65.9	65.9	58.0	76.1	79.5	90.1
Bondrating	0.95	42.0	42.0	*	*	39.2	69.5

a single point in the instance space; destroying such a distinction increases entropy. The blurring Δ captures all three factors that make concept learning difficult. In these controlled synthetic concepts, however, the only contribution to blurring is attribute interaction.

Table 1 shows accuracy results for four algorithms:

1. No feature construction and no lookahead search (symbolic greedy learning)
2. Feature construction but no lookahead search (represented by FRINGE-like algorithms)
3. No feature construction but lookahead search (as in Buntine's *IND* or Norton's [1989] *IDX*)
4. Feature construction with lookahead search, *LFC* (caching relevant attribute relationships)

Each *FRINGE-like* entry for accuracy is actually the best of multiple results using different *FRINGE* variants, such as *DCFringe* [Yang *et al.*, 1991].

The training sample size in each case was 32, with 68 instances for testing. Repeated cross-validation (usually ten runs each) were made to ensure that most differences are significant at the 0.001 level..

Table 1 shows the importance of *both* lookahead search (or its equivalent) ***and*** feature construction (or its equivalent); neither alone gives the best accuracy. For all concepts f_1 through f_4, the standard decision tree algorithm *ID3* does relatively poorly. For all these concepts, a lookahead method alone (no caching) and *FRINGE-like* feature construction alone (no lookahead), are both inferior to a system that does both (*LFC*). The divergence in accuracy increases with greater blurring, with *LFC* well ahead of its rivals. Other experiments show the same trends, often more prominently. The next section assesses more algorithms with more varied data.

3.2 Algorithm Comparisons using Boolean and Real-World Concepts

Table 2 shows results using several boolean and real-world concepts of varying difficulty as measured by the blurring Δ. Four of the concepts are the randomly generated boolean functions of the previous section, two are from the Irvine databases, and two are hard financial concepts [Ragavan *et al.*, 1993]. These financial data represent risk classification, such as to lend or not to lend.

Table 2 indicates accuracies obtained with several induction algorithms, using ten cross-validation runs for each. We also ran *C4.5* (not shown), which behaved much as *ID3*. The considerable differences are mostly significant at the 0.001 level. In cases indicated by "*", an algorithm did not converge to reliable values despite various trials.

Although speeds are not shown, the times were comparable, except that *MARS* [Friedman, 1991] was much faster. A simple lookahead algorithm for constructing decision trees was too slow (taking several days for the financial concepts, without converging). Although *LFC* is generally slower than *ID3*, its analytic technique, heuristic methods, and more concise trees made its speed competitive for the concepts we studied.[2]

Table 2 shows that the performance of all algorithms degrades with increasing Δ, except that *MARS* is somewhat anomalous, which may relate to its design (fitting different splines in different parts of instance space). The generally low Pima accuracy may indicate noise or representational inadequacy. Another discrepancy is unsurprising: the accuracy difference with *LFC* for bankruptcy prediction compared to f_4 is probably caused by the larger training to testing sample sizes for the financial concepts (300) compared with the boolean concepts (32).

All algorithms degrade partly because the fixed number of training examples in this experiment does not compensate for increasing concept complexity [Devroye and Gyorfi, 1985; Haussler, 1988]. However, a significant part of the degradation is caused by differences in the algorithms themselves.

For *BackProp*, the table shows the best results us-

[2]The current version is implemented in Prolog; we are recoding the algorithm in C++.

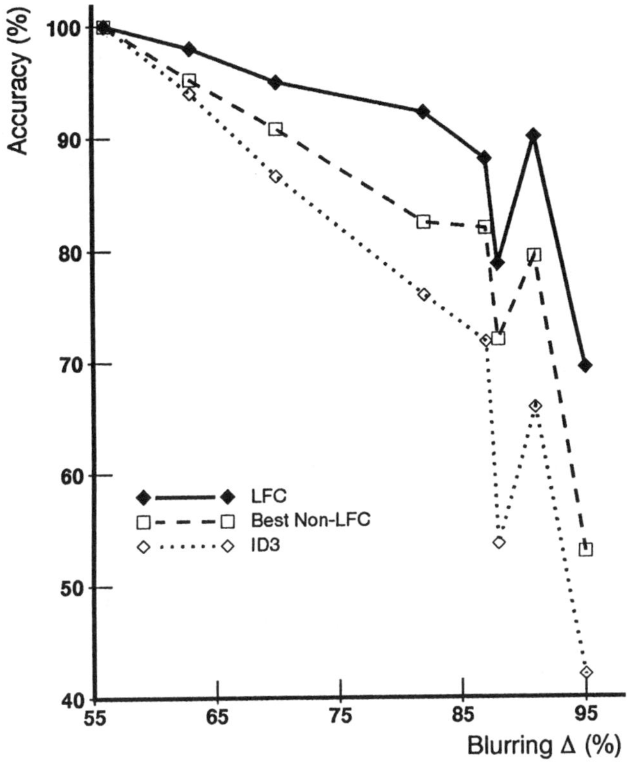

Figure 3: Accuracy of Algorithms as a Function of Concept Difficulty (Blurring).

ing several different parameter settings. We used the recommended heuristics for a fully connected network structure: initial weights selected at random and a single hidden layer whose number of nodes was half the total number of input and output nodes [Rumelhart *et al.*, 1986]. The output layer had one unit which classified an example as positive or negative. Although we had some difficulty in getting *BackProp* to converge, this method is more accurate than most other algorithms. But even compared with *BackProp, LFC* is more accurate throughout these cases, especially for high-interaction concepts.

For the bankruptcy domain, *BackProp*'s accuracy was 76% and *MARS*' accuracy was 80%, compared to 90% for *LFC.* For bondrating, *MARS* gave 39%, versus 70% for *LFC.* These results with the financial concepts, which use numeric representation, are particularly significant because *MARS* was designed expressly to handle real variables, whereas *LFC* uses logic transformations for new features. On the Pima Indian Diabetes domain, *LFC*'s 79% is better than the previous best accuracy of 76%, obtained by the *Adapt* algorithm.

3.3 Trends and Interpretation of Results

Figure 3 summarizes the accuracy results listed in Table 2. Two of the three curves represent the two learning systems *ID3* and *LFC*. The middle curve is a composite, on a point-by-point basis, of the best accuracy of any of the five algorithms *ID3, FRINGE, GREEDY3, BackProp,* and *MARS*.

This graph shows general tendencies. Except for irregularities largely caused by differing sample sizes, the accuracy distinctions among *LFC*, any otherwise best algorithm, and *ID3*, are uniform and prominent. As measured by the blurring Δ, *ID3* is inferior on hard concepts; *LFC*'s accuracy is unmatched. The algorithms may be ranked by their overall accuracy.

As concepts become harder, *LFC* scales up considerably better than the other approaches, including *BackProp* and *MARS*, which are considered able to handle attribute interaction. When the blurring is high, *LFC* is as much as thirty percentage points more accurate than *ID3*, and ten percentage points better than any other algorithm tested.

The blurring measure quantifies attribute interaction, the essence of difficulty in poorly-understood domains requiring low-level representation. Many real-world concepts (e.g., in molecular biology) have primitive representations characterized by high attribute interaction [Devijver and Kittler, 1982; Rendell and Seshu, 1990]. Although other aspects of a concept (such as scale and dimensionality) are also relevant, a measure such as Δ allows a meaningful overall assessment of algorithms. The ability of algorithms to manage attribute interaction is one of their most important functional differences. Rendell and Ragavan [1993] explore these relationships further.

Aside from accuracy, other algorithm capabilities need attention. One important capability, particularly with complex concepts, is the creation of concise and comprehensible concept descriptions. In a detailed study of the two financial concepts, Ragavan et al. [1993] show that *LFC*'s simpler outputs are easier for an expert to understand and build on.

4 Discussion and Related Work

A typical divide-and-conquer *splitter,* such as Breiman et al.'s *CART* [1984] or Quinlan's *ID3* [1986] iteratively partitions the data using the single best attribute to create a decision node. This is a greedy procedure. Although it is efficient, it may get trapped by local optima and degrade the quality of the induced decision tree [Rendell and Seshu, 1990]. This occurs when the concept is hard. Attribute interaction increases the number of original attributes (conjuncts) required to specify meaningful subclasses at the leaves. Attribute interaction also causes node *replication* [Pagallo, 1990], which degrades accuracy, consistency, and comprehensibility.

Some algorithms have extended greedy splitters. For

example, *FRINGE* [Pagallo, 1990] uses the decision tree produced by a greedy splitter to construct new features for improving tree quality. Repeated fringe patterns near the leaves of the decision tree are coalesced to give new features, which are combined with the original attributes to build a new decision tree, and the process iterates. Such strategies are insufficient for high attribute interaction. When repeated decision patterns are distributed throughout the tree rather than being confined to fringes, the replications become complex, and the original greedy procedure is insufficient.

One way to extend inductive splitters is to look ahead to observe the effects of current attribute selection further down in hypothesis construction. The best sequence may be found when all possible expansions of a decision tree are evaluated. This avoids problems of attribute interaction. Norton [1989] found that his exhaustive lookahead algorithm *IDX* gave reasonable improvement, though it does not construct new features to cache the knowledge. Although splitters can construct better hypotheses with full lookahead search, naive lookahead search is expensive, and unnecessary in many cases.

A practical cure for attribute interaction is directed lookahead search. *LFC* constructs features while building the decision tree. The system replaces a greedy algorithm for the decision tree construction phase of *FRINGE*-like algorithms, largely preventing tree patterns from repeating in the first place. A sequence of decisions down any path of a decision tree is treated as a conjunction of attributes for constructing a new feature. The features are not evaluated individually, but instead as a group (effectively projecting multi-dimensionally). Forming a new feature from the attributes economically caches this search information.

LFC guides lookahead search and feature construction by taking advantage of patterns in the training data and natural search constraints that arise using its geometric search representation. The algorithm deepens search only when necessary, stopping when it reaches the **P** axis (Fig. 2). An important property of *LFC* is that it can dynamically increase computational complexity for difficult concepts. The window filter is used for initial selection of candidate original attributes for feature construction, based on their quality. Subsequently, the beam is based upon where the features and attributes map in the geometric plane.

The *FC* subroutine uses only the coordinates of the component attributes in branch-and-bound to determine whether to eliminate new features constructed from them, so the data are not split on a feature that could then be discarded because of higher entropy than its component attributes. Although global search still requires more computation per node, it produces smaller trees for hard concepts. *LFC*'s search parameters lookahead depth l and beam width α allow a user to trade computational complexity for accuracy. For many real-world concepts, the maximum number of conjunctions in a term is small (e.g., $l \leq 5$ covers many complex interactions in chess).

The main distinction between *LFC*'s search and ***iterative broadening*** [Ginsberg and Harvey, 1992] is the way in which *LFC* focuses on essential parts of the search space and prunes irrelevant parts. Other related algorithms include *GREEDY3* [Pagallo, 1990], *CN2* [Clark and Niblett, 1989] and *STAGGER* [Schlimmer and Granger, 1986]. *LFC* differs primarily because it uses a variable representation that may change from conventional decision trees at the one extreme to decision lists at the other. Also, the system caches search information from constrained lookahead search into new features, which reduces computational requirements.

A different approach transforms decision trees for incremental induction by switching nodes in the decision tree based on frequency of attribute occurrence [e.g., *IDL,* Van de Velde, 1990]. Indurkhya and Weiss [1990] discuss a similar attribute swapping technique. These "lookback" techniques do not construct new features and are limited to the expressive power of the original attributes at each node. Although attribute swapping algorithms are useful for restructuring the decision tree in a more compact form, they do not improve the abstraction of the model.

Rendell and Ragavan [1993] relate these and other algorithms to the underlying problem of learning hard real-world concepts. Although the results reported here emphasize algorithm accuracy, conciseness and comprehensibility are also important. The general nature of the relationship between more concise hypotheses and higher predictive accuracy has been investigated both theoretically [Rissanen, 1983] and empirically [Quinlan and Rivest, 1989]. Ragavan *et al.* [1993] extend the idea to constructive induction. The function of feature construction in a learning system is to simplify descriptions by caching intermediate representations, thus abstracting appropriate features as part of an emerging domain theory.

5 Conclusion

Typical induction systems are severely limited for real-world problems. To combat the cause of the limitation, we developed, tested, and analyzed a global search technique for feature construction that improves learning for synthetic and natural domains. The algorithm reduces the complexity of lookahead search in decision trees for feature construction, through a combination of analytic and heuristic techniques. Unlike exhaustive lookahead search, *LFC*'s speed is reasonable on fairly hard concepts.

Comparative analysis of *LFC* indicated substantial improvement. Characterizing concept difficulty as attribute interaction measured using conditional entropy or *blurring*, we found that *LFC* scales up better than other symbolic methods, backpropagation, and multivariate adaptive regression splines. *LFC*'s accuracy is often ten or more percentage points better than the otherwise best method such as backpropagation, and thirty percentage points better than symbolic methods such as *ID3*.

Importantly, results with *LFC* indicate that *both* lookahead search (or its equivalent) *and* feature construction (or its equivalent) are required for accurate learning of hard concepts.

Acknowledgments

This research was supported in part by NSF grant IRI-92-04473. We wish to thank Pat Langley and Gunnar Blix for their detailed suggestions.

References

[Breiman *et al.*, 1984] L. Breiman, J. H. Friedman, R. A. Olshen, and C. J. Stone. (1984) *Classification and Regression Trees.* Wadsworth, Belmont, CA.

[Clark and Niblett, 1989] P. Clark and T. Niblett. (1989) The CN2 induction algorithm. *Machine Learning*, 3(4):261–284.

[Devijver and Kittler, 1982] P. A. Devijver and J. Kittler. (1982) *Pattern Recognition: A Statistical Approach.* Prentice Hall, Englewood Cliffs, New Jersey.

[Devroye and Gyorfi, 1985] L. Devroye and L. Gyorfi. (1985) *Nonparametric Density Estimation: The L1 View.* Wiley, New York, NY.

[Friedman, 1991] J. H. Friedman. (1991) Multi-variate adaptive regression splines. *Annals of Statistics*, 19:1–141.

[Ginsberg and Harvey, 1992] M. L. Ginsberg and W. D. Harvey. (1992) Iterative broadening. *Artificial Intelligence*, 55:367–383.

[Haussler, 1988] D. Haussler. (1988) Quantifying inductive bias: AI learning algorithms and Valiant's learning framework. *Artificial Intelligence*, 36:177–221.

[Holte, 1993] R. C. Holte. (1993) Very simple classification rules perform well on most datasets. *Machine Learning.* (in press).

[Indurkhya and Weiss, 1990] N. Indurkhya and S. M. Weiss. (1990) Iterative rule induction procedures. Technical Report LCSR-TR-145, Laboratory for Computer Science Research, Rutgers University, New Brunswick, NJ.

[Mehlsam, 1989] G. Mehlsam. (1989) *Automatisches Erzeugen von Klassifikationskriterien.* PhD thesis, Technische Universitat Wien, Vienna, Austria.

[Norton, 1989] S. W. Norton. (1989) Generating better decision trees. In *Proceedings of the Eleventh International Joint Conference on Artificial Intelligence*, pages 800–805.

[Pagallo, 1990] G. Pagallo. (1990) *Adaptive Decision Tree Algorithms for Learning from Examples.* PhD thesis, University of California at Santa Cruz.

[Quinlan, 1983] J. R. Quinlan. (1983) Learning efficient classification procedures and their application to chess end games. In R. Michalski, J. Carbonell, and T. Mitchell, (eds.), *Machine Learning: An Artificial Intelligence Approach*, chapter 15, pages 463–482. Tioga Publishing Co., Palo Alto, CA.

[Quinlan and Rivest, 1989] J. R. Quinlan and R. L. Rivest. (1989) Inferring decision trees using the minimum description principle. *Information and Computation*, 80:227–248.

[Ragavan *et al.*, 1993] H. Ragavan, L. Rendell, M. Shaw, and A. Tessmer. (1993) Learning complex real-world concepts through feature construction. Technical report, Beckman Institute, University of Illinois, Urbana, IL. Short version in *Proceedings of the Thirteenth International Joint Conference on Artificial Intelligence*, 1993.

[Rendell and Ragavan, 1993] L. A. Rendell and H. Ragavan. (1993) Improving the design of induction methods by analyzing algorithms functionality and data-based concept complexity. In *Proceedings of the Thirteenth International Joint Conference on Artificial Intelligence*, 1993.

[Rendell and Seshu, 1990] L. A. Rendell and R. Seshu. (1990) Learning hard concepts through constructive induction: Framework and rationale. *Computational Intelligence*, 6(4):247–270.

[Rumelhart *et al.*, 1986] D. E. Rumelhart, G. E. Hinton, and R. J. Williams. (1986) Learning internal representations by error propagation. In *Parallel Distributed Processing: Explorations in the Microstructures of Cognition*, volume 1, pages 318–362. MIT Press.

[Rissanen, 1983] J. Rissanen. (1983) A universal prior for integers and estimation by minimum description length. *Annals of Statistics*, 11:416–431.

[Schlimmer and Granger, 1986] J. C. Schlimmer and R. H. Granger. (1986) Incremental learning from noisy data. *Machine Learning*, 1:317–354.

[Van de Velde, 1990] W. Van de Velde. (1990) Incremental induction of topologically minimal trees. In *Proceedings of the Seventh International Workshop on Machine Learning*, pages 66–74.

[Yang *et al.*, 1991] D-S. Yang, L. A. Rendell, and G. Blix. (1991) A scheme for feature construction and a comparison of empirical methods. In *Proceedings of the Twelfth International Joint Conference on Artificial Intelligence*, pages 699–704.

Adaptive NeuroControl: How Black Box and Simple can it be

Jean-Michel Renders
Laboratoire d'Automatique
Université Libre de Bruxelles, cp. 165
Av. F. Roosevelt 50, 1050 Bruxelles – BELGIUM
renders@labauto.ulb.ac.be

Hugues Bersini and Marco Saerens
IRIDIA Laboratory
Université Libre de Bruxelles, cp. 194/6
Av. F. Roosevelt 50, 1050 Bruxelles – BELGIUM
bersini@ulb.ac.be; saerens@ulb.ac.be

Abstract

In this paper three objectives are pursued. The first one is to connect two among the seminal neurocontrol methodologies due to Jordan and Narendra, and to make clear how the first one is obtained by a simplification of the second one. The next objective is to alleviate more and more the prior knowledge about the process required to achieve its control. In particular, we propose three extensions of Jordan's method making feasible the control of processes characterized by an arbitrary time delay, and which are powerful enough to be used for a large set of applications while preserving the simplicity inherent to neural network approaches in general. Finally, we show by simulations that these methods, although resulting from an approximation of Narendra's gradient descent approach, do not suffer from any degradation regarding the control performance while relaxing the necessary prior knowledge of the process and gaining in simplicity and computer economy.

1 INTRODUCTION

There has been a recent resurgence of interest for the old cybernetic project to exploit neural networks for control applications (Miller et al. 1990, Narendra and Parthasarathy 1990, Hunt et al. 1992). It is more and more accepted that control methods based on connectionist systems could offer several advantages with respect to more classical approaches. They are simple to implement and allow constraining mathematical analysis to be bypassed by a pure algorithmic process. Also it has been established that multilayer neural networks together with an adequate adjustment of their synaptic weights are capable of approximating in a satisfactory way any function and its derivative (for a review, see White 1992). This justifies their study and use in the framework of nonlinear system theory and nonlinear control where mathematical analysis is either laborious or forced to resort to rough linear approximations.

Traditional adaptive control schemes such as MRAC (Model Reference Adaptive Control, Aström and Wittenmark 1989, Landau 1979) rely on a priori knowledge of the process to be controlled and on basic assumptions (linearity, type of perturbations, slow deviation of process parameters) which are not easily overcome. On the other hand, as a consequence of the universal approximation capacity of neural networks, neurocontrollers can become "emancipated" from a precise knowledge of the process to be controlled or from a rough linearisation. A "black box" control is then favoured departing from classical approaches in which a prior description of the process is required. In addition to their capacity to generalize and to extrapolate from reference situations, neural networks are also claimed to be robust with respect to damages affecting the control systems to a certain extent, due to the redundancy induced by the parallelism. This parallelism would allow hardware implementation yielding significant acceleration as compared with serial computer architectures. Finally, the adaptive capacity of neural networks when associated with gradient-like methods (the well known backpropagation algorithm for feedforward multilayers architecture) allows them to be used in the context of closed-loop adaptive control.

Several approaches are possible when using neural networks for process control (see Miller et al. 1990, Hunt et al. 1992, Psaltis et al. 1987, 1988 for a survey): general learning, indirect learning with plant identification, indirect learning, iterative inversion technique, etc. This contribution will be restricted to specialized learning methods which fit in perfectly with the classical adaptive control attitude since the neurocontroller relies on the error measured at the output of the process used as feedback to adjust the connection weights. In the context of specialized learning architectures where the neurocontroller is simply coupled with the process and the learning algorithm based on the difference between the actual output and the desired output, the two most influential approaches are due to Jordan (1989ab, Jordan and Jacobs 1990, Jordan and Rumelhart 1991) and Narendra and Parthasarathy (1990, 1992).

A first objective of this paper is to make the connection between these two approaches (link which can still appear unclear in the neurocontrol literature) and to show how Jordan's approach can be derived from Narendra's Dynamic Back Propagation by making certain simplifications. The paper will further discuss how these simplifications are analog to those applied in the context of recurrent neural network learning when using the backpropagation through time truncated to one (BPTT-1, Williams and Peng 1990) instead of Williams and Zipser's (1989) real time recurrent learning (RTRL).

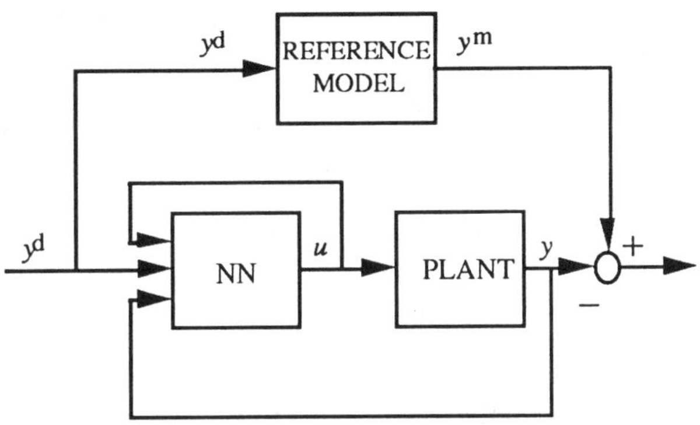

Figure 1: Architecture of adaptive control with a neural net

The second objective of the paper is to generalize Jordan's approach by allowing processes with arbitrary time delay to be controlled in the same way. These extensions still originate from Narendra's more general approach while keeping the simplicity and economy inherent to Jordan's approach. Three different methods, called the JEAN methods (Jordan Extended for Adaptive Neurocontrol), are proposed. JEAN techniques in general are extensions of Jordan's method for processes characterized by an arbitrary time delay. Due to the presence of such a delay, JEAN-1, the first method we propose, requires a number of intermediate copies of the neurocontroller to be stored (as many copies as the time delay). JEAN-2 alleviates this requirement but needs in compensation a model of the process able to predict at the current time the process behaviour after the delay. Mini-JEAN derives from works previously achieved and described by Saerens and Soquet (1991); this approach responds to the following question: how elementary the prior knowledge of a process can be in order to still enable its control. We will show that in many circumstances, given a process characterized by Jacobians of constant sign, a satisfactory control can be attained even on basis of a very crude knowledge of the process: namely the sign of these Jacobians.

The last objective is to make simulation comparisons. Five adaptive neurocontrollers are applied to a highly nonlinear process in order to show their respective advantages and limitations: Narendra's dynamic back propagation, Jordan's approach and the three further methods that we have developed and tested over the last few years: JEAN-1, JEAN-2 and Mini-JEAN.

Let us finally mention that we have also provided some theoretical support, that will not be developed here because of the lack of space, to these three proposed algorithms. Indeed, by applying the so-called hyperstability formalism and Lyapunov theory, we showed that, under some conditions, JEAN's closed-loop adaptation laws are asymptotically stable (Renders 1993; Saerens, Renders and Bersini 1993).

2 FROM NARENDRA'S APPROACH TO JORDAN'S APPROACH

Let us consider a single input / single output process (or plant, see Figure 1) which can be described by the following discrete-time equation:

$$y(k+1) = F[y(k), ..., y(k-p+1); u(k-d+1), ..., u(k-p+1)]$$
$$= F_{k+1} \tag{1}$$

where $y(k)$ is the process output at time k and $u(k)$ is the process input, also at time k. p designates the *order* of the process; d is called the *delay* of the process (or the *relative degree*) and it is the lapse of time required by the process to respond to any input.

Let us first assume a first-order delay for the process; let us suppose further that the objective of the control is to provide to the process a signal $u(k)$ which minimizes the output error:

$$e_{k+1} = \frac{1}{2}[y(k+1) - y^m(k+1)]^2 = \frac{1}{2}[y(k+1) - y^d(k)]^2 \tag{2}$$

where $y^d(k)$ is the desired output that has to be reached at time $k+1$, used at time k for computing $u(k)$. This means that the output of the reference model as showed in Figure 1 is simply the delayed desired output: $y^m(k+1)=y^d(k)$.

In this case, it can be shown that if the time delay d is one, if the reference signal is reachable in one step, and if the process inverse is stable (minimum phase system), the control of the process can be achieved by using a multilayer neurocontroller, characterized by its synaptic weight vector w and receiving as inputs: the last process outputs observed, the desired output $y^d(k)$ to be followed by the process at time $k+1$ and the last inputs injected into the process:

$$u(k) = N[y(k), ..., y(k-p+1);$$

$$u(k-1), ..., u(k-p+1), y^d(k); \mathbf{w}] = N_k \quad (3)$$

To achieve this, the neurocontroller tries to minimize the error (2) on-line by a continuous adjustment of its weights using a gradient-descent method: at time k+1, $\mathbf{w}$ is slightly modified according to:

$$\mathbf{w}^{k+1} = \mathbf{w}^k - \eta \frac{\partial e(k+1)}{\partial \mathbf{w}}$$

$$= \mathbf{w}^k - \eta\, [y(k+1) - y^d(k)]\, \frac{\partial y(k+1)}{\partial \mathbf{w}} \quad (4)$$

where $\partial y(k)/\partial \mathbf{w}$ is defined as the gradient of $y(k)$: $\partial y(k)/\partial \mathbf{w} = (\partial y(k)/\partial w_1, \partial y(k)/\partial w_2, ..., \partial y(k)/\partial w_n)^T$, and η is the learning rate. Now, according to Narendra and Parthasarathy's (1992) developments, the computation of the derivative $\partial y(k+1)/\partial \mathbf{w}$ from (1) and (3) turns out to be a laborious task:

$$\frac{\partial y(k)}{\partial \mathbf{w}} = \sum_{i=1}^{p} \frac{\partial F_k}{\partial u(k-i)} \frac{\partial u(k-i)}{\partial \mathbf{w}} + \sum_{i=1}^{p} \frac{\partial F_k}{\partial y(k-i)} \frac{\partial y(k-i)}{\partial \mathbf{w}} \quad (5a)$$

with

$$\frac{\partial u(k-i)}{\partial \mathbf{w}} = \left(\frac{\partial N}{\partial \mathbf{w}}\right)_{k-i} + \sum_{j=1}^{p} \frac{\partial N_{k-i}}{\partial u(k-i-j)} \frac{\partial u(k-i-j)}{\partial \mathbf{w}}$$

$$+ \sum_{j=1}^{p} \frac{\partial N_{k-i}}{\partial y(k-i-j)} \frac{\partial y(k-i-j)}{\partial \mathbf{w}} \quad (5b)$$

In the following, we will suppose that either a process model or a neural identifier of the process is available. Both Narendra and Jordan have proposed to incorporate the process model in a second neural network, the neural emulator, and then to link the neurocontroller with this neural emulator. Consequently, it corresponds to the classical indirect control approach in which the parameters are estimated either on-line or in a preliminary phase, and the parameters of the controller (in this case the weights of the neural controller) are adjusted assuming that the estimated parameters of the process represent the real values. Provided such a process model (or neural emulator) is available, the derivatives $\partial F_k/\partial y(k-i)$ and $\partial F_k/\partial u(k-i)$ are easily computed either directly from the model or through a "backpropagation-like" algorithm applied to the respective inputs of the neural emulator. The derivatives $\partial y(k-i)/\partial \mathbf{w}$ can be computed in the same recurrent way as $\partial y(k)/\partial \mathbf{w}$, but at time $k-i$, with $\partial y(0)/\partial \mathbf{w} = 0$.

In the same vein, the derivatives $\partial N_{k-i}/\partial y(k-i-j)$ and $\partial N_{k-i}/\partial u(k-i-j)$ can be obtained through backpropagation applied now to the respective inputs of the neurocontroller and the derivatives $\partial u(k-i)/\partial \mathbf{w}$ can be calculated in the same recurrent way as $\partial u(k-i-j)/\partial \mathbf{w}$, but at different times. Finally, the first derivative of expression (5b), $\partial N/\partial \mathbf{w}$, can be computed by the backpropagation algorithm applied, in the usual way, to the synaptic weights of the neurocontroller.

The problems raised by the recurrent calculations just described relate first to the quantity of items to store in memory so as to compute derivatives at time k+1 as a function of derivatives obtained at time k, and then to the computer time required to achieve all the operations.

The specialized learning method proposed by Jordan (1989ab, Jordan and Jacobs 1990) makes one further assumption as compared with Narendra's approach: since, at time k–1, the control $u(k-1)$ is given by a neural mapping whose only parameters to tune are the synaptic weights for whatever data received as inputs, Jordan assumes that, when adjusting the weights at time k, the only explicit function of $\mathbf{w}$ is indeed $u(k-1)$ and that all input variables of the network at time k–1 are not explicit functions of $\mathbf{w}$. In a sense, this amounts to dismiss the recurrent nature of the architecture during the learning phase and leads us to designate this assumption by "non-recurrence-in-learning". As a result, coming back to Narendra's developments (eq. 5ab), all the derivatives with respect to $\mathbf{w}$ can be suppressed except for the one containing $u(k-1)$. The two expressions (5a) and (5b) merge then in a very elementary one:

$$\frac{\partial y(k)}{\partial \mathbf{w}} = \frac{\partial F_k}{\partial u(k-1)} \left(\frac{\partial N}{\partial \mathbf{w}}\right)_{k-1} \quad (6)$$

where $\partial N_{k-1}/\partial \mathbf{w}$ is given by the classical backpropagation algorithm applied to the neurocontroller. The derivative $\partial F_k/\partial u(k-1)$ corresponds to the process reaction to slight control modifications (process Jacobian), and is obtained directly on a model of the process or by backpropagation applied to the relevant input of the neural emulator.

This assumption can be better understood in light of the studies devoted to the training of recurrent networks. Let us consider a fully recurrent network defined by the following equations:

$$x_i(k+1) = S[\sum_j w_{ij}\, x_j(k)] \quad (7)$$

where k is the current time, x_i is the activation value of unit i, S is the sigmoid function and w_{ij} the connection weights. Let us suppose that we have to train the network in such a way that some of its nodes follow a prescribed trajectory $x_i^d(k)$. At time k+1, the connection weights will be tuned in order to decrease the squared error $1/2\ [x_i(k+1) - x_i^d(k+1)]^2$, summed over the nodes i for which a prescribed trajectory is imposed. As in the control case, the gradient method brings us to compute the derivatives $\partial x_i(k)/\partial \mathbf{w}$. Williams and Zipser have derived an interesting algorithm called Real Time Recurrent Learning (RTRL, 1989) obtained by differentiation of the network equations with respect to the weights:

$$\frac{\partial x_i(k+1)}{\partial w_{lm}} = S'\ (\sum_j w_{ij} \frac{\partial x_j(k)}{\partial w_{lm}} + \delta_{il}\, x_m(k)) \tag{8}$$

where S' is the derivative of the sigmoid function. As in Narendra's approach to neurocontrol, the derivatives are computed in a recurrent way by keeping in memory every items obtained at time k that equation (8) needs in order to compute the new derivatives at time k+1. But here again, the "non-recurrence-in-learning" assumption can be made: when adjusting the weights at time k+1, the activation values at time k are just considered as exogenous inputs, not dependent on the synaptic weights. When making this assumption, the resulting algorithm turns out to be trivial:

$$\frac{\partial x_i(k+1)}{\partial w_{lm}} = S'\ \delta_{il}\, x_m(k) \tag{9}$$

and becomes equivalent to the "Backpropagtion Through Time" algorithm, truncated to an horizon of one time step (BPTT(1), Williams and Peng 1990).

We have applied this algorithm to classical recurrent network toy problems such as tracing a circle or an eight (Pearlmutter 1989) and attained the same level of performance (in number of iterations) as Williams and Zipser's algorithm, while largely reducing the computer time and load. Nevertheless, in the recurrent network context, the problem appears more subtle than a simple comparison and simplification of algorithms. In the case where the simplest algorithm is used (eq. 9), only the connections sending the signal to units explicitly appearing in the error criterion (the observable units) are flexible. All other connections (the connections between hidden units or connections joining observable units to hidden ones) are fixed. Accordingly, although presenting a richer structure than a network without hidden units, this structure is still impoverished if not using the RTRL algorithm in the sense that it exhibits a greater rigidity and less degrees of freedom. Whether such an architecture, with non-plastic connections, is still able to perform the same tasks as an architecture containing only plastic connections is an interesting question to which we plan to dedicate attention in the future.

Jordan and Narendra's approaches as exposed above remain valid as long as the process to be controlled is a minimum-phase system which presents a delay of one time unit. For instance, in the cart-pole system, a classical nonlinear control application very famous in the neurocontrol community since the pioneering work of Barto et al. (1983), the position of the pole presents a longer delay (2 time steps) with respect to the force action (controller's output). It is quite significant to see that despite the popularity of this application, Jordan's method (with an error criterion such as the one discussed before) has never been attempted as such. This probably stems from the fact that minimizing an error criterion defined on the two position variables (the angle and the linear position) is unfeasible when using Jordan's approach as such, because both variables respond with a delay 2 to a change in the force applied on the cart. However other approaches, for instance the one coupling the neuro-controller with a neural emulator, not of the process but of the reinforcement predictor (Jordan and Jacobs 1990, Gullapalli 1992), can provide quite satisfactory results, since the reinforcement is indeed a direct function (i.e. with a delay of one time step) of the control signal. Note that in these approaches the goal of the control consists of maintaining the variables in a certain zone of the state space rather than forcing the cart (or pole) position to follow a specified trajectory.

3 THREE POSSIBLE EXTENSIONS OF JORDAN'S METHOD

In this section, we propose three alternative methods, all sharing the aim to preserve Jordan's method simplicity while extending it to processes exhibiting an arbitrary time delay. In fact, we can still assume a neurocontroller of the form (3), but we have to change the error criterion (2) to take into account the time delay d of the process. At time k, the control signal $u(k)$ should be computed so as to minimize the output error at time $k+d$:

$$e_{k+\mathrm{d}} = \frac{1}{2}\, [y(k+d) - y^{\mathrm{m}}(k+d)]^2 \tag{10}$$

where $y^{\mathrm{m}}(k+d)$ is the output of a reference model (Figure 1) at time $k+d$, used at time k for computing $u(k)$. The reference model is given from the desired output by:

$$y^{\mathrm{m}}(k+d) = y^{\mathrm{d}}(k) \tag{11}$$

and expresses the fact that the closed-loop behaviour cannot present a delay inferior to d time steps (actually, the closed-loop delay is chosen equal to the process delay).

Accordingly, at time k, the connection weights vector $\mathbf{w}$ is slightly modified using a simple gradient-descent step:

$$\mathbf{w}^k = \mathbf{w}^{k-1} - \eta\, [y(k) - y^{\mathrm{m}}(k)]\, \frac{\partial y(k)}{\partial \mathbf{w}} \tag{12}$$

with (for Narendra's approach)

$$\frac{\partial y(k)}{\partial \mathbf{w}} = \sum_{i=d}^{p} \frac{\partial F_k}{\partial u(k-i)} \frac{\partial u(k-i)}{\partial \mathbf{w}} + \sum_{i=1}^{p} \frac{\partial F_k}{\partial y(k-i)} \frac{\partial y(k-i)}{\partial \mathbf{w}} \quad (13)$$

The derivatives $\partial u(k-i)/\partial \mathbf{w}$ are still computed following equation (5b). Now, let us extend Jordan's approach to this case, by making the non-recurrence-in-learning assumption discussed previously, i.e. by considering that the control input $u(k-d)$ is the only explicit function of the synaptic weights of the neurocontroller when correcting them at time k. Then equations (12) and (13) become:

$$\mathbf{w}^k = \mathbf{w}^{k-1} - \eta\,[y(k) - y^m(k)]\,\frac{\partial F_k}{\partial u(k-d)}\,\left(\frac{\partial N}{\partial \mathbf{w}}\right)_{k-d} \quad (14)$$

This constitutes, together with definition (11), the basis of our JEAN-approaches (Jordan Extended for Adaptive Neurocontrol). In order to apply this technique, one needs some prior knowledge about the process, namely the knowledge of its time delay and a model – possibly in a neural form – providing the derivative $\partial F_k/\partial u(k-d)$. Since, at time k, when backpropagating the error, the state of the neural network (including its inputs) must be the one which is responsible for this error, a further requirement for applying JEAN is to keep in memory d copies of the neurocontroller at all intermediate times between the moment $k-d$ when the action is taken and the moment k when the process reacts and the error can be computed. Our first method, JEAN-1, effectively stores d copies of the network and corrects at time k the effect of an action taken d time steps before.

One way to alleviate this need for storing intermediate copies of the neurocontroller is to be in possession of a predictor of the process which is able to predict at time k, given the action injected into the process at that time, the output of the process at time $k+d$. Our second method JEAN-2 is based on the existence of such a predictor, possibly in a neural form. In JEAN-2, the squared error to minimize is $1/2\,[y^p(k+d) - y^m(k+d)]^2$ with $y^p(k+d)$ being the prediction of the process output $y(k+d)$ realized at time k. The backpropagation can now be performed just after the action has been taken without waiting for the delay. Thus, on the one hand, JEAN-1 just needs the values of the Jacobian – even roughly approximated as we will see later – but uses a lot of computer space (the amount needed increases with the delay). On the other hand, JEAN-2 does not need any intermediate storing but in compensation requires a full model of the process and is more sensitive to the quality of this model.

The last aspect to discuss, leading to the last method we propose, Mini-JEAN, is: How elementary the knowledge of the Jacobian can be in order still to succeed in controlling the process. In case of a Jacobian of constant sign, experiments suggest that a satisfactory control can be attained even on basis of a very limited prior knowledge of the process, namely the sign of its Jacobian $\partial F_k/\partial u(k-d)$ (Saerens and Soquet 1991). Indeed, the gradient method indicates that the adjustment of the synaptic weights follows the sign and the amplitude given by $(\partial F_k/\partial u(k-d)\,.\,\partial N_{k-d}/\partial \mathbf{w})$ (eq. 14). Since replacing $\partial F_k/\partial u(k-d)$ by its sign ± 1 (if constant) just alters the amplitude, not the direction of the variation, the reduced gradient method is still valid (possibly by adjusting the learning rate). Reducing to such a minimum the knowledge of the process necessary to its control makes the resulting control more "direct". The process can remain a black-box with just few holes allowing to observe qualitatively the way it reacts to increases and decreases of its input. This type of knowledge is quite common and certainly the first shallow type of knowledge a user or observer of the process is aware of and able to communicate. It is clear that Mini-JEAN can be either of the first type (Mini-JEAN-1) or of the second type (Mini-JEAN-2); however since substituting the Jabobian by its sign makes sense mainly in case of a missing prior knowledge of the process, Mini-JEAN will be generally of the first type, i.e. running without process predictor.

4 COMPARISON OF THE FIVE METHODS

In this section, we will apply and compare the five methods (Jordan, Narendra, JEAN-1, JEAN-2, and Mini-JEAN) on a non-linear process (Narendra and Parthasarathy 1992) of delay 2:

$$y(k+2) = \frac{1}{5}\left[\frac{y(k)\,y(k+1)\,[y(k+1) + 2.5]}{1 + y^2(k) + y^2(k+1)} + u(k)\right] \quad (15)$$

The operating region has been chosen as $y \in [-1.0, 1.0]$; $u \in [-1.0, 1.0]$. The desired output is chosen as a random number between [–0.2, 0.2] (uniform distribution) in order to avoid the problem of non-persistent excitation. The reference model is: $y^m(k) = y^d(k-2)$. The neural controller consists of a Radial-Basis Function (RBF) network (see, for instance, Poggio and Girosi 1990) with tunable centers and variance parameters, with 15 hidden units (i.e. 15 centers), 4 inputs ($y(k)$, $y(k-1)$, $y^d(k)$, $u(k-1)$) and one output $u(k)$. The neural emulator, when needed, also consists of a RBF-network with 15 hidden units whose center and variance parameters are tunable.

The learning curves representing at every 100 time steps the mean output error, averaged over the last 100 time steps, are drawn on Figure 3a (both Jordan and Narendra are indicated by a continuous line, but Narendra converges while Jordan does not) and Figure 3b (JEAN-1: continuous line; JEAN-2: dashed line; Mini-JEAN: dotted line). Table 1 allows us to compare the performances of the different methods. Figure 2 shows the tracking of a sinusoidal reference signal after training with Mini-JEAN algorithm. The reference is indicated by a dashed line.

The main results of this comparative analysis are:

1) The impossibility to use Jordan's method as originally stated for processes showing a delay superior to 1.

2) The equivalence of performance attained by the four other applicable methods both in the learning speed (see Figure 3ab) and the mean error after learning (see Table 1). This second observation would tend to support the non-recurrence-in-learning assumption into play when simplifying Narendra's developments so as to obtain the more elementary and economical JEAN methods. The level of performance is identical for each approach although the computer time and load are reduced with JEAN-approaches (see Table 1).

3) JEAN-2, although requiring less computer space than JEAN-1, presents some sensitivity to the process modelling precision; in particular, its mean error after learning depends on the quality of its predictor (see Table 1).

4) In case of constant sign Jacobians (it is in particular the case for a large family of processes in which the dependency on the control parameters is linear and time independant), the simplification underlying Mini-JEAN, i.e. replacing the Jacobians by their sign, can be done without observing any degradation in the results.

Table 1: Comparison of mean error after learning and relative computation time

Method	Mean error after convergence	Relative computation time
Jordan	0.1318	1.0
Narendra	0.0032	2.8
JEAN-1	0.0032	1.0
JEAN-2	0.0048	1.8
Mini-JEAN	0.0032	0.6

5 CONCLUSIONS

In this paper, three objectives were pursued. The first one was to connect the two most influential adative neurocontrol methods due to Jordan and Narendra, and to make clear how the first one can be obtained by a simplification of the second one steming from one basic assumption called the "non-recurrence-in-learning", which consists in restricting the dependency of the synaptic weights of the neurocontroller on its most recent output. This assumption also underlies the simplification of the real time recurrent learning by the back propagation through time truncated to 1 for the training of recurrent networks.

The second objective was to propose three extensions of Jordan's approach which, while keeping the simplicity of the method due to the non-recurrence-in-learning assumption, make possible the control of processes characterized by an arbitrary delay, no longer restricted to 1 time step. The last approach makes the further commitment that, for many control applications, even a very rough qualitative knowledge of the process, namely the sign of its Jacobian, suffices to satisfy the control objectives. Such method has already been tested with good results for problems as diverse as first order processes, the cart-pole problem (Saerens and Soquet 1991, Saerens et al. 1992) and an acoustic-to-articulatory inversion of a vocal tract model (Soquet et al. 1990).

The third objective was to show empirically that JEAN methods, although resulting from a simplification of Narendra's gradient approach, do not suffer from any degradation regarding the control performance while gaining in simplicity and computer economy.

Moreover, as already mentionned in the introduction, we have also provided some theoretical support to these three proposed algorithms. Indeed, by applying the so-called hyperstability formalism and Lyapunov theory, we showed that, under some conditions, the resulting closed-loop adaptation laws are asymptotically stable (Renders 1993; Saerens, Renders and Bersini 1993).

References

Aström K.J. and B. Wittenmark (1989). *Adaptive control.* Addison Wesley.

Barto A., R. Sutton and C. Anderson (1983). Neuronlike adaptive elements that can solve difficult learning control problems. *IEEE Transactions on Systems, Man and Cybernetics*, 13 (5), pp. 834-846

Gullapalli V. (1992). Dynamic systems control via associative reinforcement learning. In B. Soucek (ed.), *Dynamic, Genetic and Chaotic Programming*, pp. 27-50, John Wiley & Sons.

Hunt K.J., D. Sbarbaro, R. Zbikowski and P.J. Gawthrop (1992). Neural network for control systems – A survey. *Automatica*, 28 (6), pp. 1083-1112.

Jordan M.I. (1989a). Generic constraints on underspecified target trajectories. *Proceedings of the IEEE International Joint Conference on Neural Networks*, Washington DC, Vol. 1, pp. 217-225.

Jordan M.I. (1989b). Supervised learning and systems with excess degrees of freedom. In D. Touretzky, G. Hinton and T. Sejnowski (eds.), *Proceedings of the 1988 Connectionist models Summer School*, pp. 62-75, Morgan Kaufmann.

Jordan M.I. and R.A. Jacobs (1990). Learning to control an unstable system with forward modeling. In Touretzky (ed.), *Advances in Neural Information Processing II*, pp. 324-331, Morgan Kaufmann.

Jordan M.I. and D.E. Rumelhart (1991). Internal world models and supervised learning. In L. Birnbaum and G. Collins (eds.), *Proceedings of the eight International Workshop on Machine Learning*, pp. 70-74, Morgan Kaufmann.

Landau Y. (1979). *Adaptive control. The model reference approach.* Marcel Dekker.

Miller T., R. Sutton and P. Werbos (eds.) (1990). *Neural networks for control.* MIT Press, Cambridge (MA).

Narendra K.S. and K. Parthasarathy (1990). Identification and control of dynamical systems using neural networks. *IEEE Transactions on Neural Networks*, 1 (1), pp. 4-27.

Narendra K.S. and K. Parthasarathy (1992). Neural networks and dynamical systems. *International Journal of Approximate Reasoning*, 6, pp. 109-131.

Pearlmutter B. (1989). Learning state-space trajectories in recurrent neural networks. *Neural Computation*, 1, pp. 263-269.

Poggio T. and F. Girosi (1990). Networks for approximation and learning. *Proceeding of the IEEE*, 78 (9), pp. 1481-1497.

Psaltis D., A. Sideris and A. Yamamura (1987). Neural controllers. *Proceedings of the IEEE first International Conference on Neural Networks*, San Diego, Vol. 4, pp. 551-558.

Psaltis D., A. Sideris and A. Yamamura (1988). A multilayer neural network controller. *IEEE Control Systems Magazine*, 8 (2), pp. 17-21.

Renders (1993, forthcoming). *Biological metaphors for process control.* Ph.D. Thesis, Université Libre de Bruxelles, Faculté Polytechnique, Brussels.

Saerens M. and A. Soquet (1991). Neural controller based on back-propagation algorithm. *IEE Proceedings-F*, 138 (1), pp. 55-62. Reprinted in R. Vemuri (ed.), *Artificial Neural Networks: Concepts and Control Applications*, pp. 484-491, IEEE Computer Society Press.

Saerens M., A. Soquet, J.-M. Renders and H. Bersini (1992). Some preliminary comparisons between a neural adaptive controller and a model reference adaptive controller. In G. Bekey and K. Goldberg (eds.), *Neural Networks in Robotics*, pp. 131-146, Kluwer Academic Press.

Saerens M., J.-M. Renders and H. Bersini (1993). Neural controllers based on backpropagation algorithm. In M. Gupta and N. Sinha (eds.), *IEEE Press Book on Intelligent Control*, forthcoming, IEEE Computer Society Press.

Soquet A., M. Saerens and P. Jospa (1990). Acoustic-articulatory inversion based on a neural controller of a vocal tract model. *Proceedings of the ESCA First International Workshop on Speech Synthesis*, Autrans, pp. 71-74.

White H. (1992). *Artificial neural networks. Approximation and learning theory*. Blackwell Publishers.

Williams R.J. and D. Zipser (1989). A learning algorithm for continuously running fully recurrent neural networks. *Neural Computation*, 1, pp. 270-280.

Williams R.J. and J. Peng (1990). An efficient gradient-based algorithm for on-line training of recurrent network trajectories. *Neural Computation*, 2 (4), pp. 490-501.

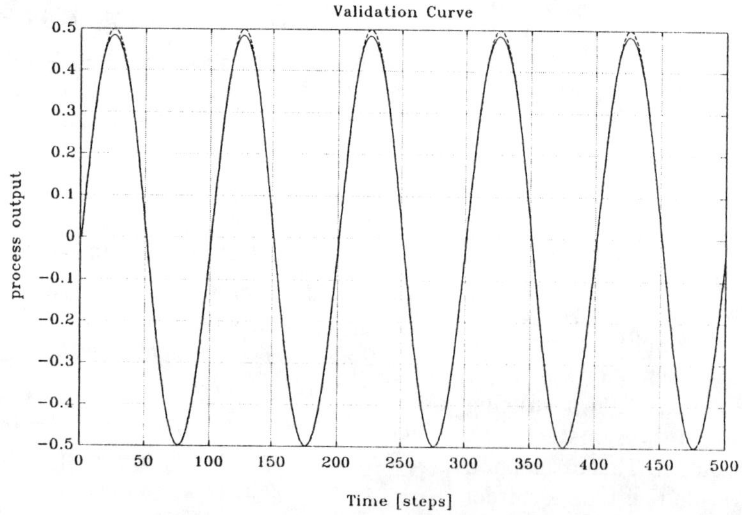

Figure 2: Validation after learning: Tracking of a sinusoidal reference

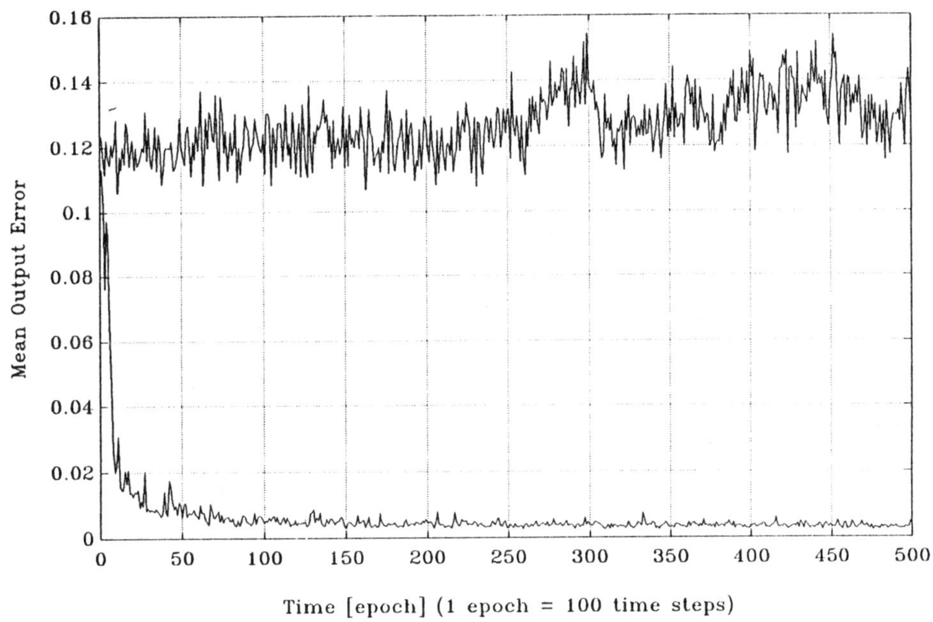

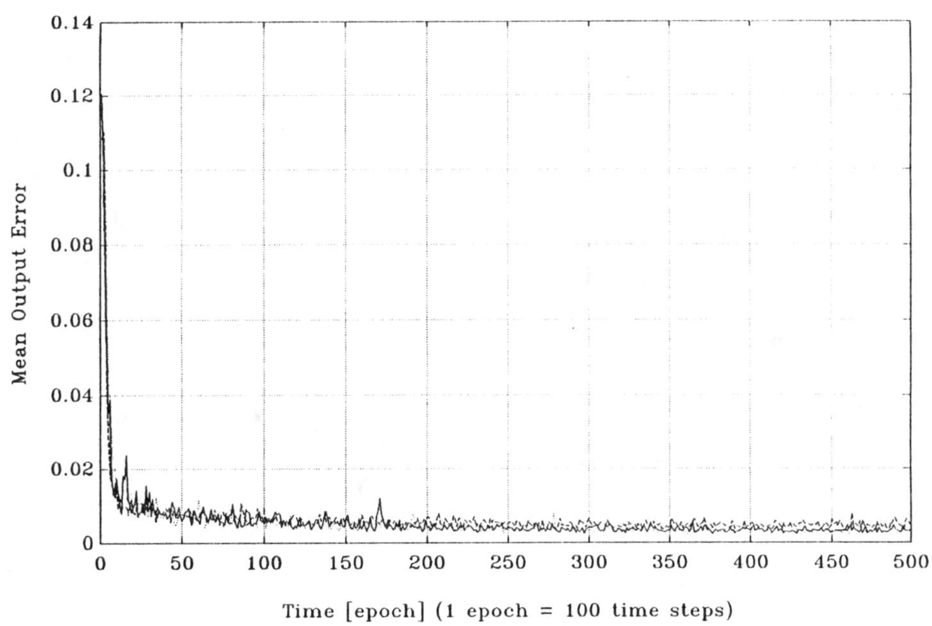

Figure 3ab: Learning curves. a. (upper figure) Narendra converges while Jordan does not. b. (lower figure) JEAN-1 is indicated by a continuous line, JEAN-2 is indicated by a dashed line, and Mini-JEAN is indicated by a dotted line

An SE-tree based Characterization of the Induction Problem

Ron Rymon
Computer and Information Science
University of Pennsylvania
Philadelphia, PA 19104
rymon@linc.cis.upenn.edu

Abstract

Many induction programs use decision trees both as the basis for their search, and as a representation of their classifier solution. In this paper we propose a new structure, called SE-tree, as a more general alternative.

1 INTRODUCTION

Many learning algorithms use decision trees as an underlying framework for search and as a representation of their classifier solutions (e.g. ID3 [Quinlan, 86], CART [Breiman *et al.*, 84]). This framework, however, is known to mix *search bias* (introduced when the algorithm decides on the order in which attributes are to be used in splitting) with *hypotheses-space bias*. To avoid being trapped by this bias, several researchers have suggested averaging over multiple trees (e.g. [Buntine, 91]). In this paper, still within a recursive partitioning framework, we propose using an alternative data structure called SE-tree [Rymon, 92]. On one hand, since the new framework shares many of the features of decision tree-based algorithms, we should be able to adopt many sub-techniques developed for the latter. On the other hand, an SE-tree embeds a large number of decision trees, thereby providing a more expressive, more flexible, representation for classifiers. Importantly, SE-tree-based algorithms can eliminate almost completely the search bias, admitting instead a *user-specified* hypotheses-space preference criterion.

Section 2 outlines a formal theory of induction where classifiers take the form of collections of rules. Sections 3 and 4 present the SE-tree, and render it useful in searching and representing such collections (the *learning* phase), and in subsequently using them for *classification*. Incorporation of user-specified bias in either stage, or in both, is described in Sections 4 and 5. Section 6 presents *general* results relating the SE-tree to decision trees, with some algorithmic implications.

2 A THEORY FOR INDUCTION

Formalizing the induction problem, we will examine collections of production rules that best model the function (concept) represented by the training data. Rules provide a common denominator for decision trees on one hand, and SE-trees on the other, since there is an obvious one-to-one mapping between rules and leaves of such trees.

Let us introduce a few useful definitions first: Let ATTRS $\stackrel{\text{def}}{=} \{A_i\}_{i=1}^{n}$ be a set of *attributes* (also called features or variables), where each attribute A_i can take values from a finite unordered discrete domain denoted $Dom(A_i)$. A *partial description* is a subset of ATTRS, each instantiated from its own domain. An *object* is a complete partial instantiation, i.e. one in which all attributes are instantiated. By UNIVERSE we refer to the collection of all objects. Consider, for example, a space of 3 binary attributes (A,B,C), hereafter called 3BIN. In 3BIN, {A=0,C=1} is a partial description. {A=0,B=0,C=1} is an object. UNIVERSE is 3BIN itself; it is made of a total of 8 objects. A training set (TSET), consisting of objects labeled by their correct *class* (π), makes an *induction problem instance*.

Example 2.1 *(The Checkers Problem)*

Consider a universe defined by two 3-valued attributes (A,B), and a set of four classes ($\alpha, \beta, \gamma, \delta$). The following figure depicts a training data, and an illustration of UNIVERSE.

A	B	π
1	2	α
2	1	β
2	3	γ
3	2	δ

		B		
		1	2	3
	1		α	
A	2	β		γ
	3		δ	

□

Having defined a problem instance, we shall try to characterize a solution. Conceptually, we assume the existence of a function (*target*) from UNIVERSE to the set of classes, and that the training data agree with this function. Our goal is to approximate *target* over the complete universe, using conjunctive rules as our elementary building blocks.

A *rule*, R, is simply a partial description such that all objects in TSET which agree with it are equally classified, i.e. for every t,t'∈TSET, if R⊆t,t' then $\pi(t) = \pi(t')$. To avoid irrelevant rules, we add the additional requirement that an object matched by a rule is provided in TSET. As a partial description, a rule defines an equivalence class within the universe, namely $[R] \stackrel{\text{def}}{=} \{t \in \text{UNIVERSE} \mid R \subseteq t\}$. Moreover, since all objects in TSET∩$[R]$ agree on their class, we can define $\pi([R])$ to be that class, and write a production rule of the form R ⇒ $\pi([R])$. Thus, from here on, we shall interchangeably talk about a rule as a set of instantiated attributes, as a region in UNIVERSE, and as a conjunction of antecedents. To model a target function, we use *collections* of rules, interpreted disjunctively for each class. In general, there may possibly be many such collections. The Checkers problem, for instance, admits 8 rules and thus 2^8 collections. The purpose of an inductive theory is to characterize ***desirable*** features of candidate collections. Bias, or preference, expresses the relative desirability of one collection versus another.

Our theory has a single bias: for the most part, we will prefer rules that are syntactically simpler. By *kernel rules* we refer to rules that are most-general (minimal set-wise). Other bias, necessary to distinguish equally simple hypotheses, is deliberately left out of the theory. Our algorithms will *modularly* implement a *user-specified* preference criterion. Consider the Checkers problem again. Only four of the eight rules are also kernel rules: (1) (A=1)⇒ α, (2) (B=1)⇒ β, (3) (B=3)⇒ γ, and (4) (A=3)⇒ δ. All other rules, e.g. (A=1)∧(B=2)⇒ α, are subsumed by one or more of the kernel rules.

Let C be a collection of rules for a problem instance P, we use Kernel(C) to denote the collection of kernel rules for P that subsume rules in C. The collection of all kernel rules, denoted KRULES, is the target of our induction algorithms. Doing so, we avoid *overfitting* of the training data. We propose that *over-generalization* be dealt with in the classification phase via resolution methods based on the user's preference criterion. Intuitively, while learning, we adopt most-general principles. Rules that are *too* general will be in conflict with others, and will then be resolved.

Definition 2.2 *Completeness*

A collection of rules C is said to be *complete* w.r.t. T⊆UNIVERSE if for every t∈T, there exists a rule R∈C such that R⊆t.

Proposition 2.3

1. Let C be a collection of rules that is complete w.r.t. some T⊆UNIVERSE, then Kernel(C) is also complete w.r.t. T;
2. KRULES is complete w.r.t. TSET, but is not necessarily complete w.r.t. UNIVERSE.

Thus, in the Checkers problem, {A=2,B=2} is not covered by any rule (including non-kernel!). In contrast, *any* decision tree *is* complete w.r.t. UNIVERSE. But is completeness desired at all? One may argue that incompleteness of KRULES is often a direct result of important incompleteness of the training data. SE-tree-based classification algorithms can, however, extend their coverage by relaxing the rule matching procedure.

Definition 2.4 *Consistency*

A collection of rules C is said to be *consistent* w.r.t. T⊆UNIVERSE, if for every t∈T, and rules R,R'∈C, if R,R'⊆t, then $\pi([R]) = \pi([R'])$.

Proposition 2.5

1. Every collection of rules is consistent w.r.t. TSET (by definition), but KRULES may be inconsistent w.r.t. UNIVERSE;
2. Every collection of rules contains a consistent sub-collection.

Thus, in the Checkers problem, each of the "corner" objects is covered by two contradicting kernel rules (e.g. {A=1,B=1} is covered by (A=1)⇒ α and (B=1)⇒ β). As per Proposition 2.5(2), KRULES may have (possibly several) sub-collections, the latter may have lesser *coverage* than KRULES. In contrast, *any* decision tree *is* consistent w.r.t. UNIVERSE. But is consistency desirable at all? KRULES is inconsistent when two rules are over-general to the point in which they contradict one another on as yet unseen parts of UNIVERSE. While ideally, one or both rules need be specialized or removed, the training data alone does *not* provide us with any suitable preference criterion. An *external* preference criteria, or *bias* [Mitchell, 80], must be applied.

Bias can be defined as the set of all factors that collectively influence hypothesis selection [Utgoff, 86]. [Buntine, 90] divides such criteria into three separate classes: *hypothesis space bias* are those criteria which specify a preference for one classifier over another; *search bias* consists of criteria used to guide the actual search for such; and finally, bias may have an *application specific* component. Adopting Buntine's dichotomy, we believe that an ideal learning system must *eliminate* search bias. Put differently, bias should be stated by the *user*, *independently* from the particular algorithm used.

We believe SE-trees represent a step in that direction. So far, we have introduced a single bias – a preference for kernel rules. Next, when presenting the *SE-Learn* family of learning algorithms, we defer the introduction of bias to the latest possible. A variety of user-defined preference criteria can be plugged into the learning and/or classification algorithms.

3 A LEARNING ALGORITHM

3.1 SET ENUMERATION TREES

Many problems in Computer Science were formalized to admit solutions in the form of *sets*, or in the form of partial instantiations of a set of variables. Typically, such sets are required to satisfy some problem-specific criterion which designates them as solutions. In addition, where multiple solutions may exist, they are often ranked by their plausibility, likelihood, or desirability. Regularly, such preference involves a minimality (or maximality) criterion, e.g. minimal entropy, maximum probability or utility, etc. *Set Enumeration (SE) trees* [Rymon, 92] were shown to be useful as the basis for a unifying search-based framework for such domains. SE-trees support complete, irredundant, and prioritized search; their special structure allows for efficient pruning and other optimizations.

Let ATTRS $\stackrel{\text{def}}{=} \{A_i\}_{i=1}^n$ be a set of attributes with domains Dom(A_i) respectively, and let *ind*:ATTRS→IN be an indexing of the set of attributes. We define the *SE-tree View* of a partial description *S* as follows:

$$\text{View(S)} \stackrel{\text{def}}{=} \{\text{A} \in \text{ATTRS} \mid \text{ind(A)} > \text{Max}_{A' \ in \ S}\text{ind(A')}\}$$

Definition 3.1 *Extended Set Enumeration Tree*

The *extended SE-tree* for a set of attributes ATTRS is defined as follows:

1. At its root is a node labeled with the empty set;
2. Recursively, let S be a node's label, It has children labeled as follows:

$$\{ \text{S} \cup \{\text{A=v}\} \mid \text{A} \in \text{View(S)}, \text{v} \in \text{Dom(A)}\}.$$

Example 3.2 Figure 1 depicts an extended SE-tree for the *complete* 3BIN space. Note that restricting a node's expansion to its *View*, ensures that *every* member of 3BIN is *uniquely* explored within the tree. □

Representing all elements of a power-set, the complete SE-tree is clearly exponential in size. However, in a large class of problems, especially where solutions are monotonic with respect to set inclusion, the SE-tree can be used to induce a complete and yet often efficient search because it allows for systematic pruning [Rymon, 92].

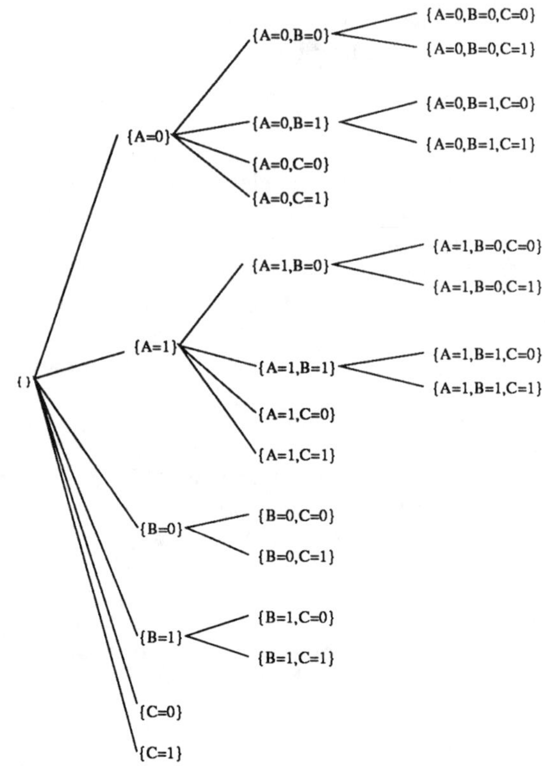

Figure 1: Complete SE-tree for 3 Binary Variables

3.2 SE-TREE-BASED LEARNING

Aimed at all kernel rules, SE-Learn (Algorithm 3.4) explores top-down an imaginary SE-tree. Nodes are explored by some predetermined priority function. In Sections 4 and 5, we show this prioritization useful in implementing various biases. In expanding open nodes, SE-Learn exploits the SE-tree structure to prune away nodes that cannot *lead* to kernel rules. SE-Learn's output is an SE-tree which leaves are labeled with kernel rules.

Definition 3.3 *Candidate and Impotent Expansions*

Let S be a node, TSET(S) $\stackrel{\text{def}}{=} \{t \in \text{TSET} \mid S \subseteq t\}$. We say that S' $\stackrel{\text{def}}{=}$ S∪{A=v} is a *candidate expansion* of S if A∈View(S), v∈Dom(A). However, S' is *impotent* if either

1. TSET(S') is empty; or
2. TSET(S')=TSET(S); or
3. all objects in TSET(S') agree on their assignment to attributes in $View(S')$, but there is not a complete agreement on the class (i.e. S' is not a rule).

Algorithm 3.4

Program SE-Learn

1. OPEN-NODES ← {ϕ};

2. Until OPEN-NODES is empty do

3. Expand (Extract-Min(OPEN-NODES))

Procedure Expand(S)

1. For every candidate expansion R $\stackrel{\text{def}}{=}$ S∪{A=v} that is not impotent and that is not subsumed by a previously discovered rule do

2. If R is a rule then mark it as such; otherwise add it to OPEN-NODES.

The algorithm works by exploring nodes along the SE-tree's current fringe (OPEN-NODES) in a best-first fashion. For that purpose, nodes are cached in a priority queue and accessed via an *Extract-Min* operation. Candidate expansions that are not subsumed by previously discovered rules (step 1) are marked as rules if they satisfy the definition or otherwise marked for expansion and added to the queue for further consideration (step 2).

3.3 EXPLORATION POLICIES

An exploration policy is simply the priority function used in Algorithm 3.4 to determine the order in which nodes are explored. It is easy to verify that if nodes are explored by their cardinality (breadth-first exploration of the tree) then the algorithm is correct, i.e. it computes all and only kernel rules. As so far described, any monotonic function ψ, i.e. such that S⊆S' implies $\psi(S) \leq \psi(S')$), results in Algorithm 3.4 being correct. A large class of interesting functions are monotonic, e.g. ones that are based on probability, utility, or information-gain measures. However, at some computational expense, SE-Learn can be modified to admit non-monotonic exploration policies as well. The sole purpose of the monotonicity restriction is to avoid recording non-minimal solutions; therefore, to remove it, we need to also check whether new rules subsume old ones.

Note however that, as so far presented, *all* exploration policies will result in the *same* tree structure. The variety of exploration policies allowed will become important next, in specifying and implementing preference criteria.

4 CLASSIFICATION ALGORITHMS

Given an SE-tree acquired as above, we want to be able to use it to classify *new* objects. As in decision tree-based classification algorithms, this is done by following matching paths from the root to class-labeled leaves (rules).

Recall however that in the SE-tree representation

1. there may be *no* such leaf (rule) (we called this incompleteness); or
2. there may be *multiple* rules (and thus leaves) matching a given object, and they may not always be equally labeled (we called this inconsistency).

The SE-tree incompleteness, we argued, is due to the incompleteness of the training data. One way to "complete" the SE-tree is to perform *partial* matching in cases where there are no perfectly matching rules.

The inconsistency property, on the other hand, gives the SE-tree its main power. Roughly, inconsistency reflects a variety of perspectives that could be adopted to logically partition the training data. In a decision tree, a *single* such perspective is decided upon at the learning phase in the choice of attribute for each branching point. Representing multiple perspectives is more expressive and allows more principled resolution. In particular, *hypotheses-space* preference, explicitly specified by the user, can be used to resolve conflicts.

Algorithm 4.1 uses such preferences directly: by searching the SE-tree best-first with respect to the specified preference, it picks the leaf which maximizes the specified preference from all those matching the object at hand.

Algorithm 4.1 *Classification via SE-tree Search*

- **Input:** (1) an object; (2) an SE-tree; and (3) an exploration policy ψ (bias).
- **Procedure:** Search SE-tree best-first (according to ψ), along paths matching the object. Stop when the first leaf is hit, or when the tree is exhausted.
- **Output:** If a leaf was hit, predict its class label. Otherwise, either respond "don't know", or guess, or re-search the tree allowing for partial matching.

A more general approach involves specifying a *resolution criterion*, e.g. weighted averaging or voting, which takes into account *all* rules matching a given object. The two approaches can, of course, be combined by applying the resolution criterion to a *subset* of the rules – those which rank highest by the preference criterion.

The following experiment, using the Monks benchmark [Thrun *et al.*, 91], demonstrates the importance of the particular choice of resolution criterion. In general, a preference and/or a resolution criterion should reflect some domain knowledge. However, given the artificial nature of the Monks problems, we experimented with three generic weight functions: simple voting; quadratic (in the rule's size) weight voting, favoring more specific rules; and inverse quadratic, favoring more general rules. In the learning phase, we simply learned all kernel rules. In classification, when the rules were incomplete, we used partial matching. Conflicts were resolved using each of the three weight functions. Figure 2 compares accuracy obtained using each of the resolution criteria to each other; to the average reported for other decision tree-based programs and to the overall average reported for all methods. Note that SE-Learn's performance is crucially dependent on the resolution criterion used.

	Monk1	Monk2	Monk3
SE-Learn (inv. quad.)	85.9%	71.3%	95.6%
SE-Learn (voting)	72.0%	69.0%	88.4%
SE-Learn (quadratic)	64.8%	67.1%	70.8%
Average decision trees	84.2%	67.6%	86.9%
Average overall	88.9%	76.4%	90.9%

Figure 2: Various Resolution Criteria

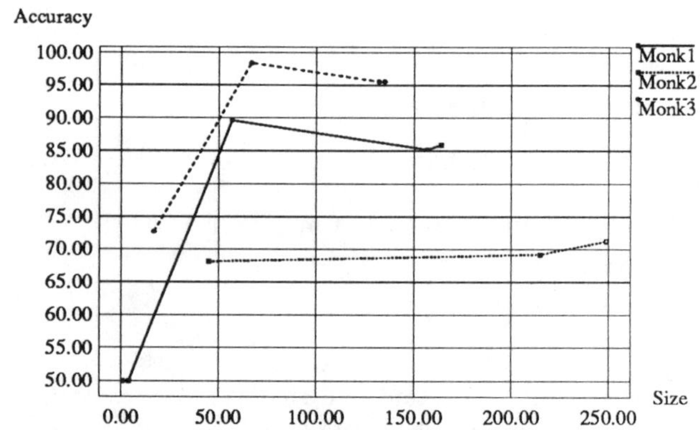

Figure 3: Complexity vs. Accuracy

5 BIAS IN THE LEARNING PHASE

5.1 PARTIALLY EXPLORED SE-TREES

It may often be intractable, or practically impossible, to explore all kernel rules. Exploration policies can then be used as early as the learning phase to prune away less promising parts of the SE-tree. Even when all kernel rules *can* be explored, added complexity may not pay in the margin. Worse, as with many other learning frameworks, more complex SE-trees can even have lower accuracy than their simpler subsets. In such instances, it is standard to use hill-climbing procedures and/or anytime algorithms which explore as time/space permit and return the best classifier seen so far. In SE-Learn, the SE-tree can be constructed gradually while testing to make sure that the added complexity of new rules is worth the marginal improvement in accuracy. When interrupted, or when it runs out of resources (particularly space) this procedure will return the best classifier it has seen so far. The particular exploration policy used plays an important role in this procedure since it determines the order in which rule nodes are seen. Using again the Monks problems, we ran an experiment in which an SE-tree was explored level by level. The change in complexity (measured by the number of rules) and in accuracy (using the inverse quadratic resolution criterion) is depicted in Figure 3.

5.2 SPECIAL COLLECTIONS OF RULES

In what follows, we briefly describe variations of SE-Learn that compute SE-trees corresponding to collections of rules with special features. Here too, the particular collection computed is determined by the exploration policy.

Consistent Sub-Collections of KRULES

A collection of kernel rules is inconsistent w.r.t. UNIVERSE iff it has rules R_1, R_2 such that $\pi([R_1]) \neq \pi([R_2])$ and no attribute appears in both $R_1 - R_2$, and $R_2 - R_1$. Thus, SE-Learn could be modified not to retain rules which are inconsistent with previously discovered rules. Since the order in which nodes are explored determines which rules are retained, the particular exploration policy used defines a bias.

Minimal Sub-Collections of KRULES

For TSET-completeness purposes, a rule R is redundant if every object in TSET that R matches is also matched by another rule R'. As before, one can modify SE-Learn so as not to retain rules deemed redundant by previously discovered rules. Another alternative is to restrict redundancy to n rules per training instance, or to rules that satisfy some other acceptance criterion such as statistical significance. Again, the particular exploration policy defines a bias.

Consistent and Complete Collections of Rules

The down side of discarding inconsistent rules, as suggested above, is that the collection of rules obtained may be incomplete even w.r.t. TSET. To avoid this, rather than discarding such rules, SE-Learn can be modified to further *expand* them. The collection of rules so obtained are guaranteed to be complete. However, individual rules may no longer be kernel.

Minimal and Consistent Collections

By removing both inconsistent and redundant rules, one may get a minimal collection of rules that is both complete and consistent.

6 SE-TREE AND DECISION TREES

A number of decision tree based algorithms have had an impact on machine learning research. Part of our purpose here is to convince researchers to look at the SE-tree as a more general alternative to decision trees. We devote this section to a broader comparison of the two data structures.

6.1 A FOREST OF DECISION TREES

One way to view a decision tree is as an SE-tree in which every possible object has exactly one path along which it can be classified, i.e. an SE-tree that is consistent and complete w.r.t. UNIVERSE[1]. Conversely, one way to view an SE-tree is as a collection, or *forest*, of decision trees. A single SE-tree can be shown to embed a large number of decision trees. In particular, let D be a decision tree in which attributes were chosen monotonically w.r.t. some indexing function. Let S be an SE-tree constructed in accordance to same indexing function, then S *embeds* D, i.e. there exists a subset of S's edges which forms a tree that is topologically and semantically equivalent to D, and that is rooted at S's root. One particular decision tree is the SE-tree's *primary decision tree*: the one in which each internal node is expanded with the first attribute in that node's SE-tree *View* that does not result in impotent expansions.

This result can be strengthened to make the SE-tree embed *any* single decision tree[2]. In particular, let D be a decision tree that is constructed by any ID3-like procedure. To create an SE-tree that embeds D we may have to slightly alter the definition of an SE-tree to allow for *dynamic re-indexing*. In particular, we will develop an indexing as we create the tree:

1. At first, we will choose an initial indexing ind_{root} in which the first attribute used in D appears first;
2. Then, while at a node labeled S, let $ind_{parent(S)}$ be the indexing used in expanding S's parent. In S, we use an indexing which coincides with $ind_{parent(S)}$ on all attributes *not* in $View(S)$, but may re-order attributes in $View(S)$ as we wish. In particular, if a node corresponding to S appears in D, we will re-order attributes in $View(S)$ so that the first attribute used in D to split that node appears first.

By construction, D will be embedded in an SE-tree created as above as its primary decision tree. It is fairly easy to verify that the SE-tree remains complete and irredundant, and that SE-Learn remains correct.

[1]An SE-tree, however, can be consistent and complete without being a decision tree.

[2]*Not* all of them at once; rather a collection that includes a specific decision tree.

6.2 IMPROVING UPON A GIVEN DECISION TREE

An important corollary of the result above is that one can *construct* an exploration policy under which SE-Learn will start off with one's favorite decision tree, and then try to improve it by adding more rule nodes. (This exploration policy may be non-monotonic though.) Of course, rule nodes will only be added to the extent in which accuracy (as tested empirically on a separate training set) is improved.

We have tested this approach on the Monks benchmark. In each of the three problems, we started with a decision tree constructed by the information-gain criterion. Then, the rest of the SE-tree was explored breadth-first. Accuracy and complexity were recorded for the primary decision tree, and for each level of the tree in which rules were added (Figure 4).

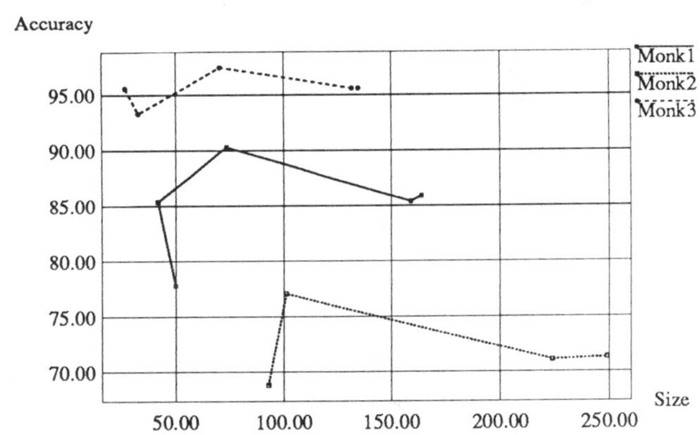

Figure 4: Starting from a Decision Tree

Note that in all three problems, the accuracy of the primary decision tree could be improved by adding SE-tree nodes, although this improvement is not monotonic. Also note that in Monk1, adding the SE-tree's first level has not only improved the accuracy, but has also *reduced* the number of rule nodes (some decision tree rules were pruned because they were subsumed by newly discovered rules).

6.3 HYPOTHESES EXPRESSIBILITY

Consider the following problem instance:

A	B	Class
0	0	0
1	1	1

		B	
		0	1
A	0	0	?
	1	?	1

While *four* different hypotheses are consistent with this training data, there are only *two* ID3-style[3] de-

[3]There are more decision trees, but only these can be generated by an ID3-like procedure.

cision trees (Figure 5). The corresponding SE-tree contains (as subset of its arcs) both trees, and can be used to represent *all four* hypotheses depending on the particular exploration policy (bias) used in a given classification session.

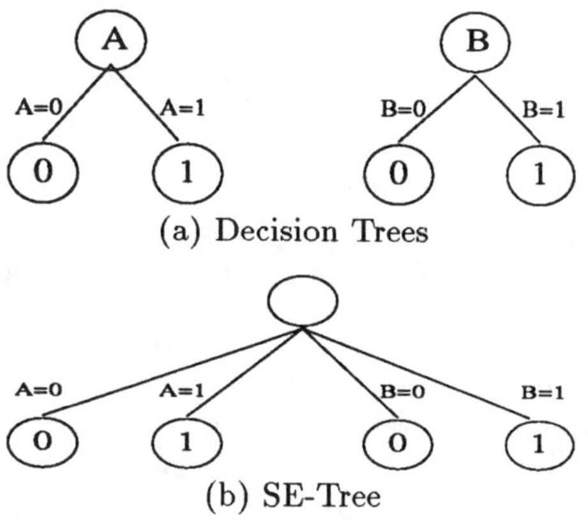

Figure 5: SE-tree versus Decision Trees

Consider, for example, an OR function (not modeled by either decision trees). In SE-Learn, if a search-based approach to classification is adopted (Algorithm 4.1), an OR function can be implemented using an exploration policy that assigns high priority to the arcs A=1 and B=1. Generalizing this problem to n attributes, each taking its values from $\{0 \ldots n-1\}$, we are given a training set with the n cases in which all attributes, and the class, are equally labeled. Now, we consider a function that takes the most frequent value among its attributes, with bias towards higher values in case of equality (for $n = 2$, we get the OR function). Such function cannot be modeled by any of the ID3-style decision trees[4], but can easily be modeled using an SE-tree with a resolution criterion based on simple voting.

6.4 COMPUTING KERNEL RULES

Considering the goal of computing all kernel rules, three problems may arise in a decision tree-based search framework:

1. The *minimality* problem – rules will often not be discovered in their minimal (kernel) form;
2. The *multiplicity* problem – each kernel rule may be discovered multiply, disguised in a number of its non-minimal supersets; and
3. The *incompleteness* problem – some kernel rules may not be discovered at all.

Both the minimality problem and the multiplicity phenomenon result from the fact that attributes used high in the tree are necessary for some, but not all, the rules. The minimality problem is often addressed by subsequently pruning the rules extracted from the decision tree (e.g. [Quinlan, 87]). The replication problem, a special case of multiplicity in which whole subtrees are replicated, has been addressed by several researchers (e.g. [Rivest, 87, Pagallo & Haussler, 90]). Incompleteness, which is only a problem if one is really interested in all kernel rules, results from the insisted mutual exclusivity of any decision tree's leaves (see [Weiss & Indurkhya, 91]). None of these problems occurs in the SE-tree-based framework:

1. Rules are always discovered in their kernel form;
2. Kernel rules are always discovered uniquely; and
3. All kernel rules are discovered.

6.5 COMPLEXITY

The SE-tree's exhaustiveness and large *initial* branching may be deceiving. Let us first compare its worst-case complexity to that of a decision tree, *independently* of their use.

Proposition 6.1 If all attributes are b-valued, then the number of nodes in a complete decision tree is $b^n + b^{n-1} + \cdots b + 1 > b^n$. The size of a complete SE-tree is $(b+1)^n$. In sharp contrast, the size of a super-tree containing all decision trees is significantly larger: $b^n \cdot n!$.

Within an induction framework, however, one rarely explores a complete decision tree (nor a complete SE-tree for that matter). In an ID3-like framework, the size of a decision tree is *linear* in the size of the training data. This is *not* true of SE-Learn! Kernel rules are close relatives of prime-implicants, and as such we know of pathological examples in which the number of kernel rules is exponential in the size of the training data. On the other hand, as just explained, one does not have to explore the entire SE-tree and one can always have the first nodes explored be those of one's favorite decision tree.

7 CONCLUSION AND FUTURE RESEARCH DIRECTIONS

We have proposed an inductive learning framework which uses an SE-tree as a basis for search and classifier representation and have presented a family of algorithms for SE-tree induction and for SE-tree-based classification. We have shown that as a representation for classifiers, SE-trees generalize decision trees in two ways: first, a decision tree is a special case of an SE-tree, and second, an SE-tree contains many decision trees. An SE-tree can also be built by improving upon one's favorite decision tree. However, unlike decision trees, most of the *search bias* can be eliminated

[4]In fact, a decision tree modeling this function is necessarily exponential.

in SE-tree-based algorithms; an independently specified ***hypothesis-space bias*** can be used instead.

Importantly, the SE-tree-based framework can borrow from techniques developed for decision trees. In particular

1. More expressive representation languages can be adopted, e.g. ordered and hierarchical variables, multi-variable tests, class probability trees, etc. Discretization techniques, and criteria developed for selecting a splitting test can be used to handle ordered variables; averaging and smoothing techniques can be used in conjunction with class probabilities representation.
2. Pruning techniques developed for decision trees, e.g. using statistical significance tests, can also be used in SE-trees.
3. Entropy-minimization and other criteria developed for selecting the next splitting attribute in decision trees will likely be useful in selecting an indexing function for an SE-tree which will minimize the number of nodes that have to be explored.

More research, however, is needed to figure ways in which these techniques can be deployed *effectively.*

Other areas of future research include general and domain-specific exploration policies and resolution criteria, termination criteria suitable for various tradeoffs between accuracy and time/space, and an incremental version of SE-Learn.

Recent advances in search algorithms lend themselves to improved implementation of the SE-tree-based framework, e.g. linear-space best-first search algorithms [Korf, 92, Russell, 92] and a SIMD version of IDA* [Powley *et al.*, 93].

Acknowledgements

The idea of using the SE-trees to learn rules originated at a talk by Tom Mitchell — I thank him for that, as well as for later suggestions. I also thank Kevin Atteson, Russ Greiner, Haym Hirsh, Alon Luss, Teow-Hin Ngair, Michael Niv, Greg Provan, Philip Resnik, Nick Short, Scott Weinstein, and anonymous reviewers for commenting on previous drafts. This work was supported in part by a graduate fellowship ARO grant DAAL03-89-C0031PRI.

References

[Breiman *et al.*, 84] Breiman, L., Friedman, J., Olshen, R., and Stone, C., *Classification and Regression Trees.* Wadsworth, Belmont, 1984.

[Buntine, 90] Buntine, W., Myths and Legends in Learning Classification Rules. *Proc. AAAI-90*, Boston, MA, pp. 736-742, 1990.

[Buntine, 91] Buntine, W., Learning Classification Trees. Technical Report, NASA Ames Research Center, 1991.

[Korf, 92] Korf, R. E., Linear-Space Best-First Search: Summary of Results. *Proc. AAAI-92*, San Jose CA, 1992.

[Mitchell, 80] Mitchell, T. M., The Need for Biases in Learning Generalizations. *Technical Report 5-110*, Rutgers University, 1980.

[Pagallo & Haussler, 90] Pagallo, G., and Haussler, D., Boolean Feature Discovery in Empirical Learning. *Machine Learning*, 5, pp. 71-99, 1990.

[Powley *et al.*, 93] Powley, C., Ferguson, C., and Korf, R. E., Depth-First Heuristic Search on a SIMD Machine. *Artificial Intelligence*, 60, 1993, pp. 199-242.

[Quinlan, 86] Quinlan, J. R., Induction of Decision Trees. *Machine Learning*, 1(1):81-106, 1986.

[Quinlan, 87] Quinlan, J. R., Generating Production Rules from Decision Trees. *Proc. IJCAI-87*, pp. 304-307, 1987.

[Rivest, 87] Rivest, R., Learning Decision Lists. *Machine Learning*, 2, pp. 229-246, 1987.

[Russell, 92] Russell, S., Efficient Memory-Bounded Search Algorithms. *Proc. ECAI-92*, Vienna, Austria, 1992.

[Rymon, 92] Rymon, R., Search through Systematic Set Enumeration. *Proc. KR-92*, Cambridge MA, 1992.

[Thrun *et al.*, 91] Thrun, S. B., Bala, J., Bloedron, E., Bratko, I., Cestnik, B., Cheng, J., De Jong, K., Dzeroski, S., Fahlman, S. E., Fisher, D., Hammann, R., Kaufman, K., Keller, S., Kononenko, I., Kreuzinger, J., Michalski, R. S., Mitchell, T., Pachowicz, P., Reich, Y., Vafaie, H., Van de Welde, W., Wenzel, W., Wnek, J., Zhang, J., The MONK's Problems – A Performance Comparison of Different Learning Algorithms. *Technical Report CMU-CS-91-197*, December 1991.

[Utgoff, 86] Utgoff, P. E., *Machine Learning of Inductive Bias.* Kluwer Academic, Boston MA, 1986.

[Weiss & Indurkhya, 91] Weiss, S. M., and Indurkhya, N., Reduced Complexity Rule Induction. *Proc. IJCAI-91*, pp. 678-684, Sydney, Australia, 1991.

Density-Adaptive Learning and Forgetting

Marcos Salganicoff
Department of Computer and Information Science
University of Pennsylvania
Philadelphia, PA 19104
sal@grip.cis.upenn.edu

Abstract

We describe a density-adaptive reinforcement learning and a density-adaptive forgetting algorithm. This learning algorithm uses hybrid k-$D/2^k$-trees to allow for a variable resolution partitioning and labelling of the input space. The density adaptive forgetting algorithm deletes observations from the learning set depending on whether subsequent evidence is available in a local region of the parameter space. The algorithms are demonstrated in a simulation for learning feasible robotic grasp approach directions and orientations and then adapting to subsequent mechanical failures in the gripper.

1 Introduction and Motivation

In many learning applications, it is often the case that the learner perceives a continuum of real-valued perceptual input attribute valuations, in which case the state-space is infinite, rather than a set of discrete-valued attributes. Additionally, it is often the case that reinforcement for a given instance (the outcome) is binary. For example, in a robotic domain, either an object is grasped successfully or dropped. Therefore, in that context, it may be more meaningful to learn the conditional probability of receiving the reinforcement value, rather than to estimate reinforcement as a real-valued quantity.

We describe a technique, *Density-Adaptive* Reinforcement Learning (DARLING), for identifying regions of a real-valued parameter space where the lower-bound probability of succeeding (receiving *immediate* reward) subject to a $1-\alpha$ confidence value is above some minimum probability required for the task.

Also, as noted previously by [18, 7, 11], an important assumption taken by many learning methods is that the concept (e.g. the environment and task) to be learned is stationary over time. By stationary, we mean that the true underlying process which maps exemplars to outcomes is unchanging. A non-stationary concept can be manifested in terms of time varying state-transition functions, or time-varying reward functions. This may, in turn, be due to gradual or sudden failures in sensors and actuators, as well as changes in the behavior of the external world.

In artificial neural-network approaches, weights are updated on-line and non-stationarity presents less of a problem, since the weight updating rules will eventually change weights so that they minimize prediction error on the most recent pool of exemplars. The problem is more acute in cases where a memory-based approach for learning is used and stored exemplars are used directly to form predictions, such as nearest-neighbor and tree based approaches. In the non-stationary case, the learning set will contain observations which are obsolete and will be significantly biased by the representative exemplars from obsolete concepts. Consider also, that often, artificial neural networks are trained on a *fixed* learning set which is repeatedly presented in random order, and therefore the same requirement to delete obsolete observations is present.

We describe a density adaptive *forgetting* technique to delete obsolete observations using exponential weight-decay based on a nearest neighbor criteria. The approach uses a decay coefficient to decrement an experience's weighting, similar to that of [8, 11, 9]. However, this coefficient is a function of the similarity of that given experience to subsequent experiences, rather than a fixed value. The weight of an exemplar is decayed and deleted when it goes below some minimum value, and is superseded by the newer observations that led to its deletion. This procedure can be used as a front-end to a variety of learning algorithms, the only prerequisite being that the input attribute space can support a distance metric. It can also be easily modified to keep the size of a learning set bounded if limited storage is available.

We demonstrate the utility of these learning and forgetting algorithms in simulation for the assessment of a robotic grasp's suitability to an object with a given parametric superellipsoid attribute description [19] and pose. However, the method can be applied to any situation where there are a fixed set of actions to evaluate, a reward and a real-valued input attribute space.

This work differs from previous efforts in learning for robotic grasping in terms of action and perceptual representation, as well as the learning methods employed. Dunn [4] employed a two dimensional polygonal representation, and a random search for successful grasps during learning, followed by a 2-D model matching during execution. Tan [20] employed a feature-based sonar depth representation and a cost sensitive extension of ID-3 with 3-D objects. Bennett [2] worked in robotic grasping of polygonal 2-D puzzle piece task using explanation-based learning and domain theories about uncertainty and grasping. Mel [10], Ritter [15] and Cooperstock have used $\Sigma - \Pi$ neural-networks, self-organizing feature maps and backpropagation, respectively, for learning visually-guided control of robot arms for grasping.

2 Learning Algorithm

First, we describe the learning algorithm, *Density Adaptive* reinforcement learning (DARLING) [16]. Here the term *Density* refers to the local density of observations in the attribute space, defined as the number of exemplars per unit volume of attribute space.

The DARLING algorithm takes inspiration from decision tree approaches embodied in Classification and Regression Trees [3] and ID-3 [14], along with the geometric learning approaches described by Omohundro [13]. The goal of the algorithm is to identify regions of the input attribute space having a lower-bound estimated probability, p_-, of succeeding (receiving reward) that is greater than some specified minimum probability p_{min} required for the task. The algorithm produces a classification tree (see Figure 1) with real-valued splits that approximates those regions. We desire that the tree approximate those regions of the parameter space with minimum over- and under-estimation.

2.1 Density-Adaptation

The algorithm first builds a *k-D*-tree [5] based on the distribution of the exemplars in the parameter space, *ignoring* the outcome labels of each exemplar. This step adaptively partitions the exemplar set into a set of bins each with a roughly uniform number of exemplars. Therefore, a *k-D*-tree takes the exemplar distribution in the attribute space, and partitions the input space such that the probability of a future observation landing in any one of the partition bins approaches equi-probability, assuming it is drawn from the same distribution as the learning set. The attribute space is effectively transformed so as to equalize the original distribution of exemplars so that it is uniform [12]. The higher the local density of exemplars, the larger the number of bins per unit volume (area) of attribute space, and the smaller the average spatial extents of those leaves. Smaller spatial extent leads to higher effective resolution (see Figure 2).

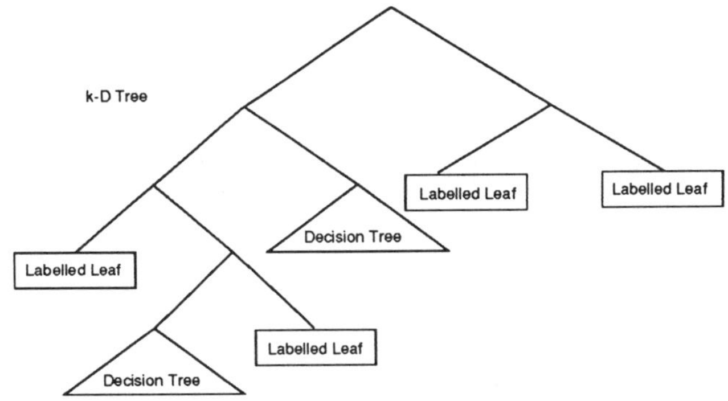

Figure 1: The DARLING Tree. It consists of a *k-D*-tree with leaf nodes that cover regions of the parameter space. The leaf nodes are either labelled classifications or the roots for shallow 2^k decision-trees that further partition and identify subregions.

Many decision-tree algorithms operating in real-valued domains are greedy, they rank the attributes and splits at the current node under construction based on some locally computable figure of merit. At one extreme are algorithms such as ID-3[14] and CART [3]. Their splitting criteria are based on the expected information gain among attributes which is purely a function of instance labelling and the orderings of these labellings as projected along the current attribute axis. They do not take into account metric information such as the physical locations of exemplars in the parameter space. The DARLING algorithm is at the other extreme since it first builds a *k-D* trees. The *k-D*-tree is also generated using a greedy algorithm for ranking attributes. However, it completely ignores the labelling of the exemplars, and picks attributes according to which attribute for the current node has the greatest spatial spread as projected onto the current attribute axis, only looking a metric information about the learning set. Immediately after this phase, the DARLING algorithm looks at outcome label information to build shallow decision trees.

2.2 Node Splitting and Labelling

As stated previously, *k-D*-tree partition does not ensure that the homogeniety of each bin is high, since its construction ignores the outcome of each exemplar, and is driven only by their locations. It may be that

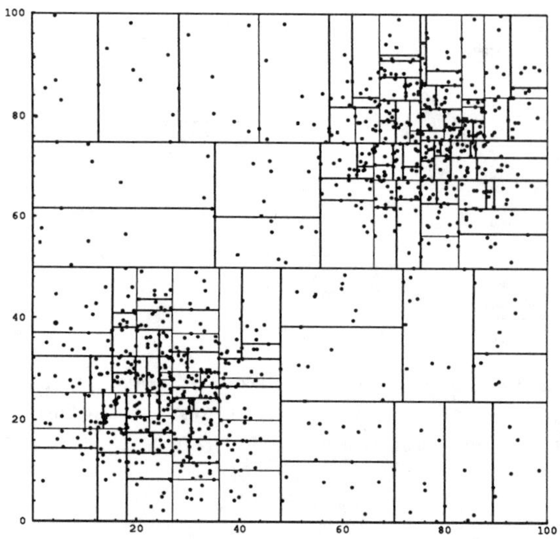

Figure 2: Density adaptation using *k-D* trees. The *k-D*-tree partition of a mixture of Gaussians and a uniform distribution. It can be seen that the size of the leaves decreases as the local density of samples increases, yielding the desired adaptive resolution property.

a node under evaluation does not meet the p_{min} stopping criteria. However upon splitting that node, it may yield a set of children nodes among which some are acceptable.

Since we are interested in finding regions of the attribute space having a pessimistic probability of success greater than some p_{min}, we use the outcome ratios to compute a probability interval estimate [6] for the underlying probability of receiving a success in that leaf. Two thresholds, p_{min} and p_{max}, are required for splitting. If the lower bound of the probability interval is above the p_{min} threshold, then it is accepted. It the upper bound p_+ is below the p_{max} value, then it is immediately rejected. If neither condition holds then the *k-D* tree leaf is further split.

This *k-D*-leaf splitting could also be accomplished using a variety of standard identification tree algorithms depending on the learning task. The critical notion is that the *effective* resolution of a decision tree of some depth *l* is greater when its domain is smaller. Because we are inserting these decision trees into the domain of *k-D*-tree leaves, the spatial distribution of exemplars governs the resolution of the individual decision trees. The decision trees may be shallow, yet still have high spatial resolution if they are embedded into a leaf with small spatial extent. In this implementation, we embed 2^k-trees (generalized quadtrees) into the *k-D*-tree. They are built to varying depths based the $(1-\alpha)$ acceptance criteria described below.

Algorithm **DARLING**(point_set)

> (* perform density adaptation *)
> Generate *k-D*-tree for point_set
> **for** all leaves of *k-D*-tree
> **begin**
>> Compute p_+ and p_- for current_leaf according to equation 2 (* can label as success *)
>> **if** $p_- > p_{min}$ **then** cur_leaf.outcome := success
>> **else if** $p_+ < p_{max}$ **then** cur_leaf.outcome := failure (* label as failure *)
>> **else** generate_2k_tree(new(2k_node), cur_leaf) (* build 2^k-tree if indeterminate *)
>
> **end**

Figure 3: **The DARLING Algorithm**

2.3 Deciding When to Split

The idea of the splitting criteria is to drive the probability interval estimates towards the extremes of 0 or 1, which indicate good homogeneity in outcome of exemplars in the current leaf partitions. The upper and lower confidence bounds for the probability estimate interval, p_+ and p_- respectively, are computed using the same $1-\alpha$ confidence bound computation utilized by Kaelbling [6].

We desire an interval that contains the true probability value with confidence $(1-\alpha)$ given x successes (rewarding outcomes) out of n exemplars in the leaf. This yields

$$p_- \leq p_i \leq p_+ \qquad (1)$$

where

$$p_\pm = \frac{\frac{g_{\frac{\alpha}{2}}^{\;2}}{2n} + \frac{x}{n} \pm \frac{g_{\frac{\alpha}{2}}}{\sqrt{n}}\sqrt{\frac{g_{\frac{\alpha}{2}}^{\;2}}{4n} + \frac{x}{n^2}(1-\frac{x}{n})}}{1 + \frac{g_{\frac{\alpha}{2}}^{\;2}}{n}} \qquad (2)$$

where, p_- and p_+ are the lower and upper bounds of the probability interval estimate, respectively and $g_{\frac{\alpha}{2}}$ is the confidence interval coefficient (either tabulated or computed). The complete algorithm is given in Figures 3 and 4.

2.4 Robustness to Noise

The difference in error immunity between *k*-nearest-neighbor algorithms and the DARLING algorithm is shown in Figure 5. The quantity p_{flip} is the probability that the outcome of a given exemplar in the learning set is mislabelled by having its labelling flipped. The quantity p_{error} is an estimate the combined misclassification rate due to false positives and false positives conditioned over all predicted and true members

Algorithm **generate_2k_tree**(cur_node, leaf cur_leaf)

> Compute p_+ and p_- for cur_leaf
> **if** $p_- > p_{min}$ **then** (* terminate *)
>   **begin**
>   cur_node.outcome := success
>   cur_node.children := λ
>   **end**
> **else if** $p_+ < p_{max}$ **then** (* terminate *)
>   **begin**
>   cur_node.outcome := failure
>   cur_node.children := λ
>   **end**
> **else** (* split further *)
> **begin**
>   **for** all cur_node.children
>   **begin**
>   cur_node.child = new(node)
>   generate_2k_tree(cur_node.child, partition(cur_leaf.child))
>   **end**
>   **end**

Figure 4: **The Adaptive 2^k-tree Construction Algorithm**

of the class. It is a normalized measure of hypothesis' agreement with the true concept, computed by taking 1000 random exemplars uniformly distributed over the input domain.

The similarity in performance is due to the fact that the labelling of a given leaf in the DARLING tree is based on a probability estimate that is pooled from a number of observations over the leaf's domain, which is similar to the mechanism employed in k-nearest neighbors. In Figure 5 the bin size is b=10, which is approximates k=10 nearest-neighbors. However, some of the k-D-tree bins are split in to 2^k trees so they have smaller bin-size. This explains why the error break-down curve of DARLING falls somewhere in between that of the k=1 and k=10 cases for the nearest-neighbor learners.

3 Density-Adaptive Forgetting

As mentioned previously, an important distinction should be made in the taxonomy of learning systems between learning in a domain with stationary concepts versus learning in a domain where concepts may change. Additionally, we cannot expect the learner to have infinite storage capacity. This implies it must have some forgetting mechanism, in order to store only a bounded number of examples at any given time.

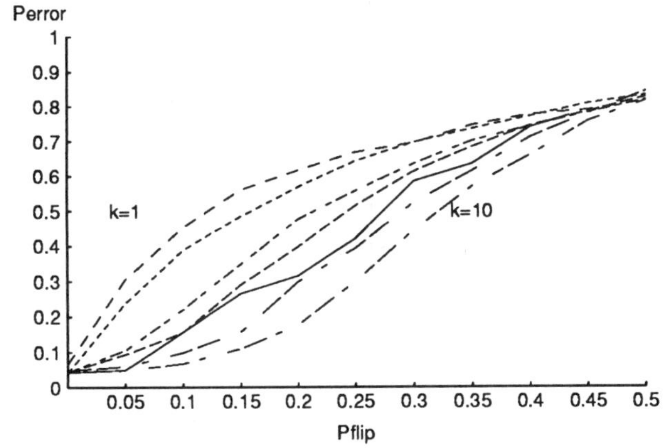

Figure 5: A comparison of several k-nearest-neighbor performance curves (dashed) to the DARLING curve (solid) for $\alpha = .5, p_{min} = .6$ and $p_{max} = .4$ and a unit circle test concept. The noise breakdown curve for the DARLING algorithm is similar to that of the 5-nn algorithm.

In particular, memory-based learning algorithms do not track changing concepts well, as noted by Moore [11]. Consider the following scenario: a learner has been collecting exemplars on line for several years and storing them (assume it has a huge store), and suddenly the dynamics of the environment change. In this case, the learner will adapt very slowly, since there will be a large number of observations from the past that are no longer representative of the current concept. In fact, the learner will have a permanent bias since the obsolete observations will always be in its database.

We develop a forgetting algorithm for accomplishing the deleting of experiences based on the principle of locality of observations. This states that observations should be forgotten *only* if there is subsequent information in their locality of parameter space.

This mechanism is implemented by associating a weight w to each observation. Each weight is decremented at a rate proportional to the number and proximity of succeeding exemplars to the corresponding observation. This is in contrast to other weighted forgetting mechanism where all weights are decremented by multiplication with factor, γ, between 0 and 1, each time a new observation is input to the system [11], independent of its location. These approaches have the disadvantage that the entire parameter space must be constantly refreshed, otherwise all data vanishes in regions not subsequently populated by exemplars. This creates an undue burden on acquiring new exemplars since, as the dimensionality of the input parameter space increases (and more exemplars are needed), the forgetting rate must be decreased which impairs track-

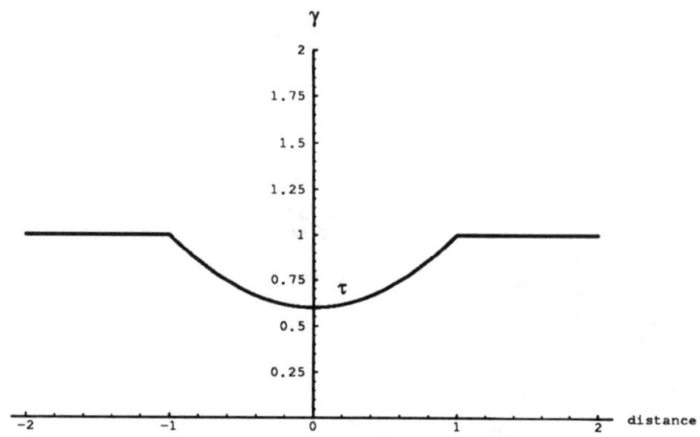

Figure 6: The influence function for decaying observation in the neighborhood of previous observations. The $\gamma = \gamma(X, X_{\{k\}})$, is used as a forgetting coefficient for the kth nearest neighbor which is at distance $d(X, X_{\{k\}})$ from the new observation X. It is a function of the scale parameter $d(X, X_{\{m\}})$ at which γ reaches unity, and τ which is the forgetting rate.

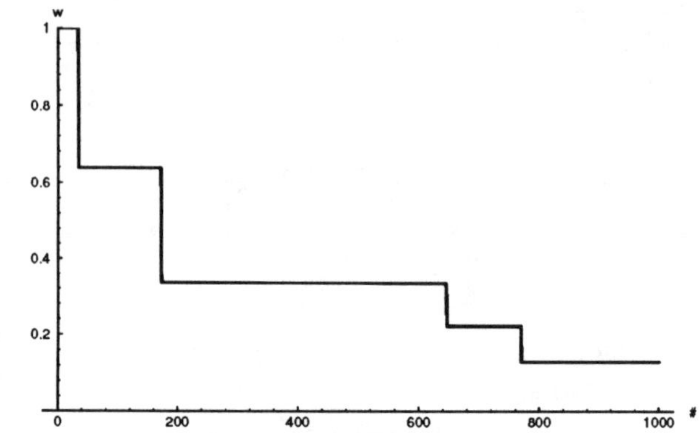

Figure 7: A plot of an actual weight decay as a function of the number of succeeding observations. Whenever the observation is within an m-th nearest neighbor interval, its weight value decreases as a function of the distance between the exemplar and the succeeding observation.

ing performance.

In our approach, we decrement each exemplar's weight by a factor γ, proportional to the proximity of a subsequent observation, based on a truncated m-nearest neighborhood influence function. A new observation is initialized with a weight $w = 1$. Each time a new exemplar is input, the weightings $w_{\{k\}}$ of kth nearest observations, $X_{\{k\}}$, $(k \leq m)$, within a neighborhood of the m nearest-neighbors of the new exemplar X are decreased by multiplication with γ.

$$w'_{\{k\}} = \gamma\left(X, X_{\{k\}}\right) w_{\{k\}} \tag{3}$$

When a given observation's weighting falls below some threshold value θ, it is deleted from the learning set. The quantity $\gamma\left(X, X_{\{k\}}\right)$ is computed based on the following truncated quadratic function (depicted in Figure 6):

$$\gamma\left(X, X_{\{k\}}\right) = \begin{cases} \tau + (1-\tau)\frac{d^2_{\{k\}}}{d^2_{\{m\}}} & \text{if } d^2_{\{k\}} \leq d^2_{\{m\}} \\ 1 & \text{otherwise} \end{cases} \tag{4}$$

Here $X_{\{i\}}$ is the location of the ith nearest neighbor, X is location of the new observation, and $d_{\{i\}} = d^2(X, X_{\{i\}})$ is the Euclidean distance from the ith nearest neighbor to the new observation. Since the radius $d_{\{m\}}$ is that of the sphere containing the m nearest neighbors, this adapts the decay radius of influence to the local density of exemplars around the new exemplar.

The parameters τ, m and θ determine how many nearby subsequent observations are necessary in the neighborhood of a previous observation before it is deleted from the learning set. The weights decay in a stochastic fashion as illustrated in Figure 7, where an observation decays only if it happens to be one of the m nearest-neighbors of a succeeding observation. A straightforward way to implement a bound on the number of exemplars stored is to set m, the number of nearest-neighbors, equal to some fixed fraction β, $(0 < \beta \leq 1)$, of the total number of observations currently in the learning set [16]. By doing this, the total number of observations that are kept in memory can be set to reach some asymptotic value based on the selection of the τ, β and θ parameters (See Figure 8).

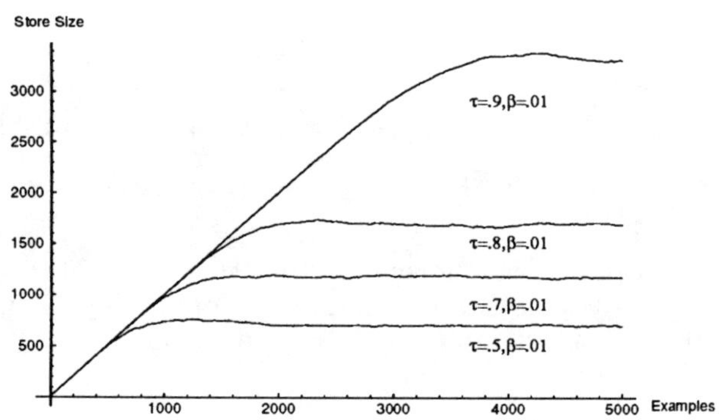

Figure 8: The asymptotic number of exemplars held in the memory store as a function of β and τ for a two dimensional domain with uniform exemplar distribution.

3.1 An Example: Adapting to Action Errors

To illustrate the algorithms discussed, we use a simple simulation developed to test the ability of the DARLING algorithm to adapt to the situation where one of the fingers on a two fingered robotic gripper is jammed at its extreme position. The task of the learner is to determine whether approaching from the object's z-axis direction when its z-axis is pointed upwards will succeed as a function of object dimensions, as schematically illustrated in Figure 9. After the failure, the gripper is still functional, it can pick up objects by squeezing with its operational finger and compressing the object against the jammed finger. However, the range of objects that can actually be picked up is decreased dramatically, and is now limited to a small interval.

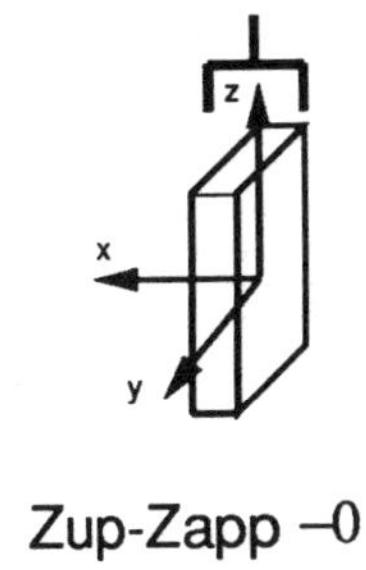

Figure 9: Approaching an object in the z-axis up configuration from the z-axis direction

The selection map (see Figure 10) for a given approach-orientation combination makes a prediction as to when the corresponding interaction will succeed. The prediction is made in terms of the parametric description of the object, its reduced superquadric description, which is essentially a bounding box representation. For example, the success or failure of the z-axis up, z-axis approach (z_{up}-z_{app}) is a function of the extents of the object perpendicular to the approach axis, namely a_x and a_y. The white areas of the selectivity map (Figure 10(a)) indicate the set of objects with a_x, a_y dimensions that are predicted to succeed in the ideal case, while the grey areas indicate objects whose dimensions would predict failure. The width of the white region is 38mm, which is the maximum width that the jaws of the gripper can open, which, in turn, determines the widest object than can be grasped.

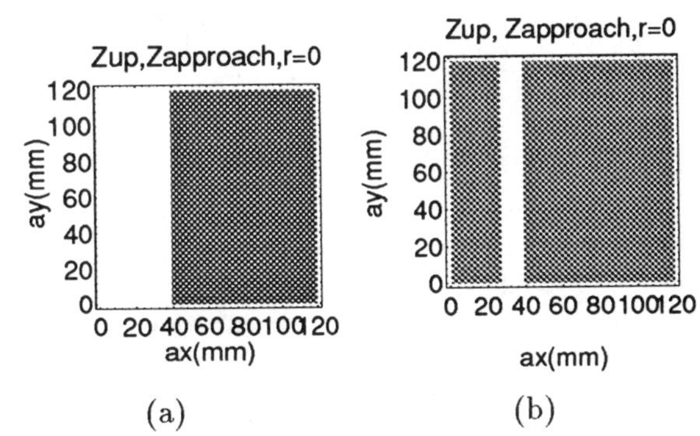

Figure 10: The beginning and ending selectivity maps

When the finger is jammed, then the underlying selection maps change so that the width of objects now graspable ranges from 25 mm to 38 mm (see Figure 10(b)), rather than 0 to 38 mm. The transition is therefore from the concept depicted in the 10 (a) to that in 10 (b). Figure 11 shows the learned selectivity maps created by the DARLING tree. The transition to the broken finger from the operational one occurs at $n = 2000$. At this point, the prediction performance is seen to degrade significantly (see Figure 12). The error then decreases with further observations as the forgetting algorithm gradually deletes the older observations and supersedes them with observations that reflect the current state of affairs of the environment.

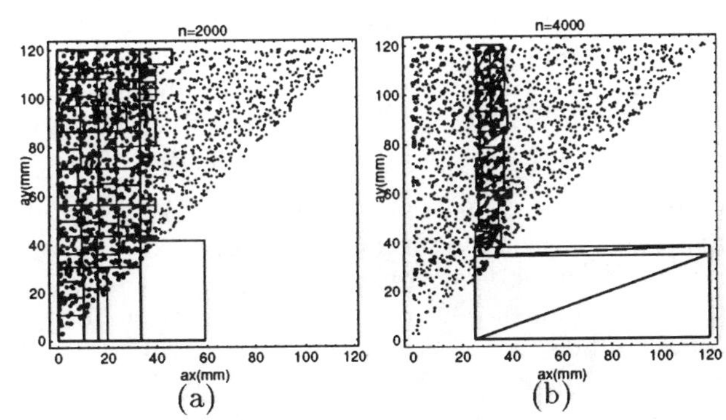

Figure 11: Adapting to a Malfunction. At $n = 2000$ in the simulation, one of the fingers in the gripper jams at its extreme position, causing the range of objects that are graspable to decrease. The selectivity map learned tracks the changes of the underlying maps depicted in 10. The learning and forgetting algorithms had the parameter values $\alpha = .5$, $p_{min} = .6$, $p_{max} = .4$, $\tau = .8$ and $\beta = .01$. The upper diagonal distribution of the points is due to the canonical superquadric representation where $a_x \leq a_y \leq a_z$.

4 Conclusion and Future Extensions

As can be seen in the simulation, a significant number of objects must be attempted (in practice around 200 are needed) before the learner begins to converge on the correct underlying selection map. This is due to the fact that the algorithm we have chosen is non-parametric in terms of the description of the concepts

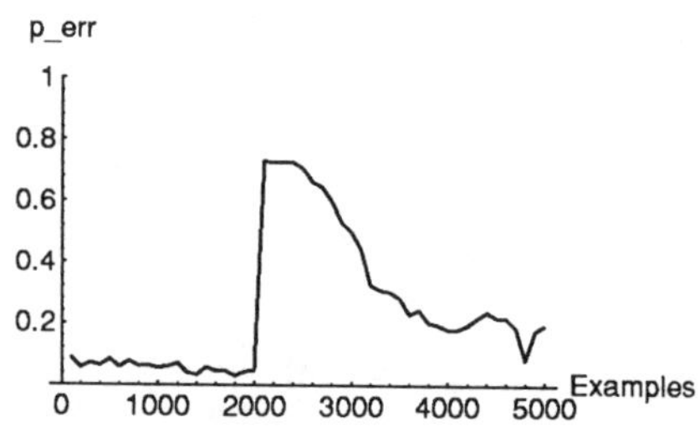

Figure 12: The learning curve for the simulation. It can be seen that the learning curve jumps upward at the $n = 2000$ point, where the finger jams, and then gradually decreases as the system forgets the obsolete observations. The error plotted is an estimate of the probability of the symmetric difference between the true and hypothesized concept.

that it creates and is therefore almost completely data driven. This is the tradeoff between inductive-bias and sample complexity. The less restrictions on the concepts that can be faithfully approximated, the larger the sample size necessary for the learner. We believe that a low-bias approach is warranted in perceptual situations where sensory distortions and miscalibrations can lead to difficult to characterize effects that may not be well approximated by methods with high inductive bias.

There are a number of immediate enhancements that can be made to the learning algorithm. The first is to embed decision trees that use non-axis parallel splits such as perceptron trees [22], or linear discriminants that might be more effective, since they will in general provide much better performance for shallow trees.

Some simple branch-and-bound tests can be implemented to prevent unnecessary subdivision. In particular, if the node's current best case split has a p_- estimate which is lower than the current node's p_- lower bound, then further subdivision will not yield an improvement and the node should be abandoned.

Additionally, by merging neighboring regions with like labellings, the resulting trees could be simplified, possibly yielding better generalization, and the error breakdown as a function of random mislabelling errors could be improved. The merging process would pool larger numbers of observations, which would yield better noise immunity.

Another drawback is that the search is greedy. It searches for partitions with sufficing pessimistic success probabilities and stops splitting when they are met, rather than for the highest possible lower bounds. It might be the case that further splitting yields a partitioning which has higher lower bound probabilities, even though the current bound is acceptable. A hill climbing lookahead search might yield better solutions.

The forgetting algorithm has the advantage of respecting locality of observations since the metric of a locale is determined by the local density of exemplars. This allows for efficient updating of the learning set so that new observations decay only their neighbors. This especially advantageous when the sampling distributions for the learning set is non-stationary and moves between different areas of the attribute space over time. Using *time-weighted* forgetting, exemplars in inactive areas would be deleted unnecessarily, whereas with density-adaptive forgetting they will persist until new evidence is available to supersede them. On the other hand, if the sampling distribution is stationary then density-adaptive forgetting behaves identically to time-weighted forgetting, so there is no penalty in adopting it over time-weighting forgetting in the first place.

Since the *k-D* tree built for the DARLING is an efficient structure for nearest-neighbor lookup, returning the nearest neighbors in time $O(\log n)$, where n is the number of observations, it is synergistic with the use of the nearest-neighbor forgetting approach.

Schlimmer *et al.* [18] point to the characteristic of *resiliency* in learning systems as a property that occurs in human and animal learning. Resiliency is the property of a learning system that the longer a behavior is trained, the longer it takes to unlearn subsequently. While algorithms which display this property may be more psychologically suggestive, resiliency can be counterproductive in rapidly changing environments. In particular, if a system operates on-line for very long periods of time before a change occurs, it will take an unacceptably long time to forget the obsolete concept. Fortunately exponentially weighted techniques that actively delete exemplars will not suffer from the same level of resiliency, since they have a natural saturation in the size of the learning set (see Figure 8) which affords turnover.

The forgetting parameters β and τ are task dependent. It is therefore important to be able to estimate the appropriate forgetting parameter for a given task. The more rapidly a task environment changes, the larger β should be and the smaller τ should be. However, there is an obvious tradeoff, the more rapid the forgetting rate, the fewer the asymptotic number of exemplars in the learning set and the worse the overall learning performance. Much work remains in devising automatic techniques for selecting these parameters. Moore suggests a technique for estimating task-specific forgetting parameters using cross-validation in [11].

Once forgetting is implemented, another important question is how often to regenerate the classification tree structures. In this work, new observations are simply inserted into their corresponding *k-D leaf* as they come in, in order to allow the nearest-neighbor forgetting queries to continue. The DARLING tree is rebuilt modulo 100 observations. If on-line performance is needed, an interleaved tree-building schedule may be used, so that the preceding decision-tree is used on-line while its successor is being built either in a background process, or on another processor. Alternatively, [17] discusses some issues in incrementally updating adaptive *k-D*-trees.

This issue might be sidestepped by using the forgetting technique together with other incremental techniques such as ID-5 [21], or using it with nearest-neighbor prediction techniques that do not form explicit decision-trees [1].

Acknowledgements

The work was supported by an NSF Postdoctoral Research Associateship in Computational Science and Engineering (NSF-CDA92-11136), Navy Grant N0014-88-K-0630, AFOSR Grants 88-0244, AFOSR 88-0296; Army/DAAL 03-89-C-0031PRI; NSF Grants CISE/CDA 88-22719, IRI 89-06770; and Du Pont Company.

References

[1] D. W. Aha, D. Kibler, and M. K. Albert. Instance-based learning algorithms. *Machine Learning*, 6:37–66, 1991.

[2] S. Bennett. Planning to address uncertainty: An incremental approach employing learning through experience. In *Proceedings of the DARPA Workshop on Advanced Planning and Control Strategies*, pages 313–324, 1991.

[3] L. Breiman, J. H. Friedman, R. A. Olshen, and C. J. Stone. *Classification and regression trees.* Wadsworth International, Belmont, CA, 1984.

[4] G. B. Dunn and J. Segen. Automatic discovery of robotic grasp configuration. In *Proceedings, 1988 IEEE International Conference on Robotics and Automation*, pages 396–401, 1988.

[5] J. H. Friedman, J. L. Bentley, and R. A. Finkel. An algorithm for finding best matches in logarithmic expected time. *ACM Transactions on Mathematical Software*, 3:209–226, 1977.

[6] L. P. Kaelbling. *Learning in Embedded Systems.* PhD thesis, Stanford University, Stanford, CA, 1990. Dept. of Computer Science.

[7] A. Kuh, T. Petsche, and R.L. Rivest. Learning time-varying concepts. In *Advances in Neural Information Processing Systems 3*, pages 183–189, Morgan Kaufmann, December 1991.

[8] P. Maes and R. A. Brooks. Learning to coordinate behaviors. In *AAAI-90*, pages 796–802, 1990.

[9] S. Mahadevan and J. Connell. Automatic programming of behavior-based robots using reinforcement learning. *Artificial Intelligence*, 55:311–365, 1992.

[10] B. Mel. *Connectionist robot motion planning: A neurally inspired approach to visually guided reaching.* Academic Press, San Diego, CA, 1991.

[11] A. W. Moore. Fast, robust adaptive control by learning only forward models. In *Advances in Neural Information Processing Systems*, Morgan Kauffman, December 1991.

[12] S. M. Omohundro. Efficient algorithms with neural network like behavior. *Complex Systems*, 1:273–347, 1987.

[13] S. M. Omohundro. Geometric learning algorithms. *Physica D, Non-Linear Phenomenon*, 42:307–321, 1987.

[14] J. R. Quinlan. *Learning efficient classification procedures and their application to chess end games*, pages 463–481. Morgan-Kauffman, Los Altos, Ca., 1986.

[15] H. Ritter, T. Martinetz, and K. Schulten. *Neural Computation and Self-Organizing Maps: An Introduction.* Addison-Wesley, Reading, Massachussetts, 1991.

[16] M. Salganicoff. *Learning and Forgetting for Perception-Action: A Projection-Pursuit and Density-Adaptive Approach.* PhD thesis, University of Pennsylvania, 1992. Dept. of Computer and Information Science.

[17] Hanan Samet. *The Design and Analysis of Spatial Data Structures.* Addison-Wesley, Reading, Massachussetts, 1989.

[18] J. C. Schlimmer and R. H. Granger. Beyond incremental processing: Tracking concept drift. In *Proceedings of the Fifth National Conference on Artificial Intelligence*, pages 502–507, Morgan Kauffman, Philadelphia, PA, 1986.

[19] F. Solina. *Shape Recovery and Segmentation with Deformable Part Models.* Technical Report MS-CIS-87-111, University of Pennsylvania, Dept. of Computer and Information Science, Philadelphia, Pa., 1987.

[20] M. Tan. A cost-sensitive learning system for sensing and grasping objects. In *Proceedings, 1990 IEEE International Conference on Robotics and Automation*, IEEE Press, 1990.

[21] P. Utgoff. ID-5: An incremental ID-3. In *Proceedings of the Fifth International WOrkshop on Machine Learning*, Morgan-Kauffman, 1988.

[22] P. Utgoff and C.E. Brodley. An incremental method for finding multivariate splits for decision trees. In *Proceedings of the Seventh International Workshop on Machine Learning*, Morgan-Kauffman, 1990.

Efficiently Inducing Determinations: A Complete and Systematic Search Algorithm that Uses Optimal Pruning

Jeffrey C. Schlimmer
School of Electrical Engineering and Computer Science
Washington State University
Pullman, Washington 99164-2752
schlimmer@eecs.wsu.edu

Abstract

Determinations are a useful type of functional knowledge representation. Applications include knowledge-based systems, analogical reasoning, database design, and robotic sensing systems. This paper presents an efficient, batch algorithm for inducing all minimal determinations from observed data. The algorithm is based on breadth-first search and runs in polynomial time and space given a user-supplied parameter limiting the maximum size of a determination. The algorithm uses probabilistic measures to induce determinations despite noisy data. One key contribution is the identification of an enumeration order in the space of possible determinations that affords a complete and systematic search. Another contribution lists axioms that relate neighboring states and allow the construction of pruning rules. A third contribution formulates a perfect hash function for states in this space and facilitates optimal use of the pruning rules. This paper also sketches an algorithm that can incrementally revise a set of determinations given additional data.

1 INTRODUCTION

Representations supporting inference play a central role in many artificial intelligence systems. One useful representation specifies only a functional form rather than specific, computable functions. Called *determinations*, this class of representation identifies which factors influence others and is compatible with probabilistic as well as logical systems of inference. Technically speaking, a determination specifies the domain and range of a function; there is exactly one element of the range for each element of the domain of the function. Intuitively, determinations specify which properties of a datum allow one to conclude other properties. For example, the country in which a child is raised determines their first language spoken; knowing that a child is raised in France allows inferring that their native language is French. The converse is not necessarily true. Knowing the first language spoken does not in general allow inferring the country; French is spoken in several countries.

Determinations are useful for several different inference tasks. The first use envisioned was as a guide for analogical reasoning (Russell, 1986). Here the domain of the determination specifies which properties of a stored datum (or source) should match the new datum (or target), and its range specifies which properties of the source should be predicted for the target. This simplifies the computationally complex process of figuring out which of the possible ways of matching the source and target is the most appropriate, and it obviates the need for a similarity metric.

Database design and verification also relies heavily on determinations. Knowledge of functional dependencies between database attributes can facilitate design-time trade-offs between retrieval speed, redundancy, and reliability. Determinations are also a special case of integrity constraints and may be used to identify inconsistencies in new or previous entries in a database (Schlimmer, 1992).

Determinations may be used to analyze the redundancies between different sensors in robotic applications. Like database design, knowledge about which sensors detect related events, and how those events are functionally related, can be used to design minimal or redundant sets of sensors. This type of knowledge could even be used for reconfiguration to compensate for sensor loss after deployment.

2 RELATED WORK

Russell (1986) presents a number of representations, including determinations, that capture different higher-order regularities and may be used to guide the formation of inductive hypotheses and analogical inference. Davies and Russell (1987) further develop the idea that a determination is an inductive bias and a template for analogical reasoning. For the latter, they note that a determination allows drawing valid conclusions by analogy with a single datum without prespecifying what the conclusions will be. Davies and Russell's notion of a determination is more inclusive than the one explored here. Their determinations may include specific constants and are therefore partially instantiated function templates. This paper explores learning "pure" determinations in which no constants other than property names appear.

Ziarko (1992) discusses an identical representation idea in the context of database dependencies. Using set-theoretic notions, Ziarko develops the notion of a "full functional dependency" which is precisely a determination. Given a range of interest, Ziarko goes on to identify the usefulness of minimal domains termed "reducts." Ziarko also defines the "significance factor" of a particular database attribute as the relative degree of decrease in functional dependency as a result of removing the attribute from a domain. This paper utilizes Ziarko's observations about minimality and presents an efficient search algorithm to induce all reducts given a range of interest and a set of data.

The principal of minimality has also been examined by Almuallim and Dietterich (1991). They note that many learning situations involve a large number of irrelevant features. In these cases, it is preferable if the learning method uses a minimum of features. Similar to Occam's razor, this bias is remarkably difficult to implement correctly. Almuallim and Dietterich analyze the sample complexity of selecting a minimum of features, and they present an algorithm for iteratively searching larger feature sets. Crucial to their algorithm is the notion that for every *insufficient* feature set, there will be at least two data that have the same value for every attribute in the set but differ in their classification. This paper adopts their search idea and expands it by identifying pruning heuristics and techniques for efficiently implementing them. The application of the idea is also slightly more general; instead of focusing on a fixed classification, the search identifies minimal domains for any range of interest.

Shen (1991) also explores learning regularities, but his work does not explicitly focus on minimality. The task is to discover regularities in a predicate knowledge base of the form $P(x, y) \wedge R(y, z) \rightarrow Q(x, z)$. His approach is to find all constants for which some predicate P is defined, then find some other predicate Q for which the relationship holds. No further search for a predicate R is necessary to discover a determination though it is for other regularities of interest. As is, the method is limited to finding determinations between pairs of predicates, but by searching for both a P and a Q, this method is searching for both a domain and a range. This paper instead assumes that a range is prespecified, and its methods then conduct a search for minimal domains, whatever their size. To find determinations for any range, the search can be repeated for each possible singleton range (as Shen does). Then the results of search can be combined by merging any determinations with a common domain.

Motivated by human categorization performance, Holland, Holyoak, Nisbett, and Thagard (1986) present an idea related to determinations. Specifically, they note that people capitalize on the distribution of properties in disjunctive categories when anticipating properties in new categories. For example, when people see that instances of one type of bird always have a needle-like beak and white, pea-sized eggs (e.g., hummingbirds) but differ in their ages, they expect that birds of a new type would also share a beak shape and egg characteristics but have differing ages; i.e., people expect that beak and egg properties are invariant within a bird type but that the age property is variant. Holland et al. review considerable psychological evidence showing that people also use information about the variation of properties across categories. Seeing that many types of birds have distinctive beak shapes leads people to identify the type of a bird based on its beak shape. These effects are often termed "variability bias." Martin and Billman (1991) present a computational implementation of variability bias in an incremental, hierarchical conceptual clustering system. Determinations are a special case of property invariance. The most notable distinction between the two is that variability information is probabilistic while determinations are inherently discrete.

A decision tree is a familiar representation that also specifies a function from a set of properties to another. Decision trees implicitly specify an order in which properties are to be tested during inference. Barring this, the decision tree representation strictly includes the determination representation; every determination is expressible as a full decision tree where subtrees at the same level test the same property. However, because the decision tree representation is free to use different properties in different subtrees at the same level, and is not constrained to be a full tree, not every decision tree can be expressed as a determination. Since there are efficient methods for inducing decision trees from data, this suggests a natural method for inducing a determination: require the same test for all subtrees at the same level and construct a full tree. It is simple to construct trees in a breadth-first manner and choose to test the property that has the highest evaluation over all subtrees at the same level. Moreover, the range of a determination may be defined by more than one property. As a decision tree, each external node must therefore consist of data that exhibit a single element of the range, whether the range is a single property or the cross-product of a number of properties. The next section gives an example decision tree that encodes a determination. The simple search performed by decision tree induction methods and the fact that only a single tree is induced limit the usefulness of the method sketched above. Specifically, there is no guarantee that the determination found is one of the simplest ones. (It may easily include unnecessary properties in the domain.) The goal of this paper is to explore a computationally efficient algorithm for inducing all minimal size determinations from a set of data.

3 VERIFYING A DETERMINATION

Before turning to algorithms that search for determinations, consider how to measure the validity of a potential determination given observed data. It is apparently quite simple: just check to see that all elements of the domain (that occur in the data) map to exactly one element in the range. This requires $O(n)$ space and at best $O(n \cdot d \cdot r)$ time, where n is the number of data, d is the number of properties in the domain, and r is the number of properties in the range.

Table 1: Simple Set of Synthetic Data

DATUM	PROPERTY NAME				
NUMBER	A	B	C	D	E
1.	i	i	i	i	i
2.	ii	ii	i	ii	i
3.	iii	i	ii	iii	ii
4.	iv	ii	ii	iv	iii
5.	i	i	i	iv	i
6.	ii	ii	i	iii	i
7.	iii	i	ii	ii	ii
8.	iv	ii	ii	i	iii
9.	i	i	iii	i	i
10.	ii	i	iii	ii	i

For example, consider the synthetic data in Table 1. If we wish to verify that Properties B and C jointly determine Property E, or $B \times C \rightarrow E$, we need only to check that every pair of values of $B \times C$ map to at most one value for E. Table 2 shows this mapping and verifies the determination $B \times C \rightarrow E$. Determinations do not specify one-to-one functions; as this example illustrates, the mapping from Property E to Properties B and C is not a function because at least one domain element maps onto more than one range element: a value of i for the former maps onto values of $\{i,i\}$, $\{ii,i\}$, and $\{i, iii\}$ for the latter.

Table 2: Mapping from B and C to E

PROPERTY		
B	C	E
i	i	i
ii	i	i
i	ii	ii
ii	ii	iii
i	iii	i
ii	iii	?

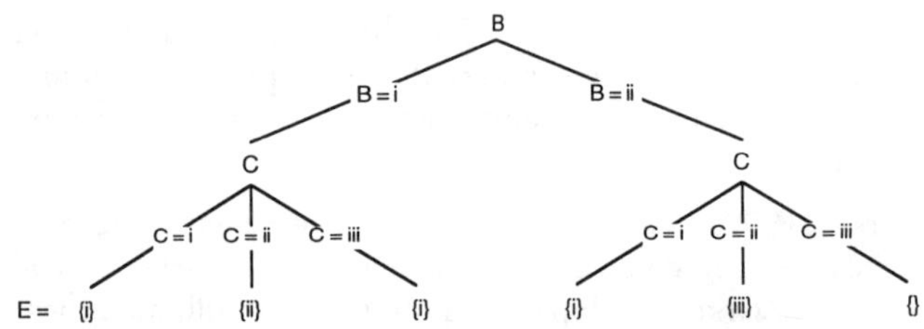

Figure 1: Decision Tree for $B \times C \rightarrow E$

To further clarify the relationship between a decision tree and a determination, Figure 1 depicts a decision tree that encodes the determination $B \times C \rightarrow E$.

If exceptions in the data yield a mapping that is not quite functional, there are three possible remedies: (a) maintain an explicit list of exceptions, (b) specialize the representation to eliminate the exception, or (c) adopt an approximate representation. From the point of view of an inference system, the first remedy is not particularly attractive since it requires inference mechanisms to reason about two different representations: the determination and its exceptions. The second remedy merely requires specializing the domain of the determination; for example, province determines first language spoken. However, this can lead to a proliferation of similar representational forms (if there are many alternative specializations) and consequently to awkward inference.

The third remedy is to treat mappings that are nearly functions as approximate determinations. In this latter vein, Russell (1986) suggested associating an integer with each determination to represent how many observed data were required for each new domain element before a confident assertion could be made about the range element. He called these "extended determinations" (because the determination had to be extended with several data). Reinterpreting the idea slightly, a determination with a lower integer could be appropriately characterized as more functional than one with a higher integer. Ziarko (1992) also suggests measuring the degree of dependency, in particular by counting for each property in the domain, the number of bounding sets each appears in. Shen (1991) combines Russell's integer cutoff with a χ^2 metric. The well known expected information measure used in decision tree learning methods (Quinlan, 1986) may also be appropriate. If the measure is perfect (in this case zero), then the mapping is a function. During verification, measures like these may be used with user-specified thresholds; the expected number of determinations that will be verified is inversely proportional to the height of the threshold. Of course there are other candidate measures, and the interested reader may wish to consult (Mingers, 1989) or (Fayyad & Irani, 1992).

Choosing between the remedies of specializing or approximating to compensate for exceptions raises the issue of overfitting. How much data is sufficient to verify a determination? Based on the definition of a function, a single datum can be used to verify any determination; indeed, any mapping that has only one instance of each domain element is a function. Such mappings are problematic because new data are likely to violate the mapping with new domain-range element combinations, and new observations may exhibit new domain elements, leaving the mapping useless for inference. Russell's integer and expected information measure the functional degree of the map given *current* data, but a reliability measure should characterize the expected functional degree of the map given *subsequent* data.

In the absence of any information to the contrary, the probability that a novel value for a property will be observed (and therefore lead to problems with the mapping) is proportional to the percentage of values that have been observed very infrequently in that mapping. Applying this idea directly leads to a simple reliability measure: the number of observed instances averaged over all domain elements. This can get a bit lopsided if a mapping has one well-populated domain element and many sparse ones, so it may be desirable to use a squashing function like logarithm, yielding

$$R(D) = \frac{\sum_i^{|D|} \log|d_i|}{|D|}$$

where D is the set of observed domain elements and $|d_i|$ is the number of instances of domain element d_i. A mapping based on a single datum will have a low log-frequency average as will one that is based on a large sample of data where each domain element has been observed just once. An important side-effect of this measure is that it berates properties that have a unique value for each datum; their unbounded values are unlikely to be useful for inference.

As with the quality measures, during verification this measure may be used with a user-specified threshold; if the base of the logarithm is set to some integer t, then the measure is greater than one if a large majority of the domain elements have been observed more than t times.

4 SEARCHING FOR DETERMINATIONS

Requiring determinations that support inference is a major design constraint on search algorithms. An inference process can gather confirming evidence by applying more than one determination to the problem, and a number of alternative determinations allow for robust inference if some properties are not observable. A complete set of determinations allows inferring meta-properties such as whether two properties are redundant (cf. Schlimmer, 1992). Moreover, having all determinations available allows closed-world reasoning and the possibility of degrading the confidence of certain inferences (cf. Martin & Billman, 1991). Therefore, the search should find all determinations. The search for determinations should also find those that have minimal domains. Omitting unnecessary properties in the domain of a determination can clarify explanations of inferences for users and other inference agents.

4.1 AXIOMS AND THE SPACE OF DETERMINATIONS

Searching for all minimal determinations requires a *complete* search, i.e., one that does not overlook any possibilities. Such a search is NP-hard (Ziarko, 1992). Intuitively, it is exponential because, given m properties that may be used in the domain of a determination, there are $O(2^m)$ possible subsets of those properties and therefore an exponential number of possible determinations. To avoid this complexity, the algorithm presented here searches only for determinations whose domains are of size $\leq k$, where k is some user-supplied parameter. (Shen, 1991 explores the case where k is 1.) The number of possible determinations is therefore limited to an exponential number in k or $\binom{m}{k}$ which is bounded by $O(m^k)$.

Just because the search must be complete does not mean that it must be exhaustive. Not every possible determination must be examined; portions of the space may be eliminated as search progresses. There are two keys to this savings. First, there are several axioms that allow inferring characteristics of a determination without directly verifying it. These are listed in Table 3. A pair of axioms are based on the nature of functions (i.e., determinations): (1) the cardinality of the domain must be at least as large as the range, and (2) specializing the domain of a function by enlarging it results in another function because there are generally more domain elements and therefore fewer range elements for each. A third axiom is based on the definition of reliability given above: (3) specializing the domain of an unreliable determination results in another unreliable determination; there are more distinct domain elements and fewer instances of each.

Table 3: Axioms About The Space of Determinations

1.	$X \rightarrow Y$	implies	$\|X\| \geq \|Y\|$
2.	$X \rightarrow Y$	implies	$X \cup \{x\} \rightarrow Y$
3.	$\neg R(X \rightarrow Y)$	implies	$\neg R(X \cup \{x\} \rightarrow Y)$
	$\neg R(X \neg \rightarrow Y)$	implies	$\neg R(X \cup \{x\} \neg \rightarrow Y)$

The second key to savings during search is the observation that the possible domains are partially ordered. The most general domain is the empty determination, implying that the range has a constant value. The most specific domain is the determination with all properties in its domain. This latter case represents nothing more than a table lookup. Most of the interesting determinations lie between these two extremes where some (but not all) of the properties are functionally related to the range. Note that mappings are more likely to be functions the more special their domain but will probably be less reliable. Conversely, mappings are less likely to be functions the more general their domain but will probably be more reliable.

Together the axioms in Table 3 and the partially ordered search space identify four pruning rules listed in Table 4. The first rule eliminates possible determinations with overly general domains and is derived from the first axiom listed in Table 3. The next two pruning rules are duals and are derived from the second axiom; one eliminates unnecessarily specific domains given a verifiable determination, and the other eliminates unrealistically general domains given a falsifiable determination. The final pruning rule is derived from the third axiom and eliminates specific domain determinations if a more general one is already unacceptably unreliable. Note that in each case, these pruning rules specify whether or not subsets or supersets of a particular determination's domain should be searched or not. Of course, the effectiveness of these pruning rules depends upon how efficiently they can be implemented and upon the regularity of the data to which the search is applied.

Table 4: Pruning Rules

1.	If	$\lvert X\rvert < \lvert Y\rvert$ in $X \rightarrow Y$ or in $X \neg\rightarrow Y$,
	Then	$X \neg\rightarrow Y$, Prune all subsets of X (i.e., more general domains)
2a.	If	$X \rightarrow Y$,
	Then	Prune all supersets of X (i.e., more specific domains)
2b.	If	$X \neg\rightarrow Y$,
	Then	Prune all subsets of X (i.e., more general domains)
3.	If	$\neg R(X \rightarrow Y)$ or $\neg R(X \neg\rightarrow Y)$,
	Then	Prune all supersets of X (i.e., more specific domains)

4.2 SYSTEMATIC SEARCH WITH PRUNING

Breadth-first search is an obvious candidate for searching the space of determinations. To simplify the discussion, assume that the determination's range is a single, known property. If the motivating inference task does not indicate which properties can be inferred as the range of a determination, the search can be iterated for each property as a singleton range. The resulting determinations are independent and can be merged by combining those with a common domain. This produces the same determinations as if all possible subsets of properties were considered as ranges because functions are independent with respect to range.

In this search, the initial state is the empty domain. Search operators add single properties to the state at the front of the queue of open states unless: (a) all available properties have already been added to the state, (b) the domain is already larger than the bound k, or (c) one of the pruning rules listed in Table 4 applies. Since the search explores successively larger domains, only Rules 2a and 3 can be used because they specify superset pruning.

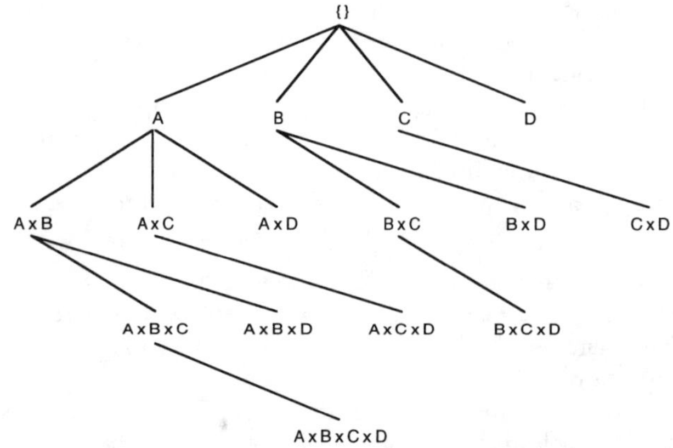

Figure 2: Systematic Enumeration of Determination Space

Without modification, this search may visit the same state repeatedly. To make the search *systematic*, successors are generated from the current state using a trie-like enumeration order. Instead of expanding a state by adding any of the remaining properties, all properties are placed in a fixed order prior to the search. Then, to expand a state, only properties appearing after the highest ranked property in the domain may be added. Assuming that properties may consist of subsets of $\{A, B, C, D\}$, Figure 2 depicts a sample space of domains; the initial state is at the top of the figure, and search operators expand the frontier downwards. Note that not all states are connected to their logical successors. For example, whereas simple generation would consider all domains of size two after examining $C \rightarrow E$, the revised generation considers only $C \times D \rightarrow E$ (if the properties were ordered alphabetically). This modification does not compromise the completeness of the search; each possibility can be expressed as the cross-product of the highest ranked property in the domain and the remaining properties.

To use the pruning rules optimally, search must be able to properly record the recommendation of a pruning rule, or equivalently be able to consult relevant recommendations when considering a new state. The most obvious solution would be to keep a list of states that either have been pruned or should be pruned. In either case, the size of the list is exponential in k. Keeping the states that *have been pruned* requires a constant update time but exponential time to consult the list and see if any subset of the current state has already been pruned. Conversely, keeping a list of states that *should be pruned* requires exponential update time (to add all supersets of a pruned state) but a significantly lower amount of time to consult the list. If a suitable hash function could be constructed, then consultation would be a constant time operation. Given the expectation that determinations are less likely than non-determinations in the space of possibilities, it seems prudent to maintain a list of states that should be

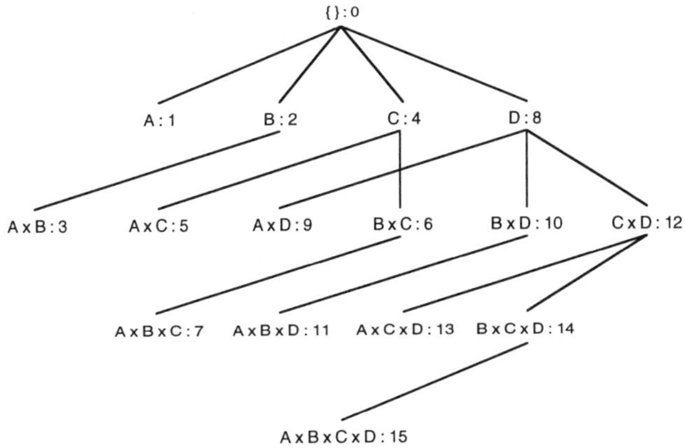

Figure 3: Hash Enumeration of Determination Space

pruned since the common, consulting operation is efficient at the expense of the infrequent, updating operation.

To be precise, an efficient way to consult whether a state should be pruned is to maintain a bit vector equal in size to the number of states in the space. Whenever a search determines that a state should be pruned, it either avoids generating it (by not putting it on the queue) or it marks the corresponding location in the bit vector. When examining a state, search first consults the bit vector, and if the corresponding location is marked, the state is skipped. To be efficient, this requires a fast computation for: (a) the exact number of states, and (b) the unique location for each state. One way to compute (a) is in terms of (b) as discussed below, so consider the construction of a hash function that maps states to unique addresses in the bit vector.

Formulation of the hash function is based on the sizes of fragments of the state space. To simplify the mathematics, assume that states are expanded using a systematic generation that adds only *lower* ranked properties. (As explained below, this will fit nicely with the actual generation using higher ranked properties.) Figure 3 illustrates a sample of the assumed generation order. Given a domain, the hash function computes when the corresponding state would be visited in pre-order, and this is used as the location for the corresponding mark in the bit vector. In short, the location of a particular domain is the sum of the sizes of each of the searches that must precede this point in pre-order traversal. Specifically,

$$Loc(D, k) = \sum_{i=1, j=k}^{i \le |D|, j \ge 1} Size(Rank(D[i]), j)$$

which is read as the location of a domain D given k is the sum of the sizes of systematic searches using properties ranked less than i with successively smaller bounds j for k, where D is the domain of the state with properties in descending order and k is the maximum size of a determination's domain. The variable i iterates over the properties in the domain from first to last. Because these properties are sorted in descending order, $D[i]$ represents them from greatest to least. The variable j takes on increasingly smaller values of k. To simplify the mathematics, properties are represented directly by their integer rank. This combines nicely with the decision to order the systematic search space based on adding higher ranked properties. During the search, new properties are easily added to the front of a list representing each domain, yielding a list sorted in descending order. This list can be efficiently processed to compute the location of the state's mark.

The size of a search using only properties ranked less than $r = D[i]$ and of a maximum domain size of k is

$$Size(r, k) = \begin{cases} r & \text{if } k=1 \\ 1 & \text{if } r=1 \\ 1 + \sum_{i=1}^{r-1} Size(i, k-1) & \text{otherwise} \end{cases}$$

where r is the rank of a property in the fixed order. In the degenerate case of k equal to one (i.e., only one property can be chosen at a time), the size is just the rank of that property. Similarly, if the rank is one, no other properties would be searched first, so the size is just one. Otherwise, if both k and r are greater than one, then the size is one (for this property) plus the sum of the sizes of searches using properties ranked less than r with a reduced maximum size $k-1$.

Though a closed form of the size computation is unknown at this time, it is easily computed by memoizing the function with a small local cache. The cache is bounded by the possible values for r and k, or $O(mk)$ because r is bounded by m the number of properties.

Computing a unique location for each search state in this manner also lends itself naturally to computing the exact number of states in the space and therefore the size of the bit vector required to store pruning advice. The location of a domain with a single property follows the location of all domains that include properties ranked less than this one. Thus, the number of states is just the location of the hypothetical property ranked $m+1$ with the same value for k or $Loc(D = (m+1), k)$. Asymptotically, the required number of bits in the vector is bounded by $O(m^k)$.

To incorporate pruning advice, the search needs to mark the corresponding bit for all states that should be pruned. When it considers a new state, it must first check the corresponding bit. If a pruning rule applies, the affected states fall into two categories: those that would be generated by the current state, and those that are supersets of the current state but are not successors in the trie-based generation order. The former states are not generated or added to the queue of open states. They do not need to be marked because they are excluded from further consideration. States in the latter category are not successors of the current state and need to have their corresponding bit marked. If the domain of the current state is of size $|D|$, then there are at most $m - |D|$ properties that could be added to the current domain, and at most $k - |D|$ of them could be added at one time. This yields a complexity proportional to the combinations of $m - |D|$ properties chosen $k - |D|$ at a time, or $O([m - |D|]^{k - |D|})$. In the fastest case, $|D|$ is close to k and the time to mark supersets is proportional to m. In the slowest case, $|D|$ is quite small, and a number of states exponential in k must be marked.

The space complexity of this search is exponential in k because the bit vector is asymptotically the same size as the queue. Given the need to maintain space for the n data, the overall space complexity is $O(n \cdot m^k)$. The time complexity is also exponential in k. If the pruning heuristics apply frequently, then considerable effort will be expended to mark states to be pruned, but fewer states overall will be added to the queue and subsequently evaluated. If pruning heuristics apply rarely, then little effort will be spent on marking the bit vector, but more states will be added to the queue. Ignoring these interactions yields a time complexity of $O(n \cdot k \cdot m^k \cdot r)$ to verify each of the m^k domains for each of the r ranges.

5 CONCLUSIONS

This paper describes a polynomial algorithm for inducing determinations from observed data. It finds all, minimally-sized determinations and incorporates heuristic measures to tolerate noise and detect unreliable correlations. There are three key contributions. The first identifies an enumeration order in the space of possible determinations that affords a complete and systematic search. The second lists axioms that relate neighboring states and allow the construction of pruning rules. The third formulates a perfect hash function for states in this space and facilitates optimal use of the pruning rules.

Inference tasks are often unstable, and the underlying representations may need to be revised frequently. To make this batch algorithm incrementally search for determinations, each new datum must be cached for verification. Revising the determinations already found is simplified by noting that smaller samples refute strictly fewer determinations than larger samples. Thus when a new datum falsifies a determination, a search is started from this point toward more specific domains.

Inference tasks may also involve continuous or numerically-valued properties. This algorithm is limited to discretely-valued properties. It does not specify what determinations would look like for the former properties. It also does not indicate what type of search would be required to induce them from data.

Acknowledgements

This research has been supported by Digital Equipment Corporation and grant IRI-9212190 from the National Science Foundation. David Benson, Dongil Shin, Leonard Hermens, and Jack Hagemeister graciously read an early draft of this paper and offered several helpful suggestions for improving the presentation. Two anonymous reviewers also identified additional related work. The faculty and students studying AI at Washington State University cultivate a stimulating intellectual environment. Jim Kirk, Mike Kibler, Karl Hakimian, and the facilities group provided a reliable computing environment.

References

Almuallim, H., & Dietterich, T. G. (1991). Learning with many irrelevant features. *Proceedings of the Ninth National Conference on Artificial Intelligence* (pp. 547–552). Anaheim, CA: AAAI Press.

Davies, T. R., & Russell, S. J. (1987). A logical approach to reasoning by analogy. *Proceedings of the Tenth International Joint Conference on Artificial Intelligence* (pp. 264–270). Milano, Italy: Morgan Kaufmann.

Fayyad, U. M., & Irani, K. B. (1992). The attribute selection problem in decision tree generation. *Proceedings of the Tenth National Conference on Artificial Intelligence* (pp. 104–110). San Jose, CA: AAAI Press.

Holland, J. H., Holyoak, K. J., Nisbett, R. E., & Thagard, P. R. (1986). Induction: Processes of inference, learning, and discovery. Cambridge, MA: MIT Press.

Martin, J. D., & Billman, D. O. (1991). Variability bias and category learning. *Proceedings of the Eighth International Workshop on Machine Learning* (pp. 90–94). Evanston, IL: Morgan Kaufmann.

Mingers, J. (1989). An empirical comparison of selection measures for decision-tree induction. *Machine Learning, 3*, 319–342.

Quinlan, J. R. (1986). Induction of decision trees. *Machine Learning, 1*, 81–106.

Russell, S. J. (1986). Preliminary steps toward the automation of induction. *Proceedings of the Fifth National Conference on Artificial Intelligence* (pp. 477–484). Philadelphia, PA: AAAI Press.

Schlimmer, J. C. (1992). Learning determinations and checking databases. In G. Piatetsky-Shapiro & W. Frawley (Eds.), *Knowledge Discovery in Databases.* Palo Alto, CA: AAAI Press.

Shen, W. (1991). Discovering regularities from large knowledge bases. *Proceedings of the Eighth International Workshop on Machine Learning* (pp. 539–543). Evanston, IL: Morgan Kaufmann.

Ziarko, W. (1992). The discovery, analysis, and representation of data dependencies in databases. In G. Piatetsky-Shapiro & W. Frawley (Eds.), *Knowledge Discovery in Databases.* Palo Alto, CA: AAAI Press.

Compiling Bayesian Networks into Neural Networks

Eddie Schwalb
Department of Information and Computer Science,
University of California at Irvine, CA 92717
eschwalb@ics.uci.edu

Abstract

The criticism on the usage of Bayesian Networks in expert systems was centered around the claim that the use of probability requires a massive amount of data in the form of conditional probabilities. This paper shows that given information easily obtained from experts, the dependence model and some observations, the conditional probabilities can be estimated using backpropagation, such that during training the Bayesian characteristic of the network is preserved. Applying the Occam's razor principal results in defining a partial order among neural network structures. Experiments show that for the Multiplexer problem, the network compiled from the more succinct causal model generalized better than the one compiled from the less succinct model.

1 Introduction

Many problems of both theoretical and practical interest can be modeled by Bayesian Networks. In this paper, the main concern is not to force the expert to estimate all the conditional probabilities. It addresses the problem of estimating and revising the conditional probabilities (quantitative) based on a given dependence model (qualitative) and some observations. The algorithm suggested can be viewed as a Bayesian Network refining method.

Evaluating how good a given neural network structure is has also proven to be an important task (Martin & Pittman 91). The model presented in this paper defines a partial order among network structures based on the succinctness of the causal model from which they were compiled.

The input to the algorithm is a dependence model, an estimate of some of the conditional probabilities and a set of observations given in the form of input/output probability vector pairs. The task is to learn a probability distribution that best approximates a given set of observations. There are input, output and hidden propositions. Input propositions are such that their prior probabilities are given. Output propositions are such that their probabilities (conditioned on the prior probabilities of the inputs) can be measured. The hidden propositions are such that their probabilities are not given and can not be measured.

In Bayesian Networks the dependence model is represented by a DAG. A *simple* and *natural* integration of Bayesian Networks with neural networks is achieved by mapping the sources of that DAG to the input propositions and the sinks to the output propositions. The rest of the nodes correspond to hidden propositions. A given Bayesian Network is compiled into a standard high-order SIGMA-PI network (Rumelhart, Hinton & Williams 86) such that the standard (with a small modification) backpropagation scheme can be used to revise it. The *weights* are equal to the conditional *probabilities*, thus learning the weights corresponds to learning the conditional probabilities and directly revising the Bayesian Network. Backpropagation is guaranteed to converge to the global minima for some structures, however, structures that are more succinct than the later are expected to generalize better. Experiments show that for the Multiplexer problem, the neural network compiled from a more succinct causal model generalized better.

The paper is organized as follows. This section briefly presents Bayesian and SIGMA-PI networks. Section 2 defines Bayesian Propagation Networks (BPNs), and Section 3 presents the learning rule. Section 4 discusses representing probability distributions while Section 5 presents empirical evaluation. Section 6 discusses related work and Section 7 concludes.

1.1 Bayesian Networks

Let $X_1, \ldots, X_n$ be a set of propositions, and $P(X_i)$ be the probability that $X_i = true$. A Bayesian Network is represented by a DAG (Pearl 88), in which every node represents a proposition, and an arc $i \rightarrow j$ exists if X_j depends on X_i, namely $P(X_j|X_i) \neq P(X_j)$. A node with m parents (indegree m) defines a distribution with 2^m elements. For example, in Figure 1 the DAG represents 4 propositions with probabilities $P(X_1)$, $P(X_2)$, $P(X_3)$, $P(X_4)$. Node X_4 has 2 parents, X_2, X_3. The conditional probabilities required for computing $P(X_4)$ are $P(X_4|X_2,X_3)$, $P(X_4|\neg X_2,X_3)$, $P(X_4|X_2,\neg X_3)$ and $P(X_4|\neg X_2,\neg X_3)$. Thus it defines a distribution of $2^2 = 4$ conditional probabilities. For a more detailed formal definition see (Pearl 91, Pearl 88)

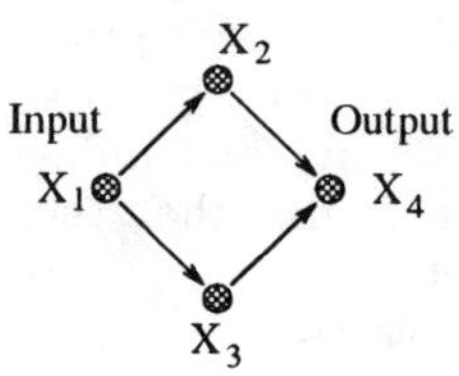

$$P(X_2) = \sum P(X_2|X_1)P(X_1)$$

$$P(X_3) = \sum P(X_3|X_1)P(X_1)$$

$$P(X_4) = \sum P(X_4|X_2,X_3)P(X_2,X_3)$$

Figure 1: An example DAG and the distributions it defines.

1.2 SIGMA-PI Networks

The use of non-linear discriminant functions in a *multinomial* model was discussed in (Rumelhart, Hinton & Williams 86, Shrier & Barron 87, Plutowski 88). The advantages of using a single High-Order-Units (HOUs) layer to do what requires several layers of first-order units are well known (Giles & Maxwell 87). It was shown that HOUs are also advantageous when used in backpropagation networks (Plutowski 88). A special type of HOUs are SIGMA-PI units, in which the expression used for the weighted sum is

$$net_j = \sum_i w_{ij} \prod_k o_{i_k}$$

where i varies over the set of activations feeding into unit j, and k varies over the elements of the conjunct (for example, see Figure 2).

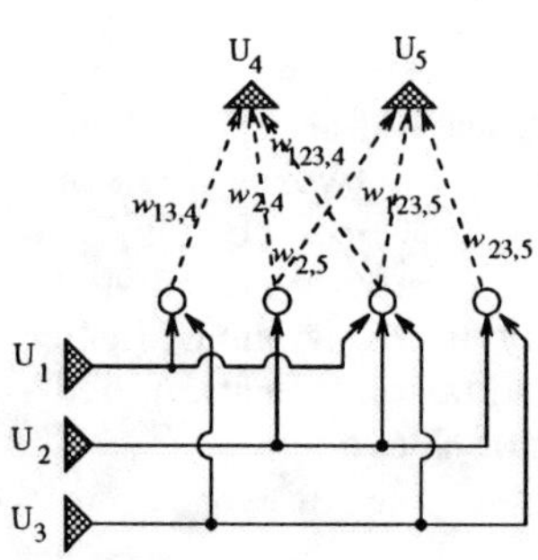

$$\begin{aligned} net_4 &= w_{13,4}o_1o_3 + w_{2,4}o_2 + \\ & w_{123,4}o_1o_2o_3 \\ net_5 &= w_{2,5}o_2 + w_{123,5}o_1o_2o_3 + \\ & w_{23,5}o_2o_3 \end{aligned}$$

Figure 2: An example of a SIGMA-PI network.

2 Bayesian Propagation Network Definition

This section presents a mapping of Bayesian Networks to a special kind of SIGMA-PI networks called Bayesian Propagation Network (BPN), such that propagation of the values will mimic the probability computation of the original Bayesian Network. Consider the DAG in Figure 1. Given $P(X_1)$, the probabilities $P(X_2), P(X_3), P(X_4)$ are evaluated as follows.

$$\begin{aligned} P(X_2) &= P(X_1)P(X_2|X_1) + P(\neg X_1)P(X_2|\neg X_1) \\ P(X_3) &= P(X_1)P(X_3|X_1) + P(\neg X_1)P(X_3|\neg X_1) \\ P(X_4) &= P(\ X_2,\ X_3)P(X_4|\ X_2,\ X_3) + \\ & P(\ X_2,\neg X_3)P(X_4|\ X_2,\neg X_3) + \\ & P(\neg X_2,\ X_3)P(X_4|\neg X_2,\ X_3) + \\ & P(\neg X_2,\neg X_3)P(X_4|\neg X_2,\neg X_3) \end{aligned}$$

The above can be generalized as follows:

$$P(X_j) = \textstyle\sum_{i=1}^{n} o_j^i w_{ij} \quad where \quad \begin{array}{l} o_j^i \equiv P(X_{i_1},\ldots,X_{i_m}) \\ w_{ij} \equiv P(X_j|X_{i_1},\ldots,X_{i_m}) \end{array}$$

Two types of units need to be defined: $\sum$-units (triangles in Figure 2), and $\prod$-units (circles in Figure 2). The output of a $\sum$-unit o_j corresponds to the probability $P(X_j)$. The output of a $\prod$-unit u_j^i corresponds to the probability of the conjunct $P(X_{i_1},\ldots,X_{i_m})$. Every $\sum$-unit is either an output unit, or feeds to $\prod$-units. Also, every $\sum$-unit is either an input unit, or being fed from $\prod$-units. Similarly, every $\prod$-unit feeds and is being fed by $\sum$-units.

Definition 1: Given a Bayesian Network, a SIGMA-PI **BPN** (Bayesian Propagation Network) is such that (see figure 3, for example)

- For every node X_j in the Bayesian Network's DAG, two $\sum$-units $u_j, u_{\bar{j}}$ in the BPN are created. The output values $o_j, o_{\bar{j}}$ of the $\sum$-units represent the probabilities $P(X_j) = o_j$, $P(\neg X_j) = o_{\bar{j}}$.
- All *input* and *output* units of the *BPN* are $\sum$-units. The **sources** of the DAG are mapped to the **input units**, and the **sinks** are mapped to the **output units**.
- The $\sum$-units u_j and $u_{\bar{j}}$ are fed from 2^m common parents which are $\prod$-units $u_j^1,\ldots,u_j^{2^m}$ (see example) where m is the number of parents of node X_j in the DAG of the Bayesian Network.
- The value o_j^i of a $\prod$-unit is $P(X_{i_1},\ldots,X_{i_m})$ where $X_{i_1},\ldots,X_{i_m}$ are the parents of X_j with 2^m different positive/negative combination (see example).
- The $\prod$-units u_j^i are fed from $\sum$-units which represent the factors for computing $P(X_{i_1},\ldots,X_{i_m})$ where X_{i_l} is a parent of X_j in the DAG.

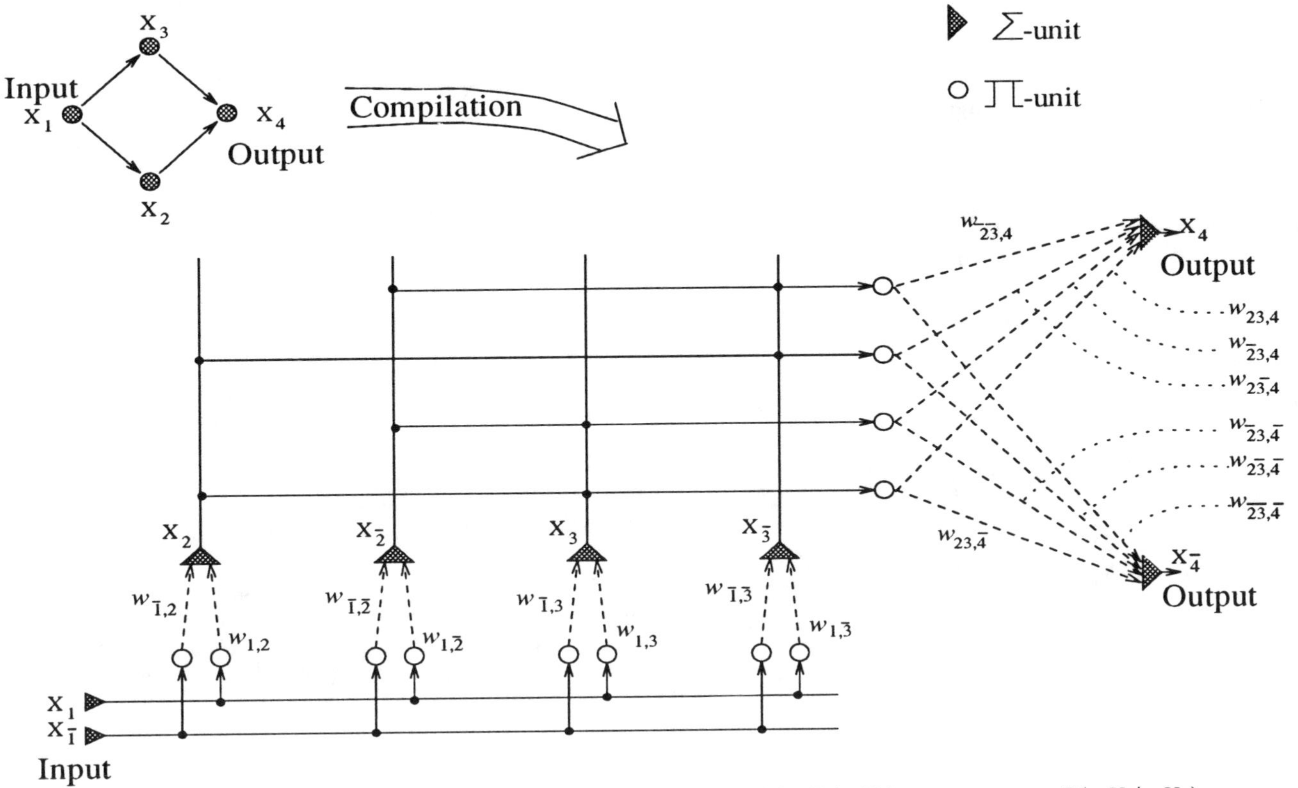

$w_{1,2} = P(X_2|X_1)$ $\quad w_{\bar{1},2} = P(X_2|\neg X_1)$ $\quad w_{1,\bar{2}} = P(\neg X_2|X_1)$ $\quad w_{\bar{1},\bar{2}} = P(\neg X_2|\neg X_1)$

$w_{1,3} = P(X_3|X_1)$ $\quad w_{\bar{1},3} = P(X_3|\neg X_1)$ $\quad w_{1,\bar{3}} = P(\neg X_3|X_1)$ $\quad w_{\bar{1},\bar{3}} = P(\neg X_3|\neg X_1)$

$w_{23,4} = P(X_4|X_2\ X_3)$ $\quad w_{\bar{2}3,4} = P(X_4|\neg X_2\ X_3)$ $\quad w_{2\bar{3},4} = P(X_4|X_2 \neg X_3)$ $\quad w_{\bar{2}\bar{3},4} = P(X_4|\neg X_2 \neg X_3)$

$w_{23,\bar{4}} = P(\neg X_4|X_2\ X_3)$ $\quad w_{\bar{2}3,\bar{4}} = P(\neg X_4|\neg X_2\ X_3)$ $\quad w_{2\bar{3},\bar{4}} = P(\neg X_4|X_2 \neg X_3)$ $\quad w_{\bar{2}\bar{3},\bar{4}} = P(\neg X_4|\neg X_2 \neg X_3)$

Figure 3: The BPN compiled from the DAG in Figure 1

If $X_{i_1} \ldots X_{i_m}$ are independent[1] then $P(X_{i_1}, \ldots, X_{i_m}) = o_j^i = \prod_{l=1}^{m} o_{i_l} = \prod_{l=1}^{m} P(X_{i_l})$. Otherwise (when dependent) we need to apply the chaining rule (along the paths), in which case the definition is more complex.

- The weights value w_{ij} correspond to the conditional probabilities $P(X_j|X_{i_1}, \ldots, X_{i_m})$
- The values are forward propagated as follows:

$$\textstyle\sum\text{-unit}: \quad o_j = \sum_{i=1}^{2^m} w_{ij} o_j^i$$
$$\textstyle\prod\text{-unit}: \quad o_j^i = \prod_{k \in parents(u_j^i)} o_k$$

- The $\prod$-units and weights must satisfy

$$\forall j \quad 1 = \sum_{i=1}^{2^m} o_j^i, \qquad 1 = w_{ij} + w_{i\bar{j}}.$$

Note that the BPN is defined with separate units for X and $\neg X$ to allow trivial generalization for representing multi-valued concepts.

Theorem 1: *Given the prior probabilities of the input propositions (sources), forward propagation of the values in the BPN computes the correct probabilities of the output propositions (sinks).*

[1]Two propositions X_{i_1}, X_{i_2} are considered independent iff there is no directed path from X_{i_1} to X_{i_2} on the corresponding DAG.

Once the BPN was revised, reconstructing the revised Bayesian Network from the BPN is immediate since the conditional probabilities are provided by the weights.

3 Backpropagation

Here the learning rule of BPNs is described. The standard backpropagation algorithm is modified by adding the constraint $\delta_k = -\delta_{\bar{k}}$ to ensure that at all steps during the training there exists a mapping from the intermediate BPN to a Bayesian Network. As a result the training process can be viewed as directly revising the Bayesian Network.

Definition 2: Let u_j be a $\sum$-unit and π_j be the set of $\prod$-units feeding into u_j. Let u_j^i be a $\prod$-unit s.t. $i \in \pi_j$, and let π_j^i be the set of $\sum$-units feeding into u_j^i. Each $\sum$-unit u_j contributes to the error of a non-output $\sum$-unit u_k as follows

$$\forall i \in \pi_j, \quad \forall k \in \pi_j^i, \quad \delta_k \leftarrow \delta_k + \delta_j w_{ij} \frac{o_j^i}{o_k}$$

In order to preserve the Bayesian characteristic of the network in which $1 = \sum P(X_{i_1} \ldots X_{i_m})$, it is sufficient to guarantee that $\forall j \;\; 1 = \sum_{i=1}^{2^m} o_j^i$ by using an enhanced δ' which is an average of $\delta_k, \delta_{\bar{k}}$.

$$\delta'_k = -\delta'_{\bar{k}} = \frac{1}{2}(\delta_k - \delta_{\bar{k}}) \;, \qquad \Delta w_{ij} = \eta \delta'_j o_j^i$$

Note that this does not effect the convergence, since the original signs are preserved.

Lemma 1: *Given that* $\forall j \;\; 1 = \sum_{i=1}^{2^m} o_j^i \quad o_j = 1 - o_{\bar{j}}$ *if* $\forall k \quad \delta'_k = -\delta'_{\bar{k}}$ *then* $\forall j \;\; 1 = \sum_{i=1}^{2^m} o_j'^i$ *where* $o_j'^i = \prod_{k \in \pi_j^i} (o_k + \delta'_k)$ *.*

Proof: *The proof recursively eliminates one elements at a time from the conjuncts of*

$$A = \sum_{i=1}^{2^m} o_j'^i = \sum_{l=1}^{2^m} \prod_{k \in \pi_j^i} (o_k + \delta'_k)$$

The above sum includes factors in which either o_k or $o_{\bar{k}}$ appear, but both can not be together (since they are complementary). Hence, we can rewrite the above as

$$A = (o_p + \delta'_p) \cdot A' + (o_{\bar{p}} + \delta'_{\bar{p}}) \cdot A' = (o_p + o_{\bar{p}} + \delta'_p + \delta'_{\bar{p}}) \cdot A' = A'$$

$$\text{where} \qquad A' = \sum_{i=1}^{2^m} \prod_{k \in \pi_j^i - \{p, \bar{p}\}} (o_k + \delta'_k)$$

At the end of the recursion $A' = 1$. □

Similarly, it can be shown that $w_{ij} + w_{i\bar{j}} = 1$ which agrees with $P(X_j | X_{i_1} \ldots X_{i_m}) + P(\neg X_j | X_{i_1} \ldots X_{i_m}) = 1$, and therefore

Theorem 2: *If we initialize the BPN such that* $\forall j \;\; 1 = \sum_{i=1}^{2^m} o_j^i$, $o_j = 1 - o_{\bar{j}}$ *and* $w_{ij} + w_{i\bar{j}} = 1$ *then using* $\Delta w_{ij} = \eta \delta'_j o_j^i$ *guarantees that at all times during the training the initial constraints are satisfied.*

Corollary 1: *Updating the weights of a BPN using* $\Delta w_{ij} = \eta \delta'_j o_j^i$ *accounts for directly revising the conditional probabilities of the original Bayesian Network.*

3.1 Example: backpropagation on two propositions

Let G be a DAG with two nodes, X_1, X_2, and let us try to learn the distribution in Figure 4. The compiled BPN consists of two input and output $\sum$-units, two $\prod$-units, and 4 weights which correspond to the 4 conditional probabilities. Suppose that initially the weights are random and that the training set consists of the instance $P(X_1) = .2$, $P(X_2) = .74$. The value of $\delta_2 = 0.74 - 0.2 w_{1,2} - 0.8 w_{\bar{1},2}$. The error surface of this example is a bowl, therefore there is a single minima to which we are guaranteed to converge by backpropagation.

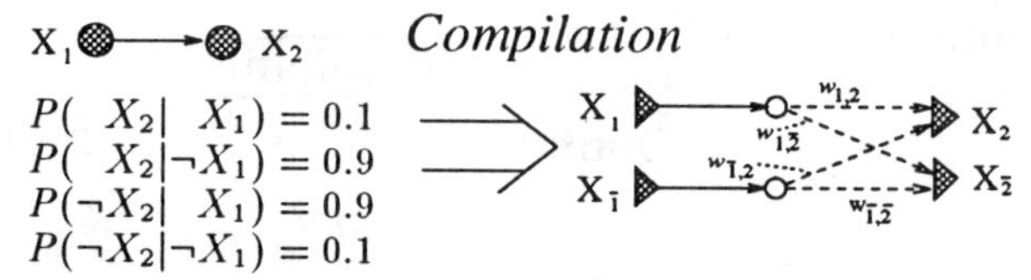

Figure 4: Example BPN of a two proposition DAG.

4 Representing Distributions

BPNs are useful for representing some probability distributions. In this section a partial order among BPN structures is defined. The most expressive structure is identified. Then, less expressive structures for which backpropagation is guaranteed to learn the distribution that best approximates the data are identified.

Definition 3: A bi-partite DAG is such that the set of vertices consists of two partitions X, Y and edges are directed from the vertices in X to the vertices in Y. A *complete bi-partite* DAG is such that there are directed edges from all vertices in X to all vertices in Y.

Lemma 2: *Any probability distribution of the output propositions (sinks) conditioned on the input propositions (sources) can be represented by a BPN compiled from a complete bi-partite DAG.*

The learning task is to find an internal representation of a distribution which best approximates a given a set of input/output vector pairs, where an input vector consists of the prior probabilities of the input propositions, and the output consists of the probabilities observed on the output propositions.

Theorem 3: *Backpropagation on a BPN compiled from a bi-partite (not necessarily complete) DAG is guaranteed to learn the probability distribution that best approximates the observations.*

Generally speaking, simpler models are more constrained, thus more falsifiable; they provide with less opportunities to overfit the data and, therefore, attain greater credibility (Pearl 78, Pearl 91). As a result, we define the structure preference criteria as follows.

Definition 4: Given two BPNs, the one compiled from the more succinct causal model is preferable.

The preference for simplicity is gauged by the expressive power of a model, not by its syntactic description. However, it is often the case that models with more concise syntactic description are more succinct. Consider the set of propositions $X_1, \ldots, X_n$. The number of parameters required to specify the Markov matrix of an internal node with m parents is $2^m - 1$. Given a set of n_i input and n_o output propositions, the complete bi-partite DAG, which is the most expressive and

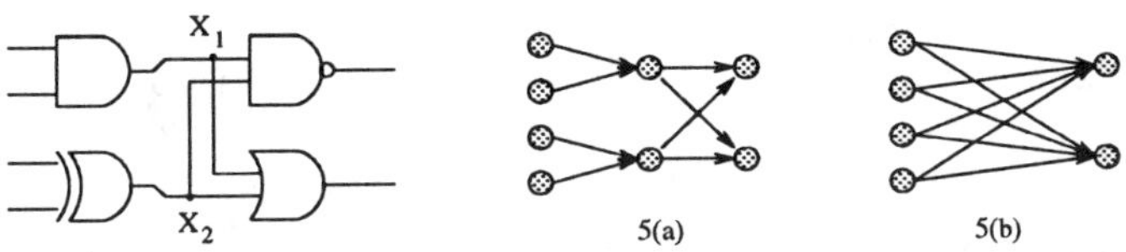

Figure 5: An example circuit with "hidden" propositions. Two possible causal models to represent that circuit: 5(a) consists of two "hidden" propositions while 5(b) doesn't (complete bi-partite DAG).

requires the maximal number of parameters to specify, is represented by $n_o(2^{n_i} - 1)$ parameters. Any consistent sparser causal model contains the same information but is more succinct.

Similarly, to achieve better generalization one should strive to reduce the neural network's capacity. That can be done by reducing the local connectivity and introducing shared weights (Martin & Pittman 91). Indeed, as observed above, reducing the connectivity of a causal model may render it more succinct. The number of weights in a BPN is closely related to the number parameters required for describing the causal model from which it was compiled. Therefore, the number of weights can be used as an easy to compute measure of succinctness of BPNs. As an example, let us consider the circuit in Figure 5 and its corresponding DAG in Figure 5(a). In case the existence of X_1, X_2 is unknown, the DAG in Figure 5(b) can be used. Using the Occam's razor principal, the model in 5(a), that consists of two hidden propositions, is more succinct. The DAG of 5(a) compiles to a BPN which consists of 32 weights, while the DAG in Figure 5(b) compiles to a BPN which consists of 64 weights.

As a result, for a given set of input/output propositions, a partial order among network structures is defined, in which the complete bi-partite DAG is the unique minimum, followed by incomplete bi-partite DAGs, followed by other more succinct structures with hidden units. Consequently, a possible heuristic for learning the structure of the neural network will be to start from a given initial structure and climb up to a more succinct structure that generalizes better. An initial neural network structure can be computed by the Inductive Causation algorithm presented in (Pearl 91). Alternatively, the most probable causal model, which can be approximated in polynomial time (Cooper & Herskovits 92), can be used.

5 Empirical Evaluation of Generalization

This section presents empirical results that lead to the conclusion that complete knowledge of dependencies and incomplete knowledge of the conditional probabilities is sufficient for the BPN to generalize, and supports the conjecture that more succinct networks generalize better.

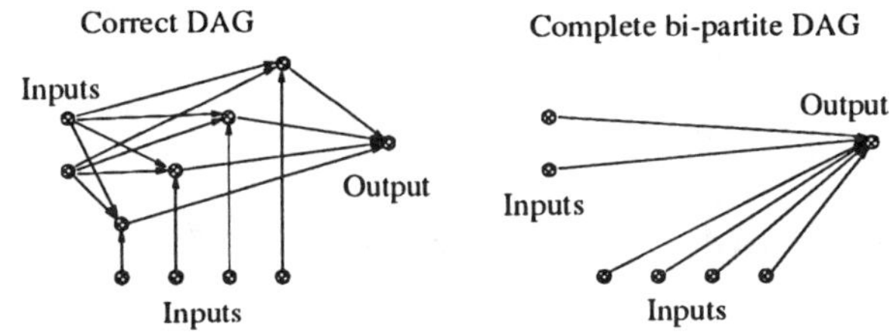

Figure 6: the Multiplexer DAG.

For empirical evaluation of the generalizing ability, *corrupted networks were generated and then revised by training on a set of examples.* The corruption (or "noise") model replaces the original weights with probability P by random ones, uniformly distributed. For symmetry breaking, all the weights (including the corrupted ones) are replaced by weights generated randomly with low variance normal distributions such that the average of that distribution is the original weight.

The experiments were conducted with the standard Multiplexer problem, in which the functionality of the logical units is to be learned, given a set of input/output pairs. The DAG which represents that problem is presented in Figure 6. There are 6 input propositions, $X_1, \ldots, X_6$, one output proposition, X_{11}, and 4 hidden propositions, $X_7, \ldots, X_{10}$. The relation represented is defined as $\rho = \{x_1, \ldots, x_6, x_{11} \mid P(x_{11}|x_1, \ldots, x_6) > P(\neg x_{11}|x_1, \ldots, x_6)\}$, namely the output is 1 iff the probability computed for X_{11} is greater than 0.5.

In this experiment, all the tuples of the concept are known. Thus, the best evaluation of the learned network will be to measure accuracy on the whole concept. Clearly, the complement of the training set is the largest possible test set.

The experiment was conducted as follows. Initially, a correct BPN was computed that represents the concept of 64 examples exactly, and corrupted by scrambling some of the weights. The resulting network was trained on a subset of the concept and *accuracy was tested on all 64 tuples.* Each point in the graph (Figure 7) represents the average of 18 training sessions of 3000 batch passes each, updated with $\eta = 0.0005$. A small η was used to ensure that the high order polynomial will not cause errors in cases of steep descent.

A satisfactory minima was obtained by repetitive runs with different initial symmetry breaking noise. On a single network, the best 3 out of 6 minimas, as measured on an independent *selecting set,* were selected and averaged. The selecting set was disjoint from the training set and contained of 40% of the remaining tuples. The network compiled from the complete bipartite DAG always converged to the same minima in

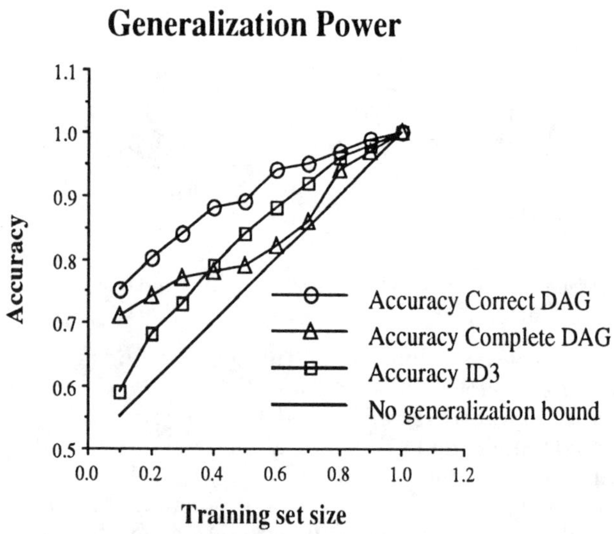

Figure 7: Generalizing distributions corrupted with $P = 0.06$, trained on various sizes of training sets. The accuracy was tested on 100% of the concept. Each point represents the average of 18 BPN training sessions and 50 ID3 runs.

all training sessions, as expected.

Three algorithms were compared (Figure 7): (1) the BPN compiled from the correct DAG, (2) the BPN compiled from a complete bi-partite DAG, and (3) the symbolic algorithm ID3, which learns decision trees. The BPN compiled from the correct DAG was consistently slightly better than ID3, but the BPN compiled from the complete bi-partite DAG generalized better only on small training sets.

6 Related Work

Several theory refinement systems that have been successfully applied to real-world problems (Ginsberg 90, Ourston & Mooney 91, Towel & Shavlik 90) have largely focused on revising *logical theories*. This work is motivated by the conjecture that many real-world domains for which logical reasoning is not adequate, require probabilistic reasoning.

KBANN (Towel & Shavlik 90) is a system that converts a propositional knowledge base represented by Horn clauses to an artificial neural network by adding new variables and links. The neural network is trained with backpropagation to correctly classify training data. However, the resulting weights do not have probabilistic meaning. More recently, RAPTURE was developed (Mahoney & Mooney 92), in which MYCIN style rules are revised. In this system the certainty factors' error was propagated and revised using backpropagation.

Successful learning of probability distributions was reported (Neal 91) for "sigmoid" and "noisy-OR" probabilistic belief networks. However, the ability of such networks to utilize dependencies and generalize concepts was not discussed.

In (Spiegelhalter & Lauritzen 90, Roizen & Pearl 86) the problem of updating conditional probabilities was discussed. The conditional probabilities are represented by parameters which account for the frequencies which can be obtained by counting. The problem addressed in this paper differs from simple derivation of the frequencies, since some of the propositions are hidden (latent), namely their probabilities are not given and can not be measured. In (Cooper & Herskovits 92) hidden (latent) variables are discussed, however, the generalization power of the resulting distribution is not discussed.

The task of determining preferable neural network structures was thoroughly discussed in the literature. A recent research (Martin & Pittman 91) suggests to use the network's capacity as measure of succinctness. Here, however, it is assumed that the causal model, which determines the neural network structure, can be obtained from experts or by other methods. Glymour suggested that discovering causal structures can be done by utilizing correlations in the data (Glymour et al. 91). A more recent development suggests that conditional independencies should be used instead (Pearl & Verma 91). Cooper & Herskovits (Cooper & Herskovits 92) have proposed a heuristic for computing the most probable causal model. Here it is suggested to evaluate how good a proposed causal model is by measuring the generalization power of the compiled neural network.

7 Conclusion

The criticism on the usage of Bayesian Networks in expert systems was centered around the claim that the use of probability requires a massive amount of data in the form of conditional probabilities. This paper presents a model that utilizes information easily obtained from experts, the dependence model and some observations, to learn the conditional probabilities using backpropagation, such that during training the Bayesian characteristic of the network is preserved. The model presented suggests that the neural network structure should reflect a causal model of the data represented. Applying the well known Occam's razor principal results in defining a partial order among network structures. The later might be useful for discovering causal structures and learning a good neural network structure.

In particular, it was shown that any Bayesian Network, in which the dependence model is represented by a DAG, can be mapped to a SIGMA-PI network, called Bayesian Propagation Network (BPN). To ensure that at all steps during the learning there exists a mapping from the intermediate partially trained BPN to a Bayesian Network, the standard backpropagation procedure needed to be modified only by adding the constraint $\delta_k = -\delta_{\bar{k}}$. As a result the training process can be viewed as directly revising the Bayesian Network. A BPN compiled from a *complete* bi-partite DAG can represent any probability distribution conditioned on the input. When the dependence model is a bi-partite DAG, the probability distribution which best approximates the observations is guaranteed to be found. Experiments show that for the Multiplexer problem, the neural network complied from a more succinct model (with hidden units) generalized better.

The drawback of the suggested method is that the resulting neural network size grows exponentially with the size of the dependence set. Clearly, in problems like deciding whether a DNA sequence codes a promoter, in which a proposition may depend on more than 10 4-valued attributes, the network will have more than 10^6 weights, thus it is not practical to implement. In the future, we hope to demonstrate the applicability of this method on some real-world problems, by refining an existing approximated Bayesian Network.

Acknowledgments

I would like to thank the AI faculty and students in UC Irvine for providing me with general support. In particular, Steve Hampson, whose intuition was of great help in the first stages of this work, Pat Murphy who was helped with ID3, Dennis Kibler who provided helpful comments, Mike Pazzani who helped to shape the paper and Rina Dechter, who helped to point out related work.

References

Cooper, G.F., Herskovits, E., 1992. A Bayesian Method for the Induction of Probablistic Networks from Data, *Machine Learning* **9**:309-347.

Dechter, R., Pearl, J., 1991. Directed constraint networks: A relational framework for causal modeling In *IJCAI'91*, Sydney, Australia, 1164-1170.

Giles, C. L., Maxwell, T., 1987. Learning invariance, and generalization in high-order neural networks *Applied Optics* **26**(23), Dec 1987.

Ginsberg, A., 1990. Theory reduction, the theory revision and retranslation In *Proc. of the 8th National Conf. on Artificial Intelligence*, 777-782, Detroit, July 1990.

Glymour, C., Scheines, R., Spirtes, P., Kelly, K., Discovering causal structure, Academic press 1987.

Mahoney, J.J., Mooney, R.J., 1992. Combining Symbolic and Neural Learning to Revise Probablistic Rule Bases. In *ML workshop 92*.

Martin, G. L., Pittman, J. A., 1991. Recognizing Hand-Printed Letters and Digits Using Backpropagation Learning, *Neural Computation* **3**:258-267.

Neal, R.M., Connectionist learning of belief networks 1992. *Artificial Intelligence* **56**:71-114.

Ourston, D, Mooney, R.J., 1991. Changing the rules: a comprehensive approach to theory refinement 1991. In *Proc. of the International Workshop on Multistrategy Learning*, 115-130, Nov 1991.

Pearl, J., Probablistic Reasoning in Intelligent Systems Morgan Kaufman, 1988.

Pearl, J., 1978. On the connection between the complexity and credibility of inferred models, *Int. J. General Systems* **4**:255-264.

Pearl, J., Verma, T.S., 1991. A theory of inferred causation, In *Proc. of the 2nd Int. Conf. on Principals of Knowledge Representation and Reasoning* 441-452.

Plutowski, M., 1988. Backpropagation with higher order units, In *IEEE International Conference on Neural Networks*, San Diego, 1988.

Roizen, I., Pearl, J., Learning Link-Probabilities in Causal Trees, In *Proc. of the 2nd AAAI Workshop on Uncertainty in AI*, Aug 1986.

Rumelhart, D. E., Hinton, G. E., Williams, R. J., Parallel Distributed Processing, Vol 1, chapter 8, MIT press, 1986.

Shrier, S., Barron, R. L., Gilstrap, L. O., 1987. Polynomial and neural networks: analogies and engineering applications, In *Proc. IEEE First International Conference on Neural Networks*(1987) Vol II, 431-439.

Spiegelhalter, D.J., Lauritzen, S.L., 1990. Sequential Updating of Conditional Probabilities on Directed Graphical Structures, *Networks* **20**:579-605.

Towel, G.G., Shavlik, J.W., Noordewier, M.O., 1990. Refinement of Approximate Domain Theories by Knowledge-Based Neural Networks, In *Proc. of the Eighth National Conference on Artificial Intelligence (AAAI-90)* 861-866.

A Reinforcement Learning Method for Maximizing Undiscounted Rewards

Anton Schwartz
Computer Science Dept.
Stanford University
Stanford, CA 94305
schwartz@cs.stanford.edu

Abstract

While most Reinforcement Learning work utilizes temporal discounting to evaluate performance, the reasons for this are unclear. Is it out of desire or necessity? We argue that it is not out of desire, and seek to dispel the notion that temporal discounting is necessary by proposing a framework for undiscounted optimization. We present a metric of undiscounted performance and an algorithm for finding action policies that maximize that measure. The technique, which we call R-learning, is modelled after the popular Q-learning algorithm [17]. Initial experimental results are presented which attest to a great improvement over Q-learning in some simple cases.

1 Introduction

In the paradigm of Reinforcement Learning (RL), an agent finds itself in an environment and must learn by trial and error to take actions so as to maximize, over the long run, rewards which it receives in return. The techniques for accomplishing this estimate the rewards that performing an action may reap over the course of time, so as to choose actions maximizing that measure. This requires summarizing a possibly infinite sequence of rewards in a finite measure. To do this, researchers have relied on *temporal discounting*, a practice of giving exponentially diminishing importance to rewards far in the future, so as to summarize the rewards in a single finite number.

While temporal discounting is convenient, it comes at a price. For one, it may make behaviors with quick but mediocre results look more attractive than efficient behaviors reaping long-term benefits. Moreover, even when it favors behaviors with adequate farsightedness, it can greatly impede the process by which Q-learning arrives at its solutions.

In this paper we outline some of the problems caused by temporal discounting, and set out to provide a workable alternative. We put forth an undiscounted measure of policy performance, and present an algorithm designed to arrive at policies which maximize that measure. The method, which we call R-learning, resembles Q-learning inasmuch as it measures the value—for a different notion of value—of state-action pairs, relative to its current policy, and in any state recommends that action which maximizes value. The key element introduced is a measure of average reward, which serves as a standard of comparison. When examined according to a measure of utility that is depends on this average, improvements to policies become more salient. This boosts performance in a number of ways.

While all of the principle ideas and techniques presented in this paper (including the formal notions of average and average-adjusted value, Theorem 3, and the R-learning algorithm) are the result of our own work, we became aware while writing that the ideas were first created and explored in the Dynamic Programming literature, often with much greater generality and elegance. As a result, this paper may serve as an introduction to the concepts of undiscounted Dynamic Programming, and as the first attempt to bring those concepts to bear on the problems and practices of Reinforcement Learning. The R-learning algorithm remains, to our knowledge, a novel technical contribution.

A more qualitative account of the ideas presented in this paper is given in [13].

2 Background

In RL, the learner's environment is modelled as a Markov Decision Process (MDP). An MDP specifies a set S of states and a set A of actions. At each step in time the process is in some state, and an action must be chosen; this action has the effect of changing the current state and producing a scalar reinforcement value. The reinforcement value, or reward, represents the extent to which we can consider the action to have had immediately desirable or undesirable consequences. Formally, an MDP is described by a 4-tuple $\langle S, A, P, r\rangle$ where $P : S \times S \times A \mapsto [0, 1]$ gives the probability (written $P_{ss'}(a)$) of moving into state s' when action a is performed in state s, and $r : S \times A \mapsto \mathbb{R}$ gives the corresponding expected reward. In this paper we will deal exclusively with finite MDP's, *i.e.*, ones with finite sets S and A. A *policy* is a mapping from S to A, suggesting which action to perform in each state.[1] The goal of RL methods is to arrive, by performing actions and observing their outcomes, at a policy which maximizes the rewards accumulated over time.

Q-learning [17] is the most widely used and studied method for RL and, like most, it uses discounted value as its criterion of optimality. The *discounted value*, or *discounted return*, of a policy π in a state s is defined as the expected value

$$V_\gamma^\pi(s) \stackrel{\text{def}}{=} E\left[\sum_{t=0}^{\infty} \gamma^t r_{s,t}^\pi\right] \quad (1)$$

where $r_{s,t}^\pi$, a random variable, represents the reward that will be received t time steps after the learner begins executing policy π in state s, and γ is a temporal discounting constant, $0 \leq \gamma < 1$.

Q-learning seeks to find a policy π^* which maximizes $V_\gamma^\pi(s)$ in all states $s \in S$. (We call such policies γ-*optimal*.) To do so, it makes particular use of the *action-value* form of (1),

$$Q_\gamma^\pi(s,a) \stackrel{\text{def}}{=} V_\gamma^{a;\pi}(s), \quad (2)$$

in which $a;\pi$ denotes the nonstationary policy which performs action a once and thereafter follows policy π. The algorithm for Q-learning is based on the relation

$$Q_\gamma^\pi(s,a) = r(s,a) + \gamma \sum_{s' \in S} P_{ss'}(a) V_\gamma^\pi(s'), \quad (3)$$

and on the fact that for γ-optimal policies π^* (and no others),

$$V_\gamma^{\pi^*}(s) = \max_{a \in A} Q_\gamma^{\pi^*}(s,a) \quad \text{for all } s \in S. \quad (4)$$

Q-learning operates by maintaining a function $\hat{Q} : S \times A \mapsto \mathbb{R}$, which initially maps all values to zero, and is updated every time an action is executed as follows. Let $x \stackrel{\beta}{\leftarrow} y$, for $0 \leq \beta \leq 1$, denote the operation of assigning to variable x the value $x + \beta \cdot (y - x)$. If action a is performed in state s, resulting in an immediate reward r_{imm} and a transition into state s', then the value of $\hat{Q}$ on input $\langle s, a \rangle$ is modified by performing

$$\hat{Q}(s,a) \stackrel{\beta}{\leftarrow} r_{imm} + \gamma \max_{a' \in A} \hat{Q}(s', a') \quad (5)$$

for an appropriate learning rate β. At any time, the Q-values induce a policy $\pi^{\hat{Q}}$ which maps each state s to the action a maximizing $\hat{Q}(s,a)$. Given certain assumptions, this procedure is guaranteed to arrive at a policy which maximizes discounted value from every state [18].

In cases where the value $V_1^{\pi^*}(s)$ exists and is finite (*cf.* Equation 1), V_1 can be used as an undiscounted measure of performance, and Q-learning with $\gamma = 1$ can be shown to converge to V_1-optimal policies [18]. But the MDP's of which the above stipulation holds are *goal tasks* in which one seeks to reach an absorbing set of "goal" states via a minimal path; and in those domains researchers tend to use discounted Q-learning for other reasons[2] (*e.g.*, [8, 16]).

[1]Except where otherwise noted, we use *policy* to refer to a stationary policy, *i.e.*, one which does not vary over time [12].

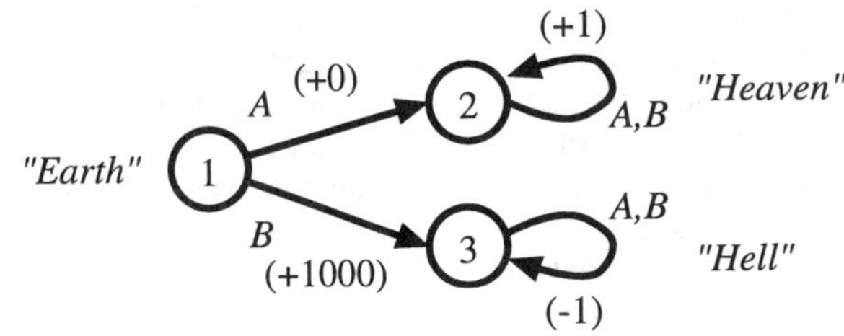

Figure 1: A trivial MDP on which discounted and undiscounted measures may disagree. States are indicated by circles, actions are given in italics, their associated state transitions are given by arrows, and their immediate rewards are given in parentheses.

3 Measures of Performance

If we look at the graphs which papers in RL use to report the performance of their systems, we find that they are almost universally graphs of undiscounted measures: either total cumulative reward or average reward per time step (*e.g.*, [6, 8, 9, 16]). But Q-Learning maximizes a future-discounted measure of reward instead. The problem is that that these criteria, in general, need not coincide.

3.1 Discounted Performance

For instance, consider the MDP of Figure 1. Here, attention to (undiscounted) future rewards will clearly mandate that a policy choose action A in state 1. But for any $\gamma < \frac{500}{501} \approx 0.998$, $Q_\gamma^\pi(1,B) > Q_\gamma^\pi(1,A)$ regardless of π—which makes methods such as Q-learning prefer action B. In fact, given any γ, there is some value we can set for $r(1,B)$ which makes the γ-discounted criterion favor action B over action A.

It is true that for any finite MDP there is some sufficiently large γ for which the discounted and undiscounted measures agree. However, proper choice of such a γ requires detailed knowledge of the domain—knowledge that we do not want to presuppose. Even with such knowledge, a parameter such as γ that needs to be tailored to suit individual domains is clearly undesirable.

In light of these observations, one may wonder why researchers use discounting at all. We address several possible answers to this question:

Discounting to compensate for rate of interest. Discounted value is the primary criterion for performance in the field

[2]These reasons, too lengthy to be presented in this paper, will be explained in detail elsewhere. They do not apply to the R-learning method.

of Operations Research, where dynamic programming has been used and studied extensively. There the motivation is economic: one assumes that interest is available on earned rewards at the rate of $(100\varphi)\%$ per unit of time. In order to compensate for the interest one can earn on rewards achieved in the present, a reward of r units t time steps into the future must be evaluated by its *present value*, $(1+\varphi)^{-t}r$. This gives motivation for using $\gamma = (1+\varphi)^{-1}$ in the above framework. However, this explanation can be dismissed out of hand by observing that RL researchers do not let interest accrue on rewards in their reportings of cumulative reward, nor do they evaluate the rewards in terms of their present value at any moment in time.

Discounting to express the finiteness of an agent's lifetime. Another possible reason to value present rewards more than future rewards is the assumption that the agent might die sometime before it is able to reap future rewards. In this case, the γ represents an assumption that the agent has a probability $(1-\gamma)$ of dying at any step in time, in which case all future rewards will be zero. A different intuition with the same mathematical interpretation is this: *Discounting to express uncertainty about the future.* Some have argued that future rewards may be uncertain because of a changing environment [1], and use discounting to reflect that any reward expected at future time t may turn out to be zero instead with a probability of $(1-\gamma^t)$. But both of these interpretations of discounting beg the following question: If researchers assume that agents may die or that rewards may turn to naught, why do they measure performance in domains where neither of these eventualities come to pass?

This paper will proceed on the premise that the reason why people use discounting is none of these but a more practical one: *By discounting future rewards, one makes their infinite sum finite.* Which is to say, researchers use a discounted value measure because there exists no workable alternative. We proceed to provide such an alternative.

3.2 Undiscounted Performance

We wish to compare total undiscounted rewards reaped by a policy from a state; but since policies are likely to accrue rewards steadily over time, it is generally impossible to merely compare the infinite sums of rewards. Naturally, we turn to some comparison of the finite cumulative sums. Define the *n-period value* of a policy as

$$V^{\pi}_{(n)}(s) \stackrel{\text{def}}{=} \sum_{t=0}^{n-1} E\left[r^{\pi}_{s,t}\right].$$

One way to obtain a finite measure is to look at the average reward per unit of time incurred by a policy over the long run. We define the *average reward* of a policy π started in state s as

$$\rho^{\pi}(s) \stackrel{\text{def}}{=} \lim_{n\to\infty} \frac{V^{\pi}_{(n)}(s)}{n}.$$

While a policy needs to maximize average reward in order for us to consider it optimal in an undiscounted sense, the converse may not be true. For example, in some state s, two policies π_1 and π_2 may yield the same average reward even though π_1 will constantly outperform π_2 in that $V^{\pi_1}_{(n)}(s) = V^{\pi_2}_{(n)}(s) + c$ $(c > 0)$ for large n. In such cases we would like to have an additional measure which is sensitive to such constants c. One possibility is

$$\lim_{n\to\infty} V^{\pi}_{(n)}(s) - n\cdot\rho^{\pi}(s),$$

the limiting difference between cumulative performance and the line through the origin with slope $\rho^{\pi}(s)$. (We may think of this line as the cumulative performance of the hypothetical reference case in which π were to reap its average reward $\rho^{\pi}(s)$ at every step.) This measure, while intuitive, may not be well defined when the policy reaches periodic limit cycles. But in such cases we can generalize it to a measure which is guaranteed to exist. We define the *average-adjusted value* [5] of policy π in state s as the Cesàro or "limit in the average" [4] version of the simpler expression above:

$$\sigma^{\pi}(s) \stackrel{\text{def}}{=} \lim_{n\to\infty} \frac{\sum_{m=0}^{n-1} V^{\pi}_{(m)}(s) - m\cdot\rho^{\pi}(s)}{n}. \quad (6)$$

If we summarize the performance of a policy π in state s by a linear function in n approximating $V^{\pi}_{(n)}(s)$, then $\rho^{\pi}(s)$ is that line's slope and $\sigma^{\pi}(s)$ the y-intercept.

These two values, then, provide us with an undiscounted standard of performance. We wish foremost to maximize $\rho^{\pi}(s)$ and secondarily (ρ's being equal) to maximize $\sigma^{\pi}(s)$. So let us define the *total value* of a policy π from state s as the ordered pair

$$V^{\pi}_{T}(s) \stackrel{\text{def}}{=} \langle \rho^{\pi}(s), \sigma^{\pi}(s)\rangle$$

and use lexicographical order as the ordering on V_T. That is, we say that $\langle\rho,\sigma\rangle > \langle\rho',\sigma'\rangle$ if and only if $(\rho > \rho')$ or $(\rho = \rho'$ and $\sigma > \sigma')$.

We define undiscounted action-values analogously to the discounted case:

$$Q^{\pi}_{T}(s,a) \stackrel{\text{def}}{=} V^{a;\pi}_{T}(s).$$

To make parallels to the discounted case clear, we will use $V^{\pi}_{\sigma}(s)$ and $Q^{\pi}_{\sigma}(s,a)$ to refer to the σ components of $V^{\pi}_{T}(s)$ and $Q^{\pi}_{T}(s,a)$, respectively. Let us write $\pi_1 \succeq_T \pi_2$ to mean that $V^{\pi_1}_{T}(s) \geq V^{\pi_2}_{T}(s)$ for all states s. We say that π is *T-optimal* whenever $\pi \succeq_T \pi'$ for all policies π'. Like γ-optimal policies, stationary T-optimal policies are guaranteed to exist for finite MDP's [5]. We will henceforth use π^* to denote T-optimal policies.

The notion of T-optimality exists under a variety of names in the literature [11]. It is a stronger condition than average-reward optimality, but weaker than other forms including Blackwell optimality [3]. Blackwell optimality, the most selective one in the literature according to which all finite MDP's have optimal stationary policies, may be viewed as lexicographically maximizing an infinite series of which ρ and σ are the first two terms. So far we have not seen the need to utilize the higher order terms.

We briefly explore an important property of average reward:

Fact 1 *If two states s and s' are such that executing policy π from either state leads to the same ergodic set*[3] *of states in S, then $\rho^\pi(s) = \rho^\pi(s')$.*

This has the following consequence:

Corollary 2 *For any finite MDP, either*
1. $\rho^{\pi^*}(s)$ is independent of s, or
2. There are states between which no policy can ever guarantee passage.

The corollary tells us that in all cases of interest to RL, the optimal policy has a single average reward, since MDP's of which the second clause holds would normally violate the frequency of visit assumptions required for the convergence of stochastic approximation methods such as Q-learning [18].

While for many MDP's there exist policies that induce multiple ergodic sets, a simplification commonly made in the Dynamic Programming literature is that all policies are *unichain*, *i.e.*, give rise to a single ergodic set [11]. In light of Fact 1, this lets one assume that all policies, not only π^*, achieve a single state-independent average reward. At times we will make this assumption so as to facilitate the presentation of R-learning. A discussion of the behavior of R-learning in the general multichain case is forthcoming.

Attention to σ may seem frivolous, as σ represents merely a constant offset to cumulative value, likely to be quickly dominated by the repeated contributions of ρ. But for terminal goal tasks, average reward is merely a function of the goal state that is reached, invariant of the behavior that leads to the goal.[4] Thus, σ is of great importance; it is the entire measure of efficiency in reaching the goal.

Moreover, even if we are only interested in maximizing average reward, σ turns out to be a crucial instrument in that maximization. For any policy π, states which lead to the same ergodic set—and all states do, given the unichain assumption—share a common value of $\rho^\pi(s)$, so their values $V_T^\pi(s)$ differ only with regard to their second component, $\sigma^\pi(s)$. Likewise, for all actions a that lead to the same ergodic set, the action-values $Q_T^\pi(s,a)$ share a constant ρ component. Clearly, then, σ is the key to policy improvement. When an action a is found for which $Q_\sigma^\pi(s,a) > V_\sigma^\pi(s)$, then changing π to choose a in s results in an improvement of V_T^π, increasing $\rho(s)$ if s is a recurrent state under π.

[3] Any policy, applied to an MDP, gives rise to a Markov chain. An ergodic set of a Markov chain is a minimal set of states which, once entered, will never be left [7].

[4] Any policy which reaches the goal, strictly speaking, remains there forever. The average reward of a policy reflects this fact, even though a researcher generally stops the simulation at that point and begins a new trial from a different state. In practice, learners are rarely if ever allowed to execute a fixed stationary policy, so $\rho^\pi(s)$ need not express the average reward observed during experimental trials.

4 The Connection Between Discounted and Undiscounted Value

Before proposing a method for learning T-optimal policies, we note a connection between discounted and undiscounted value. The main result of interest is the following [11]:

Theorem 3 *For any policy π and state s,*

$$V_\gamma^\pi(s) = \frac{\rho^\pi(s)}{1-\gamma} + \sigma^\pi(s) + \varepsilon(s,\gamma), \quad \textit{where} \lim_{\gamma\to 1} \varepsilon(s,\gamma) = 0.$$

We may read this statement as saying that for values of γ approaching 1, the discounted value $V_\gamma^\pi(s)$ is composed of two nonvanishing terms: one that is a large constant multiple of the average reward expected from starting policy π in state s, and one that is the average-adjusted value of s. We will refer to these as the ρ-term and σ-term, respectively.

So for γ close to 1, V_γ may be seen as approximating the lexicographical preference of V_T by giving much more weight to ρ than to σ. But the approximation is imperfect, as is manifest in the fact that V_γ dictates opting for a quick constant bonus in reward over a long-term improvement in average reward when $\Delta\sigma$, the gain in finite short-term reward, is greater than $\frac{\Delta\rho}{1-\gamma}$, the scaled difference in long-term average reward. This explains the faulty choice in the example of Figure 1.

Conversely, a simple corollary of Theorem 3 lets us understand average-adjusted value in terms of discounted value:

Corollary 4 *For any policy π and state s,*

$$V_\sigma^\pi(s) = \lim_{\gamma\to 1} E\left[\sum_{t=0}^{\infty} \gamma^t \left(r_{s,t}^\pi - \rho^\pi(s)\right)\right]. \qquad (7)$$

If we think of the quantities $r_{s,t}^\pi - \rho^\pi(s)$ as *average-adjusted rewards* [13], then this corollary lets us view $V_\sigma^\pi(s)$ as the expected discounted sum of average-adjusted rewards, for vanishingly little discounting (*cf.* Equation 1).

5 Learning T-Optimal Policies

When we express average-adjusted values in the form of Equation 7, it is easy to verify that they obey the following recurrence relation:

$$\sigma^\pi(s) = r(s,\pi(s)) - \rho^\pi(s) + \sum_{s'\in S} P_{ss'}(\pi(s))\,\sigma^\pi(s'). \quad (8)$$

The recurrence, like the expression for value in Corollary 4, is analogous to the discounted case, but with the following two modifications:

1. Rewards are average-adjusted by subtracting out ρ^π.
2. The effect of γ is eliminated by bringing γ arbitrarily close to 1.

We may see that first modification enables the second as follows: In the representation of V_γ given by Theorem 3, the first term is the one which blows up for γ close to 1 when $\rho^\pi \neq 0$; this is what prevents us from simply using the undiscounted sum V_1 in the first place. But average-adjusting the incoming rewards reduces the problem to one where $\rho^\pi = 0$, eliminating the first term altogether. This done, we are free to let γ approach 1 in order to eliminate the contribution of the high order term $\varepsilon(s, \gamma)$. What is left is a measure of the σ-term alone which, as we have mentioned, is precisely that upon which we wish to base action selection.

By applying these two modifications to the standard Q-learning algorithm, what results is a technique for approximating $Q^{\pi^*}_\sigma(s, a)$ instead of $Q^{\pi^*}_\gamma(s, a)$, and hence maximizing total rather than γ-discounted value. The only additional machinery needed is a mechanism for approximating the average reward of the successive policies suggested by the algorithm. The method, R-learning, is now presented:

The R-Learning Algorithm

1. Begin with a $|S| \times |A|$ table of real numbers $R(s, a)$, all initialized to zero, and a real-valued variable ρ, also initialized to zero.
2. Repeat:

   2a. From the current state s, perform an action a, chosen by some exploration/action-selection mechanism (this is an orthogonal component of the system, just as it is for Q-learning). Observe the immediate reward r_{imm} received and the subsequent state s'.

   2b. Update R according to:

   $$R(s, a) \stackrel{\beta}{\leftarrow} r_{imm} - \rho + U_R(s') \tag{9}$$

   where $U_R(s') = \max_{a'} R(s', a')$ and β is a learning rate parameter.

   2c. If $R(s, a) = U_R(s)$ (*i.e.*, if a agrees with the policy π^R), then update ρ according to:

   $$\rho \stackrel{\alpha}{\leftarrow} r_{imm} + U_R(s') - U_R(s) \tag{10}$$

   where α is a learning rate parameter.

One might wonder why we do not simply approximate ρ via exponential averaging of immediate rewards (*i.e.*, $\rho \stackrel{\alpha}{\leftarrow} r_{imm}$), performed on *every* tick. This is so as to restrict our attention to the policy π^R, uninfluenced by the conflicting behavior of the exploration mechanism that is ultimately responsible for action choice. Exploratory actions, which generally incur subaverage rewards, would skew the approximation of ρ if included in the calculation. The appearance of the term $U_R(s') - U_R(s)$ in Equation 9 plays the role of compensating for known variations in the rewards received in different states; it serves to adjust for periods of low reward when the agent is using its optimal policy to *recover* from suboptimal exploratory actions, and more generally to minimize the variance of the values used to estimate ρ.

One may easily show that whenever R-learning converges it must arrive at a T-optimal policy. But unlike the discounted methods, whose mathematics have been extensively explored (*e.g.*, [18]), a proof of the convergence of R-learning has not been established. Nonetheless, related techniques such as undiscounted Policy Improvement [5] are well understood, and work toward convergence results is currently under way.

6 Advantages of R-Learning

R-learning is designed to arrive at T-optimal policies, and we have already argued for the advantages of undiscounted performance criteria. But in addition to maximizing undiscounted performance, R-learning displays several computational advantages over existing techniques. As a result, even when one can be sure of choosing γ so as to allow Q-learning to arrive at T-optimal policies, it is often preferable to use R-learning (bearing in mind that the algorithm has not yet been *proven* to converge).

For discounted methods such as Q-learning to arrive at policies that do not overlook temporally distant rewards, they must use large values of γ. But it is well known that for successive approximation techniques the geometric rate of decay in the approximation error is proportional to γ, so that high values of γ can slow the convergence dramatically [2]. As a result, one might expect an undiscounted method such as R-learning to converge extremely slowly. In fact the opposite is generally true, for the following reasons:

6.1 Better Initial Estimates

In cases where the optimal policy π^* has nonzero average reward and γ is near 1, Q-learning spends much of its time converging to the large ρ-term of $V^{\pi^*}_\gamma$, which is invariant of s, whereas the σ-term is the one needed for action choice. During this time, the true values of σ necessary for action selection may be entirely obscured by approximation error, causing poor performance. R-values, in contrast, have no contribution from ρ. As a result, the values, which begin at zero, already reflect their ρ-term, and need only converge on σ.

6.2 Faster Propagation of Rewards

Many researchers have pointed out that information about rewards can be propagated very slowly across states by Q-learning [10, 16]. In particular, we note that the ρ-terms of the Q-values, though constant over a state space, may be updated only locally, and one state at a time. By contrast, R-learning uses ρ to effectively store a common ρ-term for all its action-values. This term is updated on every iteration, and lets information be propagated instantly throughout the state space. Section 7.2 presents experimental data attesting to the resulting speedup.

6.3 Value Disambiguation

Even for MDP's where γ-optimal policies are T-optimal for small γ—in which case one would hope for Q-learning to converge rapidly despite the above concerns—there turn out to be compelling reasons to prefer R-learning. Let us examine any case where temporal credit assignment is necessary—where some T-suboptimal action gives immediate reward as large as that of the T-optimal action. That is, for some state s of an MDP with T-optimal policy π, $Q_T^{\pi^*}(s,a) > Q_T^{\pi^*}(s,b)$, but $r(s,b) \geq r(s,a)$. Then one may show that there is a value γ_0 such that $Q_{\gamma_0}^{\pi^*}(s,a) = V_{\gamma_0}^{\pi^*}(s,b)$, and for which $Q_\gamma^{\pi^*}(s,a) > Q_\gamma^{\pi^*}(s,b)$ holds of all $\gamma_0 \leq \gamma < 1$.[5] To be sure to prefer the T-optimal action, one must choose a γ within this interval. This granted, one would like to choose a γ at the very bottom of the range so as to speed convergence. But choosing γ arbitrarily close to γ_0 will result in an arbitrarily small difference between $Q_\gamma^{\pi^*}(s,a)$ and $Q_\gamma^{\pi^*}(s,b)$.[6] This is problematic for at least the following two reasons:

First, for stochastic MDP's, approximation errors of Q-values are due not only to the process of value iteration, but also to the Monte Carlo sampling it employs. When differences in true action-values for competing actions are small they are more likely to be obscured by such errors, which may cause suboptimal actions to be chosen. An example of this phenomenon is presented in Section 7.1.

Secondly, many popular exploration methods select actions stochastically according to their relative action-values [6, 16, 17]. In such cases, an action whose Q-value differs from the optimal one by a small amount will be chosen almost as frequently as the optimal action. This may result in a substantial loss of cumulative reward.

One may see that R-learning minimizes these problems, because using average-adjusted value maximizes the differences in value in the following sense:

$$Q_\sigma^{\pi^*}(s,a) - Q_\sigma^{\pi^*}(s,b) = \sup_{\gamma_0 \leq \gamma < 1} \left\{ Q_\gamma^{\pi^*}(s,a) - Q_\gamma^{\pi^*}(s,b) \right\}$$

In summary, choosing γ to be large for Q-learning results in poor initial estimates and slow convergence, while choosing γ small, when it does not result in T-suboptimal solutions, may reduce performance dramatically for other reasons. R-learning eliminates the hazards that accompany small values of γ, while using other means to speed convergence.

[5] This follows from the proof of existence of stationary Blackwell optimal policies ([3], Theorem 5).

[6] In goal tasks where nonzero reward is given only upon achieving the goal, this is the familiar problem wherein temporal differencing causes all actions in states distant from the goal to have approximately zero value.

6.4 Linearity of Undiscounted Values

In the case of a deterministic MDP, we may read the recurrence for σ (Equation 8) as telling us that

$$\sigma^\pi(s') - \sigma^\pi(s) = \rho(s) - r(s,\pi(s))$$

where s' is the state reached by performing $\pi(s)$ in s. Since unichain policies have $\rho(s)$ constant, it follows that for regions of S where following π incurs a constant reward, average-adjusted value of successive states encountered will change linearly. By contrast, the γ present in Q-values makes increases and decreases in those values exponential, growing in magnitude with temporal proximity to rewards.

Linearity is very desirable in the case where S is a metric space, and the policy action causes uniform movement along some dimension of S. In this case the R-values for the policy action vary linearly over that dimension, potentially permitting the use of simple and accurate linear interpolation to speed up learning and even allowing learning over continuous state spaces.

Finally, the linearity of σ values can be useful in situations where we want to combine action-values for multiple individual tasks to determine values for a composite task. Singh [14] has explored this possibility for sets of goal tasks.

6.5 Q-Learning Seen as a Special Case of R-learning

Occasions might arise where temporal discounting is a useful feature for any of the reasons given in Section 3.1. As we saw, the discounted value V_γ measures total value in the case where at each point in time there is a probability $1-\gamma$ of an exogenous incident after which all rewards are zero. Given any MDP, we may introduce this assumption explicitly by adding one absorbing state s_{ab} with autotransitions yielding reward zero, to which all actions from all other states lead with probability $1-\gamma$. (Such actions receive their normal reward, since it is only the state they result in that changes.) Accordingly, we multiply all preexisting transition probabilities by γ. Now let quantities marked by a dot denote values pertaining to the modified MDP. We first observe that for all policies and all states s of the new decision problem, $\dot\rho^\pi(s) = 0$, and build this fact into the algorithm by eliminating step 2c. Now by Equation 8 we have, for all $s \in S$,

$$\begin{aligned}
\dot Q_\sigma^\pi(s,a) &= \dot r(s,a) - \dot\rho^\pi(s) + \sum_{s' \in \dot S} \dot P_{ss'}(a) \dot V_\sigma^\pi(s') \\
&= \dot r(s,a) - \dot\rho^\pi(s) + (1-\gamma)\dot V_\sigma^\pi(s_{ab}) + \\
&\quad \sum_{s' \neq s_{ab}} (\gamma P_{ss'}(a))\, \dot V_\sigma^\pi(s') \\
&= r(s,a) + \gamma \sum_{s' \in S} P_{ss'}(a) \dot V_\sigma^\pi(s').
\end{aligned}$$

In other words, $\dot Q_\sigma$ obeys the same recurrence relation as Q_γ. By modifying the R-learning update of step 2b to reflect the recurrence of $\dot\sigma$ instead of σ, we are left with precisely the Q-learning algorithm.

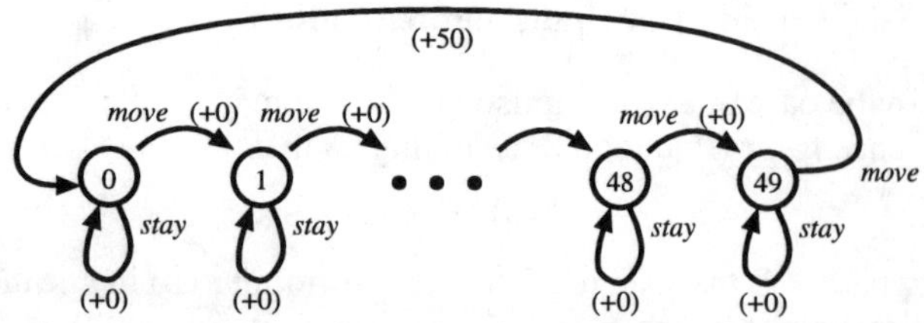

Figure 2: A simple MDP with temporally distant rewards.

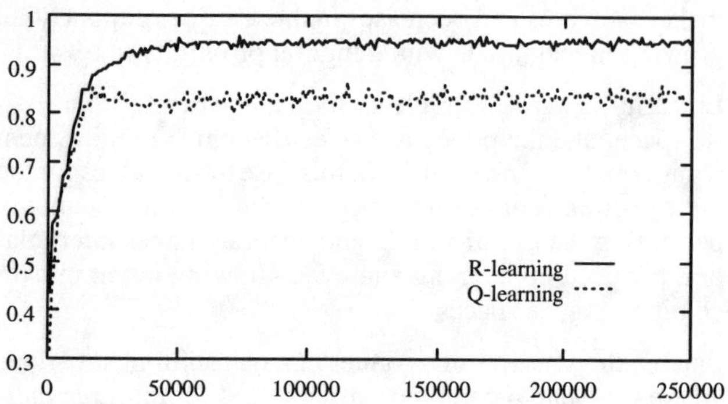

Figure 3: Performance of R-Learning versus Q-learning.

7 Experimental Results

7.1 Value Disambiguation

An initial experiment compared Q-learning and R-learning in the simple domain pictured in Figure 2, modified to yield stochastic rewards that always deviate from the values given by either +1 or -1 (with equal probability). Figure 3 shows the results. The x-axis measures number of actions performed, while the y-axis measures average reward per 5000-action interval. (The results are averaged over 50 trials.) We used random exploration with a fixed probability 0.05 of a random action at any time step; an exploration method that favors actions with near-optimal values would make the advantage of R-learning more pronounced.

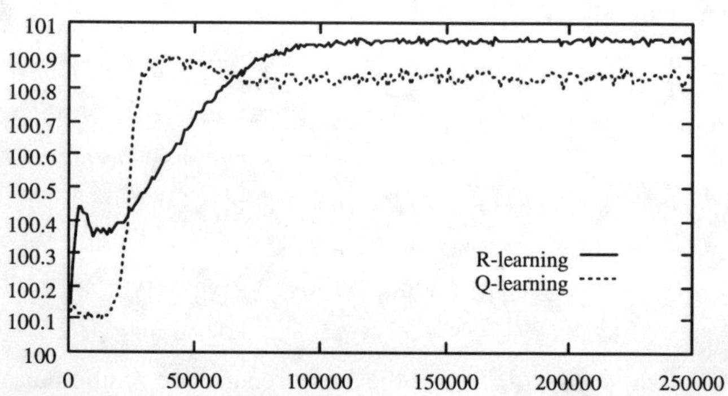

Figure 4: Performance of R-Learning versus Q-learning (all rewards increased by 100).

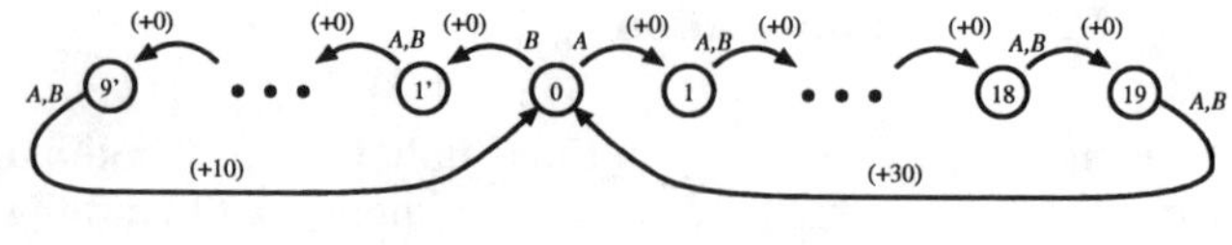

Figure 5: An MDP with two cycles. Action choice is irrelevant except in state 0.

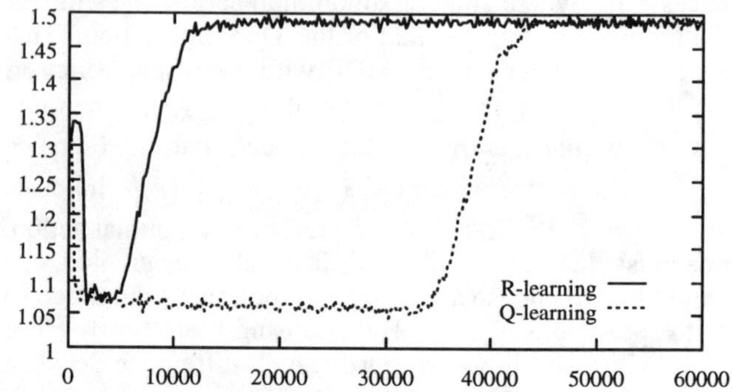

Figure 6: Comparison of learning mechanisms on a MDP with two cycles. Performance of Q-learning is poor compared to R-learning because of ramping.

Figure 4 shows a comparison of Q-learning and R-learning in the same domain with all rewards increased uniformly by 100. Notice the period in which R-learning stalls while its estimate of ρ climbs from an initial value of zero up to the final value of 101.

Both runs use $\gamma = 0.9$, $\beta = 0.2$. Because of the exploration strategy, an optimal policy will have an average reward of 0.95. Note that the fixed β is responsible for the fact that the Q-values never converge to the optimal value.

7.2 Convergence Rate

A second experiment used the double-loop domain shown in Figure 5. Average rewards of the two methods are plotted in Figure 6, compiled over 100 runs. The reason for the poor performance by Q-learning is that the shorter cycle, though it gives less per-step payoff than the longer one, allows rewards to be propagated more quickly. As a result, it's Q-values converge faster than the longer one's, making it look more favorable during the long process of convergence.

These experiments use the same parameters as the previous ones, except that here γ is increased to 0.99 to allow Q-learning to learn the T-optimal policy at all. For larger γ, the effect is even more pronounced: When $\gamma = 0.999$ instead of 0.99, the speedup of R-learning over Q-learning is more than forty-fold.

8 Related Work

In Section 2 we remarked that Q-learning may be used to find V_1-optimal policies in cases where that undiscounted measure is finite. Now we may further observe that in such cases, $V_T^\pi(s) = \langle 0, V_1^\pi(s) \rangle$ and the recurrence for V_σ reduces to that of V_1. In this sense, the theory of total value V_T subsumes that of V_1, and R-learning is a generalization of undiscounted Q-learning.

Whereas Q-learning is an asynchronous, stochastic approximation version of the well-understood dynamic programming method of value iteration, R-learning has no such precise analog in the literature. Though several successive approximation algorithms exist for computing σ, none of them approximate ρ explicitly; this added complexity present in R-learning, while making it more robust in the multichain case, necessitates new methods of analysis, which we are working to develop. We know of no successive approximation methods in the Dynamic Programming literature for handling the multichain case.

We have recently learned of the related work of Westerdale [19], who presents a bucket brigade technique based on the notions of average and average-adjusted value. Since he does not draw any connections to the Dynamic Programming or Reinforcement Learning literature, the precise contribution of this work is difficult to assess.

The general notion that performance should be viewed relative to a standard of reference, which underlies average-adjusted value and the workings of R-learning, has appeared in many places in the psychological literature, as well as in Sutton's Reinforcement Comparison algorithm [15]. A presentation of R-learning from a more psychological standpoint is offered in [13].

9 Conclusion

Until now, most of the work in RL has maintained one standard of performance while using algorithms that maximize another. The discounted algorithms have been well understood, but the performance standards have not: In goal tasks, maximal undiscounted value V_1 has been sought, while, in recurrent domains, high average reward has been the aim. The concept of total reward presented here subsumes these two criteria, and is the basis for R-learning, a method we have proposed to maximize them both. We have used total reward as a tool to gain a better understanding of some of the computational shortcomings of the discounted techniques, and have shown that R-learning may ameliorate many of those problems.

While informal tests have shown R-learning to be applicable to a variety of domains, more empirical and theoretical work is necessary to establish its viability as a robust algorithm for reinforcement learning. Some of this work is currently under way.

Acknowledgements

I wish to thank Nils Nilsson, Rich Sutton, George John, and Moshe Tennenholtz for their helpful comments. This work was supported by an IBM Graduate Fellowship.

References

[1] A. G. Barto, R. S. Sutton, and C. J. C. H. Watkins. Learning and sequential decision making. Technical Report COINS 89-95, Dept. of Computer and Information Science, University of Massachusetts, Amherst, 1989.

[2] D. P. Bertsekas and J. N. Tsitsiklis. *Parallel and Distributed Computation: Numerical Methods.* Prentice Hall, Englewood Cliffs, NJ, 1989.

[3] D. Blackwell. Discrete dynamic programming. *Ann. Math. Statist.*, 33:719–726, 1962.

[4] G. H. Hardy. *Divergent Series.* Clarendon Press, Oxford, 1949.

[5] R. A. Howard. *Dynamic Programming and Markov Processes.* MIT Press, Cambridge, MA, 1960.

[6] L. P. Kaelbling. *Learning in Embedded Systems.* PhD thesis, Stanford University, 1990.

[7] J. G. Kemeny and J. L. Snell. *Finite Markov Chains.* Van Nostrand, Princeton, NJ, 1960.

[8] L.-J. Lin. Programming robots using reinforcement learning and teaching. In *Proceedings AAAI-91*, pages 781–786. MIT Press, Cambridge, MA, 1991.

[9] S. Mahadevan and J. Connell. Automatic programming of behavior-based robots using reinforcement learning. In *Proceedings AAAI-91*, pages 768–773. MIT Press, Cambridge, MA, 1991.

[10] R. A. McCallum. Using transitional proximity for faster reinforcement learning. In *Proceedings of the Ninth International Workshop on Machine Learning*, pages 316–321. Morgan Kaufmann, San Mateo, CA, 1992.

[11] M. L. Puterman. Markov decision processes. In D. P. Heyman and M. J. Sobel, editors, *Handbooks in OR & MS, Vol. 2*, pages 331–434. Elsevier, North-Holland, 1990.

[12] S. M. Ross. *Introduction to Stochastic Dynamic Programming.* Academic Press, New York, 1983.

[13] A. Schwartz. Thinking locally to act globally: A novel approach to reinforcement learning. In *Proceedings of the Fifteenth Annual Conference of the Cognitive Science Society.* Lawrence Erlbaum, Hillsdale, NJ, 1993.

[14] S. P. Singh. Transfer of learning by composing solutions for elemental sequential tasks. *Machine Learning*, 8(3/4):323–339, May 1992.

[15] R. S. Sutton. *Temporal Credit Assignment in Reinforcement Learning.* PhD thesis, Department of Computer and Information Sciences, University of Massachusetts, 1984.

[16] R. S. Sutton. Integrated architectures for learning, planning, and reacting based on approximating dynamic programming. In *Proceedings of the Seventh International Workshop on Machine Learning*, pages 216–224. Morgan Kaufmann, San Mateo, CA, 1990.

[17] C. J. C. H. Watkins. *Learning from Delayed Rewards.* PhD thesis, King's College, Cambridge, 1989.

[18] C. J. C. H. Watkins and P. Dayan. Q-learning. *Machine Learning*, 8:279–292, 1992.

[19] T. H. Westerdale. Quasimorphisms or queasymorphisms? Modeling finite automaton environments. In G. J. E. Rawlins, editor, *Foundations of Genetic Algorithms*, pages 128–147. Morgan Kaufmann, San Mateo, CA, 1991.

ATM Scheduling with Queuing Delay Predictions

Daniel B. Schwartz*
GTE Laboratories, Inc.
40 Sylvan Rd.
Waltham MA 02254
dbs@gte.com

Abstract

High speed packet switched networks provide numerous challenges for machine learning based control. In this work we address the problem of scheduling the transmission of packets in a system supporting multiple traffic types with different delay and loss requirements. We develop an adaptive transmission scheduling algorithm, urgency scheduling, that combines elements of memory based function approximation, reinforcement learning and dynamic programming. The resulting learning algorithm should be of more general interest, especially for problems with continuous state spaces that are sensitive to rare events.

Introduction

Real world queueing systems like ATM networks are potentially a fruitful area for the application of machine learning techniques. Unlike the time invariant, uncorrelated sources characteristic of queueing theory, the pattern of arrivals in these systems are highly correlated in time. Exploiting these correlations, either directly, with a predictive model, or indirectly, as in reinforcement learning, can result in significant performance gains . Queuing systems have another property which demands the application of non-traditional control techniques – the rewards, or more often penalties, associated with control actions are delayed and very non-linear. Dealing effectively with feedback signals of this type requires control methods capable of finding optimal sequences or trajectories instead of just responding to the instantaneous state of the system.

The enormous state spaces, characteristic of all but the simplest queueing systems, suggest the use of a continuous representation of the state variables because of both the resulting decrease in complexity and the generalization that follows from inducing a topology upon the state space. However, the direct application of most connectionist approximation functions is doomed to failure due to the large bias in prior distribution of observed states. As a simple example, consider the M/M/1 queue. In this system, customers enter the queue randomly at rate λ and wait until they reach the head of the queue, at which time they occupy the server for an exponentially distributed interval of average duration τ. Under these circumstances, the probability of finding n customers waiting in the queue at any time is simply (Schwartz 1987)

$$p(n) = (1 - \lambda\tau)(\lambda\tau)^n.$$

The goal in controlling most queueing system is to avoid, subject to suitable constraints, having an excessive number of customers in the queue at any instant. Thus 'congested' states, such as those with high queue occupancies n, are the most interesting from the viewpoint of the control system but also the least frequent. This is a serious problem for most connectionist networks since the most frequent training examples tend to obliterate any memory of the rare ones, especially when trained on-line as required by many sequential decision problems.

ATM Networking

Asynchronous Transfer Mode is a networking technology defined by the telecommunications industry to provide a universal interface to a broadband public communications network. As originally conceived, the goal was to provide a single network interface and transport technology to serve a spectrum of applications ranging from conventional telephony to the interconnection of supercomputers while being parsimonious with network resources. The result is a network based on high speed packet switching of small fixed size cells, each containing 48 bytes of data and 5 bytes of routing information. Because the network is packet switched, the utilization of transmission facilities is much higher than in an equivalent circuit switched

*Now at Motorola, Inc., EL 508, 2100 E. Elliot Rd., Tempe AZ 85284

system, especially in the presence of bursty sources of traffic like data or compressed video. Due to the small size of the cells, queueing delays in an ATM switch can be controlled far more tightly than in a conventional packet switched network, where a small packet from a delay sensitive application like video or voice might have to wait behind a large packet generated by a file transfer.

Efficient control mechanisms are essential if applications with widely varying performance requirements are to share resources as is required to achieve reasonable network utilization. Control in ATM networks is a promising area for the application of machine learning because of both the number of unknowns involved in engineering such a network and the difficulty of analyzing them using traditional techniques. Universal to all control frameworks for ATM networks is the partitioning of traffic into classes based upon their *quality of service* requirements. Here a traffic class s is defined by its maximum allowable queueing delay τ^s_{max} and maximum cell loss probability ϵ^s_{max}, where cells can be lost either by exceeding the acceptable delay or by being discarded as a congestion control measure. For complex queueing systems of this type, congestion is simply defined as failure to meet the quality of service constraints. In this work, the time stamp of each cell is examined just prior to transmission and the late ones are discarded. To understand the role of traffic classes within the network, consider an outgoing link in a packet switch supporting m traffic classes as shown in figure 1. Cells waiting for transmission on the link

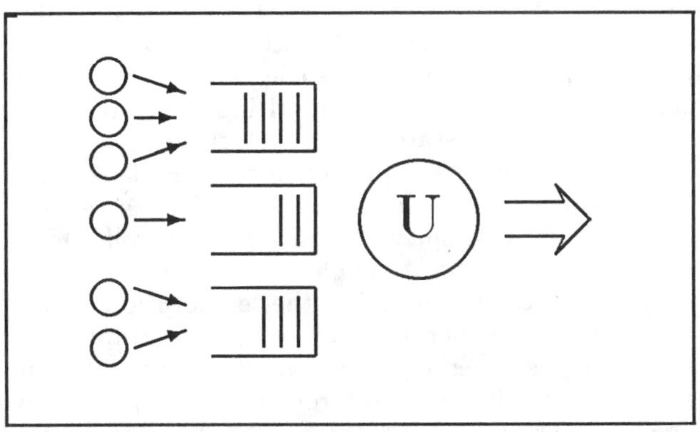

Figure 1: A schematic of an outgoing link in a packet switch with three traffic classes. The sources on the left can be viewed as being different input ports in a packet switch. Sources in the same service class are assumed to have similar characteristics and are combined in a single queue. At each time step, the number of cells entering the system can range from zero to the total number of active sources. In this work, the sources all have hidden internal states. Neither the number or internal states of the sources are visible to the controller U.

are sorted into m fifo queues, one for each traffic class. The output controller must decide in what sequence to service the queues in order to maximize the number of cells transmitted subject to the quality of service constraints and must also, in anticipation of congestion, decide which cells to discard. In this work we will address the former, the cell scheduling problem.

The most common service discipline for a system with multiple traffic classes is the use of static priorities. In a system with two service classes and worst case queueing delays $\tau^I_{max} < \tau^{II}_{max}$ the static priority service discipline is to always service class I if there are any cells in its queue regardless of how many cells are in class II. Static priorities are suboptimal because they do not take the size of the load on each queue into account; when class II is heavily loaded and class I lightly loaded, a better service discipline delays cells in class I so as to reduce the queueing delays for class II cells. A more effective service discipline is Earliest Deadline First algorithm. At each transmission opportunity, the time stamp of the cell at the head of each queue is examined and the cell that is closest to being late is transmitted. When the objective is to minimize the total cell loss regardless of class and late cells are discarded, the EDF algorithm is optimal. When objective is to satisfy separate quality of service constraints for each service class a family of optimal algorithms have been proposed (Peha 1990). However, these algorithms are primarily of theoretical interest because they assume the course of an entire busy period is know in advance and performs a sort whose computational cost is quadratic in the length of the busy period. Practical algorithms can use traffic predictors to produce causal algorithms but must also contain heuristics to reduce the computational cost. For example, the MARS algorithm (Hyman 1991) combines a first order traffic predictor with a heuristic to limit the depth and granularity of the computationally expensive sorting operation.

On-Line Dynamic Programming

In this work, rather than construct a predictor and combine it with a separate algorithm, we have incorporated the predictor directly into the service discipline using model free dynamic programming or reinforcement learning, as it is more commonly known. The resulting algorithm is a member of a class of stochastic service disciplines described by weights α^s where each traffic class s is serviced with a probability

$$P^s = \frac{\alpha^s h(n^s)}{\sum_s \alpha^s h(n^s)}$$

that is proportional to its weight. Here, h is a step function,

$$h(x) = \begin{cases} 1 & x > 0 \\ 0 & x \le 0 \end{cases}$$

and n^s is the occupancy or number of cells waiting transmission in queue s. This family of service disciplines can approximate those described earlier to any degree of accuracy; for example if $\alpha^1 >> \alpha^2 .... >> \alpha^{m-1} >> \alpha^m$ the result is static priorities. Similarly, if $\alpha^s = (\tau^s/\tau^s_{max})^\mu$, where τ^s is the elapsed time the cell at the head of the queue for traffic class s has been waiting for transmission, the earliest deadline first service discipline is obtained in the limit as $\mu \to \infty$. Regardless of the form or functional dependents of the weights α^s, the scheduling mechanism must be combined with a discard mechanism in order to maximize its performance. In all of the work discussed here we used a simple discard mechanism, dropping cells that are late from the head of each queue.

To reduce the computational cost of this algorithm, the weights α^s are only evaluated once every T time steps where time is measured in units of the transmission time of a single cell. The cost incurred in servicing traffic class s during a cycle is a function of the queuing delays incurred by that class; it can be readily described in terms of the queuing delay τ^s_t which is :

- The waiting time of the cell at the head of the queue for traffic class s if it was serviced at time t.
- τ^s_{max} if the cell at the head of queue for class s was discarded at time t.
- 0 if class s was not serviced at time t.

The cost u^s_i incurred over a cycle is then

$$u^s_i = \frac{\sum_{t=iT}^{(i+1)T-1} (\tau^s_t/\tau^s_{max})^{\mu^s}}{\sum_{t=iT}^{(i+1)T-1} h(\tau^s_t/\tau^s_{max})}.$$

where h is step function as defined above and the denominator is thus the total number of cells transmitted or discarded from class s over the cycle. When the exponent $\mu^s = 1$, u^s_t is the mean queueing delay for class s normalized to the maximum tolerable queueing delay τ^s_{max}. As $\mu^s \to \infty$ the cost u^s_t approaches the probability of a cell from traffic class s being discarded during the cycle. The delayed rewards characteristic of this problem suggests basing the service discipline directly upon the infinite horizon discounted estimate of u^s_t, a quantity we call the urgency U^s

$$U^s(\vec{x}) = < \sum_{i=t}^{\infty} \gamma^{i-t} u^s_t > . \tag{1}$$

where $\vec{x}$ is the state vector of the system, as will be defined shortly and the expectation $< \ldots >$ is computed over all possible sequences of states that start at $\vec{x}$. For reasons of convergence, the discount factor $0 < \gamma < 1$. All of the temporal indices in this expression and those that follow are measured in terms of the cycle time T. The policy or service discipline is computed directly from the urgency, $\alpha^s = U^s(\vec{x}_t)$.

To understand how the controller works it is informative to consider what happens when $\mu^s \to \infty$. In this case, the controller assigns the largest weight to the traffic class with the highest probability of discarding cells. By reducing the exponent, the risk of cell loss tolerated by the controller for a given traffic class can be reduced, allowing the loss characteristics of each class to be tailored independently of its delay requirement and the loss requirements of the other traffic classes.

The natural choice of state variables for the controller are the queue occupancies n^s, especially since this is one of the few statistics readily available in real switches. However, in early experiments we found the performance resulting from this choice of state vector to be lacking for reasons that are obvious – the queuing occupancy does not distinguish between the case where cells are just starting to build up from the start of a burst and that where the queue is coming out of congestion. In the former case, the cells can be delayed whereas in the latter they are likely to be close to their deadlines. This problem can be surmounted by adding the waiting time of the cell at the head of each queue at the start of the cycle to the state vector. The resulting state vector $\vec{x}_t = (\vec{n}_t, \vec{\tau}_t)$ is of dimension twice the number of traffic classes in the system. Even with this expanded state vector, the system still has hidden variables due to the unobservability of the sources's internal states.

Computing the Urgency

A number of factors conspire to make direct computation of the urgency intractable; the most obvious is simply the size of the state space. In this work, we discuss an experimental example with three traffic classes where both the queue occupancies and waiting times have ranges of at least 1000, resulting in a state space with at least 10^{18} states, all of which are reachable. Since the controller has no influence over the sources, the dynamics of the system are essentially a random walk through state space to which the controller must respond. Hence the controller cannot speed up the learning process by directing the 'exploration' of the state space. Furthermore, although computation of the urgency is superficially a Markov estimation problem, it is actually a control problem since the urgency directly determines policy through the weights α^s. We rely upon two key algorithms to make the computation tractable :

- The urgency is computed with an on-line learning rule based on the method of temporal differences (Sutton 1988,Barto 1990). Temporal differences learning generates the urgency directly from a sequence of observations without forming an estimate of the transition matrix $P_{\vec{x}\vec{x}'}$.
- A smooth, local representation is used for the urgency. Thus the properties of a state that has never been visited can be inferred from its neighbors.

The Learning Procedure

When compared to the computational cost of full dynamic programming, the method of temporal differences as used here is strikingly simple. At time $(t+1)T$ the change in the urgency is

$$\Delta U^s(\vec{x}_t) = \eta(u_t^s + \gamma \hat{U}^s(\vec{x}_{t+1}) - \hat{U}^s(\vec{x}_t))$$

where η is a learning rate parameter. Note that the update for $U^s(\vec{x}_t)$ is performed at time $(t+1)T$ using $\vec{x}_{t+1}$ and the cost incurred by the transition from $\vec{x}_t$ to $\vec{x}_{t+1}$ as is characteristic of the method of temporal differences. When no cells are transmitted from class s during a cycle its urgency is not updated. The tradeoff involved in using a learning rule of this type as opposed to full dynamic programming is between computation and efficiency. Because full dynamic programming keeps detailed information about past observations in the transition matrix, it can squeeze the most information out of the current observation by combining it with earlier observations of its predecessor states. Learning procedures that lie between the extremes of having no system model and building a complete model are an area of active research (Moore 1992a, Sutton 1990). As described later in this paper, we bridge this gap by keeping a limited record of past state transitions and make strategic use of them to back up rare states.

As posed, urgency scheduling is an optimization problem only in a loose sense. The objective is to transmit as many cells as possible subject to the quality of service constraints but we do not ever explicitly evaluate the link utilization let alone make control decisions on the basis of it. Instead, following the strategy assumed by the earliest deadline first algorithm and its derivatives, we attempt to maximize link utilization by delaying the transmission of each cell for as long as possible. Thus we place strong restrictions on the choice of policy and the optimality of the resulting policy is unclear. However, we can rely upon some of the theoretical results (Watkins 1989, Bertsekas 1989) on the convergence of optimal control algorithms for insight. In particular, we know the controller must occasionally take actions that are suboptimal according to the current estimate $\hat{U}^s(\vec{x})$ of the evaluation function in order to avoid being trapped by a policy that is locally optimal with respect to a restricted trajectory through state space but globally suboptimal. We follow such a program rather crudely by weakening the policy,

$$\alpha^s(\vec{x}) = (\hat{U}^s(\vec{x}))^\beta,$$

where $0 \leq \beta < 1$. This is similar in spirit to weighting the selection of actions with Boltzman factors (for example, Barto 1991 and references therein) since for small values of β, all actions are equally likely and for large values, the queue with the highest urgency is always served. As a default procedure, β follows a linear schedule, starting at zero and reaching one at the end of training. A more sophisticated learning procedure could adjust the value of β in accordance with the reliability of the current estimate of the urgency.

Representing the Urgency

Development of an on-line representation of the urgency proved to be a significant challenge due to the interaction between the service discipline and current estimate of the urgency. A CMAC (Albus 1975) failed at this task due to a pair of interrelated factors – first, instabilities resulting from interference between new and stored observations and second, the enormous skew in the prior distribution of observations as described in the introduction of this paper. The challenge is to develop a function representation and learning algorithm that efficiently utilize rare observations without being overwhelmed by the commonplace.

A powerful approach to function approximation problems of this type is to simply store every data point, generating estimates of the function by retrieving the n data points nearest to the desired point and applying some type of regression to them (Atkenson 1989, Moore 1992b). In its simplest form, a piecewise constant approximation can be obtained using the value of the data point nearest the query point as the function estimate. If the data is stored in a tree structure, like a kd tree (Bentley 1975, Sproull 1991), the retrieval cost is proportional to $\log N$ where N is the number of data points and thus acceptable.

The resulting learning rule is to simply store

$$U^s(\vec{x}_t) = u_t^s + \gamma \hat{U}^s(\vec{x}_{t+1})$$

for every observation. The rate of convergence of the controller is dominated by the frequency of rare events; in the simulations described here typical experiments were 10^8 time steps long. With a cycle length of 64 this corresponds to approximately 1.5×10^6 observations. At approximately 50 bytes per record, this is a substantial amount of storage even by contemporary standards. We circumvent this difficulty by averaging together points that are closer together than a threshold value. When a new observation $\vec{x}$ is within d_{min} of an old data point $\vec{x}_i$ the two are coalesced,

$$\begin{aligned} y' &= \frac{y + \omega_i y_i}{1+\omega_i} \\ \vec{x}' &= \frac{\vec{x} + \omega_i \vec{x}_i}{1+\omega_i} \\ \omega' &= 1+\omega_i. \end{aligned}$$

The weight ω is intialized to one when a point is created. Even with sixteen nearest neighbors in the six dimensional space of this work, the simplex formed by the retrieved data points frequently collapses in such a way that the query point lies outside of it. In this case, simple linear regression is unreliable so we use kernel regression to estimate the urgency,

$$\hat{U}^s(\vec{n}) = \frac{\sum_{i=1}^{N} K(d_i/d_N) y_i \omega_i}{\sum_{i=1}^{N} K(d_i/d_N) \omega_i}$$

where d_i is the distance to $\vec{x}$'s i'*th* nearest neighbor and $K(x) = (1 - x^2)^3$. To de-emphasize data points acquired during the early stage of training when the level of experimentation is high and reliability of the estimate of the urgency low, each data point is tagged with its acquisition time, t_{acq}, which is then used to compute an exponential weight, $\omega \propto \exp(-\alpha(t - t_{acq}))$.

The accuracy of locally weighted regression is sensitive to the choice of metric used to define the neighborhood of the query point. We restricted our attention to metrics of the form

$$||\vec{x}||^2 = \sum_i x_i^2/\sigma_i^2$$

computed using two different methods. The simpler of the two is to let σ_i^2 be the variance of the i'th coordinate of the data used to estimate the urgency. A more complicated procedure with superior performance is to allow the controller to run with the discount factor $\gamma = 0$ in which case the urgency reduces to a simple estimate of the cost u_t^s. We then use gradient descent in the form of the simplex method (Press 1989) to minimize the prediction error ε_p averaged over all those data points whose cost u^s were greater than a threshold value,

$$\varepsilon_p = \sum_{y_i > y_{min}} (y_i - \hat{U}(\vec{x}_i))^2$$

where $\hat{U}$ is the estimated value of the undiscounted urgency at $\vec{x}_i$.

Backing Up Rare States

The rate of convergence of the urgency is dominated by the frequency of occurrence of rare events with non-trivial cost. Motivated by the success of prioritized sweeping (Moore 1992a), we have developed a technique that allows rare states to be backed up without attempting to model the dynamics of the system. Instead, a history of the past behavior of the system is kept, stored without clustering in a kd tree containing every 'interesting' observation of the system. Each record in the history tree contains

- The cost u_t^s incurred in leaving the state.
- Pointers to the records corresponding to each observations predecessor and successor states.

States are added to the history tree only if one of its costs u_t^s exceeds a threshold, RecordThreshold, and states are backed up only if their costs exceed a second, higher threshold, BackUpThreshold. Due to the close correlation between the probability for the occurrence of a state and its cost, these thresholds effectively control the size of the history tree.

When the cost of new state exceeds BackUpThreshold, the first step is to update the urgency as usual and then back up those points affected by this local change in the urgency. To simplify the notation, it is helpful to define some pseudo-code in which each record is a structure whose fields are

- $\vec{x}$, the point in state space corresponding to the record.
- u^s, the costs incurred in leaving this state.
- *pred*, the predecessor of the current state.
- *succ*, the successor of the current state.

In this notation if r is a record then r.$\vec{x}$ is the state vector by which it is indexed and r.pred.$\vec{x}$ is the state vector of its predecessor. If N is the number of points used to estimate the urgency we back up a state $\vec{x}$ by finding its N nearest neighbors, R[1..N], in the history tree. We then generate an update for the predecessor of each of these states by storing

$$U^s(R[i].pred.\vec{x}) = R[i].pred.u^s + \gamma \hat{U}^s(R[i].\vec{x})$$

for i = 1 to N and R[i].pred.u^s > BackUpThreshold.

The effect is as if the new information on the urgency was available when the old transitions happened. In practice, the addition of the backing up of rare states to the learning algorithm is to speed up the convergence of the urgency by a factor of up to five as measured by the learning time required to achieve comparable performance.

Experimental Evaluation

To provide a realistic environment in which to evaluate scheduling with urgency prediction we have developed a model system with three traffic classes that might be found in an ATM switch with 155 Mbit ports serving as a hub connecting multiple ATM LANs. Traffic class I carries compressed video as found in a high performance video phone, class II supports high performance graphic applications as might be generated by CAD tools or a visualization program and class III carries TCP-IP traffic. All of these sources are very bursty, reflecting the type of traffic expected in real ATM networks.

The Video Source

Traffic class I is a video source based on measurements (Maglaris 1988) of the output of a video codec when the face of a human engaged in conversation is used as input. The characteristic feature of this source is the periodic emission of bursts, thirty times a second second, as determined by the frame rate of a video signal. The length of the bursts varies slowly as a function of time as determined by the presence or absence of motion in the subject. In all of the simulation discussed here the maximum queuing delay for this source was $\tau^{I}_{max} = 1000$ and the average link utilization 0.045.

Interrupted Poisson Sources

Both the interactive graphic application and the TCP-IP traffic were modeled by interrupted Poisson processes. Such a model has two states, **on** and **off** and three parameters, ρ, P_{off} and P_{on}. When the source is on, it transmits a cell at each time step with probability ρ. The transition from **off** to **on** occurs with probability P_{on} and from **on** to **off** with probability P_{off} resulting in an average data rate of

$$\nu_{IPP} = \rho \frac{P_{on}}{P_{off} + P_{on}}.$$

Interactive Graphics

In the absence of measurements of an interactive graphics application the parameters for sources in traffic class II were determined from typical specifications for a high performance color workstation, resulting in an average burst size of 2000 cells (approximately 100 Kbytes) with an average spacing between bursts of 100 milliseconds and average link utilization of 0.034. The maximum queuening delay was set to $\tau^{II}_{max} = 2000$.

TCP-IP Sources

The parameters for the TCP-IP traffic as modeled by traffic class III were obtained from experimental measurements of the average packet length on a campus internet (Schmidt 1992). The experimental measurements can be roughly modeled by randomly interspersing bursts with an average length of ten cells or 500 bytes. The worst case delay for this traffic class was $\tau^{III}_{max} = 5000$ and the average link utilization 0.09.

Simulations

One of the primary goals of this work was to produce a robust controller capable of performing well when presented with a broad spectrum of traffic mixes without relying upon adaptation to respond to short term fluctuations in the characteristics of the traffic. To provide the variety of traffic scenarios needed to achieve this performance the controller was trained with sources constantly being created and destroyed, just as would be caused by the diurnal variations in loading in real networks. The lifetimes of individual sources were exponentially distributed with a mean of 250,000 cell times and the source creation events were Poisson distributed with the same mean. If we imagine a three dimensional space whose axes are the number of active sources of each type, the point describing the current source configuration executes a slow random walk which will eventually fill in the space. In order to prevent gross congestion the creation of new sources was blocked if they would have made the average link utilization exceed 0.85. Typical training sessions were 10^8 time steps long at the end of which the urgency for each traffic class was dumped to disk where it could be retrieved for performance testing.

To test the controller, the performance was measured for different combinations of fixed sources and the result compared to that obtained by applying the earliest deadline first service discipline to *the identical stream of traffic.* The use of identical streams of traffic substantially reduces the variance of the ratio of the schedulable volumes when comparing the two service disciplines. The results of a single performance measurement is an ordered pair of vectors $(\vec{c}, \vec{\epsilon})$ where the components of $\vec{c}$ are the number of each type of source used in the simulation and those of $\vec{\epsilon}$ are the fraction of the cells lost from the corresponding traffic class. Overall performance is most easily compared by counting the total number of points $\vec{c}$ for which the quality of service constraints can be met, a quantity we refer to as the *schedulable volume*, following the concept of the schedulable region introduced in (Hyman 1991). Typical performance measurements consisted of 10^7 time steps per source configuration.

Controlling the Total Cell Loss Rate

In these simulations the quality of service constraint was somewhat arbitrarily chosen to be a total loss rate $\epsilon^{total}_{max} < 10^{-3}$. For this quality of service constraint, earliest deadline first is optimal. Based upon a series of experiments, the exponent μ in the definition of the urgency (equation 1) was set to eight for all three traffic classes. Experimental result are shown in table 1. The significance of these results is primarily

Service Discipline	Schedulable Volume
Earliest Deadline First	74
Urgency Scheduling	72
Naive Scheduling	49
Static Priorities	42

Table 1: Experimental results where the objective is minimizing the total cell loss rate. The 'naive' service discipline is obtained by using the queuing delay of the cell at the head of each queue exponentiated by μ as a crude estimate of the urgency to demonstrate that the urgency has significant predictive power.

to demonstrate that urgency scheduling can achieve near optimal performance, at least when the quality of service constraint is minimizing the total cell loss. The results for urgency scheduling are essentially independent of the value of the discount factor γ, an unsurprising result since the optimal algorithm requires knowledge of only the cell at the head of each queue.

Heterogeneous Service Objectives

A more interesting application of urgency scheduling occurs when the most delay sensitive traffic class, in this case video, can tolerate much higher losses than a delay tolerant traffic class like TCP-IP traffic. This is not an unrealistic scenario – video codecs that can tolerate relatively high cell losses have already been demonstrated. For these simulations the loss thresholds ϵ^s and exponents μ^s were set to $(10^{-2}, 8)$, $(10^{-3}, 4)$ and $(10^{-4}, 2)$ for video traffic, graphics traffic and TCP-IP traffic, respectively. As in the previous example, the values of the exponent were adjusted by experiment, building on the obvious assumption of $\mu^I > \mu^{II} > \mu^{III}$. Some experimental results measured as a function of the discount parameter are shown below in figure 2 Urgency based scheduling clearly out-

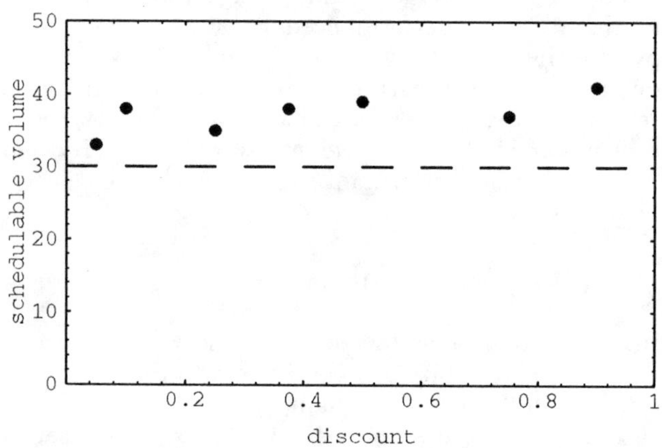

Figure 2: Performance of urgency scheduling with heterogeneous service objectives as a function of the discount parameter. The vertical axis is the size of a subset of the schedulable volume and the dotted line denotes the performance obtained from EDF. In these experiments the cell loss probability was measured over 10^6 time step windows. Failure to meet the quality of service constraints in any particular window caused that source configuration to be removed from the schedulable region.

performs the earliest deadline first algorithm for all values of the urgency, achieving a 25% improvement for $\gamma = 0.9$. In an extensive set of experiments designed to elucidate the worst case behavior we found for $\gamma = 0.9$ urgency scheduling always outperformed EDF by at least 20%.

The observed performance advantage of urgency scheduling, although modest, is of practical interest since for many configuration of sources it corresponds to a real increase in available bandwidth. Furthermore, in ATM switching equipment urgency based scheduling has a subtle performance advantage as follows. When implemented in hardware, the controller can easily be modularized hierarchally to reduce its computational cost. At the bottom and most time critical level a module would be dedicated to executing the schedule from the weights, α^s, acting on a cell-by-cell basis. This module would require dedicated, although simple, hardware. At the next level in the hierarchy, the memory based function approximator used to approximate the urgency can be replaced with a more parsimonious representation like a multi-layered perceptron or a heavily pruned kd tree that stores the regression coefficients for each region. This replacement can reduce the computational cost of evaluating the urgency to the point where, when amortized over an entire cycle, the computational cost of urgency scheduling can be comparable to or lower than simple earliest deadline first. At the top level of the hierarchy where learning takes place the memory based function approximator must be retained, but this representation of the urgency need only be updated in response to rare states and their immediate predecessors. As appropriate, this slowly changing representation of the urgency can be used to update that of the module below it.

Conclusions

We have applied on-line dynamic programming to a realistic, stochastic system and demonstrated it to be capable of matching the performance of the earliest deadline first algorithm, when the quality of service constraints are such that EDF is optimal. For more complex quality of service constraints, we have shown that our algorithm, urgency scheduling, outperforms EDF by a substantial margin. For control in ATM networks, adaptive algorithms like urgency scheduling will be critical to the deployment of complex networks due to large uncertainties in the quantity and characteristics of the traffic that will flow through them.

The combination of memory based function approximators and on-line dynamic programming to stochastic control demonstrated here should be of more general interest. Treating the state variables in these problems as continuous is essential to handling real world problems that would otherwise have intractably large state spaces. The efficient handling of rare events in on-line learning is not a problem unique to queueing systems; rather, it occurs in many control problems and memory based technques may be the only way to handle them.

Acknowledgements

The author would like to acknowledge helpful discussion with Larry Jackel, Rich Sutton and Steve Whitehead.

References

J. S. Albus (1972). A new approach to manipulator control: the cerebellar model articulation controller (CMAC). *J. Dyn. Sys. Meas. Cont.*, 97:220–227.

C. G. Atkeson (1989). Using local models to control movement. In *Advances in Neural Information Processing Systems*, volume 2, pages 316–323, San Mateo, CA. Morgan Kaufman Publishers, Inc.

A. G. Barto, S. J. Bradtke, and S. P. Singh (1991). Real-time learning and control using asynchronous dynamic programming. Technical Report 91-57, University of Massachusetts at Amherst.

A. G. Barto, R. S. Sutton, and C. J. C. H. Watkins (1990). Learning and sequential decision making. In M. Gabriel and J. Moore, editors, *Learning and Computational Neuroscience : Foundations of Adaptive Networks*, pages 539–602. MIT Press, Cambridge, MA.

J. L. Bentley (1975). Multidimensional binary search trees used for associative searching. *Comm. of the ACM*, 18:509–516.

D. P. Bertsekas and J. N. Tsitsiklis (1989). *Parallel and Distributed Computation: Numerical Methods.* Prentice-Hall, Englewood Cliffs, NJ.

J. M. Hyman, A. A. Lazar, and G. Pacifici (1991). Real-time scheduling with quality of service constraints. *IEEE J. Select. Areas Commun.*, 9:1052–163.

B. Maglaris, D. Anastassiou and P. Sen, G. Karlsson, and J. D. Robbins (1988). Performance models of statistical multiplexing in packet video communications. *IEEE Trans. on Commun.*, 36:834–843.

A. G. Moore and C. G. Atkeson (1992a). Memory-based reinforcement learning : Converging with less data and less real time. Technical report, Massachusetts Institute of Technology.

A. G. Moore and C. G. Atkeson (1992b). An investigation of memory-based function approximators for learning control. Technical report, Massachusetts Institute of Technology.

J. M. Peha and F. A. Tobagi (1990). Evaluating scheduling algorithms for traffic with heterogeneous performance objectives. In *Proc. GLOBECOM '90*, pages 21–27.

W. H. Press, B. P. Flannery, S. A. Teukolsky and W. T. Vettering (1988). Numerical Recipes in C. Cambridge University Press, Cambridge.

A. Schmidt and R. Campbell (1992). Internet protocol traffic analysis with applications for ATM switch design. Technical report, University of Illinois at Urbana-Champagne.

R. F. Sproull (1991). Refinements to nearest-neighbor searching in k-dimensional trees. *Algorithmica*, 6:579–589.

R. S. Sutton (1989). Learning to predict by the method of temporal difference. *Machine Learning*, 3:.

R. S. Sutton (1990). Integrated architecture for learning, planning and reacting based on approximating dynamic programming. In *Proceedings of the 7'th International Conference on Machine Learning.* Morgan Kaufman.

C. J. C. H. Watkins (1989). *Learning from Delayed Rewards.* PhD thesis, Cambridge University, Cambridge, UK.

Online Learning with Random Representations

Richard S. Sutton and Steven D. Whitehead
GTE Laboratories Incorporated
40 Sylvan Road
Waltham, MA 02254
sutton@gte.com swhitehead@gte.com

Abstract

We consider the requirements of online learning—learning which must be done incrementally and in realtime, with the results of learning available soon after each new example is acquired. Despite the abundance of methods for learning from examples, there are few that can be used effectively for online learning, e.g., as components of reinforcement learning systems. Most of these few, including radial basis functions, CMACs, Kohonen's self-organizing maps, and those developed in this paper, share the same structure. All expand the original input representation into a higher dimensional representation in an unsupervised way, and then map that representation to the final answer using a relatively simple supervised learner, such as a perceptron or LMS rule. Such structures learn very rapidly and reliably, but have been thought either to scale poorly or to require extensive domain knowledge. To the contrary, some researchers (Rosenblatt, 1962; Gallant & Smith, 1987; Kanerva, 1988; Prager & Fallside, 1988) have argued that the expanded representation can be chosen largely *at random* with good results. The main contribution of this paper is to develop and test this hypothesis. We show that simple random-representation methods can perform as well as nearest-neighbor methods (while being more suited to online learning), and significantly better than backpropagation. We find that the size of the random representation does increase with the dimensionality of the problem, but not unreasonably so, and that the required size can be reduced substantially using unsupervised-learning techniques. Our results suggest that randomness has a useful role to play in online supervised learning and constructive induction.

1 Online Learning

Applications of supervised learning can be divided into two types: online and offline. By *offline* supervised learning we mean the classical task in machine learning and statistics: a set of examples is obtained and used to learn a good approximating function before the function is used in the application. In *online* learning, on the other hand, data gathered during the normal operation of the system is used to continually adapt the learned function.

Online learning has several advantages over offline learning. First, online learning is potentially more robust because errors or omissions in the training set can be corrected during operation. Second, training data can often be generated easily and in great quantities when a system is in operation, whereas it is usually scarce and precious before. Being able to use this data sometimes puts online learning at a great advantage; for example, this was probably the most important reason for the success of Tesauro's (1992) champion backgammon-playing program. Finally, online training is necessary in order to learn and track time-varying functions, to continue to adapt to a changing environment. In a broad sense, online learning is essential if we want to obtain *learning* systems as opposed to merely *learned* ones.

Online supervised learning methods are also needed as components of reinforcement learning systems, for example, to learn evaluation functions, policy functions, and action models. In reinforcement learning one learns by trial and error, so it is essential to learn online. In addition, reinforcement learning usually involves some form of temporal-difference learning, e.g., to handle the credit assignment problem involved in learning an evaluation function. Temporal-difference learning inherently involves non-stationarity because the targets for learning are themselves learned quantities that change over time.

What supervised learning methods are suited to online learning? The two most important requirements are that the methods be *incremental* and able to handle *nonstationary* (time-varying) target functions.

We distinguish two degrees of incrementality. We say a method is *weakly incremental* if it requires relatively little additional memory and computation in order to process one additional example. Most classical machine learning and statistical methods do not meet this standard of incrementality. Methods such as ID3 (Quinlan, 1986), CART (Breiman et al., 1984), INDUCE (Michalski, 1983), and MARS (Friedman, 1988) all take a training set as a whole and perform a computationally intensive process that has to be repeated anew each time examples are added to the training set. Weakly incremental methods include extended decision tree methods such as ID4 (Schlimmer & Fisher, 1986) and ID5R (Utgoff, 1989), and nearest-neighbor and case-based learning methods. However, the memory and (per-example) computational requirements of all of these methods may increase without bound as more examples are seen,[1] which is problematic for long-lived online applications. We say a method is *strictly incremental* if its requirements for memory and (per-example) computation do not increase with the number of examples. Strictly incremental methods include STAGGER (Schlimmer & Granger, 1986) and most connectionist learning methods. Many weakly incremental methods can be converted into strictly incremental variants, e.g., by retaining only a limited number of examples. Such modifications usually involve some loss of the methods' simplicity, ease of use, and theoretical assurances, but are nevertheless an interesting direction of research (e.g., see Moore & Atkeson (1992), Schwartz (1993)).

The situation with regard to nonstationarity is very similar. Weakly incremental methods do not naturally handle time-varying target functions, but most can be adapted to do so. Many strictly incremental methods, on the other hand, are well suited to nonstationary problems. The approach we take in this paper is to explore a particular class of connectionist method, described in the next section, that is both strictly incremental and able to handle nonstationarity. As a challenging benchmark, we present results comparing our approach to nearest-neighbor methods on tasks well suited to nearest-neighbor methods.

Multilayer connectionist methods based on gradient descent, such as backpropagation, are typically strictly incremental and able to handle nonstationarity, but have met with mixed success in online applications. The primary problem here is that of "catastrophic interference," in which training on new examples interferes excessively with previously learned examples. This problem has been partially overcome in practice by storing old examples and retraining on them (Lin, 1992), or by learning slowly and training extensively (Tesauro, 1992), but it remains a significant limitation. We also present results comparing our approach to backpropagation in this paper.

2 Learning with Expanded Representations

The most effective and popular methods for online learning are radial-basis-function networks (e.g., Moody & Darken, 1989), CMAC networks (Albus, 1981), and closely related statistical methods such as Parzen windows (e.g., see Duda & Hart, 1973). Other important online methods are self-organizing maps (Kohonen, 1990), STAGGER (Schlimmer & Granger, 1986), and unsupervised classifiers such as COBWEB (Fisher, 1987), among many others. All of these methods are strictly incremental and able to handle nonstationarity. Moreover, all share a similar two-layer structure: The first layer expands the original input representation into a high dimensional feature space, and the second layer maps that expanded representation to the final answer. The first layer is non-linear and either fixed or learned by an unsupervised learning process, and the last layer is much simpler and is the only part affected by supervised training (see Figure 1). In a radial-basis-function network, for example, the first layer is composed of the radial basis functions, and the last layer is usually a linear mapping or a linear mapping followed by a threshold or sigmoid nonlinearity. In a self-organizing map and in COBWEB the first-layer re-representation is formed by an unsupervised process. This general architecture is the primary focus of this paper. We call it learning with an *expanded representation (ER)*.[2]

The first ER learning system was Rosenblatt's perceptron. Although ignored in most modern treatments, the original perceptron included a preprocessing layer of fixed, random, boolean functions (see also Uhr & Vossler, 1963; Klopf & Gose, 1969). More recently, Gallant and Smith (1987), Kanerva (1988), and Prager and Fallside (1988) have also advocated ER networks in which the first layer consists entirely of fixed, random functions of the original input. They proposed that the random functions be simply linear threshold functions with random weights. This approach may seem naive, but Kanerva's analytic arguments and the results by Gallant and Smith (1987) and Prager and Fallside (1988) suggest that it can perform well. We call ER systems in which the expanded representation

[1] In a sense, the memory requirements of decision-tree methods are always bounded by the size of the most complex possible tree. However, as this bound is exponential in the dimensionality of the input space, it is far to high to be useful in practice.

[2] Grouping and clustering methods such as Chapman & Kaelbling (1991), Mahadevan & Connell (1992), and Mahadevan (1992) can also be viewed as ER methods where the final layer is a lookup table rather than a linear mapping.

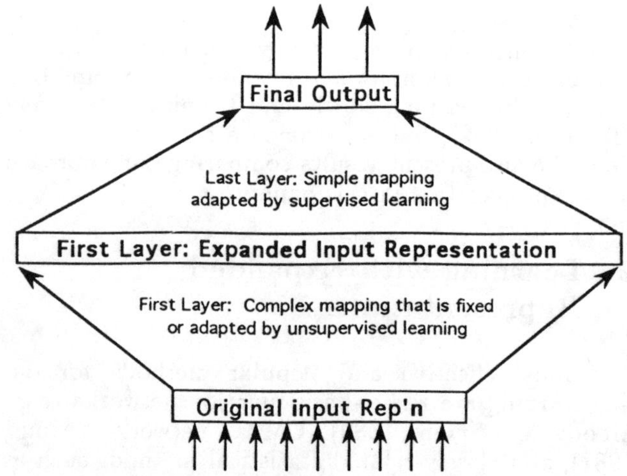

Figure 1: General architecture for learning with an Expanded Representation (ER).

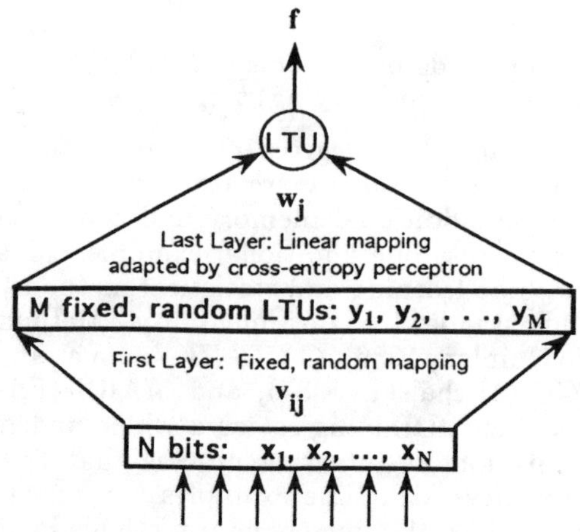

Figure 2: The basic Random Representation (RR) learning system used in this paper.

is constructed with a significant random component *random representation (RR)* systems.

In this paper, the performance of RR methods is measured along three co-varying dimensions: speed of learning, asymptotic error, and number of hidden units required (i.e., size of the random representation). If the number of hidden units is allowed to be arbitrarily large, then it is fairly easy to show that any static target function can be learned to arbitrary accuracy. A more significant result is suggested by Kanerva (1988), who concluded that the speed of learning also becomes very good as the number of hidden units increases, approaching that of nearest-neighbor methods. We present empirical results for a specific RR system that confirm this prediction.

The key question, however, is how many hidden units are needed to obtain desirable speed and accuracy properties? If the number required grows too rapidly with, say, the size of the original input space, or the complexity of the target function, then these methods would be impractical. Gallant and Smith (1987) showed that good results could be obtained with a few hundred hidden units on s set of tasks from the neural network literature such as 7-input parity and right-shift. Is a few hundred a lot? Certainly it is more than is used in typical connectionist networks, but it is no challenge to the memory capacity of today's computers, even conventional serial ones. As proponents of other memory-intensive learning methods have pointed out, memory is cheap; we should not be stingy with our hidden units. Nevertheless, we still seek to obtain the best performance possible with the fewest number of hidden units. We present several innovations that appear to improve this tradeoff for ER systems.

3 A Basic RR Network

In this section we describe a basic RR network based on linear threshold units (LTUs) which we evaluate and extend in subsequent experiments. This system is very close to that described by Gallant and Smith (1987).

The RR system is shown schematically in Figure 2, as an instance of the general architecture of Figure 1. There are n inputs denoted $x_1, x_2, \ldots, x_n$ ($x_i \in \{0,1\}$) and m hidden units. The hidden units are LTUs, meaning that each unit j is connected to each input by a weight $v_{ij} \in \Re$, and its output y_j is given by

$$y_j = \begin{cases} 1, & \text{if } \sum_{i=1}^{n} v_{ij} x_i \geq \theta_j; \\ 0, & \text{else.} \end{cases} \tag{1}$$

For now the weights v_{ij} will be fixed and chosen as either $+1$ or -1, with equal probability. Each unit has one input pattern to which it responds maximally, sometimes called its *prototype*, or address. The prototype for unit j is the input pattern with $x_i = 1$ for those i where $v_{ij} = +1$ and $x_i = 0$ where $v_{ij} = -1$. The threshold θ_j is chosen so that the unit will be active ($y_j = 1$) if slightly more than half of the input bits match the prototype, i.e.,

$$\theta_j = S_j^{min} + \beta n, \tag{2}$$

where S_j^{min} is the minimum possible value for the jth unit's weighted sum (S_j^{min} is just minus the number of the unit's negative weights) and β is the proportion of the bits that have to match the prototype ($\beta = 0.6$ in all but one of the experiments reported in this paper).

The final unit of our basic RR network is also an LTU. Its output f is given by

$$f = \begin{cases} 1, & \text{if } \sum_{j=0}^{m} w_j y_j \geq 0 \\ 0, & \text{else,} \end{cases} \tag{3}$$

where $w_j \in \Re$, $j = 1, \ldots, m$, are weights from each hidden unit to the final LTU. The 0th weight, w_0, acts as a negative threshold or bias; the corresponding input signal y_0 is defined always to be 1. All of the weights are initially zero and then adjusted according to a normalized, cross-entropy perceptron rule:

$$\Delta w_j = \frac{\alpha}{N}(f^* - p)y_j, \tag{4}$$

where $\alpha > 0$ is a learning-rate parameter ($\alpha = 1$ in all experiments reported in this paper), N is the number of hidden units that are active ($N = \sum_{k=0}^{m} y_k^2$), f^* is the target value for the current example, and p is the estimated probability that $f^* = 1$, given by

$$p = \frac{1}{1 + e^{-\sum_{j=0}^{m} w_j y_j}}. \tag{5}$$

This learning rule is a version of the perceptron suited to binary classification problems (Hinton, 1989). If the overall problem were instead one of minimizing squared error, then an LMS or normalized LMS rule would be more appropriate (see Section 7). This is an online learning procedure because the learning rule (4) is applied once to each example as it is received.

4 Performance vs Representation Size

The first experiment evaluated the learning performance of the basic RR network as a function of m, the size of the expanded representation in number of random LTUs. We designed the tasks to be suitable for solution by nearest-neighbor methods, so that these methods could serve as challenging benchmarks to the performance of the RR methods.

The tasks were generated randomly as follows. Each input consisted of 16 randomly generated bits, of which 8 were designated as relevant and 8 as irrelevant. For each task, 8 prototypical inputs were also generated and half assigned a target bit of 1 and half a target bit of 0. To determine the target for a randomly generated 16-bit input, it was compared to each of the prototypical inputs. The prototypical input that was closest in hamming distance (based only on the relevant bits) was selected and its target bit used as the target for the input. Ties were broken according to an arbitrary ordering of the prototypical inputs. Finally, noise was introduced by flipping the target bit on a random 5% of the examples.

The basic RR network was run on this problem with random representations ranging in size from $m = 25$ to $m = 5000$. We also ran a simple nearest-neighbor method called *1NN* on this problem. In this method, for each new input we first found its ***nearest neighbor***, the previously experienced input closest to it in hamming distance (using all 16 bits). The guess for the new input was then the same as the target bit stored with the nearest neighbor. Ties were broken in favor of the most recent nearest neighbor. Finally, we also ran on this problem a single cross-entropy perceptron using the original input representation. The performance of this perceptron tells us the extent to which the problem is solvable by a linear method.

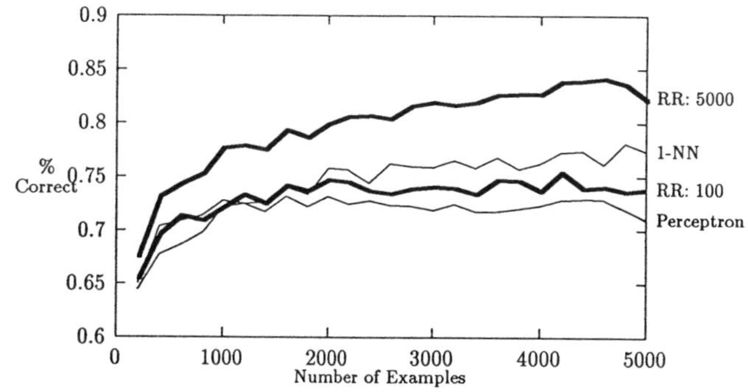

Figure 3: Learning curves on the first task.

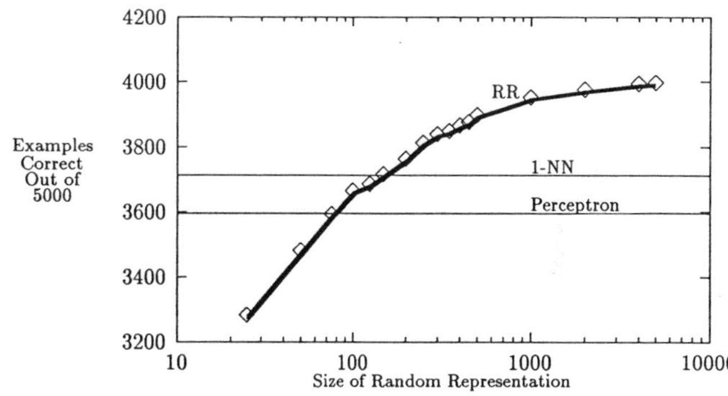

Figure 4: Performance vs. rep'n size on the first task.

Each algorithm was run for 5000 examples. The number of correct guesses by each algorithm was averaged over blocks of 200 examples and then over 20 repetitions of the whole procedure to obtain the learning curves shown in Figure 3. This figure shows the behavior of the RR algorithm with a small representation ($m = 100$) and with a large representation ($m = 5000$). In general, the performance of the method improves with larger representations. Figure 4 is a summary graph that plots the total number of examples guessed correctly by the RR methods as a function of representation size. The flat lines show the performance levels of the perceptron and of the 1NN method. The RR method performed better than both the perceptron and the 1NN method as long as the representation was larger than about 200 units.

Note that the performance of the RR method only improves as the number of hidden units increases. This behavior may be surprising to those accustoming to thinking that excessive memory results in "memorization" of the training examples and poor generalization to new ones. In all of our work with online training with RR systems we have never found this to be

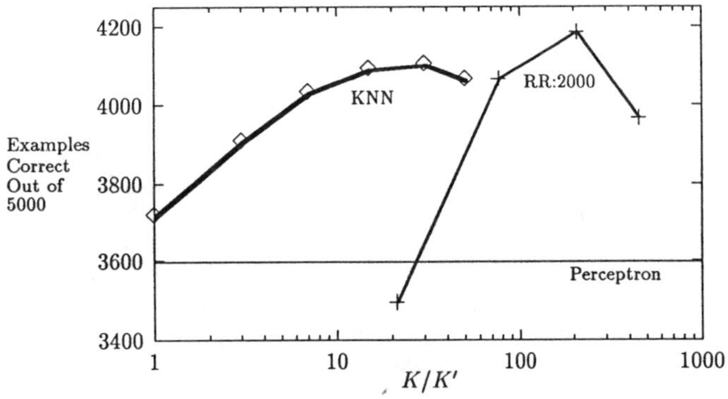

Figure 5: KNN vs. RR on the first task, varying the number of neighbors (KNN) or the average number of active hidden units (RR). For RR, the total number of hidden units was 2000.

a problem.[3] Accordingly, we have not sought ways of simplifying RR networks (e.g., removing little-used hidden units) in the hope of improving generalization.

The 1NN method performs relatively poorly on this task in part because the task is noisy and includes irrelevant input dimensions. In these cases, nearest-neighbor methods perform better if they are based not on the single nearest neighbor, but on the majority recommendation of several near neighbors. These are called K-nearest-neighbor (KNN) methods, where K is the number of neighbors considered. Figure 5 shows the total performance of a KNN method as a function of K. If K was chosen within the right range, then the KNN method performed better than the 1NN method.

The β parameter of the RR methods plays a role similar to that of K. β determines the average number of hidden units that respond to an input pattern, which we here call K'. The K' hidden units that respond together determine the network's output, much as the K nearest neighbors together determine the output of the KNN method. In fact, the effects of K and K' on the performance of the two method is very similar, as shown in Figure 5. Within the right range of their respective parameters, the two methods perform roughly equally as well.

5 Unsupervised Learning

The preceding experiments showed that randomly constructed features, if sufficiently numerous, can be useful in learning arbitrary functions. However, the method as presented so far is potentially inefficient. For example, depending on the input distribution, it is possible for many of the randomly-constructed LTUs to be always active or always inactive. Such units do not contribute to learning because they cannot discriminate between inputs. Additionally, units that are active too often can slow learning by causing excessive generalization between inputs with different targets.

[3]This is may be due more to the use of online training than to the use of RR methods

Ideally, one would like to construct hidden units whose frequency of activation is normalized to fall within a desirable range, neither too rare nor too common. Because this sort of normalization is based purely on the input distribution, without reference to the targets, it is a form of *unsupervised learning*. It is also desirable to normalize the *density* of activation, that is, the number of unit's that are active at one time. We don't want all the units to be active or inactive at the same times because then they are redundant.

In this section we explore the ability of simple unsupervised learning processes to reduce the size of the representation required by RR methods. It has long been recognized that unsupervised processes can improve the representation used by subsequent linear learning processes. Competitive learning methods (Rumelhart and Zipser, 1986; Kohonen, 1990) have been widely used for this purpose. Sanger (1992), Oja (1983), Linsker (1988), and Földiák (1990) have all argued that the activity of hidden units should be uncorrelated, and have proposed learning methods that detect and eliminate correlations. A significant disadvantage of these latter methods is that they require communication and memory between each pair of units. Generating hidden units at random, as in RR methods, can be seen as an attempt to produce a similar result with no communication at all, relying on statistical properties to ensure that no hidden units are extremely similar.

In this and the following experiments we applied two unsupervised learning techniques. Their overall goal was to keep the frequency and density of activity (as defined above) within a desirable range. Unsupervised learning occurred online, at the same time as supervised learning proceeded in the final layer.

To normalize the frequency of activation of a unit, j, we continually estimated the proportion $\bar{y}_j$ of examples on which it was active ($y_j = 1$):

$$\bar{y}_j \leftarrow \lambda \bar{y}_j + (1-\lambda) y_j, \qquad (6)$$

where $\lambda = 0.99$. Our objective was to keep the frequency of activation at $25\% \pm 5\%$. Thus, whenever the estimate $\bar{y}_j$ fell below 0.2 we decremented the threshold θ_j by ϵ, so that the unit would come on more often. Whenever the estimate rose above 0.3, we incremented the threshold by ϵ, so that the unit would come on less often. In the following experiments we used $\epsilon = 0.001$.

To normalize the density—the proportion of units active at one time—we adjusted the weights of each unit so that they would respond maximally to different portions of the input space. As with frequency, we sought to keep the density at $25\% \pm 5\%$. If the density on some time step was less than 0.2 (less than 20% of

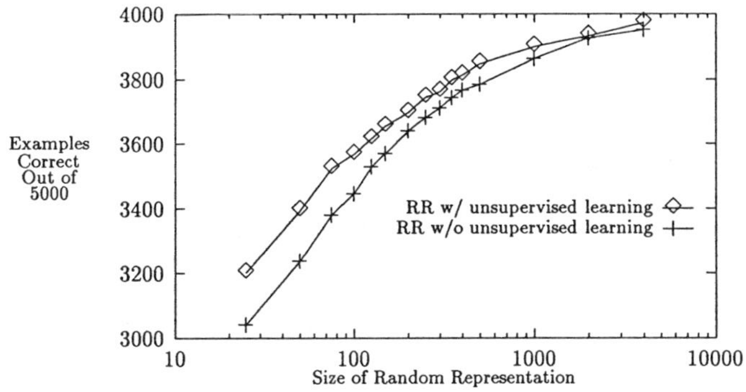

Figure 6: Comparison of RR methods with and without unsupervised learning on a task with many unchanging input bits.

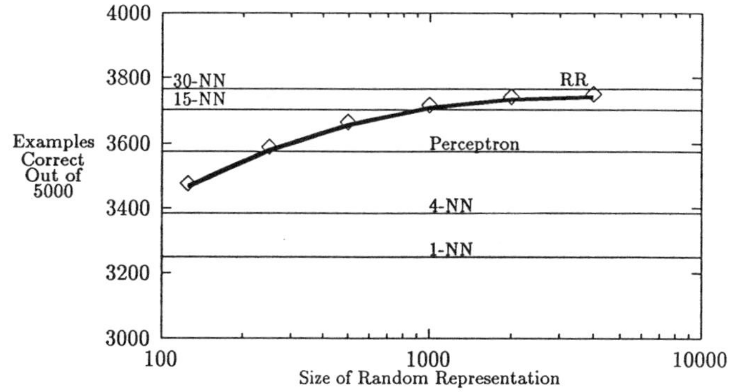

Figure 7: Performance on a task with many irrelevant input bits.

the units active) then it was considered too low, and some of the inactive units were selected and changed so as to become more responsive to that time step's input pattern. Each inactive unit was selected for being changed with a probability of 0.0001. Selected units were changed by selecting at random one of their weights that did not agree with the input pattern and flip it so that it did agree. If the selected bit was 1 and the weight was $v = -1$, then the weight was flipped to $v = +1$, and if the input bit was 0 and the weight $+1$, then the weight was flipped to -1. In either case the unit's threshold θ was decreased by 1 so that the primary effect was on density (when the unit comes active) rather than frequency. Conversely, if the density on some time step was greater than 0.3, then it was considered too high, and in a symmetrical way we picked some units at random and flipped one of their bits so that it did *not* agree with the current input. In this case the selection probability was 0.0005, and the threshold was increased by 1 rather than decreased.

The next experiment was designed to directly assess the benefits to the RR algorithm of the unsupervised adaptations. The task was the same as the first experiment (8 relevant inputs, 8 irrelevant) except that 16 additional inputs were added that were always 1. This was done as a simple way to generate tasks with a nonuniform input distribution. Note that in the first experiment all input patterns were equally likely. Such a uniform input distribution is a favorable case for RR approaches and is the case used in most of Kanerva's analyses and Gallant and Smith's experiments. When the distribution is instead *non*uniform, many of the randomly constructed units may respond most strongly to parts of the input space that never occur, or that occur too often. It is here that unsupervised learning may have a significant effect.

Figure 6 summarizes the performance of the RR algorithm with and without unsupervised learning at a variety of representation sizes. The graph shows the numbers of examples correctly guessed by the algorithm out of 5000, plotted against representation size. Within the range where the size of the representation has an effect on performance, unsupervised learning permits the representation to be reduced by roughly 40%.

6 Many Irrelevant Inputs

One of the strengths claimed for RR methods is that they are relatively unaffected by irrelevant inputs. Other online learning methods such as radial basis functions are known to have great difficulty with irrelevant inputs (e.g., Hartman and Keeler, 1991). As we show next, irrelevant inputs also cause difficulties for nearest-neighbor methods.

This experiment was identical to the first experiment (8 relevant input bits, 8 target prototypes, 5000 steps per run, 20 runs) except that it used 22 irrelevant input bits instead of 8. The summary results for the RR method with unsupervised learning and for the KNN methods are shown in Figure 7. In this experiment the KNN method performed worse than the RR method at most values of K tried, and much worse at low values of K.

7 RR vs Backpropagation

The backpropagation algorithm has been widely criticized as being poorly suited to online learning because it learns too slowly, requires repeated passes through the training set, and generalizes too much between examples. This final experiment is meant to briefly illustrate these problems and show that the RR method does not suffer from them.

We sought a simple class of problems well suited to solution by both backpropagation and RR methods. The basic idea was to learn to replicate the behavior of a randomly constructed network. This *target network* consisted of three LTUs, each of which had connections to three randomly selected inputs. The weights of the connections were set to +1 or −1 with equal probability, and each LTU's threshold was set so that the LTU was active and inactive with roughly equal probability. The LTU output values were +1 for active and −1 for inactive. The final output of the target network was determined by a linear unit with connections to each LTU (and to a constant bias input) weighted either +1 or −1 with equal probability. There were 9 binary inputs signals, which took on the values +1 and −1 with equal probability. 50 tasks were created in this way and used to test all algorithms and parameter values. All algorithms were run for 500 examples.

For the backpropagation algorithm, networks with 4, 40, and 400 hidden units were used. The RR method was run with a range of representation sizes from 10 to 4000. Unsupervised learning was not used in this experiment. For backpropagation, the final layer consisted of a single linear unit. The RR method was adapted from the binary classification form described earlier to a minimum squared error form by replacing equations (3) and (5) with a normalized weighted sum (weighted average):

$$f = p = \frac{\sum_{j=0}^{m} w_j y_j}{\sum_{i=0}^{m} y_j}. \qquad (7)$$

For the backpropagation method, many different values were tried for the learning rates for the first and second layers, and for the variance of the gaussian distribution of initial weights. The results we report are for the best values found. Momentum was not used.

Figure 8 shows average learning curves for the RR method with representation sizes of 100 and 1000, and for backpropagation with 4, 40, and 400 hidden units. The backpropagation results shown are for the best parameter values found after a substantial search. Higher numbers of hidden units were not explored due to the computational expense, but the general trend of the data was toward worse performance at higher numbers of hidden units.

On might wonder why RR methods do so much better than backpropagation on this task. A backpropagation network with a large number of hidden units, and whose initial random weights are chosen with a large variance is in fact almost equivalent to a RR network, However, in this case roughly half the units are on for each input pattern resulting in excessive generalization between input patterns. To get best performance from backpropagation, the number of hidden units must be chosen carefully, neither too small nor too big.

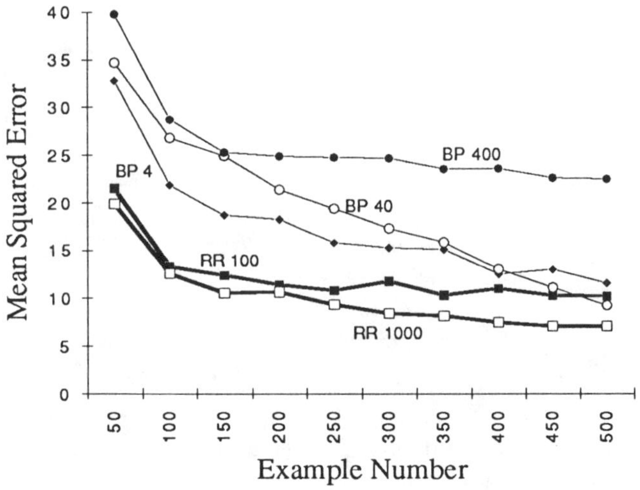

Figure 8: RR vs. Backpropagation.

8 Conclusions

In this paper we have begun to experimentally evaluate the performance and utility of random-representation methods for online learning. Our results significantly extend what was previously known about RR methods in that:

- We have shown a rough parity between the performance of RR methods and nearest-neighbor methods, without requiring unreasonably large random representations. This is a promising result because RR methods are more immediately suitable for online learning tasks than nearest-neighbor methods, which are neither strictly incremental nor easily adapted to nonstationary problems. This general result was predicted by Kanerva (1988) for a related system, but had not previously been shown.
- Our results show that RR methods can handle moderately high dimensional input spaces with many irrelevant inputs (e.g., 22 irrelevant bits out of 30) with little increase in representation size. This is in sharp contrast with other ER methods such as radial-basis-function networks, which have great difficulties with these cases.
- We have introduced two simple methods for unsupervised adaptation of randomly constructed representations and shown that they can significantly reduce the required representation size on a problem with a nonuniform input distribution.
- We have presented results showing much faster initial learning by RR methods than by backpropagation networks.

These results show that randomness can play a surprisingly useful role in the search for good representations. Random selection is easy to implement, and, suitably biased, can be an effective search strategy for high-dimensional spaces. Rather than trying to follow gradients, or proposing a small number of carefully chosen features, why not generate a great many at random? What is lost in missteps may be more than made up by the freedom to take simultaneous large steps in a wide variety of directions.

For future work, we are interested in applications to inherently online tasks, such as reinforcement learning tasks, in extensions to continuous inputs and continuous hidden-unit weights, in data-driven methods for biasing the generation of hidden-units (e.g., as in Rogers (1990)), and in multi-layer RR systems. In this paper we have shown that network and nearest-neighbor methods can yield surprisingly similar performance. Does this similarity of performance reflect a deeper similarity between these superficially very different approaches? In our current work we are exploring algorithms that further blur the distinctions between these two classes of methods, in the attempt to get all the advantages of both.

Acknowledgments

We gratefully acknowledge the helpful comments we have received from Dan Schwartz, Ming Tan, Richard Yee, Chris Atkeson, and the ML93 reviewers.

References

Albus, J.S. (1981) *Brain, Behavior, and Robotics.* Peterborough, NH: Byte Books. Chapter 6, pp. 139–179.

Breiman, L., Friedman, J., Olshen, R., Stone, C.J. (1984) *Classification and Regression Trees.* Belmont, California: Wadsworth.

Duda, R.O., Hart, P.E. (1973) *Pattern Classification and Scene Analysis.* New York: Wiley.

Fisher, D.H. (1987) Knowledge acquisition via incremental conceptual clustering. *Machine Learning 2*: 139–172.

Földiák, P. (1990) Forming sparse representations by local anti-Hebbian learning. *Biological Cybernetics 64*: 165–170.

Friedman, J.H. (1988) Multivariate adaptive regression splines. Technical Report 102, Stanford Univ. Lab. for Computational Statistics.

Gallant, S., Smith, D. (1987) Random cells: an idea whose time has come and gone ... and come again? *Proceeding of the IEEE International Conference on Neural Networks.*

Hartman, E., Keeler, J.D. (1991) Predicting the future: Advantages of semilocal units. *Neural Computation 3*: 566–578.

Hinton, G.E. (1989) Connectionist learning procedures. *Artificial Intelligence 40*: 185–234.

Kanerva, P. (1988) *Sparse Distributed Memory.* Cambridge, MA: MIT Press.

Klopf, A.H., Gose, E. (1963) An evolutionary pattern recognition network. *IEEE Transactions on Systems, Man, and Cybernetics 15*: 247–250.

Kohonen, T. (1990) The self-organizing map. *Proceedings of the IEEE 78*: 1464–1480.

Lin, L.-J. (1992) Self-improving reactive agents based on reinforcement learning, planning, and teaching. *Machine Learning 8*: 293–322.

Linsker, R. (1988) Self-organization in a perceptual network. *Computer 21*: 105–117.

Mahadevan, S. (1992) Enhancing transfer in reinforcement learning by building stochastic models of robot actions. *Proceedings ML92*: 290–299.

Mahadevan, S., Connell, J. (1992) Automatic programming of behavior-based robots using reinforcement learning. *Artificial Intelligence*: 311–365.

Michalski, R.S. (1983) A theory and methodology of inductive learning. In *Machine Learning: An Artificial Intelligence Approach*, R.S. Michalski, J.G. Carbonell, & T.M. Mitchell (Eds.). San Mateo, CA: Morgan Kaufmann.

Moody, J., Darken, C.J. (1989) Fast learning in networks of locally-tuned processing units. *Neural Computation 1*: 281–294.

Moore, A.W., Atkeson, C.G. (1992) An investigation of memory-based function approximators for learning control. MIT AI Laboratory Techical Report.

Oja, E. (1983) *Subspace Methods of Pattern Recognition.* Letchworth, Hertfordshire, UK: Research Studies Press.

Prager, R.W., Fallside, F. (1988) The modified Kanerva model for automatic speech recognition. *Computer Speech and Language 5*: 257–274.

Quinlan, J.R. (1986) Induction of decision trees. *Machine Learning 1*: 81–106.

Rogers, D. (1990) Predicting weather using a genetic memory: a combination of Kanerva's sparse distributed memory and Holland's genetic algorithm. *NIPS-2*, pp. 455–464. San Mateo, CA: Morgan Kaufmann.

Rosenblatt, F. (1962) *Principles of Neurodynamics.* New York: Spartan Books.

Rumelhart, D.E., Zipser, D. (1986) Feature discovery by competitive learning. In: *Parallel Distributed Processing: Explorations in the Microstructure of Cognition, Vol. 1*, 151–193. Cambridge, MA: MIT Press.

Sanger, T.D. (1991) Optimal hidden units for two-layer nonlinear feedforward neural networks. *Int. J. Pattern Recognition and AI 5*: 545-561.

Schlimmer, J.C., Fisher, D. (1986) A case study of incremental concept induction. *AAAI-86*: 496–501.

Schlimmer, J.C., Granger, R.H., Jr. (1986) Incremental learning from noisy data. *Machine Learning 1*: 317–354.

Schwartz, D. (1993) ATM scheduling with queuing delay predictions. *Proceedings ML-93.*

Tesauro, G. (1992) Practical issues in temporal difference learning. *Machine Learning 8*: 257–278.

Uhr, L., Vossler, C. (1961) A pattern recognition program that generates, evaluates and adjusts its own operators. *Proc. of the Western J. Computer Conference*, 555–569.

Utgoff, P.E. (1989) Incremental induction of decision trees. *Machine Learning 4*: 161–186.

Learning from Queries and Examples with Tree-structured Bias

Prasad Tadepalli
Department of Computer Science
Oregon State University
Corvallis, OR 97331
(tadepalli@cs.orst.edu)

Abstract

Incorporating declarative bias or prior knowledge into learning is an active research topic in machine learning. Tree-structured bias specifies the prior knowledge as a tree of "relevance" relationships between attributes. This paper presents a learning algorithm that implements tree-structured bias, i.e., learns any target function probably approximately correctly from random examples and membership queries if it obeys a given tree-structured bias. The theoretical predictions of the paper are empirically validated.

1 Introduction

Mitchell defined "bias" to be any prior knowledge that the learner has about the target function that enables it to generalize the examples beyond what it has already seen (Mitchell, 1980). Incorporating declarative bias into learning is an active research topic in machine learning, and has recently given rise to many useful algorithms, e.g., (Cohen, 1992), (Pazzani and Kibler, 1992), and (Shavlik and Towell, 1989). However, most of these algorithms are "general-purpose" or "weak" in that they are not designed to take advantage of the structure of the prior knowledge, and hence, do not always give good results. This paper presents a contrasting approach, which is to design special-purpose learning algorithms that effectively exploit *particular kinds* of declarative bias. In particular, it describes a learning algorithm for "determination knowledge," which is intended to capture the notion of "relevance" (Russell, 1989).

According to Valiant's Probably Approximately Correct (PAC) learning framework, one role of bias or prior knowledge in learning is to constrain or restrict the set of functions that the learner is required to learn (Valiant, 1988). The determination knowledge identifies all the attributes relevant to making predictions about a target attribute (Russell, 1989). The property of determination knowledge that is important to us here is that by identifying the relevant features for a target function, it reduces the set of functions that the learner has to consider, which in turn reduces the number of examples sufficient for learning (Mahadevan and Tadepalli, 1988).

Russell showed that the power of determinations in reducing the number of training examples is even greater when the learner has a set of determinations structured as a tree (Russell, 1989). Tree-structured bias consists of a tree of attributes such that each attribute at a node is determined by a small number of attributes represented as its children. The root of the tree represents the target attribute whose value the learner is trying to predict from the observable input attributes represented at the leaves of the tree. Only the leaves and the root of the tree are observable during training, which makes the learning problem difficult. Previous attempts to implement tree-structured bias had only limited success and restricted scope (Getoor, 1989).

This paper presents a polynomial-time learning algorithm that efficiently learns functions which obey a given tree-structured bias. The teacher provides random examples, and also gives the outputs for any inputs queried by the learner, i.e., answers "membership queries" (Angluin, 1988). The algorithm is proved correct using the PAC learning framework, and the time and sample complexities are estimated. The paper also presents empirical results that validate the theoretical predictions, illustrating the power of declarative bias and special-purpose learning algorithms designed to exploit it. We close with a discussion of related work and future research.

2 Tree-structured Bias

Russell identified a useful notion of bias called "determinations" which specifies the set of all relevant attributes to make predictions about a target attribute (Russell, 1989).

Let an object x be described by a set of input attributes $P_1, \ldots, P_n$, whose values are denoted by $P_1(x), \ldots, P_n(x)$. The task is to predict the value of the output attribute $Q(x)$.

Out of the many types of determinations Russell defined, in this paper, we are concerned with what may be called a "functional" determination (Russell, 1989). This is defined as follows.

Definition 1 *A set of attributes* $\{P_1, \ldots, P_k\}$ *determines* Q*, written as* $\{P_1, \ldots, P_k\} \succ Q$*, if there is a* k*-input function* f *such that,* $\forall x, Q(x) = f(P_1(x), \ldots, P_k(x))$.

Intuitively, the above determination says that some subset of attributes $P_1, \ldots, P_k$ are sufficient to predict the value of Q for any object x.

There are many examples of such determinations: the nationality of an individual might determine his/her language; the model, year, and make of a car determine its list price; the inputs of a combinatorial boolean circuit determine its output, etc.

The most important property of determinations that is relevant to us is that they reduce the set of functions that the learner has to consider by identifying the relevant features. If nationality of a person determines his/her language, then the learner may not consider functions which map different people of the same nationality to different languages, since they are not consistent with this determination. Since learning occurs by filtering out functions which are not consistent with the training examples, the more constraining the determination, the fewer the examples needed to filter the remaining functions.

Russell introduced "tree-structured bias" to further reduce the number of examples needed for learning (Russell, 1989). Tree-structured bias consists of a tree of attributes such that each attribute at a node is determined by at most a small constant number (k) of other attributes, which are represented as its children. The tree of attributes is called the "determination tree," and is given as prior knowledge to the learner. At the root of the determination tree is the "target attribute," whose value is to be predicted, and at the leaves are the "input attributes," whose values are given. The non-root internal nodes or "intermediate" nodes represent "intermediate"

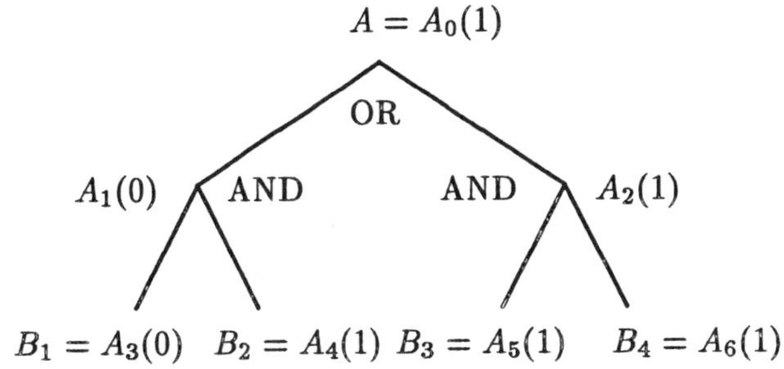

Figure 1: A Tree-structured Bias

attributes, whose values are not observable during the training or testing.

If i is a node in the tree structure T, let A_i represent the attribute at i, and let $i_1, \ldots, i_k$ represent the children of i. $A_i(x)$ represents the value of A_i for the object x. $A = A_0$ denotes the target attribute. T_i represents the subtree of T rooted at node i. We also denote the n input attributes by $B_1, \ldots, B_n$. The input attributes at the leaves of T_i are called the *terminals* of T_i.

For each internal node i, $\{A_{i_1}, \ldots, A_{i_k}\} \succ A_i$, which means that there exist a set of k-input functions f_i such that $\forall x, i, A_i(x) = f_i(A_{i_1}(x), \ldots, A_{i_k}(x))$.

In Figure 1, the numbers in the parentheses represent the values of the attributes for a particular example when the target function is OR-OF-ANDS = (OR (AND B_1 B_2) (AND B_3 B_4)). Hence, $f_1 = f_2 = AND$, and $f_0 = OR$.

Note that without loss of generality we can ignore the internal nodes with a single child. This is because the determinations $\{P_1\} \succ Q_1$, and $\{Q_1, \ldots Q_j\} \succ R$, can be replaced with $\{P_1, Q_2, \ldots Q_j\} \succ R$, getting rid of the attribute Q_1 with a single child without increasing the number of children of any node. Hence, we assume that each internal node in the determination tree has 2 to k children.

3 The PAC Learning Framework

In this paper, we will be using a version of Probably Approximately Correct (PAC) learning, introduced by Valiant, and extended by Angluin (Valiant, 1984), (Angluin, 1988). For a broad introduction, see (Natarajan, 1991).

We restrict ourselves here to learning boolean functions. An *assignment* is a mapping of attributes $B_1, \ldots, B_n$ to their values in $\Sigma = \{0, 1\}$. Σ^n denotes the set of binary strings of length n. Each string in Σ^n represents an assignment, where the ith bit of the string is the value of B_i. Let $\mathcal{F}_n$ be the set of functions from Σ^n to Σ that we are interested in learning. The set $\mathcal{F} = \{\mathcal{F}_1, \ldots, \mathcal{F}_n, \ldots\}$ is called a *function space.*

We assume an oracle called INSTANCE which takes no arguments and generates a random example (assignment) $x \in \Sigma^n$ according to some fixed, but unknown, probability distribution P. In other words, the probability of a particular example x being generated by a call of INSTANCE is $P(x)$.

We also assume another oracle called MEMBER which takes an assignment x as input and outputs $F(x)$, where $F \in \mathcal{F}_n$ is the target function. We call this a membership oracle.

Definition 2 *For a function space $\mathcal{F}$, if there is an algorithm $\mathcal{M}$ that, given an error parameter ϵ, a confidence parameter δ, and the problem size n, for all target functions $F \in \mathcal{F}_n$ and all probability distributions P,*
(i) makes polynomially many calls to INSTANCE and MEMBER, in n, $\frac{1}{\epsilon}$, and $\frac{1}{\delta}$,
(ii) runs for time polynomial in n, $\frac{1}{\epsilon}$, $\frac{1}{\delta}$, and the minimum length of F, and
(iii) with probability at least $1 - \delta$ outputs a function $G \in \mathcal{F}_n$ such that, $\sum_{x \in S} P(x) \leq \epsilon$, where $S = \{x | x \in \Sigma^n and F(x) \neq G(x)\}$

then $\mathcal{M}$ is said to PAC-learn *$\mathcal{F}$ from queries and examples.*

The parameter ϵ specifies the error of the function G when compared to the real function F the learner is trying to approximate. The error is measured by the probability that F and G differ on some example chosen randomly using the same distribution P that was used during the learning. Since the approximation is obtained using randomly chosen training examples, they might sometimes be unrepresentative, in which case the approximation learned from them may not be sufficiently accurate on representative test examples. A learning algorithm must ensure that the probability of this event is lower than the confidence parameter δ.

Definition 3 *A function G is* **consistent** *with the target function F on a set of examples S if $\forall x \in S, F(x) = G(x)$.*

Typically, learning algorithms work by finding a function which is consistent with a sufficiently large set of random examples. The results in PAC learning framework suggest that the sample size sufficient to learn a given space of functions using only random examples varies logarithmically with the number of functions in the function space (Blumer et al., 1987), (Natarajan, 1991). Russell used these results to derive an upper bound on the number of random examples sufficient to learn a function consistent with a given tree-structured bias (Russell, 1989). Since we also use queries in addition to random examples, we derive our algorithm-specific results from first principles, which also gives us a better upper bound on the number of random examples.

4 The Learning Algorithm

The learning algorithm works top-down on the determination tree, learning truth tables for the boolean functions that correspond to the internal nodes of the tree. As it recurs down the determination tree, it also constructs an effective membership oracle for each of the relevant internal nodes.

The main problem in learning with a tree-structured bias is that the intermediate attributes in the determination tree are not observable. The basic idea behind our algorithm is that an intermediate attribute A_i can be made effectively observable by finding inputs for all input attributes except for the terminals of T_i, such that the value of A_i for any input is always the same as or always the opposite of the value of the root attribute. Such an input vector is part of what is called *a distinguishing assignment d(i)* for the node i. A distinguishing assignment for a node i also makes it possible to set the value of A_i to 1 or 0 by assigning the terminals of T_i to some values.

We will see that if the algorithm is not successful in generating the distinguishing assignment for a node i using a sufficiently large sample, then, with a high probability, A_i can be ignored without losing approximate correctness in predicting the target attribute A. The rest of this section describes the algorithm and proves it correct.

We are interested in learning the set $\mathcal{F}_n$ of functions from the values of the terminals $\{B_1, \ldots, B_n\}$ of a given determination tree T to the value of its target attribute A.

The **projection** of an assignment x onto a subtree T_i, denoted by x_i, also called a **partial assignment**, is a mapping of the terminals of T_i to their values under x.

If x and y are two (partial) assignments, $x + y$ is a (partial) assignment that maps any attribute B_i to $B_i(y)$ when it is defined and to $B_i(x)$ otherwise.

Note that $x+y$ is defined exactly for those attributes which are defined for either x or y. When an attribute is defined for both x and y, the value under y overwrites that under x. Hence the operation '+' is transitive, but not commutative in general.

We use z to denote a special assignment where every input attribute is set to 0. Without loss of generality, for any target function F, we assume that the values of all intermediate attributes are 0 when the terminals of the corresponding subtrees are all set to 0, i.e., $A_i(z_i) = 0$ for all intermediate nodes i.

For a target attribute A, and an intermediate node i, an assignment x such that $A(x) \neq A(x + z_i)$, is called a **distinguishing assignment** for i, and is denoted by $d(i)$.

A distinguishing assignment $d(i)$ gives us the abilities to *control* and *observe* the value of A_i. Control, i.e., setting A_i to 1 or 0, is possible because merely changing the values of terminals of T_i can change the target attribute value only if it also changes A_i's value. Since $A_i(z_i) = 0$, $A_i(d(i)_i) = 1$.

Observing the output of A_i for any arbitrary input w_i, i.e., simulating the membership oracle for A_i, is possible since switching the value of A_i switches the target attribute value in the context of $d(i)$. To observe $A_i(w_i)$, we set the terminals of T_i according to w_i, and all other inputs according to $d(i)$. We then observe the value of A, and compare it with that obtained by changing the settings of the terminals of T_i to z_i. If the two outputs are the same, then $A_i(w_i) = A_i(z_i) = 0$, otherwise $A_i(w_i) = 1$.

For the target function OR-OF-ANDS in Figure 1, the assignment 0111 is a distinguishing assignment for node 2. This is because $A(0111) \neq A(0100) = 0$. Hence, A_2 can be set to 1 by setting its terminals to 11. Its value on any input can be observed because it is always the same as the value of A after setting the terminals of A_1 to 01.

All internal nodes i need not have distinguishing assignments. A node is called *live* for a given target function, if it has a distinguishing assignment. If a node i is not live, then, $A(x) = A(x + z_i)$ for all assignments x, which means that replacing A_i with the constant function 0 would not effect the value of A for any input. A non-live node is called *dead.*

The recursive algorithm Learn-Tree (see Table 1) takes a random example set S, a subtree T_i of the determination tree, and a distinguishing assignment for node i as inputs. It returns an approximation G_i to the target function A_i. Given a distinguishing assignment $d(i)$ for the node i, the algorithm searches for distinguishing assignments $d(i_j)$ among all possible $d(i)+c_i$, where c_i's are obtained by setting the terminals of some subtrees T_{i_j} of T_i to the corresponding projections of some example e, and setting the terminals of all other subtrees to 0's. All such assignments for a given node i and example e are called the *corners* C_i of e at node i. In other words, $C_i = \{d(i) + c_{i_1} + \ldots + c_{i_k} \mid c_{i_j} \in \{e_{i_j}, z_{i_j}\}\}$.

If Learn-Tree cannot find a distinguishing assignment for some node i_j, it is assumed to be dead, and the attribute A_{i_j} is set to the constant function 0. If it can find a distinguishing assignment for a node i_j, then it has, in effect, a membership oracle for the attribute A_{i_j}. Hence, it can call itself recursively on each node i_j with a known distinguishing assignment.

For example, consider the random training example 0111 for the target function OR-OF-ANDS of Figure 1. The corners of 0111 at node A_1 are $\{0111, 0011, 0100, 0000\}$. Since $A(0111) \neq A(0100) = 0$, 0111 (or 0011) is recognized as a distinguishing assignment for node 2. Given no other training example, node 1 does not have a distinguishing assignment, and is assumed to be dead. If another example, say 1100, is provided, then it will be recognized as a distinguishing assignment for node 1.

After finding distinguishing assignments, at each node i, the algorithm constructs a partial truth table for the function A_i, denoted by g_i, by generating all possible bit vectors $b_1, \ldots, b_k$, at nodes $i_1, \ldots, i_k$, such that $b_j = 0$ whenever $d(i_j)$ is not known. It uses the partial assignment $c_{i_j} = d(i_j)_{i_j}$ to make the bit $b_j = A_{i_j}(c_{i_j}) = 1$, and uses $c_{i_j} = z_{i_j}$ to make it 0. Then, $g_i(b_1, \ldots, b_k)$ is assigned to $A_i(c_{i_1} + \ldots + c_{i_k})$, which is inferred using a simulated membership oracle for A_i.

In the above example, assuming that no distinguishing assignment has been found for A_1, the first input of g_0 is always assumed to be 0. The truth table of g_0 will only consist of two entries: $g_0(00) = A(0100) = 0$. and $g_0(01) = A(0111) = 1$.

It then calls itself recursively on each node i_j with a known distinguishing assignment by passing itself the distinguishing assignment $d(i_j)$ and the projections of the examples in S onto T_{i_j}. The recursion terminates at the leaves of the tree and returns the values of the input attributes.

In our example, Learn-Tree will be called on node 2 with the distinguishing assignment 0111 and the single input 11. 0111 is found to be the distinguishing assignment for both the nodes 5 and 6. All possible inputs are generated at nodes 5 and 6 to generate the truth table for A_2. The output of A_2 on any input is the same as the output of A with the first two input bits set to 01. For example, $g_2(00) = A(0100) = 0$; $g_2(11) = A(0111) = 1$; Finally, the program terminates at the leaf nodes 5 and 6 by returning the values of the input attributes.

Hence, given a single example 0111, the program learns the function (AND B_3 B_4) for A. This gives incorrect output on 3/16 cases. Given two examples $\{0111, 1100\}$, it will be able to distinguish node 1 as well, and learns the OR-OF-ANDS function.

Theorem 4 *The function output by Learn-tree is consistent with the target function on the input example set S.*

Proof: The proof is by contradiction. Note that if an algorithm finds a distinguishing assignment for a node, it must be correct. However, the algorithm assumes that any node for which it has not found a distinguishing assignment to be dead and stops the recursion at that level. The only inconsistencies between the target function and the learned function are due to this assumption.

Assume that the output function is not consistent with some example $e \in S$. Hence, some node in the determination tree which is assumed to be dead must be responsible for the inconsistency. Let i be one of the farthest nodes from the root such that the distinguishing sequence $d(i)$ has been found, but some of its children are assumed dead. Without loss of generality, let $Q_i = \{i_1, \ldots, i_l\}, l \leq k$ be the set of children of i assumed dead. Since i is one of the farthest such nodes, all the live children of i would be free of dead descendents, and hence their values always match those of the target function.

When called on the subtree T_i, Learn-Tree would have looked for distinguishing assignments for nodes in Q_i in the set $C_i = \{d(i)+e_i+c_{i_1}+\ldots+c_{i_l} \mid c_{i_j} \in \{e_{i_j}, z_{i_j}\}, 1 \leq j \leq l\}$, and failed. This means that

$A(d(i)+e_i) = A(d(i)+e_i+z_{i_1}) = A(d(i)+e_i+z_{i_1}+z_{i_2}) = \ldots = A(d(i)+e_i+z_{i_1}+\ldots+z_{i_l})$.

Since changing the value of A_i always changes the target attribute value in the context of $d(i)$, it follows that $A_i(e_i) = A_i(e_i+z_{i_1}+\ldots+z_{i_l})$.

In other words, assuming that the values of A_{i_1} through A_{i_l} are 0 does not change the value of A_i, and hence, none of the attribute values of ancestors of i. We can now remove nodes i_1 through i_l from possible reasons for the inconsistency, and repeat the same argument for the remaining such nodes. This means that none of the nodes assumed dead is responsible for the inconsistency, which contradicts our initial observation. •

```
Procedure Learn-Tree (S, T_i, d(i))

; Takes the random example set S,
; a subtree T_i of the determination tree, and
; a distinguishing assignment d(i) of i as inputs, and
; finds an approximation G_i to A_i.

; Terminal condition

  If i is a leaf node, Then return a function G_i = A_i

; Find distinguishing assignments for i's children

  For each example e_i ∈ S
    C_i := {d(i) + c_{i_1} + ... + c_{i_k} | c_{i_j} = e_{i_j} if d(i_j)
      has already been found, else c_{i_j} ∈ {e_{i_j}, z_{i_j}};}
    For each i_j s.t. d(i_j) has not been found
      If ∃x, y ∈ C_i s.t. y = x+z_{i_j}, and A(x) ≠ A(y)*
        Then d(i_j) := x;
    End For;
  End For;

; Generate the truth table for i, denoted by g_i

  For each possible bit vector ⟨b_1, ..., b_k⟩ s.t.
      b_j = 0 whenever d(i_j) is not defined
    g_i(b_1, ..., b_k) := A_i(c_{i_1} + ... + c_{i_k})*,
        where, c_{i_j} = d(i_j)_{i_j} if b_j = 1, and
          c_{i_j} = z_{i_j} if b_j = 0;
  End For;

; Recursively call Learn-Tree on subtrees of T_i

  For each child i_j of i
    If d(i_j) is defined Then
      G_{i_j} := Learn-Tree({e_{i_j} | e_i ∈ S}, T_{i_j}, d(i_j));
    Else G_{i_j} := The constant function 0;
  End For;

Output G_i := ⟨g_i, ⟨G_{i_1}, ..., G_{i_k}⟩⟩;
End Learn-Tree;

* A_i(w_i) := If A_i is the target attribute A
              Then MEMBER(w_i)
              Else If MEMBER(d(i) + w_i) =
                        MEMBER(d(i) + z_i)
                   Then 0 Else 1;
```

Table 1: Learning Algorithm for Tree-structured Bias

Theorem 5 *If the number of input attributes in a determination tree is n, then Learn-Tree PAC-learns the function class consistent with a determination tree from queries and examples if it is called with a random example set of size* $m \geq \frac{1}{\epsilon}(\frac{n}{2}\ln 2 + \ln\frac{1}{\delta})$.

Proof: Note that we are only interested in finding a function G such that the probability of its disagreeing with the target function on a randomly chosen example $\sum_{G(x)\neq F(x)} P(x) < \epsilon$. Call all other functions 'bad'.

Since the only discrepancies between the target function and the learned function are due to assuming that some nodes are not live, for a given target function, the function output by *Learn-Tree* is determined by the set of nodes in the determination tree assumed to be dead.

Denote the set of internal nodes which are parents of leaf nodes in the determination tree by L. Since each internal node has at least degree 2, $|L| \leq \frac{n}{2}$. Note that the number of potential subsets of internal nodes assumed to be dead by *Learn-Tree* is bounded by the number of possible subsets of L. A node which is not in L being dead is equivalent to all its descendents in L being dead.

Let $b \subseteq L$ be a set of internal nodes of the determination tree which are assumed to be dead by *Learn-Tree* while learning a target function F. Let G be the function learned. Assume that G is 'bad,' so that for any example e, $P(G(e) = F(e)) \leq (1 - \epsilon)$. However, by Theorem 4, G is consistent with all m examples in S. Since the training examples are chosen independently randomly, the probability of this event is $\leq (1-\epsilon)^m$. Since there is potentially a function G for each subset $b \subseteq L$, the probability of some bad function being consistent with all the random examples is upper bounded by $2^{|L|}(1-\epsilon)^m$.

If we choose m such that $2^{|L|}(1-\epsilon)^m < \delta$, we can ensure that our algorithm does not output a bad function with probability greater than δ. This can be done by making $m \geq \frac{1}{\epsilon}(|L|\ln 2 + \ln\frac{1}{\delta})$.

Since $|L| \leq \frac{n}{2}$, it suffices to bound the number of examples by $\frac{1}{\epsilon}(\frac{n}{2}\ln 2 + \ln\frac{1}{\delta})$.

In the worst case, to find the distinguishing assignments, one query is generated for each possible corner of each example at each internal node. In addition, a query may be generated to fill each entry in the truth table at each internal node. Hence the number of queries is bounded by $(n-1)2^k(1 + \frac{1}{\epsilon}(\frac{n}{2}\ln 2 + \ln\frac{1}{\delta}))$. Since this is also the most expensive part of the algorithm, its complexity is polynomial in n, $\frac{1}{\epsilon}$, and $\frac{1}{\delta}$, satisfying all our requirements. •

5 Experimental Results

The above algorithm was implemented as a program called TSB. There were two previous implementations of tree-structured bias (Getoor, 1989). However, both of them are inadequate to compare with TSB. One of them assumes that the boolean functions at each node are monotone. The other is a neural network implementation which uses Backprop for learning and is too slow to be used on trees of a few dozen nodes. Hence TSB is compared with with ID3, which is knowledge-free and hence cannot be expected to perform as well (Quinlan, 1986). However, the comparison is useful to demonstrate the power of tree-structured bias and special-purpose learning algorithms designed to exploit it.

TSB was tested on a determination tree with $k = 3$. For concreteness, we can think of the target concept as a combinatorial boolean circuit, with a maximum fan-in $k = 3$. The circuit has $n = 20$ inputs. Each training episode consisted of generating a random circuit consistent with the determination tree, training it on a set of random examples (selected using the uniform distribution), and testing it on 25, separately generated, test examples. Results were averaged over 50 randomly generated circuits for each random training sample size, which varied from 0 to 50 with increments of 5.

Figure 2 shows the relationship between the size of the random training sample and the number of queries generated by TSB. The number of queries increased with the size of the random sample, but not too sharply. The total number of queries raised from 8, with no random examples, to 557, with 50 random examples. However, using a hash table that caches the results of previous queries reduced the number of queries considerably. The number of unique queries raised to 158 with 45 random examples and then declined slightly to 148 with 50 random examples. This shows that the number of unique queries, although larger than the number of random examples, is still quite reasonable.

Figure 3 shows the relationship between the number of unique queries and the accuracy on the test sample for TSB. It also shows the performance of ID3 on a training example set which was collected from the unique queries asked by TSB. Hence ID3 and TSB used the same training data, although ID3 did not have the determination knowledge.

Each successive point on the two curves of Figure 3 represents a random training sample of size 5 more than the previous point. With no random examples at all, both the programs learn a function which al-

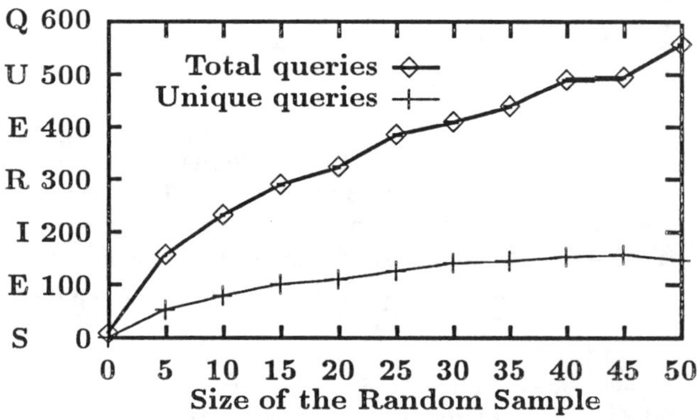

Figure 2: Growth of queries with random examples

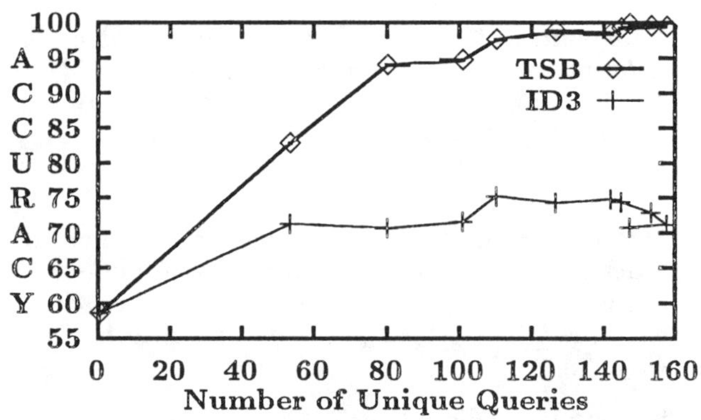

Figure 3: Learning curves: TSB vs. ID3

ways outputs a 0. That gives 60% accuracy in this domain. In TSB, the accuracy reached 94% with approximately 80 (unique) queries (corresponding to 10 random examples). The prediction on the test sample was more than 99% accurate after making 145 queries (corresponding to 35 random examples). In contrast, ID3's performance only increased to a maximum of 75% with 111 examples and then declined with more training. ID3 was run without pruning. C4.5 with information gain heuristic and with pruning performed similarly (not shown here). This shows that TSB effectively exploits its tree-structured bias, and ID3 suffers from not being able to take advantage of this knowledge.

As can be expected, the experimental results of TSB were also much better than the worst-case theoretical predictions. For the above domain, to achieve a 90% accuracy with 90% probability ($\epsilon = \delta = 0.1$), the theory predicts upper bounds of 92 random examples and 13,984 queries, which are much higher than the experimentally determined values of ≈ 10 and ≈ 230 respectively.

6 Discussion and Related Work

It appears that both the oracles used by our algorithm are necessary to implement tree-structured bias. Learning with tree-structured bias from classified random examples is reducible to learning arbitrary boolean formulas (Pitt and Warmuth, 1990), which in turn is reducible to some apparently hard cryptographic problems (Kearns and Valiant, 1989). To see that tree-structured bias cannot be implemented with membership queries alone, consider the class of boolean functions which output 1 on exactly one input and output 0 on all others. This function class can be represented with a tree-structured bias. However, it cannot be learned with membership queries alone, because the program does not get any information unless it chances upon the single input that gives rise to an output of 1. In the worst case, this involves trying each possible input, which is not allowed.

Our algorithm shares some features with the read-once formulas studied in the Computational Learning Theory literature, e.g., (Hancock and Hellerstein, 1991). Read-once formulas are boolean formulas where each variable appears exactly once. If we write down the function described by a determination tree using the functions $f_1, \ldots, f_n$ that correspond to the internal nodes of the tree, each input feature appears exactly once in such a formula. However, read-once formulas only allow a 'base' set of functions such as AND, OR and NOT (and perhaps a few more) to appear in them, and do not allow arbitrary functions described by truth tables. The algorithms for learning read-once formulas first learn the tree structure, and then adopt methods similar to Learn-Tree to learn the functions at the nodes in the tree.

Angluin studied the problem of exact identification of a target concept from membership and equivalence queries (Angluin, 1988). Equivalence queries are in the form of "is the target function the same as G?" If G is the target function, the teacher answers 'yes'; otherwise the teacher responds with a counter-example, i.e., an example where G and the target function disagree. We can design a learning algorithm that exactly identifies the target function for tree-structured bias from membership and equivalence queries using Learn-Tree as a subroutine. In each iteration, the top-level algorithm runs Learn-Tree on all the counter-examples provided by the teacher thus far. It then asks an equivalence query on the learned function. Either the function is correct, or the teacher provides yet another counter-example, and the cycle repeats. Each iteration makes at least one non-live node live, because otherwise the counter-example would have been classified correctly by the previously learned function. Hence the process terminates in at most n iterations.

7 Conclusions and Future Work

This paper is another attempt to bridge the gap between the theoretical tools developed in the computational learning theory, and the problems addressed and ideas developed in the experimental machine learning. We saw that the idea of learning from examples and membership queries can be utilized to learn effectively when the function space is constrained by declarative knowledge in the form of a tree of determinations. This illustrates the power of tree-structured bias in constraining learning, and the effectiveness of special-purpose learning algorithms in exploiting this bias.

One limitation of our results is that they do not generalize to determination *graphs*, where a node might have multiple parents. Multiple parents make it difficult or impossible to independently control their attribute values and find their distinguishing assignments. It is also unclear, whether the determination tree itself can be learned, and under what conditions. The work on read-once formulas is interesting in this context. Another generalization is to allow restricted classes of non-boolean functions at the nodes of the tree. It would also be interesting to look for practical applications of tree-structured bias to a real world task.

Acknowledgments

This research was supported by the National Science Foundation under grant number IRI:9111231. I thank Hussein Almuallim, Sridhar Mahadevan, Balas Natarajan, Stuart Russell, and Manfred Warmuth for interesting discussions on this topic. I thank Sridhar Mahadevan, Chandra Reddy, and the reviewers of this paper for many useful comments on previous drafts.

References

Angluin, D., Queries and concept learning, *Machine Learning*, 2, 1988.

Blumer, A. Ehrenfeucht, A., Haussler, D., and Warmuth, M. K., "Learnability and the Vapnik-Chervonenkis Dimension," *Journal of the ACM*, 36:4, 1989.

Cohen, W. W., Compiling Prior Knowledge Into an Explicit Bias, In Proceedings of Machine Learning Conference, Morgan Kaufmann, 1992.

Getoor, L., *The instance description: How it can be derived and the use of its derivation.* MS report, Computer Science Division, University of California, Berkeley, CA, 1989.

Hancock, T. and Hellerstein, L., Learning Read-Once Formulas over Fields and Extended Bases, In Proceedings of the Fourth Annual Workshop on Computational Learning Theory, Morgan Kaufmann, 1991.

Kearns, M. and Valiant, L. G., Cryptographic Limitations on Learning Boolean Formulae and Finite Automata, In Proceedings of 21st Annual ACM Symposium on Theory of Computing, Assoc. Comput. Mach., 1989.

Mahadevan, S. and Tadepalli, P., On The Tractability of Learning from Incomplete Theories, In Proceedings of the Fifth International Machine Learning Conference, Morgan Kaufmann, 1988.

Mitchell, T. The Need for biases in learning generalizations. In *Readings in Machine Learning* (Ed) Shavlik, J. and Dietterich, T. G., Morgan Kaufmann, 1990.

Natarajan, B., *Machine Learning: A Theoretical Approach*, Morgan Kaufmann, 1991.

Pazzani, M. and Kibler, D., The Utility of Knowledge in Inductive Learning, *Machine Learning*, Kluwer Academic, 9:1, 1992.

Pitt, L. and Warmuth, M. K., Prediction Preserving Reducibility, *Journal of Computer and System Sciences*, Academic Press, 41:3, 1990.

Quinlan, R., Induction of Decision Trees, *Machine Learning*, Kluwer Academic, 1:1, 1986.

Russell, S., *The Use of Knowledge in Analogy and Induction.* Morgan Kaufmann, 1989.

Shavlik, J. W. and Towell, G. G., An Approach to Combining Explanation-Based and Neural Learning Algorithms, *Connection Sciences*, 1:3, 1989.

Valiant, L. G., A Theory of the Learnable, *Communications of the ACM*, 27:11, August 1984.

Multi-Agent Reinforcement Learning: Independent vs. Cooperative Agents

Ming Tan

GTE Laboratories Incorporated
40 Sylvan Road
Waltham, MA 02254
tan@gte.com

Abstract

Intelligent human agents exist in a cooperative social environment that facilitates learning. They learn not only by trial-and-error, but also through *cooperation* by sharing instantaneous information, episodic experience, and learned knowledge. The key investigations of this paper are, "Given the same number of reinforcement learning agents, will cooperative agents outperform independent agents who do not communicate during learning?" and "What is the price for such cooperation?" Using independent agents as a benchmark, cooperative agents are studied in following ways: (1) sharing sensation, (2) sharing episodes, and (3) sharing learned policies. This paper shows that (a) additional sensation from another agent is beneficial if it can be used efficiently, (b) sharing learned policies or episodes among agents speeds up learning at the cost of communication, and (c) for joint tasks, agents engaging in partnership can significantly outperform independent agents although they may learn slowly in the beginning. These tradeoffs are not just limited to multi-agent reinforcement learning.

1 INTRODUCTION

In human society, learning is an essential component of intelligent behavior. However, each individual agent need not learn everything from scratch by its own discovery. Instead, they exchange information and knowledge with each other and learn from their peers or teachers. When a task is too big for a single agent to handle, they may cooperate in order to accomplish the task. Examples are common in non-human societies as well. For example, ants are known to communicate about the locations of food, and to move objects collectively.

In this paper, I use reinforcement learning to study intelligent agents (Mahadevan & Connel 1991, Lin 1991, Tan 1991). Each reinforcement-learning agent can incrementally learn an efficient decision policy over a state space by trial-and-error, where the only input from an environment is a delayed scalar reward. The task of each agent is to maximize the long-term discounted reward per action.

Although most work on reinforcement learning has focused exclusively on single agents, we can extend reinforcement learning straightforwardly to multiple agents if they are all independent. They together will outperform any single agent due to the fact that they have more resources and a better chance of receiving rewards. Recently, Whitehead (1991) has also demonstrated the potential benefit of multiple "complete-observing" cooperative agents over a single agent. However, the more practical study is to compare the performance of n independent agents with the one of n cooperative agents and to identify their tradeoffs. Yet, no such study has been done previously. It is the subject of this paper.

How can reinforcement-learning agents be cooperative? I identify three ways of cooperation. First, agents can communicate instantaneous information such as sensation, actions, or rewards. Second, agents can communicate episodes that are sequences of (sensation, action, reward) triples experienced by agents. Third, agents can communicate learned decision policies. This paper presents three case studies of multi-agent reinforcement learning involving such cooperation and draws some related conclusions that are not limited to multi-agent reinforcement learning. The main thesis of this paper is that *if cooperation is done intelligently, each agent can benefit from other agents' instantaneous information, episodic experience, and learned knowledge.*

Specifically, in case study 1, I investigate the ability of an agent to utilize sensation input provided by another agent. I demonstrate that sensory information from another agent is beneficial only if it is relevant and sufficient for learning. I show one instance where cooperative agents were not able to efficiently learn decision policies (compared with independent agents) due to insufficient sensation from other agents.

Case study 2 focuses on sharing learned policies and episodes. I show that in these cases cooperation speeds up learning, but does not affect asymptotic performance. I also provide upper bounds on their communication costs incurred during cooperation. While sharing policies is limited to homogeneous agents, sharing episodes can be used by heterogeneous agents as long as they can interpret episodes.

Case study 3 concerns joint tasks which require more than one agent in order to be accomplished. I demonstrate that cooperative agents who sense their partners or communicate their sensations with each other can learn to perform the tasks at a level that independent agents cannot reach even though they start out slowly. If a cooperative agent must sense other agents, the size of its state space can increase exponentially in terms of the number of involved agents.

Ideally, intelligent agents would learn when to cooperate and which cooperative method to use to achieve maximum gain. This paper is a starting point for the examination of these fundamental open questions.

2 RELATED WORK

Several multi-agent learning systems have been developed for speed and/or accuracy. GTE's ILS system (Silver et. al 1990) integrates heterogeneous (inductive, search-based, and knowledge-based) learning agents by a central controller through which the agents critique each other's proposals. The MALE system (Sian 1991) uses an interaction board (similar to a blackboard) to coordinate different learning agents. DLS (Shaw & Sikora 1990) adopts a distributed problem-solving approach to rule induction by dividing data among inductive learning agents. Recently, Chan and Salvatore (1993) advocate meta-learning for distributed learning. Most of these systems deal with inductive learning from examples, rather than autonomous learning agents that involve perception and action. One exception to this is the complexity analysis of cooperative mechanisms in reinforcement learning by Whitehead (1991). His main theorem is that n reinforcement-learning agents who can observe everything about each other can decrease the required learning time at a rate that is $\Omega(1/n)$.

Recent work in the field of *Distributed Artificial Intelligence* (DAI) (Gasser & Huhns 1989) has addressed the issues of organization, coordination, and cooperation among agents, but not for multi-agent learning. In the terms of DAI, my case studies 1 and 2 explore reinforcement learning in *collaborative reasoning systems* (Pope et. al 1992) which are concerned with coordinating intelligent behavior across multiple self-sufficient agents, and my case study 3 studies reinforcement learning in *distributed problem-solving systems* (Durfee 1988, Tan & Weihmayer 1992) in which a particular problem is divided among agents that cooperate and interact to develop a solution. Unlike DAI, this work does not deal with issues such as communication language, agent beliefs, resource constraint, and negotiation. It also mainly focus on homogeneous agents.

3 REINFORCEMENT LEARNING

Reinforcement learning is an on-line technique that approximates the conventional optimal control technique known as *dynamic programming* (Bellman 1957). The external world is modeled as a discrete-time, finite state, Markov decision process. Each action is associated with a reward. The task of reinforcement learning is to maximize the long-term discounted reward per action.

In this study, each reinforcement-learning agent uses the one-step *Q-learning* algorithm (Watkins 1989). Its learned decision policy is determined by the state/action value function, Q, which estimates long-term discounted rewards for each state/action pair. Given a current state x and available actions a_i, a Q-learning agent selects each action a with a probability given by the Boltzmann distribution:

$$p(a_i|x) = \frac{e^{Q(x,a_i)/T}}{\sum_{k \in actions} e^{Q(x,a_k)/T}} \tag{1}$$

where T is the temperature parameter that adjusts the randomness of decisions. The agent then executes the action, receives an immediate reward r, moves to the next state y.

In each time step, the agent updates $Q(x,a)$ by recursively discounting future utilities and weighting them by a positive learning rate β:

$$Q(x,a) \leftarrow Q(x,a) + \beta(r + \gamma V(y) - Q(x,a)) \tag{2}$$

Here γ $(0 \leq \gamma < 1)$ is a discount parameter, and $V(x)$ is given by:

$$V(x) = \max_{b \in actions} Q(x,b) \tag{3}$$

Note that $Q(x,a)$ is updated only when taking action a from state x. Selecting actions stochastically by (1) ensures that each action will be evaluated repeatedly.

As the agent explores the state space, its estimate Q improves gradually, and, eventually, each $V(x)$ approaches: $E\{\sum_{n=1}^{\infty} \gamma^{n-1} r_{t+n}\}$. Here r_t is the reward received at time t due to the action chosen at time $t-1$. Watkins and Dayan (1992) have shown that this Q-learning algorithm converges to an optimal decision policy for a finite Markov decision process.

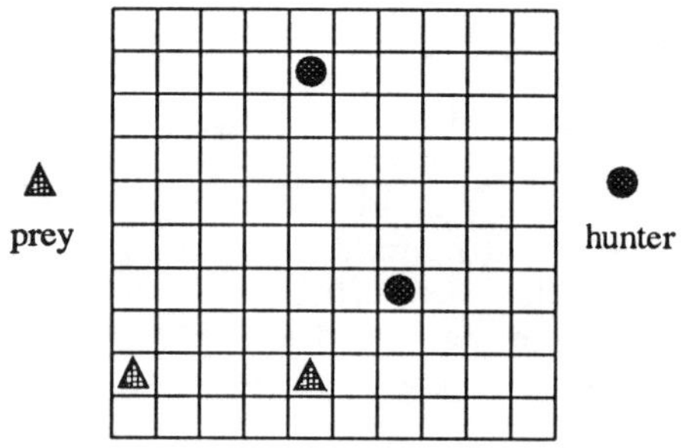

Figure 1: A 10 by 10 grid world.

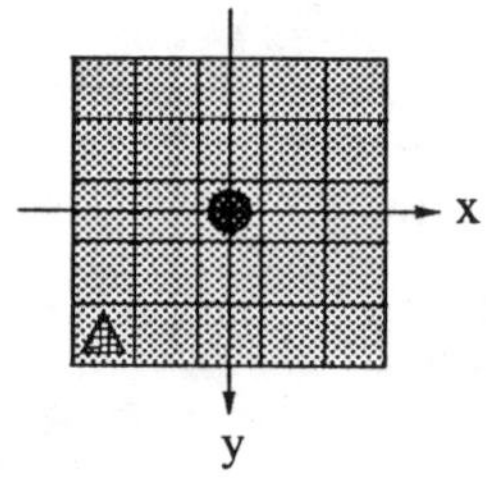

A perceptual state represented by (-2, 2)

Figure 2: A visual field of depth 2.

4 TASK DESCRIPTION

All the tasks considered in this study involve hunter agents seeking to capture randomly-moving prey agents in a 10 by 10 grid world, as shown by Figure 1. On each time step, each agent (hunter or prey) has four possible actions to choose from: moving up, down, left, or right within the boundary. Initially, hunters also make random moves as they have equal Q values. More than one agent can occupy the same cell. A prey is captured when it occupies the same cell as a hunter (in case study 1 and 2) or when two hunters either occupy the same cell as the prey or are next to the prey (in case study 3). Upon capturing a prey, the hunter or hunters involved receive +1 reward. Hunters receive −0.1 reward for each move when they do not capture a prey. Each hunter has a limited visual field inside which it can locate prey accurately. Figure 2 shows a visual field of depth 2. Each hunter's sensation is represented by (x, y) where x (y) is the relative distance of the closest prey to the hunter according to its x (y) axis. For example, (-2, 2) is a perceptual state when the closest prey is in the lower left corner of the hunter's visual field (see Figure 2). If two prey are equally close to a hunter, only one of them (chosen randomly) will be sensed. If there is no prey in sight, a unique default sensation is used.

Each run of each experiment consisted of a sequence of trials. In the first trial of each run, all agents were given a random location. Afterwards, each trial began with only rewarded hunters in random locations. Each trial ended when the first prey was captured. Each run was given a sufficient number of trials until the decision policies of hunters converged (i.e., the performance of hunters stabilized). I measured the average number of time steps per trial in *training* where actions were selected by the Boltzmann distribution, at intervals of every 50 trials. After convergence, I also measured the average number of time steps per trial in *test* where actions were selected by the highest Q value, over at least 1000 trials. Results were averaged over at least 5 runs.

The Q-learning parameters were set at $\beta = 0.8$, $\gamma = 0.9$, and $T = 0.4$. These values are reasonable for these tasks. Task parameters include the number of prey, the number of hunters, and the hunters' visual-field depth.

Without learning, hunters move randomly with baseline performances for four different prey/hunter tasks given in Table 1. The table shows the average number of steps for random hunters to capture a prey over 200 trials. I also tested the performances of independently learning hunters for the corresponding tasks. Table 1 gives their average number of steps to capture a prey in training calculated after a sufficient number of trials, where the hunters' visual-field depth was 4. Clearly, learning hunters significantly outperform random hunters. The real question is whether or not cooperation among learning hunters can further improve their performance.

5 CASE 1: SHARING SENSATION

First, I study the effect of sensation from another agent. To isolate sensing from learning, I choose the one-prey/one-hunter task and add a scouting agent that cannot capture prey. Later I extend this concept to hunters that perform both scouting and hunting. I demonstrate that sensory information from another (scouting) agent is beneficial if the information is relevant and sufficient for learning.

The scout makes random moves. At each step, the scout send its action and sensation back to the hunter. Assume that the initial relative location between the scout and the hunter is known. Therefore, the hunter can incrementally update the scout's relative location and also compute the location of the prey sensed by the scout. For example, if the relative locations of a prey to the scout (known) and the scout to the hunter (sensed) are (-2, 2) and (2, 5) respectively, then the relative location of the prey to the hunter is (0, 7). To keep the same dimension of a state representation (i.e., still use (x, y)), I combine sensation inputs from the hunter and the scout as follows: use the hunter's sensation first, if the hunter cannot sense any prey, then use the scout's sensation.

Table 2 shows the average numbers of steps to capture

Table 1: Average Number of Steps to Capture a Prey: Random vs. Independently Learning Hunters.

N-of-prey/N-of-hunters	1/1	1/2	1/2 (joint task)	2/2 (joint task)
Random hunters	123.08	56.47	354.45	224.92
Learning hunters	25.32	12.21	119.17	100.61

Table 2: Scouting vs. No Scouting.

Hunter Visual Depth	Scout Visual Depth	Average Steps to Capture a Prey	
		Training	Test
2	no scouting	47.14 (±1.28)	49.49 (±1.60)
2	2	46.33 (±1.39)	42.91 (±1.48)
2	3	39.78 (±1.06)	32.08 (±1.22)
2	4	32.67 (±1.03)	25.07 (±0.89)

a prey in training after 2000 trials and the ones in test after convergence with or without a scout. Their 90% confidence intervals calculated by a *t-test* are listed in the parentheses. The hunter with a scout took fewer steps in both training and test to capture a prey than the one without.[1] As the scout's visual-field depth increases, the difference in their performances becomes larger. This observation held when the hunter's visual-field depth was given other values (other than 2). Based on this state representation, the maximum number of perceptual states in the 10 by 10 grid world is 442 (= $(2\times10+1)^2+1$). After introducing a scout, the size of the state space for the hunter was effectively increased from 26 (= $5^2 + 1$) to 442. This increase was traded for extra sensory information and paid off in the end. In fact, when the scout's visual-field depth was 4, no obvious slowdown was observed after only 50 trials.

Once establishing the benefit of additional sensory information from a scout, I then extended this concept to the one-prey/two-hunter task with each hunter acting as a scout for the other hunter. Table 3 gives the similar measures for both independent and mutual-scouting agents. Their 90% confidence intervals calculated by a *t-test* and the resulting *t-test* comparisons within each pair are given in the parentheses. As their visual-field depth increases, (a) both independent and mutual-scouting agents take fewer and fewer steps to capture a prey; (b) mutual-scouting agents gradually outperform independent agents; and (c) the advantage of mutual-scouting agents over independent agents shows up sooner in test than in training. As an example, when the visual-field depth was 4, mutual-scouting hunters took, on the average, 8.83 steps in test to capture a prey comparing with 11.53 steps for independent hunters. However, when the visual-field depth was limited to 2, sharing sensory information hindered *training*, because a short-sighted scouting hunter could not stay with a prey long enough for the other hunter to learn to catch up with the prey. This suggests that sensory information from another agent should be used prudently, and extra, insufficient information can interfere with learning. Scouting also incurs communication cost. The information communicated from a mutual-scouting agent to another agent per step is bounded by the size (in bits) of its sensation and action representation. In this experiment, it is $2\log_2(2V_{depth}+1)+2$ where V_{depth} is the visual-field depth.

[1] Although the average steps of the hunter in training with a scout whose visual-field depth was 2 (= 46.33) is less than the one of the hunter without a scout (= 47.14), the difference is not significant according to the *t-test*.

6 CASE 2: SHARING POLICIES OR EPISODES

Assume that agents do not share sensation. If each agent is adequate to accomplish a task (e.g., each hunter can capture a prey by itself), is cooperation among agents still useful? I studied several ways of sharing learned policies and episodes in the one-prey/two-hunter task. Hunters can either (1) use the same decision policy or (2) exchange their individual policies at various frequencies. Episodes can be exchanged (a) among peer hunters or (b) between peer and expert hunters. I will show that such cooperative agents can speed up learning, measured by the average number of steps in training, even though they will eventually reach the same asymptotic performance as independent agents. This study presents the experimental results when the hunters' visual-field depth is

Table 3: Two Independent Agents vs. Two Mutual-Scouting Agents.

	Visual Depth	Average Steps to Capture a Prey	
		Training	Test
Independent agents	2	20.38 (±0.57)	24.04 (±1.00)
Mutual-scouting agents	2	25.20 (±0.79) (worse)	24.52 (±1.24) (same)
Independent agents	3	14.65 (±0.53)	16.04 (±0.56)
Mutual-scouting agents	3	14.02 (±0.75) (same)	12.98 (±0.65) (better)
Independent agents	4	12.21 (±0.65)	11.53 (±0.61)
Mutual-scouting agents	4	11.05 (±0.56) (better)	8.83 (±0.78) (better)

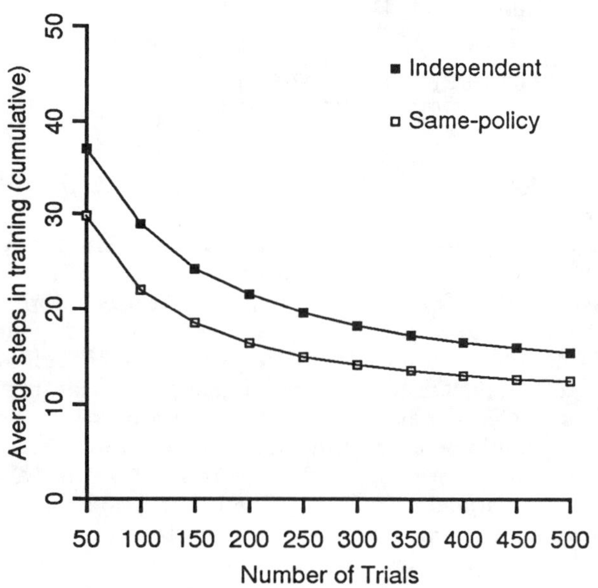

Figure 3: Independent agents vs. same-policy agents.

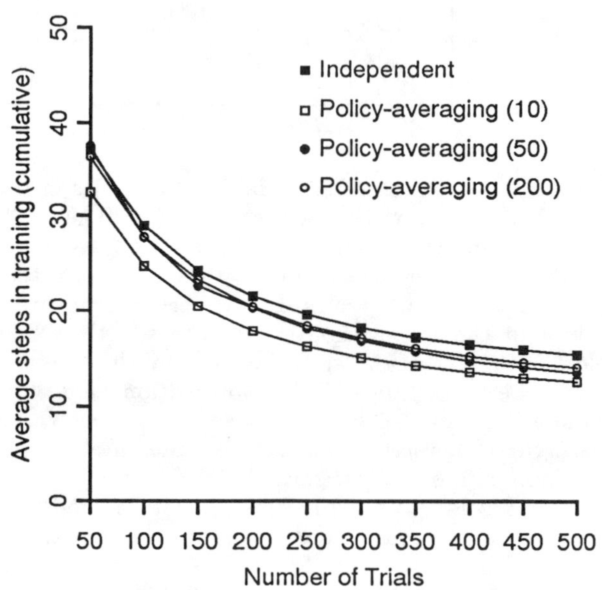

Figure 4: Independent agents vs. policy-averaging agents.

4. The conclusions when the visual-field depth is 2 or 3 are similar to 4.

One simple way of cooperating is that hunters use the same decision policy. Although each hunter updates the same policy independently, the rate of updating the policy is multiplied by the number of hunters per step. Figure 3 shows that when two hunters used the same policy, they converged much quicker than two independent hunters did. The average information communicated by each same-policy hunter per step is bounded by the number of the bits needed to describe a sensation, an action and a reward.[2] In this experiment, it is $2\log_2(2V_{depth}+1)+3$.

[2] I assume that only one agent keeps a decision policy. At each step, the rest of the involved agents send their current sensation to the policy-keeping agent, receive corresponding actions in return, and then send the rewards of their actions back to the policy-keeping agent.

If agents perform the same task, their decision policies during learning can differ because they may have explored the different parts of a state space. Two hunters can complement each other by exchanging their policies and use what the other agent had already learned for its own benefit. Assume that each agent can simultaneously send its current policy to other agents, I adopted the following policy assimilation: agents average their policies at certain frequency. Figure 4 shows the performance results when two hunters averaged their policies at every 10 steps, 50 steps, or 200 steps. All of them converged quicker than two independent hunters. One interesting observation is that when the visual-field depth was 4, the best frequency was every 10 steps (see Figure 4) while when the visual-field depth was 2, the best frequency was every 50 steps (not shown here). In general, the information communicated by each policy-exchanging hunter per step is bounded by $(N-1)\cdot P\cdot F$ where N is the number

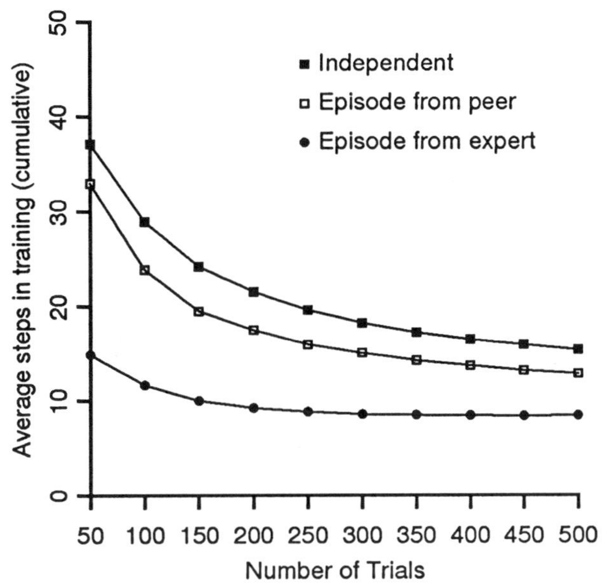

Figure 5: Independent agents vs. episode-exchanging agents.

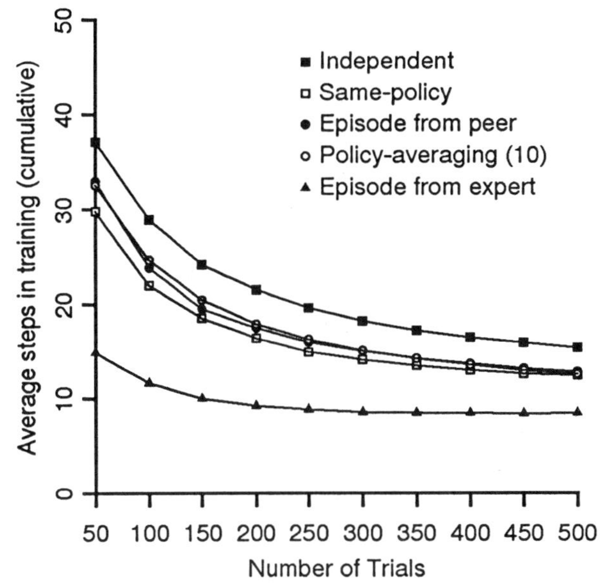

Figure 6: Summary.

of participating hunters, P is the size of a policy (i.e., number of perceptual states $\times$ number of actions $\times$ number of bits needed to represent a sensation, an action and a Q value), and F is the frequency of policy exchanging. When P or F is large, communication can be costly. On the other hand, unlike same-policy agents, a policy-exchanging agent can be selective in assimilating another agent's policy. For example, an agent could adopt another agent's decision only when it did not have confidence in certain actions.

Instead of sharing learned knowledge such as a policy, agents can share their episodes. An episode is a sequence of (sensation, action, reward) triples experienced by an agent. I used the following episode exchanging: when a hunter captured a prey, the hunter transferred its entire solution episode to the other hunter. The other hunter then "mentally replayed" the episode forward to update its own policy. As a result, two hunters doubled their learning experience. The middle curve in Figure 5 shows the speedup in training of two hunters after exchanging their episodes. The average information communicated by each episode-exchanging hunter per step is bounded by $(N-1) \cdot E$ where E is the number of bits needed to represent a sensation, an action, and a reward ($E = 2\log_2(2V_{depth}+1)+3$ in this experiment). In addition to the flexibility of assimilating episodes, exchanging episodes can be used by heterogeneous reinforcement-learning agents as long as they can interpret episodes (e.g., hunters can have different visual-field depths). To demonstrate this point, I let two hunters learn from an expert hunter that always moves towards the prey using the shortest path. Figure 5 shows significant improvement for the two novice hunters when the episodes they received were from an expert hunter (see the bottom curve). Note that an expert hunter could be just another hunter who has already learned hunting skills. This result demonstrates another benefit of learning in a cooperative society where novices can learn quickly from experts by examples (Lin 1991, Whitehead 1991).

Figure 6 summarizes the experimental results of this case study. Generally speaking, during the early phase of training, cooperative learning outperforms independent learning, and learning from an expert outperforms both. Their differences in performance are statistically significant according to *t-tests*. However, among different ways of cooperation (excluding learning from an expert), there is no conclusive evidence that one performs better than the others. In terms of the average information communicated, if the number of participating agents is limited to 2, exchanging episodes is comparable to using the same policy. Exchanging policy is plausible if the size of a policy is small and the proper frequency of policy exchanging can be determined.

7 CASE 3: ON JOINT TASKS

In the previous two case studies, each hunter can capture prey by itself. Here, I study joint tasks where a prey can only be captured by two hunters who either occupy the same cell as the prey as or are next to the prey. Hunters cooperate by either passively observing each other or actively sharing their sensations and locations. I demonstrate that cooperative agents can learn to perform the joint task significantly better than independent agents although they start slowly.

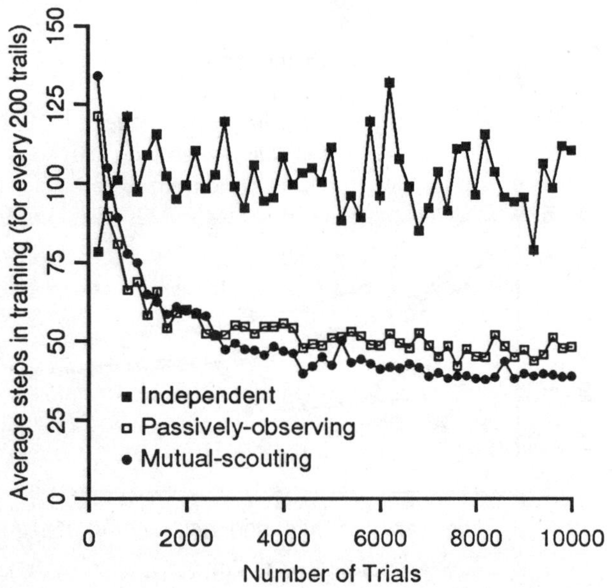

Figure 7: Typical runs for the 2-prey/2-hunter joint task.

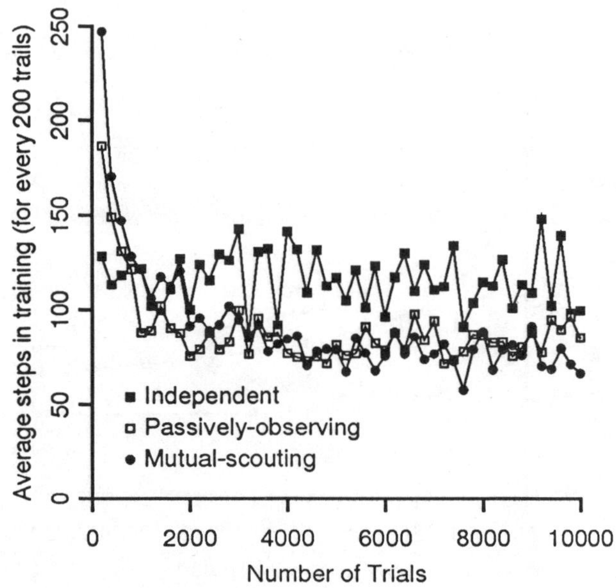

Figure 8: Typical runs for the 1-prey/2-hunter joint task.

Assume that the hunters' visual-field depth is 4 (again, the conclusions are similar when the visual-field depth is 2 or 3). Let us first consider the two-prey/two-hunter joint task. When two independent hunters were given this task, each hunter tended to learn to approach a prey directly. When both hunters approached the same prey, they succeeded and received rewards. When they chased two different prey, they failed and were penalized. As training continued, their performance fluctuated noticeably around the level of taking, on the average, 101 steps to capture a prey (see the top curve in Figure 7).

The problem with independent hunters is that they ignore each other. They cannot distinguish the situation where another hunter is nearby from the one far away. If each hunter can also sense the other hunter, cooperative behavior can emerge from greedy learning hunters. To address this problem, I extended the sensation of a hunter to two pairs $\{(x_{prey}, y_{prey})(x_{ptn}, y_{ptn})\}$ where (x_{prey}, y_{prey}) is the relative location ($\leq$ visual-field depth) between a prey and the hunter, and (x_{ptn}, y_{ptn}) between a partner and the hunter. Note that the state space is increased exponentially in terms of the number of agents. A large state space means more state exploration for a hunter, and slower learning. Nevertheless, although starting slowly, such passively-observing hunters began to overtake independent hunters soon after 400 trials, and eventually reduced the average number of steps to only 49 (see the middle curve in Figure 7).

Two hunters can cooperate passively by observing each other in addition to prey. Given the encouraging results from case study 1, I proceeded to let hunters also actively share their sensory information. This means that the state space is further enlarged although there is no increase in the dimension of a state representation. This enlargement made initial learning even slower than passively-observing hunters. Yet, mutual-scouting hunters soon outperformed passively-observing agents after about 1400 trials, and settled down at average 39 steps in training (see the bottom curve in Figure 7). The average number of steps per trial in test for independent, passively-observing and mutual-scouting hunters are 49, 42 and 34, respectively.

People may wonder what would happen if there was only one prey in the joint task. Independent hunters might do well because both hunters can just learn to approach the prey directly. This, however, is not the case. By knowing where its partner is, a hunter can learn better approach (herding) patterns. Figure 8 shows the typical runs of the three types of hunters when there was only one prey. As you can see, independent agents, passively-observing agents, and mutual-scouting agents settled down at average 116, 84, and 76 steps in training, respectively. Although it is difficult to analyze the hunters' specific approach patterns, the fact that cooperative hunters outperformed independent hunters by at least 32 steps per trial suggests the existence of such patterns.

8 CONCLUSIONS AND FUTURE WORK

This paper demonstrates that reinforcement-learning agents can learn cooperative behavior in a simulated social environment. Although this paper's results are based on simulated prey/hunter tasks, I believe the conclusions can be applied to cooperation among autonomous learning agents in general. This paper identifies three ways of agent cooperation, i.e., by communicating instantaneous information, episodic experience, and learned knowledge. Specifically, cooperative reinforcement-learning agents can learn faster and converge sooner than independent agents via sharing learned policies or solution episodes. Cooperative agents can also broaden their sensation via mutual scouting, and can handle joint tasks via sensing other partners. On the other hand, this paper also shows that extra sensory information can interfere with learning, sharing knowledge or episodes comes with a communication cost, and it takes a larger state space to learn cooperative behavior for joint tasks. These tradeoffs must be taken into consideration for autonomous and cooperative learning agents.

This research raises several important issues of multi-agent reinforcement learning. First, sensation must be selective because the size of a state space can increase exponentially in terms of the number of involved agents. One heuristic used here is that each hunter only pays attention to the nearest prey (or hunter). Can such selective sensation strategies be learned? Second, on a related issue, one needs to use generalization techniques to reduce a state space and improve performance for complex, noisy tasks. Third, learning opportunities are hard to come by for nontrivial cooperative behavior. If a prey were smart enough to know how to escape, it could take a long time for hunters to get enough learning experience. How can learning be more focused (e.g., by learning from a teacher)? Fourth, information exchanging among agents incurs communication costs. Can agents learn to communicate? This learning task gets complicated when the content of communication can be instantaneous information, episodic experience, and learned knowledge. Fifth, other cooperative methods need to be explored. For example, what if hunters share their action intentions to avoid collision, or share their rewards to sustain hunger? Finally, can homogeneous agents learn to have job division and to specialize differently? Can heterogeneous agents (such as scouting agents vs. blind hunting agents) learn to cooperate? These are directions for future work.

Acknowledgments

I am grateful to Rich Sutton, Steve Whitehead, and Chris Matheus for useful discussions and careful comments. I would like to thank Shri Goyal for his support of this research.

References

Bellman, R. E. (1957). *Dynamic Programming.* Princeton University Press, Princeton, NJ.

Chan, P. K. & Salvatore, J. S. (1993). Experiments on parallel and distributed learning by meta-learning. Submitted for publication.

Durfee, E. H. (1988). *Coordination of Distributed Problem Solvers*, Kluwer Academic Publishers, Boston.

Gasser, L. & Huhns, M. (1989). *Distributed Artificial Intelligence, 2*, (eds.) Pitman, London.

Lin, L. J. (1991). Programming robots using reinforcement learning and teaching. In Proceedings of AAAI-91. (pp. 781-786).

Mahadevan, S. & Connel, J. (1991). Automatic programming of behavior-based robots using reinforcement learning. In Proceedings of AAAI-91. (pp. 768-773).

Pope, R., Conry, S., & Meyer, R. (1992). Distributing the planning process in a dynamic environment. Proceedings of the 11th International Workshop on Distributed AI, Glen Arbor, MI.

Shaw, M. J. & Sikora, R. (1990). A distributed problem-solving approach to rule induction: learning in distributed artificial intelligence systems. Technical Report, CMU-RI-TR-90-28, The Robotics Institute, Carnegie Mellon University.

Sian, S. S. (1991). Extending learning to multiple agents: issues and a model for multi-agent machine learning. In Y. Kodratoff (Ed.), *Machine Learning – EWSL 91.* Springer-Verlag, pp. 440-456.

Silver, B., Frawely, W., Iba, G., Vittal, J., & Bradford, K. (1990). A framework for multi-paradigmatic learning. In Proceedings of the Seventh International Conference on Machine Learning, 348-358. Austin, Texas.

Tan, M. (1991). Cost-sensitive reinforcement learning for adaptive classification and control. In Proceedings of AAAI-91. (pp. 774-780).

Tan, M. & Weihmayer, R. (1992). Integrating agent-oriented programming and planning for cooperative problem solving. Proceedings of the AAAI-92's Workshop on Cooperation among Heterogeneous Intelligent Agents, San Jose, CA,

Watkins, C. J. C. H. (1989). Learning With Delayed Rewards. Ph.D. thesis, Cambridge University Psychology Department.

Watkins, C. J. C. H. & Dayan, P. (1992) Technical Note: Q-Learning. *Machine Learning*, 8(3/4), Kluwer Academic Publishers.

Whitehead, S. D. (1991). A complexity analysis of cooperative mechanisms in reinforcement learning. In Proceedings of AAAI-91. (pp. 607-613)

Better Learners Use Analogical Problem Solving Sparingly

Kurt VanLehn
Learning Research and Development Center
University of Pittsburgh
Pittsburgh, PA 15260
VanLehn@cs.pitt.edu
(412)624-7458

Randolph M. Jones
Artificial Intelligence Laboratory
University of Michigan
1101 Beal Av.
Ann Arbor, MI 48109-2110
rjones@engin.umich.edu
(313)764-0683

Abstract

When solving homework exercises, human students often notice that the problem they are about to solve is similar to an example. They then deliberate over whether to refer to the example or to solve the problem without looking at the example. We present protocol analyses showing that effective human learners prefer not to use analogical problem solving for achieving the base-level goals of the problem, although they do use it occasionally for achieving meta-level goals, such as checking solutions or resolving certain kinds of impasses. On the other hand, ineffective learners use analogical problem solving in place of ordinary problem solving, and this prevents them from discovering gaps in their domain theory. An analysis of the task domain (college physics) reveals a testable heuristic for when to use analogy and when to avoid it. The heuristic may be of use in guiding multistrategy learners.

1 WHEN TO ANALOGIZE?

When doing homework exercises, human learners often notice that the problem they are about to solve is similar to an example, then deliberate over whether to refer to the example or to solve the problem without its aid. As one of our subjects said, "this looks very much like the one I had in the examples. Okay. Should I just go right to the problem, which I distinctly remember? Or should I try to do it without looking at the example?" A multistrategy machine learning program could face the same decision. The objective of this paper is to find out what heuristics good human learners use for deciding whether to do analogical problem solving, then determine when those heuristics would be good for a machine learning program to use.

Because we use protocol data, the only evidence we have of analogical problem solving is episodes where a person explicitly refers to an example, typically by flipping pages in a textbook in order to expose the page on which the example is printed. Thus, analogical problem solving, in this paper, means the process of referring to a written example rather than a mentally held one. As will be seen later, nothing in our conclusions relies on this restriction, so the results may apply to analogies that refer to mental examples (or cases?) as well as written ones.

The protocol data come from subjects learning Newtonian physics. The subjects worked with textbook physics problems and examples, such as the one in Figure 1. The protocol data were collected as part of a study by Chi, Bassok, Lewis, Reimann & Glaser (1989). The subjects were 9 college students selected to have similar backgrounds (Chi & VanLehn, 1991). The subjects first refreshed their mathematical knowledge by studying the first 4 chapters of Halliday & Resnick (1981), a popular physics textbook. They then studied the expository part of chapter 5, which introduces the basic principles of Newtonian mechanics, its history and some classic experiments. Student were tested at this point and had to re-study parts of the material that they did not understand. After they had mastered the mathematical prerequisites and the basic principles, they studied 3 examples and solved 19 problems while talking aloud. They were allowed to refer to the examples at any time while solving problems, but they were not allowed to refer to their own previous problem solutions. The 9 subjects' protocols, which averaged 5 hours each, are the raw data for the findings reported here. They contain many instances of analogical problem solving. The goal is to discover which ones helped learning and which ones hurt it.

We used a contrastive protocol analysis technique pioneered by Chi et al. (1989). The basic idea is to split the subjects into two groups—effective learners and ineffective learners—then determine what the effective learners did differently from the ineffective learners. Because the students were trained to have the same prerequisite knowledge, the scores on their problem solving reflect their learning rate during example

Problem: The figure on the left below shows a block of mass *m* kept at rest on a smooth plane, inclined at an angle of 45 degrees with the horizontal, by measn of a string attached to the vertical wall. What are the magnitudes of the forces acting on the block?

Solution:
(1) We choose the block as the body.
(2) The forces acting on the block are shown in the free-body diagram on the right.
(3) Since the block is unaccelerated, we obtain T+N+mg=0.
(4) It is convenient to choose the x-axis of our reference frame to be along the incline and the y-axis to be normal to the incline.
(5) With this choice of coordinates, only one force, mg, must be resolved into components.
(6) The two scalar equations obtained by resolving mg along the x- and y-axes are:
T - mg sin 45 = 0 and N - mg cos 45 = 0.
(7) From these equations, T and N can be obtained if m is given.

Figure 1: A physics example, with line numbers added

studying and problem solving. The 4 highest scoring subjects constitute the effective learners (called Good solvers by Chi et al.), and the 4 lowest scoring subjects constituted the ineffective learners (called Poor solvers). The middle subject's protocol was not analyzed (until later: see below).

The next section presents a learning mechanism and argues that it is the main source of learning by subjects in this study. The argument uses new protocol analyses as well as analyses published earlier. With this as background, the subsequent sections present the main result, which is that effective learners use analogical problem solving sparingly. A discussion section speculates on why this policy was better for human solvers in this experiment, and suggests conditions under which this policy would be good for any multi-strategy learner.

2 GAP FILLING

Given that errors are used to determine when learning was not effective, a direct way to uncover dominant learning mechanisms is to examine the subjects' errors. If errors of a certain type are much less common among Good solvers than Poor solvers, we can assume that a learning mechanism employed by the Good solvers and not the Poor solvers is reducing those errors. From the characteristics of such errors we can infer the characteristics of the learning processes. We classified errors into 5 types, which are listed below:

- *Inappropriate analogies.* Sometimes subjects fetched an example that was inappropriate for the problem being solved. At other times, subjects fetched appropriate examples but applied them in inappropriate ways. Both types of errors are classified as inappropriate analogies.
- *Gap errors.* Subjects often lacked a piece of physics knowledge, such as the fact that the tension in a string is equal to the magnitude of a tension force exerted by that string. Sometimes errors would occur when the subject reached an impasse caused by their lack of knowledge, and used some ineffective repair strategy (VanLehn, 1990) to work around it. At other times, the gap would cause an error (such as a missing minus sign) without the subject ever becoming aware of the gap.
- *Schema selection errors.* All subjects knew several methods or schemas for solving physics problems. One method was to draw forces, generate equations and solve the equations. Another method was simply to generate equations that contained the sought and/or known quantities without considering what forces or other physical quantities might be present. On some problems, subjects chose the equation-chaining schema instead of the force schema, and this caused them to answer the problem incorrectly.
- *Mathematical errors.* A typical mathematical error was to confuse sine and cosine, or to drop a negative sign.
- *Miscellaneous errors.*

The error classification was done separately by two coders, with an intercoder reliability of 82%. Differences were reconciled by collaborative protocol analysis.

Table 1: Mean errors per subject for each error category

Error type	Good	Poor
Inappropriate analogies	1.00	2.25
Gap errors	**0.25	**7.75
Schema selection	0.50	1.75
Math errors	0.25	0.75
Miscellaneous errors	1.25	1.75
Totals	**3.25	**14.25

Table 1 shows the average number of errors of each type per subject. Although the Good solvers had fewer errors than the Poor solvers in every category, the difference was significant only for gap errors ($t(6) = 5.36, p < .01$). Moreover, the difference was quite large (3.8 standard deviations), and accounts for most (68%) of the difference in the total error rates of the Good and Poor solvers.

These results suggest that Good solvers were more effective learners than Poor solvers because they employed some kind of learning process that filled in the gaps in their knowledge.[1] There are many kinds of mechanisms in the literature that can detect and rectify incomplete domain theories. For handy reference, let us refer to the process(es) that Good solvers use as *gap filling* even though we do not know what it is. Table 1 suggests that gap filling is the main learning process that differentiates effective from ineffective learners in this study.

This suggestion is consistent with findings from Chi et al.'s (1989) analysis of the same data. They found that during example studying, Good solvers tended to thoroughly explain the examples to themselves, while the Poor solvers tended to read them rather casually. Further examination of the protocols suggested that self-explanation consisted of actually rederiving the lines of the solution (VanLehn, Jones & Chi, 1991). If the main learning process is gap filling, then this method of studying the example should cause the subjects to detect gaps in their knowledge. If a piece of physics knowledge is required for deriving a line of the example's solution, and students lack that knowledge, then they will be unable to fully explain the line. The resulting impasse might cause them to seek the missing knowledge and fill their gap. Thus, the gap-filling hypothesis is consistent with the finding that Good solvers self-explain examples more than Poor solvers. Moreover, it explains why self-explanation causes better learning (VanLehn & Jones, in press-b).

The computational sufficiency of gap-filling has been tested by implementing a simulation of human learning, called Cascade, that is based a particular gap filling mechanism and comparing Cascade's behavior to the protocols (VanLehn, Jones & Chi, 1991; VanLehn & Jones, 1991; in press-a). Gaps can cause Cascade to reach impasses (i.e., be unable to achieve a goal) while trying to solve problems or rederive examples. When Cascade's "official" domain knowledge is insufficient to achieve a goal, it tries to apply overly general knowledge that captures regularities common to many types of scientific and mathematical problem solving. For instance, one overly general rule is that scientific concepts often correspond roughly to common sense concepts. Cascade uses this rule during a problem where a block rests on a spring. Cascade lacks the knowledge that a compressed spring exerts a force on the objects at its ends, so it reaches an impasse. The overly general rule applies, because Cascade knows that springs push back when you push on them. The overly general rule justifies creating an instance of a scientific concept ("force") because it involves the same objects as an instance of a lay concept ("push back"). As a side-effect of the application of this overly general knowledge, a new domain rule is proposed: If a block rests on a spring, the spring exerts a force on it. If this rule is used successfully enough times, it becomes a full-fledged member of the domain theory. In this fashion, Cascade fills gaps in its domain knowledge.

Cascade's behavior compares well with both aggregate findings (VanLehn, Jones & Chi, 1991) and individual protocols (VanLehn & Jones, 1993). This establishes that with plausible assumptions about subjects' prior knowledge, there is enough information present in the environment to allow a gap filling process to learn everything that the Good solvers learn, to do so without implausibly large computations, and to generate outward behavior that is similar to the subjects' behavior. In short, gap filling is a computationally sufficient account for the Good solvers' learning.

None of the results show that gap filling is the *only* learning process going on. There could be others as well. However, Table 1 suggests that gap filling is the most important learning process, because it accounts for most of the difference in the learning of the Good and Poor solvers.

3 AVOIDING ANALOGY

There is already some evidence that the Good solvers avoid analogical problem solving. This section reviews those findings, then tries to ascertain whether this is a just a correlation or whether avoiding analogy actually causes more effective learning.

Chi et al. (1989) counted episodes of analogical prob-

[1] An alternative explanation is that the Good solvers never had the gaps because they learned the knowledge before studying the examples. Analyses of pre-test data (Chi et al., 1989), the instructional material (VanLehn, Jones & Chi, 1991) and the subjects' backgrounds (Chi & VanLehn, 1991) fail to support this interpretation of the data.

lem solving during the first 3 problems. They found that Good solvers used analogy only 2.7 times per problem, whereas the Poor solvers used analogy 6.7 items per problem. Thus, the Good solver use analogical problem solving less often than the Poor solvers. Chi et al. also found that the Good solvers used analogy in a more focused way. When the Good solvers referred to an example, they tended to jump into the middle of it and read only a few lines (1.6 lines per episode, on average). The Poor solvers tended to start at the beginning of the example and read until they found something they could use (13.0 lines per episode). This suggests that Good solvers are basically solving the problem on their own, but they occasionally use analogical problem solving to get specific information from the example. The Poor solvers, on the other hand, seem to use analogical problem solving instead of regular problem solving. These findings indicate that effective learning co-occurs with avoiding of analogy, but it is not clear which way the causality runs.

Our first hypothesis was that the Poor solvers used more analogical problem solving because they lacked domain knowledge so they had to refer to the example if they were to make any progress. Cascade embedded this hypothesis. It did analogy (called transformational analogy in earlier reports) only when it reached an impasse (VanLehn, Chi & Jones, 1991; VanLehn & Jones, in press-a). On this account, the Chi et al. correlation is due to ineffective learning causing analogy.

However, when we fitted Cascade to individual protocols, we found that we sometimes had to force it to do analogy even though it had the knowledge to do regular problem solving (VanLehn & Jones, 1993). While simulating all 9 subjects, Cascade used analogy 231 times, and 196 of these were caused by impasses while 35 (15%) were caused by our intervention. If we believe the modeling, then these 35 analogies were "optional" in that the subjects did not have to do them. They could have used their knowledge of physics principles instead. In most of these cases (30 of 35), the subjects copied the example's force diagram rather than generate their own. Copying the force diagram was also frequent among the 196 impasse-driven analogies.

Upon reflection, it occurred to us that some of these supposedly impasse-driven analogies may not actually be caused by trying to generate forces, failing, and reaching an impasse. If this were the case, then one would expect the analogy to yield new knowledge about the missing force (or whatever the missing knowledge was), thus filling the gap and allowing the person to draw their own force diagram the next time it was needed. We examined all 196 cases of analogy and found no cases were this kind of learning occurred. If a person had an gap that caused an impasse-driven analogy, then they would use analogy on every subsequent occasion (if any) when that piece of knowledge was required. It could be that what people learn from such an impasse is that "analogy works here," so they continue to use it. However, it could also be that our modeling was incorrect, and they never had such any impasses for that gap. Instead, when they go to certain sections of the problem (typically, the force diagram), they would use analogy without ever considering using their domain knowledge. Perhaps some of those 196 cases of impasse-driven analogy were really optional analogies. Indeed, two of the subject never tried to draw a force diagram on their own—they always copied an example's diagram.

While investigating the gap-filling hypothesis, we discovered additional support for this conjecture. According to the gap-filling hypothesis, gaps in the textbook become gaps in the student's domain knowledge, which cause errors until they are detected and remedied. In order to check this story, we carefully analyzed the first 5 chapters of Halliday and Resnick (1981) and discovered 9 pieces of knowledge that are required by the problems and are not in the text (VanLehn & Jones, in preparation). Using Cascade, for each of the 9 subjects, we located the places in the protocols where the 9 pieces of knowledge could appear if they were known, or cause errors if they were unknown. For each of the 9 pieces of knowledge, we created a chart, such as the one shown in Table 2, that summarizes what happened at each possible occurrence of the gap. The particular piece of knowledge referenced by Table 2 is "Projecting a vector onto the negative portion of an axis yields a negative formula." This piece of knowledge is relevant 5 times during example studying and 16 times during problem solving. At each place, for each subject, we classified the protocol fragment into one of the categories shown below (the symbol in parentheses corresponds to the code used in Table 2).

- (E) The subject omited use of the knowledge, which resulted in an error.
- (O) The subject omited use of the knowledge, but no error occurred. For instance, one sign error might compensate for another.
- (blank) During example studying, the subject did not explain the part of the example where this piece of knowledge would be used. During problem solving, the subject used analogical problem solving to avoid the line of reasoning that would use the piece of knowledge.
- (U) The subject used the piece of knowledge without hesitation or other signs of unusual processing.
- (L) The subject seemed to learn the knowledge. Episodes received this code if the subjects expressed puzzlement or commented on their lack of knowledge, but eventually came up with the right action (e.g., writing a negative sign). For instance, subject P2 overlooked the first minus

Table 2: Places where the negative-projection rule could be used

Subj.	Examples					Problems															
	1	2	3	4	5	1	2	3	4	5	6	7	8	9	10	11	12	13	14	15	16
P2		L			U	?	?	U	U	U	U	U	U	U	U	U	U	U	U	U	U
S101								L	L			O	U			U					U
P1	L	L	U	O	U	U		U	U		U	U		U	U		U		U	U	
S110								O					U	O	O	U	O			U	R
S102		L				U							U	U	O		U				
S109																					
S105	U							U			U		U		U		U				E
S103									E					O	E						
S107	U							E	R			U		U	U	O	U				

sign in the first example, but on the second minus sign she said, "Hmm, why is [it] minus? Uh Huh.... Because these axis are starting here so this is minus." She then went back to the first minus sign and said, "How about the X's. It should also be a minus. Yah, that was a minus." Subject S102 paused after seeing the second minus and said, "Negative W.... It's because it's going in a negative direction it points...they give it a negative value [if] it's below the Y-axis. I mean the X-axis." Subject P1 (quoted at length in VanLehn, Jones & Chi 1991), took several garden paths before discovering the correct rule for explaining the minus sign, which is clear evidence of her lack of knowledge. However, her verbal behavior at the time of the discovery was just as brief and cryptic as the verbal behavior of P2 and S102. Such limited verbal evidence is typical of discovery events in protocol data (VanLehn, 1991; Siegler & Jenkins, 1989). They nonetheless seem to reliably mark transitions in the subjects' knowledge.

- (R) The subjects' verbal behavior indicates that they are learning the piece of knowledge, but they used it at least one before. We believe these are cases of relearning.
- (?) Protocol missing.

The blanks in the problem solving part of Table 2 shows that for this piece of knowledge, many gaps are not detected because the student used analogical problem solving. When we constructed similar analyses for all 9 gaps and all 9 subjects, we found that of the 81 (= 9x9) cases where a piece of knowledge could be learned, in 44 cases (54%) the subject avoided *all* places where the gap could be detected (as did S109 in Table 2). This analysis clearly indicates that analogical problem solving is thwarting gap filling by avoiding lines of reasoning that would cause the gap to be detected.

This finding makes intuitive sense. Most problems can be solved by a 4 step process: select some objects as the "bodies" (line 1 of Figure 1), draw a diagram for each body showing the forces acting on it (lines 2 and 3 of Figure 1), produce a set of equations (line 6 of Figure 1), then solve the equations for the sought quantity (omitted in Figure 1). The last step cannot usually be replaced by analogy because the problems seldom seek the same quantities. However, the first 3 steps can often be achieved by analogy. The student can find an analogous problem and copy either its force diagram, its equations or both. A student who does this avoids using the force laws (which generate forces) and Newton's laws (which generate the equations). Missing physics knowledge can remain undetected as long as one uses analogy to copy force diagrams and equations. To put it bluntly, analogical problem solving often preserves ignorance.

We can now understand part of Chi et al.'s finding about the use of analogy by Good and Poor solvers. The Poor solvers displayed more episodes of analogical problem solving and read more lines during each episode because they generally avoided generating their own forces and equations by copying them from the examples. This is not just a coincidence, but seems to have caused them to learn much less than they would otherwise. On the other hand, the Good solvers generally tried to generate their own forces and equations and only referred sporadically and briefly to the examples. Thus, they could still detect their gaps and remedy them.

4 USING ANALOGY SPARINGLY

We suspect that the Good solvers' use of analogy does more than just allow gap-filling to operate. It may actively aid gap-filling by helping to both detect and fill gaps. This section presents a few pieces of protocol data to support our conjecture. However, more data are clearly required.

There were 6 cases in the protocols where, according to the analysis above, knowledge was learned during problem solving. During 4 of the 6 episodes, the subject clearly referred to an example. These 4 cases, discussed below, are different enough that they begin to show that analogy can assist gap filling in several ways.

Subject P2 reached an impasse and filled it with the aid of analogy. The subject needed to know whether water exerted a force on a block floating on it. She referred to an example where a string held up a block instead of water. The close similarity of the problems convinced her that water can exert a force. This conjecture both filled a gap in the subject's knowledge and resolved a problem solving impasse. ACT* (Anderson, 1990) and other theories claim that analogy is often used to resolve impasses and thereby acquire new knowledge.

Subject S105 used analogy to detect a knowledge gap. While drawing forces for an inclined plane problem, the subject omitted one force (the surface normal—a notoriously unintuitive force). He had never produced that force in earlier problem solving, nor had he self-explained the line in the examples that was intended to teach it. Thus, we assume he had a knowledge gap. After finishing his force diagram, the subject fetched an example, viewed its force diagram, said, "That's the force I wasn't thinking of," and drew a normal force on his diagram. Thereafter, the subject regularly drew normal forces on his diagrams. In this case, analogy was used to *check* a step in the problem solving, and that revealed a knowledge gap. Whereas the preceding case illustrates how analogy can help in *filling* gaps, this case illustrates how analogy can help in *detecting* gaps. There was a second case of analogy-based checking causing detection of a gap, but it will not be presented here. These cases are consistent with a finding of Chi et al. (1989), who classified analogical episodes as either reading, checking or copying. Good solvers had many fewer episodes of reading and copying than Poor solvers, but they actually had more episodes of checking.

Subject 101 learned a rule while engaged in a mixture of analogical problem solving and self-explanation. While trying to project forces onto axes, the subject decided to see what a similar example had done. He could partially explain the example's equations, but he could not self-explain the negative signs. He gave up, copied the negative signs and said, "Well let's see if I can just push these in.... This is called copying too much from the book. I hate that." This is clearly a case of analogical problem solving of the worst kind. However, after solving the equations and producing a negative formula, he said, "So, according to this, my x-component is equal to −9, which means, okay. That makes sense. That makes sense. One of these has to always be negative, doesn't it?" Apparently, the subject figured out why there is a negative sign. His reasoning appears to be based on some kind of symmetry argument, which is an overly general line of mathematical reasoning, but not the best one for learning this rule. A bit later in the protocol, he failed to use his new knowledge, but corrected his oversight a few lines later (we coded this as a learning event in Table 2). After that, he used the rule fairly consistently. This case illustrates how analogy can combine with self-explanation to produce learning via a kind of justified analogy (Kedar-Cabelli, 1985).

We believe that these cases are just a few of the many ways that analogy can support learning. Note that all these uses of analogy only briefly interrupt regular problem solving in order to achieve a specific meta-goal, such as detecting a gap or filling one. Wholesale analogy, the kind used by the Poor solvers, avoids detecting gaps and thus tends to retard learning. Thus, we hypothesize that learning is most effective when analogy is used sparsely, as an augmentation to regular problem solving rather than a replacement.

5 DISCUSSION

The preceding sections showed that in one study, effective human learners used analogical problem solving sparingly. With a little bit of computational common sense, we can generalize this result and formulate a heuristic for when such sparse analogical problem solving should be effective.

There are four steps to solving a Newtonian mechanics physics problem:

1. *Define a system.* One must (a) select an idealization of the physical world consisting of idealized bodies that have idealized relationships to other objects and move in idealized trajectories, and (b) decide whether to base the analysis on forces, energies or momenta. In Figure 1, line 1 corresponds to part *a* (albeit, tersely), and part *b* is missing because the text has only introduced one type of analysis (forces) at this point.
2. *Explicate physics quantities.* For each body in the system, one notes the forces, energies or momenta associated with that body. Often, a diagram is drawn to help one remember them. In Figure 1, this occurs during line 2.
3. *Generate equations.* The equations are instances of general principles. In Figure 1, the equations are produced on line 6. They are instances of Newton's first law.
4. *Solve the equations for the sought quantity.*

Although logically distinct, these steps are often intermingled in an solver's work. Solvers have no trouble learning this basic procedure. It is often printed in the textbook. It is a specialization of the general 3-step procedure (define a system, formulate a mathematical model, solve it) that is used for all mathematical analysis problems, from lowly arithmetic and algebraic word problems to esoteric branches of science and engineering (see any textbook on systems theory, e.g., Shearer, Murphy & Richardson, 1971).

The system definition step is quite different from the others. There are no real principles for defining a system. Sometimes a chain is treated as a single body, sometimes as an infinite sequence of infinitely small bodies, and sometimes as two bodies. Textbooks give few heuristics for defining systems. Although the problems used in our data are too simple to reveal how the subjects learn about system definition, it is plausible that system-defining can be learned by analogical problem solving and/or and case-based reasoning.

All the steps except system definition are governed by well-known principles, such as the force laws (for step 2), Newton's laws (for step 3) and mathematical transformations (for step 4). Moreover, once the system has been defined, the analysis is completely determined. In step 2 (explication of physics quantities), one produces all the forces (or energies or momenta) acting on the system's bodies. In step 3 (equation generation), one produces all the equations implied by those physics quantities.[2] In step 4, the equations are solved mechanically. The point here is that in physics and many other mathematical analysis task domains, the most important decisions are made during system definition, and the rest of the analysis follows more or less deterministically from those choices. Although analogical problem solving would be useful for learning search control, search control is not very important for steps 2 and 3.

Although principles can be used for steps 2 and 3, it may be that case-based reasoning is more efficient than principle-based reasoning. If so, analogical problem solving would be an effective way to master those steps. The output of step 2 is completely determined by the output of step 1, and case-based reasoning appears to be the most effective way to define systems (step 1), so case-based reasoning should be just as effective for delineating forces and other quantities (step 2). However, generation of equations (step 3) depends only only on the earlier steps, but on the exactly which quantities are sought and which are given. Even when problems have very similar systems, they rarely have similar givens and soughts, so case-based reasoning should seldom be helpful generating equations. In addition, it is much easier to remember the diagrams produced by steps 1 and 2 than the systems of equations produced by step 3.

It is worth recalling that our top-level goal is to determine when analogical problem solving is advisable for effective learning. So far, we have argued that case-based reasoning and/or analogy should be used during the system defining step and possibly during the quantity delineation step, whereas principle-based reasoning should be used instead of analogy during the equation generation step (we ignore the equation solving step, since it involves skills acquired prior to studying the task domain). We next consider how principles can be learned during steps 2 and 3.

Suppose the learner already knows many principles, so the learning problem is to detect a gap (missing principle) and fill it, rather than to learn a whole batch of principles at once. In order to detect a gap, one must try to use principles instead of analogies to achieve goals, for otherwise the body of knowledge containing the gap will not be referenced and detecting the gap would be impossible.

Although impasses in principle-based problem solving will uncover some gaps, not all gaps cause impasses. Thus, it is good to check intermediate results because early detection of an error will facilitate locating the gap that caused it. Analogy is one way to check intermediate results.

By considering the nature of the task domain, one can predict which intermediate results should be checked. In physics, missing knowledge of physics quantities will cause step 2 to produce too few forces, energies, etc., but this will not causes impasses until much later, if at all. Consequently, it is good to use analogical problem solving to check the results of step 2 before moving on to step 3. This is just what subject S105 did in the case mentioned earlier.[3] In general, when the goal is "generate all X that you can think of," where X in S105's case is "forces," then gaps will not cause impasses, so it is wise to use analogy to check the outcome of generate-all-X goals. Experienced learners of mathematical analysis may know this heuristic for increasing their learning rate. They may know other heuristics as well.

Once a gap is detected, analogy is certainly one possible way to fill it, but it is not easy to predict whether one should use analogy or some other technique, such as instantiating an overly general rule (VanLehn, Jones & Chi, 1991) or explanation pattern (Schank, 1986). A heuristic for this decision would be hard to formulate.

We have arrived finally at our goal, which are heuristics for deciding when to use analogical problem solving. The heuristics are:

1. If the task domain, or some part of the task domain (e.g., steps 2 and 3), has principles, and they are more effective knowledge than cases, and they require little search control, then the target knowledge should be principles.

[2] Actually, there are choices to make during step 3 regarding how to rotate the coordinate axes or whether to omit certain equations. These choices affect the difficulty of step 4, but not the ultimate outcome.

[3] In order to fill such gaps, Cascade 3 used analogy essentially as a check of step 2, although the implementation was rather baroque (VanLehn & Jones, 1991; in press-a).

2. If the target knowledge is principles, they should be acquired by gap filling, which implies:
   (a) Gap detection: Try to use principles instead of analogies, as a gap may show up as an impasse. Use analogy to check the intermediate results derived via principles, as this may uncover gaps that do not produce impasses.
   (b) Gap filling: Analogical problem solving is one possible technique for filling gaps. Others should be considered as well.
3. If the target knowledge is not principles but cases or search control, then analogical problem solving may be useful.

This conclusion was suggested by human data. There is evidence that the Poor solvers use analogy "wholesale," as a replacement for principle-based solutions to steps 1, 2 and 3. There is also evidence that Good solvers avoid analogical problem solving in general. There is some evidence, albeit only a few protocol excerpts, that when Good solvers do use analogy, it is used as an aid to gap filling. In this last section, we have reflected on the human data and, supported by common sense, derived a heuristic for when analogical problem solving should aid learning. This heuristic could have several uses. (1) It helps explains why the Good solvers learned more than the Poor solvers. (2) It is a prescription for effective learning that could perhaps be taught to human students. (3) It could be embedded in a multi-strategy learning.

Clearly, all these implications are testable in their own fashions. A good next step would be to augment Cascade so that we can experimentally test whether the heuristic does increase learning. If this succeeds, one could try teaching human students the heuristic and see if their learning increases as predicted.

Acknowledgements

This research was supported by grant N00014-88-K-0086 from the Cognitive Sciences Division of the Office of Naval Research. We appreciate Joel Martin's and Ted Rees' critiques of the manuscript.

References

Anderson, J.R. (1990). *The adaptive character of thought.* Hillsdale, NJ: Lawrence Erlbaum Assoc.

Chi, M.T.H., Bassok, M., Lewis, M.W., Reimann, P. & Glaser, R. (1989). Self-explanations: How students study and use examples in learning to solve problems. *Cognitive Science*, 13, 145-182.

Chi, M.T. H. & VanLehn, K. (1991) The content of physics self-explanations. *Journal of the Learning Sciences*, 1(1), 69-106.

Halliday, D. & Resnick, R. (1981). *Fundamental of physics, Second edition.* New York: Wiley.

Kedar-Cabelli, S. (1985). Toward a computational model of purpose-directed analogy. In A. Prieditis (Ed.) *Analogica.* San Mateo, CA: Morgan Kaufman. Reprinted in J. W. Shavlik & T. G. Dietterich (Eds.) *Readings in machine learning.* San Mateo, CA: Morgan Kaufman.

Schank, R.C. (1986). *Explanation patterns: Understanding mechanically and creatively.* Hillsdale, NJ: Lawrence Erlbaum Assoc.

Shearer, J.L., Murphy, A.T. & Richardson, H.H. (1971). *Introduction to systems dynamics.* Reading, MA: Addison-Wesley.

Siegler, R.S. & Jenkins, E. (1989). *How children discover new strategies.* Hillsdale, NJ: Lawrence Erlbaum Assoc.

VanLehn, K. (1990) *Mind bugs: The origins of procedural misconceptions.* Cambridge, MA: MIT Press.

VanLehn, K. (1991) Rule acquisition events in the discovery of problem solving strategies. *Cognitive Science, 15*, 1-47.

VanLehn, K., Jones, R.M. & Chi, M.T.H. (1991). A model of the self-explanation effect. *Journal of the Learning Sciences, 1*, 69-106.

VanLehn, K. & Jones, R.M. (1991). Learning physics via explanation-based learning of correctness and analogical search control. In L. Birnbaum & G. Collins, (Eds.), *Machine Learning: Proceedings of the eighth international workshop.* San Mateo, CA: Morgan Kaufman.

VanLehn, K. & Jones, R.M. (1993). Learning by explaining examples to oneself: A computational model. In S. Chipman & A. L. Meyrowitz (Eds.) *Foundations of knowledge acquisition: Cognitive models of complex learning.* Boston: Kluwer Academic Publishing.

VanLehn, K. & Jones, R.M. (in press-a). Integration of analogical search control and explanation-based learning of correctness. In S. Minton & P. Langley (Eds.) *Machine learning methods for planning and scheduling.* Los Altos, CA: Morgan Kaufman.

VanLehn, K. & Jones, R.M. (in press-b). What mediates the self-explanation effect? Knowledge gaps, schemas or analogies? To appear in M. Polson (Ed.) *Proceedings of the 15th Annual Conference of the Cognitive Science Society.* Hillsdale, NJ: Erlbaum.

VanLehn, K. & Jones, R.M. (in preparation). Self-explanation and analogy.

AUTHOR INDEX

SUBJECT INDEX